T
BRITISH RAJ
IN INDIA

AN HISTORICAL REVIEW

Frontispiece: Shah Alam II handing Robert Clive sovereign rights in Bengal in 1765, by Benjamin West. (India Office Library, London)

THE
BRITISH RAJ
IN INDIA

AN HISTORICAL REVIEW

S. M. Burke

and

Salim Al-Din Quraishi

KARACHI

OXFORD UNIVERSITY PRESS

OXFORD   NEW YORK   DELHI

Oxford University Press, Great Clarendon Street, Oxford OX2 6DP
Oxford New York
Athens Auckland Bangkok Bogotá Buenos Aires Calcutta
Cape Town Chennai Dar es Salaam Delhi Florence Hong Kong Istanbul
Karachi Kuala Lumpur Madrid Melbourne Mexico City Mumbai
Nairobi Paris São Paulo Singapore Taipei Tokyo Toronto Warsaw
and associated companies in Berlin Ibadan

Oxford is a registered trade mark of Oxford University Press

First published by Oxford University Press, 1995
This edition in Oxford Pakistan Paperbacks, 1996

fourth Impression 2000

ISBN 0 19 577734 4

Printed in Pakistan at
Mueid Packages, Karachi.
Published by
Ameena Saiyid, Oxford University Press
5-Bangalore Town, Sharae Faisal
PO Box 13033, Karachi-75350, Pakistan.

CONTENTS

page

Acknowledgements xi

Preface xiii

PART I

1. European Traders in India 3
2. The British Conquest of India 9
3. The Great Rebellion of 1857 27

PART II

4. Strangers in India 51
5. The Hindu Community 62
6. The Muslim Community 71
   Sir Syed Ahmed Khan 76
7. The Indian National Congress (The First Twenty Years) 90
   The Complexity of Indian Nationalism 90
   The Foundation of the Indian National Congress 94
   The Indian National Congress (1885-1905) 98
   The Partition of Bengal 109
   Congress Propaganda in England 112
   The Limitations of Congress 113

PART III

8. The Aftermath of the Partition of Bengal 119
   Moderates Versus Extremists 119
   The Morley-Minto Reforms 123
   The Aga Khan Delegation and the Foundation of
   the Muslim League 128
   Mohammad Ali Jinnah, the Early Years 135

page

9. **Hindu-Muslim** *Rapprochement*   **140**
   The Annulment of the Partition of Bengal   140
   Congress and the Muslim League in Harmony   142
   India's Reaction to World War I   148
   Indian Demands (The Lucknow Pact)   157
   The British Response to Indian Demands   165

PART IV

10. **India in a Ferment**   **177**
    The Rowlatt Bills   179
    Mahatma Gandhi   181
    The Rowlatt Agitation and the Outbreak of Violence   201

11. **The Non-Co-operation Movement**   **215**
    The Khilafat Question   215
    Jinnah Breaks with Congress   226
    Non-Co-operation in Action   229
    The Abolition of the Khilafat   237
    The Rise of Hindu-Muslim Tension   238
    Muslim Politics in the Doldrums   239

PART V

12. **Communal Antagonism**   **245**

13. **The Working of the Reforms**   **251**
    The Hindu Mahasabha   257
    The Akali Movement   257
    The Communist Party of India   258

14. **Appointment of the Simon Commission and its**
    Repercussions   **260**
    The Nehru Report   264
    The Calcutta Congress   270
    Lord Irwin's Statement of 31 October 1929   271
    The Lahore Congress   275

page

15. **Appointment of the Simon Commission and its Repercussions (continued)**   **278**
    The Civil Disobedience Movement   278
    The Simon Report and the First Session of the Round
       Table Conference   281
    The Gandhi-Irwin Pact and the Second Session of the
       Round Table Conference   285
    The Resumption of the Civil Disobedience Movement
       and its End   292
    The Third Session of the Round Table Conference   296

16. **The Act of 1935**   **297**
    Response of Congress to the Reforms of 1935   300
    Congress and Provincial Autonomy Under the Act of 1935   306
    Muslim Politics and the Rise of the Muslim League   307
    Toward Pakistan   321

Part VI

17. **World War II**   **333**
    Indian Reaction to International Tension and World War II   334
    The Pakistan Resolution   348
    The German Blitzkrieg and its Repercussions in India   351

18. **The Cripps Mission**   **361**
    The Quit India Movement   378
    The Muslim League and the Quit India Movement   390

19. **Wavell's Initiatives**   **393**
    The Indian National Army   393
    Wavell Succeeds Linlithgow   396
    Gandhi-Wavell Correspondence   398
    Gandhi-Jinnah Negotiations   403
    The Jinnah-Khizar Rift   409
    The Simla Conference   410

20. **The Labour Party Takes Office in the United Kingdom**   **418**
    The Trial of the Indian National Army Officers   419
    Political Ferment in India   422
    The Parliamentary Delegation   422
    Wavell's Appreciation of the Political Sitaution   423

	page
The Cabinet Mission's Negotiations with the Indian Leaders	425
The Cabinet Mission's Proposals of 16 May 1946	435

21. Toward Transfer of Power — **451**
The Interim Government — 451
Mountbatten's Appointment and Attlee's Statement of
    20 February 1947 — 468
Congress Accepts Partition of India — 479
Liaquat's Budget — 482

22. Toward Transfer of Power (continued) — **485**
Mountbatten: The Opening Phase — 485
'Plan Balkan' — 495
Developments in the North-West Frontier Province — 497
Proposal for a United Independent Bengal — 499
Formulation of the New Plan — 499
The Plan of 3 June 1947 — 508
The Constitutional and Legal Formalities of
    Partition and Independence — 513

23. The Transfer of Power — **518**
The Process of Partition — 518
The Partition Committee — 518
The Partition Council — 519
The Arbitral Tribunal — 521
Division of the Armed Forces — 521
Reconstitution of the Interim Government — 525
Compensation to the Services — 527
The International Status of the Two New Dominions — 528
The Governor-Generalships of India and Pakistan — 530
The Radcliffe Boundary Awards — 536
Postscript — 560
The Andaman and Nicobar Islands — 561

Appendices (between pages 562-3)

a) Letter of 23 January 1946 from V. P. Menon to
    George Abell, Private Secretary to the Viceroy.
b) Enclosure to V. P. Menon's letter to George Abell
    of 23 January 1946.

c) Telegram from the Secretary of State for India
   to the Viceroy.
d) Reply from the Viceroy to the Secretary of State.
e) Note of 25 February 1948 from Philip Noel-Baker,
   Secretary of State for Commonwealth Relations,
   to Clement Attlee, Prime Minister of the
   United Kingdom.
f) Note of 28 February 1948 from Noel-Baker to Attlee.

24. **The Integration of the Princely States**   **563**
    Bhopal   576
    Travancore   576
    Dholpur   577
    Rampur   578
    Jodhpur   579
    Junagarh   580
    Hyderabad   581
    Kashmir   584

25. **The Dawn of Freedom**   **609**
    Law and Order   612
    Mountbatten Appraised   625

    Epilogue I   **633**

    Epilogue II   **647**

    Bibliography   **659**

    Index   **671**

ACKNOWLEDGEMENTS

Next only to the two authors, this book owes its completion to Professor Burke's daughter Pamela, who has not only diligently typed the manuscript but has also assisted in research and continuously given useful advice.

The authors are grateful to Mr D. M. Blake of the India Office Library and Records, who was a member of the editorial team responsible for the preparation of the *Transfer of Power* series. He has generously collaborated in the preparation of the treatise from the very beginning and perused the manuscript as it progressed. His continuous suggestions, made in writing as well as in personal discussions, have been most helpful.

Research material on Muslim nationalism is not as abundant as on the Congress and British points of view. The authors are indebted to Syed Sharifuddin Pirzada for making available to them his rich collection of documents on the Pakistan movement and for exchanging views with them on many occasions.

Finally, they wish to thank Mr R. H. Belcher, CMG, a retired member of the Indian Civil Service and a former Deputy High Commissioner for the UK in India, and Professor Burke's daughter Robin, both of whom have read the manuscript and made constructive suggestions.

PREFACE

Why yet another book on the raj in India?

First, it has not yet been sufficiently recognized that the emotional gap separating the British rulers from their subjects made their departure from India only a question of time. In retrospect it seems amazing that so many persons on both sides should ever have believed that the British would hold on to their Indian empire indefinitely. The number of the British in India was too small for them to have been able to form a citizen ruling class after the fashion of their Muslim predecessors. Owing to their natural arrogance as the conquering race, and their habit of segregating themselves from the natives, they remained strangers in India whose ultimate resting place was the distant land from which they had come. The superficiality of their roots in India was vividly demonstrated by the speed with which they were able to pack up their bags in 1947 and quit India for good and all.

Secondly, the existing literature on the subject is largely self-justifying and hero-orientated. Gandhi is praised for 'winning' independence from unwilling hands by the unique method of a non-violent struggle; Jinnah is credited with wresting Pakistan from the Hindus as well as the British by getting the better of them; and Attlee and Mountbatten are lauded for their statesmanship in 'granting' freedom to India. World events and developments inside India, which influenced the conduct of the leaders as well as the course of events, have not received the amount of attention they deserve.

Thirdly, the present seems to be an appropriate juncture at which to examine the nature of British rule in India. One of the authors, Professor S. M. Burke, spent half his life under British rule and has passed the other half in freedom. Hopefully, the former circumstance has given him a direct feel of the subject and the latter has provided time for cooler reflection. He has had the privilege of personally meeting several of the major figures in this book including Gandhi, Jinnah, the Aga Khan, Jawaharlal Nehru, Liaquat Ali Khan, Vallabhbhai Patel, Muhammad Ali, Dr Khan Sahib, Abdul Ghaffar Khan, Muhammad Iqbal, Churchill, Attlee, Cripps, Lord Willingdon and Lord Mountbatten. At the time of partition he was Chairman of the First Elections Petitions Commission of the Punjab, which was

xiv PREFACE

constituted to hear disputes arising out of the 1946 provincial elections
in which the main issue had been whether or not there should be a
Pakistan.

The authors have devoted proportionately greater space to the
crucial transfer of power period because it is the happenings of those
days which call for greater investigation. They have had the privilege
of having free access to the unique archives of the India Office Library
and Records.

The division of labour between the two authors has been that Burke
has done most of the writing and Quraishi has done most of the
research, and they met weekly to evolve the argument presented in
these pages.

In spelling place names such as Sind and Baluchistan, we have
followed *The Imperial Gazetteer of India,* New and Revised edition
published under the authority of the Government of India at Oxford,
The Clarendon Press, 1931.

S. M. Burke
21 August 1994   Salim Al-Din Quraishi

PART I

'It is an old maxim of "divide and rule". But there is a division of labour here. We [Indians] divide and you [British] rule'.

Maulana Muhammad Ali

CHAPTER 1

EUROPEAN TRADERS
IN INDIA

The early sixteenth century did not only witness the foundation of the Mughal dynasty in India, but it also saw the forging of the first link in the chain of events which led to the termination of Mughal supremacy and its replacement by the British Empire. On 22 May 1498 Vasco da Gama completed his discovery of the sea route from Europe to India via the Cape of Good Hope when he landed at Calicut on the Malabar coast. The Portuguese were unable to gain a foothold in Calicut but they took Goa from the Sultan of Bijapur in 1510, sixteen years before Babur occupied Delhi and Agra, following his victory at Panipat. Da Gama declared that he had come to India to seek 'spices and Christians'.

Spices from the East were a necessity in Europe before the invention of refrigeration. They were required to preserve meat and to make it palatable and to mull wine. Though the spice trade had never ceased, the problem of transit through the numerous intervening states had become increasingly difficult after the decline of the Roman Empire in the fifth century and the rise of Islamic power in the seventh. With improvements in shipbuilding and navigational skills, European sailors were able to embark upon voyages for the discovery of a sea route to India. One of these ventures took Christopher Columbus accidentally to America and another brought da Gama successfully to India.

With Goa as the capital of their eastern possessions, the Portuguese established a chain of trading-posts at Socotra and Ormuz (to control the Red Sea and the Persian Gulf), at Diu on the western coast of India, at Colombo in Ceylon, at Malacca (to control the trade routes of the East Indies) and at Macao in China. The East Indies were the main source of spices, especially cloves. The Indian and Ceylonese settlements were a convenient staging post and introduced some spices of their own—such as pepper, cinnamon and cardamom—to the cargo. India was still the main supplier of cotton textiles to the world.

For nearly a hundred years the Portuguese monopolised the traffic in Indian waters. They earned the hatred of the Indian people and princes by levying a toll on all non-Portuguese vessels sailing from Indian ports, including even those carrying pilgrims on the way to Mecca, and by their religious intolerance and zeal to make converts to Catholicism. Hindu temples were forbidden in Goa and the frightful Inquisition was introduced. The overzealous da Gama and his companions readily swallowed the tales that Hindu temples at Calicut were Christian churches and that a (Hindu) Nayar wore a top-knot to denote that he was a Christian.

In a letter written to Abdullah Khan Uzbeg in 1586, Akbar stated that, had circumstances permitted, he would have personally undertaken 'the destruction of the Feringhi infidels' who had 'stretched out the hand of oppression upon the pilgrims to the holy places'

But in the end, the Portuguese position in the east was overwhelmed by two north European Protestant sea-faring peoples, the Dutch and the British. When Portugal became a part of Spain under Philip II in 1580, the Dutch were already in revolt against Spanish rule. The British also became bitter enemies of Philip when he sent the 'Invincible' Armada to conquer their country. After the destruction of the Armada (1588) the Dutch as well as the British felt bold enough to take the offensive and to attack Philip's newly acquired Protuguese possessions, and eventually the Portuguese presence in the East was reduced to insignificance. In India, the Portuguese settlement of Goa lingered on harmlessly till the forces of independent India invaded and occupied it on the midnight of 17-18 December 1961.

However, the Portuguese did leave some permanent traces of their connection with India. First, by intermarrying with local people they contributed a small but distinct community to the population of India known as the Goans. Though principally Indian by blood, the Goans have retained the Catholic religion and a veneer of Portuguese culture. Secondly, the Portuguese introduced from the New World the cultivation of potatoes, maize and tobacco into India. Lastly, they added a surprisingly large number of words to the vocabulary of the Indian languages—for example, the Urdu words *achar* (pickle), *mez* (table), *baramda* (verandah), *almari* (cupboard), *qamiz* (shirt) and *nilam* (auction) are derived from Portuguese.

At least in one respect the Dutch and the British were preferable to the Portuguese. They did not force Christianity upon the natives but concerned themselves mainly with making profits by trade. To the Muslims, in particular, the Dutch and British places of worship caused less offence than the Portuguese churches which had contained images ('idols').

The Dutch were the first to confront the Portuguese in the east. They made the East Indies their principal objective, sailing there for the first time in 1595. Other voyages followed and, despite Portuguese opposition, they established themselves at Batavia (Jakarta), expelled the Portuguese from Ceylon and Malacca, established themselves at the Cape of Good Hope and took Sumatra. In India they ejected the Portuguese from Malabar and acquired trading posts on the Coromandel coast, and also at Chinsura and at Agra, but they continued to concentrate on trade with the East Indies and regarded India as of secondary importance. Their cultural impact, therefore, was deeper and more enduring in the East Indies than in India. They did besiege Goa, but in the end did not bother to conquer it, evidently because they thought the Portuguese already had been rendered sufficiently ineffective.

It was on the last day of the year 1600 that Queen Elizabeth I bestowed a charter upon the British East India Company which granted it a monopoly to trade everywhere to the east of the Cape of Good Hope. At first, the British merchants also tried to establish themselves in the East Indies, but the Dutch had little desire to put up with them. The ensuing rivalry culminated in the massacre of Amboyna (1623), when the Dutch stormed the British post there and slaughtered the occupants. This horrible setback had momentous long-term consequences. The British were compelled to concentrate on the trade with India, which eventually resulted in their succeeding the Mughals as the rulers of India. Wars in Europe, chiefly against France, and sometimes also against England, weakened the Dutch, and in time Britain and France became the main contenders for power in Europe as well as in India.

It was the third voyage commissioned by the East India Company that brought a British ship to the shores of India for the first time. On 24 August 1608 Captain William Hawkins dropped anchor at the mouth of the Tapti river, about fourteen miles below Surat. The British had never conceded the Portuguese claim to a monopoly of the sea trade with the East. They therefore had no hesitation in trading with Surat. Hawkins travelled to the court of Jahangir to obtain formal permission to trade within his dominion but failed in his mission, mainly because the British had not yet demonstrated that they could successfully challenge the supremacy of the Portuguese in the Indian seas. It was only after Captain Thomas Best's victories over a Portuguese squadron off Surat in 1612 that they were granted temporary rights to trade in Surat under a *firman* issued by Prince Khurram (afterwards the Emperor Shah Jahan), Viceroy of Gujarat.

Hawkins had been a servant of the Company, not his King's ambassador. Hoping that a formal treaty between the two monarchs— James I and Jahangir—would expand the Company's trade in the Mughal Empire and win them the active support of the Mughals against the Portuguese, the East India Company successfully petitioned their King to send an ambassador, at their expense, to the court of Jahangir. The appointee, Sir Thomas Roe, resided in India from 1615 but was unable to achieve the desired treaty. However, he did manage to obtain another *firman* from Prince Khurram in 1618 extending the Company's right to trade.

Having taken Ormuz from the Portuguese with Persian help in 1622, the British proceeded to expand their presence on the peninsular coastline of India. A trading post at Masulipatam (1633) was followed by one at Madras on land leased from the local Hindu ruler (1640), and another at Bombay, which Charles II had received in 1660 as a part of his dowry for marrying Catherine of Portugal. Bombay was made available to the Company in 1668 in return for a large loan and the small annual rent of £10 in gold. In 1674 the headquarters of the Company were transferred from Surat to Bombay. Calcutta, in Bengal, was founded in 1690.

During the chairmanship of Sir Josiah Child, who entertained visions of a British dominion in India 'for all time to come', the Company's servants ventured to fight a small war against the Mughals (1687-91) but, with the formidable Aurangzeb on the throne, the Mughals had no difficulty in curbing this ambition. The trouble had originated in differences between the Mughal Viceroy of Bengal and the traders of the Company over customs and other taxes. The British sacked the Mughal town of Hooghly and, at the instigation of Sir Josiah, James II dispatched a naval expedition to conquer Chittagong. The enterprise ended disastrously. On the west coast English pirates seized some pilgrim ships, and it was suspected that the British authorities at Bombay were issuing their own rupees. Under orders from the Mughal Emperor, the British were then expelled both from Bengal and from Surat. In the end, the Company obtained forgiveness on payment of one and a half lakh[1] rupees as a fine and by promising to stop piracies. The Mughal display of leniency was no doubt influenced by the fact that the British controlled the Arabian Sea across which the pilgrim ships had to sail (in 1632 a Portuguese settlement at Hooghly, which practiced piracy and forcible conversions in addition to trade, had been similarly chastised by Shah Jahan: a large number of

---

[1] One lakh equals 100,000.

prisoners were taken to Agra and ignominiously paraded before the Mughal Emperor).

After its humiliation by Aurangzeb, the Company was content to bide its time, and revived its political ambitions only when the Mughal Empire was in the process of disintegration.

In the meantime, the Company's trade prospered. The British purchased from India chiefly cotton yarn and cloth, silks, indigo, salt-petre (for making gunpowder), spices, and sugar, and they sold lead, quicksilver, tin, ivory, tapestries and sundries. The balance of trade was heavily in favour of India and the difference had to be paid in the form of silver bullion. In 1740 imports from India, amounting to £1,795,000, constituted more than ten per cent of the revenue of Britain. A profitable trade with China was also developing. Because of the Company's prosperity, it was said that Sir Josiah in London 'by his great annual presents could command both at Court and in Westminster Hall what he pleased'.

In the decades following Aurangzeb's death, opportunities for political adventure had opened up in India, but before the British could aspire to becoming a continental power instead of remaining simply coastal traders, they had to contend with a major European rival. The French East India Company, founded in 1664 during the reign of Louis XIV, established posts at Pondicherry, Chandernagore and Masulipatam, and on the Malabar coast.

For some decades the English and the French Companies remained at peace with each other, but the eighteenth century was one of frequent conflict between England and France. They were on opposite sides in the War of the Austrian Succession (1740-48), in the Seven Year's War (1756-63) and in the Napoleonic Wars which ended in 1815 when the French were defeated at Waterloo.

It was as part of the larger struggle for power between their two nations that the British and the French fought their wars in India.

The opening rounds in India went to the French. A French fleet captured Madras in 1746 but it was returned under the Peace of Aix-la-Chapelle. Hostilities were renewed when the French and the British supported rival candidates for the Nawabship of the Carnatic and the throne of Hyderabad (the Carnatic was nominally a part of the dominions of the Nizam of Hyderabad). The French at that time were led by Dupleix, who had been appointed Governor of Pondicherry in 1742. He lived in oriental splendour and had not only a shrewd grasp of the power politics of the region, but also the diplomatic skills to manipulate them. He managed to install his nominees in both the disputed positions and, in consequence, the French dominated the scene for some years.

It was a brilliant manoeuvre by Robert Clive in 1751 that transformed the situation. Clive had enlisted as a clerk in the service of the Company but turned out to be a military genius. At that moment, Muhammad Ali, whom the British supported as the Nawab of the Carnatic, was besieged at Trichinopoly by a superior force and was expected to capitulate any day. Instead of following the obvious course of going to Muhammad Ali's relief directly, Clive audaciously marched to Arcot, the capital of the Carnatic, and took it. This had the desired effect. The enemy removed a large number of troops from Trichinopoly to win back Arcot, but Clive held on to the prize against heavy odds. From this point on, the initiative passed to the British. Their candidate was installed as Nawab of the Carnatic, and Dupleix was recalled.

The Anglo-French rivalry in the south yielded certain lessons which were relevant to the future. It became apparent that the soldiers of the native chiefs were no match for the better-drilled and disciplined British soldiers, who also carried superior firearms. Experience had shown that native men too, with proper training and equipment, made good fighting machines. It was learnt further that, in the rivalry for power between Indian chiefs, foreign intervention on a small scale could tip the balance in the desired direction. These lessons were soon to stand Clive in good stead in Bengal, which was to be the next scene of his activities.

CHAPTER 2

THE BRITISH CONQUEST
OF INDIA

The Province of Bengal at that time comprised Bengal, Bihar and a part of Orissa. It was the richest province of the Mughal Empire because of its natural resources and flourishing trade. It was ruled by a Muslim Viceroy (Nawab) who owed nominal allegiance to the Mughal Emperor, but its people were predominantly Hindu and its trade was mostly in the hands of Hindu merchant princes who had close business ties with European merchants.

In 1740, Alivardi Khan appointed himself Viceroy of Bengal by force of arms. Upon Alivardi's death in 1756, he was succeeded by his grandson, Siraj-ud-Daula, a young man of twenty. Before his death Alivardi Khan had ordered the British and the French to desist from fortifying their settlements in preparation for the imminent war between their two countries. He had feared that his territory would become a theatre of war, just as the Carnatic had in the south. The French complied with Alivardi's orders but the British remained evasive. The newly installed Nawab, Siraj-ud-Daula, therefore attacked Calcutta. Most of the British residents managed to escape, but those who were captured were crammed into a small room. It was the month of June and the summer heat was at its worst. Most of the captives perished during the night. The incident is known as the Black Hole of Calcutta (Black Hole being the name for a lock-up where the British confined offenders belonging to their own community). Some British historians later exaggerated the scale of the occurrence. The tragedy did take place though it was caused more by lack of consideration than by deliberate brutality. The correct figures seem to have been sixty-four persons confined and twenty-three dead.

Clive and Admiral Watson easily recovered Calcutta in January 1757 and made peace with the Nawab. Clive also took the French settlement of Chandernagore as a precaution. The future, however, remained uncertain. The Nawab's throne was being contested by members of his own family, and some of the most powerful Hindu merchants also desired his fall. There was also the possibility that the Nawab might ally himself with the French.

Clive did not wait for events to overtake him but moved to take control of the situation himself. He first undermined the Nawab's position by entering into a conspiracy with Mir Jafar, a relation of the Nawab and his commander-in-chief, and with the wealthy Hindu merchants Jagat Seth and Omi Chand. He then defeated the Nawab in the Battle of Plassey on 23 June 1757—the battle was a mere skirmish in which the British lost twenty-two men. The Nawab was later apprehended and executed under the orders of Mir Jafar's son. The Company now assumed the role of kingmakers in Bengal.

During the same period the British were able to foil an attempt by the Dutch to revive their position in India. The Dutch sent an expedition from Batavia but were beaten off. The French too, tried to recover lost ground in the south but were defeated at Wandiwash (1760) and lost Pondicherry.

With rich Bengal at their feet, the British were in a position to enter the contest between the Indian princes and to fill the growing vacuum resulting from the progressive deterioration of Mughal power. First, though, the Company's servants in Bengal proceeded to fill their own pockets with all the loot they could lay their hands on. Their activities took two forms. As kingmakers they made and unmade nawabs, exacting 'presents' from each new incumbent (four nawabs in the eight years after Plassey). Secondly, they indulged in private trade with unbridled rapacity.

When Mir Jafar was enthroned in place of Siraj-ud-Daula, Clive personally received £234,000 in cash and a land grant which brought him an annual income of £30,000. His subordinates were also handsomely paid. Mir Jafar was replaced by Mir Kasim, but when Mir Kasim was dismissed, Mir Jafar was made Nawab again. Jafar this time agreed to pay £300,000 to the Company, £530,000 to the members of the Council and £250,000 to the armed forces.

After his retirement from the Company's service, Clive was accused of extortion, and put forward the following famous defence before a committee of the House of Commons:

A great prince was dependent on my pleasure; an opulent city lay at my mercy; its richest bankers bid against each other for my smiles; I walked through vaults which were thrown open to me alone, piled on either hand with gold and jewels! Mr Chairman, at this moment I stand astonished at my own moderation.

It had always been understood that the Company's servants would supplement their meagre salaries by private internal trade so long as the Company's official monopoly of trade with Europe was not infringed. After installing Mir Jafar as Nawab, the Company's servants claimed exemption from all tolls and taxes, which put the native traders at a ruinous disadvantage. The abuse was carried to such an extreme that 'anyone who could show a pass with an Englishman's signature, could buy, sell or transport without duty, whatever he liked, wherever he liked'. In vain did Mir Kasim complain to the Governor and his council that, 'they, [the Company's servants] forcibly take away the goods and commodities of the peasants, merchants, etc., for a fourth part of their value, and by way of violence and oppression they oblige the peasants to give five rupees for goods which are worth but one rupee...' Unable to change the ways of the British, Mir Kasim exempted his own people also from all trade dues. This was the affront that lost him the throne.

After amassing fortunes in India, the Company's servants returned to England as 'nabobs', lived ostentatiously and could influence the policy of the Company by buying the Company's stock and seats in parliament. One of them, Thomas Pitt, ancestor of two prime ministers of England, laid the foundation of his family's fortune by acquiring the Pitt Diamond during his career in India, first as a merchant and then as Governor of Madras. In general, the 'nabobs' were not accepted by the hereditary landed gentry of England as real aristocrats but were looked down upon as *nouveaux riches*.

Clive left India in 1760 and returned to England. In 1765 he was sent back to check the rampant corruption as a kind of 'poacher turned gamekeeper'. He succeeded to some extent, and after him Warren Hastings went a step further, but the root of the problem was tackled only under Cornwallis, when officers were given adequate salaries. Clive advanced the Company's political status by taking advantage of the situation that had developed during his absence from India.

Mir Kasim, in his continuing hostility to the British, had enlisted the support of Shuja-ud-Daula, the Nawab of Oudh. The Mughal Emperor, Shah Alam, was at that time also under the shelter of the Nawab of Oudh, who constitutionally was his vassal. On 22 October 1764, the combined forces of Mir Kasim, Shuja-ud-Daula and Shah Alam were defeated at Buxar by Major Munro.[1]

---

[1]Prince Ali Gauhar, afterwards the Emperor Shah Alam, had been the heir-apparent of his father, the Emperor Alamgir II. Alamgir's unscrupulous minister, Ghazi-ud-din, had completely dominated the emperor and kept Ali Gauhar under surveillance. After a daring

Continued on the next page

The victory at Buxar enabled Clive to extract concessions for the Company from the Mughal Emperor as well as from the Nawab of Oudh. The Emperor granted the *diwani* (right to collect revenue) of Bengal—which included Bihar and Orissa—in return for an annual tribute of twenty-six lakhs of rupees. Police and judicial functions were left in the hands of the Nawab, but since military control was exercised by the British they became the virtual rulers of Bengal. From the Nawab of Oudh, Clive obtained fifty lakhs of rupees as compensation, and also the districts of Allahabad and Corah which were made over to the Emperor. Clive finally left for England in 1767 and died by his own hand in 1774.

Shah Alam took up residence at Allahabad and no doubt could have passed his life peacefully there, but he longed to get back to Delhi to capture bygone glory. His opportunity came when the Marathas, having occupied Delhi, invited him there to re-occupy the throne of his forefathers. He left Allahabad in May 1771 and in December reached the imperial capital. He had consulted the British and they had advised him not to trust the Marathas. Warren Hastings, who had been appointed Governor of Bengal in 1772, discontinued the tribute of twenty-six lakhs and also made over the districts of Allahabad and Corah to the Nawab of Oudh. These measures where understandable as *realpolitik,* but had no moral or legal justification. They amounted to a repudiation of the Company's vassalage as *diwan* and the annexation of Bengal.

In 1788, Sindia lost control of Delhi. He was defeated by the Rajputs and was forced to retreat to Gwalior. During his absence the Rohilla chief, Ghulam Qadir, occupied Delhi. He treated the royal family brutally and in a fit of rage blinded the Emperor himself. Sindia returned to the north the following year, prevailed over Ghulam Qadir, and tortured him to death by cutting him down limb by limb.

The three Presidencies of Bombay, Madras and Bengal each had a Governor, independent of the other two, who was directly responsible to the Company in London. But the British Parliament had begun to take an interest in the administration in India and decided to change its structure. Although Clive was not impeached, his conduct and that of others who had enriched themselves by doubtful means had stirred public opinion. Moreover, in spite of its great expectations, the Company found itself on

---

escape from Delhi, Ali Gauhar had appeared in the eastern provinces of his father's empire in 1759, hoping to strengthen his position by gaining control over Bengal and Bihar. Upon the assassination of his father caused by Ghazi-ud-din in the same year, he had proclaimed himself Emperor, assuming the title of Shah Alam. After the battle of Buxar, Shah Alam pitched his camp beside that of the British and sought their protection.

the point of bankruptcy and was compelled to solicit a loan from the government. The reason for this was that the manipulations of the Company's servants ensured that its earnings enriched only themselves and their associates at home. So low was the reputation of the Company's employees in India that during the great famine of 1770, in which millions died, 'it was rumoured that the Company's servants had created the famine by engrossing all the rice of the country; that they had sold the grain for eight, ten, twelve times the price at which they had bought it'.

Although the provisions of the Regulating Act of 1773 (which came into force in 1774), did not go far enough to be really effective in curb-   ing abuses, it was important inasmuch as it was the first evidence of Parliament's new concern with the administrative machinery in India, and thus its first step towards governing that country. The Governor of Bengal was elevated to the status of Governor-General and a Supreme Court of Justice was established at Calcutta. The Governor-General was given the authority to 'superintend and control' the Governors of Bombay and Madras but it was not stated how he could enforce his wishes. He was also saddled with a council of four in which he could be out-voted. Hastings' Councillors gave him endless trouble. The state of politics in England also meant that he could not always count upon the desired degree of support from the home government.

These handicaps were particularly unfortunate because the times were difficult. The American War of Independence broke out in 1775, and on 4 July 1776 the American Colonies declared independence and France aligned itself with the Americans. A French fleet, under the dashing Admiral de Suffren, appeared off the coast of India and generally had the better of the British navy in several engagements. But the contest on the whole was indecisive and led to no permanent results. The Governors of Bombay and Madras involved the Company in wars with the Marathas, the Nizam of Hyderabad and Hyder Ali of Mysore. It is a measure of Hastings' tenacity that he not only managed to hold on to the existing territory but enlarged it slightly and left the Company in a much stronger position.

But wars cost money and this caused Hastings to extort large sums from Raja Chet Singh of Benares and from the Begums of Oudh, and to hire out the Company's soldiers for cash to assist the Nawab of Oudh in crushing the Rohillas. Hasting's influence was also seen by the popular mind as being behind the hanging for forgery of Nandakumar, a wealthy Hindu, by the Supreme Court. Nandakumar had been cited as a witness against Hastings by the faction in the Governor-General's Council which accused Hastings of misdeeds.

After his retirement in 1795, Hastings was impeached in Parliament. Although he was finally acquitted, the proceedings dragged on for eight years and ruined him financially. With regard to Nandakumar, it was felt that he had been tried and sentenced by a court of law, and that there was nothing to connect Hastings with the verdict. In other cases it was felt that he had not acted for personal gain but for the good of the state as he saw it during those stressful years.

In the administrative field, Hastings established a Board of Revenue in Bengal and appointed collectors for the districts, thus laying the foundation of the system of revenue collection which eventually evolved in India. He also tried to curb private trade by the Company's servants by abolishing the practice of 'free passes'.

By reason of his respect for the people and their culture, Hastings, in Macaulay's words, 'enjoyed among the natives a popularity such as no other governor has been able to attain'. He was conversant in Persian, Arabic and Bengali and was responsible for the foundation of an Arabic College at Calcutta. He also encouraged Sanskrit studies and enabled Sir William Jones to found the Asiatic Society of Bengal in 1784. He thought of Hindus as a 'gentle and benevolent' people who, though superstitious, 'do not think ill of us for not behaving as they do'. He believed that 'among the natives of India, there are men of as strong intellect, as sound integrity, and as honourable feelings as any of this Kingdom'. He was quick to recognize the soundness of the system of government established by Akbar, and under his patronage Francis Gladwin translated the *Ain-i Akbari* into English because 'it will serve to assist the judgements of the court of directors on many points of importance'.

The impeachment of Warren Hastings had reflected the continuing disquiet prevailing in political circles in England concerning the way in which India was governed, and Pitt's India Act of 1784 was passed to remedy the situation. In India, the Governor-General could now supersede the administrations of Bombay and Madras in time of war and he could override the majority in his own council. In England, the Board of Directors was brought under parliamentary supervision by the setting up of a Board of Control answerable to Parliament. Of the six members of the Board, two were Ministers of the Crown. The official title of the President was 'President of the Board of Commissioners for the Affairs of India'. No dispatch could be sent to India without the sanction of the President. Appointments to the offices of Governor-General, Governor and Commander-in-Chief in India had to be approved by both boards and each could recall an incumbent. The Governor-General could no longer declare war against any Indian Prince without the authority of the directors and it was laid down that 'to pursue schemes of conquest and extension of dominion in India are measures repugnant to the wish, the honour and the policy of this nation'. Time was soon to show how unrealistic these guidelines really were.

Hastings' successor, Sir John Macpherson, held office for twenty months. Then came Lord Cornwallis (1786-93). Cornwallis was a landed aristocrat, much respected for his stoical integrity. He enjoyed Pitt's confidence and his reputation had remained unscathed by his surrender at Yorktown during the American War of Independence. He was sent out to India to inaugurate the cleaner administration envisaged by Pitt's Act, after the much-publicised excesses of the days of Clive and Hastings.

In 1789 Cornwallis was drawn into a war with Tipu Sultan of Mysore when the latter attacked Travancore, which was entitled to British protection under a treaty. Tipu had succeeded to the throne of Mysore upon the death of his father, Hyder Ali, in 1782. Luckily for Cornwallis, Tipu had roused the fears of the Nizam of Hyderabad and the Marathas by his expansionist policies so they joined the British in the fight against him. The war lasted three years and Tipu fought hard but in the end was compelled to surrender half his dominion under the Treaty of Seringapatam, signed on 18 March 1792. The spoils were divided between the three victorious allies. The British received territories covering some 20,000 square miles.

Cornwallis' administrative reforms were far-reaching and the outlines of the governmental machinery drawn by him endured till the end of British rule in India. Having secured higher salaries for the Company's officers, he proceeded vigorously to suppress private trade and other objectionable practices. He set up district courts, from which appeals could be made to the higher courts. The Police and the army were also reorganized. The Company's officers were required to sign covenants when they entered service. Enhanced emoluments, greater security of service, and the challenge to govern what was becoming an empire, not only a market for trade, began to attract a higher type of professional civil servant.

Previously the Company had made use of Indians up to the status of deputy nawab for revenue collection and general administration. Cornwallis believed that 'every native of India' was corrupt, and accordingly reserved all the higher posts in the civil, military, and judicial departments for Europeans. This monopoly became a source of grievance when Indians with Western education began to aspire to a share in the governance of their own country.

Another unfortunate measure introduced by Cornwallis was the Permanent Settlement of Bengal. Influenced, no doubt, by the status of landlords in England, Cornwallis in effect turned *zamindars*, who essentially had been collectors of revenue, into landowners, and the cultivators, who had enjoyed hereditary rights, into tenants-at-will.

Nothing of importance took place during the five-year tenure of the sedate Sir John Shore who succeeded Cornwallis.

It was the French threat in Europe and its possible repercussions in India which caused the British to adopt a 'forward' policy and to strive to regain the custody of Shah Alam. Napoleon Bonaparte, the 'son' of the French Revolution and a military genius of the highest order, conquered Egypt in 1798, and made no secret of his fascination for the east and his ambition to march to India. In India, several French adventurers had been employed by the native rulers to improve the efficiency of their armies. A French general named Perron had obtained from Sindia the position of commandant of the fortress of Delhi, and had thus secured possession of the person of Shah Alam. The formidable Tipu had actually been negotiating for French help against the British. The British feared that the French military officers might overthrow Maratha power and use the authority of the Mughal emperor to further French ambitions in India.

To frustrate French designs in India, the London authorities in 1789 appointed Lord Mornington (better known by his later title of Marquis of Wellesley) as Governor-General. At the age of thirty-seven he was in the prime of life. He was strong-willed, energetic and a deep-dyed imperialist. It was his 'conscientious conviction' that 'no greater blessing' could be 'conferred on the native inhabitants of India than the extension of British authority, influence and power'.

Wellesley decided to eliminate Tipu first, and started by taking advantage of a recent defeat which the Nizam had suffered at the hands of the Marathas, with considerable loss of territory. He concluded a Subsidiary Alliance with the Nizam in 1798, the terms of which became the standard form of relationship between the British and the Indian rulers. The prince was guaranteed protection from external aggression, and was to have no relationship with a foreign power. He was promised non-interference in internal affairs but had to receive troops supplied by the British, for which he had to pay either by surrendering some territory or by cash. In addition, a Resident, representing the paramount power, was stationed in the state.

The Governor-General now ordered an attack on Tipu, who was eventually killed fighting bravely in defence of his capital, Seringapatam (1799). He annexed half of the territory which Tipu still possessed (after it had been halved by Cornwallis) and returned the rest to the scion of the Hindu dynasty which had been dispossessed by Hyder Ali. He deprived the Nawab of the Carnatic of his state on the ground that he had been conspiring with Tipu. He also took possession of Surat and pensioned off its Nawab. Taking advantage of the succession disputes in Tanjore and Arcot, he annexed both those territories as well.

The Nawab of Oudh was compelled to cede more than half of his kingdom on the ground that it was essential for the British to maintain a large subsidiary force to guard against the Afghan threat. This new area, measuring some 30,000 square miles, brought under Company rule the Lower Doab (between the Ganges and the Jumna), Allahabad and the territory along the Ganges and the Gogra right to the neighbourhood of Benares.

Wellesley now felt in a position to confront the Marathas. Taking advantage of the Peshwa's flight after his defeat by Holkar in 1802, Wellesley concluded a Subsidiary Alliance with him. Sindia and Bhonsla of Nagpur were next attacked. The main campaign was led by General (afterwards Lord) Lake, the Commander-in-Chief, and was directed towards taking Delhi; he succeeded in this objective in September 1803, after defeating Sindia's forces commanded by French officers. Shah Alam thus came under British protection once more. In the Deccan, Arthur Wellesley (brother of the Governor-General and himself the future Duke of Wellington) and other commanders won notable victories. Sindia and Bhonsla saw no alternative to accepting British terms and had to part with a considerable part of their territories.

Holkar, who had not entered the contest so far, evidently believed that the British had been exhausted by their long and arduous campaigns and that it was an opportune moment for him to challenge them. He was a redoubtable fighter and at one stage advanced dangerously close to Delhi. It seemed that another strenuous campaign was necessary to subdue him. At this stage Lord Wellesley was recalled and left India in August 1805.

When Shah Alam's grandson, the emperor Bahadur Shah, was tried by the British authorities in 1858 for his role in the Great Rebellion of 1857, it was asserted that 'the kings of Delhi' had become British subjects from 14 September 1803, on which date British troops entered Delhi and Shah Alam had come under British protection, and that Bahadur Shah had traitorously proclaimed himself sovereign of India and had seized Delhi unlawfully. But by no stretch of the imagination, can Shah Alam be said ever to have become a British subject. The mere fact that the British were protecting him did not mean that he was not their overlord, for it is the bounden duty of a vassal to protect his lord. Hitherto this precisely had been the relationship between the Marathas and the Emperor.

The Marathas had acknowledged that constitutionally they were servants of the emperor. The arrangement had been that Shah Alam appointed the Peshwa as his *Vakil-i-Mutlak* (Sole Regent of the Empire) *in absentia,* with Sindia as the working minister with the rank of deputy regent. In fact, Wellesley instructed General Lake to treat 'His Majesty and the Royal family' with such reverence that they 'should immediately experience the benefit' of the change from Maratha to British protection. The promised change for the better could scarcely mean the degradation of the Emperor to the status of a British subject.

Reflecting Wellesley's directions, Lake, in a letter dated 8 August 1803, assured the emperor, 'I am cordially disposed to render your Majesty every demonstration of my loyalty and attachment and I consider it to be a distinguished honour as it is a peculiar happiness to execute your Majesty' commands'. In his *History of the Sepoy War in India* (Vol. II, p. 3) J. W. Kaye rightly observed, 'Even in the depths of his misery and humiliation, he (Shah Alam) was regarded by the most magnificent of English viceroys (Wellesley) as a mighty potentate, whom it was a privilege to protect and sacrilege to think of supplanting'. The British thus gave every indication that they had returned to the Emperor's obedience and that the breach caused by his abandonment of Allahabad for Delhi had been healed.

The Mughal Emperor no longer had the military power to enforce his will, but the aura of the House of Timur still lived in the length and breadth of the country. The nawabs and *subedars* still sought formal sanction of the Emperor on their accession and valued the titles he bestowed upon them; they struck coins in his name; and prayers in mosques were read in his name. The British were not yet strong enough to claim sovereignty on their own account. Such a step might very well have created a platform for the Indian princes to unite against them.

Wellesley had never been on good terms with the Directors of the Company, whom he called 'the cheesemongers of Leadenhall Street'. While he was winning glory, they were suffering deficits instead of reaping profits. England was still engaged in a desperate fight with Napoleon and William Pitt the Younger, who returned to power in 1804, decided that the veteran Lord Cornwallis should replace the youthful Wellesley. A letter dated 30 August 1805 from Cornwallis to Lord Lake indicates the feeling that prevailed at the time in England with regard to the question of expansion of British power in India: 'It is not the opinion only of ministers or of a party, but of all reflecting men of every description, that it is physically impracticable for Great Britain, in addition to all other embarrassments, to maintain so vast and so unwieldy an empire in India, which annually calls for reinforcements of men and for remittances of money, and which yields little other profit except brilliant gazettes'. But Cornwallis died only two months after the commencement of his second term and was succeeded by Sir George Barlow, a civil servant of the Company.

Barlow's brief tenure was marked by a sizeable mutiny by the sepoys at Vellore (1806) in the Madras Presidency. The origin of this outbreak was not far different from the one which started at Meerut in 1857 and grew into the terrible Rebellion of 1857. It is surprising that its lesson should have been lost on the next generation of the Company's officers. The garrison at Vellore comprised 370 Europeans and some 1500 sepoys. At three o'clock one morning the sepoys suddenly attacked the Europeans, who were asleep. Thirteen European officers and eighty-two soldiers were killed and ninety-one wounded by the sepoys, who murdered several other Europeans as well. The survivors held out in the fortress until help arrived from Arcot. Between three and four hundred sepoys were killed, a large number were taken prisoner and the rest absconded. And the cause of the mutiny? Certain regulations which the sepoys saw as a deliberate attempt to deprive them of their caste and make them Christians. They were forbidden to paint the marks of their caste on the forehead or to wear earrings when in uniform, and were ordered to be clean-shaven on the chin. The last straw was the order to wear a headgear with a leather cockade which could be compared to a European hat. This mutiny led to the demotion of Barlow to the governorship of Madras and the appointment of Lord Minto as Governor-General in his place.

Minto's term (1807-13) did not see any expansion of the Company's territories though the country was restive and it was obvious that it was only a question of time before the Company would be involved in wars again. First there were the Pindaris, who were freebooters, the product of the general lawlessness caused by numerous wars. From their lairs in the mountainous areas of central India they emerged to ravage Malwa, Rajputana, Berar and beyond. 'By rapid marches they reached some peaceful region, against which their expedition was intended. Terror and dismay burst at once on the helpless population; villages were seen in flames'. In the north-west Ranjit Singh, Maharaja of the Punjab, having consolidated his rule north of the Sutlej, was poised to strike at the Sikh principalities south of that river. Here Minto scored a diplomatic success by making a treaty with Ranjit Singh in 1809 which fixed the Sutlej as the boundary. The Sikh states south of the river became a protectorate of the British and Ranjit was given a free hand to its north. Holkar was still unsubdued and the Peshwa and Sindia were smarting under their recent humiliation. In the north the frontier with the Gurkhas of Nepal was undefined and these doughty highlanders were descending on the areas to their south. Minto had served notice on the Gurkhas to withdraw from the disputed territory but was recalled soon afterwards, and it was left to his successor Lord Moira (afterwards the Marquis of Hastings) to cope with this and other looming problems.

Apart from tensions within India itself, some external factors also served to create a climate more favourable to the resumption of a forward policy. The menace of Napoleon had receded with his disastrous retreat from Moscow in 1812 and disappeared altogether when he was finally defeated at Waterloo three years later. After Nelson's victories, Britain had become the undisputed mistress of the seas, and the industrial revolution was turning her into a nation of shopkeepers looking for bigger markets. America was not yet industrialised and the European countries had been disorganized by the Napoleonic wars. There was a new mood of optimism in Britain and a strong urge for world-wide free trade. It was believed that trade with India, with its vast size and large population, would yield rich dividends only if the Company's monopoly could be brought to an end and political stability there could be achieved by bringing the whole country under British sway. Consequently, when the Company's charter was renewed in 1813, its monopoly of trade with India was abolished, though it was permitted to continue trading there along with others for another twenty years. However, its monopoly of trade with China (mostly China tea for Indian opium) was continued on the plea that the profits from that source were essential for keeping it solvent at home and enabled it to meet the expenses of its establishment in India.

Hastings (1813-23) was thus able to carry forward the empire-building policies of Clive and Wellesley and made Britain the supreme power in India up to the Sutlej. His first war was against Nepal, where trouble had been brewing since the time of his predecessor. After a hard fight, the Gurkhas were compelled to accept British terms and to cede the province of Kumaon and the Terai (lowlands to the south of Nepal).

These acquisitions included Simla, the future summer capital of British India.

In the meantime the Pindaris had begun to extend their raids into British possessions. When Hastings moved to hunt down those agile predators he called upon the Marathas to join in the operation, but the Marathas, fearing that after eliminating the Pindaris the British would crush them, chose the path of war. In a series of campaigns the British wiped out the Pindaris and also broke the power of the Maratha chiefs, who had failed to unite against the common danger. The Peshwa, Baji Rao, surrendered on 18 June 1818. The office of Peshwa was abolished, his territories were annexed and Baji Rao was pensioned off and permitted to reside at Bithur, on the Ganges near Cawnpore. His adopted son, Nana Sahib, joined the Great Rebellion of 1857 because his late father's pension had been stopped.

During the tenure of Lord Amherst (1823-8), who succeeded the Marquis of Hastings as Governor-General, the most notable event was war with Burma. The Burmese at that time were under the rule of an expansionist regime whose conquests included Assam, which gave them the valley of the Brahmaputra from which they were poised to invade Bengal. So confident of victory was the invading force that it was carrying a set of gold fetters in which the Governor-General was to be taken to Ava. Instead of fighting a defensive war, the British took the offensive and struck at Rangoon by sea and took it on 7 May 1824. From there, they laboriously marched northwards through swamps and jungles suffering heavy casualties, mostly from disease. It was only when they approached Ava that the Burmese sued for peace. Under the treaty signed on 26 February 1826, the Burmese agreed to pay one million pounds as compensation for the war and also handed over Assam, Manipur, and the coastal areas of Arakan and Tenasserim to the victors. Lower Burma was taken by Lord Dalhousie in 1852, following a commercial dispute, and the rest of the country by Lord Dufferin in 1886, as a bulwark against the French in Indo-China.

The fear of losing caste led to another sepoy mutiny during the preparations for the 1824 naval assault on Rangoon. A regiment of sepoys at Barrackpore refused to cross the 'black water'. Some sixty sepoys were shot and a dozen or two were hanged.

Hitherto, the Company had been content to impose political control over its Indian possessions but had as yet not interfered with the socio-religious life of its subjects. Warren Hastings, for one, had actually admired Indian culture and civilization. But quite a new mood dawned under Lord William Bentinck (1828-35).

In his Indian policy, Bentinck reflected the urge for reform prevailing in England at that time. The American and the French Revolutions had spread the philosophy of equality and freedom and the responsibility of governments for the welfare of the people. In Britain, the abolition of the slave trade was followed by other measures, such as the Reform Bill, abolition of slavery in the British colonies, the Factory Act and the New Poor Law. Economics and medicine were entering the modern age. Mechanical inventions and technical achievements were the order of the day. James Watt had invented the steam engine (1769), the semaphore telegraph from Lille to Paris had been constructed (1794), and the Stockton and Darlington Railroad, the world's first railway line, had been opened in England (1825). The spirit of enquiry and adventure was manifesting itself also in hazardous voyages and perilous explorations. Their great achievements were inspiring Europeans with a new spirit of self-confidence—a superiority complex—causing them to assume the 'white man's burden' of having to convey the blessings of their civilization to peoples they deemed backward.

In the enthusiasm of the moment, the British Parliament's Charter Act of 1833 boldly declared that 'no native of India nor any natural-born subject therein, shall by reason only of his religion, place of birth, descent, colour, or any of them, be disabled from holding any place, office or employment under the Company'. Since this reckless promise was never really redeemed it became, in the long run, more of an irritant than a palliative between educated Indians and the British Government.

Besides throwing open the trade with India to everyone, the Act of 1813 had made an annual grant of £10,000 toward education in India. It had further, under pressure from Wilberforce, the champion of freedom for slaves, permitted missionaries to go to India to propagate Christianity. The Christian missionaries were appalled at customs such as caste, female infanticide and *suttee* (self-cremation by Hindu widows on the pyre of their husbands), and became crusaders for social reform in addition to their proselytizing activities.

Bentinck was an ardent admirer of Jeremy Bentham, the philosopher of utilitarianism, which seeks to achieve the greatest happiness of the greatest number, and upon his assignment to India assured his mentor, 'I shall govern in name, but it will be you who will govern in fact'. He forbade the practice of *suttee* (1829) and suppressed the *thugs,* who disguised themselves as travellers and strangled their unwary companions to death, robbing them of their belongings in the name of the goddess Kali.

The horrible custom of child sacrifice in Sangor Island was stopped and measures against infanticide were adopted.

In 1834, English replaced Persian as the official language and the language of the higher courts. In the lower courts, vernaculars replaced Persian. Thomas Babington Maculay, who had arrived in India in 1834 as the Law Member, started the codification of Indian law which completed the process, inaugurated by Cornwallis, of introducing the principles and procedures of English law into India.

Macaulay was also largely responsible for the victory of the 'anglicists' in their long debate with the 'orientalists'. On 7 March 1835, Bentinck announced that 'the great object of the British government ought to be the promotion of European literature and science among the natives of India' and that this would be done through the medium of the English language. It needs to be stated that English was to be the medium of only higher education; in the lower classes, the vernacular was to continue as the medium of teaching.

In his famous minute on education dated 2 February 1835, Macaulay confessed that he had 'no knowledge of either Sanskrit or Arabic'. Nevertheless, he proceeded to aver that he had 'never found one among them [the orientalists] who could deny that a single shelf of a good European library was worth the whole native literature of India and Arabia'. He argued that 'whosoever knows that language [English] has ready access to all the vast intellectual wealth which all the wisest nations of the earth have created and hoarded in the course of ninety generations'. Speaking on the Charter Bill of 1833 in the House of Commons, Macaulay had already made his perceptive prophecy that 'having become instructed in European language, they [the Indians] may, in some future age, demand European institutions' and added that, 'whenever it comes, it will be the proudest day in English history'.

Two events of constitutional significance during Bentinck's time were the annexation of Coorg and the virtual placing of the administration of Mysore under the control of the British Resident. The stated reason in both cases was misgovernment. It was a warning to the Indian princes that the British Government, as the sovereign authority, reserved the right to take extreme measures against them if, in its judgment, circumstances called for them.

Bentinck's immediate successor was a civil servant, Sir Charles Metcalfe, but a tradition was growing that the highest post in India should be held by a distinguished public figure from England, and Lord Auckland was appointed Governor-General in 1836. By this time Russia, in British eyes, had replaced France as the outside danger to the British Empire in India. Turkey had come under Russian influence and in 1833 had agreed to keep the Dardanelles closed to all foreign ships. In 1837 the Persians, backed by Russia, attacked Herat. The East India Company as well as Ranjit Singh felt that it would be expedient at this time to have a friendly ruler in the buffer state of Afghanistan. A tripartite treaty was accordingly signed on 25 July 1838 between the Company, Ranjit Singh and Shah Shuja, who had been ousted from the Amirship of Afghanistan by Dost Muhammad. The idea was to expel Dost Muhammad and retrieve the throne for Shah Shuja.

Ranjit Singh displayed no inclination to join the British in a military invasion of Afghanistan; the British had therefore to proceed alone. Shah Shuja was duly installed as Amir (August 1839) but the British had not yet learnt that the freedom-loving Afghans would not put up with the occupation of their homeland by any foreign troops. In November 1841 the Afghans rose in revolt and compelled the British force to retreat leaving behind some persons, chiefly women and children, as hostages. Only one survivor, Dr Brydon, reached Jalalabad in January 1842. All others fell victim to Afghan guerillas and the terrible highland winter.

It fell to the lot of Lord Ellenborough (1842-44) to retrieve British honour. An invading force rescued the British hostages in Kabul but wisely decided to retreat after saving face. Dost Muhammad again became Amir.

The conquest of Sind by the British, which followed in the wake of the Afghan war, was an act of naked imperialism. Sind had been the base of operations for the British army which had marched to put Shah Shuja on the throne of Kabul. For fear of Sikh interference, the route taken was through the Bolan Pass in Baluchistan. When the Afghan war was over, the British, instead of vacating Sind, mounted a campaign against it and annexed it (1843). It would appear that the chief reason was to restore British prestige and demonstrate that they were still invincible. After the Kabul disaster it was believed that the Muslims of India, whom the British had replaced as the supreme power, might become restive. Elphinstone likened the British assault on Sind to the act of 'a bully who has been kicked in the streets and goes home to beat his wife in revenge'. There was also the desire to use the entire length of the river Indus for trade and to strengthen security against the Afghans and the Sikhs.

Hitherto, the Company had ritually acknowledged allegiance to the Mughal Emperor by offering *nazar* (a present) to him by the hand of the Governor-General or his deputy. In 1843 Ellenborough discontinued this courtesy. Ellenborough's flamboyant manner and his high-handed annexation of Sind were criticised in the British Parliament and Press and he was recalled though only two years of his term had expired.

The next Governor-General, Lord Hardinge (1844-48), was a veteran of Waterloo. The chief event of his regime was the annexation of the Punjab. Ranjit Singh, who had united the Sikhs under his banner and built the Punjab into a powerful state, had died in 1839. He had left behind an army of 90,000, trained by Italian and French officers and possessing powerful artillery. The Sikhs were formidable soldiers but given to internal rivalry and divisions. Intrigues and confusion followed the death of Ranjit Singh. Nominally, the throne was occupied by Dalip Singh, a minor son of Ranjit Singh under the regency of his mother, but the controlling force in the country was the army. As a precaution against any eventualities, Hardinge moved troops to the British side of the Sutlej. The Sikhs, believing that, after Sind, their turn to be conquered had come, took the offensive and crossed the Sutlej (December 1845). After some hard-fought battles the British managed to take Lahore, the capital, on 20 February 1846. Dalip Singh was allowed to retain the major portion of his territory but the administration was to be supervised by a British Resident.

By another arrangement following this First Sikh War, Kashmir was detached from the Punjab by the British and handed over to Raja Gulab Singh of Jammu for the sum of rupees seventy-five lakhs. This sale of a Muslim country to a Hindu ruler sowed the seeds of the Kashmir dispute which erupted between India and Pakistan when the British left the Subcontinent in 1947.

Lord Dalhousie took over as Governor-General on 12 January 1848. At thirty-five years of age he was in the prime of life and he ruled India for eight years. He had already served as vice-president and president of the Board of Trade in Peel's cabinet. A great believer in the superiority of Western civilization, he strove to spread its benefits by bringing under British rule all the territory he could. His annexations totalled nearly twice the area of England and Wales and more than twice the area acquired by any other Governor-General.

The murder of two British officers during an uprising in Multan and disturbances elsewhere developed into the Second Sikh War. Again, the Sikhs gave a good account of themselves in the fighting but were decisively defeated at Chilianwala and Gujrat on 13 January and 21 February 1849 respectively. Dalhousie annexed the Sikh kingdom by proclamation on 29 March 1849. His critics have pointed out that, at the time of the rebellion, the administration was under the control of the

British and Maharaja Dalip Singh was a helpless minor under their guardianship. It was hardly just to deprive him of his throne.

After another war, Dalhousie took Lower Burma by proclamation on 19 December 1852. Under the already known excuse of misgovernment, the masterful Governor-General deposed the Nawab of Oudh, the last Muslim ruler of any consequence, and took the state. He invented the Doctrine of Lapse under which, if an Indian prince died without a direct heir, the succession lapsed to the British as the supreme power. In this way Satara, Jhansi, Nagpur and some minor states were taken. When the Maratha Peshwa died in 1851, Dalhousie disallowed the continuation of his pension to his adopted son Nana Sahib. He also reduced the status of some other princes. The rulers of the Carnatic and Tanjore had lost their territories to Wellesley but had been allowed to retain the rank of Nawab and Raja respectively. Upon the deaths of the incumbents, Dalhousie abolished these titular sovereignties. He also obtained an agreement from Prince Fakhr-ud-Din, the heir apparent of Bahadur Shah II, that though he would be recognized as king upon his father's death, he would leave the palace-fortress of Delhi and take up residence at Qutb some miles away. After Fakhr-ud-Din's death in 1856, Canning, the new Governor-General, not only confirmed the decision to remove the royal family from Delhi, but went further and decided that on Bahadur Shah's demise his eldest surviving son, Muhammad Quresh, would be recognized as the head of the family but instead of the title of king, he should be designated and have the title of *shahzada*.

Dalhousie was equally zealous in bringing to India the advantages of western education and technological advances. Road-building and canal irrigation programmes were undertaken, the first railway line was opened (1853), a telegraph line up to Delhi was installed, and a cheap postal service was inaugurated. The system of western education was invigorated by the foundation of three universities and the famous Engineering College at Roorkee. Dalhousie was succeeded by Lord Canning (1856-62).

CHAPTER 3

THE GREAT REBELLION
OF 1857

'The Great Mutiny' was much more than a revolt of the sepoys against their British officers, though the fuse that caused the wide conflagration was lit by units of the Bengal army stationed at Meerut. The Bombay and the Madras Armies for the most part remained loyal to the British.

At the time of the outbreak, the Bengal army comprised 128,000 'Hindustani' sepoys and 23,000 Europeans. Some 40,000 sepoys hailed from Oudh, which until 1856 was a feudatory state, and the rest were mostly from the North-Western Provinces (later the United Provinces). They were mainly high-caste Hindus—Brahmins and Rājputs—and Muslims. The responsibilities of the Bengal army covered the area from Calcutta to the north-western frontier of India. The European element in the Indian army had been depleted by wars in Iran and the Crimea, and the ratio was now seven and a half sepoys to one European.

There had been trouble in the ranks of the sepoys several times before. Of the main incidents, the mutinies at Vellore and Barrackpore have already been described. Subsequently, there had been disaffection during the First Afghan War and after the conquest of Sind. When ordered to march to Afghanistan, the Hindu sepoys thought they had lost face by having to cross the Indus and go outside India, while the Muslims were resentful at having to fight fellow Muslims. A Muslim *subedar* was shot and a Hindu *subedar* was dismissed for giving voice to these sentiments. With regard to Sind, the grievance resulted from the fact that during the Afghan War the sepoys had been paid a special allowance (*batta*) for crossing the Indus, but after the conquest of Sind their claim to *batta* was disallowed on the grounds that Sind was no longer a foreign country but a province of British India. The sepoys argued that they still had to cross the Indus. On pay day, the 64th Regiment threw stones at their officers and assaulted them. Thirty-nine ringleaders were apprehended of whom six were executed and the rest imprisoned. Another regiment, the 34th, was disbanded for refusing to march to Sind.

Between the sepoys and their British officers there existed an emotional gulf. The former were mercenaries without a tradition of permanent loyalty to anyone. Their officers belonged to a different religion which permitted the consumption of pork and beef, and they belonged to a different race, spoke a foreign language, and belonged to a totally different culture. The sepoys knew they could never rise to be officers and could see that their salaries and standard of living were lower than those of the European soldiers. Such loyalty as existed between them and their officers was founded on personal trust and respect and could be shaken by the transfer of an officer, a lack of tact on the part an officer, or real or imagined grievances of various kinds.

After the British conquest of the Punjab, the sepoys' pride reached new heights. They boasted that they had enabled the British to conquer India from Burma to Kabul. It was the wrong time for any thoughtless regulations to be introduced, but this is precisely what happened. First came the General Service Enlistment Act in 1856, decreeing that all recruits must swear that they would be willing to cross the sea if so required. Then followed the issue of the Enfield Rifle in January 1857. The cartridges for this rifle were greased with tallow containing cow and pig fat and had to be bitten to pour out the powder. Asking the sepoys to use such ammunition was an act of amazing carelessness because it was universally known that the cow is sacred to the Hindu and the pig impure to the Muslim. The mistake was hastily rectified: on 27 January 1857 it was ordered that the offending cartridges were to be used only by the British soldiers and the cartridges for the sepoys would be greased with a vegetable lubricant. But it was too late. The sepoys were convinced that yet another blatant attempt had been made to deprive them of their religion so that they would have no option but to turn Christian. This was not surprising because, as will be explained, the fear that the British Government was endeavouring in all possible ways to convert everyone in India to Christianity was widespread.

On 26 February the 19th Native Infantry at Berhampore refused to take delivery of their percussion caps and on 29 March a sepoy of the 34th Native Infantry at Barrackpore openly incited mutiny. He was executed and both regiments were disbanded. Soon the entire Bengal army was in a state of turmoil, but it was the mutiny of the sepoys at Meerut, forty miles from Delhi, which developed into the Great Rebellion. On 24 April eighty-five sepoys of the Third Cavalry refused to touch the cartridges under the mistaken belief that they still contained the objectionable grease, and rejected the assurance that this was not so. They were sentenced to long terms of imprisonment by a court martial. On 9 May they were brought to the parade ground and subjected to the disgrace of being publicly fettered like ordinary felons. This proved to be the straw that broke the camel's back. On the following day, which happened to be a Sunday, the comrades of the imprisoned sepoys rose in revolt, released their friends as well as all the other prisoners from the jail and, along with the roughs of the town, killed all the Europeans they could find, including women and children. Then they marched to Delhi, arriving on the morning of 11 May, and proclaimed the eighty-two year old Bahadur Shah Emperor of India. At his subsequent trial for treason Bahadur Shah pleaded, and his defence seems plausible, that 'I did whatsoever they required, otherwise they would immediately have killed me.'

The capture of Delhi by the rebels had been made easy by the fact that no European soldiers were stationed there at the time. The sepoys at Delhi killed their European officers and welcomed their comrades from Meerut. Those European men, women and children who failed to escape were savagely slaughtered.

That the sepoys had first overcome the European officers and men at Meerut and then taken the imperial city of Delhi so easily had an electrifying effect on the minds of anti-British elements in the country and started the process of turning the sepoy mutiny into a general rebellion. Meerut at that time had, proportionately, more European soldiers than anywhere else in India—1700 Europeans to 2700 Indians—and the Europeans controlled the guns and had a battalion of riflemen (the sepoys had only muskets). Yet not only did the Europeans fail to put up a fight at Meerut, they also made no attempt to pursue the sepoys and intercept their march to Delhi.

Though it was the sepoys who had taken the plunge, they were by no means the only part of the population seething with discontent. The sepoys dared to be the first because they had arms and were an organized body capable of joint action. 'It is evident', wrote Karl Marx, 'that the allegiance of the Indian people rests on the fidelity of the native army, in creating which the British rule simultaneously organized the first general centre of resistance which the Indian people was ever possessed of'.

Perhaps the greatest apprehension of all in the minds of the Indians, whether Hindu or Muslim, was that their religion was in danger. Once this suspicion was born, there was hardly any move of the British government that was not seen as a part of the design to convert the people to Christianity. It was not uncommon to think that the main reason why the British wished to conquer the whole of India was that it would make it easier for them to convert the people to their faith.

The abolition of *suttee* and the Hindu Widow's Remarriage Act of 1856 were regarded as violations of the Hindu religion. Attacks on the purity of caste were seen in the regulation requiring the sepoys to cross the sea in ships where they would be huddled with non-caste people, in the common eating arrangements in jails, and in railway travel where the high had to rub shoulders with the low. Railways not pulled by any animals and telegraph wires mysteriously transmitting messages over long distances were seen as the work of the devil.

Lord Dalhousie's Emancipation Act (1850), which laid down that no one would be deprived of his inheritance on account of a change of religion, deeply alarmed the Hindus. Under Hindu law, succession to property was linked with the duty of performing religious rites for the salvation of the deceased's soul. This ceremony could not be performed by a non-Hindu. The new law meant that even during his lifetime a Hindu could no longer disinherit a child who had abandoned his ancestral faith.

European missionaries were regarded with special suspicion. Some high officials openly assisted them. 'Many covenanted officers and many military men', complained Sir Syed Ahmed Khan, 'have been in the habit of talking to their subordinates about religion; some of them would bid their servants come to their houses and listen to the preaching of missionaries, and thus it happened that in the course of time no man felt sure that his creed would last even his own lifetime.' Lt. Col. Wheeler, Commanding Officer of a sepoy regiment at Barrackpore, for instance, was known to have distributed religious material among the sepoys and to have invited them to his bungalow with a view to convert them. It was thought that the missionaries would not have dared to condemn customs such as purdah without the encouragement of the government.

Western education, especially the teaching of English, was also suspect, and with good reason. The belief that western education would make the Indians recognize the superiority of Christianity was not confined to the missionaries. Even Macaulay, in a letter to his father, ventured to predict that 'if our plans of education are followed up, there will not be a single idolator among the respectable classes in Bengal thirty years hence and this will be effected without efforts to proselytize'. Female education was repugnant to orthodox Hindus as well as to Muslims. The former suffered from the superstition that an educated woman was destined to become a widow and believed that sending girls to educational institutions would interfere with the custom of early marriage. The Muslims believed that attendance at schools would lead to discarding the veil.

Sanskrit, the sacred language of the Hindus, and Arabic, the sacred language of the Muslims, were being superseded by English, which had also replaced Presian as the court and cultural language of India. Muslim *madrassas* had always made religious instruction a necessary part of the curriculum, but western education was biased in favour of Christian values, and in missionary schools the principles of Christianity were openly taught. Some high officials visited the schools and encouraged people to enrol in them.

It is not surprising that brahmins and *maulvis* were amongst the bitterest enemies of British rule. Their religions were in danger, and their own centuries-old pre-eminence in the community was threatened. For the *maulvis,* the fact that a Christian power had extinguished a Muslim Empire and taken its place was galling in the extreme. They believed that India had become *dar-ul-harb* (literally the abode of strife, denoting a territory not governed by Muslim laws, i.e., not having a Muslim government) since the battle of Plassey, when the British defeated the Muslim Nawab of Bengal and virtually became the rulers of that principality. According to them, it was sufficient that the infidel rulers were now possessed of the power to interfere with the religious observances of their Muslim subjects; whether they did interfere or not was immaterial. It was, therefore, incumbent upon the Muslims to wage a holy war (jihad) against the British to reconvert the country into *dar-ul-Islam* (literally the abode of peace, meaning a territory where Muslim laws prevail, i.e., having a Muslim government). The efforts of Hindu and Muslim religious leaders helped to win popular support for the rebellion.

Dalhousie's annexation of Oudh on the charge of misgovernment created nervousness among princes of all denominations and his denial of the right of adoption was a clear violation of an ancient right exercised by all Hindus, whether princes or commoners. A Hindu must have a son to perform the obsequies without which his soul would be condemned to perdition.

Two victims of Dalhousie's Doctrine of Lapse became the most prominent leaders of the rebellion. These were Lakshmi Bai, the Rani of Jhansi, and Nana Sahib, the adopted son of the last Peshwa, Baji Rao. The Rani's grievance was that Dalhousie had disallowed the adoption made by her husband and had annexed the state, and Nana Sahib was angry because Dalhousie had refused to pay him the pension which his father had received. His contention was that since the annuity had been granted to the late Peshwa in lieu of territories ceded by him in perpetuity, the pension was also due to the Peshwa and his successors for the same duration.

Land reforms, first in the North-West Provinces and then in Oudh, had proceeded on the assumption that it would be to the benefit of the exploited peasant as well as the state if the cultivator was brought into a direct relationship with the government and restored to his rightful status as a freeholder. This policy dispossessed many *talukdars* and landlords who were regarded as parasitic middlemen. The laws resulting in the resumption of lands which were held free of land revenue were, according to Sir Syed Ahmed Khan, 'most obnoxious' and 'nothing disgusted the natives of this country more with the English Government than this resumption of revenue-free lands...Many lands which had been held revenue free for centuries were suddenly resumed on the flimsiest pretexts'. When the rebellion broke out, the *talukdars* of Oudh forcibly resumed possession of the lands they had recently lost and defended them with the help of their armed retainers. In fact the members of the aristocracy as a whole were a highly resentful segment of society. No longer could their ability and ambition find a satisfying outlet in the higher ranks of the civil and military services of the country. All important government positions were now monopolised by the foreign rulers. This situation was especially humiliating for the Muslims, who had been the privileged community for several centuries before the arrival of the British.

A declaration issued on 25 August 1858 by the insurgents who had captured Azamgarh, a town sixty miles from Benares, makes an overall assessment of the situation. Though it purports to be the proclamation of the Emperor Bahadur Shah, it must be treated as a statement representing the mutineers' own point of view and thus of special significance:

> The people of Hindostan, both Hindoos and Mohammedans, are being ruined under the tyranny and oppression of the infidel and treacherous English...the British Government in making zamindary settlements have imposed exorbitant jumas, and have disgraced and ruined several zamindars, by putting up their estates to public auction for arrears of rent, in so much, that on the institution of a suit by a common Ryot, a maid servant, or a slave, the respectable zamindars are summoned into court, arrested, put in gaol and disgraced...the British Government have monopolized the trade of all fine and valuable merchandise, such as indigo, cloth and other articles of shipping, leaving only the trade of trifles to the people...under the British Government, natives employed in the civil and military service, have little respect, low pay, and no manner of influence...the Europeans, by the introduction of English articles into India, have thrown the weavers, the cotton dressers, the carpenters, the blacksmiths, and the shoemakers, &c., out of employ...The pundits and fakirs being the guardians of the Hindoo and Muhammedan religions respectively,

and the Europeans being the enemies of both the religions, and as at present a war is ranging against the English on account of religion, the pundits and fakirs are bound to present themselves to me, and take their share in the holy war...

In Oudh the rebellion was more pervasive than anywhere else. Resentment there was fresh because the Nawab had been deposed only a year before and his disbanded army readily entered the fray. A large part of the Bengal Army came from Oudh and its members were able to excite sympathy for their cause.

Once it was seen that the sepoys, the main prop of the foreign government, had begun to crumble, all sorts of adventurers—disbanded soldiers of deposed princes, freebooters, thugs, prisoners released by the rebels and other bad characters—took a hand in the game. Some people who normally would have remained loyal or neutral came down off the fence just to be on what they perceived to be the winning side. The government treasuries at district and sub-district headquarters, full of silver rupees and guarded by the sepoys themselves, presented irresistible and easy targets.

After the fall of Delhi a series of mutinies took place elsewhere—at Cawnpore on 4 June and at Jhansi and Allahabad on 7 June, for example. At Lucknow, the capital of Oudh, the British barricaded themselves in the Residency and heroically defended it against overwhelming odds until relieved in March 1858. At the height of the rebellion, British control was totally lost in Hindustan, i.e., in the North-West Provinces, Oudh and Bihar.

Since the deposed Nawab of Oudh was in Calcutta, his cause at Lucknow was taken up by his wife who proclaimed their minor son Nawab on 7 July. At Cawnpore the leadership was assumed by Nana Sahib who had been in residence at Bithur a few miles away; he was proclaimed Peshwa on 30 June. At Jhansi, the Rani took up the cudgels on behalf of her minor son. Numerous other persons declared themselves either independent rulers or feudatories of the Mughal Emperor. Nana Sahib and the Rani of Jhansi pleaded afterwards that they joined the mutineers because the sepoys would have turned against them if they had refused to do so.

Everyone regarded Delhi and Lucknow as the crucial cities and Nana Sahib and the Rani of Jhansi as the leaders most likely to prevail against the British. Once the fate of these cities and these leaders had been decided in favour of the British the rebellion became a lost cause.

British troops from Simla and Meerut marched jointly to Delhi in the early part of June (1857) and carried the Ridge by assault. They dug themselves in at that vantage-point and held on for the months of June, July and August against vastly superior numbers. Strengthened by instalments of supplies and reinforcements from the Punjab, they stormed and carried the city on 20 September. On 21 September Bahadur Shah surrendered to Captain Hodson and after a trial was deported to Rangoon where he died in 1862.[1] Bahadur Shah seems to have been a harmless old man more interested in sufism and composing Urdu poetry than in affairs of state, and enjoyed considerable personal respect because of his piety and his descent from the Great Mughals.

Sir Henry Lawrence, the Chief Commissioner, had gathered in the Lucknow Residency British soldiers, civilians, women and children and those sepoys who had remained loyal. The effective defenders—British men and sepoys—numbered about 1,700. They were surrounded by six thousand rebel sepoys who were continuously reinforced by *talukdars* and their armed followers till the total strength rose to a hundred thousand or more. The Residency consisted of a main building and several other residences and buildings. It was protected on one side by the river Gumti and on the other sides by mud walls and trenches. The defenders held their ground and were reinforced on 25 September, but the newly arrived force and the original garrison, even together, did not feel strong enough to take the offensive and remained besieged. At last a force, about 50,000 strong, marched to Lucknow in March (1858) and advanced step by step against stiff resistence. The last post of the mutineers fell on 19 March and British control over Lucknow was firmly established once more. Among the losses during the ordeal was Henry Lawrence himself, who was wounded on 2 July and died two days later.

Another siege heroically resisted by the British was that of Agra fort, where the Lieutenant-Governor and a large number of men, women and children took shelter in the early part of July 1857 and remained in safety until the storm blew over.

Nana Sahib is better known for being responsible for the savage murder of the English men, women and children at Cawnpore than for any prowess on the battlefield. He was roundly defeated by General Havelock in a battle outside Cawnpore on 16 July. He managed to escape with his life and henceforth it was his resourceful righthand man, Tantia Topi, who carried on the fight in his name. Tantia Topi

---

[1] For a fuller account of the last phase of the Mughal Empire in India, *see*, S. M. Burke and Salim Al-Din Quraishi, *Bahadur Shah the Last Mughal Empror of India* (forthcoming).

was defeated by the British more than once and failed to take Cawnpore. Chased by the British troops, Nana Sahib and the Begum of Oudh ultimately took shelter in Nepal.

Of the rebel leaders, the ablest and the most valiant was the Rani of Jhansi. Sir Hugh Rose, against whom she had fought, acknowledged that she was 'the best and bravest military leader of the rebels'. She appealed to Tantia Topi for help and he marched toward Jhansi with a large force, but he was routed by Sir High Rose near Jhansi on 1 April (1858) and on 3 April, Rose took the city. The Rani escaped.

The Rani and Tantia now joined forces and conceived the daring plan of seizing Gwalior, the seat of the Sindia, who was loyal to the British. They reached Gwalior on 30 May. On 1 June, when the Sindia marched out to fight them, his army refused to fight. He fled to Agra and the Rani and Tantia took Gwalior. This exploit created a sensation but Sir Hugh Rose promptly invested Gwalior and retrieved the loss. Clad as a man, the Rani personally led her troops to battle and died fighting valiantly outside Gwalior (17 June). Tantia fled the scene and on 20 June the British took the fort of Gwalior and restored the Sindia to the throne.

This important setback was the beginning of the end of the rebellion. There was no longer any concerted resistance to British arms. The mopping up took a long time because the British were not fighting a central command against whom a pitched battle or two would have decided the issue. They were putting down numerous small revolts and were opposed by elusive bands of irregular fighters, some of whom concealed themselves in the jungles. Tantia waged guerilla warfare for several months but was eventually captured. He was publicly hanged on 18 April 1859.

Though control was not effectively established everywhere until the end of 1859, the Great Rebellion may be taken to have ended officially on 2 August 1858, when Queen Victoria signed the Act which transferred the responsibility for ruling India from the East India Company to the Crown.

Of the causes of the failure of the rebellion, the most important was the disunity of the Indian people. From the very first steps of the British conquest of India, far more Indians than Englishmen had fought on the side of the British. The British had defeated the Gurkhas and the Sikhs with the help of Hindustani sepoys, and during the rebellion of 1857 they were helped by the Gurkhas and the Sikhs to subdue the Hindustanis; nor had the Indian princes scrupled to side with the British, even against princes of their own denomination.

No Indian prince of any consequence made common cause with the rebels in 1857. Most princes, including the Nizam of Hyderabad, held their peace, while several visibly leaned toward the British. To the latter category belong the Sikh rulers of East Punjab, Sindia of Gwalior, Holkar of Indore and the Raja of Jodhpur. Even in the area most affected by the upheaval, some chiefs, including the Nawab of Rampur, remained loyal to the British. Dost Muhammad of Kabul carefully watched the struggle but stood on the sidelines. The Sikh rulers of East Punjab not only rendered positive help to the British, but also made it possible for reinforcements from the Punjab and the tribal areas to flow smoothly to Delhi. To assist in the re-conquest of Delhi the Raja of Jindh personally led his contingent, and the ruler of Kashmir sent 2,200 men and four guns.

Territorially, the British lost control over no more than about one-fourth of their Indian Empire. Only the swathe from Patna to Delhi went up in flames.

To call the insurrection of 1857 a War of Independence, as some Indian nationalists of the twentieth century have done, is manifestly absurd. Had it been a truly national revolt the British would certainly have been thrown out of the country. It would have been impossible for them to bring reinforcements to the crucial points over long distances.

In 1857 there was no Indian nation and consequently no country-wide feeling of nationalism. The recipients of western education, who later became the standard-bearers of Indian nationalism, were, at this stage, tiny in number, without an organization of their own to given them weight, and too full of admiration for the blessings of British rule to oppose it. Amongst the people of India the Muslims, the Marathas and the Sikhs can be said to have had some rudiments of nationalism. The Muslims had two reasons: firstly, their religion required them to form a brotherhood of the faithful, and secondly, they were a minority in the land of the Hindus, which instilled a feeling of communal solidarity in them. Among the Marathas and the Sikhs, their bitter conflict with the Mughals had generated a religious, racial and territorial cohesion within their respective communities. But there was no feeling of an all-India unity. The Sikhs and the Marathas would certainly not have welcomed the revival of Mughal rule under Bahadur Shah. Nana Sahib and the Rani of Jhansi were not fighting for the freedom of the whole of India but for the restoration of the dynastic rights they had lost. The rebels were not fighting for a common cause, they were only fighting a common enemy.

Though there was no Indian nationalism at the time of the rebellion, an event of such magnitude and emotional intensity could not but influence future developments. The horrible atrocities, committed first by the sepoys and local ruffians and then by the British, both of which will soon be described, left permanent scars on the minds of the British as well as the Indians. Hatred of foreign domination has been the cause of the birth of nationalism in many lands. The traumatic events of 1857 may thus have assisted the birth of nationalism in India. In India, though, matters are always complicated by religious diversity. Hindus and Muslims had risen against the British in the defence of their own respective religions. It was, therefore, a Hindu nationalism and a Muslim nationalism toward which the upheaval of 1857 contributed. The rebellion also provided inspiration for the Indian freedom fighters of the twentieth century. They drew strength from the fact that Hindus and Muslims had made common cause against the British and had nearly succeeded in expelling them from their motherland.

Lack of unity among the rebels was not, however, the only cause of their failure. The sepoys had no professional military leaders to match the British generals. They had no central command nor an overall strategy. In the entire course of the rebellion, the losses in terms of British soldiers amounted only to 586 killed in battle or dead as the result of wounds received.

The mutineers succeeded in creating chaos but did not possess the capacity to restore order even in the short term, let alone to make plans for an orderly administration in the future. In the general disorder looting was common and old scores were freely settled. A favourite target was the money-lenders, who were robbed of their money and whose books were burnt to destroy evidence of debt. The mutineers did not hesitate to join the free-for-all and enrich themselves as best as they could. Bahadur Shah's queen, Zinat Mahal, complained that the sepoys who had come to Delhi from Meerut were as ready to rob her as anyone else. She said that the mutineers robbed the palace and that her own jewels were saved only because they had been buried.

Of course, the insurgents were not following any well-laid plans, and the conspiracy theory advanced by some writers has no reliable basis. Had it been otherwise, there would have been a designated military commander, a fixed date on which the rising would have taken place everywhere instead of occurring piecemeal at different places on different dates, and the rebels would not have chosen to fire the first shots at Meerut, where the British military presence, as compared to that of the sepoys, was the strongest in the whole of India. In a recently discovered letter bearing the date 14 December 1869, Sir Syed Ahmed Khan wrote to Sir John William Kaye, the historian of the mutiny, that, had the Meerut sepoys been given the option of resigning instead of being so severely punished for refusing to bite the new cartridges, they would 'undoubtedly have peaceably withdrawn themselves from the Company's service'.

There certainly was communication between the various units of the Bengal Army, especially after the rumour regarding the greased cartridges had spread in January 1857 and trouble had broken out at Barrackpore on 29 March. However, the subject was greased cartridges, not a general all-India revolt. A relay system was employed to spread the word with speed: a man would hand over a lotus flower to a senior member of a sepoy regiment, it would be passed from hand to hand to all the members of the regiment and then sent off to the next station where the same process was repeated. This happened in every regiment of the Bengal army, but there is no suggestion that the lotus flower was distributed to anyone outside the Bengal army.

The civil counterpart of the circulation of the lotus flower was the passing of *chapatis* (flat wheaten bread) from village to village over a large part of the country early in 1857. Contemporary British administrators suspected that someone who wished to foment a rebellion had adopted this seemingly innocent device to spread his message, but none of them could say what the message was and who was behind the whole thing.

Some British writers have underrated the significance of the Great Rebellion by calling it a mutiny of sepoys against their officers, while others have held that its psychological effect has been over-stated. This is due to a natural desire to show that the British occupation of India was not as widely resented by the population at large as latter-day Indian nationalists have alleged. Moreover, it is always easier for the winning side to subscribe to the noble doctrine of forgive and forget. On the Indian mind, the sanguinary days of 1857-8 left behind a lasting and humiliating wound.

To be able to comprehend the unforgettable depths of savagery to which both sides sank, it is essential to describe at least some of the atrocities that were perpetrated. Of course, instances of mercy toward the British were not lacking. Some officers were permitted to leave unmolested, others were escorted to safety. Many Indians risked their own lives by providing succour and safety to fleeing English women and children. Also there was only one proven case of an English woman having been violated—Miss Wheeler, the Eurasian daughter of General Wheeler, was abducted by a sepoy from Cawnpore to be his wife or mistress. But the pervading atmosphere was one of unspeakable murder and rapine.

The indiscriminate slaughter of European men, women and children by the Indians at Meerut and Delhi has already been mentioned. At Jhansi some officers were killed or injured when trouble broke out. The remaining Europeans took shelter in a fort outside the town. They were lured out of it by the mutineers with the promise that they would not be harmed provided they left the fort unarmed. However, immediately upon exposing themselves, they were herded into a garden and slaughtered in cold blood. Horrible atrocities took place at Allahabad and Bareilly as well. An eyewitness to what happened at Allahabad wrote: 'A gang of upwards of two dozen sepoys...cut into two an infant boy of two or three years of age, while playing about his mother; next they hacked into pieces the lady and while she lay crying out of agonizing pain for safety...felled, most shockingly and horribly, the husband'.

Cawnpore earned especial notoriety for being the scene first of depraved brutality by the Indians and then by the avenging Britons. The British garrison there surrendered on receiving a written assurance from Nana Sahib that boats and food would be provided for their safe passage to Allahabad by river, but as soon as they had got into the boats they were attacked (27 June 1857). Most of them were killed, others were captured. Only four escaped. An even more gruesome massacre took place in July in a building called Bibighar. The prisoners in Bibighar consisted of the survivors of the riverside tragedy plus others who had come to Cawnpore to seek safety. On 15 July the Nana, hearing that General Havelock was approaching Cawnpore, had the four or five male prisoners killed in his presence and ordered the massacre of the women and children in Bibigarh. The sepoys, who were ordered to carry out the deadly assignment, shrank from the task. Thereupon, some butchers went into the building and mercilessly slashed the hapless inmates with long knives. On the following day they returned to the scene accompanied by a few sweepers. The latter began to throw the dead, as well as some women who were still alive, into a nearby well. Three little boys aged between five and seven, who were evidently unhurt, could do nothing but run round the well. They were caught and thrown into the well like the others.

On 17 July, General Havelock captured Cawnpore. A few days later he left for Lucknow, leaving General Neill in charge at Cawnpore. How Neill avenged the massacre of Bibigarh is best related in his own words:

Whenever a rebel is caught he is immediately tried and, unless he can prove a defence, he is sentenced to be hanged at once; but the chief rebels or ringleaders, I make first clean up a certain portion of the pool of blood, still two inches deep, in the shed where the fearful murder and mutilation of women and children took place. To touch blood is most abhorrent to the high-caste natives;

they think, by doing so, they doom their souls to perdition. Let them think so. My object is to inflict a fearful punishment for a revolting, cowardly, barbarous deed, and to strike terror into these rebels. The first I caught was a subahdar, or native officer—a high-cast Brahmin, who tried to resist my order to clean up the very blood he had helped to shed but I made the provost-marshall do his duty and a few lashes soon made the miscreant accomplish his task. When done, he was taken out and immediately hanged, and after death, buried in a ditch at the road-side.

Lieutenant V.D. Majendie has left behind an eyewitness account of what happened when the British forces captured Lucknow: 'the unfortunate who fell into the hands of our troops was made short work of—Sepoy or Oude Villager, it mattered not—no questions were asked; his skin was black, and did not that suffice? A piece of rope on the branch of tree, or a rifle bullet through his brain, soon terminated the poor devil's existence'.

At Delhi, Bahadur Shah's two sons and a grandson had stationed themselves in Humayun's tomb near Delhi. When Lieutenant Hodson, commander of an irregular cavalry unit called Hodson's Horse, arrived there, they voluntarily surrendered to him after two hours' discussion in the expectation that their conduct would be investigated by a properly constituted court of law. But when their cart was one mile from Delhi Hodson halted it, ordered the princes to get down, strip themselves and climb back into the cart. He then shot them with his own hand. Upon arrival in Delhi, Hodson exposed the dead bodies at the exact spot where forty-nine Europeans and persons of mixed blood had been murdered by the mutineers. Hodson gloried in having made 'the last of the House of Timur eat dirt'. In one of his letters to his wife, he also referred to 'the turquoise armlet and signet-rings of the rascally princes whom I shot' which he had sent her. Robert Montgomery, judical commissioner of the Punjab, congratulated Hodson in these words: 'All honour to you (and your 'Horse') for catching the king and slaying his sons. I hope you will bag many more'. Montgomery, it may be added, was strongly in favour of spreading Christianity in India and after the mutiny ascribed British victory not to soldiers but to 'the Lord our God'.

An English gentleman described the situation in Delhi on 21 September in these words:

All the city people found within the walls when our troops entered were bayoneted on the spot; and the number was considerable, as you may suppose, when I tell you that in some houses forty or fifty persons were hiding. These were not mutineers, but residents of the city, who trusted to our well-known mild rule for pardon. I am glad to say they were disappointed.

The Punjab was a special case. The majority of the population, the Muslims, had only recently been rescued by the British from Sikh rule and had no special reason for hostility toward the newcomers, and while the Sikhs may have resented being conquered by the British, they resented even more the fact that the Bengal Army had helped the British in that achievement. Further, the Sikhs had no wish to be ruled once more by the Mughals who had suppressed them in the past. Finally, all Punjabis... Muslim, Sikhs and Hindus...considered themselves a superior breed of men and looked down upon the Poorbias (men from the eastern provinces). Thus those units of the Bengal army which happened to be stationed in the Punjab cantonments when the rebellion broke out lacked the popular support that was available to them in their own homeland. The actual and potential mutinies in the Punjab were consequently easily put down. But it is the manner in which they were crushed that is relevant to the topic of atrocities.

There were in the Punjab 18,920 sepoys of the Bengal army compared to 5,620 European troops The mutineers at Meerut and Delhi had forgotten to cut off the telegraphic connection with the Punjab. Consequently, the news of the happenings at Meerut reached Lahore on 11 May, and of those at Delhi on 12 May. On 13 May, all the four sepoy regiments at Lahore were marched out and disarmed as a matter of precaution. Similar action was taken at some other military stations but a unit at Hoti Mardan mutinied and absconded. They were hunted down. Of those who were captured alive, forty were brought to Peshawar and blown to pieces from the mouths of guns at a ceremonial parade.

The most gruesome incident involved the sepoys of the 26th Native Infantry, which was one of the units that had been disarmed and incarcerated at Lahore. During a duststorm on 30 July they made an attempt to escape. Those who had remained behind were killed in a cannonade on their lines by Europeans and Sikhs. Of the fugitives, some 150 were killed by Sikh villagers. The main body retreated into a river and managed to swim to an island on pieces of wood. At this juncture Mr Frederick Cooper, Deputy Commissioner of Amritsar, arrived at the scene and took command of the situation. Exhausted and demoralised by their experiences and exertions, the hunted men, in Cooper's own words, were 'crouching like a brood of wildfowl. It remained to capture this body, and having done so, to execute condign punishment at once...the doomed men, with joined palms [a gesture of submission] crowded down to the shore...They evidently were possessed of the sudden and insane idea that they were going to be tried by court-martial, after some luxurious refreshment'. Cooper took the 282 prisoners who had surrendered, and confined them in the bastion of the police station at Ajnala six miles away. Next morning the men were brought out tied together in batches of ten and shot. When the number of the slain reached 237, it was reported that the remainder refused to come out. 'The doors were opened,' to quote the exultant Cooper again, 'and behold! Unconsciously the tragedy of Holwell's Black Hole had been re-enacted...Forty-five bodies, dead from fright, exhaustion, fatigue, heat, and partial suffocation, were dragged into light'. A dry well had been discovered near the police station and was used for the disposal of the bodies. This inspired Cooper to proclaim gleefully 'There is a well at Cawnpore, but there is also one at Ajnala.'

Cooper's acts were not the only ones which were particularly disgusting. Neill systematically burnt the bodies of Muslims and buried those of the Hindus so that the souls of both might suffer eternal damnation. Nor were examples lacking of sewing Muslims in pig-skin and smearing them with pork-fat before execution.

The British were frenzied because the sepoys and the *goonda* elements had slaughtered not only men but also helpless women and children. The horrors perpetrated by the British, therefore, are understandable as the acts of ordinary human beings but negated their claim to be the torchbearers of a higher civilization, upholders of legal justice and practitioners of Christian values. Their object was not only to punish the guilty but to strike terror in the minds of Indians at large so that none of them would ever dare to rise against them again. It was, in essence, the panicky response of a small alien minority whose main prop in ruling a huge majority of natives was prestige.

After the madness had cooled down, both sides felt so disgusted by their respective excesses that they said little about them openly for some decades. At a personal level there were innumerable life-long friendships and genuine feelings of mutual respect between individuals of the two races, but the British never again felt quite secure in India and the Indians never really forgot the degradation their forbears had suffered. How close to the surface this antagonism was became manifest when the moderate phase of Indian politics ended and some elements among the nationalist movement began to think in terms of a violent struggle to win freedom. The bloody events of 1857 began then to be extolled as the first War of Independence.

Long after the Great Rebellion, a ballad in praise of the Rani of Jhansi was still recited in the small towns of the United Provinces. Its concluding lines were:

> You fought well. If you lost, what does it matter?
> You fought for your right, of which you were so cruelly deprived by the
>   Firangis.
> You fought well. If you lost your life it does not matter.
> You earned immortality for your name.

After Independence both India and Pakistan celebrated the centenary of the Rebellion. A deputation of citizens of Karachi travelled to Rangoon to honour the grave of Bahadur Shah, and a street in Karachi was named after him.

The Act transferring the responsibility for governing India to the Crown was followed by Queen Victoria's famous Proclamation of 1 November 1858 enunciating the principles on which the administration of India would in future be based. The Queen had personally taken a keen interest in the wording of the proclamation, and in a memorandum had insisted that 'such a document should breathe feelings of generosity, benevolence, and religious toleration, and point out the privileges which the Indians will receive in being placed on an equal footing with the subjects of the British Crown...' The proclamation was not a stubborn defence of British policies. In fact the redresses promised in it implicitly admitted that the administration previously had been seriously flawed in some important respects and assured the Indians that the offending features would be modified. This is clear from the extracts that follow:

> ...we desire no extension of our present territorial possessions and...we shall sanction no encroachment on those of others. We shall respect the rights, dignity, and honour of native princes as our own...

> Firmly relying ourselves on the truth of Christianity...we disclaim alike the right and desire to impose our convictions on any of our subjects...

> And it is our further will that, so far as may be, our subjects, of whatever race or creed, be freely and impartially admitted to offices in our service, the duties of which they may be qualified, by their education, ability and integrity, duly to discharge...

We know and respect the feelings of attachment with which the natives of India regard the lands inherited by them from their ancestors, and we desire to protect them in all rights connected therewith, subject to the equitable demands of the State; and we will that, generally in framing and administring the law, due regard be paid to the ancient rights, usages, and customs of India...

It is our earnest desire to stimulate the peaceful industry of India...

Thus, though the upheaval of 1857 failed to drive the British out of India, it succeeded in the limited purpose of making them acknowledge what had gone wrong and made them promise to behave more considerately in the future.

That India would henceforth be directly governed by the Crown was the final touch to a process that had been visible from the time of the Regulating Act of 1773. In 1813 Lord Grenville had declared: 'The British Crown is *de facto* sovereign in India'. The Government of India Bill of 1833 had asserted the sovereignty of the Crown in India and declared that the territory was held by the Company in trust for Her Majesty. It also forbade the company to engage in trade any more, thus removing the taint of profit-making from the Government of India. Under the Act of 1858 the Secretary of State for India replaced the Board of Control and the India Council superseded The Board of Directors. The Secretary of State was a cabinet minister and the members of the India Council, who were his advisers, were persons with experience of India. To emphasize the monarch's direct constitutional link with the Indian princes, the Governor-General was given the additional title of Viceroy.

Under the Charter Act of 1833, the Government of India had remained purely official in structure. The Governor-General and his Council were the sole legislative authority, and executive power was wielded by the Governor-General and his Council as well as by the Governors of the Presidencies and their Councils. All the members of the various Councils were British. But the lesson of the Great Rebellion, in the words of Sir Bartle Frere, was that it would be dangerous to continue 'to legislate for millions of people with few means of knowing, except by a rebellion, whether the laws suit them or not'.

Under the Indian Councils Act of 1861 the Governor-General's Council was enlarged to form a Legislative Council and the Councils of the Governors of Bombay and Madras were similarly expanded to become Legislative Councils. It also created legislative councils in Bengal, the North-Western Provinces and the Punjab. At least half the additional members were to be nominated non-officials, most of whom in practice were Indians of high status such as princes and landed gentry. The majority in all the Councils was still official. Their functions were purely legislative. They could not discuss executive business or even ask questions about it. The administration was the responsibility solely of the officials. Frere compared the councils to 'the durbar of a native prince...the channel from which the ruler learns how his measures are likely to affect his subjects, and may hear of discontent, before it becomes disaffection'. Even so, it was the first appearance of Indians in the top echelons of the government of their own country.

As a logical sequel to bringing India directly under the Crown, the Queen, on 1 January 1877, assumed the title of Empress of India. She had already endeared herself in India by displaying a genuine concern for the welfare of her Indian subjects. The new title made her personal relationship with India seem still closer. The use by the mutineers of the hapless Bahadur Shah as their symbolic head had reminded the British that monarchy in the Indian mind carried a special mystique. Despite growing Indian disenchantment with her representatives in India later, the conscientious Queen retained the loyalty and affection of the India peoples till the end of her days.

Perhaps the greatest beneficiaries of the rebellion were the Indian princes. Some of them had only recently been unceremoniously toppled by Dalhousie but they were all now acclaimed by Canning as 'breakwaters in the storm'. Their right to adoption was conceded, and their territorial integrity was guaranteed. A more friendly policy toward the landed gentry, such as the *talukdars* of Oudh, was also adopted. One unfortunate result of this alliance between the British administration and the conservative elements of society was that scant respect was shown by the powers that be to the members of the rising Western-educated middle class, who ultimately were accepted by the masses as their leaders.

Another victory for conservatism was that the British Government abandoned the mission of improving the socio-religious tone of Indian life. They thought it safer to confine themselves to improving material facilities—such as railways, roads and irrigation works—than to touching the contentious field of practices purporting to be sanctioned by religion and tradition.

That the army in India should have been subjected to a thorough reorganization was not surprising. The old Bengal Army had disintegrated by its own action. In the reconstituted Bengal Army there was a parity of numbers between the European and the sepoy elements, and in the army as a whole the goal was to have one European to two Indians. The number of Brahmins from Hindustan was greatly reduced and their place was taken by Sikhs, Punjabi Muslims, Gurkhas, Pathans and Hindu Rajputs and Jats... 'the martial classes'. The artillerymen henceforth were all to be British.

Sir Syed Ahmed Khan, in analysing the causes of the Great Rebellion, stated that the British government had made the mistake of putting 'the two antagonistic races'—Hindus and Muslims—into the same regiments. This had smoothed their differences and created a feeling of brotherhood between them. Had each community had its own separate regiments, such a feeling would not have arisen. The British authorities evidently came to the same conclusion, because it was decided that the Indian regiments in future would be communal in composition and every two battalions of sepoys would be linked to one battalion of Europeans.

Finally, the failure of the Great Rebellion made it clear to the Indians that they would not be able to expel the British from India by force of arms, at least for some time to come. Their thoughts, therefore, turned inwards with a view to diagnosing the reasons that made the Indians so weak and the British so superior. The Hindus had taken to learning the English language and adopting the Western system of education without compunction from the moment it became possible to do so. After the Great Rebellion, they followed that course even more vigorously than before. The Muslims, proud of their past and still smarting from their recent eclipse, at first disdained to co-operate with the British. But the collapse of the Great Rebellion brought home to them the fact that it was not possible for them to revive Muslim rule in India. Under the powerful persuasion of Sir Syed Ahmed Khan, they too began to learn English and cultivate friendly relations with the British. For the time being, thus, Indians of all complexions adopted the maxim 'if you can't beat 'em, join 'em'.

There were outpourings of loyalty by the Indian intelligentsia and professions of goodwill to the British authorities. As individuals, many Britons were fascinated by India's ancient and rich culture and civilization and loved India. All Indians who had received a Western education admired English literature, British political institutions and the outstanding all-round achievements of the British people, and most of the Indians who had visited the United Kingdom, breathed the air of its lush countryside and seen her inhabitants at their natural best, loved Britain. But the racial barrier in India was never crossed (See Chapter 4). As E.M. Foster said, the Englishman and the Indian were always posing to each other and naturally they felt uncomfortable in each other's company. Each bored the other and was glad to get away from him to breathe freely and move naturally again. Even during their most loyal years, Congress and the Muslim League passed resolutions that were a mixture of assurances of loyalty to the British Crown, complaints against the way India was administered by the representatives of the Crown, and demands for greater control by Indians over their own affairs. The picture began to darken from the eighteen-nineties when Tilak raised the cry of *swaraj* (self-government) and violent revolutionaries began to function underground and became a permanent, though small, component of Indian politics.

PART II

'We appeal to England gradually to change the character of her rule in India, to liberalise it, to shift its foundations, to adapt to the newly-developed environments of the country and the people, so that, in the fullness of time, India may find its place in the great confederacy of free states, English in their origin, English in their character, English in their institutions, rejoicing in their permanent and indissoluble union with England.'

Surendranath Banerji

And suppose the British withdraw from India. Who would rule the country? 'Is it possible that under these circumstances the two nations—the Muhammadans and the Hindus—could sit on the same throne and remain equal in power? Most certainly not. It is necessary that one of them should conquer the other and thrust it down.'

Sir Syed Ahmed Khan

CHAPTER 4

STRANGERS IN INDIA.

No one seriously disputes that the British maintained their own racial, cultural and social identity despite their long connection with India, but opinions differ as to which of the two parties—the Indians or the British— was more responsible for this separation. Indian writers have tended to heap most of the blame on British shoulders. The British, being less emotional and therefore better able to see both sides of the question, do not deny their own insularity but point out rightly that Indian society, too, has always presented insurmountable barriers of its own.

Hinduism and Islam represent two irreconcilable civilizations. Liaquat Ali Khan, the first Prime Minister of Pakistan, emphasized the fact that the lives of a Hindu and a Muslim differ in every respect from the cradle to the grave. Even after death, the body of one is burned and that of the other buried. The concept of existence after death is also different. When the British first arrived in India the two communities had already shared a common motherland for several centuries without becoming a homogenous community. After the birth of nationalism, they both wanted the British to leave India, but the majority of the Muslims demanded an independent country of their own, on the grounds that the Hindus and Muslims constituted two separate nations.

In fact, the Hindus were hardly a nation even by themselves. As K. M. Panikkar points, out, 'The caste system, originally a process of integration, degenerated early into a system of division and sub-division till at last the broad four castes disappeared into innumberable sub-castes thereby rendering the development of a common Hindu feeling or a realisation of a sense of Hindu community difficult.' Radhakrishnan concedes that 'while it's [India's] culture produced individuals who had something undeniably attractive and superior, it did not develop a high civic or national sense.'

Hindu prejudice against mixing with foreigners is well illustrated by the fact that even after more than a hundred years of dealings with the British, the Hindu considered an overseas voyage a religious offence. On the eve of his departure for England for his studies, young Gandhi was summoned before a caste meeting. The verdict was that 'this boy shall be treated as an outcaste from today. Whoever helps him or goes to see him off at the dock shall be punishable with a fine of one rupee four annas. ' When Gandhi returned home, his brother had to pacify those who had disapproved of the trip by giving Gandhi a bath in the sacred river and by giving a dinner to the members of the caste. Similar experiences befell Bishan Narayan Dar and Motilal Nehru, who later became presidents of the Indian National Congress.

Muslims too create a gulf between themselves and non-Muslims by their belief that the Muslims of the world belong to a brotherhood distinct from the rest of humanity.

If the Hindus and the Muslims refused culturally and socially to become one society after sharing the same land for so long, what chance had the British, representing yet another race and civilization, to mix on equal terms with them? Even today, when the flow of population has been reversed and thousands of South Asians have taken up permanent residence in the United Kingdom, the Hindus, the Muslims and the Sikhs live as distinct minorities, tenaciously holding on to their own modes of worship, cultural values, and social customs. The British towns of Bradford and Southall, for example, where people from the Subcontinent have settled in large numbers, have lost their original character. Their city centres are now more like Indian bazaars than English shopping streets.

However superior the British in India might have felt as conquerors and rulers, the Hindu caste system reduced them to the status of untouchables. Newcomers were advised not to shake hands with a Brahmin because the resulting pollution would compel the Brahmin to undergo a purification ritual. Eating together was out of the question. Between the Muslims and the British, social relations were inhibited because the British disapproved of polygamy and the custom of keeping women in purdah, which prevented them from participating in mixed functions. In addition there was the lingering 'cross and crescent' hostility of the days of the crusades, plus the underlying fact that the British had destroyed a Muslim dynasty.

For their part, the British themselves never seriously tried to come to terms with the Indian way of life. At first they came to India simply as traders, and later also as administrators, soldiers, and professional persons, but never as immigrants. It was understood from they very beginning that on retirement they would go back ' home' to Britain. What need then was there for them to get Indianized? It is entirely possible that, if they had behaved less arrogantly, they might have prolonged the duration of their Empire. But human beings being what they are, was it possible for the

British in India not to feel that they belonged to an altogether superior breed of mankind? After all, they were but a small number of persons from a distant island who had managed to lord it over an entire subcontinent in which lived millions of peoples and hundreds of princes.

To start with, since their status was that of ordinary traders, their safety and prosperity naturally hung on the good will of the Indian authorities. The great Mughals were magnificent and their country was fabulously rich. The traders' own island was small, not yet particularly rich and not yet a great power even in Europe.

Communications between India and England in those days were by sailing-ships via the Cape. A voyage seldom took less than six months and sometimes nearly a year. The entire working lives of the traders were therefore usually spent in India and they had to make themselves physically as comfortable as possible during this long exile. Some of them married Goan women or kept Indian mistresses. They wore loose Indian clothes in the privacy of their quarters, included spiced Indian dishes in their menu, imbibed Indian spirits along with imported wines, smoked *hookahs*, enjoyed performances by *nautch* girls and watched firework displays. The Governor lived in considerable pomp and led noisy processions in imitation of the local notables. But there were no close friendships between the British and the Indians as equals. What the British borrowed from India was trivial and superficial and they themselves were too few and too self-centred to have had any effect on the Indian mind and culture.

The number of the Company's servants greatly increased when they expanded their role to encompass power politics in addition to trade. Soldiers, as well as civilians, were needed in ever-increasing numbers, turning their settlements into small towns including Indian sections. The process started with the Anglo-French wars in the south and greatly accelerated when the British became the military masters of Bengal and then also its revenue collectors. The senior servants of the Company were no longer content to retire just as well-off merchants; they aspired to return home as nabobs. A much larger number of Europeans and Indians were inevitably thrown together as a result of these changes.

The British were still only one of the several powers picking up the fragments of the disintegrating Mughal Empire. Their pride was growing but was not yet overweening. But the contacts remained at a business level. They were not sufficiently intimate to penetrate and touch the basic outlook of either side. The British nabobs, as well as their less well-off compatriots, still regarded Britain as their home and India as the place where they worked and made money. The only healthy feature of the period was that there was no marked racial tension between the white foreigners and the dark natives.

It was from the time of Cornwallis that the rift between the British and the Indians really began to open up. It was ironic that such a man as this should have followed Warren Hastings, who had held the Indian character and culture in such high esteem. We have already noted elsewhere that Cornwallis excluded Indians from all important civil and military positions because he believed that they were all corrupt. He further alienated the higher classes by his lack of courtesy and imagination, so essential in a country like India where formal politeness and ostentation is a way of life. He lived simply himself and cut back on ceremonial honours to princes. *Nazars* in person were to be presented only to members of the Mughal royal family. Some princes were denied the customary honours when visiting Calcutta.

Bentinck later earned praise for permitting Indians to drive to Government House in carriages, but the extolling of the English language and Western education and the belittling of Oriental languages and learning during his time, characterized by Macaulay's pungent minute, retarded the process of building up mutual understanding which the respect shown to the Indian languages by Warren Hastings and Sir William Jones had inaugurated. Jones, a judge of the Calcutta High Court and a Sanskritist, looked upon Asia as 'the nurse of sciences'. In fairness to the British, it must be added that responsible Indians too showed far greater enthusiasm for the English language then for the languages of their own country. It would have been healthier if the growth of the one had not been at the cost of the others. The credit for reviving Sanskrit belongs to the Germans.

The lofty Wellesley, who did not suffer gladly even his own employers, the Directors of the East India Company, was not the man to lay great store by Indians, whether people or princes. The distance between Indians and the British became even more marked during his regime. With the annexation of the Punjab in 1849 the British completed the conquest of India. They were no longer just traders, no longer just one of the powers jockeying for position in the Subcontinent; they were the new Mughals, except that they did not make India their home. They were not only supreme in India but, following the industrial revolution and the victory at Waterloo, had become the richest and the most powerful people in the world. In their eyes, even fellow Europeans belonged to a lower class of human being than themselves, and the coloured peoples, of course, ranked below all the whites.

In analysing the causes of the Great Rebellion of 1857, Sir Syed Ahmed Khan observed,

> One great source of stability of a Government is undoubtedly the treating of its subjects with honour, and thus gaining their affections...In the first years of the British rule in India the people were heartily in favour of it. This good feeling the Government has now forfeited, and the natives very generally say that they are treated with contempt. A native gentleman is, in the eyes of any petty official, as much lower than that official as that same official esteems himself lower than a duke. The opinion of many of these officials is that no native can be a gentleman.

The appalling atrocities of the Rebellion alienated the Indians and the British from each other irretrievably. Even in 1904, Malcolm Darling, a member of the Indian Civil Service, felt that the mutiny was 'a kind of phantom standing behind the official chairs'.

Meanwhile, improvements in communications were bringing their 'home' closer to the English exiles in India. From the eighteenth century, the travellers could choose the shorter route and avoid going round the Cape. They could cross the Mediterranean by boat, travel overland through Egypt to the Red Sea and finally take a boat to India. In 1830 a steamship service was inaugurated between Suez and Bombay, and the opening of the Suez Canal, on 16 November 1869, made it possible to travel by the shorter route without changing ship. This made it even less necessary than before for the British to put down any roots in India. Visits to England became more frequent.

Another result of the easier and speedier travel between the two countries was the arrival, in increasing numbers, of British women in India; this further complicated social relations between the two races. The British thought that the Indians treated their own womenfolk abominably: a woman who could not produce a son was looked down upon; Muslims practiced polygamy and kept their women in seclusion. A common fear was that oriental men lusted after white women and that some English women might respond favourably to their overtures. Lord Curzon explained the Government of India's reluctance to send Indian troops to participate in the Queen's Diamond Jubilee celebrations in 1901 in these words: 'the ÷woman√ aspect of the question is rather a difficulty, since strange as it may seem Englishwomen of the housemaid class, and even higher, do offer themselves to these Indian soldiers, attracted by their uniform, enamoured of their physique, and with a sort of idea that the warrior is also an oriental prince'. The Indians for their part considered Englishwomen to have loose morals: they danced in the embrace of strange men and behaved immodestly in the company of men.

At the age of about seven, children were sent off to England for their education, and ultimately everyone left India on retirement. This absence of old persons, young children and a British working class made British society in India unnatural.

Added to all these features was the well-known British preference for their own company wherever in the world they might be. At District Headquarters they lived in a section called the Civil Lines and ran clubs from most of which Indians were excluded. When alone on tour, they preferred loneliness to the company of locals. Anyone who mixed with Indians on equal terms was considered odd. Women remained more ignorant about India than men because they lacked the opportunity which men had of having to meet a large number of Indians of different classes and denominations in the course of their duties. For women, daily contact with Indians was limited to servants. British men too, now having a family to go to after working hours, felt less need for other diversions.

There were conscientious British administrators in India and there were politicians in England who respected the Indian people and culture. There were also scholars, writers, and archaeologists who brought India's past greatness to light. The prevailing mood, however, especially among the British in India, was one of racial superiority, and this more than anything else made it impossible for the Indians and the British ever to become fully reconciled to each other. Even the most respectable Indians were sometimes subjected to degrading insults, and despite the lavish promises contained in the Act of 1833 and the Queen's Proclamation of 1858, Indians were never given an equitable share in the top civil and military positions in their own country.

Even a person of the status of Raja Ram Mohan Roy, of whom more will be said in these pages, was once publicly humiliated by a British district officer. On the afternoon of 1 January, 1809, the Raja was being carried in a palanquin in Bhapolpur. Sir Frederick Hamilton, the Collector, shouted abuse and ordered the Raja to get down from his palanquin. The Raja complied, saluted Sir Frederick and apologized, explaining that the omission to show him proper respect before was due to the fact that he had not seen him.

W. S. Blunt, who travelled in India in 1883, related several instances of insults inflicted by Englishmen on Indians. Blunt's host at Patna was the elderly local aristocrat, Nawab Vilayat Ali Khan, whom the British

Government had made a Companion of the Star of India for his loyal services. When Blunt went to the railway station to catch a train at the end of his stay, the Nawab and some thirty other respectable people of Patna accompanied him as a mark of honour. After Blunt had entered his railway carriage, the Nawab and his companions remained on the platform 'as orderly and respectable a group of citizens as need be seen', but an English passenger in the adjoining compartment took umbrage at the presence of so many Indians on the platform. He thrust out his head from the window, abused them and told them to be off. When they took no notice, he struck at them with a stick. When Blunt tried to interfere the Englishman was most indignant and calmed down only after Blunt had secured the aid of the police.

If Indians of such high rank as Raja Ram Mohan Roy and Nawab Vilayat Ali Khan could be insulted by Englishmen with impunity, the plight of Indians of humbler status can be imagined. The crudest members of the British community in India were the common soliders and the planters; and they were the worst offenders.

It goes to Lord Curzon's credit that as Viceroy he was appalled at the fact that Englishmen could ill-treat Indians without fear of punishment and he tried his best to improve matters. He describes the problem in a letter dated 17 September 1900 to the Secretary of State for India, Lord George Hamilton, in these words:

I meet with nothing but tacit discouragement and sublatent antagonism from the soliders. They are banded together throughout India in a compact body, animated by the fiercest *esprit de corps*. They will wink at things done by a fellow solider, which they would denounce if committed by a civilian. The moment one is censured, all the rest are up in arms. They cannot see why the poor solider should not be allowed to go out and shoot and harry at his own sweet will and if in the course of the excursion a Native is killed, their attitude is that of a very fast bowler at cricket whom I once met, and who having killed a man by the ball jumping up and striking him on the temple, said to me, 'why did the d...d fool get his head in the way?'

With regard to tea-planters and their coolies in Assam, Curzon wrote to Hamilton on 5 August 1903:

These managers are drawn from a most inferior class of Englishmen and Scotsmen; they do not know the language, they have a profound comtempt for the Natives and they are sometimes guilty of serious acts of lust and oppression. The planters actually allege in public meetings that they can be certain of no justice, though what they mean by this is that they regard it as the greatest of hardship if a planter is find Rs. 100/- for an assault that terminates in the death of a coolie, while the coolie gets a term of rigorous imprisonment of from three to six years if he so much as lifts his hands against a European.

The lobbying power of the British community in India was vividly demonstrated in 1883 when the Viceroy, Lord Ripon, was so compelled to water down the Ilbert Bill that it lost its purpose. That bill, introduced by Sir Courtenay Ilbert, the Law Member of the Viceroy's Council, had aimed at racial justice. Under the existing law, European British subjects could be tried only by judges of their own race. Indian magistrates and sessions judges were thus barred from trying any European for a criminal offence. The Government of India published proposals 'to settle the question of jurisdiction over European British subjects in such a way as to remove from the Criminal Procedure Code at once and immediately every judicial qualification which is based merely on race distinction'.

The agitation against the bill was carried to ridiculous lengths. In Bengal effigies of Ilbert and Ripon were burnt and even a plot to kidnap the Viceroy was hatched. The head of the Criminal Investigation Department reported that, 'to make their grievance a general one, they raised the cry of danger to European women'. There were stories that in Calcutta, Indians emboldened by Ripon's liberal policies had tried to rape European women. An Englishwoman wrote, 'It is not the colour of their skins, it is the colour of their minds we object to.' It was argued that until Indians liberated their own women, they had no business to judge 'civilized women'. English ladies held public meetings. Seven hundred ladies from Bihar dispatched a petition to the House of Commons and nearly six thousand sent one to the Queen herself. Henry Cotton, a member of the Indian Civil Service, lamented that, 'it is with a feeling of shame that I am bound to add that the opposition to the Ilbert Bill was headed by members of my own Service, and that the practical unanimity of opposition to that measure was as complete among civil Magistrates and Judges as it was among planters, merchants and members of the legal profession'.

That the Indians wholly supported the bill was of no avail. The vociferous European minority carried the day, but the damage to race relations was grievous. Responsible Indians realized more than ever before that, unless the system of government was drastically changed, they would continue to occupy a humiliatingly subject position.

In obvious violation of the pledges that Indians would not be barred from holding any office under the crown, all sorts of obstacles were placed in the way of their entering the higher services. The promise of equal employment opportunities was regarded as more of an embarrassment than a solemn undertaking. In a confidential minute to the Secretary of State in 1878, Lord Lytton, the Viceroy, wrote, 'No sooner was the Act of 1833 passed than the Government began to devise means for practically evading the fulfilment of it...The application to Indians of the competitive examination system as conducted in England, and the recent reduction in the age at which candidates can compete, are all so many deliberate and transparent subterfuges for stultifying the Act, and reducing it to a dead letter'.

Lord George Hamilton, Secretary of State for India, wrote to the Viceroy, Lord Elgin, on 7 May 1897, 'I do not think we should put very prominently forward Queen Victoria's Proclamation of 1858. As a piece of English it is fine, but 40 years' practice has shown the extreme difficulty of giving effect to the academic utterances as to equality of races...' The memory of the Great Rebellion obviously rankled in Hamilton's mind for he said in the House of Commons, 'In India, almost without warning, an apparently peaceful population might suddenly become as dangerous as criminal lunatics, but with one object before them—to murder the class alien to them'. Not surprisingly, he wrote to Curzon on 17 May 1900, 'the large scale preponderances of Natives in appointments above a certain grade as compared with Europeans always fills me with apprehension as regards the future... One of the greatest mistakes ever made was the issue in the Proclamation annexing India of the principle that perfect equality was to exist, so far as all appointments were concerned, between European and Native'. He wrote hopefully to Lord Elgin on 16 September 1879 that, 'If we can keep the affection of the fighting races and higher orders of society in India, we can ignore the dislike and disaffection of the intellectual non-fighting classes, the baboos, students and pleaders.'

Lord Curzon had no compunction in telling the Legislative Council on 30 March 1904 that, 'the highest ranks of civil employment in India, those in the Imperial Civil Service, though open to such Indians as can proceed to England and pass the requisite tests, must, nevertheless, as a general rule, be held by Englishmen, for the reason that they possess, partly by heredity, partly by up-bringing, and partly by education, the knowledge of the pinciples of Government, the habits of mind, and the vigour of character, which are essential for the task...'

From 1853 entrance to the Indian Civil Service was by open competition. Indians were eligible to sit for the examination but, since it was held only in London, they were under a serious handicap. Not many could afford the long and expensive journey or comtemplate with equanimity a long separation from their families. The Hindus had the fear of losing caste if they travelled to the country of the Untouchables. In 1878 the age at which candidates could compete was reduced from 21 to 19, which made it even more difficult for Indians to try. By this time an increasing number of Indians had become qualified to sit for the examination and in India the new rule was seen as a deliberate obstruction in their path. From 1892 the age limit was raised to 21-23 and from 1906 to 22-24. But it was not till 1920 that examinations began to be held in Delhi as well as in London.

The coming of the 'competition wallah' had a good as well as a doubtful side. He was the new Brahmin, proud of his intellectual prowess, conscious of the superiority of his own caste and anxious to reserve its purity by keeping undesirables out. He was incorruptible and industrious but he was also a self-righteous know-all and believed that he knew what was good for the Indian peasant better than the city-bred Indian-educated class. He strengthened the conservative character of the administration and, as the 'man on the spot', was able to render powerful support to forces that retarded the processes of political advance and the Indianization of the higher services. India had already been conquered and the framework of the administration had been laid. The age of the heroic Empire builders had passed. 'We do not want heroes to preside over drainage committees', observed H. G. Keene, himself a civil servant, in 1882.

The failure of the British Government to live up to its promises of providing equal opportunities for Indians to enter the services had serious consequences. Not only did it contribute to the alienation of Western-educated Indians from the government but it also had a pernicious effect on the Indian character. Sir Thomas Munro, who arrived in India in 1780 and died as Governor of Madras in 1827, perceptively observed:

None of them [natives of British India] can look forward to any share in the civil or military government of their country. It is from men who either hold or are eligible for public life that nations take their character; where no such men exist, there can be no energy in any other class of the community. No elevation of character can be expected among men who in the military line cannot attain to any rank above that of subedar, where they are as much below an ensign as an ensign is below the Commander-in-Chief, and who in the civil line can hope for nothing beyond some petty judicial revenue office in which they may by corrupt means make up their slender salary.

A Brahmin member of the Viceroy's Legislative Council complained to Joseph Chailley, a member of the French Chamber of Deputies who

visited India in 1900-1 and again in 1904-5, that, 'The [British] Indian
Civilian does not wish us to rise. When we learn his language, understand
his ideas, and attain his intellectual level, he regards this not as a homage
which he sould welcome, but as an encroachment to be resented. We used
to esteem them for their character, and we flattered ourselves that they
would welcome in us just and independent men, but they only want
baseness and servility, and their favours go out to flatterers and time-
servers'.

Those who resisted the admission of an increasing numbers of Indians
to the services often took shelter behind the words 'so far as may be' in the
Queen's proclamation, but they never satisfactorily explained why the
Indian aspirants to public service could not be recruited and trained in
India. The British government made things easy only for the British
candidates. Not only could they pass the qualifying examination in their
own country, but they also received training there before coming out to
India. The directors founded 'The East India College, Herts.' in 1806 for
preparing British civilians destined for India (it was moved to Haileybury
in 1809). For the military cadets there was a corresponding institute at
Addiscombe.

In the period 1861-85 only 12 Indians were recruited to the Indian Civil
Service, and only 68 Indians as compared to 1,235 Europeans in the period
1886-1910. No less than 42.46 per cent of the Indian total of 68 was taken
by the Bengalis. After 1920, when the competitive examination began to
be held in India as well, the number of Indians increased noticeably. In
1933 the cadre consisted of 478 Indians out of a total of 1,297 and in 1940,
502 Indians out of 1,284. But the strength of the Indians never equalled that
of the Europeans. In April 1947, just before Independence, Indians
numbered 510 and Europeans 668.

CHAPTER 5

THE HINDU COMMUNITY

It was but natural that the Hindu reaction to British supremacy should have been different from that of the Muslims. The Hindus welcomed it as an improvement on the Muslim rule which it had replaced, while the Muslim resented it because it had ended their domination.

The Hindus, therefore, were the first to be reconciled to the new rulers and to take to Western education, while the Muslims realized only upon the extinction of the Mughal Empire that the British were in India to stay and that they had better make the best of the situation.

In truth, Hindu society had been stagnant for the last several centuries and was panting for a breath of fresh air. The revival of orthodox Brahmanism during the classical age had increased the rigidity of the caste system and sanctioned certain undesirable socio-religious practices. At the beginning of the eleventh century, al-Biruni had found the Hindus arrogant, self-satisfied and isolated from the rest of the world, but added that Mahmud's plundering raids had further blighted the prosperity and culture of the country.

The seven hundred years of India's subjugation by the Muslims following Mahmud's incursions were hardly a period during which the Hindus could be expected to reverse the process of decadence. It was the British conquest of India that not only ended the long period of Hindu suppression and inequality, but also brought with it a variety of invigorating Western values, including the spirit of inquiry which encouraged the challenging of outmoded concepts.

In Bengal, which was the first part of India to come under British control, the Hindus enthusiastically turned their attention to Western learning. Institutions with Western curricula were established even before Macaulay and Bentinck had made the encouragement of Western learning a part of official policy, In 1817 the Hindu College was founded at Calcutta. This had resulted from a meeting held at the residence of Sir Hyde East, Chief Justice of the Supreme Court, which had been attended by more than fifty leading Hindus. Nearly half a lakh of rupees were subscribed on the spot and many more donations were pledged. The college was to promote the teaching of English and other secular subjects such as history, astronomy and mathematics. In 1823 Raja Ram Mohan Roy protested against the proposal by the government to establish a Sanskrit School under pandits and represented that it would be more beneficial to promote the teaching of mathematics, natural philosophy, chemistry, anatomy and 'other useful sciences'. By 1835 Calcutta had twenty-five schools offering liberal education and in 1836 Macaulay came across 1400 boys learning English in one town alone in Bengal.

It was in the religious and social fields that the impact of Western education first manifested itself. This is because in India religion and politics are inseparable: the one nourishes the other. In Islam the state is governed by religious law (hence the need for Pakistan) while Mahatma Gandhi enjoyed a greater mass following among the Hindus than other leaders because he was seen to be their spiritual superior.

Even in Europe, before the age of nationalism, religion was the dominant force in national life as well as in international relations. The Pope's authority was recognized in Christendom and the Cardinals, Archbishops and Bishops wielded no less political influence than the pandits and *maulvis* of India. Christian kings conducted crusades against the Muslims and Protestant countries fought against Catholic ones.

Before the Hindus could muster sufficient self-confidence to demand the right to govern themselves, they had to go through the process of reviving their pride in their own religion and history. For the rediscovery of their past greatness they were beholden to European linguists and archaeologists, just as they had to thank the English language and Western example for stimulation in all the other fields. It exhilarated them to know that their ancestors had developed a rich civilization centuries before the Britons and West Europeans had modernized themselves, and it reassured them to learn that linguistically and racially the Aryans shared a common ancestry with West Europeans.

The merging of religious awakening into political awakening can best be traced by reference to the careers of the leading Hindus of the nineteenth century. Raja Ram Mohan Roy, the first notable Indian to personify the rationalizing influence of Western ideas, was born of orthodox Brahmin parents in a village in West Bengal in 1772. As a young man he studied Persian and Arabic at Patna, which was then a centre of Muslim learning, and became a confirmed monotheist, rejecting all forms of idol worship. He also studied Sanskrit and Hindu scriptures as well as English and the Bible. For some time he served under his friend John Digby, a covenanted servant of the East India Company. Digby has recorded that the Raja took a keen interest in European politics, in particular the French Revolution. Ram Mohan Roy had to leave the Company's service in 1814 because he was not made permanent. Thereafter he settled down in Calcutta and in 1828 founded the Brahmo Samaj (Society of God) with the object of providing a meeting-ground for all sects for the worship of One True God.

Worship of images was not the only feature of Hindu society which Ram Mohan Roy tried to reform. He disliked the abuses of the caste system, and he was a champion of equal rights for women. He opposed *suttee,* polygamy, and the ban on widow remarriages. He registered his disapproval of the prohibition against crossing the seas by personally travelling to England. His object was not to found a new religion but to restore what he believed to be the Vedic purity of Hinduism so that it could weather the challenge posed by Christian missionaries.

Ram Mohan Roy's liberal outlook made him an enthusiastic supporter of Western education and an admirer of civil liberty. The latter trait was vividly illustrated by an incident during his voyage to England. He left for England in November 1830. At the Cape of Good Hope, despite the poor state of his health, he insisted upon going aboard a French vessel to pay tribute to the land which had given to the world the revolutionary message of 'Liberty, Equality and Fraternity'. Being in feeble health, he stumbled and injured his leg and was left with a permanent limp. He died in Bristol in 1833.

The Raja's ideas were too revolutionary for the orthodox members of his community, who opposed him vehemently. Though the Brahmo Samaj never became a mass movement, its founder's endeavours stirred up a vigorous controversy in a society that had long been hidebound, and started an era of bold debate and inquiry which progressed inevitably to cover political issues as well. The official history of the Indian National Congress calls Raja Ram Mohan Roy 'the prophet of Indian nationalism and the father of Modern India'.

After the Brahmo Samaj, the most important movement was the Arya Samaj. It represented the reaction from Ram Mohan Roy's over-zealous acceptance of Western values and sought a greater adherence to traditional Hinduism. Its founder, Swami Dayanand, was born in 1824 in a small town in Gujrat. His family, too, were orthodox Brahmins. At the age of fourteen his father took him to a temple to keep an all-night vigil before the statue of Siva. During the night a mouse climbed the image of the god and stole the offerings with impunity. The helplessness of the mighty Siva made a deep impression on the young observer and he embarked upon an independent search for truth. After wandering far and wide for years as an ascetic, practicing yoga and studying, he founded the Arya Samaj in 1875. He died in October 1883.

Dayanand spent the last eight years of his life preaching, writing, and setting up branches of the Arya Samaj in different parts of India. He never learnt English but preached in Hindi, the language of north India. He believed in the sanctity of the cow and in the doctrines of transmigration and Karma. He preached that the Supreme God should be worshipped in spirit and not through images. The institution of four castes and the wearing of the sacred thread by the three upper castes were retained but he favoured inter-caste marriages and denounced child marriage. In his book *Satyartha-Prakasa* he bitterly attacked some aspects of Islam and Christianity.

Dayanand's basic message was that the Vedas contained all the knowledge that mankind required for its spiritual guidance and nourishment, and enjoined his followers to study them diligently. He broke entirely fresh ground by promoting *suddhi*, i.e., welcoming back to the fold of Hinduism those of its children who by coercion or conviction had turned Muslim or Christian. Hinduism hitherto had refused to readmit those of her children who had strayed away. Dayanand's proselytizing activities angered the Muslims but he earned a mass following in his own community for injecting new ideas without departing from fundamentals, such as the ancient scriptures and the caste system. The Arya Samaj acquired a large membership in northern India, especially the Punjab.

The mystic Ramakrishna demonstrated that 'God can be worshipped and realized by following the traditional methods of India, which the Christian missionaries had characterized as superstitious'.He was born in a village in the Hooghly district of Bengal in 1836. His parents were poor Brahmins. In 1855 he took up a position as priest in a temple near Calcutta. From childhood onward he was of a deeply religious and contemplative turn of mind and is said to have experienced trances from the age of six. His visions of God continued to occur for the rest of his life and his fame as a true saint spread far and wide, attracting crowds of admirers to his temple. During one of his ecstacies he fell on a live coal which burned deep into his flesh but he became aware of it only after the condition had run its course. He had a complete disregard for material possessions and entertained a *bhakta*-like respect for all religions as different paths leading to the same Almighty. He had been schooled only up to the primary standard, but the other-worldly serenity of his character won the homage of those educated and well-to-do persons whose minds had remained restless despite the achievement of worldly success. He passed away in August 1886.

Ramakrishna's mission was continued by his favourite disciple, Vivekananda, but in an altogether new spirit. Vivekananda was born to a Kayastha family in Calcutta in January 1863. He had received an English education, with a BA from Calcutta University. He also broadened his mind by extensive travels within his own country, the USA and Europe. He combined religious fervour with a practical wisdom which recognized the causes responsible for India's political and economic decay and for the West's progress in those fields.

Vivekananda had the moral courage to acknowledge that it was not the British but the Indians themsleves who were primarily responsible for India's degradation. Poverty, neglect of the masses and Hindu India's conquest by foreigners caused him much anguish. In his view India was superior to the West spiritually while the West excelled India materially. It would benefit both sides if India gave some of its spirituality in return for 'western science, technology, methods of raising the standard of life, business integrity and techniques of collective effort'. He chided his countrymen for thinking that they could do without the rest of the world and said that they had paid for this 'foolishness...by about a thousand years of slavery'.

Educated Hindus hitherto had been on the defensive against allegations by the Muslims and the Christians that their religion was supersititious and their society afflicted by social evils. Vivekananda led the counter-attack by asserting that, in some important respects, Hinduism was superior to both those religions. A Parliament of Religions was due to convene at Chicago in September 1893. The Indian revivalist made his way there and managed to address no less than five meetings.

He immediately captivated the hearts of the audience with the greeting 'sisters and brothers of America'. The word intolerance, he claimed, cannot be found in the dictionary of Hinduism. His most telling discourse contained the following argument:

We who come from the East have sat here on the platform day after day and have been told in a patronizing way that we ought to accept Christianity because Christian nations are the most prosperous. We look about us and we see England, the most prosperous Christian nation in the world, with her foot on the neck of 250,000,000 Asiatics. We look back into history and see that the prosperity of Christian Europe began with Spain. Spain's prosperity began with the invasion of Mexico. Christianity wins its prosperity by cutting the throats of its fellow men. At such a price the Hindu will not have prosperity. I have sat here today and I have heard the height of intolerance. I have heard the creeds of the Moslems applauded, when today the Moslem sword is carrying destruction into India. Blood and sword are not for the Hindu, whose religion is based on the laws of love.

Vivekananda's exposition of the humane aspect of Hinduism convinced many that it really had something special to offer to the world and he was able to establish several centres for the study of Vedanta in America. During his tour of Europe he conferred with Max Muller, the celebrated orientalist who afterwards signalled his approval of what he had learnt by writing a biography of Ramakrishna.

On his return to India in January 1879, Vivekananda was greeted as a national hero. In the summer of 1899 he embarked on a second tour of America and Europe, returning home in December 1900. The Swami breathed his last on 4 July 1902. His positiveness had infused the Hindus with a new sense of pride and self-confidence.

Dayanand's orthodoxy had strengthened Hinduism's backbone but it had also sharpened its differences with other religions. The Ramakrishna-Vivekananda mission's message of tolerance, love and peace presented Hinduism in a universally acceptable form.

Indian authors, too, began to write in a new vein under the influence of English literature. The most popular and politically influential writer of the early period was the novelist Bankim Chandra Chatterjee. His novel *Ananda matha* (Abbey of Bliss) contains the famous song 'Bande Mataram', which the Hindus used as a national anthem during the struggle for independence. The novel depicts a band of *sanyasis*, called Santanas or children, whose objective was to annihilate Muslim rule in Bengal. They called themselves children because in their temple they placed three images of the goddess Kali as a representation of the motherland. They followed the principle that the end justifies the means, and did not shirk from lawlessness and roguery. The children put an end to Muslim rule but had to put up with British rule in its place. The novel denounces the former but praises the latter. Bankim Chandra's other writings also display a galling resentment against the Muslim conquest of India. Clearly, Bankim Chandra's nationalism, though fervent, was Hindu in dimension, not Indian. The adoption of 'Bande Mataram' as the national song of the Hindus deeply offended the Muslims.

The Indian National Congress had been founded in 1885; its early history is related in Chapter 7. It did not become a mass movement until Mahatma Gandhi took charge of it in 1919. India's first nationalist leader to command a mass following was Bal Gangadhar Tilak (1856-1920), who earned the title of *Lokmanya* ('respected by the people'). In 1885 he wrote in his paper *Kesari*, 'The birth of patriotism among us is due to English rule and the English education... The spirit of patroitism has not as yet permeated all classes. It is only those who have come under the influence of English education and begun to realise the defects of British administration that have been inspired by that spirit.'

Tilak, a Chitpavan Brahmin of Poona, utilized history and religion to whip up nationalist feelings and represented that section of the political leadership which had come to believe that it would be the strength of the people of India that would attain the desired results, not the policy of 'mendicancy' followed by the Congress party. While Congress, at this stage, was asking for a share in the administration, Tilak, and others of his way of thinking, demanded *swaraj* (self-government). He coined the famous slogan '*Swaraj* is my birthright and I will have it'.

Tilak had graduated with honours from the Bombay University. He was learned in Hindu scriptures and was a competent journalist. He first achieved prominence by his vigorous opposition to the Age of Consent Act (1891) which prohibited the consummation of marriage until the wife had reached the age of twelve. He stated, somewhat ambivalently, that he did not take exception to the contents of the Act but to the right of a foreign government to interfere with the social customs of the Hindus. The strong agitation against the Act had an unfortunate long-term effect. Since the Great Rebellion the British government had been loath to pass any measures which would ruffle the religious susceptibilities of the Indians. After the hue and cry raised by the Age of Consent Act, they became still more reluctant to attempt any social reform.

It was the inauguration by Tilak of the Ganapati and Shivaji festivals and the part that he played during the plague epidemic that brought him to the forefront of political life. The Ganapati festival was an old religious event to which Tilak gave national flavour when he reorganized it in 1893; after that it was celebrated as a popular *mela* (fair) with processions, lectures and songs. The first celebration of the Shivaji festival took place on 15 March 1895 at Raigarh, which had been Shivaji's capital. The festival became an annual event and began to be celebrated at many places besides Raigarh. Lectures were delivered and discussions took place. Public processions featured volunteeers displaying their skill in fencing and national sentiments were roused by religious and patriotic songs.

In the meantime a terrible famine broke out in Bombay, and while it was still raging, plague arrived in epidemic form. Several cases of plague occurred in Poona in September 1897 and by the end of the year 11,882 persons had died in Bombay. House-to-house searches had to be made to segregate those stricken by the disease from others; in Poona British soldiers were employed for some time on search parties. An official report acknowledged that 'the repressive measures, which were absolutely necessary to stamp out the plague, came in conflict with caste prejudices of the Hindus'.

Tilak urged the people to demand the benefits available to them under the Famine Relief code. He said they should pay the government dues if they could but should not sell their lands and cattle to do so out of fear of government officials. This 'no rent' campaign earned Tilak the disapprobation of officialdom, but more was to follow.

On 4 May 1897, Tilak published an article in his newspaper *Kesari* accusing the British soldiers employed on plague duty of excesses and the whole government of deliberately oppressing the people. He described Rand, the Collector of Poona who was also the Plague Commissioner, as tyrannical. On 15 June two further items appeared in the same paper. The first was a poem entitled 'Shivaji's Utterances'. In it Shivaji soliloquized that he had delivered the country by establishing *swaraj* but now foreigners were depriving it of wealth, and famine and epidemic stalked the land. The second article reported discourses by two professors who defended Shivaji's murder of the Mughal General Afzal Khan. In his summing-up Tilak himself raised the question, 'did Shivaji commit a sin in killing Afzal Khan or not?' and said that the answer could be found in the Mahabharata itself—Krishna's advice in the Gita is to kill even our own teachers and our kinsmen, thus Afzal Khan was killed for the good of others.

A week after the publication of these articles, Collector Rand and another British officer, Lt. Ayers, were murdered by two Brahmin brothers who were subsequently tried and executed.

Tilak himself was prosecuted on the charge of inciting disaffection towards the government on the basis of the articles of 15 June. Six European jurors found him guilty and three Indians jurors declared him not guilty. The judge accepted the verdict of the majority and sentenced him to eighteen months' imprisonment. Leave to appeal to the Privy Council was refused. Six months of the term were subsequently remitted.

Tilak's incarceration raised a storm of protest and made him a hero. By bringing politics from the rarified debating halls of Congress to the man in the street, he had struck a new note. Willingness to suffer imprisonment henceforth became a badge of true leadership. His nationalism, of course, was manifestly Hindu. He saw 'nothing wrong in providing a platform for all the Hindus of all high and low classes to stand together and discharge a joint national duty'. While the religion and history which he invoked inspired the Hindus, it enraged the Muslims. To the Muslim mind, Hindu gods such as Ganapati denoted idolatory, and Shivaji was an arch rebel who undermined the Mughal Empire. Tilak's further career is considered in Part III.

CHAPTER 6

THE MUSLIM COMMUNITY

After the death of Aurangzeb, the rapid decline of Mughal power had a demoralizing effect on the Muslims who had ruled India for so long. There was a general feeling that it was the weakening of the moral fibre of the community that had led to its political decline. At this juncture there appeared a theologian who was notably successful in reviving the Muslim community spiritually. Shah Wali-Ullah (1703-62) was the son of a scholarly Sufi who had founded a college. Wali-Ullah read at the college and, after his father's death, taught there for twelve years. Thereafter he performed *hajj* and studied at Medina for nearly fourteen months.

Shah Wali-Ullah diagnosed that it was the schisms within the Muslim family that had done it the greatest harm. He made a deep study of various schools of thought and wrote extensively to harmonize the different points of view. He opposed fellow-Sunnis who thought that the Shias were not true Muslims.

He believed that a better understanding of the Quran by the people at large would reduce the differences resulting from the variety in the interpretations of the original message. Accordingly, he translated the holy book into simple Persian, which was then the literary language of the Indian Muslims. This was a bold step because many Muslims were opposed to the circulation of the Quran in any language other than the original Arabic. Finally, he advocated that to be healthy, society must eliminate economic injustice.

To a large measure, the success attained by Shah Wali-Ullah's mission was due to the fact that his work was continued by a band of devoted followers, including four learned sons. Of Wali-Ullah's sons, the most celebrated was Shah Abdul Aziz (1746-1824), who became the leader of the movement founded by his father and wrote several books presenting Wali-Ullah's philosophy in popular form. One of Abdul Aziz's brothers translated the Quran into Urdu freely, and another did the same literally, thus reaching an even larger number of readers than their father's Persian rendering had done. The brothers attracted a large number of disciples who spread Wali-Ullah's message in all parts of India.

Shah Abdul Aziz issued a *fatwa* that India had become *dar-ul-harb* which made it incumbent upon the faithful to restore Muslim political supremacy by waging jihad (holy war). One pupil of Abdul Aziz, Saiyid Ahmad, proceeded to do just that. He was born in 1786 to a family of Saiyids of Rai Bareilly, about forty-nine miles from Lucknow.

After studying under Abdul Aziz at Delhi, Saiyid Ahmad Barelvi joined the forces of Amir Khan, the Pindari leader. This military experience was to stand him in good stead in the time to come. In 1821 he went to Arabia for *hajj*. He did not sail from the west coast but chose the longer route via Calcutta. He had already started to preach and gathered a following. Four hundred persons attended him during his leisurely journey to Calcutta during which he preached and enrolled more disciples. At Calcutta so many persons wished to join his movement that he had to forgo the custom of initiation by placing his hand into their hand; instead he spread out his turban so that the disciples could touch it as a token of accepting his leadership.

Barelvi returned to India, again via Calcutta, and devoted himself to organizing jihad against the Sikhs. His plan was first to liberate the Muslim-majority province of the Punjab from the Sikhs, and then to use it as a base for operations against the British. Since the British were on friendly terms with Ranjit Singh, he decided to establish his headquarters in Pathan territory and launch an attack on the Sikh kingdom from the north-west. He arrived there in December 1824 and commenced operations. That he and his companions were able successfully to negotiate the tortuous route from India to the tribal area through Rajputana, Sind, Baluchistan, Kandahar, Ghazni and Kabul is clear proof of their determination and sound organization.

It had been Barelvi's hope that the Pathans, who were resisting Sikh expansion, would wholeheartedly side with him but he had not made allowances for their tradition of inter-tribal rivalries and unrestrained way of life. His attempts to set up an organized administration, including the imposition of taxes, to sustain long-term effort were not well received by his allies and Ranjit Singh was able to buy some of them off. After a brave start, including the occupation of Peshawar for a short time, the Saiyid was decisively defeated at Balakot in May 1831 and killed along with nearly six hundred *mujahidin*[1].

Though an organized campaign was no longer possible, the *mujahidin* did not abandon the effort and continued to trouble the Sikhs and the

---

[1] Plural of *mujahid*. *Mujahid* : one who fights in a holy war.

British when they conquered the Punjab from the Sikhs. Between 1850 and 1857 the British government was forced to mount sixteen distinct expeditions, aggregating 33,000 regular troops, and by 1863 the number rose to twenty separate expeditions, aggregating 60,000 regular troops, besides irregular auxiliaries and police. Though there were cells of the *mujahidin* all over India, their chief spiritual centre was Patna and their chief recruiting area was East Bengal. Their success in keeping their camp on the frontier supplied with men and money across two thousand miles of enemy territory is convincing proof of their fanatical courage and resourcefulness.

British military operations on the frontier were supplemented by suppression of the movement at its source in India and by 1870 the situation had been brought under control. But the danger had by no means disappeared. In his book, *The Indian Mussalmans*, Sir William Hunter, a senior member of Her Majesty's Bengal Civil Service, thus voiced British fears in 1871 : '[The organization] still continues the centre towards which the hopes alike of our disloyal subjects and of our enemies beyond the Frontier turn...and no one can predict the proportions to which this Rebel Camp, backed by the Mussalman hordes from the Westward, might attain to weld together the nations of Asia in a Crescentade'. Later, in 1918, the Rowlatt Report noted that the colony of the *mujahidin*, 'although small, had survived many vicissitudes and remains until now'. In fact there were *mujahidin* in the tribal areas right up to the establishment of Pakistan. When a subsequent generation of the Indian Muslims demanded Pakistan, they were following in the footsteps of the *mujahidin* who had endeavoured to re-establish *dar-ul-Islam*.

The nineteenth century also witnessed a Muslim revival in Bengal. Its sponsors were persons who availed themselves of the improved facilities for travel to Arabia. Haji Shariat-Ullah (1781-1840) was born in Faridpur District and visited the Islamic holy land from 1799 to 1818. There he was influenced by the teachings of Shaikh Muhammad Abdul Wahhab and on his return home sought to purge Islam of the beliefs and practices it had imbibed by its long contact with Hinduism. His followers were called 'Faraizis' on account of their insistence that everyone must perform the duties (*faraiz*, obligations) enjoined by their religion. The popularity of his movement among the peasants alarmed the landlords who were predominantly Hindu since the Permanent Settlement. They harassed him in various ways. But his mission was carried forward even more vigorously by his son Mohsin-ud-Din, popularly called Dadu Miyan (1819-1862), who had visited Arabia at a young age. He organized his followers into a popular force and resisted the excesses of Hindu landlords and European indigo planters. He was jailed several times.

An even more militant leader of Muslim peasants, who had been influenced by Saiyid Ahmad Barelvi, was Mir Nasir Ali whose popular name was Titu Mir. He had visited Mecca with a member of the Mughal royal family. His followers vigorously rejected all Hindu rites. They refused to pay a tax levied on beards by one of the Hindu *zamindars*. Their efforts to obtain justice through the usual channels failed because of the influence of the landlords. Titu Miyan and fifty of his disciples were killed in a battle against British troops on 18 November 1831.

Another disciple of Saiyid Ahmad was Maulvi Karamat Ali (1800-1873). He was born at Jaunpur and carried out his missionary work in East Bengal travelling by boat on the waterways. His outlook was conciliatory in the tradition of Shah Wali-Ullah. He vehemently opposed the Faraizi view that, India having become *dar-ul-harb*, the Muslims should suspend offering Friday and Id prayers there. He belonged to that section of the Muslims who held that, since the British did not interfere with the practice of religions, India was not *dar-ul-harb* but *dar-ul-aman* (abode of safety).

The Muslim revival movements in Bengal had an important result. They saved Islam from being swamped by a resurgent Hinduism.

A movement which profoundly affected the political future of the entire Subcontinent was one instituted by Sir Syed Ahmed Khan (1817-1898). It came to be known as the Aligarh movement because it was there that Sir Syed established his headquarters and founded the college which for the Muslims in India became equivalent to the English universities at Oxford and Cambridge. He has rightly been called the First Pakistani, because he was the first Muslim leader of consequence who said that the Hindus and the Muslims of India constituted two separate nations. To appreciate the magnitude of his achievements it is necessary to gauge the depth to which the fortunes of the Muslims had sunk at the time when he undertook the task of rehabilitating them.

There were, at that time, two main prerequisites for worldly success in India. The first was the favour of the British government, the new rulers of the country. The second was proficiency in the English language—the language in which the administration as well as trade and commerce were conducted. In both these respects the Hindus had the advantage.

As already stated, it was natural that there was little love lost between the Muslims and the British to start with. It was a Muslim empire that the British had conquered; it was the Mughal Emperor that the rebels in 1857 had proclaimed as their king. Even before the Great Rebellion, Reginald

Heber, Bishop of Calcutta, who journeyed through northern India during 1824-5, had felt that 'if fair opportunity offered, the Musalmans, more particularly, would gladly avail themselves [of it] to rise against us'. And when the rebelling actually happened, the Muslims, in British eyes, were the main culprits. 'The most obvious, popular and pressing theory', wrote Sir George Campbell in a letter to *The Times*, 'is that the Muhammadans have rebelled'.

With regard to language, the first great shock received by the Muslims was the replacement of Persian by English as the court language in 1837. The *ulema* believed that the British wanted the Indians to learn English to wean them away from their own culture and religion and convert them to Christianity. They employed their considerable influence to prevent the members of their flock from learning English, and shunned as *kafirs* the few Muslims who had received Western education. As a community, the Muslims steered clear of schools imparting Western education because they had a tradition of educating their children privately if they could afford to do so, or of sending them to *madrassas* where religious education was compulsory. As Sir Syed pointed out, the Muslims 'could never be brought to admit that sound and useful learning existed in any language except Arabic and Persian...I still remember the days when, in respectable families, the study of English, with the object of obtaining a post in Government service or of securing any other lucrative employment, was considered highly discreditable'.

It is no wonder that in all branches of government service, the British preferred to employ Hindus who were considered to be more loyal and had learnt English so readily. The plight of the Muslims was vividly and authoritatively described by William Hunter in his famous book, *The Indian Mussalmans, Are They Bound in Conscience to Rise Against the Queen?* He wrote the book at the behest of Lord Mayo, the Viceroy. The object was to diagnose the causes of Muslim disaffection so that steps could be taken to reconcile the Muslim community to British rule. 'The greatest wrong', to use Hunter's own words, 'that the English can do to their Asiatic subjects is not to understand them'. Hunter's book (1871) was the first sign of a change of heart by the British towards the Muslims and was of considerable assistance to Sir Syed in his task of bringing about a rapport between the Muslims and the British

Referring to the past, Hunter stated that the Muslim aristocracy once 'were conquerors and claimed as such the monopoly of Government... Three distinct streams of wealth ran perennially into the coffers of a noble Mussalman House—Military command, the Collection of the Revenue, and the Judicial or political Employ. These were its legitimate sources of greatness, and besides them were Court-Services, and a hundred nameless avenues to fortune'. He rejected the suggestion that the Hindu 'monopoly of official preferment' was due to their inherent superiority and pointed out that 'when the country passed under our rule, the Mussalmans were the superior race, and superior not only in stoutness of heart and strength of arm, but in power of political organization, and in the science of practical government'. Nor was the Muslim superiority limited to the sphere of political power; they were also 'the intellectual power in India' and he quoted an Indian statesman, E. C. Bayley, to the effect that the Muslims possessed a system of education which 'was capable of affording a high degree of intellectual training and polish'. Hunter argued that the Muslims had suffered because of the hostile attitude of the British government towards them: 'Nobody takes any notice of their helpless condition, and the higher authorities do not deign even to acknowledge their existence'. So much so that 'there is now scarcely a Government office in Calcutta in which a Muhammadan can hope for any post above the rank of porter, messenger, filler of ink-pots and mender of pens'. Only a hundred years before' 'the Mussalmans had monopolized all the important offices of state. The Hindus accepted with thanks such crumbs as their former conquerors dropped from their table, and the English were represented by a few factors and clerks'.

As the ruling class the Muslims in their heyday had preferred to occupy prestigious government positions and had left trade and commerce mostly in Hindu hands. They had neither the expertise nor the capital to make a quick change from state employment to business. In the economic field too, therefore, they now came a very poor third, after the British and the Hindus.

SIR SYED AHMED KHAN

It was after the Great Rebellion of 1857, when the fortunes of the Muslims of India were at their lowest ebb, that Sir Syed Ahmed Khan entered the political field and took up the cudgels on their behalf. He was born at Delhi on 17 October 1817 and was of noble stock. As a Saiyid he could claim descent from the Prophet through his daughter Fatima, the wife of Ali. His ancestors had migrated to India from Iran. His paternal grandfather was a titled courtier and his maternal grandfather was prime minister to the Mughal Emperor Akbar II. Sir Syed's father was a religious recluse and a close friend of Shah Ghulam Ali, a sufi saint. It was under the influence of these two pious men that Sir Syed acquired his devotion to religion.

Upon the death of his father in 1838, Sir Syed entered the service of the East India Company and, having qualified for the post of *Munsif* (Sub-Judge), was posted as such at Fatehpur Sikri in 1841. In 1846 he was transferred to Delhi and remained there until 1855. During his stay at the capital, he wrote a book on the historic buildings under the title *Asar-ul-Sanadid*.

In 1855 he was transferred to Bijnore and there edited Abdul Fazl's *A'in-i-Akbari,* Jahangir's autobiography and Zia-ud-Din Barni's history of the early Muslim rulers of India. His historical writings earned him an honorary Fellowship of the Royal Asiatic Society of London in 1864.

When the Great Rebellion broke out, Sir Syed was still at Bijnore working under Shakespeare, the Collector. A large force under Nawab Mahmud Khan threatened the lives of the local Europeans, who had assembled in the Collector's bungalow. With great presence of mind, Sir Syed negotiated with the Nawab and convinced him that it would be wise for him to let the Europeans depart in peace. That Sir Syed's intervention was the decisive factor in saving the lives of the beleaguered Europeans was afterwards acknowledged by Shakespeare in his official report on the happenings at Bijnore.

The terrible massacres during the Great Rebellion and its immediate aftermath, during which the Muslims were singled out by the British as the main culprits, awakened in Sir Syed the qualities of statesmanship, political foresight and public service that hitherto had lain dormant. His immediate task was to save his fellow Muslims from the wrath of the British government. To this end he wrote a pamphlet entitled *The Causes of The Indian Revolt*. This remarkable essay boldly places on the shoulders of the British govennment its share of the blame for the Rebellion and shows clearly that the author was not given to mincing words. The main cause of disaffection, he argued, was the ignorance of the government of the feelings of their subjects. This was because the people were not allowed a share in the deliberations of the Legislative Council. He also criticised the government for the resumption of revenue-free lands and for its encouragement to the spread of the Christian faith. And he blamed the tactless handling of the situation at Meerut for the general outbreak that followed. He called the disgracing of the prisoners who had declined to use the objectionable cartridges 'most wrong and most inopportune...the prisoners, on seeing their hands and feet manacled, looked at their medals and wept'. The news of this punishment angered the whole army.

The principal reasons why the British government blamed the Muslims for the Great Rebellion was that the rebels had proclaimed Bahadur Shah as their leader. Sir Syed called the Emperor such an imbecile that 'had one assured him that the angels of heaven were his slaves, he would have welcomed the assurance...' 'His object, of course, was to show that Bahadur Shah was in his dotage and a mere puppet in the hands of the insurgents.

Sir Syed's criticism of the policies of the government so offended the Foreign Secretary in the Viceroy's council that he labelled the pamphlet as 'highly seditious' and called for the punishment of the author. But no action was taken because the Viceroy and others regarded the author as basically a well-wisher of the British government.

Sir Syed supplemented *The Causes of the Indian Revolt* with a series of pamphlets on *The Loyal Mohammedans of India*. In these, while characterizing the conduct of those Muslims who had joined the rebellion as 'criminal', he deplored the wholesale denunciation of the Muslims as a race.

It has been suggested in some quarters that Sir Syed originally was a 'nationalist' Indian and turned 'communal' later under the influence of the British, especially under that of Theodore Beck, the principal of Aligarh College. The truth of the matter, as will become increasingly clear in the subsequent pages, seems to be that Sir Syed from the very beginning regarded the Hindus and the Muslims as 'the two antagonistic races' but at first believed that it was possible for them to cultivate friendly relations with each other on an equal footing. However, the Hindi-Urdu controversy convinced him that co-operation between the two peoples as equals was impossible and that the Muslims must take the necessary steps not to be overwhelmed by the larger community. As mentioned in the chapter on the Great Rebellion the term 'two antagonistic races' had already been used by him in *The Causes of the Indian Revolt*.

Sir Syed's emphasis in the same pamphlet on the necessity of the rulers being aware of the feelings of their subjects had another momentous result. A. O. Hume, the Scotsman who after retirement from the Indian Civil Service founded the Indian National Congress, told Sahibzada Aftab Ahmad Khan in London in 1892 that, 'It was after reading Syed Ahmed's book on *The Causes of The Indian Revolt* that I first felt the need for having a forum of public opinion in India, and eventually the Indian National Congress came into existence. But the amazing thing is that when it was started, Syed was the first to oppose it'.

Sir Syed recognized that it was not enough just to plead the Muslim cause with the British. It was even more important for the Muslims to have access to Western knowledge so that they could stand on their own feet and catch up with the Hindus. At this stage, however, he did not favour learning the English language. As he confessed later, 'I am the person who had first entertained the idea that the acquisition of the knowledge of European science through the medium of the vernacular would be more beneficial to the country...But I could not help acknowledging the fallacy of my opinion at last'. It was in consonance with his earlier preference for the vernacular that he established the Scientific Society in 1846, which translated several historical and scientific works from English into Urdu. The Society also published a magazine under the title of *The Aligarh Institute Gazette.*

Two year later he started the British India Association, with the purpose of keeping British public opinion, especially Parliament, informed of Indian opinion and grievances.

Hitherto, he had striven for the good of Hindus and Muslims alike. The Scientific Society was managed by him in association with Raja Jai Kishen Das, and the British India Association had been open equally to both Hindus and Muslims. But in 1876, when he was at Benares, a sudden change came over him. Some Hindu leaders there resolved that the use of Urdu, written in Persian script, should be replaced in the lower courts by Hindi, written in Devanagari script. Sir Syed used to recall that this was the first occasion on which he felt that it was now impossible for the Hindus and the Muslims to progress as a single nation and for anyone to serve them both.

The Hindi-Urdu controversy inflamed the members of both the major communities. The Muslims argued that Urdu was not their national or religious language; it had not been imported from a foreign land but had originated in India itself as the result of the joint efforts of the Hindus and the Muslims. But the Hindus said it was 'a pure and simple survival of the old Muslim tyranny in India' and it did not accord with the religious and social aspirations of the Hindus because its script was Arabic, which was the sacred language of the Muslims. Sir Syed felt so strongly on the subject that he said that adoption of Hindi in Devanagari characters would cause the Muslims 'the greatest injury save deprivation of their religion'. The bitter Hindi-Urdu agitation significantly contributed to the development of nationalism on communal lines.

In 1869 Sir Syed went to England accompanied by his sons Syed Mahmud and Syed Hamed and stayed there for seventeen months. Syed Mahmud had been awarded a scholarship to study at Cambridge. Sir Syed was treated with respect by many British officials who had served in India and had a prolonged meeting with Carlyle. However, he did not spend his time sightseeing but laboured hard in the India Office and British Museum libraries doing research for his *Essays on the Life of Muhammad*. This was a refutation of Sir William Muir's unfavourable *Life of Mahomet*. Sir Syed was greatly impressed with the character and way of life of the British people and felt that the key to their superiority was education. He visited several British universities and resolved to establish one in India on the same lines for the benefit of his own community.

Soon after his return home, he started a magazine under the title of *Tahzibul Akhlaq* (Social Reformer). Though the avowed object of the periodical was to improve the manners and social customs of the Muslims, Sir Syed did not refrain from including religious topics in its pages and expressed himself in a characteristically forceful manner. His views enraged the orthodox, who hurled insults such as *'kafir'* at him.

Sir Syed's most concrete service to his community was the foundation at Aligarh of the Muhammadan Anglo-Oriental (MAO) College. The college started in 1875; in the following year he retired from Government service and settled down at Aligarh to tend the infant institution. Lord Lytton, the Viceroy, formally laid the foundation stone of the college in 1877. Sir Syed had the college managed by carefully-selected Englishmen who ensured that the education of the pupils was not confined to the class room but included those extra-curricular activities which go to make up an all-round gentleman.

In their address of welcome to Lord Lytton, the College Committee stated that the objective of the college was to '...dispel those illusory traditions of the past which have hindered our progress; to remove those prejudices which have hitherto exercised a baneful influence on our race; to reconcile Oriental learning with Western literature and science; to inspire in the dreamy minds of the people of the East the practical energy which belongs to those of the West; to make the Mussalmans of India worthy and useful subjects of the British crown...' Loyalty to the British government was an important plank of Sir Syed's programme because he realized that British goodwill was essential for the Muslims to save them from being overwhelmed by the numerically and educationally superior Hindus. The MAO. College graduates played an effective role in the regeneration of the Muslims of India. In 1920 the college attained university status.

For a greater spread of education, Sir Syed in 1886 founded the Mohammedan Educational Conference which met at different places in the country. This body, besides laying stress on education, became an important literary forum where Muslim writers and poets could express themselves and stimulate the audience intellectually and politically. It continued to flourish after its founder had passed away. Its twentieth session was held at the end of December 1906 at Dacca, the capital of Eastern Bengal, a province which had recently come into existence as the result of the partition of Bengal. After conducting their normal business, the delegates reconvened as an independent assembly and decided to found the All-India Muslim League.

Sir Syed's political philosophy started the trend which ultimately convinced the Muslims that they and the Hindus constituted two irreconcilable nations. His main argument is contained in two famous speeches, one made on 15 January 1883 on Lord Ripon's Local Self-Government Bill (he had been nominated to the Imperial Legislative Council in 1878), and the other publicly at Lucknow on 28 December 1887.

Lord Ripon's Bill established Municipal Councils and Rural District Boards whose members...in some cases a majority of them—were directly elected, but it reserved to the government the right to nominate one third of the members. Sir Syed voted for the Bill and heartily approved the first step toward self-government which the Bill represented. He also praised, in principle, the representative institutions which had made England great. He agreed, further, that the 'local boards and district councils should consist, as far as possible, of persons whom the voice of the people has elected as their representatives', but he considered that 'the principle of election pure and simple', which worked admirably in England, was not suitable for the conditions prevailing in India:

> I am convinced that no part of India has yet arrived at the stage when the system of representation can be adopted in its fullest scope...in borrowing from England the system of representative institutions, it is of the greatest importance to remember those socio-political matters in which India is distinguishable from England... India, a continent in itself, is inhabited by a vast population of different races and different creeds: the rigour of religious institutions has kept even neighbours apart: the system of caste is still dominant and powerful... The system of representation by election means the representation of the views and interests of the majority of the population... So long as differences of race and creed and the distinctions of caste form an important element in the socio-political life of India, and influence her inhabitants in matters connected with the administration and welfare of the country at large, the system of election,

pure and simple, cannot be safely adopted. The larger community would totally override the interests of the smaller community.

He welcomed the provision that one third of the members should be nominated because it would secure 'that due and just balance in the representation of the various sections of the Indian population which the system of election, pure and simple, would fail to achieve'.

The main purpose of Sir Syed's Lucknow speech was to oppose those demands of the Indian National Congress which, he thought, would place the Muslim under Hindu domination. The Congress had been founded in 1885 (see the next chapter) and, at the time of Sir Syed's speech, was meeting at Madras for its third annual session. On earlier occasions it had demanded the introduction of representative institutions; the holding of the competitive examination for recruitment to the Indian Civil Service and other higher services, not only in London, but both in England and India simultaneously; and the filling of 'all other first appointments (excluding peonships and the like)' by competitive examinations to be held in India. Conscious of the criticism that the first two sessions had failed to attract any important Muslims, the conveners of the third session had invited Badruddin Tyabjee, a prominent Muslim who later became a judge of the Bombay High Court, to preside over the proceedings. A month before the second session of Congress, Sir Syed had condemned that body as 'seditious' in an editorial in the Aligarh Institute Gazette. The efforts of Congress to entice more Muslims into its ranks evidently made Sir Syed feel that he must oppose it publicly.

He repeated, in even stronger terms than he had done in 1883, his opposition to the introduction of universal suffrage in India without paying heed to the Hindu-Muslim problem: 'Let us suppose that we have universal suffrage as in America, and that all have votes. And let us also suppose that all the Muhammadan electors vote for a Muhammadan member and all the Hindu electors for a Hindu member, and now count how many votes the Muhammadan member will have and how many the Hindu. It is certain that a Hindu member will have four times as many, because their population is four times as numerous...it is like a game of dice in which one man had four dice and the other only one'. And suppose the British withdraw from India, who would rule the country? In another speech at Meerut in 1888 he said, 'Is it possible that under these circumstances the two nations—the Muhammadans and Hindus—could sit on the same throne and remain equal in power? Most certainly not. It is necessary that one of them should conquer the other and thrust it down.'

He further pointed out that if the members of the services were recruited by competitive examinations all the vacancies would be filled by the Hindus, especially the Bengalis, who had stolen a march on the Muslims in Western education.

Sir Syed's Lucknow speech was severely criticised by the Hindu Press but the *Muslim Herald* wrote, 'We proudly accept the Syed as our leader... His speech sounds the keynote of our policy'. Most Muslims applauded Sir Syed and acknowledged that he was leading the community in the right direction.

Even the Hindus were not unaimous in their support of the Indian National Congress. Taking advantage of this, Sir Syed started the United Indian Patriotic Association in collaboration with some Hindus (1888). Its chief object as stated in the rules was:

To publish and circulate pamphlets and other papers for information of Members of Parliament, English journals, and the people of Great Britain, in which those misstatements will be pointed out by which the supporters of the Indian National Congress have wrongfully attempted to convince the English people that all the nations of India and the Indian Chiefs and Rulers agree with the aims and objects of the National Congress.

Another aim was 'To strive to preserve peace in India, and to strengthen the British Rule...'

The proceedings of the fifth session of Congress, which convened at Bombay on 26 December 1889, roused special anxiety in the mind of Sir Syed. It was presided over by Sir William Wedderburn, who had come from England specially for the purpose. Together with William Digby, he had been promoting Congress demands in England through the Congress Agency there. An even more important guest at the meeting was Charles Bradlaugh, MP, who had earned the title of 'Member for India' because he often spoke for India in Parliament. He had prepared and circulated a bill embodying the views of Congress as known till then and had come to India to ascertain their latest opinions so that they could be included in the bill.

From its very first session Congress had been demanding the expansion of the Governor-General's Council as well as the Provincial Councils by the admission of elected members, and also the conferment on them of the right to discuss the budget and 'interpellate the Executive in regard to all branches of the administration'. At the fifth session it resolved that 'the imperial and provincial Councils' should 'consist respectively of Members

not less than one half of whom are to be elected, not more than one-fourth
to sit *ex-officio*, and the rest to be nominated by Government'.

Since the Muslims had no agency of their own in England, Sir Syed
feared that the Congress lobby there would ensure the success of Bradlaugh's
bill. To show that the majority of the Muslims were opposed to the
Congress demands, he caused a petition, signed by 49,000 Muslims from
about seventy cities and towns, to be presented to the House of Commons
in April 1890. The petition prayed that '... your Honourable House will not
introduce the principle of election into the constitution of the Indian
Councils as requested by the Indian National Congress' because 'the
effect of introducing this principle would be to destroy that even-handed
justice which had been hitherto the basis of British Rule and would place
them (the petitioners) and other minorities in an almost intolerable
subjection to classes actively hostile to their welfare'. The petition
emphasised that the Muslims were not a small minority; they numbered
50,000,000 strong. It stated, further, that the demand for the introduction
of an elective system proceeded from English-educated Hindus, 'a class
that is exceptionally well able to make its voice heard both in England and
in India while the Mohammedans, being very backward in English
education, have been unable to give equal prominence to their views'.

In the end Bradlaugh dropped his bill but the government-sponsored
Councils Act of 1892 granted some of the Congress wishes in part. It
expanded only the Provincial Councils and granted only the Provincial
Councils the right to discuss the budget and question the executive on
administrative matters, but it denied them the right to vote on them. The
system of election was not directly conceded. A few of the non-official
members were still to be nominated but for the majority 'recommendations'
were to be invited from local bodies or corporations such as religious
communities, municipalities, universities and chambers of commerce.
Since the recommendations were never turned down, the rule was election
in all but name. On the face of it, only Congress seemed to have gained
ground, but the concession that religious communities could recommend
their own candidates meant that the Muslims had won the right to separate
representation. This first step, little noticed at the time, was to develop into
the system of separate electorates, with momentous consequences. A
Government of India dispatch of 1892 explained that Indian society was
'essentially a congeries of widely separated classes, races and communities
with divergences of interest and hereditary sentiment' which could be
properly represented only by those who knew and shared their sectional
opinions.

Hindu-Muslim riots have always been an all-too familiar feature of the Indian scene. Those in the summer of 1893 were especially wide-spread and vicious. In Bombay alone, sixty-five persons lost their lives and more than 500 were hurt during disturbances that continued for a whole week. It was the year in which Tilak had put the Ganapati festivals on a new footing. The significance of these festivals was discussed in a 1918 report by the Sedition Committee, presided over by Justice Rowlatt, in these words: 'Public Ganapati festivals appear to have arisen out of an anti-Mohammadan movement started after riots which broke out in the city of Bombay in 1893 between Hindus and Mohammadans. Agitators who were interested in widening the breach between these two communities encouraged the holding of public celebrations in honour of Ganapati, the elephant-headed god of wisdom and success, on a much larger scale than in previous years. The idea appears to have been to make the procession in which the god is carried to this final resting place in the water as offensive as possible to Mohammadans. During the ten days' celebrations of the festival, bands of young men paraded the streets of Poona, singing verses calculated to intensify the feeling against Mohammadans and government'. The activities of the Cow-Protection Societies also added to the tension between the two communities.

Sir Syed evidently felt that the Muslims needed an organization of their own to protect their interests. For this purpose he started the Muhammadan Anglo-Oriental Defence Association of Upper India in December 1893. Its objects were declared to be: '(1) To protect the political interests of Mohammadans by representing their views before the English people and the Indian Government, (2) to discourage popular political agitation among Mohammadans, (3) to lend support to measures calculated to increase the stability of the British Government and the security of the Empire; to strive to preserve peace in India; and to encourage sentiments of loyalty in the population'.

In 1896 Sir Syed prepared a memorandum for the Anglo-Oriental Defence Association. The demands in this remarkable document formed the basis of those put forward ten years later by the famous Aga Khan delegation to the Viceroy. It is generally agreed that the achievement of those concessions by the Muslim community greatly facilitated their march on the road to Pakistan (more on the Aga Khan delegation later). Sir Syed's Memorandum set out Muslim requirements as follows: (1) In the North-Western Provinces, the Muslims should be given representation equal to the more numerous Hindus because of their history and political importance, (2) the Muslims should be allowed communal electorates so that only Muslims would vote to elect Muslim candidates, (3) in the allotment of seats in the municipal councils, district boards and the like, the Muslims should be given weightage.

It was also Sir Syed's belief that for real Muslim-British understanding, it was necessary to show that Islam and Christianity were compatible with each other and the differences between them minor. His earliest major effort in this direction was his commentaries on the Old and New Testaments; his journal *Tahzibul Akhlaq*, by promoting a rational approach to Islam, also served the same purpose. After retirement he wrote a massive (seven volume) *Commentary on the Koran* in which he tried to prove that the contents of the Quran were not incompatible with modern science: that the Quran was the word of God and nature was the work of God. In the process of doing so he challenged many traditional ideas and made the orthodox *ulema* angrier with him than ever. Though his religious views did not attract a large following, his example encouraged the acceptance of new ideas by rational debate.

But it is not as a theologian that Sir Syed is remembered. His lasting services to his community were in the realms of education and politics, which we have already noted, and in the field of the Urdu language, which remains to be discussed. Sir Syed wrote exclusively in Urdu; his own prose was utilitarian, not literary or ornate. He was more concerned with making his message clear than with impressing the reader with the finery of his words and idioms. By his example he discouraged the trend toward cumbersome phraseology and artificiality. His writings influenced, among others, Maulana Abul Kalam Azad, the 'nationalist' Muslim who presided over Congress in his later years. Azad states in his memoirs, *India Wins Freedom*, that he 'came across the writings of Sir Syed Ahmed Khan' during his teens and 'was greatly impressed by his views on modern education' and decided that he 'must learn English'.

Sir Syed's service to the language resulted from the magnetism of his leadership, which attracted to his circle the greatest contemporary masters of Urdu poetry and prose. The scholars, who translated English works under the auspices of the Scientific Society and who contributed to the columns of the *Tahzibul Akhlaq*, pioneered a new style in Urdu suited to their purpose: direct and free of bombast. Sir Syed thus not only gave the Muslims a sense of nationhood, but was also instrumental in modernizing their language to express it.

Perhaps the most notable of Sir Syed's admirers was Altaf Husain Hali, who preceded Muhammad Iqbal as the national poet of the Indian Muslims. He came under Sir Syed's spell from the moment he saw the latter, and described their first meeting in graphic terms: 'All of a sudden I saw a man of God, a hero among men, going ahead on a hazardous path... I was drawn to him, almost within an instant... ' Hali's best known poem, *Musaddas*, written at Sir Syed's instance, first appeared in the *Tahzibul Akhlaq*. It poignantly portrays the past glories and contemporary decline of the Muslims. Iqbal paid due tribute to Sir Syed and Hali for inspiring the Indian Muslims and giving them confidence:

> The Tulip of the Desert [the Muslim nation]
> encountered autumn and withered away.
> Syed [Ahmed] gave it a new life,
> with the dew of his morning tears,
> And Hali did not cease his heart-warming melodies,
> Until the bedewed tulip had once again got its shining spot.

Among the other literary collaborators of Sir Syed were Mohsin ul Mulk, who kept the Aligarh movement alive after Sir Syed had passed away; Maulvi Nazir Ahmad, the famous prose writer and novelist; Maulvi Zaka Ullah, the versatile scholar and translator; and Shibli Nomani, who wrote eruditely on historical and religious themes. They differed in varying degrees from Sir Syed's ideas but respected him as the political teacher of their community.

Sir Syed's influence was strongest in northern India. The credit for encouraging the Muslims of Bengal to take to Western education belongs mainly to the scholar-jurist Ameer Ali and to Nawab Abdul Latif, a founder of the Presidency College and a Fellow of Calcutta University. But their achievement was not nearly as great as Sir Syed's.

Some critics of Sir Syed have alleged that he followed an anti-national communal line to please the British and also that he was greatly influenced by Theodore Beck, Principal of the Aligarh College. In this connection it is well to remember that Sir Syed was the scion of an aristocratic family and was very jealous of his self-respect. This was well demonstrated by two incidents. In 1876, while he was still in government service, he left a *durbar* in protest because the chairs for the Indian invitees had been placed at a level lower than those for the Europeans. The second incident arose out of an article which Sir Syed wrote criticising the educational policy of the government. Sir William Muir, the Lieutenant-Governor, took issue with Sir Syed, and the Urdu version of his speech suggested that he had accused Sir Syed of a lack of veracity. Sir Syed thereafter did not call on Muir and the latter had to assure him by a personal letter that he could 'never have dreamt of imputing to you anything approaching to a mis-statement of facts'. In the opening phase of his political career he had, in his *Causes of the Indian Revolt*, warned the British government that they had 'forfeited' the goodwill of the people of India because they treated them with contempt.

Today, Sir Syed's attitude toward the British government undoubtedly sounds excessively sycophantic, but this was the general characteristic of the time. Raja Ram Mohan Roy and the leaders of the Indian National Congress were no less vocal in their assurances of loyalty to the government and in singing the praises of the benefits conferred by British rule.

There is still less substance in the charge that Sir Syed's conduct was moulded by Beck. It is true that Beck was zealously pro-Muslim and was the moving spirit of the Muhammadan Anglo-Oriental Defence Association of Upper India, but this seems to have been due to the facts that he was an employee of Sir Syed's college and genuinely sympathetic to the Muslim cause.

When Beck arrived to take up the position of Principal in the beginning of 1884, he had just left the university and was only twenty-four years of age. Sir Syed then was already sixty-six years old and had given ample proof of his strong will by disregarding criticism levelled against him by the Hindus as well as by the *ulema* of his own community. He had also already made his famous speech on Lord Ripon's Local Self-Government Bill spelling out his political philosophy. Considering all the circumstances, it is more logical to conclude that Beck fell under Sir Syed's spell than the other way round. In Beck's eyes Sir Syed was 'the noblest and most gifted man with whom I have ever enjoyed intimate personal intercourse'.

Sir Syed has also been compared to Raja Ram Mohan Roy, and indeed there is some resemblance between them. Both favoured Western education as the means to uplift their respective communities. But Sir Syed's task as well as his achievements were far greater than the Raja's. Roy's attempts at social reform met with the opposition of the orthodox Hindus, but in the tasks of promoting Western education and loyalty to the British government he had the enthusiastic support of his people. Sir Syed, on the other hand had to fight hard for every aspect of his programme.

In changing the face of Indian politics and shaping the destiny of the entire subcontinent he ranks not with Ram Mohan Roy but with Mahatma Gandhi and Quaid-i-Azam Mohammad Ali Jinnah. He was certainly the predominant political figure of nineteenth century India.

He passed away on 27 March 1898, honoured alike by the British government (he had been knighted in 1888) and by much the greater majority of his own people, especially the intelligentsia. C. F. Andrews, a disciple of Gandhi, has endorsed the estimate of a lifelong friend of Sir Syed: 'Other men have written books and founded colleges; but to arrest, as with a wall, the degeneration of a whole people—that is the work of a prophet'.

CHAPTER 7

THE INDIAN NATIONAL CONGRESS—THE FIRST TWENTY YEARS

THE COMPLEXITY OF INDIAN NATIONALISM

A variety of circumstances together began to create the consciousness among Western-educated Indians that the geographical unit south of the Himalayas constituted a nation. India under British rule was governed as one country; it owed allegiance to one monarch.

An extensive railway system and cheap postal and telegraph services made communication between persons living in different parts of the vast subcontinent easy for the first time in their long history.

They had a common language in English, which not only enabled them to understand one another but also made them aware of the institutions and freedom movements of other lands. The American and French revolutions, the attainment of freedom from foreign rule by Greece and Italy, and the growth of nationalism in Europe and South America, were all watched with interest and excitement. The revelations that India's ancient civilization vied with the other great civilizations of old, and that the Aryans had sprung from the same stock as the West Europeans, made them feel second to none.

Thanks to some features of British rule and the racial tension between the white rulers and their non-white subjects (see Chapter 4), there was also present the usual spur to nationalism—dislike of foreign domination. It is true that many British politicians in England, and administrators in India, were benevolently disposed towards India, but the basic fact was that the British were in India more for the good of their own country than for that of India. It was the age when capitalist exploitation was rampant in England. One has only to read the works of Dickens to realise the squalor in which the working-class men, women and children in England had to labour to enrich the rising middle class of industrialists and bankers. It was unrealistic to expect that the Indians—a subject race—

would be treated more generously than England's own citizens. India was a temptingly huge market. The doctrine of 'free trade' enabled manufactured goods from England, especially from Lancashire, to flood the Indian market free of duty, destroying local village industries and upsetting the balance of its traditional rural economy.

It was equally unrealistic to expect that the promise of equal opportunity to join the services, reiterated at the end of the Great Rebellion, would be honoured. Feeling more insecure in India than ever before, the prevailing mood among the British was to hold on, and, if possible, to strengthen their monopoly of the higher civil and military positions in the country.

Lord Lytton's Viceroyalty (1876-80) made its own peculiar contribution to the growth of nascent Indian nationalism. The Second Afghan War was seen as an expedition in which Indian lives were being sacrificed to further the cause of imperialism; the Vernacular Press Act of 1878 was deeply resented because it gagged the Indian papers while it left the European press untouched; and the lowering of the age limit for appearing in the London competitive examination for entering the Indian Civil Service was regarded as a deliberate move to make it even more difficult for Indians to join the ranks of the ruling elite. Lord Ripon personally won plaudits from the Indians for repealing the Vernacular Press Act and supporting the Ilbert Bill and for his Local Self Government Bill, but the bitter and successful agitation against the Ilbert Bill by the British community in India resulted in increased racial hatred between the Europeans and the Indians.

Though both the major communities of India—the Hindus and the Muslims—were experiencing a political awakening, their perceptions were not the same. The discovery of India's ancient greatness stirred Hindu pride and fuelled Hindu nationalism. The Muslims found inspiration in the greatness of the more recent Arab and Ottoman Empires and the Muslim Empires in India. Prithvi Raj, Rana Partap and Shivaji were heroes in the eyes of the Hindus because they had fought valiantly against the Muslims. Muhammd bin Qasim, Mahmud of Ghazni and Muhammad Ghori were heroes in the eyes of the Muslims because they had vanquished the Hindus.

Hinduism, moreover, being a 'search after truth', is receptive to new ideas and change. Islam, on the other hand, has a well-developed polity of its own. The state is governed according to *shariah,* or Islamic law. The Muslims had governed India for several hundred years and the Ottoman Empire was still in existence. They felt that they needed no lessons from the West in the art of government. What they desired was to learn where they had gone wrong so that they could compete with Hindus on equal terms under the changed conditions. The Hindu intelligentsia derived its theory of nationalism from the British example and from English literature. It craved representative institutions as practised in England and the British colonies. To the Muslims, the parliamentary system in Indian conditions meant their permanent subjection to the Hindus. It was bad enough for them to be ruled by the British; to be ruled by their erstwhile subjects, the Hindus, was unthinkable. Not surprisingly, the Muslims largely held aloof from the Indian National Congress, which adopted British democracy as the model for India.

There was also an unbridgeable gulf between Hinduism and Islam. The Muslims of India felt closer to the Muslims of other lands than to the Hindus with whom they physically shared Hindustan. Sir Abdur Rahim, who rose to be the president of the National Assembly, once complained that, while the Muslims of India felt quite at home in the Muslim countries, in India they found themselves 'in all social matters total aliens' as soon as they crossed the street and entered that part of the town where their Hindu fellow-townsmen lived. Sir Sultan Muhammad Shah Aga Khan III has written in his *Memoirs* that his mother throughout her long life 'had been animated by one simple, sincere desire', which was 'that when the time came she should be buried on Muslim soil, by which she meant a land ruled by a free, independent and sovereign Muslim government'. She was, accordingly, taken to Iraq during her fatal illness, died there, and was buried near her husband at Najaf, near Karbala. Pursuant to his own expressed wish, Aga Khan III himself was buried in Egypt when he died.

This feeling of not completely belonging to India made it emotionally impossible for the Muslims to subscribe to Indian nationalism in the same way as the Hindus. The Muslims felt that they were Muslims first and Indians afterwards. Sheikh Muhammad Abdullah of Kashmir, a 'nationalist' Muslim, likened Islam to the sun and all other religions to the stars and declared that he was 'Muslim first and Muslim afterwards.' Fazlul Haq, while leading a coalition government in Bengal, made it clear that he was a Muslim first and Bengali afterwards.

In fact, if they had the choice, the Muslims of India would have liked nothing better than to have formed one large Muslim nation together with Muslims of other lands. Dr M. A. Ansari, who had led a medical mission to Turkey during the Balkan War, lamented that, 'it is difficult for any non-Muslim Indian to realise what Pan-Islamism means to Indian Muslims...Pan-Islamic sentiment has been one of the

Indian Muslim's most sacred and exalted passions'. When the Ansari medical mission returned to India, among those who went to receive it at the railway station was Shibli Nomani, the eminent scholar who, for some years, was a member of the faculty of the Aligarh Muslim University. Shibli was so overcome with emotion that he bent down, kissed Ansari's feet, and wept for the Turks who were struggling for their existence.

Muhammad Ali recalled: 'My feelings during the disastrous war in the Balkans were at one time so overpowering that I must confess I even contemplated suicide. The latest message of Reuter that had reached me was that the Bulgarians were only twenty-five miles from the walls of Constantinople—from Constantinople, a name that had for five centuries been sacred to every Muslim as the centre of his highest hopes.'

Hindu-Muslim tension, ever lurking below the surface, often broke out in violence. The earliest recorded Hindu-Muslim riot after the coming of the British took place at Benares in 1809, when the Hindus avenged the insult inflicted by Aurangzeb nearly a century before by allegedly building a mosque on a sacred Hindu site. Several hundred persons lost their lives and some fifty mosques were destroyed. When Reginald Heber journeyed through northern India in 1824-5 he found Benares in a state of tension. He found that the two communities there were 'literally armed' against each other and 'the fury which actuated both was more like that of demoniacs than rational enemies... It began by the Mussalmans breaking down a famous pillar, named Shiva's walking-staff, held in high veneration by the Hindoos. These last in revenge burnt and broke down a mosque, and the retort of the first aggressor was to kill a cow, and pour her blood into the sacred well. In consequence every Hindoo able to bear arms, and many who had no other fitness for the employment than the rage supplied, procured weapons, and attacked their enemies with frantic fury wherever they met them.' At Allahabad the bishop found that the local people there regarded Bengalis 'as no less foreigners than the English and even more odious than Franks.'

Communal riots took place at Bhiwindi (Bombay) in 1837, and at Broach in 1857. There were outbreaks at different places in 1871, 1872 and 1877. Violent riots occurred at Lahore and Karnal in 1885, at Delhi in 1886, at Dera Ghazi Khan in 1889, at Palakod in 1891 and in the United Provinces and Bombay in 1893.

THE FOUNDATION OF THE INDIAN NATIONAL CONGRESS

The birth of political consciousness, naturally, also saw the birth of various political organizations, especially in Bengal, where nationalism first became a serious force. In 1876 Surendranath Banerji founded the Indian Association at Calcutta. He had been dismissed from the Indian Civil Service for what is now generally acknowledged to have been an insufficient reason, and had won sympathy as a martyr to the racist policy of the foreign government. A gifted orator with a good command of the English language, he plunged into the political life of the country and promoted nationalism with vigour and distinction.

According to Surendranath himself, the Indian Association had been set up because 'the conception of a united India, derived from the inspiration of Mazzini, or at any rate of bringing all India upon the same common political platform, had taken possession of the minds of the Indian leaders in Bengal'. The Association protested against the reduction of the age limit for appearing in the Indian Civil Service examination, and against the Vernacular Press Act, and its members took an active part in countering the vicious agitation launched by the European community in India against the Ilbert Bill. Despite its significant nationalist activities, the Indian Association had the appearance of being a Bengali organization. To attain all-India status, it called the First National Conference in Calcutta in the last week of December 1883. This was done to take advantage of the expected presence in Calcutta at that time of a large number of leading Indians as visitors to an International Exhibition sponsored by the government.

The Conference was attended by upwards of one hundred delegates from several towns in India. Among the topics discussed were greater employment of Indians in the Civil Service, separation of the judicial from the executive authority, and representative government. The National Conference held its second session, again in Calcutta, from 25 to 27 December 1885, and expanded its agenda to include the question of reducing government civil and military expenditure and the 'home charges'.

At exactly the same time as the National Conference was meeting in Calcutta, the Indian National Congress was holding its inaugural session in Bombay. Before long, the Indian National Congress came to the forefront and the Indian National Conference faded away. This calls for a word of explanation because the programme of the new organization was not far different from that of the old.

The main reason for the immediate acceptance of the Indian National Congress as a desirable institution by the Indian intelligentsia—who at that time were largely moderate in outlook, enamoured of Western institutions and professed loyalty to the British government—was that it had been founded by a Scotsman, Allan Octavian Hume (1829-1912), who had retired from the Indian Civil Service to devote his life to Indian political regeneration. This was explained by G. K. Gokhale in London in 1913:

> No Indian could have started the Indian National Congress. Apart from the fact that anyone putting his hand to such a gigantic task had need to have Mr Hume's commanding personality, even if an Indian had possessed such a personality and had come forward to start such a movement, embracing all India, the officials would not have allowed it to come into existence. If the founder of Congress had not been a great Englishman [Scotsman] and a distinguished ex-official, such was the distrust of political agitation in those days that the authorities would have at once found some way or the other of suppressing the movement.

Surendranath, the moving spirit of the Indian National Conference, was regarded in official circles with a certain amount of suspicion because of his dismissal from the Civil Service and the Conference itself had been unable to shake off its provincial image. W. S. Blunt, who was present at the first session of the Conference, found it 'very provincial in its interests as quite three parts (three quarters of the hundred) of the delegates are Bengalis'. Surendranath was not even consulted by Hume when he was planning the first session of Congress and, naturally, did not attend it. His own explanation is that he was invited to attend the congress by W. C. Bonnerjee, who presided over the opening session, somewhat late. At that stage he could not suspend the conference, which was due to convene at Calcutta on the same dates as the congress at Bombay. Bonnerjee, who 'lived the life of an Englishman', was not an admirer of Surendranath and it is possible that he invited Surendranath at the eleventh hour simply to keep up appearances.

It has been suggested that Hume originally intended that Congress should concern itself with social reform but accepted the suggestion of the Viceroy, Lord Dufferin (1884-8), that it should discuss political matters so that the government could learn in what way the administration could be improved. Another suggestion is that Hume wished to carry out agitation in England to rouse the conscience of the people there, but was persuaded by Lord Dufferin that it would be more fruitful if this was done in India and a national organization was founded for the purpose. Both these surmises are conclusively refuted by an open letter which Hume addressed to the graduates of Calcutta University before Lord Dufferin had arrived in India as Viceroy.

This remarkable letter was written on 1 March 1883, after Hume had retired from government service in the previous year. It shows clearly how Hume's mind was working:

> Whether in the individual or the nation, all vital progress must spring from within, and it is to you, her most cultured and intelligent minds, her most favoured sons, that your country must look for the initiative. In vain may aliens, like myself, love India and her children...but they lack the essential of nationality and the real work must ever be done by the people of the country themselves...Scattered individuals, however capable and however well-meaning, are powerless singly. What is needed is union, organization...having for its object to promote the mental, moral, social and political regeneration of the people of India...If you, the picked the men, the most highly educated of the nation, cannot, scorning personal ease and selfish objects, make a resolute struggle to secure greater freedom for yourselves and your country, a more impartial administration, a larger share in the management of your own affairs... then, at present at any rate, all hopes of progress are at an and, and India truly neither lacks nor deserves any better government than she now enjoys...

That Hume was genuinely interested in the welfare of India is undoubted. He had obviously inherited his penchant for public service from his father, who had founded the Radical Party in England. Before retirement from service, he had spent £20,000 on a museum of ornithology and £4,000 on the preparation of the book *Game Birds of India*. Lord Lytton had offered him the Lieutenant-Governorship of the Punjab but he declined.

He was not only the father of Congress; he was also its guardian angel, serving as its General Secretary for twenty-one years and often travelling to England to further its cause there. Even the *Pioneer,* no friend of Hume, paid him a rich tribute for his long services to Congress in its issue dated 31 January 1891, 'Now everyone in India knows that Congress would have died a natural death some time ago had it not been for Mr. Hume's persistence and unflagging energy in keeping the movement alive...He has cheered the faint-hearted, stormed at the back-sliders, threatened withdrawal in case of his appeals for funds being disregarded, and, to his credit be it said, contributed largely from his private means in order to provide the sinews of war. "The

Congress c'est moi" has been his cry throughout...' He was truly selfless. Though he put his heart and soul into the work of Congress, he let the Indians enjoy the limelight.

From this it does not follow that Hume loved Great Britain less than India. That he was a deeply loyal subject of the Queen was amply demonstrated at the end of the proceedings of the very first session of Congress. According to the official report, 'Mr Hume, after acknowledging the honour done him, said that as the giving of cheers had been entrusted to him, he must be allowed to propose—on the principle of better late than never—giving of cheers, and that not only three but three times three, and if possible thrice that, for one, the laces of whose shoes he was unworthy to loose, one to whom they were all dear, to whom they were   all as children—need he say, Her Most Gracious Majesty The Queen-Empress...The rest of the speaker's remarks were lost in the storm of applause that instantly burst out, and the asked-for cheers were given over and over.'

Hume's motive for setting up an organization of influential Indians was to create a healthier and, therefore, lasting relationship between India and Great Britain; to strengthen the foundations of the British Empire in India, not to weaken them. As an intelligent observer and as a highly placed official, having access to secret reports, he felt convinced that a storm similar to the Great Rebellion was brewing. He had seen reports that the poor classes were 'convinced that they would starve and die' and were determined to resort to violence and would be joined by those members of the educated class who felt bitter against the government. Sir William Wedderburn, in his biography of Hume, writes, 'These ill-starred measures of reaction combined with Russian methods of police repression brought India under Lord Lytton within measurable distance of a revolutionary outbreak, and it was only in time that Mr Hume and his Indian advisers were inspired to intervene.'

The organization founded by Hume was first called the Indian National Union. It held a preliminary meeting in March 1885 and decided to convene a conference at the end of that year. A circular invitation stated:

A conference of the Indian National Union will be held at Poona from the 25th to the 31st December 1885...composed of Delegates—leading politicians well acquainted with the English language—from all parts of the Bengal, Bombay and Madras Presidencies. The direct objects of the conference will be: (1) To enable all the most earnest labourers in the cause of national progress to become personally known to each other; (2) to discuss and decide upon the political operations to be undertaken during the year. Indirectly this conference will form the germ of a native parliament and, if properly conducted, will constitute in a few years an unanswerable reply to the assertion that India is still wholly unfit for any form of representative institutions...'

In the event the venue of the conference had to be changed from Poona to Bombay because of an outbreak of cholera at Poona a few days before the conference was due to meet. The word 'Congress' was also substituted for 'Conference' in the description of the assembly on the eve of its meeting.

THE INDIAN NATIONAL CONGRESS (1885-1905)

Congress met in a different city each year. During the first twenty years of its existence it met at Calcutta and Madras four times each; at Bombay thrice; at Lahore and Allahabad twice each; and at Nagpur, Poona, Amroti, Lucknow, Ahmedabad and Kashi (Benares) once each. A resolution was passed at the sixth Congress (1890) to make provisional arrangements for holding a session of Congress, of not less than 100 delegates, in England in 1892 but in fact no meeting of Congress ever took place outside India.

During the same period, the number of delegates was the smallest—seventy-two—at the first session at Bombay and the largest—1889—at the fifth annual session, also held at Bombay, when the main attraction was the presence of Charles Bradlaugh, MP, and Sir William Wedderburn. At the twenty-first session (1905) at Kashi the delegates numbered 758.

This was also the phase during which Congress professed loyalty to the British Government and Crown, though from 1897, with famine and plague in Bombay, the assassination of Rand and Ayers, Tilak's imprisonment, and the slow pace of constitutional and administrative reforms, some extremists began to lose patience with the government. This mood was dramatically intensified with the Partition of Bengal in 1905 and two years later the extremists openly parted company with the moderates, who still constituted the majority. The extremists were led by Tilak and the moderates by Gopal Krishna Gokhale who, like Tilak, was an able Chitpavan Brahmin of Poona.

We will describe the first session, which set the scene for subsequent meetings, in some detail, and then generally deal with the salient features of the proceedings during the years that followed.

At the first meeting of Congress, seventy-two persons registered themselves as delegates, while another thirty attended as 'friends' because they were government servants and could not attend a political assembly as delegates. The official report claimed that, 'all the leading native political associations and the principal Anglo-native newspapers were represented; there were members of Legislative Councils, presidents and members of Municipal Committees and Local Boards'. The session convened at noon on 28 December 1885 in the hall of the Gokuldas Tejpal Sanskrit College, Bombay. The opening words were uttered by A. O. Hume, who proposed W. C. Bonnerjee as President.

Of the nine resolutions passed, the more important demanded :

1. The appointment of a Royal Commission to inquire into the working of the Indian administration.

Subrahmanya Iyer, who supported this resolution, pointed out that in the days of the East India Company such an enquiry was regularly made but, 'in many respects India has been a loser by the transfer of the government to the crown instead of a gainer. Since that time, the condition of the people has undergone a most distressing deterioration. They have been subjected to a less sympathetic despotism, and the expenditure and indebtedness of their Government have increased in a ratio utterly disproportionate to all improvement in its financial resources'.

2. The abolition of the Council of the Secretary of State for India 'as at present constituted'.

Mr Ananda Charlu, who seconded the resolution, referred to the Council as an 'oligarchy of fossilized Indian administrators' who had been 'superannuated for service in India'.

3. The reform and expansion of the Supreme and existing Local Legislative Councils by the admission of a 'considerable' proportion of elected members; the creation of Councils for the North-West Provinces and Oudh, and the Punjab; the referral of all budgets to these Councils; the empowerment of the members of the Councils to interpellate the Executive in regard to all branches of the administration; the creation of a Standing Committee of the House of Commons to consider protests recorded by the majorities of the Councils.

During the debate on this resolution Dadabhai Naoroji said that they had learnt from 'the English people how necessary representation is for good Government'.

4. That the competitive examination held in England, for appointment in the various civil departments, should, henceforth, be held simultaneously, one in England and one in India. Further, that all other first appointments (excluding peonships and the like) should be filled by competitive examinations held in India. Also, that the maximum age of candidates for entrance into the covenanted Civil Service be raised to not less than twenty-three years.

5. That the proposed increase in the military expenditure is unnecessary and excessive.

P. Rangiah Naidu pointed out that military expenditure had increased from £11,463,000 in 1857 to £16,975,750 in 1884 and urged the government to accept the offers of the people to enrol as volunteers so that no more European soldiers would be needed.

6. That the increased demands for military expenditure ought to be met by the reimposition of customs duties (which had been abolished in the interests of imports from Lancashire).

It is clear that the men who participated in the debate during the first session of Congress were intelligent and well-informed and fully qualified to partake in the administration of their own country.

Though their demands were bold, there was no hint of disloyalty to the British Government. Subrahmanya Iyer acknowledged that, 'by a merciful dispensation of Providence', Britain had rescued India from centuries of external aggression and internal strife and that 'for the first time in the history of the Indian populations there is to be beheld the phenomenon of national unity among them, of a sense of national existence'. There was a naive belief in the British sense of fair play. 'If we are true to ourselves and perseveringly ask what we desire', declared Dadabhai Naoroji, 'the British people are the very people on earth who will give us what is right and just'.

It is possible that, had the process of liberalizing the government been set in motion in the early years of Indian nationalism, the Raj would have run a smoother, perhaps even a longer, course than it did; it certainly would have left behind a far greater reservoir of experienced native politicians and administraters to sustain the newly independent government. At the same time, though, it must be conceded that it is too much to expect human beings willingly to relinquish power and forgo the opportunity of enriching their country and themselves. Nor was the path of political progress clear. India presented extraordinary racial, religious and regional complexities, and a straightforward adoption of the British system of government, which Congress desired, was impracticable. In fact, the British were unable to find any real solution to the Indian problem before they left the country. Nor could the Indians themselves, at that crucial juncture, put forward any agreed plan which could keep the country united.

Verbally, British statesmen protested that the Westminster parliamentary system did not suit Indian conditions, but in practice, they edged towards it because it was the only form of government with which they were familiar.

The second session of Congress (1886) was held at Calcutta and was attended by 434 delegates. Its special feature was the consensus that Congress should confine its attention to political matters and leave the contentious problem of social reforms to other organizations.

The rationale for this policy was expounded by Dadabhai Naoroji, who presided over the second session. He pointed out that each community had its own social needs but the political needs of all the communities were similar and they could unite on a common political platform: 'A National Congress must confine itself to questions in which the entire Nation has a direct participation, and it must leave the adjustment of social reforms and other class questions to class congresses.' This policy of steering clear of the thorny problems of social reform was adhered to by Congress throughout its history, except that after the advent of Gandhi it called upon the Hindu community to eradicate the evil of untouchability.

Political advance, naturally, occupied the first place in Congress deliberations in all its meetings. Broadly, the demand was for the introduction in India of representative institutions similar to those in Britain and its major colonies, such as Canada and Australia.

At the second Congress, Pandit Madan Mohan Malaviya, making his maiden speech, said, 'Representative institutions are as much a part of the true Briton as his language and his literature. Will anyone tell me that Great Britain will, in cold blood, deny us, her free-born subjects, the first of these, when, by the gift of the latter, she has qualified us to appreciate and incited us to desire it? No taxation without representation. That is the first commandment in the Englishman's political bible...' At the next

Congress, Malaviya backed up the plea for the admission of Indians to the Legislative Councils in these words, 'The British Government has already made this concession to so many countries... Canada, the Cape, the Australian Colonies, innumerable smaller places, even the so-called Crown Colonies, except perhaps the Fiji Islands and some purely military posts, all enjoy some measure, and most of them the fullest measure, of Representative Government... Why should she withhold it from the people of India? Does she think that we are less loyal than her subjects in other lands?'

From the presidential chair at the eleventh Congress (1895) Surendranath Banerji pleaded :

We appeal to England gradually to change the character of her rule in India, to liberalise it, to shift its foundations, to adapt it to the newly-developed environments of the country and the people, so that, in the fullness of time, India may find its place in the great confederacy of free states, English in their origin, English in their character, English in their institutions, rejoicing in their permanent and indissoluble union with England....'

The interesting suggestion that India should be represented in the British parliament was made at the fourteenth Congress (1898) by Ananda Mohan Bose, and the twenty-first Congress (1905) formally passed a resolution that each of the Provinces of India should return at least two members to the British House of Commons.

In addition to the demand for representative institutions, the 'hardy annuals' were the pleas for the separation of executive and judicial functions (such that in no case should the two functions be combined in the same officer); for the admission of a larger number of Indians to the higher ranks of the civil and military services; for the holding of the competitive examination for recruitment to the services in India as well as in England, instead of in England only; and for the reduction of the military expenditure by increasing the Indian element in the army and the shouldering by the British Government of a fair share of the expenditure, especially when the Indian army was deployed beyond the borders of India to further imperial interests.

On the subject of admitting more Indians to the ranks of the superior services, D.E. Wacha had this to say at the nineteenth Congress, 'We do not grumble at Europeans having a share of the loaves and fishes, but we do grumble and make it a strong grievance that the bigger and most numerous loaves are deliberately allowed, in defiance of charters, pledges and proclamations, to go to the whites, and smaller and fewer loaves to the blacks'. At the twentieth Congress, Surendranath Banerji complained that, 'Only 14 or 17 per cent of the higher appointments fall to our lot, although the country is ours, the money is ours, and the bulk of the population is ours'. Malaviya at the eighth Congress emphasised the injustice of holding the examination for admission to the Indian Civil Service only in England: 'It is singularly unjust to compel the people of this country to go 10,000 miles away from their country to pass an examination for service in their own country.'

Interestingly, the House of Commons passed a non-official resolution on 2 June 1893 in favour of holding the competition for entering the Indian Civil Service simultaneously in India and England. But the recommendation came to nothing because the Government of India expressed themselves against it. They felt 'that material reduction of the European staff then employed was incompatible with the safety of British rule' and argued further 'that the system of unrestricted competition in examinations would not only dangerously weaken the British element in the Civil Service, but would also practically exclude from the service Mohammedans, Sikhs and other races accustomed to rule by tradition and possessed of exceptional strength of character, but deficient in literary education'.

India's growing poverty under British rule was the subject of regular discussion in Congress sessions. The ninth Congress (1893) noted 'that fully fifty millions of the population, a number yearly increasing, are dragging out a miserable existence on the verge of starvation, and that in every decade, several millions actually perish by starvation.' During his speech Malaviya lamented:

Where are the weavers, where are those men who lived by different industries and manufactures, and where are the manufactures which were sent to England and other European countries in very large quantities year after year? All that has become a thing of the past: every one sitting here is clothed in cloth of British make—almost every one—and wherever you go, you find British manufactures and British goods staring you in the face. All that is left to the people is to drag out a miserable existence by agricultural operations, and make infinitesimal profit out of the little trade left to them. In the matter of the Services, in the matter of trade, our people are not enjoying one-hundredth part of the profit and gain which they used to enjoy fifty years ago.

Gopal Krishna Gokhale, who presided over the twenty-first Congress (1905), had this to say on the same theme:

For a hundred years and more now India has been for members of the dominant race a country where fortunes were to be made, to be taken out and spent elsewhere. As in Ireland the evil of absentee landlordism has in the past aggravated the racial domination of the English over the Irish, so in India what may be called absentee capitalism has been added to the racial ascendancy of Englishmen. A great and ruinous drain of wealth from the country has gone on for many years, the net excess of exports over imports (including treasure) during the last forty years amounting to no less than a thousand millions sterling. The steady rise in the death-rate of the country—from 24 per thousand, the average for 1882-84, to 30 per thousand, the average for 1892-94, and 34 per thousand, the present average—is a terrible and conclusive proof of this continuous impoverishment of the mass of our people.

It was urged that it was essential for Indians to have a voice in the making of government policy if the scourge of poverty was to be efficiently tackled. The second Congress recorded 'its fixed conviction that the introduction of Representative Institutions will prove one of the most important practical steps towards the amelioration of the condition of the people.' The official report of the third Congress stated, 'The Indian community despair of obtaining any material alleviation of the misery they see around them, until they can secure a potential voice in the administration, and it is this conviction, more than anything else, that is giving such an intense earnestness to their efforts in the direction of representation.'

From the tenth Congress (1894), a new topic began to figure in deliberations: the plight of the Indians in South Africa.

Indians had first gone to South Africa in 1860 as indentured labourers to work in sugar, tea, and coffee plantations. Initially they had gone under a five-year contract, but many chose to stay on in South Africa after the expiry of that term. Others went as immigrants to earn their livelihood by trade, or as members of other professions. The inequitable conditions under which they laboured were first formally reported to the Congress at the tenth session by V. Madanjit, a delegate from Natal, and a resolution was passed requesting His Majesty's Government to veto the Bill of the Colonial Government disenfranchising Indians living in the South African Colonies.

When the lot of Indians in South Africa was discussed during the fourteenth Congress (1898), it was noted that Gandhi already had begun his agitation to improve the condition of his countrymen there. Gandhi's role in South Africa has a special significance in that it was there that he first formulated and practiced the technique of non-violent non-co-operation which he subsequently employed during the struggle for freedom in India.

There was a general feeling among members of Congress that the chief impediment to constitutional progress in India was the bureaucratic government of India and that things would improve if the fair-minded public in England could be apprised of the true state of affairs. For this reason they made arrangements for propaganda in England and never wavered in their professions of loyalty to the Queen and her government.

The fourth Congress at Allahabad (1888) was held in a tense atmosphere. Sir Auckland Colvin, Lieutenant-Governor of the North-West Provinces, as well as Lord Dufferin, the Viceroy, had recently expressed open disapproval of the activities of Congress, and officialdom had striven hard to deny Congress a site in Allahabad for holding the assembly.

In one of the letters he exchanged with Hume in October 1888, Colvin had expressed the view that : '.... no nation, least of all a nation in the East, can be trusted, within less than the life-time of a living man, to adopt and put into practice conceptions of political life, confined at present mainly to the Anglo-Saxon race—and only by them elaborated after long and painful centuries.' Dufferin, similarly, at a St Andrew's Day dinner at Calcutta on 30 November 1888, had said that 'by the application to India of democratic methods of government, and the adoption of the parliamentary system, which England herself has only reached by slow degrees and through the discipline of many centuries of preparation', the 'well-meaning' Congress spokesmen were not taking 'a further step in advance but a very big jump into the unknown.' He asserted that Congress represented a 'microscopic minority' of their countrymen and that it was 'a groundless contention that it represents the people of India.'

Due to the opposition of the civil and military authorities, the chairman of the Reception Committee for the fourth Congress found it hard to procure a place for holding the meeting. The problem was solved just seven weeks before the Congress was due to convene: the Maharaja of Darbhanga purchased Lowther Castle, not far from the government house where Sir Auckland Colvin resided, and placed it at the disposal of Congress.

The official report of the fourth Congress declared that, 'Official opposition and persecution will not only add to its growth, but will operate to convert an open, above-board, constitutional movement into a secret, underground, and, therefore, unconstitutional one... It will be the fault of the bureaucracy—and bureaucracy alone—if...they back into the old, disused and illegitimate channels'. It quoted with obvious approval what 'a great Indian Prince' had recently said after hearing the resolutions passed at the several Congresses: 'If only these things be conceded, the rule of the British in India will last forever.' Pandit Bishan Narayan Dhar heartened his hearers by assuring them that, 'if you go on making your appeal with fairness, courage and moderation to the great English Nation, they will assuredly respond to your prayers, for as the harp responds to the harper's touch, so does the great deep heart of England respond to every reasonable prayer for justice and freedom.'

W. E. Gladstone, the Liberal statesman, came in for special attention at more than one session of Congress. During the third Congress, Pandit Bishan Narayan Dhar quoted from a speech of Gladstone which contained the following sentence: 'Our title to be there (in India) depends on a first condition, that our being there is profitable to the Indian nations; and on a second condition, that we can make them see and understand it to be profitable.' It was Gladstone who had selected the conciliatory Ripon as Viceroy to succeed the abrasive Lytton. Gladstone's birthday—29 December—happened to fall during the annual meetings of the Congress, which sent him birthday greetings on several occasions. Upon his death the fourteenth Congress passed a resolution—the very first of the session—expressing its grief at his passing and expressing its 'sense of gratitude for the sympathy he uniformly evinced towards the efforts of the Indian people in securing a more liberal and progressive government in India'.

When Queen Victoria was about to complete fifty years of her reign, Congress (second session) passed a resolution 'humbly' offering 'its dutiful and loyal congratulations... on the approaching completion of the first half century of her memorable, beneficent and glorious reign...' The twelfth Congress placed on record 'its humble congratulations on Her Gracious Majesty, the Queen Empress, having attained the sixtieth year of her reign, the longest and the most beneficent in the annals of the Empire— a reign associated with the most important advances in human happiness and civilization.' When the Queen died, the seventeenth Congress expressed 'its profound sorrow and its sense of irreparable loss' and recalled 'with gratitude Her late Majesty's deep personal sympathy with the people of India as evidenced by her gracious proclamation and by various other measures and personal acts, conceived in the same spirit of anxious solicitude for the welfare of the people of India.' In his opening speech, the Chairman of the Reception Committee had said that the Queen's Proclamation was 'the Magna Carta of India' and that her successor had already 'won the hearts of his Indian subjects by his charming personality'. Although the twenty-first Congress met under the shadow of the Partition of Bengal, Congress gave proof of its unflagging loyalty to the Crown by 'most humbly and respectfully' offering 'its loyal and dutiful welcome' to the Prince and Princess of Wales, who were on a visit to India.

At first, the attitude of the Government of India toward Congress was one of benevolent neutrality. Lord Dufferin had invited the delegates to the second Congress at Calcutta to his garden party and Lord Connemara, the Governor of Madras, did the same when Congress met within his jurisdiction in the following year. On the eve of the fourth Congress, however, both Colvin and Dufferin expressed open disapproval of Congress activities, as already noted. The reason for the change of attitude seems to have been that Congress discussed awkward political questions and put forward unpalatable political demands. In his St Andrew's Day dinner speech, Dufferin explained the reason why he felt disappointed in Congress. When Congress first started, he said, he had hoped that 'it might render valuable assistance to the government' by dealing with social questions 'with which it was either undesirable for the government to interfere, or which it was beyond their power to influence or control'. He expressed his regret that they should consider such topics beneath their notice and 'should have concerned themselves instead with matters in regard to which their assistance is likely to be less profitable to us'.

At the unofficial level, however, *The Times,* the mouthpiece of the British establishment, editorially sounded an alarm immediately after the first session. If India was ripe for the political transformation demanded by the Congress resolutions, 'the days of English rule are numbered... (But) if we were to withdraw, it would be in favour not of the most fluent tongue or of the most ready pen, but the strongest arm and the sharpest sword...'

Lord Curzon's Viceroyalty (1898-1905) is a turning point in Indian political history. It started well but ended disastrously. India was never the same again. At the twenty-first Congress, President Gokhale's verdict was that 'even the most devoted admirer of Lord Curzon cannot claim that he has strengthened the foundations of British rule in India... To him India was a country where the Englishman was to monopolise for all time all power, and talk all the while of duty.' In a letter dated 10 November 1900, Curzon had written to the Secretary of State, Lord Hamilton, that he believed that Congress was 'tottering to its fall' and it was one of his 'greatest ambitions while in India to assist it to a peaceful demise', but in fact nationalist feeling in India both inside and outside Congress was far stronger when he left than it had been when he arrived.

Curzon was fascinated by India and by the pomp of his own office. He said that, next to his own country, India was 'nearest' to his heart, but his actions were guided by the conviction that the Indians needed an indefinite period of British tutelage before they could be expected to run their own affairs. He believed that Englishmen were superior in character to Indians and, therefore, better fitted to hold the highest positions in India, and that amongst Englishmen, he himself occupied a special position. A popular verse ran:

My name is George Nathaniel Curzon,
I am a most superior person.

His motto was: 'It is no good trusting a human being to do a thing for you. Do everything yourself.' His appetite for pageantry and imperiousness of manner were not likely to win the heart of a people who give their love to a mahatma far more readily than to a maharaja.

In his limitless capacity for work and insatiable appetite for administrative reform, Curzon closely resembled Dalhousie. He founded an agricultural research institute at Pusa in Bihar, added 6,000 miles to the railway network and planned a sizeable extension of the irrigation system. His high regard for India's historical and cultural heritage was demonstrated by the establishment of an Archeological Department which was destined to achieve brilliant results in the fields of discovery and preservation of historical sites and monuments. In an address to the Asiatic Society of Bengal, he highlighted the role of the new department by reminding the audience that 'in the days of Lord William Bentinck the Taj was on the point of being destroyed for the value of its marbles...In 1857, after the Mutiny, it was solemnly proposed to raze to the ground the Juma Masjid at Delhi...' He had a strong sense of justice and was the only Viceroy who had the courage to condemn openly the ill-treatment of Indians by Europeans. After the Boer War he refused to permit the recruitment of Indian indentured labour for the gold mines in the Transvaal. He was able to claim further that, 'We have now finally established the principle (disputed till a few years ago) that when we lend troops from India to fight campaigns for the Imperial Government in different parts of Asia and Africa, every rupee of the charge, from embarkation to return, shall be defrayed by the Imperial Government.' He won the 'gratitude' of the

Congress of 1900 'for the benevolence of his famine policy' but was severely censured by the same body for holding the dazzling Durbar at Delhi in 1903 to celebrate the Coronation of Edward VII. Lalmohan Ghosh, president of the Congress session that year, rhetorically asked, 'Do you think that any administration in England, or France, or the United States, would have ventured to waste vast sums of money on an empty pageant, when Famine and Pestilence were stalking over the land, and the Angel of Death was flapping his wings almost within hearing of the light-hearted revellers?'

It was Curzon's 'anti-national' measures, however, that caused the deepest resentment. A privilege conferred and then reduced causes even more pain than a privilege deferred. His reform of the Calcutta Corporation and the universities, which tightened official control over their management, was seen by Indian nationalists as a curtailment of the limited amount of self-government already granted by the British Government.

THE PARTITION OF BENGAL

Of all Curzon's acts, the partition of Bengal had the most unfortunate results, but Bengal was not the only province divided by him. In 1901 he had taken away from the Punjab five districts and the tribal area to create The North-West Frontier Province. This brought the affairs of the turbulent frontier directly under the Central Government. The cavalier manner in which the partition of the Punjab had been effected did not please its Lieutenant-Governor and his senior colleagues but there was no public hue and cry against it.

The partition of Bengal, however, was an altogether different matter and had lasting political results. That Bengal was an unwieldy province is undeniable. The boundary of the Presidency of Bengal had reached the river Sutlej in 1803. The North-West Provinces were detached from it in 1835 and Assam in 1874. Nevertheless, Bengal still consisted of Bengal proper, plus Bihar and Orissa. It had a population of 78,000,000 and an area of 190,000 square miles. Its terrain was covered with numerous forests and streams which made it difficult to travel from one part to another. The eastern part of Bengal was backward and distant from Calcutta, the capital. Plans for the partition of the unwieldy provice had been mooted before Curzon's time, but in the end it was he who had the courage to grasp the nettle. Despite protests voiced after the proposal became known, partition took effect on the appointed day— 16 October 1905.

Bengali Hindus had every reason to be alarmed at the consequences of the partition. From being a majority in the undivided province, they became a minority in both the new provinces. The new province of East Bengal and Assam, with a population of thirty-one million, with Dacca as its capital, was preponderantly Muslim. In the residuary province of forty-seven million, the Bengalis were outnumbered by Biharis and Oriyas.

Curzon called partition 'a mere readjustment of administrative boundaries', but the Bengali Hindus believed that Curzon had resorted to partition to curb their rising nationalism. By cutting the language area into two and separating Muslims from Hindus, he had split the 'Bengali nation'. It was nothing but the age-old device of divide and rule. At first, some Muslims joined in the agitation against partition but before long, most of them came out in its favour because they realised that in the new province of East Bengal and Assam they would enjoy a majority of more than sixty per cent and would therefore have a much greater say in their own affairs than they could ever have had in a united Bengal.

The partition of Bengal took place during a period in which Indian nationalist opinion was already in a ferment for various reasons. Famine and plague were prevalent when Curzon arrived and the Extremists led by Tilak were already clamouring for stronger action against the government to win constitutional reforms rather than merely passing 'mendicant' resolutions at Congress sessions. Events outside India had demonstrated that the European powers were not as invulnerable as they seemed. Italy had suffered severe reversals at the hands of the Ethiopians (1895-6); the Boers had put up a gallant fight against the British during the Boer War (1899-1902); and even more significantly, the small Asian country of Japan had utterly defeated the European giant, Russia, both on land and at sea (1904-5). In Lord Curzon's own words, 'The reverberations of that [Japan's] victory have gone like a thunderclap through the whispering-galleries of the East.'

It was not difficult at a time like this for the anti-partition leaders to whip up public support for their cause. Moreover, the occurrence of famine and plague—scourges which had hit not only the thin layer of Western-educated 'agitators' but also the poor masses—made such public support easier to secure.

The official policy of Congress was still controlled by the Moderates under the leadership of G. K. Gokhale. It was, therefore, at popular level that the fiercest agitation against partition was carried on. An open rebellion, after that of 1857, was impracticable; it was therefore decided to hurt the British economically by the complementary movements of a boycott of British goods and the promotion of indigenous products (*swadeshi*)[1]. From Bengal, the boycott-*swadeshi* movement soon spread to other parts of India. Its most powerful supporter in Western India was Tilak and in the Punjab, Lajpat Rai. Congress contented itself with formally passing resolutions endorsing what was being done at a public level. These resolutions will be discussed in the next chapter.

The boycott-*swadeshi* movement was vigorously promoted by innumerable meetings, processions, and speeches and by an assiduous campaign in the press. A large number of students took part in it and added to its vigour. Bonfires were made of foreign cloth. Shops selling foreign cloth were picketed.

The help of religion was enlisted to make the agitation a mass movement. During the festival of Durga Puja in 1905, a crowd of almost 50,000 collected at a temple of Kali near Calcutta. On 16 October 1905, the day on which partition took effect, all the shops in Calcutta were closed and all business activity came to a halt. Parties paraded the streets singing 'Bande Mataram' and throngs of people bathed in the holy water of the Ganges. Thousands performed the *rakhi-bandhan* ceremony which henceforth was performed on every sixteenth of October. The ritual entailed the tying of a woollen thread by a sister round her brother's wrist and his taking the vow to undo the partition of Bengal.

These religious outpourings further emphasised the Hindu character of the agitation. Jawaharlal Nehru recalled in his *Autobiography* that 'the background of these movements [boycott and *swadeshi*] was religious nationalism.'

With passions running high, clashes between the demonstrators, especially young students, and the forces of law and order, were inevitable. Repression and violence became locked in a vicious circle. Gurkha troops were stationed in East Bengal. The movement was driven underground and terrorism, which had first manifested itself during the plague, became more wide-spread. Though Bengal was their stronghold, terrorist cells existed in western India and the Punjab as well. Some Europeans were murdered. Secret societies increased in number. The cult of the bomb had arrived. Maulana Abul Kalam Azad tells us in his memoirs that during the partition agitation he had found that 'the revolutionary groups were recruited exclusively from the Hindu middle classes... The revolutionaries felt that the Muslims were an obstacle to the attainment of Indian freedom

---

[1] *Swadeshi* : made in, or belonging to, one's own country.

and must, like other obstacles, be removed'. It was with great difficulty that he was able to join a revolutionary group.

Boycott and *swadeshi* were the first movements in which the common people all over India agitated to gain political ends. The concept of the boycott of goods manufactured by foreigners was in time expanded to include the boycott of institutions created by them. And the love for the material products of one's own country promoted by *swadeshi* was but a step towards the love for everything Indian. The Indian struggle for freedom from British domination had entered a new era. Surendranath Banerji urged that agitation should not stop till partition was cancelled, and this is what actually happened.

CONGRESS PROPAGANDA IN ENGLAND

From the very beginning of its existence, Congress placed more hope for the success of its demands on British public opinion and Parliament than on the bureaucracy in India. Dadabhai Naoroji, a Parsee who normally resided in England as a merchant but visited India from time to time, proved to be a pillar of strength for the work in England. He was well respected there and was elected Member of Parliament for Central Finsbury in 1892. In recognition of his capability and services, he was thrice elected to preside over Congress.

An Agency in England was established under William Digby in 1889 and in the following year, the British Committee of the Indian National Congress was formed to advise and assist the Agency. Sir William Wedderburn was elected chairman of the Committee and held the position until his death in 1918. Charles Bradlaugh, among others, gave substantial support to Congress activities in Britain. From time to time, British members of the Committee attended Congress sessions in India and Congress also sent deputations to Britain to advance its interests.

Congress workers in Britain issued pamphlets, contributed articles to newspapers and magazines, addressed public meetings, sought interviews with influential persons and held social functions. One year they were able to organize more than a hundred meetings. To counteract unfavourable articles on India in the British Press and to supply authentic information, a journal, *India*, was started in 1890. Its first editor was Digby. Among others who edited it afterwards was Gordon Hewart, who later became Lord Hewart, the Lord Chief Justice.

But Congress endeavours in Britain achieved only marginal success. Several liberal-minded individuals were sympathetic to the people of

India but the majority of the business and ruling classes, who dictated the policy of their government, naturally placed their own interests and the interests of their country above all other considerations. The authors of *The Rise and Growth of the Congress in India* (C. F. Andrews and Girija Mookerjee) sum up the position as follows :

> It was during these closing years of the nineteenth century that the field which India gave for safe investments of capital under Government security, at a higher rate of interest than gilt-edged securities in England itself, began to bind India to the City of London—the greatest share market in the world. These bonds became stronger and tighter every year. Finance in Great Britain began to regard India more as a profitable market for investment than anything else. The coming into power of one party or another in the British Parliament, when this had happened, made little material difference in fundamental policy. For India became less and less a party question. An India Debate emptied the House of Commons. More and more the economic issue took precedence over everything else. Only on such a basis can the imposition of an excise duty on cotton goods made in India by Indian mills be understood. Lancashire's interests overruled every other consideration.

With the rise of nationalism, Congress' work in Britain lost its earlier importance. Less emphasis began to be placed on 'petitioning' the British than on self-help by direct action.

THE LIMITATIONS OF CONGRESS

Dadabhai Naoroji claimed that Congress represented 'the aristocracy of intellect', and some of the best brains in India attended its annual sessions. The standard of debate at its meetings was high and the speakers had a good grasp of the issues facing the country, but these was a certain amount of artificiality about the whole affair—it resembled more a university debating society than a political party which incessantly carries its message to constituencies all over the country and enlists the support of the people to achieve its goals. The belief of the Congress leadership, that in the end they would obtain their wishes from the British people by merely knocking at their door, was naive. They failed to appreciate the elementary fact that Britain would not willingly relinquish control over India, which was the main contributor to its wealth and greatness.

Some of the strongest critics of Congress came from its own ranks. 'The Congress movement', pointed out Lajpat Rai, 'was neither inspired by the people, nor devised or planned by them. It was a movement not from within'. The Congress leaders had, he said, certain political opinions, but not beliefs for which they were willing to suffer. Aswini-Kumar Datta of Barisal (Bengal) complained during the Congress session of 1897 that its activities amounted to no more than a three days' *tamasha* (show).

It was not until Gandhi took charge of Congress and, with his loin cloth, plain living and long tours on foot in rural areas, identified himself with the poor of the land, that Congress became a mass party. Till then the members of Congress had to put up with the charge that they were just a small number of city *baboos*, mostly lawyers, whose only tangible service to the villager was to involve him in litigation and extract a fat fee. The person who really knew the problems of the cultivator at first hand, the argument went, was the Civil Servant who constantly toured his district on horseback.

That the Muslims, under Sir Syed's influence, by and large held aloof from Congress, further diminished the validity of the claim that it represented all the people of India. At the first congress only two Muslims registered themselves as delegates. Both belonged to Bombay, where the session was held, and neither of them had a following in his own community. The Reception Committee of the second congress invited the two leading Muslim organizations—the Central National Muhammadan Association and the Muhammadan Literary Society—to send representatives but both of them declined to do so. Out of 413 delegates at that congress, twenty-seven were Muslims but, once again, those who attended enjoyed but little influence among fellow Muslims. To meet the charge of being mainly a Hindu movement, the third congress successfully invited Badruddin Tyabji, a well-known Bombay Muslim, to preside over it. This session was attended by eighty-one Muslims.

At the 1889 congress, the number of Muslim delegates rose to 254 out of a total of 1502, but in 1892 the strength of the Muslims fell to 20 out of 1,118. At the Bombay congress of 1904, which protested against the proposed partition of Bengal, and the Kashi congress (1905), which deplored that partition had been carried out, the number of Muslim delegates was 30 out of 1,010 and 20 out of 757 respectively.

Badruddin Tyabji and Sir Syed discussed the status of Congress by correspondence. Sir Syed wrote, 'I do not understand what the words "National Congress" mean. Is it supposed that the different castes and creeds living in India belong to one nation or can become [one nation]; and their aims and aspirations be one and the same? I think it is quite impossible...' Tyabji's reply is quite revealing. It shows that even an ardent Muslim supporter of Congress like himself did not believe that all the people belonged to a single nation: 'No one regarded the whole nation as one nation; but there were some questions which touched all communities or nations of India', and Congress was 'nothing more than an assembly of educated people from all parts of India and representing all races and creeds meeting together for the discussion of only such questions as may be generally admitted to concern the whole of India at large.'

R. C. Majumdar, the doyen of Indian historians and himself a Hindu, is refreshingly objective in his criticism of the Hindu leaders for their failure to conciliate the Muslims by taking note of their genuine fears :

There can be no gainsaying the fact that the Muslim apprehensions were well-founded, that in all human probability every advance in democracy in India would increase the dominance of the Hindus, and an open competitive examination would give preponderance to the Hindus over Muslims in all higher posts under the Government...It may be argued, with a great deal of plausibility that...a fusion of Hindus and Muslims into one nation was not an impossible ideal. Even if this be admitted, it must not be forgotten that what was at best merely a possible ideal should not have been mistaken for an actual fact... In the voluminous political literature of the period one looks in vain for a just assessment of the Muslim point of view on the part of the Hindus.

PART III

'Not one whit more than you do I think it desirable or possible, or even conceivable, to adapt English political institutions to the nations who inhabit India. Assuredly not in your day or mine. But the spirit of English institutions is a different thing, and it is a thing that we cannot escape even if we wished...because British constituencies are the masters, and they will assuredly insist—all parties alike—on the spirit of their own political system being applied to India'.

Morley to Minto, June 1906.

'The policy of His Majesty's Government, with which the Government of India are in complete accord, is that of increasing association of Indians in every branch of the administration and the gradual development of self-governing institutions with a view to progressive realisation of responsible government in India as an integral part of the British Empire'.

Secretary of State Montagu, 20 August 1917.

CHAPTER 8

THE AFTERMATH OF THE
PARTITION OF BENGAL

MODERATES VERSUS EXTREMISTS

The anger generated by the partition of Bengal greatly strengthened the
position of the Extremists and widened the rift between them and the
Moderates. Gokhale, the leader of the Moderates, was principally supported
by Surendranath Banerji, Pherozeshah Mehta and Dadabhai Naoroji;
Tilak, the leader of the Extremists, by Arabindo Ghose, Bipin Chandra Pal
and Lajpat Rai. The differences between the two wings related to the
nature of the goal as well as the method of achieving it.

The Moderates did not wish to break with Britain and aimed at a
colonial form of self-government, while the Extremists desired complete
freedom from foreign control. Gokhale believed that the government
possessed enormous power and would have no difficulty in crushing any
untoward moves by the Extremists, and also that, should the British leave
India in a hurry, the country would relapse into anarchy. The Extremists
deprecated the Moderates' policy of petitioning and persuasion and
advocated resistance to foreign rule and willingness to make sacrifices in
the course of the struggle.

Both sides agreed that the partition of Bengal was an evil which must
be reversed and that *swadeshi* was a legitimate programme, but they
differed sharply with regard to 'boycott'. Gokhale said, 'Boycott has a
sinister meaning—it implies a vindictive desire to injure another.' In his
view 'we would do well to use only the expression *swadeshi* to describe
our present movement, leaving alone the word "boycott" which created
unnecessary ill-will against ourselves.'

The Extremists were not only strongly in favour of retaining boycott as
a part of their movement, but they also wished to extend its scope far
beyond merely refusing to use foreign goods.

The brilliant Arabindo, an idealist who suddenly appeared on the
political scene at this juncture, was the most passionate exponent of

the Extremists' point of view. The programme spelled out by him anticipated the one adopted by Gandhi some years later. He advocated passive resistance in order 'to make administration under present conditions impossible by an organized refusal to do anything which shall help either British commerce in the exploitation of the country or British officialdom in the administration of it—unless and until the conditions are changed in the manner and to the extent demanded by the people. This attitude is summed up in the one word, "Boycott".'

He went on to elaborate that, if the government-aided and controlled system of education was calculated to discourage patriotism and encourage loyalty to the government, people should refuse to send pupils to government schools; if the people were dissatisfied with the bureaucratic system of justice because of the ruinous costliness of civil litigation and the political bias of criminal justice, they should refuse to have anything to do with the alien courts; if the people disapproved of the arbitrariness and repression of the executive administration, they should refuse to go to the executive for help, advice or protection; and finally, they should refuse to pay taxes and rents.

He equated nationalism with religion and said that the cause of nationalism should be championed with the same enthusiasm and disregard for consequence as that of religion. Nationalism, he said, was not a mere political programme; it was 'a religion that has come from God'. It was the prime duty of Indians 'to rush headlong' to save the Motherland without pausing to think whether they will succeed or fail. Lajpat Rai was of the same mind: 'Our first want...is to raise our patriotism to the level of religion and to aspire to live or to die for it.'

The differences between the Moderates and the Extremists became noticeable during the very first session of Congress after the partition of Bengal (December 1905, at Benares). The Moderates wished to send a loyal message of welcome to the Prince and Princess of Wales who were soon to visit India, but the Extremists were opposed to it; the Extremists, for their part, desired to pass a resolution in support of the boycott, which the Moderates did not relish. An open break was prevented by the Extremists absenting themselves during the passage of the motion relating to the welcome, and by the Moderates consenting to the following watered-down resolution on boycott:

> Resolved: That this Congress records its earnest and emphatic protest against the repressive measures which have been adopted by the authorities in Bengal after the people there had been compelled to resort to the boycott of foreign goods as a last protest, and perhaps the only constitutional and effective means

left to them of drawing the attention of the British public to the action of the Government of India in persisting in their determination to partition Bengal, in utter disregard of the universal prayers and protests of the people.

The resolution protesting the partition of Bengal and appealing for its reversal was passed without a hitch. There was no resolution on *swadeshi*.

The next session of Congress (1906) was to be held at Calcutta, an area where the Extremists prevailed, and the Moderates feared that their opponents would carry the resolutions of their own choice. It was rumoured that the Extremists wished to sponsor Tilak as president.

To have a president of their own choice, and at the same time a person of such eminence that the Extremists would not dare to oppose him, the Moderates nominated the eighty-two-year-old 'Grand Old Man', Dadabhai Naoroji.

Naoroji did not feel strong enough to deliver his presidential address in person. After thanking the audience for the honour they had done him he handed over his speech to Gokhale to read. Though a Moderate, he was sagacious enough to realise that the national movement in India had entered a new era. Tilak had already made *swaraj* a household word in India. Naoroji made that magic expression his own and voiced the demand for *swaraj* from the Congress platform. 'We do not ask for any favours', he said, 'we want only justice. Instead of going into any further divisions or details of our rights as British citizens, the whole matter can be comprised in one word—"self-government" or *swaraj*, like that of the United Kingdom or the Colonies.' *Swaraj* soon became the battle-cry of Indian nationalists.

On the whole, the Extremists had more cause for satisfaction at the outcome of the Calcutta Congress than the Moderates. They were especially pleased with the resolutions relating to self-government, boycott and national education. The resolution on self-government demanded that the system of government obtaining in the self-governing British colonies should be extended to India, and urged that the following reforms should immediately be carried out as steps leading to it: all higher appointments in India should be by competitive examinations which should be held simultaneously in India as well as England; Indians should be adequately represented in the Council of the Secretary of State as well as in the Executive Councils of the Viceroy and the Governors; the Supreme and Provincial Legislative Councils should be expanded to allow more effective representation of the people and a larger control over the financial and executive administration of the country; and the powers of the Local and Municipal bodies should be extended.

With regard to national education it was resolved that the people of the country should organize a system of education suited to the requirements of the country on 'National lines and under National Control'. The Bengali orator Bipin Chandra Pal in supporting the resolution on boycott tried to widen its scope. He urged that not only Bengal but the other provinces also be asked to practise boycott and further, that it should include matters other than just goods. His proposals were rejected, but the resolution that emerged was less apologetic than that passed a year earlier:

> That having regard to the fact that the people of this country have little or no voice in its administration, and that their representations to the Government do not receive due consideration, this Congress is of opinion that the Boycott Movement inaugurated in Bengal by way of protest against the Partition of that Province, was, and is, legitimate.

The resolution on *swadeshi*, which figured in the proceedings of Congress for the first time, called upon the people of the country 'to promote the growth of indigenous industries and to stimulate the production of indigenous articles by giving them preference over imported commodities even at some sacrifice.' The resolution on the partition of Bengal specified the manner in which Congress desired the division to be modified. It demanded that 'the entire Bengali-speaking commu-nity' be brought 'under one undivided administration'.

Though the Extremists managed to have the better of the Moderates at the 1906 session, both sides were aware that the fight was unfinished.

In preparation for the showdown, the Moderates managed to score two tactical successes. It had been decided at the Calcutta session that Congress would assemble next at Nagpur. The Moderates regarded Nagpur as a stronghold of the Extremists and caused the All-India Congress Committee to change the venue to Surat where the influence of the moderate Pherozeshah Mehta prevailed. Secondly, there was a difference of opinion with regard to the office of the president of the Surat Congress. The Extremists favoured Lajpat Rai and the moderates Rasbihari Ghosh. Lajpat Rai commendably refused to participate in the controversy and let the Moderates have their way.

On the eve of the Surat Congress a rumour spread that the Moderates intended to renege on the resolutions relating to self-government, boycott and national education. It was, therefore, in a tense atmosphere that the Surat session convened on 26 December 1907. The meeting had to be adjourned because the president was unable to maintain order. On the following day, pandemonium broke out when Tilak mounted the platform and insisted upon addressing the meeting even after the president had ruled him out of order. The platform was invaded by men carrying sticks, a shoe was flung and struck Pherozeshah and Surendranath, the meeting was adjourned *sine die* and the hall had to be cleared with the help of the police.

The Moderates called a Convention which met at Allahabad in April 1908 and decided that Congress would abide by the following 'creed':

> The objects of the Indian National Congress are the attainment by the people of India of a system of Government similar to that enjoyed by the self-governing members of the British Empire, and a participation by them in the rights and responsibilities of the Empire on equal terms with those members. These objects are to be achieved by constitutional means, by bringing about a steady reform of the existing system of administration, and by promoting national unity, fostering public spirit, and developing and organising the intellectual, moral, economic and industrial resources of the country.

It was laid down, further, that every member of Congress must subscribe to the prescribed creed in writing. These conditions were not acceptable to most of the Extremists, who left Congress. Two factors strengthened the position of the Moderates during the years that followed. The first was the change of government in England, which raised the expectation that a more liberal policy toward India would be initiated; secondly, the repressive policy of the government removed the leading Extremists from the political scene for various durations, which left the stage clear for the Moderates. The Moderates controlled Congress till Tilak returned to its ranks in 1916.

THE MORLEY-MINTO REFORMS

Curzon had been succeeded as Governor-General in India by Lord Minto in November 1905. In January 1906, the Liberals won an overwhelming victory at the polls in Britain and John Morley became Secretary of State for India. Minto was a Tory aristocrat, being the grandson of the Lord Minto who had been Governor-General of India from 1807 to 1813. He had seen military service in the Second Afghan War, in Egypt and in Canada, and was a highly skilled rider, having competed in the Grand National and won the Grand Steeplechase of Paris. On hearing that he would be the new Governor-General, Curzon said, 'Imagine sending to succeed me a gentleman who only jumps hedges'. But Minto did have administrative experience; he had served as Governor-General of Canada for six years. Intellectually, Morely was the opposite of Minto. He had studied Voltaire and Rousseau, was a disciple of John Stuart Mill, had been Gladstone's supporter in the campaign for Home Rule in Ireland and was his biographer. The Moderates had high hopes that Morley would inaugurate a more sympathetic era in India. Gokhale conferred with him no less than five times when he went to England in 1906 as the spokesman for Congress.

When Minto arrived in India the agitation against the partition of Bengal was at its height. Apart from angry articles in the Press and speeches from the platform, there were underground revolutionary activities. The unrest continued despite an instalment of reforms in 1909 and a series of repressive measures. Unsuccessful attempts were made to murder the Lieutenant-Governors of Eastern Bengal and Bengal. A bomb meant for Kingsford, the judge at Muzaffarpur, killed the wife and daughter of another European. A public prosecutor and a deputy superintendent of police were shot dead. During the period 1907-17 twelve bombs were thrown and three attempts were made to derail trains. The most prominent targets were Sir Curzon Wyllie, Morley's political secretary, who was shot dead at the Imperial Institute in London on 1 July 1909; Lord and Lady Minto, who were bombed on 13 November 1909 while on tour in Ahmadabad, but escaped injury; and Lord and Lady Hardinge, at whom a bomb was thrown on 23 December 1912 as they were passing through Chandni Chowk on an elephant while making a state entry into Delhi, which had replaced Calcutta as the capital of India.

Both Minto and Hardinge earned respect and praise for their exemplary conduct under attack. Minto remained utterly unruffled. The bomb thrown at the Hardinges was quite powerful; Lady Hardinge was lucky enough to remain unhurt but Lord Hardinge was badly wounded and fainted from loss of blood (the man standing behind him holding the state umbrella was killed). On regaining consciousness Hardinge gave orders that the programme was to be carried out as planned and gave the text of his speech to be read at the ceremony by the senior member of his Council.

Hardinge was a popular Governor-General (see Chapter 9) and the attack on him aroused much genuine sympathy. Gokhale, the leader of the 'opposition' in the Legislative Council, told Hardinge's private secretary that he and his party would never oppose any measure that the Governor-General considered necessary. For his part, Hardinge announced that his policy in India would not 'deviate a hair's breadth' on account of the attempt on his life.

Minto had tried to suppress the unrest by punitive legislation and action. Lajpat Rai from the Punjab and Bipin Chandra Pal from Bengal were briefly deported in 1907. Nine Bengalis were deported in 1908. On 22 July of the same year Tilak was sentenced to six years' transportation (which he passed in Mandalay goal writing his famous commentary on the *Gita*). Lajpat Rai went off to England in 1908, returning in 1909. In 1913 he again went abroad to escape harassment and did not return till 1920. Arabindo was arrested in August 1907 but the charge against him failed. He was again arrested in May 1908 along with thirty-eight other revolutionaries and spent a year in jail as an under-trial prisoner, but in the end was acquitted. In 1910, he left politics and secluded himself at Pondicherry, where he spent his days in spiritual contemplation.

This vicious circle of agitation and suppression with a periodic dose of constitutional advance formed the pattern of British rule till its end in 1947. Congress passed resolutions condemning both terrorism and repressive measures in the same breath, but never explained how else the government could deal with the inflammatory activities of the extremists and their acts of violence. The real problem was that a comparatively small number of British officials and soldiers were required to rule a huge country containing several hundred million people of a different race and culture. The Great Rebellion of 1857 had made it amply clear that if a sufficient number of Indians ever wanted the British to leave, they would have to go. Indeed, the British in India could never get rid of the feeling that their position was no better than that of an army of occupation whose safety lay in a perpetual show of strength. 'We are here a small British garrison', wrote Minto to Morley in a letter dated 23 May 1906, 'surrounded by millions composed of factors of an inflammability unknown to the Western world, unsuited to Western forms of Government, and we must be physically strong or go to the wall.' The endless concocting and peddling of rumours, a favourite Indian addiction, made political unrest and the threat of insurrection seem far more ominous than they actually were. It is not surprising that the authorities often over-reacted to the situation. For their part, the Indian nationalists conveniently heaped all the blame on the British. They overlooked the fact that the actual instruments of oppression were mainly fellow Indians. The laws enacted by the government in many cases were necessary and were meant to curb and punish only those who were guilty. Most of the spies, the informers, the witnesses, the police and the soldiers were Indian. It was they who actually committed the fabrications and excesses to win the favour of their foreign rulers. We have already seen that the Indians themselves had materially helped the British to conquer India. It must be added that they afterwards also helped the British to rule the country. Lajpat Rai confessed that he had left India in 1913 in disgust because 'I began to suspect that I was being spied on by my own servant who lived with me in the same compound. Life became intolerable and I lost my sleep and appetite, so I decided to leave India.'

Both Morley and Minto recognized that punishment of seditious and violent persons was only one half of the policy. It was equally essential to encourage and reward the loyal elements. After prolonged deliberation they produced the 'Morley-Minto Reforms' in the shape of the Indian Councils Act of 1909 which received Royal Assent on 25 May of that year.

When the reforms were in the offing, the Calcutta Congress (December 1906) reiterated Congress' demand for 'the system of government obtaining in Self-Governing British Colonies'. But the Muslims had Sir Syed's warning—that the Western system of election 'pure and simple' would place them under Hindu domination—very much in mind. A delegation of thirty-five leading Muslims led by Aga Khan III waited on Lord Minto on 1 October 1906 and spelled out the protective measures they considered necessary for their political safety.

They pleaded that the position accorded to the Muslims 'in any kind of representation...should be commensurate not merely with their numerical strength, but also with their political importance and the value of the contribution which they make to the defence of the Empire' and expressed the hope that due consideration would be given in that connection 'to the position [of rulers] which they occupied in India a little more than a hundred years ago, and of which the traditions have naturally not faded from their minds.' More specifically they demanded first, that the Muslims should be allotted a definite number of seats in the Municipal and District Boards, in the Provincial Councils and in the Imperial Legislature ('reserved seats'); secondly, that in fixing the number of seats for the Muslims, factors other than their numerical strength should also be considered in their favour ('weightage', i.e., a larger number of seats than warranted by their proportion in population); and thirdly, that only Muslims should vote for candidates for the Muslim seats ('separate electorates'). The Aga Khan explained at a later date that his deputation, in effect, had 'asked that the Muslims of India should not be regarded as a mere minority, but as a nation within a nation whose rights and obligations should be guaranteed by statute.' The Viceroy conceded that the position of the Muslims should be estimated not merely on their numerical strength but also with respect to their 'political importance'. He further agreed that in any electoral system the Muslims 'should be represented as a community'.

The Indian Councils Act of 1909 increased the size of the legislative councils to 60 members for the Imperial Council, to 50 for the Councils of the major provinces and to 30 for the rest. Some members were to be elected and others nominated. They could discuss budgets, ask questions and introduce resolutions on matters of general public interest. A small official majority was retained at the centre but in all the provinces the non-official-elected, plus nominated members, were in the majority, and in Bengal the purely elected members had a majority.

The Act left it to the Government of India 'subject to the approval of the Secretary of State, to make regulations, among others, for laying down the procedure for election and nomination of members of all Councils and determining their qualifications'. The resultant regulations continued the practice that the constituencies would be communities and groups of various kinds and not general constituencies of the Westminster type. They also granted all the three main concessions which the Aga Khan delegation had demanded.

Congress had reposed high hopes in the promised reforms. When the twenty-third Congress, which had been suspended at Surat, reconvened at Madras (December 1908), it gave 'expression to the deep and general satisfaction with which the Reform proposals formulated in Lord Morley's dispatch have been received throughout the country.' But the mood of unqualified approval did not last long. The Regulations were issued five weeks before the twenty-fourth Congress met at Lahore on 27 December 1909. In a resolution moved by Surendranath Banerji, Congress protested that the Regulations had caused 'widespread dissatisfaction... by reason of:(a) the excessive and unfairly preponderant share of representation given to the followers of one particular religion; (b) the unjust, invidious, and humiliating distinctions made between Muslim and non-Muslim subjects of His Majesty in the matter of electorates, the franchise and the qualifications of the candidates...' Indian nationalists have alleged that the Aga Khan deputation was stage-managed by the British bureaucracy in India in furtherance of their policy of divide and rule. We shall discuss this charge in the next section.

To Lord Curzon's apprehension that the new Councils could become 'parliamentary bodies in miniature', Morley vehemently replied that, 'if it could be said that this chapter of reforms led directly or indirectly to the establishment of a parliamentary system in India, I for one would have nothing at all to do with it'. But he had already confessed in a letter to Minto in June 1906 that while it was inconceivable to adapt English political institutions to the 'nations who inhabit India...the spirit of English institutions is a different thing and it is a thing that we cannot escape, even if we wished...because the British constituencies are the masters, and they will assuredly insist...all parties alike...on the spirit of their own political system being applied to India.' He never got down to explaining how the spirit of the British system of government could be achieved without its body.

Independently of the Act but as a part of the package of reforms, two Indians were nominated to the Secretary of State's Council, one to the Governor-General's Executive Council, and one to each of the Provincial Executive Councils. An Indian was also made a member of the Privy Council. These appointments caused unmixed satisfaction in India.

Though Congress denounced the communal aspect of the system in the terms already quoted, it did not refuse to work the reforms. In its view the Act embodied 'a fairly liberal measure of constitutional reforms' but the Regulations had undermined the spirit in which the scheme had originally been conceived. The blame did not rest with Parliament but with the 'bureaucracy' in India—'Is the bureaucracy having its revenge upon us for the part we have played in securing these concession?' asked Surendranath rhetorically.

THE FOUNDATION OF THE MUSLIM LEAGUE

Sir Syed had believed that the Muslims should eschew agitational politics and rely on the British Government to save them from being engulfed by the rising tide of Hindu nationalism. If they concentrated upon educating themselves they would eventually be able to compete with the Hindus on equal terms for political and administrative spoils. But after his death, the Muslims increasingly felt that they needed an organization of their own to offset Congress. A leader who tried to set up such an organization was Nawab Viqar-ul-Mulk, who had worked as Reader (Clerk of Court) to Sir Syed when the latter was a sub-judge and had assisted him in his educational and literary activities. He took up service in Hyderabad in 1875 and held responsible positions till his resignation in 1892.

After that, he did not take any active part in public affairs, but sprang into action when the Government of the United Provinces passed an order in April 1900 ending the special position which Urdu had enjoyed till then, by elevating Hindi to the same position as Urdu for official purposes.

Among other things, he wrote an article in the *Aligarh Institute Gazette* (15 August 1901) on 'What should be done by Muslims to safeguard their political interests'. He urged that after the death of Sir Syed, who had grown to be a powerful institution in his own person, it was becoming increasingly necessary for the Muslims to establish an organization to further their cause. Some other influential Muslims expressed similar views. At a meeting at Lucknow in October 1901, Viqar-ul-Mulk outlined a scheme for a Muslim political organization but his efforts led to no permanent result.

It was the clamorous agitation against the partition of Bengal which really shocked the Muslims into action. Nawab Salimullah of Dacca said in a speech on the day it took effect that partition had 'aroused us from inaction and directed our attention to activities and struggle'.

Muslim fears as to their future were increased when the Liberals took office in England. On 20 July 1906, Morley stated in the House of Commons that the Governor-General would soon appoint a committee to consider what reforms in the direction of 'the extension of the representative element in the Legislative Council...can be expeditiously carried forward'. The Muslim reaction was expressed in a letter which Mohsin-ul-Mulk, the Secretary of MAO College, Aligarh, wrote on 4 August to W.A.J. Archbold, Principal of the college, who was vacationing in Simla:

> You must have read and thought over Mr John Morley's speech...It is very much talked of among the Mohammedans of India and is commonly believed to be a great success achieved by the 'National Congress'... If the new rules now to be drawn up introduce 'election' on a more extended scale, the Mohammedans will hardly get a seat, while the Hindus will carry off the palm by dint of their majority, and no Mohammedan will get into the Councils by election... It has been proposed that a memorial be submitted to His Excellency the Viceroy to draw the attention of Government to a consideration of the rights of Mohammedans...Will you therefore inform me if it would be advisable to submit a memorial from the Mohammedans to the Viceroy, and to request His Excellency's permission for a deputation to wait on His Excellency to submit the views of Mohammedans on the matter?

Minto forwarded a copy of the letter to Morley on 8 August saying, 'I have not had time to think over the advisability of receiving the proposed deputation, but am inclined to do so.'

Two days later, Archibold was able to write to Mohsin-ul-Mulk that, 'Colonel Dunlop Smith, Private Secretary to His Excellency the Viceroy, informs me that His Excellency is agreeable to receive the Muslim deputation. He advises that a formal letter requesting permission to wait on His Excellency be sent to him.' Accordingly, a delegation of thirty-five leading Muslims of India led by the Aga Khan waited on the Viceroy on 1 October. The main points of their submission and of the Viceroy's reply have already been described in the previous section.

There is general agreement that the right of communal representation won by the Aga Khan deputation meant that the British formally accepted that the Muslims in India formed a political entity separate from the Hindus. It became a feature of all future enactment and culminated in the constitutional recognition of the Muslims as a separate nation entitled to a homeland of their own.

We have used the word 'formally' above advisedly because in principle, British statesmen had never made any secret of the fact that India was made up of diverse peoples to which an unadulterated British system of government was inapplicable. In his letter of June 1906 to Minto, quoted in a previous page, Morley had referred to 'the nations who inhabit India'. Lord Salisbury, when Prime Minister, had stated that elective and representative government was 'not an Eastern idea' and puts 'an intolerable strain' on a society divided into hostile sections. Even the twentieth congress (December 1904), protesting against the proposed partition of Bengal on the ground that it would divide 'the Bengali nation', implied that India had more nations than one.

Though in the long run, the grant of separate electorates to the Muslims contributed to the establishment of Pakistan, in the short run, it cleared the way for the introduction of representative institutions which Congress as well as the British desired. What the Muslims had said in effect was that 'we are willing to accept the system of elections provided it is accompanied by the safeguards we are requesting'.

Under the Lucknow Pact (to be discussed later) Congress also agreed to allow the Muslims the assurances they desired. Had that spirit of give-and-take been continued, there might very well have been no Pakistan.

Was the Aga Khan delegation a brain-child of the British? The documentary evidence just cited makes it amply clear that the Muslim deputation was a spontaneous effort by the Muslims to protect their interests. They had consistently believed from the days of Sir Syed that in a system of election 'pure and simple', the Hindus would overwhelm them. They realized that it was impossible for them to prevent the introduction of the system altogether. They therefore accepted the inevitable but pressed for provisions which would make the situation acceptable to them. There was nothing extraordinary in their wish to wait on the Viceroy to make their point of view known, nor in their action to sound out the Viceroy beforehand whether he would be willing to receive the deputation, nor in their use of Archbold as the intermediary.

That some Britons were sympathetic to the Muslim viewpoint is not any more reprehensible than that many more of them backed the Hindu-dominated Congress. It should not be overlooked that Congress was the creation of the former civil servant Hume, who continued to tend it for many years; also that in the process of founding Congress, Hume had obtained the advice and blessing of the Viceroy, Lord Dufferin.

Some sessions of Congress were presided over by invitees from Britain, and Congress enjoyed the support of a large number of people in that country. The official *History of the Indian National Congress* by B. Pattabhai Sitaramayya pays tribute to some of these in the chapter entitled 'Our British Friends', of which the the introductory sentence acknowledges that 'some members of the British Parliament and certain other eminent Englishmen played a notable part in the evolution of Indian politics.'

Indian writers, in the main, advance two arguments in support of their contention that the Aga Khan deputation was a put-up show. In the first place they quote from the speech delivered by Maulana Muhammed Ali as president of the thirty-eighth session of the Indian National Congress at Cocanada[1], in the course of which he referred to the Aga Khan delegation as a 'command performance'. Secondly, they refer to an entry in Lady Minto's diary dated 1 October 1906 which reads: 'This evening I have received the following letter from an official: "I must send Your Excellency a line to say that a very big thing has happened today. A work of statesmanship that will affect India and Indian history for many a long year. It is nothing less than the pulling back of sixty-two millions of people from joining the ranks of the seditious opposition.' The extract from Muhammad Ali's speech which the critics of the Aga Khan quote runs as follows:

> To follow the fashion of British journalists during the War, 'there is no harm now in saying' that the Deputation's was a 'command' performance! It was clear that Government could no longer resist the demands of educated Indians, and, as usual, it was about to dole out to them a morsel that would keep them gagged for some years. Hitherto the Mussalmans had acted very much like the Irish prisoner in the dock who, in reply to the judge's inquiry whether he had

---

[1] The Cocanada session was held from 28 December 1923 until 1 January 1924.

any counsel to represent him in the trial, had frankly replied that he had certainly not engaged counsel, but that he had 'friends in the jury'! But now the Muslims' 'friends in the jury' had themselves privately urged that the accused should engage duly qualified counsel like all others.

Muhammad Ali does not reinforce his witty and cryptic observations with any hard facts and names. In fact his speech read as a whole justifies the appearance of the Aga Khan delegation before the Viceroy to convey the Muslim requirements to him. In the very next lines to those quoted above he says:

> From whatever source the inspiration may have come, there is no doubt that the Muslim cause was this time properly advocated. In the common territorial electorates the Mussalmans had certainly not succeeded in securing anything like adequate or real representation, and those who denounced and deplored the creation of separate electorates for which the Mussalmans had pleaded should have remembered that separate electorates were the consequence, and not the cause, of the separation between Mussalmans and their more numerous Hindu brethren.

He argued that in fact 'the creation of separate electorates was hastening the advent of Hindu-Muslim unity. For the first time a real franchise, however restricted, was being offered to Indians, and if Hindus and Mussalmans remained just as divided as they had hitherto been since the commencement of British rule, and often hostile to one another, mixed electorates would have provided the best battle-ground for inter-communal strife, and would have still further widened the gulf separating the two communities.'

He paid high tribute to Sir Syed who was the father of Muslim nationalism: 'Reviewing the actions of a bygone generation to-day, when it is easier to be wise after the event, I must confess I still think the attitude of Syed Ahmed Khan was eminently wise, and much as I wish that some things which he had said should have been left unsaid, I am constrained to admit that no well-wisher of Mussalmans, nor of India as a whole, could have followed a very different course in leading the Mussalmans... and it is my firm belief that his advocacy succeeded mainly because of the soundness of the policy advocated'.

There is also nothing sinister in the observation in Lady Minto's diary that the rapport between the Aga Khan delegation and her husband had pulled back the Muslims from joining the ranks of the seditious elements. No one at that stage could tell whether the Moderates or the Extremists in Congress would gain control of that organization, and the agitation against the partition of Bengal was supported by disorder and terrorism. If the milder Hindus could make things so difficult for the government, there was no knowing what the more warlike Muslims would do if their pleas were turned down. Lady Minto's diary does not say that the Muslim delegation had been inspired by the British officials; it simply expresses the relief felt in official circles that the Muslims had been propitiated and their loyalty had been retained. The British had already greatly pleased Congress by the promise of constitutional reform. But the expected nature of the changes had deeply alarmed the Muslims. It is not surprising that the British should have striven to appease them as well.

Though the idea of the Muslims having a party of their own had been in the air for some time, the Muslim League, which became a permanent institution and ultimately achieved Pakistan, was the child of the Simla delegation. The members realized that it was not sufficient to plead the Muslim case before the Viceroy at a single meeting. It was essential for the community to have a standing political organization, constantly to propagate and press their claims at all levels. Three days after they had waited on the Viceroy they conferred at the local Nabha House and agreed in principle to give practical shape to the idea.

Influential Muslim delegates from all parts of India were due to gather at Dacca during the forthcoming Christmas holidays to attend the twentieth session of the Mohammedan Educational Conference and it was decided to make use of that occasion to finalize the question of setting up a political body. After the Conference, a meeting was called on 30 December 1906 under the presidency of Viqar-ul-Mulk. It discussed the scheme for 'The Mohammedan All-India Confederacy' which Nawab Salimullah of Dacca had framed and circulated some time previously. Ultimately, at the motion of Salimullah, it was decided that

a Political Association be formed, styled All-India Muslim League, for the furtherance of the following objects:

(a) To promote, among the Mussalmans of India, feelings of loyalty to the British Government, and to remove any misconception that may arise as to the intention of Government with regard to any of its measures.

(b) To protect and advance the political rights and interests of the Mussalmans of India, and to respectfully represent their needs and aspirations to the Government.

(c) To prevent the rise, among the Mussalmans of India, of any feeling of
     hostility towards other communities, without prejudice to the other
     aforementioned objects of the League.

While moving the above resolution, Salimullah said, 'Had the party
now in power in England been familiar with the position and rights of the
Mohammedans of India, and had those among our countrymen who have
hitherto been taking a prominent part in the public life of this country been
consistently just in asking for the allotment of their respective shares to the
various communities in India, it is not improbable that the League which
it is now proposed to form would not have been heard of for a long time,
if at all; and that we would have gone on pursuing the traditional policy
of our people and attending solely to our educational needs... It is only now
that I, for one, have been forced, by the practical needs of our community
during the crisis through which we in Eastern Bengal are passing, to
believe in the urgent necessity of a separate political organization for the
Mohammedans of India...only after a central League like the one proposed
to be formed today comes into existence, can the Government find a
representative body to which to turn for ascertaining the views of the
Mussalmans of India, and to which the Mussalmans themselves can turn
for consistent and firm support, sensible and sincere advice, and a true
interpretation of the wishes of the Government.'

In March 1908 the Aga Khan was elected 'permanent' president of the
Muslim League, and in May of that year the London branch of the League
was founded with Syed Ameer Ali as President. The Aga Khan served as
president till his resignation in 1913.

The inaugural session at Dacca welcomed the partition of Bengal in
these words:

 Resolved: that this meeting, in view of the clear interest of the Mussalmans of
 Eastern Bengal, considers that the Partition is sure to prove beneficial to the
 Mohammedan community which constitutes the vast majority of that Province,
 and that all such methods of agitation as boycotting should be strongly
 condemned and discouraged.

The first session of the League was held in two parts, at Karachi in
December 1907 and at Aligarh in March 1908. At the latter a resolution
put forward the demands that a Muslim Judge be appointed to each of the
high courts and chief courts of the country where such appointments had
not already been made; that the Muslims be given their proper share of

appointments in the public service; that it was of 'vital importance' that the Muslims be adequately represented 'as a distinct Community' in the Legislative Councils as well as in the various local bodies by 'enabling Mohammedan voters to elect their own representatives'; that the Muslims should be given due representation on the syndicates and Senates of the Universities and 'on the Textbook Committee connected with the Department of Public Instruction'.

At the second session (Amritsar, December 1908), Syed Ali Imam made some lively observations in the course of his presidential address. He said that,

> Home rule under the aegis of the British Crown in India is possible only when racial, religious, social and intellectual disparities are removed and a fusion has levelled down characteristics of separate denominations to a plane where the pulsations of a common national life are the most prominent features... When I find the most advanced province of India (Bengal) put forward the sectarian cry of 'Bande Mataram' as the national cry, and the sectarian *rakhi-bandhan* as a national observance, my heart is filled with despair and disappointment; and the suspicion that, under the cloak of nationalism, Hindu nationalism is preached in India becomes a conviction.

The Amritsar session also expressed its 'grateful thanks' to Morley and Minto 'for the broad and general policy foreshadowed in the Despatch dealing with the reform scheme'. Similarly the third session, at Delhi in January 1910, placed on record 'its deep sense of appreciation of the just and beneficial scheme of reform embodied in the Indian Councils Act and the regulations framed thereunder...'

MOHAMMAD ALI JINNAH, THE EARLY YEARS

Mohammad Ali Jinnah's background had some interesting features in common with Gandhi, his principal opponent in the struggle for Pakistan during the closing period of British rule in India. The ancestral homes of both of them were in Kathiawar, Western India—Jinnah's at Paneli in the princely state of Gondal and Gandhi's at Porbander in the princely state of Rajkot; the mother-tongue of both, thus, was Gujrati. Both, moreover, belonged to mercantile communities. Jinnah's family were Khojas of the Ismaili sect of Shiahs who accept the Aga Khan as their spiritual leader. Not long after his return to India from England, Jinnah joined the Khoja sect of Isna Asharis, who are also Shiahs but have no religious head. Gandhi was a member of the Modh Bania subcaste of the Vaisa caste. Both went to England at an early age and qualified as barristers, and both were ardent admirers of Gokhale and started their political careers as Moderate members of the Indian National Congress.

However, their lifestyles and political styles were totally different. Jinnah dressed immaculately and lived elegantly; Gandhi took to wearing a loin-cloth and led a life of austerity. Jinnah's approach to a problem was sharply direct and easy to comprehend. Gandhi's message was couched in moral terms and his conduct was guided by his 'inner voice' and often puzzled even his most intelligent and devoted followers. Gandhi captivated the masses by his saintliness. Jinnah never courted popularity. He was more respected and trusted than loved. His greatness resembled that of a surgeon or a lawyer who possessed the brilliant skill to prevail against impossible odds. Gandhi inspired faith, Jinnah confidence; Gandhi was the right leader for the contemplative Hindus, Jinnah for the more practical Muslims. Jinnah became a mass leader late in life, when the Muslims of India began to look upon him as a modern Moses who would lead them to the Promised Land. As the demand for Pakistan gathered strength, he became Pakistan personified, and everyone who loved Pakistan loved Jinnah too.

With the opening of the Suez Canal, Karachi had begun to grow and prosper. It was to that town that Jinnah's father, Jinnabhai, migrated in 1875 to seek his fortune. There on 25 December of the following year was born the eldest of his four sons. He named him Mohammad Ali. He also had four daughters, the third of whom was Fatima, who was to keep house for her widowed brother Mohammad Ali Jinnah.

At birth Jinnah was underweight but normal in other respects; he remained slim all his life. As a boy he was not studious. This troubled his father but his mother was fully confident that he was destined to be a great man. From his ancestors, and more immediately from his father, he inherited the faculty of being careful with money. His high income as the leading light of the Bombay Bar, and his careful investments, in time brought him real affluence.

In the course of his business, Jinnah's father had come to know Sir Frederick Croft, General Manger of the British firm of managing agents who traded under the name of Douglas Graham and Company. In 1892, Croft secured an apprenticeship for Jinnah at the London office of his firm. Jinnah's father was pleased but his mother was heart-broken at the thought of parting with her son. She finally agreed to let him go provided he agreed first to get married to a girl of their own community as an insurance against acquiring a foreign wife. The arranged marriage took place at Paneli, from where the bride hailed. Soon afterwards, in November 1892, Jinnah sailed for England. Both his mother and his young bride died while he was away.

Not long after his arrival in England, Jinnah forsook routine commercial apprenticeship and embarked on the more exciting pursuit of the legal profession. In May 1896 he was called to the bar. His father's business, which had prospered in Karachi at first, had failed and he had already moved to Bombay. So it was to Bombay that Jinnah went to start his practice as a barrister.

During his three and a half years' stay in London, Jinnah had imbibed some of the liberalism that was in the air in those days, and he attended the House of Commons where he heard, among others, Dadabhai Naoroji, for whom he had campaigned during the parliamentary elections. He also developed a passion for the theatre and confessed at a later date that he had nursed the ambition to star as 'Romeo' at the Old Vic playhouse. After he had completed his course for the bar, he successfully auditioned for a theatrical job, but had to return home at the insistence of his father. His proficiency as a performer no doubt stood him in good stead as a practioner in law and politics.

By 1900 he had shown sufficient promise as a barrister to be invited by John Molesworth MacPherson, the Bombay Advocate General, to work in his office and use his library. The MacPherson connection secured him the position of temporary Third Presidency Magistrate but he refused the offer of a permanent post on the then handsome salary of fifteen hundred rupees per month, confidently predicting that he would soon be earning that much in a single day freelancing. His practice flourished and he helped his family both generally, and, in particular, by bearing the expenses of the education of his brothers and sisters.

Politically, the liberalism he had acquired in London continued to grow in Bombay, which has always been the most cosmopolitan of the Indian cities, not least because the Parsees, who are the most cosmopolitan of all the Indian peoples, form an important element of its population. It therefore bred less orthodox Muslims, like Tyabji, than did northern India, which produced those of a stricter kind, such as Sir Syed.

It was not surprising that the outlook of young Jinnah should have been affected by the circles in which he moved. In England he had already come under the powerful influence of Dadabhai Naoroji. In Bombay, he worked for some time in the chambers of another influential Parsee, Pherozeshah Mehta, who was a pillar of moderation in Congress, and established a close relationship with him based on mutual respect.

Friendship with yet another Parsee family, that of the socialites Sir Dinshaw and Lady Petit, resulted in their beautiful sixteen-year-old daughter Rutti and the much older Jinnah falling in love with each other. Petit was bitterly opposed to Jinnah's proposal to marry his daughter and the couple had to wait for two years till the girl attained majority and could marry without parental consent. The bride was converted to Islam in the Jamia Masjid, Bombay, and the marriage took place on 19 April 1918. Jinnah shaved off his moustache to smarten up his appearance as a bridegroom. In January 1928 the couple separated 'due to temperamental differences and difference in age'. Rutti died in 1928 and Jinnah never remarried. Dina, the only issue of their union, married a Parsee-born Christian of Bombay named Wadia against the vehemently expressed disapproval of her father, who urged her to seek a Muslim husband.

To return to Jinnah's political complexion in the early years, his model was the Maratha Gokhale, the most highly regarded Moderate, so much so that he openly vowed to become 'a Muslim Gokhale'. Some years later, Gokhale returned the compliment by saying that Jinnah 'has true stuff in him and that freedom from all sectarian prejudice which will make him the best ambassador of Hindu-Muslim unity'. When Dadabhai Naoroji, by now the Grand Old Man of Indian Politics, was invited to preside over the 1906 session of Congress, he selected Jinnah as his private secretary for the event. This was Jinnah's first recorded participation in a Congress meeting.

The Aga Khan recalled that period in his *Memoirs* in these words, 'Who then was our doughtiest opponent in 1906? A distinguished Muslim barrister in Bombay, with a large and prosperous practice, Mr Mohammed Ali Jinnah... he said that our principle of separate electorates was dividing the nation against itself...' The Allahabad Congress (1910) passed the following resolution at Jinnah's motion: 'This Congress strongly deprecates the expansion or application of the principle of Separate Communal Electorates to Municipalities, District Boards or other Local Bodies', but in his brief speech he said, 'I am not prepared to make a long speech on this resolution as I did not intend to speak at all, but in response to the wishes of a great many leaders of the Congress, I have agreed to move this resolution before you. Gentlemen, I wish it to be made quite clear that I do not represent the Mohammedan community here nor have I any mandate from the Mohammedan community. I only express my personal views here and nothing more'. It is evident that he was uncomfortably conscious that he was out of tune with the majority of his co-religionists.

In 1909, Jinnah was elected to the Governor-General's Legislative Council from a Muslim constituency and took his seat in January 1910. His first speech as member was in support of a resolution demanding an end to the export of indentured labour from India to South Africa, where Gandhi was championing the same cause on the spot. The following year Jinnah sponsored the Wakf Validating Bill and skilfully piloted it to the statute books. The necessity for this bill had arisen from the rulings of the Privy Council which had invalidated the right of the Muslims to create tax-free *wakfs* (trusts) in favour of their families under Muslim law. In 1906 the Congress Party, which claimed to be the guardian of the interests of all the communities of India, had passed a resolution calling for the appointment of a commission to examine the question. If it found that the Privy Council had erred, the situation had to be rectified by legislation. Two years later the Muslim League also passed a resolution demanding legislation to validate *wakfs,* and it continued to press the issue till redress was achieved by Jinnah through his bill. Though Jinnah's efforts won the gratitude of all Muslims and were appreciatively mentioned in the proceedings of the Muslim League, he was at that time a member of the Congress Party.

CHAPTER 9

HINDU-MUSLIM
RAPPROCHEMENT

THE ANNULMENT OF THE PARTITION OF BENGAL

When the year 1910 closed, both the major political parties of India, Congress and the Muslim League, were in loyal hands. Congress continued to pass resolutions for the revision of the partition of Bengal but displayed its moderation by not including the weapon of boycott in its programme. The very first resolution of the 1910 Congress session, which was passed with everyone standing in silence, gave expression to 'profound grief at the sudden and untimely demise of His Most Gracious Majesty King Edward VII, whose beneficient reign will ever be memorable in the annals of India'; the second resolution offered Congress's 'humble homage and duty to the King Emperor George V on his accession' and begged 'to tender to His Majesty an assurance of its profound loyalty and attachment to his august throne and person'.

The Muslims had been shocked in the early part of Minto's regime by the resignation under pressure of Sir Bampfylde Fuller, Lieutenant Governor of Eastern Bengal, who was noted for his pro-Muslim bias, and by Morley's promise of extending the electoral system in India; but they were pacified by the declaration that the partition of Bengal was a settled question, and by the grant of communal representation under 1909 legislation. Upon the death of King Edward VII, therefore, the Muslim League vied with Congress in the expression of loyalty to the British crown. Its first two resolutions at the December 1910 session ran parallel to those of Congress quoted above. Resolution I 'voicing the feeling of 60 million loyal Muslims of India' expressed 'profound sorrow at the lamented demise of His Majesty Edward VII who...was justly regarded as a friend and promoter of peace throughout the civilized world'; Resolution II tendered 'loyal and respectful homage to His Majesty King George V'. H. M. Malak, President of the Reception Committee, in his speech of welcome to the delegates, said that 'the British Crown has no more loyal and devoted subjects than the Mussalmans of India; to them the British Sovereign is not a foreign ruler but like their own Emperor, the continuance of whose beneficial sway is essential to the peace and prosperity of India'.

But at the people's level, especially in Bengal, disruptive agitation, including acts of terrorism, by Hindus continued. The disorder was not serious enough to subvert the government, but its persistence and the fear that the situation might get out of hand was a source of continuous worry. In *My Indian Years* Lord Hardinge, who succeeded Minto in November 1910, has stated that 'even before I arrived in India I was well aware that the Province of Bengal was seething with sedition, the outcome of the policy of partition. Dacoities and assassinations of police and informers were an almost daily occurrence in Calcutta and its neighbourhood and it was practically impossible to secure a conviction by the ordinary process of law.' Within a few months of his arrival in India he realized 'that if nothing were done we would have to be prepared for even more serious trouble in the future than in the past in Bengal.' That King George V and his Queen were due to hold an Imperial Durbar in India in December 1911 made Hardinge and the British Government even more anxious to calm things down.

Hardinge had been specially selected for the post of Viceroy by Morley and Asquith, who realised that the situation in India demanded a more tactful and imaginative Chief Executive than Minto had been. His family had a tradition of service in India going back more than a hundred years. He himself was a career diplomat and had held the post of permanent Under-Secretary of State at the Foreign Office for nearly six years immediately before coming out to India. His real ambition, though, had always been to follow in the footsteps of his grandfather, the first Viscount Hardinge, who had been Governor-General of India from 1844 to 1848. Lord Kitchener, who had been Commander-in Chief in India during the viceroyalty of Curzon, was extremely keen to be Viceroy, and was bitterly disappointed when Hardinge was appointed in preference to him.

The exchanges between Calcutta and Whitehall which undid Curzon's partition of Bengal were opened by Lord Crewe, the new Secretary of State for India, who wrote to Hardinge on the subject in January 1911. Hardinge replied to Crewe on 19 July 1911, explaining the scheme he favoured and also giving the views of the members of his Council. Approval was granted in less than a month but the scheme was kept secret until the King's announcement at the Durbar. The partition of Bengal was revoked and the two parts of Bengal were made into a new Governor's

Province with the same status as the Presidencies of Bombay and Madras; Bihar and Orissa were created a Lieutenant-Governor's Province and Assam reverted to Chief Commissionership; at the same time, the capital of India was transferred from Calcutta to Delhi.

Hardinge had proposed the removal of the capital from Calcutta mainly because 'the presence of the Legislative Assembly in Calcutta created an undue and inevitable Bengali influence upon the Members which was detrimental to their legislative impartiality, and presented a field for intrigue, in which the Bengali excelled.' The idea was not new but had not been pressed before for fear of the consequences. Hardinge had rightly judged that the main source of expected trouble, the Bengali Hindus, would peacefully swallow the change if it was coupled with the annulment of the partition of Bengal, which in their mind overshadowed all other issues. That left the British mercantile community of Bengal as the main objectors. They bitterly resented the fact that Calcutta would lose all the glitter and ceremony and prestige which it had enjoyed as the imperial capital. Their most illustrious residents—the Viceroy and Commander-in-Chief and their staffs, the members of the Viceroy's legislative council, and the departments of the central government and their staffs—would all move to Delhi. In spite of support from some influential voices in England, Hardinge was able to ride out the storm because the measure was welcomed by all the peoples of India, other than the Bengalis, and by the ruling princes, who appreciated that Delhi enjoyed a more central position in India than Calcutta and had been the seat of some glorious empires in the past.

The announcement that the two Bengali-speaking regions would be united was received by the Hindus with acclaim but it deeply shocked the Muslims and powerfully influenced their thinking and conduct in the years to come. The Muslims, who had been assured by the British Government that the partition of Bengal was a settled question, felt betrayed when it was suddenly undone. Their confidence that their interests were safe in British hands was shaken. It was not their loyalty but Hindu subversion that had paid off.

CONGRESS AND THE MUSLIM LEAGUE IN HARMONY

Already at the third annual session of the Muslim League at Delhi in January 1910, the Aga Khan had expressed the hope that the attainment of separate electorates, which the Muslims had 'deemed to be an absolute necessity', would 'result in a permanent political sympathy and a genuine working entente cordiale between the members of the two great sister communities'. At the fourth session of the League at Nagpur in December of the same year, Syed Nabiullah in his presidential address endorsed the Aga Khan's sentiments, and declared that the achievement of separate electorates 'has happily put us in a position effectively to look after our interests.. (and) put us in the proper frame of mind to co-operate cordially with our Hindu brethren for the advancement and glory of our common country... barring the question of employment in the public services of the State and the Urdu-Hindi question, there is hardly any question of public importance, so far as I can see, on which the Mohammedans are not in substantial agreement with their Hindu brethren. That being so, I venture to suggest that Hindu and Mohammedan leaders, and especially our Hindu and Mohammedan legislators, should from time to time meet each other in formal conferences, for the purpose of exchanging notes and holding friendly discussions on all questions affecting the general well-being of the country.' With regard to this initiative for Congress-League rapport, which reached its climax in the Lucknow Pact of 1916, it is pertinent to emphasis two facts because they generally have not received the recognition they deserve. The first is that it was taken by the Muslim League and not by the Indian National Congress. The second is that its originator was the Aga Khan and not Jinnah, who embarked on his role as 'ambassador of Hindu-Muslim unity' at a later stage.

The growing feeling among the Muslims that they should move closer to the Hindus received a strong impetus when the British let them down by depriving them of the Muslim-majority province of Eastern Bengal. 'If we cannot trust the British, why not join hands with the resourceful Hindus who know how to get the better of the British?' they began to ask themselves. This trend in Muslim thinking was strengthened by threats posed to independent Muslim powers, especially to the Ottoman Empire, whose Sultan was the Caliph of Islam. This calls for a brief explanation.

We have already noted that the failure of the Great Revolt brought home to the Indian Muslims the lesson that there was no forseeable prospect of reviving a Muslim empire in India. Increasingly, therefore, the eyes of the Indian Muslims turned towards Turkey, which alone in the world at that time seemed capable of becoming the focus of universal Muslim regeneration. That the Ottoman Sultan had also held the title of Khalifa since 1517 made him especially qualified to stand forth as the champion of Islam.

During the Russo-Turkish war of 1877, the Muslims of India for the first time demonstrated their sympathy for the Turks on a large scale.

Religious services were held in some mosques in Calcutta and subscriptions were collected for the succour of the wounded and sick Turks. Many expressed a desire to fight in the ranks of their Turkish comrades. Similar feelings were roused during the Greco-Turkish war of 1897. Henceforth, all Turkish causes evoked agitation in India.

The fate of neighbouring Afghanistan and Iran served to confirm the fear of the Indian Muslims that the Christian powers were determined to subdue the world of Islam—Afghanistan was dominated by Britain and in 1907 the conclusion of the Anglo-Russian Entente had made Iran a dependency of the two contracting powers.

By a coincidence, the year 1911 was not only the year in which the partition of Bengal was revoked, but was also the year in which Italy invaded Tripoli. This was followed by the war between Turkey and the Balkan league (1912), during which a medical mission under Dr M. A. Ansari was dispatched to Turkey. Money was subscribed more readily for the Turkish cause than for any proposal for the betterment of the Indian Muslims themselves. At the sixth session of the Muslim League at Nagpur (March 1913), even the well-known moderate Mian (afterwards Sir) Muhammad Shafi noted with concern in the course of his presidential address that 'the victories of the Balkan States were acclaimed by some of the European races as triumphs of the Cross over the Crescent. Even the Liberal Prime Minister of the greatest Muslim power in the world [1], regardless of the feelings of 100 millions of His Majesty's Mussalman subjects, rejoiced at the fall of Salonica on the ground of its having been the gate through which Christianity had entered Europe... For the first time in modern history, a section of the European Press openly proclaimed the startling doctrine that the Turks had no right to remain in Europe.'

A Muslim League Council meeting held at Bankipore on 31 December 1912, under the presidency of the Aga Khan, recommended a change in the creed of the Muslim League. A resolution, which was passed unamended after a debate, declared that the League should aim at 'the attainment, under the aegis of the British crown, of a system of self-government suitable to India by bringing about, through constitutional means, a steady reform of the existing system of administration, by promoting national unity and fostering public spirit among the people of India and by co-operating with other communities for the said purposes.'

During the debate two amendments were suggested, but both were lost because they were opposed by Jinnah, who was not yet a subscribing

---

[1] Great Britain then ruled over an empire containing more Muslims than any other country.

member of the League and was evidently attending the session as an invited guest.

The first proposal was made by Mazhar-ul-Haque of Bankipore, who objected to the words 'self-government suitable to India' and said that India wanted self-government on colonial lines. This amendment, if carried, would have made the creed of the League identical with that of Congress. But Jinnah argued that the resolution as worded represented the right ideal for the League and, though he himself was a member of Congress, he believed that Congress was wrong in this matter. He did not spell out the kind of constitution he considered suitable for India. Was he already convinced that the Muslims of India would not accept the colonial model without the safeguards which they had been demanding from the days of Sir Syed?

The second objection to the resolution was made by Viqar-ul-Mulk, who said that the time had not yet come for the attainment of self-government. Jinnah observed that 'nobody asked for it to be given tomorrow or the day after. It was the goal and ideal of the nation, and might be attained say a century hence.' Jinnah's rejoinder illustrates the belief then prevalent that the British would govern India for a long time to come.

The resolution of the Council that the ideal of the Muslim League should be the attainment, under the aegis of the British crown, of a system of self-government suitable to India, was ratified at the sixth session of the League at Lucknow in March 1913. Jinnah once again attended as an invitee. There were also two further indications at that session of the League's wish to co-operate with the Hindus in matters which were of common interest to all Indians. The first was that Mrs Sarojini Naidu, the Hindu poetess and afterwards a devoted follower of Gandhi, was invited to address the League session. At the conclusion of her speech she was honoured by three cheers and the audience stood up to show respect to her. Secondly, the following resolution was passed:

The All-India Muslim League places on record its firm belief that the future development and progress of the people of India depends exclusively on the harmonious working and co-operation of the various communities; deprecates all mischievous attempts to widen the unfortunate breach between the Hindus and Mussalmans; and hopes that the leaders on both sides will periodically meet together to restore the amicable relations prevailing between them in the past and find a *modus operandi* for joint and concerted action in questions of the public good.

Later in 1913, Jinnah yielded to the argument that, since self-government had become the chief aim of both Congress and the League, there was no longer any reason why he should not belong to both organizations, and formally joined the League on the condition that his 'loyalty to the Muslim League and Muslim interests would in no way and at no time imply even the shadow of disloyalty to the larger national cause to which his life was dedicated'. His status as a respected member of both Congress and the Muslim League now uniquely qualified him to take on the responsibilities of 'ambassador of Hindu-Muslim unity'.

At the seventh session of the League at Agra (December 1913), Sir Ibrahim Rahimtoola said in his presidential address: 'Our policy towards the British Government should be one of unswerving loyalty, and towards the Hindus one of brotherly love and regard.'

Congress welcomed the new trend in the League's policy and at the twenty-eighth session at Karachi (December 1913) responded by the following resolution:

This Congress places on record its warm appreciation of the adoption by the All-India Muslim League of the ideal of Self-Government for India within the British Empire, and expresses its complete accord with the belief that the League has so emphatically declared at its last sessions that the political future of the Country depends on the harmonious working and co-operation of the various Communities in the country which has been the cherished ideal of the Congress. This Congress most heartily welcomes the hope expressed by the League that the leaders of the different communities will make every endeavour to find a *modus operandi* for joint and concerted action on all questions of national good and earnestly appeals to all the sections of the people to help the object we all have at heart.

Though the Muslims were moving closer to the Hindus at this time, they were still a backward minority educationally as compared to the latter and were not quite sure how things would turn out. Everyone believed that the British would rule India for a long time to come, and the Muslims did not wish to lose their protection and goodwill. Lord Hardinge was a tactful Governor-General and tried in a number of ways to assuage Muslim feelings, which had been hurt by the annulment of the partition of Bengal. East Bengali Muslims welcomed his announcement that a tea-ching and residential university—the first of its kind in India—would be founded at Dacca.

He also resolved an ugly dispute relating to a mosque at Cawnpore to the satisfaction of the Muslims. This had resulted from a decision of the local authorities to widen a road. The original plan was abandoned because it would have involved the destruction of a Hindu temple. In accordance with the revised alignment a corner of the courtyard of a mosque was demolished on 1 July 1913. When the Muslims tried to rebuild it they were fired upon by the police. Some fifty persons were wounded or killed. The provincial government turned down all requests to rebuild the destroyed part. Hardinge personally went to the spot, overruled the Lieutenant-Governor, and ordered the reconstruction of the razed part with a passage under it for public use. He also ordered the release of the arrested Muslims. At its Agra session that year, the Muslim League expressed 'its deep sense of gratitude' to Hardinge for 'bringing peace to Cawnpore and the Muslim community in a manner which has enhanced the faith of the people of India in British justice'. Hardinge won further praise for extending Jinnah's term as a member of the Legislative Council to enable the latter to pilot the Wakf Validating Bill till it became law.

He was even able to neutralize, to some extent, Muslim anxiety with regard to the policy of the British cabinet toward Turkey. In the very speech in which he criticised the British Prime Minister, Mian Muhammad Shafi said, 'fortunately for Muslim interests, at this critical juncture there is at the helm of the Indian administration a far-sighted statesman who has felt the pulse of Muslim feeling with a precision which has won him our sincere respect and admiration. The active sympathy shown by Lord Hardinge and his noble consort for our suffering Turkish brethren, the lead taken by their Excellencies in collecting subscriptions for the relief of the wounded and the distressed in this unrighteous war and the wise pronouncements made by His Excellency from time to time have gained for him the deep gratitude of 70 millions of His Majesty's Mussalman subjects in India.'

This capacity of keeping in close touch with the feelings of the people of India also enabled Hardinge to win the hearts of all Indians by his attitude toward the plight of Indians in South Africa. He sent Gokhale on a visit to South Africa (October-November 1912) where the Indian leader's tour put new heart into the campaign which Gandhi was waging. Gokhale also conferred with General Smuts and his colleagues and elicited promises of reform. In India, Hardinge publicly declared his 'deep and burning sympathy' for Indians in South Africa 'in their resistance to invidious and unjust laws' and successfully demanded the appointment of a commission of inquiry in South Africa to examine the Indian question. After the passage of the Indian Relief Act in July 1914,

Gandhi felt he could leave South Africa and return home. A few weeks before Hardinge relinquished office in India, he had the satisfaction of receiving an assurance from the British Government that Indian indentured labour for the colonies would be abolished.

In *My Indian Years*, Hardinge recorded that he had also attained 'an assurance from the Home Government that as soon as the war was over, the economic position of India would be reconsidered with a view to abolishing the excise duty on cotton. This excise duty on cotton goods was imposed on India as a protective measure for the cotton industries of Lancashire rather than of India. To this reproach there was absolutely no reply and I felt its injustice so keenly that I left no stone unturned during my term of office in India to obtain its removal.'

Both Congress and the Muslim League requested His Majesty's Government to extend Hardinge's term of office. He was due to vacate office after five years but was allowed to serve for an extra five months, until 4 April 1916. He was succeeded by Lord Chelmsford.

INDIA'S REACTION TO WORLD WAR I

Thanks to Hardinge's conciliatory policies, India on the whole was in loyal mood when World War I broke out on 4 August 1914 and responded generously to Britain's call for help. The Allies—Britain, France and Russia—were joined by Japan. At the end of October, Turkey threw in its lot with the Central Powers—Germany and Austria. In 1915 Italy decided to side with the Allies and Bulgaria with the Central Powers. Allied victory was assured after the United States declared war on Germany on 6 April 1917. Germany surrendered on 11 November 1918. Soon after Turkey had entered the war, a British army consisting mainly of Indian soldiers, including Muslims, was dispatched to Mesopotamia and Palestine. Indian troops also fought in Europe, Egypt, East Africa and other theatres of war.

At first Britain was not sure how India would react to the war. In a speech in the House of Commons on 12 July 1917, the Secretary of State Edwin Montagu recalled: 'We did not know whether India should co-operate in this war or not; we did not trust them; we dare not trust them...' But help from India in men and money was generous and prompt and for the first two years of the war the Indian political scene remained relatively calm. The only direct taste of war that India had was the shelling of Madras by the German cruiser *Emden* in September 1914.

Lord Hardinge described India's response in these terms:

During the twenty months of war that elapsed while I was still in India, there were no serious disturbances and merely a few isolated plots, most instigated from outside India...

Within six months of the outbreak of war seven divisions of infantry and two divisions and two brigades of cavalry were sent from India overseas. But in addition to these organized forces no less than 20 batteries of artillery and 32 battalions of British infantry, 1,000 strong and more, were sent to England. Altogether 80,000 British officers and troops and 210,000 Indian officers and men were sent from India overseas during the first six months of the war. I would here remark that the largest Indian expeditionary force ever previously sent from India overseas amounted to 18,000 men. It is interesting to note as regards the army in India that of nine British cavalry regiments seven were sent overseas, of 52 British infantry battalions 44 went overseas, and of Royal Artillery batteries 43 out of 56 were sent abroad. Twenty out of 39 Indian cavalry regiments and 89 out of 138 Indian infantry battalions were also sent overseas. It is a fact that for several weeks before the arrival of some untrained Territorial battalions from England the total British garrison in India, a country bigger than Europe and with a doubtful factor on the North-West frontier, was reduced to less than 15,000 men.

At the same time, India supplied England in her need within the first few weeks of the war with 560 British officers of the Indian Army who could ill be spared, 70 million rounds of small-arm ammunition, 60,000 rifles, more than 550 guns of the latest pattern, together with enormous quantities of material such as tents, boots, clothing, saddlery, etc., every effort being made to meet the increasing demands of the War Office. All the Indian aeroplanes with the personnel of the Indian Air Force were sent to England or Egypt, and the later demands of India for aeroplanes in Mesopotamia when the need was great, were entirely ignored.

The foregoing is a brief summary of the great military effort made by India at the beginning of the war, but this was almost overshadowed by the splendidly loyal and patriotic response of all the Ruling Princes and Chiefs to the appeal that I addressed to them for their loyal support and assistance. Every one of them without exception offered personal service, troops, hospital ships, one of them, the Maharaja of Rewah, as I have already stated, offering all his personal jewels. A telegram I sent home, recounting their loyal offers, provoked the greatest enthusiasm when read in the two Houses of Parliament. I accepted from them every offer of a practical nature and a large number of them went overseas to the war with their own contingents.

Indian troops arrived in France in September 1914, just when the Allied forces were waging a desperate struggle to stem the German sweep toward the English Channel. In Hardinge's words 'these fine divisions arrived in

France just in time to fill a gap in the British line that could not otherwise have been filled...In spite of the severity of the weather and their unfamiliar surroundings they behaved with great gallantry but suffered terrible losses in the trenches. I had previously succeeded in obtaining the right of Indian soldiers to receive the Victoria Cross for bravery and they won two Victoria Crosses within their first month in France. Very few survived to return to India.'

In his introduction to Colonel Merewether's *Indian Corps in France*, Lord Curzon stated that 'the Indian Expeditionary Force arrived in the nick of time, that it helped to save the cause both of the Allies and of civilization after the sanguinary tumult of the opening weeks of the war, has been openly acknowledged by the highest in the land from the Sovereign downwards. I recall that it was emphatically stated to me by Lord French himself. The nature and value of that service can never be forgotten.'

During the war altogether 1,161,789 Indians were recruited, 1,215,338 were sent overseas, and they suffered 101,439 casualties.

India also made a handsome financial contribution to the war effort. In September 1914 the Central Legislative Assembly, on the motion of non-official members, resolved that 'in addition to giving military assistance, the people of India would wish to share in the heavy financial burden of the war'. In all some $100 million were donated.

After the war, Indian nationalists were to claim that the whole of India had fully supported Britain during her hour of need and had earned the right to a substantial advance toward self-government. The British Government acknowledged India's generous contribution to the war effort and they granted a degree of self-government in the shape of the Montague-Chelmsford Reforms, but the Indians found the concessions disappointingly inadequate. These questions will be examined at a later stage. Let us first examine the real nature of India's response to the war. To state simply that 'India' helped Britain to its utmost capacity is to over-simplify the position. India has always been a complex society and its reaction to World War I was not as clear-cut as the vocal Western-educated Indians tried to make out. Broadly, Indian society consisted of four classes, each one of which responded to the war in its own peculiar fashion. These classes were (1) the Indian ruling princes (2) the Western-educated classes who, during the short period under review, disregarded communal differences and voiced similar views (3) the villagers who constituted the bulk of the Indian peoples and (4) the revolutionaries who sought Indian freedom by a violent overthrow of British rule; their number was not large but their potential for subverting the government was larger than is generally realised.

The ruling princes were aware that their future was tied up with that of British rule in India. They were, therefore, fighting as much for the preservation of their own thrones as for that of the British crown. Their princely tradition had also infused them with a sense of chivalry and honour.

The Western-educated Hindus and Muslims formed a small portion of the total population of the country. The majority of those of them who wished to take part in politics belonged to Congress or the Muslim League, neither of which at this stage had acquired a popular following. These members of the intelligentsia did not flock to the recruiting centres, but their voice was the loudest in the land. When the first session of Congress after the outbreak of the war met at Madras (28-30 December 1914), in a specially-erected pavilion, the premises were draped in white, the pillars were wreathed in flowers, and the portraits of the King and Queen and the royal arms were proudly displayed. Resolution IV expressed Congress' 'unswerving allegiance to the British connection, and its firm resolve to stand by the Empire, at all hazards and at all costs'. The introduction, consideration, and passage of the resolution were artfully timed to coincide with the visit to Congress by a representative of the British Crown. The Muslim League did not meet during 1914, but in its first session after the outbreak of the war (Bombay 30 December 1915- 1 January 1916), it too assured the British government that it 'may continue to rely upon the loyal adhesion to and support to the Imperial cause by the Mussalmans of India'. The Lieutenant-Governor of the province paid a goodwill visit to the League when it next met at Lucknow in December 1916. That the government kept the Muslim Press relatively quiet by recourse to the Press Act, and interned the more fiery Muslim leaders, such as the brothers Muhammad Ali and Shaukat Ali, Abul Kalam Azad and Hasrat Mohani, helped the Moderates in their efforts to keep their community loyal.

Congress and the League never wavered in their formal expressions of unconditional loyalty to the British crown and their promises of whole-hearted support in the war. But a full reading of their proceedings makes it evident that their utterances were not—indeed they could not have been—the outpourings of the unalloyed patriotism of a free people fighting for the defence of their own motherland, but were the response of a subject people thankful for some aspects of British rule and resentful of others and hoping that the winds of change released by World War I and the gratitude accruing from their own share in the allied victory would bring them closer to the cherished goal of self-government.

There was a unanimous opinion that Western education and the example of British political institutions had sown and nursed the seeds of nationalism in India. There was agreement also that Indian nationalism was still a tender plant that needed the protection of orderly British administration until it could stand independently. When Hardinge asked Gokhale what he would do if he, the Viceroy, and all the British officials left for England, Gokhale unhesitatingly replied that he would telegraph them, before they reached Aden, to come back. And indeed they were realistic enough to accept that the Indians were not at that stage strong enough to expel the British by force. The only course open to them was to make the best of the situation in which Providence had placed them.

The members of Congress and the Muslim League were also generally agreed upon the features of British rule which they found unacceptable. They protested against the repressive use of the Press Act and the Defence of India Act. The latter superseded the provisions of criminal law and set up Special Tribunals which could hold summary trials, and conferred on the executive arm of the government the power to intern persons without trial. In his presidential address to the Bombay session of the League (30 December 1915-1 January 1916), Mazhar-ul-Haque said, 'repression generally defeats its purpose. To the terrorists among our own people I can say with confidence that they can never hope to terrorise a powerful nation like the British. To the coercionists among our rulers, I can say with equal confidence that they can never hope to repress the rising hopes and aspirations of 315 million people. The policy of repression is an insult to God...But it is no less an insult to the countrymen of Shakespeare and Milton to think that repression could ultimately and finally succeed in cowing those whose only crime was that they fearlessly "spake the tongue" that Shakespeare spoke and held "the faith and morals" that Milton held.'

The complaints that the Arms Act denied the freedom to carry arms, that enlistment in the army was by selective recruitment and not open to all volunteers, and that Indians were barred from holding commissions in the armed forces, gathered added force during the war. Mazhar-ul-Haque alleged that 'India has been so maimed and crippled in her manhood that she can help neither herself nor Great Britain.' M. V. Joshi, speaking at the Bombay session of Congress (27-29 December 1915), regretted that Indians were denied military training and were not allowed to volunteer, otherwise 'we could easily have spared 1 to 10 millions. Perhaps Germany might never have begun the war.' At the same meeting the president, S. P. Sinha, complained that though Indians had won Victoria Crosses, not one of them could obtain a commission in the army even if qualified by virtue of 'birth or bravery, education or efficiency'.

Another speaker quoted with approval from a speech Surendranath Banerji had made in another forum: 'A Shivaji, a Hyder Ali, a Ranjit Singh, a Madhaji Sindia could not now have risen to the position of a colonel of a regiment or the captain of a company.' A resolution passed at the thirty-first session of Congress (Lucknow, December 1916) urged that 'an army may be raised immediately in India from the civil population under Indian commissioned officers.' The various speakers do not seem to have paused to think how the British government, on whom they were pressing these demands, viewed the prospect of continuing to govern India with the help of a comparatively small number of British officials and soldiers in the presence of a huge army composed entirely of Indian officers and men.

Both Hindus and Muslims resented equally bitterly that Indians exercised almost no control over the administration of their own country. Mazhar-ul-Haque, in the presidential address already referred to, complained that, 'the children of the soil had no real share in the government of their own country. Policy is laid down and carried on by non-Indians, which oftener than not goes against the wishes of the people and ignores their sentiments'. Bhupendranath Basu, president of the twenty-ninth session of the Congress (December 1914), said even more forcefully:

> Viceroys and Governors may come and go, but the Great Service remains, dominating the life of the people and practically free from all responsibility except what it owes to itself. They form the Executive Council of the Viceroy, with the exception of one solitary dumb Indian member of recent origin. They also form the Council of the Secretary of State with the addition of two Indian members. They furnish rulers to six provincial Governments out of nine. The great departments of state including education are under their control and the inspiration and the motive power of Government comes from them. Influence, patronage, authority, power, dominion, the government itself, are all in their hands.

Indian political leaders had high hopes that the war would bring them substantial political gains. During a meeting of Congress in December 1915, a speaker expressed the hope that 'British statesmanship will... rise equal to the occasion and make England's response to India after the war as generous and whole-hearted as India's response has been to England in the hour of her sorest trial.' A year later Jinnah observed from the platform of the League that 'after such colossal upheavals as this war, the world cannot quietly slip back into its old grooves of life and thought'. Soon after the conclusion of the war, Madan Mohan Malaviya, in his presidential address to the Indian National Congress (Delhi, December 1918), described the peace programme consisting of fourteen points which President Wilson had presented to the Congress of the USA on 8 January 1918, and drew the attention of the audience especially to the concluding words of Wilson's message: 'An evident principle runs through the whole programme I have outlined. It is the principle of justice to all people and nationalities and their right to live on equal terms of liberty and safety with one another.'

Jawaharlal Nehru's assertion in his *Autobiography* that 'there was little sympathy with the British in spite of loud professions of loyalty' is an exaggeration. In fact there was considerable genuine sympathy for the British cause. Nehru's own future idol, Gandhi, was supporting the war effort whole-heartedly and was working as a recruiting agent. Politically conscious Indians wanted Britain to win the war for emotional as well as realistic reasons. Emotionally they admired the British people and their values. Realistically, they were aware that they were not yet united and strong enough to protect their independence and would be far worse off under the rule of any other power.

The fighting men that India supplied came from its rural areas. Though the villagers comprised no less 75 per cent of the total population, they were the least vocal of their countrymen. They lived in countless small communities scattered over the vast expanse of their motherland. Not conversant with the principles of economics, they were not conscious that their country was being impoverished by the foreign rulers, and not having read Shakespeare and Milton, they were not excited by the feeling that the whole of India was or could become a nation. They concentrated, as they had done for countless centuries, on the problem of eking out a living by tilling the soil. Their view of British rule was utterly different from that of their Western-educated countrymen. The foreign bureaucracy, which irked the politically-conscious Indians so much, in the estimate of the villagers consisted of rulers who were incorruptible; who were not swayed by considerations of caste and creed; who, not having a local axe to grind, were neutral and just in resolving local disputes and problems; and who listened sympathetically to the complaints of the weak against the strong. That the British district chief was a white man from a distant land endowed him with a special mystique. Far from being disliked, he was looked upon by the cultivators as their *mai-bap* (literally mother and father; meaning guardian or protector). While this huge sea of human beings, in numbers the real India, remained benign, the foundations of British rule remained virtually unshaken. It was only when the masses began to be stirred by movements such as non-co-operation and *Khilafat* that real danger made its appearance.

The 'martial races' towards whom the recruiting officers usually directed their efforts had a tradition of military service. Not only did it bring extra income to the family and a pension if the serviceman became a casualty, it also enhanced the status of the uniformed warrior in village society. Though village officials, with the connivance or encouragement of their superiors, specially in the Punjab, were apt to use strong-arm tactics to enhance their quota of recruits and loans, most men came forward willingly and most financial contributions were voluntarily made. To dismiss these valiant men as mercenaries is a calumny. They were men of honour and would never have fought for a cause they considered ignoble. They and their ancestors had always fought on the side of the rulers of the day without question. The Raja of Mahmudabad, while presiding over the special session of the Muslim League at Bombay in September-October 1918 explained: 'I do not say that every man who has enlisted in India since the war broke out has done so after a severe process of reasoning respecting the rights and wrongs of the war. No, manifestly not. But the national mind of India has instinctively felt the justice of England's cause.'

To the revolutionaries, desirous of immediate independence by overthrowing the British government violently, the war seemed to offer a unique opportunity. The number of troops in India had been greatly reduced and it was hoped that Germany would supply weapons for an armed rising in India, and that Turkey would incite the Indian Muslims to rebel against British rule. There was already a cell of Indian revolutionaries, mostly students, in Germany, and many thousands of immigrants, mostly Sikhs, on the West coast of Canada and the USA. The latter had organized themselves into the Ghadar (mutiny) Party in 1913. Indian peasants had also migrated to Burma, Malaya, Singapore, Hong Kong and some parts of China.

The German effort took the form of a committee in Berlin with a mixed membership of Germans and Indians which established contact with the Ghadar Party. The German embassy in the then neutral USA was to supply funds and arms, but plans by the embassy to ship arms to India ended in a muddle. The Ghadar Party did succeed in inducing some 3,000 men from Canada, the USA, South-East Asia and the Far East to steal into India in different ways to ignite a rebellion, but they soon realised that reports that India needed only a match to explode had been misleading. Their efforts remained fruitless for want of local support and because of police vigilance. Attempts by other Indian revolutionaries to win over their compatriots fighting against Turkey or to form a regiment from Indian prisoners of war in Turkish hands also came to nothing.

An Indo-German mission to Kabul made an impressive start. The main actor in this episode was Raja Mahendra Pratap of Hathras in the United Provinces, who had gone to Berlin soon after the outbreak of the war. He was granted an interview with the Kaiser and was given a pledge of help in writing by the German Chancellor, Bethmann-Hollweg, who also wrote to several Indian princes. A mission was dispatched to Kabul. Its leader was the Raja and the members were a German diplomat and a Muslim revolutionary named Maulvi Barkatullah. They arrived in Kabul on 2 October 1915 and were received in audience by King Habibullah. A provisional Government of India was set up with the Raja as president, Maulvi Barkatullah as prime minister and another Muslim named Obeidullah Sindi as home minister. The provisional Government sent out several missions and issued numerous proclamations but was unable to drum up any real support anywhere. The Raja returned to Berlin in frustration.

Though the Amir of Afghanistan remained friendly to the British government, the tribesmen made several incursions into the north-west frontier of India during the first twelve months of the war. Retaliatory measures, however, had the effect of restoring calm in the area. When Lord Hardinge talked with some Pathans who had come to India to trade, they said that they had stopped fighting because 'the use of aeroplanes, armoured cars, bombs and live wires was not playing the game'.

Two incidents in the early phase of the war resulted in bloodshed. One related to the s.s. *Komagata Maru*, a Japanese ship which a Sikh businessman had chartered to take a large number of Punjabis, mostly to Canada, early in 1914. The would-be immigrants were not allowed to land in Canada and the ship returned to India, anchoring at Budge-Budge near Calcutta at the end of September 1914. The Government of India regarded the returning Sikhs as sympathisers of the Ghadar Party and ordered them to travel to the Punjab immediately in a special train which had been provided for the purpose. Some sixty persons complied but the rest refused to board the train. They were fired upon by the Fusiliers. Eighteen

Sikhs were killed, some disappeared and the rest were arrested. The government party also lost six men. The second incident took place in Singapore, where half the men of a purely Muslim regiment, the Fifth Light Infantry, mutinied on 15 February 1915 under the mistaken belief that they were about to be dispatched to Mesopotamia to fight against the Turks. They stormed the German internment camp but the German prisoners refused to join them. The native population also displayed no inclination to assist them and the revolt was completely suppressed after three days of fighting. The British casualties were 8 officers, 1 lady, 9 soldiers and 16 civilians killed and a number of persons wounded. Of the mutineers, 2 were hanged and 38 were shot, but some three hundred disappeared in the jungle.

INDIAN DEMANDS (THE LUCKNOW PACT)

Two personalities injected some excitement into the calm that had marked Indian political life in the first part of the war. These were Mrs Annie Besant and Tilak. That Gokhale had died on 19 February 1915 made it easier for these Extremists to attain prominence.

Mrs Besant, a spirited Irish lady, had come under the spell of Madame Blavatsky, who had founded the Theosophical Society in 1875. When Gandhi was a student in London he visited Blavatsky Lodge in Bayswater and met both of them. Mrs Besant had always been interested in the welfare of the poor and was attracted by socialism. For some years she worked with Charles Bradlaugh and became interested in Indian affairs. She arrived in India in 1893 to work for the Theosophical Society. At first she concerned herself with only educational, social and religious work, but she later realised that for a real improvement in the general condition of the people, it was necessary for India to exercise greater political control over its affairs. She signalled her arrival in the political arena by joining the Congress Party in 1914 and declared that 'India claims the right, as a Nation, to justice among the peoples of the Empire...not as a reward but as a right...' A good organizer, full of energy and already a well-known international figure, she immediately enlivened Indian politics. She started a weekly, *The Commonweal,* and a daily, *New India.* On 25 September 1915 she announced the foundation of the Home Rule League 'with Home Rule for India as its only object, as an auxiliary to the National Congress here and its British Committee in England'. In demanding Home Rule immediately, she outpaced Tilak as well as Congress. Consequently, her wish to affiliate her Home Rule League with

Congress was ruled out at the Bombay session (1915) of Congress on the ground that the party's creed restricted the scope of the demand for self-government by the words 'bringing about a steady reform of the existing system of administration'. In the end she decided to go it alone, and announced the inauguration of her Home Rule League in September 1916 at Madras.

Branches of the Home Rule League were established at various places and Mrs Besant launched a propaganda offensive by personal tours and through her two papers. Her oratory, literary capacity, sincerity, and indefatigability attracted wide attention and respect. Government measures such as forfeiture of security under the Press Act, demanding a larger sum as security and prohibition from entering the Bombay Presidency and the Central Provinces, failed to curb her. In June 1917 Mrs Besant and two of her colleagues were interned, but the order was withdrawn in September under pressure from Secretary of State Montagu, who wished to improve the political climate for his forthcoming visit to India.

In recognition of her heroic efforts in the political field, Mrs Besant was elected as President of the Calcutta session of Congress (December 1917). One of the main reasons for her popularity, in the words of Subhas Chandra Bose (*Indian Struggle*) was that she 'became the great champion of Hinduism against all attacks. Even the errors and abuses of Hinduism she would explain away, rather than attack. Thereby she helped to bring back into the hearts of the people faith in their own culture and civilization, which had been badly shaken as a result of the impact of the West.' In her 1917 presidential address she said, 'Home Rule has become so intertwined with religion by the prayers offered up in the great southern temples—sacred places of pilgrimage—and spreading from them to village temples, and also by its being preached, up and down the country, by Sadhus and Sanyasis, that it has become in the minds of the women and of the ever-religious masses, inextricably intertwined with religion.' Her relations with Gandhi had never been smooth and her popularity plummeted when she sharply disagreed with Gandhi with regard to his attitude toward the Rowlatt Bills and their aftermath. She declared that there was nothing in the Bills which an honest citizen could object to. On 18 April 1919, less than a week after the Jallianwalla massacre, she wrote that 'when the mob begins to pelt them (soldiers) with brick-bats, it is more merciful for soldiers to fire a few volleys of buckshot'. The slogan 'bullets for brick-bats' further tarnished her image, but in her heyday she had enjoyed the admiration and support of worthies such as Jinnah, Motilal Nehru and Motilal's son Jawaharlal Nehru.

Tilak was released from confinement in Mandalay on 16 June 1914, and set about reorganizing the Nationalist Party. He convened a conference of Nationalists at Poona in December 1915 which appointed a committee to suggest a political programme. The committee's report was considered by the conference in April 1916 and it was decided to start the Indian Home Rule League with a view 'to attain Home Rule or self-government within the British Empire by all constitutional means and to educate and organize public opinion in the country towards the attainment of the same'. He worked for the League with characteristic zeal. The authorities tried to curb him in various ways but that only increased his popularity. On his sixtieth birthday in 1916, Tilak was presented with a purse of one lakh rupees which he promptly earmarked for furthering the work of the Nationalist Party. For two years, the ceaseless propaganda in the Press and from the platform at popular level of the two Home Rule Leagues eclipsed the periodic debating sessions of Congress and the Muslim League at city centres. By tacit agreement, Tilak spread his message in Maharashtra and the Central Provinces while Besant did so in the rest of the country. In 1916 Tilak rejoined the Congress party, thus repairing the rift between the Moderates and the Extremists that had occurred at Surat in 1907.

In the changing political climate, Congress too increased its demands. During his address Sir S. P. Sinha, who presided over the Bombay session in December 1915, said that if a definite constitutional advance was not forthcoming, 'it will be difficult to believe that the war has changed the angle of vision of our rulers. It will be impossible to retain faith in what was proclaimed by the present premier Mr Asquith "that the Empire rests, not upon the predominance, artificial and superficial, of race or class, but upon the loyal affection of free communities built upon the basis of equal rights". ' A resolution passed at that session said that 'the time has arrived to introduce further and substantial measures of reform towards the attainment of self-government...so as to secure to the people an effective control over' the system of government. Among the specific proposals listed in the resolution the first was 'the introduction of provincial autonomy, including financial independence'.

But the most remarkable development of those years was the fruition of the movement toward a co-operative relationship between Congress and the Muslim League. We have already taken this story up to the end of 1913. There was no meeting of the League during the year 1914. Largely through the efforts of Jinnah, the Muslim League and Congress held their respective sessions of 1915 at the same place—Bombay—and at the same time—the end of December. There was much fraternizing between the

Hindus and the Muslims. The volunteers of the League helped the volunteers of Congress in running the Congress session and vice versa. At a Hindu-Muslim dinner, the organizers wore a brilliant badge which symbolised Hindu-Muslim unity by depicting the lotus as well as the crescent. The two political organizations passed parallel resolutions authorizing their respective representatives to prepare a scheme of reforms in consultation with each other.

As already stated, it was the League that had taken the first steps towards a *rapprochement* with Congress because it felt that Muslim interests had been sufficiently safe-guarded by the attainment of communal representation. Such representation had been granted in the Legislative Councils. The League had regularly demanded that the system should be extended to all local bodies also but Congress had always opposed the demand. How strongly the majority of the members of the League felt about the question was demonstrated in 1913.

In its proceedings that year, Congress, out of deference to Muslim feelings, had for the first time omitted to pass a resolution opposing the extension of separate communal representation to local institutions, but when the League met less than a week later, the usual resolution asking for the extension of communal representation was proposed by Maulvi Rafi-ud-Din, who said that the resolution was very important and should be passed without much discussion, and pointed out that for the previous six years it had always been passed unanimously. To reciprocate the courtesy shown by Congress, Muhammad Ali moved the following amendment to the resolution: 'the All-India Muslim League is of the opinion that the consideration of the question of communal representation in self-governing bodies should be postponed for a year'. Though the amendment had the influential backing of the Aga Khan and Jinnah, it was lost by 89 votes to 40. In vain did the Aga Khan plead that the question was not whether the Muslims should renounce what they had got; it was only whether 'the time was propitious to pass a resolution this year'. Evidently piqued by the League's attitude, Congress in 1914 reverted to its practice of passing a resolution opposing the League demand. Its resolution read:

> Resolved: that this Congress while deprecating the creation of Separate Electorates in the Imperial and Provincial Legislative Councils urges on the Government that the said system should not in any case be extended to the Local Bodies, as it will prove injurious to the development of national unity and the fostering of the national ideal.

The resolution on communal representation was again proposed during the Bombay session of the League. It was opposed by Hasrat Mohani on the grounds first, that it was 'superfluous', and second, that it might harm the endeavour of the Congress and League committees to frame an agreed scheme. Another member, A. M. Khwaja, moved that the question should be deferred until the two committees had carried out their deliberations. Jinnah indicated that though he personally did not agree with 'the overwhelming majority of his co-religionists in the matter', he recognized 'that there was a very strong opinion and feeling among the Mohammedans about the question of communal representation'. He said the proposals of Mohani and Khwaja were 'sure to be lost' and he successfully requested those gentlemen to withdraw them. The original resolution was then carried by a large majority. But at its own Bombay session during the same week, Congress refrained from passing a resolution opposing the League's demand. This was a clear sign that it had begun to waver in its standpoint on the contentious issue.

Jinnah's logical mind had by now accepted that the Muslims would not forgo the right to communal representation under any circumstances and that Congress would have to accept that fact if it really wanted to come to an understanding with the League. He therefore turned his attention to persuading the Congress leadership to let the Muslims have their way. While presiding over the Bombay Provincial Conference at Ahmadabad in October 1916, he pleaded:

> This question of separate electorates from the top to bottom has been before the country ever since 1909 and, rightly or wrongly, the Muslim community is absolutely determined for the present to insist upon separate electorates. To most of us the question is no more open to further discussion or argument as it has become a mandate of the community. As far as I understand, the demand for separate electorates is not a matter of policy but a matter of necessity to the Muslims who require to be roused from the coma and torpor into which they had fallen so long [ago]. I would therefore appeal to my Hindu brethren that in the present state of position they should try to win the confidence and trust of the Muslims who are, after all, in the minority in the country. If they are determined to have separate electorates, no resistance should be shown to their demands.

That Jinnah had succeeded in his efforts to persuade Congress to let the Muslims have the right to communal representation became clear when Congress and the League again held their respective sessions at the same place and at the same time (Lucknow, December 1916), and approved the unanimously-agreed scheme presented by their respective committees. The Congress-League scheme, popularly known as the Lucknow Pact, laid down that the Muslims would be elected to the Imperial Legislative Council as well as to the Provincial Legislative Councils by separate electorates.

Two other terms of the Lucknow Pact also gave assurance to the Muslims that their rights would be protected. The first was that no bill in any of the Councils affecting one or the other community would be passed if three-fourths of the members of that community opposed it. Secondly, the Muslims were given one-third of the seats in the Imperial Legislature, although their population in British India was not more than one-fourth.

The principle of more seats than warranted by population (weightage) could not very well be applied only to provinces where the Muslims were in a minority; it was applied also to provinces where the Hindus were in a minority. In Bengal and in the Punjab, the Muslims were given only three-quarters and nine-tenths respectively of the seats to which they were entitled according to their numerical strength (but this was more than they had been given under the Morley-Minto Reforms). In the remaining provinces, the Muslims were allotted more seats than they had occupied till then or would have on a population basis.

The main reforms which Congress and the League wanted the British Government to enact were the following:

Provincial Legislative Councils shall consist of four-fifths elected and one-fifth nominated members.

The members of Councils should be elected directly by the people on as broad a franchise as possible.

A resolution passed by the Provincial Legislative Council shall be binding on the Executive Government unless vetoed by the Governor-in-Council, provided, however, that if the resolution is again passed by the Council after an interval of not less than one year, it must be given effect to.

Not less than one-half of the members of the (Provincial) Executive Councils shall be Indians elected by elected members.

The strength of the Imperial Legislative Council shall be 150 [and] four-fifths of the members shall be elected.

All financial proposals [in the Imperial Legislative Council] relating to sources of income and items of expenditure, shall be embodied in Bills. Every such Bill and the Budgets as a whole shall be submitted to the vote of the Imperial Legislative Council.

When the Crown chooses to exercise its power of veto in regard to a Bill passed by the Provincial Legislative Council or by the Imperial Legislative Council, it should be exercised within twelve months from the date on which it is passed.

The Imperial Legislative Council shall have no power to interfere with the Government of India's direction of military affairs and the foreign and political relations of India, including the declaration of war, the making of peace and entering into treaties.

[The Government -General of India] will have an Executive Council, half of whom shall be Indians [to be] elected by the elected members of the Imperial Legislative Council.

The Government of India shall not ordinarily interfere in the local affairs of a Province, and powers not specifically given to a Provincial Government shall be deemed to be vested in the former. The authority of the Government will ordinarily be limited to general supervision and superintendence over the Provincial Governments.

The Council of the Secretary of State for India should be abolished [and he] should be assisted by two Permanent Under-Secretaries, one of whom should always be an Indian.

The demands embodied in the Lucknow Pact were the first ever put forward jointly by the two major political organizations of India. Unfortunately, they were also the last. The Muslims naturally felt delighted that the highly emotive issue of separate electorates had been settled in their favour. They were pleased also that the provinces had been promised virtual autonomy from the centre in internal affairs. This would ensure that their interests, including religious and cultural interests, would be safe in the Muslim majority provinces.

It was when Congress, in the Nehru report of 1928, reneged on the Lucknow agreement that the Muslim League concluded that Congress promises could not be relied upon. The rift thus opened was fuelled by other causes as the years rolled on, and in the end resulted in the division of Britain's Indian Empire into two independent countries.

Jinnah had, for the time being, succeeded in his mission as 'ambassador of Hindu-Muslim unity', but in his presidential address at the Lucknow session of the League in 1916, he made certain observations which indicated that he was edging away from his original stance that Congress was the national party of India representing Hindus and Muslims alike and he himself an impartial peacemaker between the two communities. His view now was that the Muslim League alone represented all the Muslims of India and that his own role was that of an advocate of their views. Though personally he would have felt happier if communal representation could have been avoided, he no longer doubted that the grant of this safeguard to the Muslims was essential in the larger interests of the country. 'Gentlemen of the All-India Muslim League,' he declaimed, 'the decisions that you may take...at this historic session of the League will go forth with all the force and weight that can legitimately be claimed by the chosen leaders and representatives of 70 millions of Indian Mussalmans...And, whatever my individual opinion may be, I am here to interpret and express the sense of the overwhelming body of Muslim opinion of which the All-India Muslim League is the political organ'. He argued that 'a minority must, above everything else, have a complete sense of security before its broader political sense can be evoked for co-operation and united endeavour in the national tasks. To the Mussalmans of India that security can only come through adequate and effective safeguards as regards their political existence as a community.'

On the Hindu side, it was the powerful support of Tilak that had facilitated the acceptance by Congress of the Lucknow Pact. He had arrived on the scene with a large following in a 'Home Rule Special' and was carried shoulder-high to the meeting by his admirers. When he rose to speak he was loudly cheered. Gandhi, who also attended the proceedings, took no part in them. The question arises, why did Tilak, an orthodox Hindu who would normally have felt unsympathetic towards the Muslims, so readily let the Muslims have the concessions they desired? The reason is quite simple. Tilak's own nationalism was inspired by Hindu religion, culture and history. He was a realist, not a visionary, and had no problem in accepting that the nationalism of the Muslims was similarly inspired by their own rich past.

The *National Paper*, the organ of the Hindu Mela, which met fourteen times from 1867 to 1880, asserted that 'Hindus...certainly form a nation by themselves'. In 1924, Lala Lajpat Rai, an orthodox Hindu like Tilak and one-time president of the Indian National Congress, despairing of Hindu-Muslim unity, proposed a division of India on religious lines. 'Under my scheme', he said, 'the Muslims will have four Muslim states: (1) The Pathan province, or the North-West Frontier; (2) Western Punjab; (3) Sind; and (4) Eastern Bengal...It means a clear partition of India into a Muslim India and a non-Muslim India'. V. D. Savarkar, president of the Hindu Mahasabha, admitted that 'the Hindu Mahasabha is pledged to protect and promote all that contributes to the freedom, strength and glory of the Hindu Nation'. From the belief that the Hindus formed a nation, it was a logical step to concede that the Muslims formed another nation. 'It is safer,' said Savarkar, 'to diagnose and treat deep-seated disease than to ignore it. Let us bravely face unpleasant facts as they are. India cannot be assumed today to be a unitarian and homogeneous nation, but on they contrary these are two nations, in the main the Hindus and the Muslims in India.'[1]

It is unfortunate that Hindu-Muslim antagonism was a blind spot for both Gandhi and Nehru, who played such decisive roles in the independence movement. Gandhi believed that the antagonism was the result of British rule and would disappear when the British left India. Nehru, the agnostic, thought religion had no place in politics.[2] If a problem is not diagnosed properly, it is not possible to devise appropriate measures to eradicate it. Gandhi and Nehru in the end had to yield to the reality of Hindu-Muslim differences and agree to the division of the subcontinent on communal lines. By ignoring these differences for so long, they only allowed tension to build up and thus made an amicable settlement impossible. 'There were...some politicians,' writes R. C. Majumdar, 'who ignored the great differences between the two communities and talked and behaved as if there were none and these two [communities] constituted a common brotherhood. This attitude was carried to an extreme—almost absurd— length by Gandhi and his followers while carrying on the struggle against the British.'

THE BRITISH RESPONSE TO INDIAN DEMANDS

While ratifying the Lucknow Pact in 1916 Congress had stressed that 'the time has come when His Majesty the King-Emperor should be pleased to issue a proclamation announcing that it is the aim and intention of British policy to confer self-government on India at an early date' and that 'in the

---

[1] However, when the Muslim League demanded Pakistan, Savarkar insisted that India must not be divided. In his *Pakistan or The Partition of India*, Ambedkar made this comment: 'He [Savarkar] wants the Hindu nation to be the dominant nation and the Muslim nation to be the servient nation. Why Mr Savarkar, after sowing this seed of enmity between the Hindu nation and the Muslim nation, should want that they should live under one constitution and occupy one country, is difficult to explain'.

[2] *See*, pp. 635-6 and 638.

reconstruction of the Empire, India shall be lifted from the position of a dependency to that of an equal partner in the Empire with the Self-Governing Dominions.' For their part, the British government were fully aware that the rise in the tempo of Indian nationalism and the expectations created by the world war made it impossible to maintain the *status quo* in India.

Lord Chelmsford was a classical scholar and had been a Fellow of All Souls, Oxford. He had held the governorships of Queensland and New South Wales, but he lacked the diplomatic touch of Hardinge and did not possess the imagination and forcefulness to take initiatives and provide strong leadership. Altogether he was not equipped to handle the momentous problems that marked his tenure. During the first two years of the war, when the Indians were in a loyal mood and were offering enthusiastic support, Hardinge had been the Viceroy. It was Chelmsford's lot to deal with the complicated question of India's political reward for its services and to face the angry mood generated by the Rowlatt Bills, the Punjab atrocities, including the Jallianwala massacre, and the Khilafat (Caliphate) Movement. He took over as Viceroy on 5 April 1916. Three developments in that year progressively increased the pressure on the British Government to come up with new ideas. First, there was the Home Rule agitation whipped up by the firebrands Besant and Tilak. Secondly, Hussain, the Sharif of Mecca, revolted in June, with British blessing, against the Sultan of Turkey who was also the Caliph of Islam. In October he was proclaimed King of the Arabs, and was recognized as such by the British Government in December. The Muslims of India considered Hussain a stooge of the British and feared that the holy places of Islam had in fact fallen under the control of a Christian power. And lastly, at the end of the year, Congress and the Muslim League put forward the joint demand for political reforms described above.

After long consultations with his advisers, Chelmsford forwarded his ideas to the Home Government in November 1916. Austen Chamberlain, the Secretary of State, found Chelmsford's proposals inadequate. He believed that the British Government should boldly state that the aim of their rule in India was 'the development of free institutions with a view to ultimate self-government' although it had at the same time to be made clear that this was a distant goal, and that the stages by which it was to be reached would be determined by the British Government. Before these ideas could be translated into policy, Chamberlain resigned and was succeeded by Edwin Montagu, a former Under-Secretary of State for India.

On 20 August 1917 Montagu made his famous statement in the House of Commons. It bore a striking resemblance to Chamberlain's thinking. Its most important passage ran:

The policy of His Majesty's Government, with which the Government of India are in complete accord, is that of the increasing association of Indians in every branch of the administration and the gradual development of self-governing institutions with a view to the progressive realisation of responsible government in India as an integral part of the British Empire... I would add that progress in this policy can only be achieved by successive stages. The British Government and the Government of India, on whom the responsibility lies for the welfare and advancement of the Indian people, must be the judges of the time and measure of each advance, and they must be guided by the co-operation received from those upon whom new opportunities of service will thus be conferred and by the extent to which it is found that confidence can be reposed in their sense of responsibility.

'Responsible government' in British constitutional parlance could only mean the Westminister type under which the executive government is responsible to the elected members of the House of Commons and can hold office only while it enjoys their confidence. So the British Government finally decided in favour of the parliamentary system as practised in Britain. It is true that the Lucknow Pact had not used the expression 'responsible government' but, since the Indians were asking that they should be given the same constitutional status as the other self-governing members of the British Empire, it was implied that they wanted 'responsible government' of the same type. Complete independence in the sense of control over foreign affairs and defence was not a live issue in 1916-17. But if, and when, the other dominions reached that status, the Indians automatically would reach it too. It was the Imperial Conference in 1926 that summed up the position which the self-governing Dominions had attained by then *vis-a-vis* Britain: the United Kingdom and the Dominions 'are autonomous communities within the British Empire, equal in status, in no way subordinate to one another in any aspect of their domestic or external affairs, though united by a common allegiance to the Crown, and freely associated as members of the Commonwealth of Nations'. This status was formalized by the Statute of Westminister passed by the British Parliament in December 1931.

Montagu personally visited India from November 1917 to the following April for the stated purpose of consulting the Viceroy and public opinion, but no doubt also to sell what he personally had in mind with regard to the constitutional changes. When he landed in Bombay, he was accorded a warm welcome by Tilak and others, and garlanded on behalf of the Home Rule League. At Delhi he received a joint delegation of Congress and the Muslim League as well as the Home Rule delegation, which included Mrs Besant and Tilak. He also received representatives of several other organizations and conferred with individual political leaders. An entry in his diary shows how deeply he was impressed by Jinnah in particular: 'Young, perfectly mannered, impressive-looking, armed to the teeth with dialectics, and insistent upon the whole of his scheme...Chelmsford tried to argue with him and was tied up into knots. Jinnah is a very clever man, and it is, of course, an outrage that such a man should have no chance of running the affairs of his own country.' The Montagu-Chelmsford Report was signed by the two authors on 22 April 1918 but it was not published till 8 July 1918, after Montagu had returned to England.

To mollify public opinion some other concessions were announced while the reforms were under consideration: the recruitment of Indian indentured labourers for the sugar colonies was prohibited; the import duty on cotton goods was raised without any corresponding increase in excise duty on Indian-made cotton goods; and the ban on Indians receiving the King's Commission in the army was lifted.

The Montagu-Chelmsford Report was a skilfully drafted document. It sought to convey the general impression that Britain wished India well and would gladly relinquish power. It even vouchsafed a glimpse of India's rosy ultimate destiny:

> Our conception of the eventual future of India is a sisterhood of States [federation] self-governing in all matters of purely local or provincial interest...Over this congeries of States would preside a central Government...representing the interests of all India on equal terms with the self-governing units of the British Empire.

Unfortunately, however, the desired goal would take an indefinite period to reach because Indian society contained insurmountable impediments to advance on democratic lines. 'The immense masses of the people are poor, ignorant, and helpless far beyond the standards of Europe. The knowledge of English was confined to less than two million people, a fractional percentage of the entire population'. But though the educated Indian had 'assumed the place of leader' his authority was 'by no means universally acknowledged and may in an emergency prove weak'.

Another main feature of Indian society was its division by races, creeds and castes. The authors of the report quoted Lord Dufferin to the effect that 'perhaps the most potent characteristic of our Indian cosmos is its division into two mighty political communities [the Hindus and the Muslims] as distant from each other as the poles, asunder in their religious faith, their historical antecedents, their social organization, and their natural aptitudes'. The Lucknow Pact was worthy of praise as testimony to the growing force of nationalism and the last thing they desired was to see it broken, but 'we are bound to ask ourselves what sure guarantee it affords that religious dissensions between the great communities are over'. Their own verdict on the point was that 'the Hindus and Muhammadans of India have certainly not yet achieved unity of purpose or community of interest. They have yet a long road to pursue before that end is reached'. The reader may be permitted to point out that these centuries-old features of Indian society were not likely to disappear in the measurable future, and to ask whether this meant that Britain must continue to hold India indefinitely. As we all know, in the end Britain had to concede independence to the subcontinent less than thirty years later while all these problems were still outstanding and when, in fact, Hindu-Muslim enmity had escalated to its highest pitch, necessitating the partition of the country into the separate states of India and Pakistan. One may ask whether it would not have been wiser to have granted a generous instalment of self-government at a time—never to occur again—when the Hindus and the Muslims had reached a concord and both of them still genuinely admired the British and bore so much goodwill towards them. As Shakespeare said:

There is a tide in the affairs of men,
which, taken at the flood, leads on to fortune.

Perhaps the least ingenuous parts of the report were its references to communal representation. The authors rejected the view that 'communal representation is an inevitable and even a healthy stage in the development of a non-political people'. This stand directly contradicted the policy laid down by the Government of India in 1892 when representative institutions were first introduced. It was then argued that the various classes, races and communities could be properly represented only by those who shared their respective views[1]. In 1906, on the eve of the next instalment of constitutional reforms, Lord Minto, in his reply to the Aga Khan delegation, said even

---

[1] *See*, p. 84.

more emphatically, 'I am as firmly convinced as I believe you to be, that any electoral representation in India would be doomed to mischievous failure which aimed at granting a personal enfranchisement regardless of the beliefs and traditions of the communities composing the population of this continent.'

Thus the British authorities in the past had wholeheartedly, and independently of what the Muslims had to say on the subject, subscribed to the view that communal representation was the only correct form of representation suitable for the conditions prevailing in India and they had unhesitatingly given legislative effect to it. The Hindus were the only dissenting voice at that time. Even they had now conceded the Muslim right to special representation. In effect, the Hindus and the Muslims were saying to the British Government: 'In the past you have used Hindu-Muslim antagonism as an excuse for the continuation of your paternal rule in India. We have composed our differences. So, how about a big step towards the independence of our country?'

Instead of using the Hindu-Muslim agreement as a springboard for an imaginative constitutional reform, Montagu and Chelmsford invoked the abstract principle that 'division by creeds and classes means the creation of political camps organised against each other, and teaches men to think as partisans and not as citizens'. But on the very next page they pleaded: 'At the same time we must face the hard facts' and proceeded to give reasons why they were permitting communal representation to continue: 'How can we say to them [the Muslims] that we regard the decision of 1909 as mistaken, that its retention is incompatible with progress towards responsible government, that its reversal will eventually be to their benefit; and that for these reasons we have decided to go back on it?' The Muslims 'regard separate representation and communal electorates as their only adequate safeguards' and 'the Hindus' acquiescence is embodied in the present agreement between the political leaders of the two communities [the Lucknow Pact].' The authors of the report went on to say that communal representation was yet another reason for 'slower progress towards the realization of a common citizenship' [and, therefore, towards the time when Indians would be fit for self-government]. But despite their expressed disapproval of separate representation, they proceeded to recommend its extension to the Sikhs because 'they are a distinct and important people: they supply a gallant and valuable element to the Indian Army but they are everywhere in a minority, and experience has shown that they go virtually unrepresented'.

Not surprisingly, the Montagu-Chelmsford report concluded that Indians were not ready for self-government. They recommended that the question of further constitutional changes be examined by a commission ten years after the institution of the reforms proposed by them and thereafter by commissions at intervals of twelve years. The vision of several periodic commissions did not materialize. World events allowed time only for one commission—the Simon Commission—to report on India's political future. After that, World War II released the forces that brought freedom to India and other countries.

Montagu and Chelmsford formulated four general principles on which to base their proposals:

(1) There should be, as far as possible, complete popular control in local bodies and the largest possible independence for them from outside control.

(2) The provinces are the domain in which the earlier steps towards the progressive realization of responsible government should be taken. Some measure of responsibility should be given at once, and our aim is to give complete responsibility as soon as conditions permit. This involves at once giving the provinces the largest measure of independence, legislative, administrative, and financial, of the Government of India which is compatible with the due discharge by the latter of its own responsibilities.

(3) The Government of India must remain wholly responsible to parliament, and saving such responsibility, its authority in essential matters must remain indisputable, pending experience of the effect of the changes now to be introduced in the provinces. In the meantime the Indian Legislative Council should be enlarged and made more representative, and its opportunities of influencing Government increased.

(4) In proportion as the foregoing changes take effect, the control of Parliament and the Secretary of State over the Government of India and Provincial Governments must be relaxed.

The main recommendations of their report were: a greater delegation of powers to the provinces to pave the way for an all-India federation; the replacement of official majorities in the legislatures by elected majorities; the introduction of 'dyarchy' in the provinces, i.e., the division of portfolios into 'transferred' and 'reserved' subjects, the former to be entrusted to ministers, the latter retained by the Governor in Council; the establishment of a second chamber at the centre to be called the Council of State; and the setting up of a Council of Princes presided over by the

Viceroy. The report also recommended that recruitment to the superior services, which hitherto had been carried out only in England, should also be carried out in India to the extent of a fixed percentage. The proportion for the Indian Civil Service would start at 33 per cent and rise annually by 1.5 per cent.

It was not till 23 December 1919 that the Bill, mainly based on the recommendations of the Montagu-Chelmsford Report, received Royal Assent. Elections to the new legislatures were held in November 1920 and the Act of 1919 came into force on the first day of 1921.

Both the Houses at the centre had elected majorities. The Legislative Assembly (previously the Legislative Council) consisted of 145 members of whom 103 were elected; the Council of State had 60 members out of which 33 were elected. The Governor-General's Executive Council, which till now had had only one Indian member, was to have three Indians out of a total of six. The Governor-General could enact any law he considered essential by 'certification'. He could also disallow the consideration of any bill if, in his opinion, it affected 'the safety or tranquillity of British India or any part thereof'. The relationship between the centre and the provinces was little changed, but the distribution of the sources of revenue between the two were more clearly set out. To the centre went customs, income tax, posts, salt and railways, and to the provinces land tax, excise, irrigation and stamps.

The principle of communal representation was accepted. Indeed, it was extended, not only to the Sikhs as recommended by the Montagu-Chelmsford report but also to Europeans, Anglo-Indians and Christians. The seats in the provinces were divided between the communities in accordance with the Lucknow Pact.

By lowering the qualifications of the voters, the size of the electorate for the provinces was increased, but even so it totalled no more than 5.5 million out of a total population in British India at that time of some 250 million.

The most novel feature of the new constitution was the introduction in the provinces of the system of 'dyarchy'. The 'reserved' subjects were to be administered by Executive Councillors who were nominated by the Governor entirely at his discretion, and the transferred subjects by ministers to be chosen by the Governor from the members of the legislature. In theory, the ministers held office during the Governor's pleasure, but in effect, they could continue only while they enjoyed the confidence of the House, which could withhold their salary, or censure their administration, or throw out the budgets of their departments. This was the only concession to the concept of 'responsible government' in the entire scheme. Broadly, the reserved subjects were law and order and revenue, and the transferred subjects (the 'nation-building' departments) were local self-government, education, public health, public works, agriculture and co-operative societies. At the centre, despite the elected majority in the Legislative Assembly, the real power still lay with the Viceroy. He governed with a wholly nominated Executive Council and could legislate and impose taxes at will under his powers of 'certification'.

A Royal Proclamation, ceremoniously read in February 1921 by the Duke of Connaught in Delhi Fort on behalf of his nephew King George V, brought the Chamber of Princes into existence. It consisted of 108 members sitting in their own right and twelve elected by the rulers of the less important states. In its annual sitting, the Chamber was to consider questions of general interest to all the States as well as those of common interest to the States and British India, but it was a purely consultative body and its recommendations were not binding on any State or prince. Some major States, such as Hyderabad and Mysore, did not deign to join it.

PART IV

'That [Jallianwala massacre] is an episode which appears to me to be without precedent or parallel in the modern history of the British Empire. It is an event of an entirely different order from any of those tragical occurrences which take place when troops are brought into collision with the civil population. It is an extraordinary event, a monstrous event, an event which stands in singular and sinister isolation... "I was confronted," says General Dyer, "by a revolutionary army". What is the chief characteristic of an army? Surely it is that it is armed. This crowd was unarmed.'

The Secretary of State for War, Winston Churchill, on 8 July 1920, in the House of Commons Committee of Supply, during the motion for the reduction of the salary of the Secretary of State for India.

CHAPTER 10

INDIA IN A FERMENT

The solidarity achieved by Congress and the Muslim League by the Lucknow Pact continued in their attitude towards the Montagu-Chelmsford scheme of reforms. Both the political parties held their sessions in the same city and in the same week, in order to co-ordinate their responses to Montagu's declaration of 20 August 1917, as well as to the Montagu-Chelmsford Report after its publication.

Montagu's statement was discussed by Congress and the League at their respective meetings at Calcutta in December 1917. Both organizations welcomed Montagu's promise of responsible government but demanded that a parliamentary statute should promptly introduce the Congress-League Scheme of Reforms (the Lucknow Pact), and lay down the time limit within which complete responsible government would be established in India.

Congress and the League convened special sessions at Bombay in August 1918 and made the following concerted response to the Montagu-Chelmsford Report: while conceding that some of the recommendations constituted an advance on the existing conditions, they labelled them as unsatisfactory on the whole; they repudiated the assumption that India was not fit for responsible government; they desired that constitutional advance should proceed simultaneously in the Centre and the provinces; they asked for the same freedom in fiscal matters for the Indian Legislature as that enjoyed by the self-governing dominions of the Empire; and they demanded full provincial autonomy in six years. Congress insisted that a statutory guarantee should be given that responsible government in British India would be established within a period not exceeding fifteen years, while the League declared that the grant of self-government within the Empire was essential to strengthen the bond between England and India and also to satisfy the legitimate aspirations of the Indian people.

At this stage, neither of the two parties held out the threat that they would refuse to co-operate in the working of the forthcoming constitution if their wishes were not granted. Even so, the Moderates kept away from the Bombay special session of Congress. They viewed the Montagu-

Chelmsford proposals more favourably than the Extremists, who, led by Tilak and Mrs Besant, controlled the majority in Congress. An All-India Moderate Conference was convened at Bombay on 1 November 1918 under the chairmanship of Surendranath Banerji to appraise the Montagu-Chelmsford Report. Congress ranks were thus split for the second time, except that at Surat it had been the Extremists who had left while this time it was the Moderates who did so. The new Moderate party called itself The All-India Liberal Federation. At a popular level, it was referred to as the Liberal Party, or simply as the Liberals. In Jawaharlal Nehru's words 'truth for them [the Liberals] indeed always lies between two extremes. By criticising everything they consider extreme, they experience the feeling of being virtuous and moderate and good.' Holding the middle position between the British Government and Congress and being on speaking terms with both, they were at some difficult junctures able to act as intermediaries between the two. Though possessed of considerable intellect they lacked the charisma to attract a mass following. Their most illustrious spokesmen were Srinivasa Sastri, Sir Tej Bahadur Sapru and M. R. Jayakar.

It was a period of great expectation. World War I had wrought a revolution in people's ideas of equality and liberty everywhere. The claim that the white man was superior to other races was undermined by the sight of the British and the Germans viciously at each other's throats. Indian soldiers had fought as valiantly as any other. Britain, hitherto indisputably the greatest power on earth, was nearly defeated by Germany and had to be saved by America, which preached democracy and self-determination. The mighty Czar of Russia had succumbed to people's power. In India, the Home Rule agitation had heightened political awareness and ambition, and the Lucknow Pact had demonstrated that Hindus and Muslims were united in the demand for a substantial instalment of self-government and were capable of working together harmoniously in the cause of their country's freedom.

After a heroic start, the ugly side of war had begun to manifest itself. The Indians suffered heavy casualties abroad, and shortages of food and clothing and rising prices at home. On 29 April 1916, the Indian troops under General Townshend were forced to surrender at Kut, in Mesopotamia, mainly because of poor leadership and bad management (though the position was retrieved later and Baghdad was taken in March 1917). After the war ended, prices rose still further instead of falling. The fate of defeated Turkey deeply stirred the Muslim masses. A devastating epidemic of influenza in the winter of 1918-19, coincident with a poor harvest, carried away millions of ill-nourished, ill-clad Indians. Officially the dead numbered six million, but unofficial estimates put the number at some sixteen million or more. One of the authors remembers that almost every family in the Punjab mourned the loss of loved ones. He personally lost two uncles and an aunt. India was deeply troubled and expected liberality and consideration from Britain in recognition of its sacrifices during the war. The moment demanded imagination and generosity, not bureaucratic stolidity. Unfortunately, it was the latter which the Government of India displayed by its stubborn persistence with the Rowlatt Bills in the face of unanimous opposition by the Indian intelligentsia. This touched off an agitation leading to bloody consequences.

THE ROWLATT BILLS

On 10 December 1917, the Government of India appointed the Sedition Committee (popularly called the Rowlatt Committee after its chairman Mr Justice Rowlatt) to report on the nature and extent of conspiracies connected with the revolutionary movement in India, and to recommend legislation to deal with them. It was felt that the war was nearing its end and some legislation was needed to take the place of the Defence of India Act which would automatically expire six months after the war.

The committee held all its sittings *in camera*. The public had no knowledge of the nature of the evidence tendered before it nor of the names of the witnesses. Since the public was unrepresented, the witnesses were not cross-examined on its behalf. The committee submitted its report to the government on 15 April 1918 and two bills based on it were introduced in the Imperial Legislature on 6 February 1919. One of them was dropped but the other was passed on 18 March 1919. Originally it was intended to be a permanent measure but an amendment limited its life to three years. The punitive part of the Act provided for a speedy trial of offences by a Special Court presided over by three High Court Judges who would sit *in camera* and could take into consideration evidence inadmissable under the Indian Evidence Act. There was no right of appeal. Under preventive measures the Provincial Government could order any person to reside in a particular place and desist from any specified act. It could also arrest a person without warrant and detain him in confinement. The popular view of the Act was summed up in the slogan *'na appeal, na dalil, na vakeel'* ('no appeal, no argument, no advocate').

When the recommendations of the Rowlatt Committee became known there was a storm of protest all over the country. There had been some revolutionary activity during the war but, as already related, it was easily suppressed because it found practically no popular support. Indian politicians at this juncture were in no mood to brook any new repressive legislation. In the Imperial Legislative Council the bill was opposed by all the non-official Indian members and three of them...M. A. Jinnah, Madan Mohan Malaviya and Mazhar-ul-Haque...resigned. During the proceedings Jinnah warned that if the Rowlatt Bills were passed, 'you will create in the country from one end to the other a discontent and agitation, the like of which you have not witnessed.' And Srinivasa Sastri, a moderate, protested: 'a bad law once passed is not always used against the bad...I have known the best, the noblest Indians, the highest characters amongst us, brought under suspicion, standing in hourly dread of the visitations of the Criminal Investigation Department...No section of public opinion supports you.' The Commissioners appointed by the Punjab Sub-Committee of the Indian National Congress to report on the Punjab atrocities expressed their indignation in these terms:

> The crime of the government became complete when they persisted in the face of unanimous popular opposition. We would note, too, that the Viceroy has sufficient powers by means of ordinances to deal with extraordinary situations. The government were wholly unjustified in placing on the Statute book, on the eve of liberal reforms, an extraordinary measure to deal with anarchy, as if anarchy had been endemic instead of being rare in India. That the provisions of the Act were never actually invoked was seen as proof that the Government of India had exaggerated the necessity for them.

The wide-spread indignation called for a leader to formulate a programme of protest. Tilak had sailed for England on 19 September 1918 to sue Sir Valentine Chirol for defaming him and did not return to India till 27 November 1919. It was Mohandas Karamchand Gandhi who stepped forward and assumed supreme leadership, which he retained till India won independence in 1947, despite periods of formal detachment from politics and resignation from membership of the Congress party. He was assassinated on 30 January 1948 but is still revered by his countrymen as the saintly father of the nation. Before we discuss his role in the turmoil resulting from the Rowlatt legislation, it would be pertinent to introduce to the reader this man and his remarkable philosophy.

MAHATMA GANDHI

Gandhi was the son of Karamchand and Putlibai who belonged to the Modh Bania sub-caste of the Vaisa caste. He was born on 2 October 1869 at Porbandar, in the princedom of Kathiawar, now in the Indian state of Gujarat. Though Gandhi's own grandfather had been Chief Minister of Porbandar and his father that of Porbandar as well as of the states of Rajkot and Vankaner, the traditional occupation of the members of their caste was trade and agriculture. Thus, good account keeping and the capacity to strike a bargain (i.e., to arrive at compromise) were in Gandhi's blood. Speaking of his leadership at a later date he was able to claim that he had left the accounts of every movement he had led in surplus, never in the red.

He did not distinguish himself as a student. After passing the matriculation examination he joined a college but returned home having failed to get through the first examinations. He sailed for England on 4 September 1887, where he qualified as a barrister in June 1891, and then returned home. He also managed to pass the London Matriculation but had to sit for it twice because he failed in Latin at the first attempt.

As a child and young man he was painfully shy. At the farewell dinner given in his honour by fellow vegetarians in London, he could bring himself to utter only one sentence of thanks. After returning to India he tried to practice in Bombay but at the very first appearance in court was so overcome by shyness when he rose to cross examine a witness that he sat down and made over the case to a colleague. He never again appeared as a barrister in an Indian court. He returned to Rajkot in Kathiawar and earned a modest living by drafting documents till he left for South Africa in April 1893. He began to speak in public there but never became an orator.

Shortly before leaving for South Africa he learnt how different a British official in India was from his countrymen in their native land. Gandhi's brother was accused of having given wrong advice to his former employer, the Rana of Porbandar, and the complaint was pending before the Political Agent, whom Gandhi had met in England and found quite friendly. Gandhi's brother believed that the Political Agent was prejudiced against him and asked Gandhi to intercede for him. When Gandhi called on the official, the latter simply refused to listen to him and ordered his servant to throw him out. Gandhi felt deeply humiliated and said 'this shock changed the course of my life.'

He never participated in sports but in London he regularly walked to his destination. His original purpose probably was to save fares, but tramping developed into a life-long form of exercise and relaxation and became the means of delivering his message personally to countless villagers.

At the age of sixteen Gandhi lost his father, but from the very beginning it was his mother who had influenced him most strongly. He learnt from her the habits of fasting, praying and taking religious vows, and evidently it was her influence that caused him to derive satisfaction from nursing the sick and to take pleasure in playing with children. Mother and son loved each other dearly and the she consented to his departure for England only after he had vowed not to touch wine, women and meat. He left behind his wife, Kasturbai, whom he had married when he was thirteen and she slightly younger. His mother passed away while he was abroad but he was not told about it till his return to India. This bereavement grieved him deeply.

His nurse taught him to ward off his childish fear of the dark and of ghosts by repeating the name of Ram (God). This became a life-long habit. A few months before his assassination he said, 'call Him Ishwar, Allah, God, Ahura Mazda...There is none greater than He...Such is my Rama... He alone is my Lord and Master'. (When fatally shot his only words were 'Ram, Ram'.) The Ramayana became a constant source of inspiration to him.

Another literary work that greatly influenced him in his boyhood was the play *Harishchandra*. 'Why should not all be truthful like Harishchandra'? he would constantly ask himself. While in London he read the *Gita* in the original with the help of two Theosophist brothers. At the same time Sir Edwin Arnold's *The Light of Asia* deepened his appreciation of the teachings of the Buddha. His favourite text in *The New Testament* was the Sermon on the Mount, in which Christ preached the doctrine of returning good for evil: 'Resist not evil: but whosoever shall smite thee on thy right cheek, turn to him the other also...Love your enemies, bless them that curse you, do good to them that hate you, and pray for them which despitefully use you, and persecute you...' 'Hate the sin and not the sinner' was the precept which Gandhi practised.

Among the philosophers whose ideas specially attracted him were Tolstoy and Ruskin. Tolstoy was interested in Indian literature and culture and his conception of non-violence was an amalgamation of Christian and Buddhist ideas. Gandhi corresponded with him and wrote an introduction to his *Letter to a Hindu*. Tolstoy called Gandhi's movement in the Transvaal 'the first attempt to apply the principle of *satyagraha* to masses or bodies of men'. Tolstoy also believed that the village was the only unit in which the principle of 'loving thy neighbour as thyself' could be practised. From Ruskin's *Unto This Last* Gandhi drew the lesson that the good of the individual is contained in the good of all, that a life of labour is most commendable and that all labour is of equal worth. Gandhi founded the first of his settlements in South Africa at Phoenix, where everyone was to lead a simple life and work for the benefit of all. He named his second settlement Tolstoy Farm. In India too, after his return from South Africa, he mostly resided with chosen followers in settlements not far different from India's age-old *ashrams* (retreats where the inmates live a life of monastic discipline and labour). Gandhi was aware that Thoreau had refused to pay taxes as a protest against slavery but there is no tangible evidence that he consciously followed his example. From Passive Resistance and Sinn Feinism he positively distanced himself, on the ground that they did not rule out violence.

In fact his inspiration from foreign sources was highly selective, and was limited to conceptions which accorded with his personal beliefs, which were derived from India's own ancient and rich religious and cultural heritage, which contains something for everyone, and in particular from the Jain tradition of *ahimsa* which was strong in his native Gujarat. In an article on *The Doctrine of the Sword* in 1920 he wrote:

I believe that non-violence is infinitely superior to violence, forgiveness is more manly than punishment... Strength does not come from physical capacity. It comes from an indomitable will... The religion of non-violence is not meant merely for the *Rishis* and saints. It is meant for the common people as well. Non-violence is the law of our species as violence is the law of the brute... The dignity of man requires obedience to a higher law. I have, therefore, ventured to place before India the ancient law of self-sacrifice. For *satyagraha* and its off-shoots, non-co-operation and civil resistance, are nothing but new names for the law of suffering... The *Rishis* who discovered the law of non-violence in the midst of violence were greater geniuses than Newton. They were themselves greater warriors than Wellington. Having themselves known the use of arms, they realised their uselessness and taught a weary world that its salvation lay not through violence but through non-violence... It does not mean meek submission to the will of the evil-doer, but it means the pitting of one's whole soul against the will of the tyrant.

Gandhi said the word *satyagraha* was coined to describe his unusual technique for combatting various forms of injustice.[1] *Sat* meant truth and

[1] Gandhi confessed that he had learnt his earliest lessons in non-violent resistance from his wife. He was an overbearing young husband and his wife silently resisted some of his unreasonable demands.

agraha meant firmness. 'Its root meaning', he explained 'is holding on to truth, hence truth-force. I have also called it love-force or soul-force. In the application of *satyagraha*, I discovered in the earliest stages that pursuit of truth did not admit of violence being inflicted on one's opponent but that he must be weaned from error by patience and sympathy. For what appears to be truth to the one may appear to be error to the other. And patience means self-suffering. So the doctrine came to mean vindication of truth, not by infliction of suffering on the opponent, but on one's own self.' The very insistence on truth, he claimed, had taught him to appreciate the beauty of compromise and to recognize that this was an essential part of *satyagraha*. Before resorting to *satyagraha*, he would always offer to meet his opponent so that the possibilities of an amicable settlement could first be explored. 'In *satyagraha*', explains an Indian analyst colourfully, 'it is not a question of capturing a particular outpost, isolating and overwhelming an army corps, or bombing an industrial town or a military target out of existence. *Satyagraha* seeks to initiate certain psychological changes first in those who offer it and then in those against whom it is directed'. In other words, *satyagraha* does not endeavour to floor an adversary physically by the conventional method of using superior force but aims at converting him to one's way of thinking by overwhelming him with a sort of 'moral jiu-jitsu'.

Much as he disliked violence, Gandhi disliked cowardice even more. 'Where there is only a choice between cowardice and violence, I would advise violence,' he said. He rejected the suggestion that non-violence was the weapon of the weak, arguing that its practice was founded on strength of character and required courage, physical endurance and strict discipline. But the standard of discipline and physical endurance prescribed by the Mahatma was impossible for ordinary human beings to live up to. In his weekly *Young India* (20 October 1921) he deplored the fact that the members of the gathering in Jallianwala Bagh had scattered and started to run for their lives when the soldiers opened fire on them. 'If the message of non-violence had reached there,' he wrote, 'they would have been expected when fire was opened on them to march towards it with bare breasts and die rejoicing in the belief that it meant the freedom of their country'.

As a matter of fact, the commitment to non-violence of even Gandhi's closest followers was not as absolute as Gandhi's own. They have confessed that they did not consider non-violence as a sacrosanct principle of morality but regarded it simply as good tactics in the existing circumstances. Nehru unequivocally stated: 'For us and for the National

Congress as a whole the non-violent method was not, and could not be, a religion or an unchallengeable creed or dogma. It could only be a policy and a method'. Rajendra Prasad explained: 'We were disarmed; we were unable to fight with arms, and not a few of us saw in Gandhiji's method a way out of our difficult position.' And Maulana Abul Kalam Azad plainly said: 'For me, non-violence was a matter of policy, not of creed. My view was that Indians had the right to take to the sword if they had no other alternative.' When Gandhi's attention was drawn to the fact that even in his own favourite scripture, the *Gita*, Krishna urged Arjuna to do his duty by fighting in a just war, he replied that Krishna was talking symbolically of the conflict between good and evil.

Indeed, it was impossible for a mass political agitation in India to remain non-violent. This was demonstrated at the very first non-co-operation movement launched by Gandhi. The effort had hardly commenced when a horrible incident took place at Chauri Chaura in the United Provinces near Gorakhpur on 5 February 1922. After firing at a procession the members of the police force took shelter in a building but were forced to come out when a mob set fire to the premises, All of them, twenty-one policemen and an inspector, were hacked to death and their bodies were thrown into the flames. Gandhi decided to end the movement and undertook a five-day fast by way of repentance. This exasperated his political colleagues. Jawaharlal Nehru described their feelings in these terms:

If this was the inevitable consequence of a sporadic act of violence, then surely there was something lacking in the philosophy and technique of a non-violent struggle. For it seemed to us to be impossible to guarantee against the occurrence of some such untoward incident. Must we train the three hundred and odd million of India in the theory and practice of non-violent action before we could go forward? And, even so, how many of us could say that under extreme provocation from the police we would be able to remain perfectly peaceful? But even if we succeeded, what of the numerous *agents provocateurs,* stool pigeons, and the like who crept into our movement and indulged in violence themselves or induced others to do so? If this was the sole condition of its function, then the non-violent method of resistance would always fail... a few odd persons...maybe even our opponents in the guise of friends...had the power to upset or end our movement by their rash behaviour.

Non-violent civil disobedience was not a suitable programme for mobs for they easily got out of hand. Physical pain and suffering are difficult to bear peacefully. Only disciplined and dedicated persons can remain calm under such provocation. *Satyagraha* was seen at its best in South Africa and during the salt campaign of 1930, where the numbers involved were comparatively small and the volunteers acted under the Mahatma's personal supervision and direction. It always led to violence when practiced by the people at large.

It was even less easy to subscribe to Gandhi's views on sex, his cry of 'back to the village', and his rejection of Western civilization with its urbanization and its emphasis on industrialization and material possessions.

He took a vow of celibacy for life in South Africa in 1906. He was at that time commanding a volunteer Indian stretcher-bearer company in the Zulu war. This involved long separations from his wife. 'It was borne in on me,' he explained, 'that I should have more and more occasions for the service of the kind I was rendering, and I should find myself unequal to my task if I were engaged in the pleasures of family life.' But he carried his attitude to absurd lengths as shown by some of his utterances: 'I must declare with all the power I can command that sensual attraction, even between husband and wife, is unnatural'; and 'the adoption of artificial methods must result in imbecility and nervous prostration'. In 1945 and again in 1947 he tested his chastity by sleeping naked with women for brief periods.

His fasts for the improvement of health, for self-purification and for penance to atone for the sins of others conformed to accepted traditions, but those he undertook to get his own way in political causes were regarded by most observers as a form of moral coercion contrary to his total commitment to non-violence.

One well-known fast of his to gain a political objective took place in 1932 while he was in prison at Poona. It resulted from the fact that in the Communal Award made by Prime Minister Ramsay MacDonald, the Untouchables...officially described as the Depressed Classes...had been given separate electorates along with other minorities. MacDonald, however, had declared that any alternative arrangement agreed upon by the Untouchables and the caste-Hindus would be acceptable to the government. Gandhi regarded the Untouchables as an integral part of the Hindu family and on 20 September commenced a fast which he vowed would continue unto death unless the Award was modified. When charged with having resorted to coercion, he explained:

> It [the fast] is intended to sting the Hindu conscience into right religious action. Fasting stirs up sluggish consciences and fires loving hearts to action. Those

who have to bring about radical changes in human conditions and surroundings cannot do it except by raising ferment in the society. There are only two methods of doing this—violence and non-violence. Non-violent pressure exerted through self-suffering by fasting... touches and strengthens the moral fibre of those against whom it is directed.

Under pressure from a country-wide uproar Dr Ambedkar, the leader of the Untouchables, who had originally derided the fast as a 'political stunt', and the principal Hindu leaders hastened to conclude a compromise—the Poona Pact (25 September)—acceptable to Gandhi, who thereupon broke his fast. The pact considerably increased the number of seats for the Untouchables at the cost of caste-Hindu seats; but the principle of separate electorates applied only to the first stage of the election, in which the Untouchable voters would select a panel of four candidates for each seat reserved for the Untouchable voters. A joint electorate composed of Caste Hindu voters and Untouchable voters would then elect a person from each panel to sit in the legislature. This scheme was endorsed by the British Government.

With regard to village life, Gandhi wrote in 1909, 'India's salvation consists in unlearning what she has learnt during the last fifty years. The railways, telegraphs, hospitals, lawyers, doctors and such-like have all to go; and the so-called upper classes have to learn consciously, religiously and deliberately the simple peasant life, knowing it to be a life-giving true happiness.' He believed that Western civilization tended 'to propagate immorality' and that towns bred vice. He thought hospitals were 'institutions for propagating sin' and was utterly opposed to vaccination against smallpox. A firm believer in nature cure, he insisted upon utter cleanliness in his surroundings, mainly to prevent disease but also because he was stung by the knowledge that white South Africans regarded Indians as a lower species of humanity because they lived in dirty conditions. He readily cleaned the latrines personally and expected others to do the same. He did not think that this important task should be left to scavengers (generally called *bhangis* or 'sweepers'in India). Some friends jokingly labelled him *mahabhangi* (*maha*, great).

He was a strict vegetarian but frequently carried out dietary experiments by varying the menu. He gave up cow's milk in South Africa because he believed it stimulated the lower passions. Even after a serious illness in 1918 he refused to eat a nourishing diet and agreed to take goat's milk only after his wife's constant pleading. His vow, she argued, prohibited only cow's milk.

Despite his great concern for the poor, Gandhi was against disturbing the existing economic order. Addressing a deputation of big landowners he said:

> I shall be no party to dispossessing propertied classes of their private property without just cause. My objective is to reach your hearts and convert you so that you may hold all your private property in trust for your tenants and use it primarily for their welfare...But supposing that there is an attempt unjustly to deprive you of your property you will find me on fighting on your side...the socialism and communism of the West is based on certain conceptions which are fundamentally different from ours. One such conception is their belief in the essential selfishness of human nature...Our socialism and communism should therefore be based on non-violence and on the harmonious co-operation of Labour and Capital, landlord and tenant.

He believed that big landowners, rich industrialists and princes held their wealth as trustees for the benefit of the poor.

Jawaharlal Nehru, who believed in industrialization and in the compulsory distribution of wealth by state socialism, differed strongly from Gandhi in these matters. He believed that Gandhi's glorification of village life was based on a false view of history; there had been no 'golden past' in village life. 'All history tells us,' he wrote, 'that the great masses of the people lived in utter misery in those past days, lacking food and the barest necessaries of life.' He believed that the industrial age had 'laid down a basis of material well-being which makes cultural and spiritual progress much easier for large numbers.' With regard to Gandhi's theory of trusteeship, Nehru asked whether it was reasonable to give unchecked power and wealth to an individual and to expect him to use it entirely for the public good: 'Are the best of us so perfect as to be trusted in this way?'

Gandhi claimed to be a democrat. True democracy according to him was to go down to the level of the masses, mix with them on equal terms and thus help to improve them. 'Many have despaired of resisting me,' he wrote in September 1934. 'This is a humiliating revelation to me, a born democrat. I make that claim, if complete identification with the poorest of mankind, longing to live no better than they, and a corresponding conscious effort to approach that level to the best of one's ability, can entitle one to make it.' But in fact Gandhi controlled Congress like a dictator. His main instrument was the Working Committee, which in the Congress hierarchy performed the same decision-making role as the Cabinet in the parliamentary system of government. Subhas Chandra

Bose, who called him the 'virtual dictator' of Congress, pointed out that the Working Committees since 1929 had been elected according to Gandhi's wishes and that no one could aspire to a place in that committee who was not thoroughly submissive to him.

Bose had personally tasted this reality. He had been elected president of Congress in 1938 with Gandhi's approval, but during the ensuing year it became evident that Bose wished to follow a more militant policy towards the British Government than Gandhi and his followers. Consequently, when Bose stood for re-election in 1939, Gandhi caused Pattabhai Sitaramayya to oppose him and when Sitaramayya was defeated Gandhi said the defeat was more his own than Sitaramayya's, thus making the issue one of confidence in himself. This had the desired effect of alarming the members of Congress and the country at large. Thirteen members of the Working Committee resigned, leaving only Bose and his elder brother in place. When Bose requested Gandhi to suggest replacements for the vacant places, the latter refused to put forward any names. Bose, finding it impossible to function, had no option but to tender his resignation (29 April 1939). Even Jawaharlal Nehru, who revered Gandhi much more than Bose, concedes that 'a mere suggestion from him [Gandhi] that he would retire has always been enough to upset the Working Committee as well as the country'. He called him the 'super-president' of Congress and approved of the appellation 'beloved slave-driver' which another politician had coined. Bose's forced resignation had demonstrated Gandhi's own continuing supremacy over Congress. It also had the important consequence that Bose lost prestige in Congress circles and was eliminated from a possible contest with Jawaharlal Nehru for the Mahatma's political mantle.

It is interesting to note that in 1951 Gandhi's tactics were repeated by Prime Minister Nehru. In order to get rid of the right-wing Purushottamdas Tandon, who had been elected as president of the Congress with the backing of Sardar Vallabhbhai Patel, Nehru resigned from the Working Committee. This created a crisis during which all the remaining members of the Working Committee also resigned, thus forcing Tandon's own resignation. At the request of the party Nehru then took over the presidency.

The Mahatma had never displayed any marked interest in the fine arts and architecture. He regarded the Taj Mahal as no more than an embodiment of forced labour. He was not an orator but spoke in public gently and smoothly. He impressed the multitude with the honesty and sincerity of a saint, not with the histrionics of a politician. Thousands felt happy just because they had his *darshan* ('sight', the beholding of holy men, kings and the like which earns merit). In ordinary conversation, however, he joked and laughed easily. 'His smile is delightful,' said Jawaharlal Nehru, 'his laughter infectious and he radiates light-heartedness. There is something childlike about him which is full of charm. When he enters a room he brings a breath of fresh air with him which lightens the atmosphere.' When he was in London in 1931 to attend the Round Table Conference, he humorously told a reporter who had questioned him about his dress, 'You people wear plus-fours, mine are minus-fours.' During the same visit he went to Buckingham Palace dressed in his usual loincloth and shawl. When asked whether he had been sufficiently clad for his meeting with the King, he replied, 'The King had enough on for both of us.'

As a student in London he had dressed meticulously like an English gentleman and his sartorial possessions included a silk hat. In South Africa he continued to don English suits but wore a cap-like ready-made turban. He started to wear Indian dress just before leaving South Africa and in 1921 finally adopted the garb by which he is most remembered…a loin cloth and a shawl. He explained the significance of his meagre covering to a member of the London Press in these words: 'If I came here to live and work like an English citizen, then I should conform to the customs of the country and should wear the dress of an Englishman. But I am here on a great and special mission [to attend the Round Table Conference], and my loincloth, if you choose so to describe it, is the dress of my principals, the people of India'. The 'Gandhi cap' made of white cloth, which became a badge of Congress membership in India, was a Gandhi import from South Africa. When in prison in that country, Gandhi, like all Indians, was classed as a Negro. He was confined in the Negro ward and was required to wear Negro uniform. The Gandhi cap was a reproduction of the headpiece in that outfit.

Now we come to the important question: What magic did this half-naked, insignificant looking man, who at times weighed only a little over seven stone, possess that made even sophisticated Western-educated persons like Jawaharlal Nehru, who did not always agree with his philosophy, seek his leadership during the most crucial phases of the struggle for independence?

The main reason was that his saintliness and identification with the poor of India had made him the darling of the masses. By his tireless and frequent tramping through rural India he had, moreover, acquired a unique insight into the mind of village India. 'He is the great peasant,' wrote Jawaharlal Nehru, 'with a peasant's blindness to some aspects of life. But India is peasant India, and so he knows his India well and reacts to her

lightest tremors, and has a knack of acting at the psychological moment...
Always we had the feeling that while we might be more logical, Gandhiji
knew India far better than we did, and a man who could command such
tremendous devotion and loyalty must have something in him that
corresponded to the needs and aspirations of the masses.' Referring to the
fact that the some 'parlour Socialists' called Gandhi 'the arch-reactionary',
Nehru pointed out that the 'fact remains that this "reactionary"...has
shaken up India as no so-called revolutionary has done'.

Jawaharlal Nehru believed that Gandhi followed his instinct (which the
Mahatma himself called his 'inner voice') and 'later, for the benefit of his
surprised and resentful colleagues, tries to clothe his decision with
reasons' which were not always convincing. When Nehru told him that his
way of springing surprises frightened him and filled him with apprehension,
Gandhi admitted the presence of this unknown element in him, and said
that he himself could not answer for it or foretell what it might lead to. To
the charge that he was sometimes inconsistent, the Mahatma answered
that his aim was not to be consistent with his own previous statements but
to be consistent with truth as it may present itself at a given moment.

Subhas Chandra Bose, who did not belong to Gandhi's inner circle and
was, therefore, less respectfully inclined towards him than Nehru, described
the secret of the Mahatma's popularity in these words: 'The asceticism of
Gandhiji, his simple life, his vegetarian diet, his adherence to truth and his
consequent fearlessness...all combined to give him a halo of saintliness.
His loincloth was reminiscent of Christ, while his sitting posture at the
time of lecturing was reminiscent of Buddha. Now all this was a tremendous
asset to the Mahatma in compelling the attention and obedience of his
countrymen.' Bose recalled that in 1922 when he was in prison 'Indian
warders in the service of the Prisons' Department would refuse to believe
that the Mahatma had been cast in prison by the British Government. They
would say in all seriousness that since Gandhiji was a Mahatma, he could
assume the shape of a bird and escape from prison any moment he liked.'

Even his fads endeared him to the masses because they were Indian fads
conforming to the country's ancient culture. To his Westernized colleagues
they were a source of some amusement, and Jawaharlal has recorded in his
Autobiography that they would half-humorously say that after independence
had been achieved these fads must not be encouraged.

Indeed, it was Gandhi's power to sway the masses that made him
indispensable to his colleagues, No movement could carry much weight
without him. Also, when the principal figures in Congress fell out with
each other, they had no alternative but to turn to Gandhi as the super-leader

to devise a compromise and restore unity. 'He dominates the Congress and the country', Nehru wrote, 'not so much because of any opinions he holds, and which are generally accepted, but because of his unique personality' which was much bigger than his writings and sayings convey.

He was the national movement's greatest propaganda asset. His life-style, mode of dress, philosophy and technique were so utterly different from those of all other political leaders of world stature that he became a magnet for writers, journalists, photographers and interested visitors from all over the globe. By becoming a world figure he gave the Indian problem a world dimension. He walked through more villages than anyone had done before, spreading his meassage of nationalism, uplift of Untouchables and universal use of the *charka* (spinning wheel) and *khadi* (hand-woven cloth, also called *khaddar*). He edited newspapers and called his daily political platform a 'prayer meeting'. This latter was another public relations masterpiece for collecting crowds because the proceedings opened with recitations of Hindu, Muslim and Christian spiritual texts.

Not surprisingly, the British Government placed Gandhi in a class of his own. They appreciated that but for him, the Indian struggle for freedom might have become more revolutionary and violent. He prevented leaders like Nehru and Bose from causing Congress to take up extreme positions. Communism had overwhelmed peasant Russia at about the same time as Gandhi assumed leadership in India, and his conservatism and devotion to religion made him a powerful bulwark against the spread of the new contagion to peasant India. Miss Ellen Wilkinson, a former Member of Parliament, who visited India in 1932 as a member of the India League Deputation,[1] considered that 'Gandhi was the best policeman the Britishers had in India.'

The Congress party had the Mahatma to thank for being able to hold together and survive in periods of severe conflict with the British Government, for it was he who had placed its structure on a sound country-wide basis and made it a mass party. This achievement had the immensely important consequence that upon attaining independence, Congress was able to form a more stable government than other independent countries, including Pakistan, whose political parties lacked the long experience and maturity of the Indian National Congress.

It was at its special session at Amritsar in September 1920 that Congress requested Gandhi to frame a new constitution for the party; this he successfully did at the Nagpur session in December that year. Congress

[1] In the summer of 1945 she become Minister of Education in Attlee's Labour Government.

was now reorganized to conform to the various tiers of the civil administration of the country. With the Village Congress Committee at the base there would rise successively the Sub-divisional, the District, the Provincial and the All-India Congress Committees. The only difference was that the Congress provinces followed linguistic boundaries, not those drawn by the British Government. The All-India Congress Committee was to have a membership of 350 and would elect fifteen persons who together would function as the Cabinet or the executive arm of the party. It would meet frequently and take the initiative in all important matters. Each province was to contribute delegates to the Congress sessions proportionate to its population. This was meant to remove the unfair advantage which the local politicians had enjoyed of being able to pack the sessions with their local followers. Finally, the creed of Congress was also redefined as 'the attainment of *swaraj* by peaceful and legitimate means'— the previous term 'constitutional means' was dropped. *Swaraj* literally means self-government, but the Congress resolution deliberately avoided controversy within its ranks by not indicating whether *swaraj* meant self-government within the British Empire or outside it. To Gandhi it denoted 'self-government within the empire, if possible, and outside, if necessary'.

The Mahatma instilled pride, courage and hope into the mind of India's poor and made them independence-conscious. Poverty no longer was a mark of inferiority; going to prison in the national cause became a signal honour. He eroded the fear of the foreign government in the public mind, thus weakening one important element of its control over India's millions.

Gandhi's emphasis on non-violence and the right means enhanced the moral tone of the Indian struggle for independence and gave it a unique character among the freedom movements of the time. The period of his leadership witnessed two devastating world wars which showed western civilization in the worst light. The moral basis of the right of the European races to rule 'backward' non-white peoples was shattered. In a world sick of bloodshed, Gandhi's voice struck a sympathetic chord. Perhaps the ancient land of India did have a healing message for humanity after all.

The women of India also owe a debt of gratitude to Gandhi for enlisting them in the political movement and thus raising their status above that of mere housewives. This first happened in South Africa when a judgement of the Supreme Court (1913) declared illegal all marriages other than those performed according to Christian rites and those which were monogamous and registered by a Registrar of Marriages. This meant that Indian wives who had married their husbands according to the laws of their own country were nothing more than mistresses and that their children were illegitimate. Indian women, including Kasturbai Gandhi herself, offered *satyagraha* of their own and several went to prison. Afterwards, in the non-co-operation movements in India, women, including those from the most respectable families, came forward and joined the men; they suffered the *lathi* [1] blows of the police and cheerfully went to prison. Among those who were incarcerated in 1931, for instance, were members of the family of Madan Mohan Malaviya, a prominent orthodox Brahmin. In Delhi alone, 1600 women went behind bars that year. On 8 April 1932, the elderly mother of Jawaharlal Nehru was badly injured in an ugly incident. He described the occurrence in these poignant words:

> In Allahabad my mother was in a procession which was stopped by the police and later charged with *lathis*. When the procession had been halted someone brought her a chair, and she was sitting on this on the road at the head of the procession. Some people who were especially looking after her, including my secretary, were arrested and removed, and then came the police charge. My mother was knocked down from her chair, and was hit repeatedly on the head with canes. Blood came out of an open wound in the head; she fainted, and lay on the roadside, which had now been cleared of the processionists and public. After some time she was picked up and brought by a police officer in his car to Anand Bhawan...slowly she recovered, and when she came to see me next month in Bareilly Gaol she was still bandaged up. But she was full of joy and pride at having shared with our volunteer boys and girls the privilege of receiving cane and *lathi* blows. Her recovery, however, was more apparent than real, and it seems that the tremendous shaking brought into prominence deep-seated troubles, which a year later assumed dangerous proportions.

That women in India have enjoyed the same political status as men is in no small measure due to Gandhi and others who shared his views. Two of his close associates, Sarojini Naidu and Rajkumari Amritkaur, became Governor of a province and a Cabinet Minister respectively in newly independent India. Earlier, in 1925, Mrs Naidu had presided over the Congress session at Cawnpore. However, Gandhi stopped short of allowing women the right of birth control except by abstinence from sex. Two women—the English suffragist Mrs How Martyn and an American, Mrs Sanger—travelled all the way to India to plead with him to allow artificial methods of birth control but he remained adamant.

But the Mahatma's leadership suffered from one major shortcoming.

---

[1] *Lathi* : a staff, the tip of which is usually clad with iron.

It was Hindu in character and unsuited to cure the Hindu-Muslim discord which was India's most serious political malady. Even his most notable endeavour—to unite Hindus and Muslims by championing the cause of the Khilafat—served, in the long run, to drive the two communities further apart. Some of the 'nationalist Muslims' whom Congress was able to attract were men of high personal worth. The most prominent among them were Hakim Ajmal Khan, Dr M. A. Ansari and Maulana Abul Kalam Azad, each one of whom was elected president of the Congress, but like their earlier counterparts, such as Tyabji, they did not enjoy any significant popular following. The politically unsophisticated masses of India, whether Hindu or Muslim, could be fully roused only by the familiar cry of religion which had governed their daily lives for centuries past.

Gandhi never made any secret of the fact that he was a devout Hindu nor that he believed religion was inseparable from politics. 'Every fibre of my being is Hindu', he affirmed. That he respected other religions as much as his own did not make him less of a Hindu, for Hinduism is defined by its followers as a perpetual search for truth. Followers of other religions stoutly maintain that their own particular religion is the only true one, though they may be tolerant of the other faiths.

Gandhi's aim in wishing to end discrimination against the Untouchables—whom he called 'Harijans' or children of God—was not to violate Hinduism but to reform it by removing a blot which he believed had no sanction. Morever, it would have been a substantial political loss to the Hindus if the Untouchables were treated as a separate minority (there were 50 million of them). So strongly did he feel on the issue that when an earthquake devastated Bihar in January 1934, he said that the catastrophe was a divine punishment for 'the sin of Untouchability'. He made no answer to the poet Tagore's question why God had punished so many innocent children including Untouchables. Jawaharlal Nehru endorsed Tagore's criticism and observed that it was 'an astounding thing'

[1] Though he is most famous for his role in the Indian freedom movement, his activities covered all aspects of human welfare…spiritual (religious and ethical life); economic (self-sufficient villages); educational (he sponsored what he called 'Basic Education'); social (removal of Untouchability and other abuses); health (improved hygiene, nature cure, correct diet and temperance). His conception of *swadeshi* was a wide one. He defined it in these terms: 'After much thinking I have arrived at a definition of *swadeshi* that perhaps best illustrates my meaning: *Swadeshi* is that spirit within us which restricts us to the use and service of our immediate surroundings, to the exclusion of the more remote. Thus (1) in the matter of religion I must restrict myself to my ancestral religion...If I find my religion defective, I should serve by purging it of its defects. (2) In the domain of politics I should

Continued on next page

to suggest that 'a human custom or failing had its reactions on the movements of the earth's crust.'

That religion and politics are inseparable was a part of Gandhi's belief that all aspects of human life constitute one inextricable whole.[1] 'To see the universal and all-pervading Spirit of Truth, face to face', he explained, 'one must be able to love the meanest of creation as oneself. And a man who aspires after that cannot afford to keep out of any field of life. That is why my devotion to Truth has drawn me into the field of politics; and I can say without the slightest hesitation, and yet in all humility, that those who say that religion has nothing to do with politics do not know what religion means.' On another occasion he vehemently averred: 'Those who say that religion has nothing to do with politics do not know what religion means...for me there are no politics devoid of religion.'[2]

'Gandhiji, indeed, was continuously laying stress on the religious and spiritual side of the movement,' wrote a troubled Jawaharlal Nehru, 'his religion was not dogmatic, but it did mean a definitely religious outlook on life, and the whole movement was strongly influenced by this and took a revivalist character so far as the masses were concerned.'

In truth, the secret of Gandhi's hold over the masses, and therefore the main reason for his success as a political leader, was his religious appeal. 'When the Mahatma speaks,' explained Subhas Chandra Bose, 'he does so in a language that they comprehend—not in the language of Herbert Spenser and Edmund Burke, as for instance Sir Surendranath Banerji would have done, but in that of the *Bhagavad Gita* and the *Ramayana*. When he talks to them about *swaraj*, he does not dilate on the virtues of provincial autonomy or federation, he reminds them of the glories of *Rama-rajya* (the kingdom of king Rama of old)[2] and they understand. And when he talks of conquering through love and *ahimsa* (non-violence), they are reminded of Buddha and Mahavira and they accept him.'

It is obvious that such a style of leadership was not likely to appeal to the Muslims. Adherence to non-violence under all circumstances was not consistent with the Islamic injunction that the faithful must fight in a just

---

make use of the indigenous institutions, and serve them by curing them of their proved defects. (3) In the field of economics, I should use only those things that are produced by my immediate neighbours, and serve those industries by making them efficient'.

[1] Those who later blamed Jinnah for introducing religion into politics conveniently overlooked the fact that it was Gandhi who was the first to do so.

[2] This naturally meant a Hindu kingdom.

cause and would be rewarded in the hereafter should they perish in the line of duty.

Gandhi's admirers such as Jawaharlal Nehru said 'he was the movement itself' and 'he was almost India'. That this leader, who so clearly drew his inspiration from ancient Hinduism, became the personification of Congress, inevitably gave that party a Hindu complexion.

It seems that Gandhi did not think that the fusion of the peoples of India into one homogeneous nation by any meaningful measures, such as inter-marriage or inter-dining, was necessary. On one occasion he was asked by what criterion one could judge that the last trace of Untouchability had been eradicated from the heart. He said, 'Have you an unmarried son or daughter? If you have one, get him or her a Harijan for a bride or bridegroom, as the case may be, in the spirit of a sacrament and I shall send you a wire of congratulations at my expense.' But he was not prepared to use the same prescription for easing Hindu-Muslim disunity. He was deeply distressed when his second son, Manilal, fell in love with a Muslim girl in 1926, and said that such a match would contravene the Hindu religion. He was equally shocked in 1936 when his eldest son, Harilal, turned Muslim, and referred to him as a ne'er-do-well who had sold himself 'to the highest bidder'. On the question whether Hindus and Muslims should inter-marry or eat together, Gandhi said, 'In my opinion the idea that inter-dining and inter-marrying are necessary for national growth is a superstition borrowed from the West.'

Gandhi's latent qualities of leadership first came to the surface in South Africa. He was not doing well as a legal practioner in India so he gladly accepted a lucrative offer from an Indian firm to go to South Africa to instruct and assist their counsel in a case against another Indian firm. He reached Durban in May 1893. Instead of pursuing the case in court, he persuaded the parties to arrive at a friendly compromise and save themselves further worry and expense. His tact was noticed appreciatively by the members of the Indian community and he was able to build up a good practice. He always strove to get disputes settled out of court on fair terms for both sides. But professional success was not the main reason for his decision to stay on in South Africa.

He had intended to return to India after his initial assignment had been completed, but in the meantime his concern had been deeply roused by the racial discrimination to which his countrymen were being subjected by the white South Africens, and he stayed on to fight the evil. Not long after his arrival he had personally tasted what it meant to be an Indian in South Africa. He was travelling first class in a train—for which he had the necessary ticket—but a European passenger complained at having to share a compartment with a coloured person. Gandhi was forcibly ejected and had to spend the night on the cold platform. He also suffered similar humiliating experiences later and went to prison three times for his championing of the Indian cause. Altogether, he stayed in South Africa for two decades, and it was there that he originally formulated and practiced *satyagraha* with success. At that time he was thoroughly loyal towards the British Government. He laid the entire blame for the ill-treatment of Indians on the shoulders of the South African authorities.

During the South African (Boer) War he organized an Indian Ambulance Corps consisting of more than a thousand volunteers. He and thirty-six other Indians received war medals for their services. His argument for helping the British Government in the war was that if Indians demanded equal rights as British subjects they must discharge their responsibilities in time of need. He deeply admired British values and sense of justice and placed high hopes in it. In the Zulu War too, he raised an Indian stretcher bearer company and commanded it with the honorary rank of sergeant-major.

In was on 18 July 1914 that Gandhi said farewell to South Africa and sailed to London *en route* for Bomby. He arrived in London a day before the start of World War I. While he was there, he was instrumental in the formation of an Indian Field Ambulance Training Corps. He rejected the suggestion that Britain's danger was India's opportunity and argued that, if Indians expected to improve their status with British help, it was their duty to help Britain in its hour of need. He said the British Empire had certain ideals with which he had 'fallen in love.' According to him the best government was the one that governed the least and he had found that 'it is possible for me to be governed least under the British Empire'. In the New Year's honours list of 1915 Lord Hardinge conferred upon him the *Kaisar-i-Hind* gold medal for services in South Africa.

After staying in London for some time he sailed for India, landing at Bombay on 9 January 1915. When Gandhi returned home he was already a much respected personality. One of his strongest admirers was Gokhale. They had first met in 1896 when Gandhi came to India on a visit. Their mutual liking was instantaneous and lasted till Gokhale's death. At a public meeting in 1909 Gokhale said that Gandhi could 'mould heroes out of common clay' and went on to say that Gandhi's struggle in South Africa was 'in furtherance of the future interests of our motherland.' During the Lahore session of Congress later that year, he observed that Gandhi was 'a man among men, a hero among heroes, a patriot among patriots, and we may well say that, in him, Indian humanity at the present time has really reached its high-water mark.' During his visit to South Africa in 1912, Gokhale had seen Gandhi's work at first hand and their mutual respect had increased still further. Soon after Gandhi's return to India, the poet Rabindranath Tagore described Gandhi as a 'Mahatma (great soul)'. Before long the title was on everybody's lips.

Not surprisingly, Gandhi's first important journey in India was a trip to Poona to visit his *guru*, Gokhale. Gokhale died a few days later (19 February 1915) but not before he had advised Gandhi to spend his first year in India bringing himself up to date with the prevailing conditions and to take no active part in the affairs of the country till he had done so. Gandhi faithfully obeyed his *guru's* injunction and travelled far and wide. He always rode third class in the train and publicised the degrading conditions in which the poor rail passengers in India had to travel. At a later stage, when he began to collect crowds at every stop and delay the scheduled service, the government decided to place a special train of third class carriages at his disposal. He attended the Congress sessions at Bombay (1915) and Lucknow (1916), but played no important part in the proceedings.

However, Gandhi's attendance at the Lucknow session led to his first involvement in a matter of public concern in India. Congress passed a resolution urging the government to appoint a committee 'to enquire into the causes of agrarian trouble and strained relations between the Indian *ryot* and the European planter in North Bihar and suggest remedies as well.' What the resolution referred to was the deplorable conditions to which the white planters were subjecting the Indian workers on the indigo plantations in Champaran district. A villager from Champaran had attended the Congress meeting and at his persistent urging, Gandhi accompanied him to Champaran.

At first the local authorities adopted a tough attitude and ordered Gandhi to leave the district. He replied that he would not do so till he had completed his investigation. He was put on trial but remained adamant. At this stage the Lieutenant-Governor, who happened to be an unusually sensible official, intervened and Gandhi was released. After studying the situation for several months Gandhi demanded that the grievances of the peasants should be redressed and if not, an official enquiry must be held. A committee of enquiry was appointed and Gandhi was given a seat on it. It recommended the refund of illegal exactions and the abolition of the compulsory growing of indigo. Gandhi's success greatly added to his fame. He also made life-long friendships with two persons who had collaborated with him in Champaran—Rajendra Prasad, who rose to be

President of independent India, and Mahadev Desai, who became the
Mahatma's secretary.

The scene of Gandhi's next success was Kaira district in his native
Gujarat. The crops having failed, the peasants there demanded a
suspension of land revenue. To put pressure on a reluctant government,
Gandhi obtained a declaration from a large number of peasants that
they would not pay the demand even if their lands were forfeited.
During the impasse, an act of non-violent resistance was performed
by some volunteers under Gandhi's direction. They removed the onion
crop from a field that had been attached by the authorities. When
tried for theft and sentenced, they became heroes. In the end, the
government offered a compromise acceptable to the peasants. Once
again Gandhi acquired a powerful life-long colleague from among those
who had helped him: Vallabhbhai Patel, the famous first Home Minister
of independent India.

Gandhi's next success was to bring about the settlement of a wage
dispute between the mill-owners of Ahmadabad and their employees. This
time he decided to undergo a fast till the reasonable demand of the workers
was conceded. He broke the fast on the fourth day, after the employers had
yielded to country-wide pressure.

In 1918 Gandhi attended a war conference at Delhi. He was then
persuaded by the Viceroy to support a resolution on recruiting and
followed it up by volunteering as a recruiting officer in Kaira, where he
had recently earned much influence.[1] He was severely criticised for this
positive contribution to the war effort while preaching non-violence under
all circumstances. His previous wartime assistance, having been in the
form of ambulance work, had been humanitarian in character. Even less
defensible was the argument he employed in a leaflet to attract recruits:
'Among the many misdeeds of the British rule in India, history will look
upon the Act depriving a whole nation of arms as the blackest. If we want
the Arms Act to be repealed, if we want to learn the use of arms, here is
a golden opportunity.' During his trial for sedition in March 1922 Gandhi
explained that his help to the British Government during the Boer and Zulu
Wars and World War I had been 'actuated by the belief that it was possible
by such services to gain a status of full equality in the Empire for my
countrymen.'

---

[1] It is interesting to note that Jinnah, at a war conference presided over by over the
Governor of Bombay, said, 'If you wish to enable us to help you, to facilitate and stimulate
the recruiting, you must make the educated people feel that they are citizens of the Empire
and the king's equal subjects'.

In August 1918, during his recruiting campaign, Gandhi fell seriously ill with dysentery and thought he was going to die. The war, and with it his recruiting duties, came to an end in November. His recovery was slow because of dietary fads and his belief in natural cures. He also had to undergo an operation for a fistula and was still feeling unwell when the agitation against the Rowlatt Bills erupted in the early part of February, but he felt so strongly about the matter that he decided to take action.

THE ROWLATT AGITATION AND THE OUTBREAK OF VIOLENCE

Gandhi, as usual, tried persuasion first and wrote to the Viceroy on 20 February but to no effect. Thereupon he decided to launch a countrywide public protest and drew up a *satyagraha* pledge which was published in the Press on 2 March along with a manifesto explaining why he wanted the Rowlatt legislation to be withdrawn. The pledge to which the opponents of the Rowlatt Bills were invited to subscribe ran as follows:

> Being conscientiously of the opinion that the Bills known as the Indian Criminal Law (Amendment) Bill No. I of 1919 and the Criminal Law (Emergency Powers) Bill No. II of 1919, are unjust, subversive of the principles of liberty and justice and destructive of the elementary rights of individuals on which the safety of the community, as a whole, and the State itself, is based, we solemnly affirm that, in the event of these Bills becoming law and until they are withdrawn, we shall refuse civilly to obey these laws and such other laws as a Committee, to be hereafter appointed, may think fit, and we further affirm that in this struggle we will faithfully follow truth and refrain from violence to life, person or property.

In the manifesto he described the step he had taken as 'probably the most momentous in the history of India'.

On 11 March he sent a telegram to the Private Secretary to the Viceroy in which he pleaded for the last time: 'Even at this eleventh hour I respectfully ask His Excellency and his Government to pause and consider before passing Rowlatt Bills.' But the objectionable legislation was passed on 18 March.

In the meantime, Gandhi had been visiting different parts of the country prior to launching the mass movement. While at Madras (according to his own version), in the moment between sleeping and waking his inner voice told him what to do. Accordingly, he issued a message from Madras on 24

March calling for the following programme on 30 March (the date was later changed to 6 April). He desired that the day be observed 'as a day of humiliation and prayer'. More concretely, he recommended that a twenty-four hour fast should be observed on that day; that all work, except such as may be necessary in the public interest, should be suspended for the day and markets and other business places should be closed (*hartal*[1]); and that public meetings should be held everywhere at which resolutions asking for the rescinding of the Rowlatt Act should be passed.

The information with regard to the change of date did not reach Delhi and the Punjab in time and in some places the *hartal* was observed on the earlier date. But disorder and violence made their appearance in Delhi, the Bombay Presidency, and the Punjab during the week following 6 April. The infamous Jallianwala Bagh massacre happened at Amirtsar on 13 April 1919. Martial Law was declared in Lahore and Amritsar districts on 15 April, in Gujranwala district on 16 April, in Gujrat district on 19 April and in Lyallpur district on 24 April. It was withdrawn from Gujrat on 28 May, from Amritsar, Gujranwala and Lyllpur at midnight on 9 July and from Lahore at midnight on 11 July.

Sir Michael O'Dwyer, Lieutenant-Governor of the Punjab at the time, was an Irishman who believed in governing the natives with a firm hand. In *My Indian Years*, Lord Hardinge relates how he had to overrule Sir Michael in a conspiracy case in which a Special Tribunal set up under the Defence of India Act had condemned twenty-four men to death: 'I went to Lahore to see the Lieutenant-Governor Sir M. O'Dwyer and told him categorically that I absolutely declined to allow a holocaust of victims in a case where only six men had been proved to be actually guilty of murder and dacoity. He recommended that only six of the twenty-four should have their sentences commuted.' After consulting his Law Member, Hardinge used his powers as Viceroy (there was no other appeal from the Tribunal) and commuted the sentences of eighteen of the twenty-four men.

Sir Michael was especially contemptuous of the educated, politically vociferous Indians. In his memorandum on the forthcoming constitutional reforms in 1919 he wrote, 'We must, if we are faithful to our trust, place the interests of the silent masses before the clamour of the politicians...

---

[1] In his presidential address at the Amritsar Congress (December 1919) Motilal Nehru described the significance of *hartal* in these words: 'The *hartal* in India is a spiritual weapon, the old-time method of showing sorrow, of having grievances redressed by patient suffering. It has from time immemorial been resorted to to express grief at a national calamity, sorrow at the loss of a loved citizen. It is not used as a threat, nor as a weapon against the forces of law and order'.

Apply any practical test—the prevention of religious riots, the composing of sectional differences, the raising of recruits for the combatant army or the Defence Force—when any of these questions is to the fore, the politician usually retires into the background. His influence for good is generally nil, but he can, and sometimes does, add to the trouble by injudicious or malicious interference. It is often stated as an argument for self-government, that there are no religious riots in Native States. For this there are many reasons but a leading one is that the professional politician does not exist there, or, if he does, is not allowed to interfere.'

The Lieutenant-Governor's attitude towards Indian politicians is relevant to our purpose because it was alleged that he had aggravated the situation by having Gandhi arrested on his way to the Punjab and by deporting two popular leaders of Amritsar—Dr Satyapal, a Hindu medical practioner, and Dr Kitchlew, a Muslim barrister who was a Doctor of Philosophy from Munster. It was not until October 1919 that the Government of India under public pressure appointed a committee under Lord Hunter, later Solicitor-General for Scotland, to investigate the disturbances in the Bombay Presidency, Delhi and the Punjab. It had four other British members and three Indian members. The committee split on racial lines, with the British members submitting a Majority Report and the Indians a Minority Report. The reports were published on 28 May 1920. In November Congress appointed an enquiry committee of its own ('Commissioners'). The unanimous report of this committee of four, one of whom was Gandhi himself, was published on 25 March 1920.

1. DELHI: The earliest disturbance took place at Delhi where a *hartal* was observed on 30 March 1919. The police and the troops had to open fire in self-defence at two places, resulting in eight deaths.

By 9 April shops had gradually opened but on the evening of that day Gandhi, who was travelling northwards from Bombay by train, was arrested at the small station of Palwal in the Punjab in pursuance of orders excluding him from Delhi and the Punjab, and confining him to the Bombay Presidency. He was escorted by the police to Bombay and released. On 10 April, Delhi again observed a *hartal* because of Gandhi's detention, and feelings rose still higher when on the evening of that day news spread of serious happenings at Lahore and Amritsar. The shops remained closed but no violence took place until 14 April, when a CID Inspector was seriously assaulted. On 17 April, a police picket fired when under attack, wounding eighteen, two of whom died later. No further disturbances took place at Delhi. The Majority Report observed that 'the disturbances at Delhi never took the form of an anti-European and anti-

Government movement' nor was there any trace of any organised conspiracy against the government.

There was impressive fraternization between Hindus and Muslims at Delhi. On 30 March an orthodox Hindu leader, Swami Shradhanand, was invited to address a big meeting in the Jamia Masjid.

2. BOMBAY PRESIDENCY : (a) *Ahmadabad* : The *hartal* on 6 April passed off peacefully at Ahmadabad but disorder broke out on 10 April upon receipt of news of Gandhi's arrest. Two Europeans were assaulted while driving through the town and took shelter in a mill, where a small party of police joined them. The mob destroyed a part of the mill. To avoid further destruction the people in charge of the mill expelled the two Europeans, who came out accompanied by four policemen. When attacked by the mob, the police fired, wounding twelve persons. In the fracas that followed all the attacked persons escaped but one. The unlucky one, a policeman, was captured and beaten up and subsequently died.

Several acts of incendiarism and violence took place on 11 April. Some government buildings were burned. Trouble continued despite police firing. During the attack on the electric power station the officer in charge, Brown, was injured but escaped alive. A European police officer, Sergeant Fraser, who took shelter in a shop, was murdered. Though troops had arrived and fired to assist the civil authorities, the rioting was not quelled.

It was only when 200 British troops arrived on the afternoon of 12 April that the situation began to improve. The last occasion on which the troops opened fire was at midday, 13 April. Twenty-eight rioters are known to have been killed and 123 wounded.

Gandhi arrived in Ahmadabad on 13 April and on the next day addressed a huge meeting at which he upbraided the people for resorting to violence. Thanks to his influence, the disturbances at Ahmadabad virtually ended on 14 April.

(b) *Virangam* (Ahmadabad District): Disorder broke out in Virangam on 12 April. On the following day a Hindu third-class magistrate was burned to death and Traffic Inspector MacIlvride was beaten unconscious. The railway station was gutted, the treasury was looted, the telegraph wires were cut and some other government property was destroyed. A detachment of troops which arrived in the evening controlled the situation and the shops opened on 13 April. Six persons were killed and eighteen were wounded by police firing.

(c) *Nadiad* (Kaira District): A rail was removed from the permanent way which derailed a troop train on the night of 11 April but there were no casualties. On 12 April the railway line was again damaged and telegraph wires were cut. To prevent further trouble, troops were posted at some places but there was no clash between them and the public.

(d) **Bombay City** : Tension began to rise in Bombay when the news of Gandhi's arrest was published on the evening of 10 April. Stones were thrown at the police on 11 April but with Gandhi's appearance in the afternoon, the situation calmed down.

As a mark of Hindu-Muslim unity Gandhi and Sarojini Naidu were invited to speak in a mosque. For a Hindu lady this was an unprecedented honour.

3. AMRITSAR : The first outbreak in the Punjab occurred at Amritsar on 10 April 1919. The two parts of the city, the Civil Lines and the city proper, were separated from each other by the railway line.

Following two public meetings, one on 23 and the other on 29 March, Satyapal was served with an order of the Punjab Government prohibiting him from speaking in public. On 30 March the city observed a complete *hartal* and on 4 April, Kitchlew too, was ordered not to speak in public. On 6 April another successful *hartal* took place. There was no clash with the police till then and no indication of any anti-European feeling.

Fearing disorder, the Deputy Commissioner of Amritsar on 8 April asked for military reinforcements. The Punjab Government on 9 April passed an order deporting Satyapal and Kitchlew from Amritsar.

The Hindu festival of *Ram Navami* fell on 9 April and this time not only Hindus but also the Muslims joined in the celebrations. As a striking demonstration of unity, Hindus and Muslims drank out of the same cups. But there was still no indication of hostility towards Europeans.

On the evening of 9 April, the Deputy Commissioner asked Kitchlew and Satyapal to come to his residence in the Civil Lines at 10 a.m. on the following day, which they did. About half-an-hour later they were driven away under police escort. The news of the deportation of the two leaders and the fact that their destination was kept secret from the public, caused great excitement. Shops were closed and crowds attempted to make their way to the Civil Lines to see the Deputy Commissioner and demand the release of the two deported leaders. They clashed with troops and police twice on Hall Bridge which spanned the railway line. According to the Hunter Committee Majority Report 'three or four individuals...[were] killed or wounded' at the first firing and 'between twenty and thirty casualties' resulted from the second incident. The maddened crowd rampaged through the city. They murdered five Europeans and attacked and burned buildings. Among premises which were partly or wholly destroyed were the telephone exchange, the Town Hall, two banks, a church and parts of the railway station. A European missionary teacher, Miss Sherwood, while bicycling through a street, was assaulted and left for dead. She was carried home by some Indians who tended her and safely delivered her to her friends.

Brigadier-General Dyer arrived at Amritsar on the evening of the 11th and took charge of the situation. (He had been educated at the Bishop Cotton School in India, where most of his fellow-students had been Anglo-Indians or Eurasians who were notorious for carrying the chip of racial prejudice on their shoulders). On the next day, a strong column under Dyer marched round the city but there was no clash with the public.

On the morning of 13 April, Dyer went through the city and had a proclamation read out by the *naib-tahsildar* at different places. The people were summoned by drum to hear it. The original was in English but the *naib-tahsildar* explained it in the vernacular. It read in part: 'No procession of any kind is permitted to parade the streets in the city or any part of the city or outside it at any time. Any such processions or any gathering of four men would be looked upon and treated as an unlawful assembly and dispersed by force of arms if necessary.' At about the same time a counter-proclamation was made by a boy beating a tin can, that a meeting would be held at Jallianwala Bagh at 4 p.m.

Though the word *bagh* means a garden, Jallianwala Bagh was in fact an open piece of waste land with only three trees on it. It was an irregular quadrangle surrounded by houses. The main entrance was a narrow passage. There were no other regular entrances but at four or five places it was possible to get out through narrow openings. The ground near the main entrance was at an elevation, suitable for soldiers to fire from.

At about 4 p.m. Dyer received information that a meeting was being held at Jallianwala Bagh. He arrived at the spot with fifty riflemen: twenty-five Gurkhas and twenty-five Baluchis. He also had two armoured cars but these had to be left in the street because the entrance was too narrow for them to get through. The meeting was in progress at the other end of the Bagh about 100 yards from the raised ground where Dyer stationed his troops. The number of those present was variously estimated from 6,000 to 20,000.

Without giving the crowd any warning, Dyer ordered the troops to open fire. The people began to disperse immediately but the attack continued for about ten minutes and stopped only when the ammunition was on the point of exhaustion, enough being retained to ensure the safe retreat of the force. In all 1650 rounds were fired. The Hunter Committee Majority

Report put the number of the dead at approximately 379 and the wounded at about three times that number, but the Indians believed the casualties were far more numerous. After the Jallianwala Bagh firing no serious outbreak took place in Amritsar.

April 13 was the Hindu New Year's Day (*Baisakhi*) and had attracted people from surrounding villages to Amritsar to partake in the festival. This was clear because the Hunter Committee Majority Report noted that among the Jallianwala dead no less than 87 were strangers who had come into Amritsar from the neighbouring district. It was not denied that these strangers, as well as many of the Amritsar people who had assembled in the Bagh, might not have known about Dyer's proclamation. The Majority Report therefore observed: 'Notice to disperse... should have been given'. It said, further, that 'in continuing to fire for so long...General Dyer committed a grave error' but added that 'he honestly considered that he was called upon in discharge of his duty to take the extreme step which he did.' In his evidence Dyer conceded that it was 'quite possible that I could have dispersed them perhaps even without firing,' and explained that he did not adopt that course because 'I could disperse them for some time; then they would all come back and laugh at me, and I considered I would be making myself a fool.' Asked whether he would have opened fire with machine guns if the entrance had been wide enough for the armoured cars to pass through he replied, 'I think, probably yes.' To the question whether he took any measures for the relief of the wounded he emphatically answered 'No, certainly not. It is not my job.' He said that he wished to 'punish' those who were holding the meeting and his 'idea from the military point of view was to make a wide impression,' and he admitted that from time to time he changed the firing and directed it to places where the crowds were thickest.

In his report to the General Staff (25 August 1919) Dyer wrote:

> I fired and continued to fire until the crowd dispersed and I consider this is the least amount of firing which would produce the necessary moral and widespread effect it was my duty to produce if I was to justify my action. If more troops had been at hand the casualties would have been greater in proportion. It was no longer a question of merely dispersing the crowd, but one of producing a sufficient moral effect from a military point of view not only on those who were present, but more especially throughout the Punjab.

In the opinion of the Majority Report 'this was unfortunately a mistaken conception of his duty.'

The general verdict of the Hunter Committee's Minority Report on Dyer's conduct was that 'General Dyer by adopting an inhuman and un-British method of dealing with the subjects of His Majesty the King-Emperor, has done great disservice to the interest of British rule in India.' He was asked, 'did this aspect of the matter strike you, that by doing an act of that character you were doing a great disservice to the British Raj?' He promptly responded, 'I thought it would be doing a jolly lot of good and they would realize that they were not to be wicked '.

Another much condemned action of Dyer's was the 'crawling order' which he gave verbally on 19 April. It related to the 150 yard long street, with houses on both sides, in which Miss Sherwood had been assaulted. Dyer felt 'the street ought to be looked upon as sacred; therefore I posted pickets at both ends and told them, no Indians are to be allowed to pass along here,' and he added, 'if they had to pass they must go on all fours.' The order was countermanded on 26 April by the Punjab Government, but in the meantime about fifty persons had fallen foul of it. 'The order is certainly open to the objection,' the Hunter Committee Majority Report observed, 'that it caused unnecessary inconvenience to a number of people and that it unnecessarily punished the innocent as well as the guilty. Above all from an administrative point of view, in subjecting the Indian population to an act of humiliation, it has continued to be a cause of bitterness and racial ill-feeling long after it was recalled.'

4. LAHORE : There was no *hartal* in Lahore on 30 March. On 6 April there was a complete *hartal* and considerable excitement, but no violence. The situation became acute on the afternoon of 10 April when news of Gandhi's arrest at Palwal and the occurrences at Amritsar arrived. Police fired at a mob on the Mall because it wished to force its way to Government House where the Lieutenant Governor resided. One man had caught hold of the Deputy Commissioner and the mob was getting out of hand. The firing killed one person and wounded about seven. Near the Lohari Gate also, buckshot was fired twice after the mob stoned officials and the police. About eighteen persons were wounded and of these, three died later.

The mob controlled the city for two days and a mixed column of some 800 police and military under Colonel Frank Johnson arrived on the morning of 12 April to regain control. At Hira Mandi that day the police fired when the mob threw stones at them. One man was killed and about 18 wounded. On 13 April the railway station at Wagah, about fourteen miles from Lahore, was burnt, telegraph wires were cut, the railway track was damaged and an armoured train was derailed. On 14 April three prominent Hindu leaders were deported. The *hartal* which had commenced on 11 April ended on 18 April as the result of action by the military under Martial Law, which had been imposed on 15 April.

In the words of the Hunter Committee Majority Report, the administration of Martial Law in Lahore's civil area by Colonel Johnson 'was more intensive than elsewhere.' He commandeered motor cars and vehicles of all descriptions from Indians but issued exemption certificates to Europeans. He made it unlawful for more than two Indians to walk abreast and gave the following interesting reason for the order:

If more than two natives come and do not give way to a European, that is likely to lead to a breach of the peace.

Question-Who would commit the breach of the peace, the European?
Answer-Undoubtedly.
Question-Do you think he would be justified in doing so?
Answer-Certainly.

Another of Johnson's orders read:

All orders to be issued under martial law will be handed to such owners of property as I may select and it will be the duty of such owners of property to exhibit and to keep exhibiting all such orders. The duty of protecting such orders will, therefore, devolve on the owners of property and failure to ensure the proper protection and continued exhibition of my orders will result in severe punishment.

The selection of the properties to be required to exhibit the orders was made on the recommendation of the Criminal Investigation Department on the ground that the owners of those properties were not 'notoriously loyal.' When asked whether this was a reasonable order he proudly replied, 'Quite. I would do it again. It was one of the few brain-waves I had.' A notice stuck on the wall of the Sanatan Dharm College was torn down by an unknown person. As punishment, between 50 and 100 students and their professors were forced to march to the fort three miles away and interned there for about 30 hours. In order to keep the students 'out of mischief' he ordered the students of three other colleges to muster for a roll-call four times a day, which for medical students meant a walk of 16 miles a day. This programme was enforced daily for three weeks. The number of students so punished was over 1,000.

Johnson 'laid the greatest importance' on the notice that if any bomb was thrown on his troops, it would be deemed to have been thrown by all persons living within a radius of 100 yards, and proclaimed that after allowing an hour's time for the inhabitants to leave, he would dismantle and demolish all buildings within that area except mosques and temples.

5. KASUR : No *hartal* had occurred in Kasur either on 30 March or on 6 April, but one took place on 11 April when the news of Gandhi's arrest was received. It continued on 12 April, on which date the telegraph office and the railway station were attacked. One of the three trains which had halted at the signals contained several European passengers. All but two left the train and escaped with their lives, though some were injured. The two who remained in the train were Warrant Officers. They were armed with revolvers. When the train was driven into the station they stationed themselves on the platform near the door. They were pelted with stones by the crowd and fired their revolvers, wounding one man. When the crowd closed in upon them they tried to escape but were pursued, caught and beaten to death. When the mob began to attack government buildings, the police fired on them, killing four. Disorder subsided after troops had arrived in the afternoon.

During the Martial Law regime some unusual punishments were devised. When a schoolmaster reported that his boys had got out of control the school authorities were asked to send six boys for punishment, but the Martial Law officers thought the selected boys were too miserable-looking. So a parade was held and the six biggest boys were chosen and received six stripes each. All persons convicted of any offence, including not greeting a European, were required to put their foreheads on the ground. Some men were stripped and flogged in the presence of prostitutes.

6. GUJRANWALA DISTRICT : (a) *Gujranwala* : A *hartal* on 6 April passed off without violence but on 14 April the body of a calf was found hanging on a bridge near the railway station. The rumour spread that the police had killed and exposed the calf to create bad blood between Hindus and Muslims. Two or three men were hurt. The post office, the *tahsil*, the church, the *dak* bungalow and the district court were all burnt. The police fired more than once to disperse the mob.

Four aeroplanes flew over Gujranwala in the afternoon and troops arrived in the evening. One of the aeroplanes dropped eight bombs and also used its Lewis gun, two others used machine-guns and the fourth made no attack. In all, ten bombs were dropped but two did not explode. Nine persons were killed by attacks from the air.

(b) Disturbances resulting in damage or destruction of telegraph wires, railway lines and other property were also reported from some smaller towns in Gujranwala district.

7, 8. GUJRAT and LYALLPUR : Similar disturbances were reported from these cities as well as from some towns in those districts.

The Salaaming Order. A Martial Law order calculated to humiliate Indians was passed in Gujranwala district on 22 April and was extended to Lyallpur and Gujrat districts later:

We have come to know that Gujranwala District inhabitants do not usually show respect to the gazetted commissioners, European Civil and Military officers of His Imperial Majesty, by which the prestige and honour of the Government is not maintained. Therefore, we order that the inhabitants of Gujranwala district should show proper respect to these respectable officers, whenever they have occasion to meet them, in the same way as big and rich people of India are respected.

Whenever anyone is on horseback or is driving any kind of wheeled conveyance, he must get down. One who has opened or got an umbrella in his hand should close or lower it down, and all these persons should salute with their right hand respectfully.

Orders were also issued that students of the districts of Gujranwala, Gujrat and Lyallpur should attend roll-calls once a day, or more often as determined by the area officer, and salute a British flag. These orders were enforced even upon boys of five or six. An order of 19 May punished all boys over fourteen years of age from four schools in Lyallpur because two of them had contravened the *Salaaming* Order. They were to parade daily at 8 a.m. until the two offenders were given up, or until such time as the Martial Law authority considered necessary.

Sir Michael O'Dwyer told the Hunter Committee that 'General Dyer's action at Jallianwala Bagh was the decisive factor in crushing the rebellion, the seriousness of which is only now being generally realized.' But the Majority Report disagreed with this view: 'The action taken by General Dyer has also been described by others as having saved the situation in the Punjab and having averted a rebellion on a scale similar to the Mutiny. It does not, however, appear to us possible to draw this conclusion, particularly in view of the fact that it is not proved that a conspiracy to overthrow British power had been formed prior to the outbreaks.' As a matter of fact the official evidence itself showed that the rural population, as a whole, had nothing to do with the disturbances. Nevertheless, the Majority Report, in justifying the declaration of Martial Law and its continuance, found that the disturbances had developed into 'a state of open rebellion against the authority of the Government'. The Minority Report on the other hand said,

'We are unable to agree in the view that the riots in the Punjab were in the nature of rebellion' and concluded that the 'introduction of Martial Law and its continuance for the period for which it was continued were not justified.'

The Punjab Government attempted to defend the prolongation of Martial Law by suggesting a connection between the Punjab disturbances and the war with Afghanistan (which had been declared on 8 May). But there was no real evidence that Indian political leaders had been in touch with the Amir of Afghanistan (Amanullah). An official witness told the Hunter Committee, 'The position we take up is that we put you in possession of the evidence we have, but we do not claim really that it proves anything more than that the Amir took advantage of the troubles in India and that he had certain emissaries in India'. The Afghan troops who had crossed the border were repulsed. An armistice was followed by a treaty which recognized the complete independence of Afghanistan by removing British control over the country's foreign affairs. The British subsidies were also discontinued.

A Report by the Congress Committee on the Punjab disturbances concluded *inter alia* that:

The arrest and internment of Mr Gandhi, and the arrests and deportation of Drs Kitchlew and Satyapal were unjustifiable, and were the only direct cause of hysterical popular excitement.

The mob violence which began at Amritsar was directly due to the firing at the Railway overbridge, and the sight of the dead and wounded at a time when the excitement had reached white heat.

Whatever the cause of provocation, the mob excesses are deeply to be regretted and condemned.

So far as the facts are publicly known, no reasonable cause has been shown to justify the introduction of Martial law.

In each case, Martial Law was proclaimed after order had been completely restored.

Even if it be held that the introduction of Martial Law was a state necessity, it was unduly prolonged.

Most of the measures taken under Martial Law, in all the five districts, were unnecessary, cruel, oppressive and in utter disregard of the feelings of the people affected by them.

The Jallianwala Bagh massacre was a calculated piece of inhumanity towards utterly innocent and unarmed men, including children, and unparalleled for its ferocity in the history of modern British administration.

The authors of the Congress Report named Sir Michael O'Dwyer, General Dyer and Colonel Johnson and four other persons as having been guilty of such illegalities that 'they deserve to be impeached, but we purposely refrain from advising any such course, because we believe that India can only gain by waiving the right. Future purity will be sufficiently guaranteed by the dismissal of the officials concerned'. They also demanded the recall of Lord Chelmsford, the Viceroy.

The Congress report made much of the over-zealous methods of recruitment and collection of war funds employed by Sir Michael O'Dwyer and his administration, and indeed the Lieutenant-Governor himself admitted: 'no doubt some had exceeded the limits and may have used pressure'. But the implication that this had caused general unrest in the province and contributed to the outbreak of the disturbances was repelled by the Hunter Committee Majority Report, which rightly pointed out that 'Recruits were...mainly obtained from country districts. Comparatively few [had] joined the army from the towns where the disturbances broke out.'

Gandhi was conscious that his own followers had contributed to the tragic events. After being forcibly brought back to Bombay from Palwal he visited the various places in the Presidency where violence had recently erupted and confessed that he had made a 'Himalayan miscalculation' in thinking that the people were ready for a non-violent campaign; he therefore imposed a three-day penitential fast upon himself. On 18 April he called off the campaign and decided not to start it again without first creating a team of disciplined volunteers who understood his ideals. At the Amritsar Congress (December, 1919) he said:

> I can produce before you chapter and verse from Virangam, from Ahmedabad and from Bombay that there was violence on our part intended and committed. I agree that there was grave provocation given by the government in arresting Dr Kitchlew and Dr Satyapal and in arresting me who was bent on a mission of peace at the invitation of Dr Satyapal and Swamiji...But the Government went mad also at the time. I say, do not return madness with madness, but return madness with sanity and the whole situation will be yours.

The Hunter Committee investigations were still proceeding and Gandhi had not yet lost faith in the ultimate triumph of British justice.

At the Amritsar Congress, the party reiterated its earlier condemnation of the Montagu-Chelmsford reforms. It declared them to be 'inadequate, unsatisfactory and disappointing,' but the leaders were sharply divided on the question whether the reforms should be rejected out of hand or should be worked while asking for improvement. C.R.Das of Bengal, a formidable intellectual and brilliant barrister, strongly urged rejection but Gandhi successfully opposed him and the following resolution was passed: 'This Congress trusts that, so far as may be possible, the people will so work the Reforms as to secure an early establishment of full responsible Government, and this Congress offers its thanks to the Rt. Hon. E. S. Montagu for his labours in connection with the Reforms.'

This was the first time that Gandhi had taken a vigorous part in Congress proceedings. That his point of view prevailed against the advocacy of a leader of the stature of Das was a clear notice to everyone that he was the man of the future. As Jawaharlal Nehru said: 'The Amritsar Congress was the first Gandhi Congress. Lokamanya Tilak was also present and took a prominent part in the deliberations, but there could be no doubt about it that the majority of the delegates, and even more so the great crowds outside, looked to Gandhi for leadership. The slogan *"Mahatma Gandhi ki jai"* began to dominate the Indian political horizon.'

On 31 December 1919 Gandhi pleaded in his weekly, *Young India*, 'The Reforms Act coupled with the Proclamation[1] is an earnest of the intention of the British people to do justice to India and it ought to remove suspicions on that score...Our duty therefore is not to subject the Reforms to carping criticism but to settle down quietly to work so as to make them a success.'

How Gandhi before long was transformed from a co-operator into a hard non-co-operator is the subject of the next chapter.

The Muslim League also held its annual session at Amritsar at the same time as Congress. On the opening day of the League meeting, a number of prominent Hindus—including Gandhi and Motilal—were present. The League resolution on the reforms ran parallel to the resolution by Congress. It described the reforms as 'inadequate and unsatisfactory' and expressed the hope that Parliament would soon establish full responsible government in India. In the meantime, it called upon Indians to avail themselves of the opportunity which was now being offered to them.

---

[1] On the very day on which the Government of India Act received Royal Assent (23 December 1919), a Royal Proclamation, as a gesture of conciliation, had granted amnesty to political prisoners in India resulting in the release of leaders such as the Ali brothers, Satyapal and Kitchlew.

CHAPTER 11

THE NON-CO-OPERATION MOVEMENT

THE KHILAFAT QUESTION

Turkey's decision to side with Germany in World War I had posed a dilemma for Indian Muslims, but on the whole they had thought it expedient to support the allied war effort and had hoped that they would be able to plead for lenient terms for Turkey, should it be defeated. The British Government was well aware of this and Prime Minister Lloyd George had placated Muslim fears by a statement on 5 January 1918: 'Nor are we fighting to deprive Turkey of its capital or of the rich and renowned lands of Asia Minor and Thrace which are predominantly Turkish in race.'

After the war, the question of defeated Turkey caused the Indian Muslims grave concern. They wished that the Ottoman Sultan should retain all his territory because only then would he be able to command the resources to enable him to maintain his status as the Khalifa of the Muslim world and the keeper of the holy places of Islam. However, the first blow to the institution of the Khilafat had already been struck in 1916 by some of the Khalifa's own Muslim subjects, the Arabs, who, stimulated by the wartime ideas of self-determination, and assisted by the British, had raised the banner of revolt against their imperial master under the leadership of no less a person than Hussain, the Sharif of Mecca, a descendant of the Prophet (PBUH) and the guardian of Muslim shrines. On 15 December 1916 the British Government had recognized him as King of the Hijaz. But the Indian Muslims regarded him as a stooge of the British and believed that the holy places of Islam had in fact passed under non-Muslim control.

During the delay in settling the status of Turkey after the war, the reports appearing in various journals in Europe as to the punishment of Turkey for allying itself with Germany fed the anxiety of the Indian Muslims. An organization for the support of Turkey, the Khilafat Conference, came into being in the middle of 1919 and held a public session at Delhi on 23 and 24 November 1919. As explained in the previous pages, Hindu-Muslim relations during recent years had been exceptionally cordial. The Muslim League and Congress had held their respective annual meetings at the same towns, and had taken a concerted position on India's political ambitions. They had also fraternized during the Rowlatt agitation.

Gandhi had displayed his sympathy for the cause of Turkey as early as 1918. After the Delhi War Conference he had written to the Viceroy bracketing the cause of Turkey with India's own cause of self-rule: 'In the most scrupulous regard for the rights of those (Mohammedan) States and for the Muslim sentiment as to their places of worship, and your just and timely treatment of India's claim to Home Rule, lies the safety of the Empire.' He attended the Khilafat Conference at Delhi and on 24 November presided over it. Another Hindu leader, Swami Shradhanand, also attended the Conference. On Gandhi's advice the Conference passed a resolution refusing to co-operate with the government unless the Khilafat and holy places were treated in accordance with Muslim wishes.

The failure of the rebellion of 1857 had reduced the influence of the *ulema* in Muslim politics, but the Khilafat movement offered them the opportunity to stage a come-back. A new Muslim organization, the Jamiat-i-Ulema-i-Hind, came into being. At the end of December 1919, no less than four parties held their sessions simultaneously at Amritsar to demonstrate Hindu-Muslim solidarity. These were Congress, the Muslim League, the Khilafat Conference and the Jamiat. The League session was presided over by Hakim Ajmal Khan, who was also a prominent leader of the Congress party.

Congress passed a resolution urging the British Government 'to settle the Turkish question in accordance with the sentiments of Indian Muslims'. Most of the prominent Congress men also attended the opening meeting of the League: Gandhi, Motilal Nehru, and Malaviya among others.

The League expressed 'its deep disappointment' at the attitude of the British Government toward the question of the Khilafat and warned that 'under the circumstances the Mussalmans would be fully justified to carry on all the possible methods of constitutional agitation open to them, including a boycott of the British Army, if it is likely to be used outside India for imperial and anti-Islamic purposes.' It also placed on record 'its deep-seated and unshakable devotion to the sacred person of His Imperial Majesty [the Ottoman Sultan] as successor of the Prophet (PBUH) and head of Islam'. Another resolution ran: 'With a view to reciprocating the good feelings shown towards the Mussalmans by their Hindu brethren and to strengthening the growing unity between them, the Mussalmans of India should, on the occasion of the *Bakar-Eid* festival, substitute, as far as possible, the sacrifice of other animals in place of cows'.

Both Congress and the Muslim League also strongly condemned the military excesses in the Jallianwala Bagh and elsewhere and demanded the punishment of the main culprits. We thus have a picture of all shades of public opinion in India united on the twin issues of the Khilafat and the Punjab atrocities. Gandhi was able to persuade Congress and the League to pass resolutions in favour of giving a chance to the reforms principally because the final determination of both the questions which troubled them was still pending...the Hunter Committee had not yet produced its report and the Turkish peace terms had not yet been officially formulated.

On the second day of the League session, the brothers Muhammad Ali and Shaukat Ali, who had been interned in May 1915 and had only just been released, joined the proceedings; when they addressed the gathering 'the audience was moved to tears.' These two colourful and passionately religious brothers...especially the Oxford educated Muhammad Ali who had a good command of spoken and written English...soon enlivened the Khilafat Conference, which eclipsed the more sedate Muslim League during the following years. In the course of his presidential speech at the Cocanada Congress, Muhammad Ali revealed that no beef was consumed in their household but with characteristic outspokenness pointed out 'that by far the most numerous owners of cows are the Hindus, and that if they did not sell cows after they had ceased to give milk, there would be much less cow-killing than there is today'.

Why did Gandhi, an orthodox Hindu, decide to champion so whole-heartedly the cause of the Caliphate, which was a purely Muslim question without any direct link with India's own movement for self-government? It is best to seek the answer to this question in Gandhi's own pronouncements on the subject. His approach, as usual, was a mixture of religion and practical politics. He wrote in *Young India* (20 October 1921): 'I claim that with us both the Khilafat is the central fact, with Maulana Mohammad Ali because it is his religion, with me because in laying down my life for the Khilafat I ensure the safety of the cow, that is my religion, from the Mussalman knife. Both hold *swaraj* equally dear because only by *swaraj* is the safety of our respective faiths possible.'

At another time he said that the Khilafat movement offered an opportunity, which would not recur for another hundred years, to prove that the Muslim was the brother of the Hindu. Again, 'We talk of Hindu-Mohammedan unity. It would be an empty phrase if the Hindus held aloof from the Mohammedans when their vital interests are at stake.'

On 19 January 1920 a Khilafat deputation of thirty-five persons waited on the Viceroy. It was led by Ansari, who read the address, and included

the Ali brothers, Abul Kalam Azad, Jinnah, Kitchlew, Gandhi and
Shradhanand. The Viceroy was unable to hold out any real hope that
Turkey would escape punishment for its defeat. In February a Khilafat
delegation led by Muhammad Ali sailed for Europe. On 17 March they met
Prime Minister Lloyd George. Muhammad Ali reiterated that, if the
Khalifa was to defend the faith adequately, his pre-war territorial status
must be restored. Asked whether he was opposed to the independence of
the Arabs, Muhammad Ali replied in the affirmative. Lloyd George said
that Turkey could not be treated differently from the defeated Christian
powers. The principle of self-determination would be applied to all
equally.

While the Muhammad Ali delegation was still in Europe, the terms of
the Treaty of Sevres were published (15 May 1920). The Sultan's empire
was to be dismembered: the Arab lands were to become independent;
Syria was to become a mandate of France, and Mesopotamia and Palestine
of Britain; Smyrna and Thrace were to be made over to Greece. But Turkey
was allowed to retain Constantinople.

On 28 May the Muhammad Ali delegation sent an appeal to the
Sultan not to accept the peace terms which contained the following
argument:

> The Khalifa is the repository of the sacred Traditions of our Prophet [PBUH],
> and, as your Majesty is aware, according to the most authentic reports, he
> commanded the Mussalmans on his death-bed not to permit or tolerate any sort
> or kind of non-Moslem control over any portion of the Jazeerat-ul-Arab, which
> includes Syria, Palestine and Mesopotamia as well as the region known to
> European geographers as the peninsula of Arabia. No Mussalman can therefore
> agree to the exercise of any control by mandatories of the powers in Syria,
> Palestine or Mesopotamia, and what no Mussalman can submit to consistently
> with his creed, the Successor of our Prophet [PBUH] can submit to still less.

It so happened that it was also on 28 May 1920 that the Hunter
Committee Majority and Minority Reports were published in India. The
Majority Report raised a storm of protest. A special session of Congress
was summoned and convened at Calcutta in September.

In the meantime, an All-Parties Conference met at Allahabad under the
auspices of the Central Khilafat Committee to formulate a response to the
Treaty of Sevres; on 2 June they decided to launch a non-co-operation
movement and appointed a sub-committee to give practical effect to the
programme. The sub-committee consisted of six Muslims and Gandhi.

On 22 June a memorial signed by a large number of leaders and *ulema* was sent to the Viceroy stating that if their demands were not heeded they would resort to non-co-operation on 1 August. On the same date Gandhi also personally wrote to the Viceroy to explain 'my connection with and my conduct in the Khilafat question' . He said he had begun to interest himself in the question from the earliest stage of the war because during his stop at London on his way from South Africa to India he had noticed 'how deeply moved the little Mussalman world in London was when Turkey decided to throw in her lot with Germany.' The peace terms and 'Your Excellency's defence of them have given the Mussalmans of India a shock from which it will be difficult for them to recover...I consider that, as a staunch Hindu wishing to live on terms of the closest friendship with my Mussalman countrymen, I should be an unworthy son of India if I did not stand by them in their hour of trial... The report of the Majority of the Hunter Committee, Your Excellency's despatch thereon and Mr Montagu's reply have only aggravated the distrust. In these circumstances the only course open to one like me is either in despair to sever all connection with British rule or, if I still retained faith in the inherent superiority of the British constitution to all others at present in vogue, to adopt such means as will rectify the wrong done, and thus restore confidence. I have not lost faith in such superiority and I am not without hope that somehow or other justice will yet be rendered if we show the requisite capacity for suffering.'

This letter makes two important points clear. First, the main issue at this stage was the Khilafat; the Punjab atrocities were a subsidiary question which merely aggravated the main issue. Secondly, Gandhi still subscribed to the common Indian nationalist view that it was the die-hard bureaucracy in India that was chiefly responsible for the harshness of British rule in India and that Indians could obtain redress by appealing to the fair-minded British people and parliament.

Yet less than two and a half months later, when Congress met in an emergency session at Calcutta, Gandhi had lost all hope in British justice, and the Punjab grievances had become the main issue. It was the attitude of the British people and government toward the Jallianwala massacre and toward Dyer, who perpetrated it, that quickly transformed the erstwhile loyal Mahatma into a rebel.

After the submission of the Hunter Committee Majority and Minority reports, and the acceptance by the government of the Majority Report, the only official who received any punishment was

General Dyer,[1] who was compulsorily retired although he received considerable support in parliament as well as outside it. On the crucial question of responsibility, the opinion of the Secretary of State, Montagu, was that Dyer had acted to the best of his understanding and with sincerity of purpose, but he had committed an error of judgement.

An interesting debate on Dyer's conduct took place in the House of Commons Committee of Supply[2] on 8 July 1920. Winston Churchill, Secretary of State for War, told the Committee that Dyer's appeal had been dismissed by the Army Council in England and explained that retirement from service was the lightest punishment that could have been awarded. Dyer could have been stripped of his rank or criminally prosecuted. Though Dyer's admirers failed to carry the day in the Commons, they were victorious in the Upper House. On 20 July the House of Lords ('the blue and brainless blood of England', to use Jinnah's description) passed a resolution by 129 to 86 deploring the action taken against Dyer as 'unjust to that officer and as establishing a precedent dangerous to the preservation of order in face of rebellion'.

Immediately after the defeat of the motion in the Commons, the *Morning Post* opened a fund to reward Dyer for his role as 'Saviour of India'. It received more than the target of £26,000. Dyer was also presented with a sword of honour. One third of the purse was subscribed in India. And from Bengal, 6,250 British women sent a petition to the Prime Minister in London protesting against the treatment meted out to the General. That so many British people regarded Dyer as a national hero deeply shocked public opinion in India. The approval of the General's conduct by the House of Lords, whom the Indian intelligentsia regarded as the mouthpiece of the British ruling classes, was especially shocking. It was the last straw that destroyed Indian hopes of ever receiving racial justice at British hands.

The Punjab atrocities, in fact, created far more bitterness than the rebellion of 1857: the Indians who had figured in the 'mutiny' had mainly been sepoys and other persons with vested interests, plus the riff-raff. Indian nationalism was then still unborn and Indians with Western education were negligible in number and influence. In 1919, on the other hand, India was politically alive and its leaders considered themselves the

---

[1] O'Dwyer's role in the Punjab disturbances was not forgotten. On 13 March 1940 he was shot by a Sikh in London just as a public meeting in Caxton Hall was dispersing.

[2] The matter was discussed in the Committee of Supply because those who wished to censure the government for its treatment of Dyer had chosen the procedure of moving resolutions for the reduction of the salary of the Secretary of State for India.

equals of the best Britain could produce. It was the pride and self respect of this new and sensitive India that had been galled. Even those Indians who valued the British connection were disenchanted. Dyer had not saved the British Empire in India, he had maimed it, and it became only a question of time before the Indians would shake off the yoke of foreign rule. Had the Hindus and the Muslims, who had displayed such solidarity in recent years, not fallen out with each other, the British would have been compelled to quit India much earlier than 1947.

From now on, the Punjab wrongs became increasingly important and, since they were a genuine Indian grievance, took a permanent and prominent place in Indian consciousness. The Khilafat question, which directly concerned only the Muslims, was before long extinguished by the Turks themselves.

For the time being, however, the momentum of the Khilafat movement carried it forward. In the summer of 1920 it had a tragic offshoot...the *hijrat* movement. Some 18,000 Muslims, mostly from Sind and the North-West Frontier Province, sold their land and belongings and sought asylum in Afghanistan, which was the nearest *dar ul-Islam*. They had been encouraged to do so by Amir Amanullah but in the event he refused to admit them. Many of the pilgrims perished by the roadside; others returned broken and destitute.[1]

On 1 August the khilafatists under Gandhi formally launched their non-co-operation campaign. The Mahatma on that date returned his war medals to the Viceroy stating, 'I cannot wear them with an easy conscience so long as my Mussulman countrymen have to labour under wrong done to their religious sentiment. I venture to return these medals, in pursuance of the scheme of non-co-operation inaugurated today in connection with the khilafat movement.'

While the Muslims had enthusiastically embraced Gandhi's non-co-operation programme, he still had to obtain the support of the predominantly Hindu Congress. When Congress met in special session at Calcutta (4-8 September 1920), the only prominent Hindu leader who supported Gandhi was Motilal Nehru, the leading light of the Allahabad bar and Congress leader of the United Provinces. Lajpat Rai, who presided over the sessions, was an avowed opponent of non-co-operation and was strongly supported by other Congress veterans such as Das, Bipin Chandra Pal, Annie Besant, Malaviya and Jinnah. But Gandhi carried the day with

---

[1] Jinnah, Shafi, Iqbal and Fazl-i-Husain were opposed to *hijrat*.

the help of Muslims and Hindus at the popular level.[1] Tilak, who with his grass-roots popularity might have made a difference to the outcome, had breathed his last on the very day on which Gandhi had inaugurated the non-co-operation campaign (1 August).

Since the resulting resolution, which was passed by 1886 votes to 884, explains the spirit of the non-co-operation programme, it needs to be quoted in full.

In view of the fact that on the Khilafat question both the Indian and Imperial Governments have signally failed in their duty towards the Mussalmans of India, and the Prime Minister has deliberately broken his pledged word given to them, and that it is the duty of every non-Muslim Indian in every legitimate manner to assist his Mussulman brother in his attempt to remove the religious calamity that has over-taken him;

And in view of the fact that in the matter of the events of April of 1919, both the said Governments have grossly neglected or failed to protect the innocent people of the Punjab and punish officers guilty of unsoldierly and barbarous behaviour towards them, and have exonerated Sir Michael O'Dwyer who proved himself, directly or indirectly, responsible for most of the official crimes, and callous to the sufferings of the people placed under his administration, and that the debate in the House of Commons and specially in the House of Lords betrayed a woeful lack of sympathy with the people of India, and showed virtual support of the systematic terrorism and frightfulness adopted in the Punjab and that the latest Viceregal pronouncement is proof of entire absence of repentance in the matter of the Khilafat and the Punjab;

This Congress is of opinion that there can be no contentment in India without redress of the two aforementioned wrongs and that the only effectual means to vindicate national honour and to prevent a repetition of similar wrongs in future is the establishment of *swarajya*. This Congress is further of opinion that there is no course left open for the people of India but to approve of and adopt the policy of progressive, non-violent non-co-operation inaugurated by Gandhiji until the said wrongs are righted and *swarajya* is established.

And inasmuch as a beginning should be made by the classes who have hitherto moulded and represented public opinion, and inasmuch as Government consolidates its power through titles and honours bestowed on the people, through schools controlled by it, its law courts, and its legislative councils, and inasmuch as it is desirable in the prosecution of the movement to take the minimum risk and to call for the least sacrifice compatible with the attainment of the desired object, this Congress advises:

---

[1] For Pal's amendment to Gandhi's resolution and Jinnah's support to it, *see,* p. 226.

(a) surrender of titles and honorary offices and resignation from nominated seats in local bodies;

(b) refusal to attend Government levees, durbars, and other official and semi-official functions held by Government officials or in their honour;

(c) gradual withdrawal of children from schools and colleges owned, aided or controlled by Government, and in place of such schools and colleges, establishment of National schools and colleges in the various provinces;

(d) gradual boycott of British courts by lawyers and litigants, and establishment of private arbitration courts by their aid, for the settlement of private disputes;

(e) refusal on the part of the military, clerical and labouring classes to offer themselves as recruits for service in Mesopotamia;

(f) withdrawal by candidates of their candidature for election to the reformed councils, and refusal on the part of the voters to vote for any candidate who may, despite the Congress advice, offer himself for election;

(g) boycott of foreign goods.

And inasmuch as non-co-operation has been conceived as a measure of discipline and self-sacrifice without which no nation can make real progress, and inasmuch as an opportunity should be given in the very first stage of non-co-operation to every man, woman and child, for such discipline and self-sacrifice, this Congress advises adoption of *swadeshi* in piece-goods on a vast scale, and inasmuch as the existing mills of India with indigenous capital and control do not manufacture sufficient yarn and sufficient cloth for the requirements of the nation, and are not likely to do so for a long time to come, this Congress advises immediate stimulation of further manufacture on a large scale by means of reviving hand-spinning in every home and hand-weaving on the part of the millions of weavers who have abandoned their ancient and honourable calling for want of encouragement.

The first open clash between Gandhi and Jinnah took place when the Home Rule League met at Bombay on 3 October 1920. Mrs Besant had resigned as President of the League and Gandhi, the new President, chaired the meeting. To bring the goal of the League in line with the programme just adopted by Congress, Gandhi wished to change its creed and also to re-name it Swaraj Sabha. Jinnah opposed him without success and in protest resigned along with some others. Gandhi invited him back to share in 'the new life that has opened up before the country'. Jinnah's reply showed how worried he felt over Gandhi's agitational politics: 'If by "new life" you mean your methods and your programme, I am afraid I cannot accept them; for I am fully convinced that it must lead to disaster...your extreme programme has for the moment struck the imagination mostly of the inexperienced youth and the ignorant and the illiterate. All this means complete disorganisation and chaos.'

The annual session of Congress at Nagpur (26-31 December 1920) witnessed some remarkable developments. Das had brought a strong contingent from Bengal and Assam to reverse the defeat he had sustained at Calcutta. But Das, Jinnah, Malaviya, Lajpat Rai and their supporters were all once more overwhelmed by the Gandhi juggernaut. In the end not only was the Calcutta resolution on non-co-operation accepted but, in the interests of maintaining a united front, the affirming motion was proposed by Das and seconded by Lajpat Rai.

The Nagpur Congress displayed its loss of faith in the British people and parliament by deciding to wind up the British branch of Congress and discontinue the publication of its paper *India*. 'We have no friends outside India; let there be no mistake about that,' one delegate explained, 'we must make or mar our future.' Congress also broke its tradition of professing loyalty to members of the British royal family. It passed a resolution to boycott the 'functions or festivities' during the forthcoming visit of the Duke of Connaught.[1] It also changed the creed of Congress and reorganized its structure.[2]

But the most extraordinary resolution was the one which envisaged the attainment of *swaraj* within one year. The reader must be given this curiously worded resolution in full:

---

[1] The aged Duke was the last surviving son of Queen Victoria and was coming to India in January 1921 to inaugurate the Legislative Council and the Chamber of Princes set up under the Montagu-Chelmsford reforms. Originally the King had nominated the Prince of Wales for this ceremony but the prince could not make the trip at the required time for reasons of health.

When the Prince of Wales's visit in connection with the reforms was announced, Gandhi was still a co-operator. So at the Amritsar Congress, at which Gandhi got through his resolution in favour of working the reforms, a resolution also welcomed 'the announcement that His Royal Highness the Prince of Wales will visit India next winter' and assured him of 'a warm reception by the people of this country'. But when the Prince of Wales arrived in November 1921, his visit was boycotted by Congress despite the Viceroy's assurance that this time it had no political purpose.

[2] See, pp. 192-3.

In order that the Khilafat and the Punjab wrongs may be redressed and *swarajya* established within one year, this Congress urges upon all the public bodies, whether affiliated to the Congress or otherwise, to devote their exclusive attention to the promotion of non-violence and non-co-operation with the Government and, inasmuch as the movement of non-co-operation can only succeed by complete co-operation amongst the people themselves, this Congress calls upon public association to advance Hindu-Muslim unity and the Hindu delegates of this Congress call upon the leading Hindus to settle all disputes between Brahmins and non-Brahmins, wherever they may be existing, and to make a special effort to rid Hinduism of the reproach of Untouchability, and respectfully urges the religious heads to help the growing desires to reform Hinduism in the matter of its treatment of the suppressed classes.

At the Calcutta Special Session, Gandhi's favourite pursuit, handspinning, had become a part of the Congress programme. At the Nagpur session his favourite goal, the removal of Untouchability, was now elevated to the same position.

The impossible dream of *swaraj* within one year was not realized but it did induce many persons to participate in the non-co-operation campaign because they believed that their suffering would be shortlived and would be followed by the bliss of freedom. Subhas Bose, who had been successful in the competitive examination for the Indian Civil Service in England, resigned his position and hurried back to India to participate in the national struggle. He landed at Bombay on 16 July 1921 and managed to secure an interview with the Mahatma on the same day. His object was to get from the leader of the campaign a clear conception of his plan of action. He summed up his disappointment as follows:

What was to him a question of faith...namely, that *swaraj* would be won within one year...was by no means clear to me and personally speaking, I was prepared to work for a much longer period. However, I had no other course but to feel thankful for what I had been able to learn after an hour's conversation. But though I tried to persuade myself at the time that there must have been a lack of understanding on my part, my reason told me clearly, again and again, that there was a deplorable lack of clarity in the plan which the Mahatma had formulated and that he himself did not have a clear idea of the successive stages of the campaign which would bring India to her cherished goal of freedom.

JINNAH BREAKS WITH CONGRESS

Another occurrence of far-reaching consequences at the Nagpur Congress was the walk-out, in disgust, of Jinnah. Ultimately, by attaining the same status among the Muslims as Gandhi had achieved among the Hindus, he became Gandhi's most powerful adversary and successfully led the movement for Pakistan.

It is important to remember that Jinnah and Gandhi at that stage both stood for *swaraj*, they both stood for the preservation of the pre-war territorial and spiritual status of the Sultan of Turkey, and they were both equally angry that the officers responsible for the Punjab atrocities had got off so lightly. They even agreed in principle that non-co-operation was a suitable weapon for paralysing the government. But they differed violently about the timing of the non-co-operation movement. Gandhi stood for launching it immediately. Jinnah believed that the country was not ready for it and its premature start would only harm the participants without bringing down the government. He believed that careful preparations were necessary before taking action. Let us elaborate.

That Jinnah was as deeply concerned about the fate of the Sultan as anyone was demonstrated in the summer of 1919 when he led a deputation of the All-India Muslim League to London to plead the Sultan's cause. He forwarded a memorandum to Prime Minister Lloyd George with a letter dated 4 September 1919. The memorandum warned that 'if Great Britain becomes a party in reducing HIM the Sultan of Turkey and the Khalifa of the Muslim world to the status of a petty sovereign, the reaction in India will be colossal and abiding'. In 'his letter Jinnah had also asked for an interview, but there is no record to show that Lloyd George acceded to the request.

Gandhi's non-co-operation resolution, as already stated, was passed at a special session of Congress at Calcutta (4 to 8 September 1920). During the debate on the resolution Bipin Chandra Pal moved an amendment aimed mainly at delaying the launch of the movement until the Prime Minister of the United Kingdom had been requested to receive a deputation from India 'to lay before him the statement of India's grievances coupled with a demand for immediate autonomy' and until preparations for launching of the non-co-operation movement had been made. He asked the audience whether they felt convinced that Gandhi's programme was practicable. Jinnah supported Pal's amendment because, while accepting non-co-operation as the ideal to be aimed at, it recommended a course of preparation before putting the ideal into practice: 'Make preparation,' he pleaded, 'have your national schools and a court of arbitration. Find out in what other directions you are able to practice non-co-operation. When you have understood the whole situation you could begin to practise led by the best brains amongst you.'

The All-India Muslim League also met in special session at Calcutta at the same time (7 September 1920). In his presidential address there, Jinnah said:

> We are not going to rest content until we have attained the fullest political freedom in our own country. Mr Gandhi has placed his programme of non-co-operation, supported by the authority of the Khilafat Conference, before the country. It is now for you to consider whether or not you approve of its principle; and approving of its principle, whether or not you approve of its details. The operations of this scheme will strike at the individual in each of you, and therefore it rests with you alone to measure your strength and to weigh the pros and the cons of the question before you arrive at a decision. But once you have decided to march, let there be no retreat under any circumstances.

Speaking of the Punjab atrocities and the destruction of the Ottoman Empire, Jinnah stated, 'the one attacks our liberty, the other our faith.' The Khilafat question, he emphasised, was a matter of life and death from the Muslim point of view.

Jinnah's criticism of Gandhi's non-co-operation movement soon became stronger. In the first week of October, as already described, he angrily disagreed with Gandhi when the latter changed the creed of the Home Rule League. On 19 December 1920, Jinnah gave an address to the students of Ferguson College, Poona. Gandhi's non-co-operation movement had by then been in operation for some months and Jinnah was now in a position to comment on the extent of its efficacy in practice. He said that though he was a believer in the policy of non-co-operation, Gandhi's programme could not be put into practice 'today' with a view to paralysing the government because the requisite materials for its enforcement were lacking. The contemplated boycott of foreign goods was impracticable; the Congress decision to boycott the councils was unfortunate because there was no dearth of other candidates; to undermine existing educational institutions before new ones could be built was going the wrong way about the business; and a few lawyers who had given up their practice could not by themselves paralyse the system. In his opinion, the whole programme was harmful and impracticable in the current state of political consciousness.

Then came the annual session of Congress at Nagpur, where Gandhi's non-co-operation resolution from the Calcutta special session was Confirmed and the creed of Congress was changed to 'the attainment of *Swarajya* by the people of India by all legitimate and peaceful means.' Of the thousands who attended, only Jinnah had the courage to walk to the rostrum and oppose both the items. He explained that he did not dispute the fact that 'the government have done us repeated wrongs of an enormous character which have made our blood boil', but that was not the issue before the people. He said that his objection to the new creed was that it did not make it clear whether *swarajya* meant severance of all connection with Britain or not. Personally he wanted 'to keep the British connection.' With regard to non-co-operation he said 'Let me tell you once more, that that weapon will not destroy the British Empire...it is neither logical nor is it politically sound or wise, nor practically capable of being put in execution'. He said that he knew that Gandhi commanded the majority in that gathering but he appealed to him 'to pause, to cry halt before it is too late'.

The crowd had persistently interrupted Jinnah with hostile shouts. At one point, when he referred to Gandhi as 'Mister,' the crowd cried 'Mahatma'. At another, when he called Muhammad Ali 'Mister', he evoked shouts of 'Maulana.' This time he remonstrated, 'if you will not allow me the liberty to address you and speak of a man in the language in which I think it is right, I say you are denying me the liberty which you are asking for.' After having his say he left the meeting in protest.

Among the audience during Jinnah's speech was Colonel Wedgwood, who had come to attend the session as a fraternal delegate of the British Labour Party. He was so deeply impressed with Jinnah's courage that he openly praised him to his hecklers' face: 'I do not know enough about Mr Jinnah's politics to say whether I agree with him or not, but I do know that a man who has the courage to come to this audience and tell you what he has told you is a man for my money.' He exclaimed with satisfaction that India was on the road to freedom as she was capable of producing at least one man who had enough strength of character to stand by his conviction in the face of huge opposition, and no support whatsoever.

The Muslim League session, which was convened at Nagpur immediately after the Congress session there in December 1920, was presided over by the veteran Congress leader M. A. Ansari. He asserted that 'so far as the Mussalmans are concerned the principle of non-co-operation is not a new idea; rather it is a clear and definite injunction of the divine *Shariat* which the Mussalmans of India had in their forgetfulness consigned to oblivion.' A resolution affirmed the League's support for non-co-operation and expressed satisfaction at the progress of the movement. Another resolution, echoing the Nagpur Congress resolution regarding the change of creed, declared that one of the objects of the League 'shall be the attainment of *swaraj* by the people of India by all peaceful and legitimate means.' Jinnah, realizing it was not his day, did not even bother to attend the meeting. He had left Nagpur on the very day he had walked out of the Congress meeting.

So it was not Jinnah's logic that prevailed but the emotional appeal of Gandhi and his disciples, the eloquent Urdu-speaking Muslim 'nationalists' such as the Ali brothers, Abul Kalam Azad, Ansari, Kitchlew and Hasrat Mohani. For the time being everyone followed Gandhi. Choudhry Khaliquzzaman, afterwards a prominent League leader, recalled in his book, *Pathway to Pakistan,* 'I was wholeheartedly for Gandhiji's policies at the time and knew too well that but for him both the Khilafat and Congress would suffer a reverse.' While addressing the League session at Lahore in May 1924, Jinnah explained that since 1920, the League had been forced to the background because 'the policy and the programme of non-co-operation enunciated and formulated by Mahatma Gandhi was the order of the day'.

NON-CO-OPERATION IN ACTION

Defenders of non-co-operation said that the movement was not only negative...renunciation of titles and the triple boycott of legislatures, law courts and educational institutions in receipt of government funds...but that it also had a positive side. The positive side consisted of the establishment of national colleges and schools; the formation of arbitration courts; the promotion of *swadeshi*, especially the expansion of handspinning and weaving; the removal of Untouchability; the promotion of temperance for the dual purpose of the moral uplift of the people and the loss of liquor revenue to government; and the building up of Hindu-Muslim unity. 'Moreover, critics forget', declared M. A. Ansari from the presidential chair of the Muslim League session at Nagpur, 'that non-co-operation is not an end in itself, but simply a means to attain *swaraj*, which surely is the most constructive of all constructive things'.

The look and spirit of India certainly underwent a rapid change. Fashionable men discarded European suits and fashionable women their silks and satins. *Khaddar* cloth became respectable and the Gandhi cap became a symbol of nationalism. In Jawaharlal Nehru's words, 'a new class of delegate, chiefly drawn from the lower middle classes, became the type of Congressman...and a new life and enthusiasm and earnestness became evident in Congress circles.' Many sincerely believed that the Mahatma's promise of *swaraj* within one year would be fulfilled.

But human nature being what it is, when it came to making practical sacrifices, non-co-operation achieved only a limited amount of success. Gandhi had aimed at enlisting a crore (ten million) of members, collecting a crore of rupees for the Tilak Memorial Swarajya Fund and introducing twenty lakhs (two million) of *charkhas* (spinning wheels). The membership reached only half the desired number; the fund exceeded the target; and the charkhas almost reached the prescribed figure.

The boycott of Councils was a success in the sense that Congress candidates withdrew their candidature and most of the voters kept away from the polling booths. On the other hand, all the seats were captured by non-Congress men, most of whom were responsive to government wishes.

Several hundred lawyers at first renounced their practice but most of them drifted back. The functioning of the official courts was not disrupted. The attempt to set up rival arbitration courts was a failure. However, some of the most eminent lawyers who had given up their profession did not resume it and became invaluable full-time stalwarts of Congress. Prominent among them were Das, Motilal Nehru and his son Jawaharlal, and Rajendra Prasad.

Only a negligible number of title holders renounced their honours[1] and only a negligible number of government servants left their posts. Most importantly, the army and the police were not affected. Titles, however, lost must of their glamour. Vigorous picketing led to a decline in the consumption of liquor but sales returned to normal when the pickets were removed.

Though the movement for the boycott of educational institutions created much youthful excitement at first, it had no appreciable effect on the existing system of education. Of the newly-started national universities the most notable were that at Ahmadabad, with Gandhi as its Chancellor, and the National Muslim University (Jamia Millia Islamia) at Aligarh,

---

[1] The poet Rabindranath Tagore did renounce his knighthood but this was before Gandhi and Congress sent out their call for the renunciation of titles. Tagore had acted independently after the Amritsar killings. In fact he did not subscribe to the Gandhian conception of non-violent non-co-operation. He believed that non-violence was for those who sought spiritual perfection and that it was not safe to impose it on everyone for the furtherance of political ends.

with Muhammad Ali as its principal. The latter was afterwards moved to Delhi and is still flourishing.

There were impressive bonfires of foreign cloth but the boycott of foreign cloth did not achieve much success. Several leaders, including Patel and Tagore, were against the wanton destruction of valuable cloth when it could have been used to clothe some of the poor millions who went half-naked. Nor did the efforts to remove Untouchability make any discernible headway.

The worst setbacks, of course, were the failures to practice non-violence and to achieve Hindu-Muslim solidarity. The Ali brothers kept up the fiery temper of the Khilafat movement. While they were touring jointly with Gandhi, Muhammad Ali said at Madras on 2 April 1921 that if the Amir of Afghanistan were to invade India not to subjugate it, but to attack those who wished to subjugate it, those who held the holy places of Islam and who wished to crush Islam and to destroy the Muslim faith, then it would be the duty of Muslims not only to refuse to assist the government but to gird up their loins and fight for Islam. This speech naturally alarmed most Hindus, but some leaders tried to limit the damage it could do to Hindu-Muslim unity. Gandhi said that if Afghanistan invaded India he would tell Indians not to assist the government. The government should expect no assistance from them unless it promised *swaraj*. They wanted to mend or end the government which had ordered the Punjabis to crawl (at Amritsar). Lajpat Rai said they could never co-operate with this government under any circumstances. It would be better for Hindus to be the slaves of Muslims than of another nation. It was preferable to die fighting one another than to live under foreign rule.

As a meeting of the *ulema* at Karachi on 10 July it was argued that as Indian Muslims were not in a position to undertake jihad they should continue to participate in the non-co-operation movement. At the same time and place the Khilafat Conference, presided over by Muhammad Ali, passed a resolution at his instance, a part of which read:

> This meeting further emphatically declares that in the present circumstances the Holy Shariat forbids every Mussalman to serve or enlist himself in the British Army or to raise recruits for it; that it is incumbent on all Muslims in general and all *ulemas* in particular to carry this religious commandment to every Muslim soldier in the British Indian Army. This meeting further declares that in case the British Government directly or indirectly, secretly or openly, resumes hostilities against the Government in Angora, the Indian Muslims will be compelled, in co-operation with the Congress, to resort to civil disobedience

and at the next session of Congress at Ahmadabad to declare India's independence
and the establishment of an Indian Republic.

In September the Ali brothers, Kitchlew and some others were prosecuted
for their part in the Karachi conference and were each sentenced to two
years rigorous imprisonment. A statement by Gandhi published on
2 October praised the Ali brothers and declared: 'We must remain non-
violent but we must not be passive. We must repeat the formula of the [Ali]
brothers regarding the duty of soldiers and invite imprisonment...We must
declare from a thousand platforms that it is sinful for any Mussalman or
Hindu to serve the existing government whether as soldier or in any
capacity whatsoever.' Gandhi's suggestion was endorsed by the Congress
high command and Muhammad Ali's speech was recited on 16 October
(1921) from innumerable platforms as a challenge to the government.

While this display of Hindu-Muslim alliance was in progress, a
grievous blow to Hindu-Muslim relations was struck by the Moplahs, a
Muslim community on the Malabar coast of South India. These people,
mostly poor ignorant peasants and fishermen, who were the descendants
of Arab settlers, were a fanatical and unruly lot and had had fierce clashes
in the past with the authorities as well as with their more prosperous Hindu
landlords and money-lenders. Inspired by the Khilafat propaganda they
rose in revolt in August (1921) as described by the following official
report:

> During the early months of 1921, excitement spread speedily from mosque to
> mosque, from village to village. The violent speeches of the Ali brothers, the
> early approach of *swaraj* as foretold in the non-co-operating Press, the July
> resolutions of the Khilafat Conference...all these combined to fire the brain.
> Throughout July and August innumerable Khilafat meetings were held, in
> which the resolutions of the Karachi Conference were fervently endorsed.
> Knives, swords, and spears were secretly manufactured, bands of desperadoes
> collected, and preparations were made to proclaim the coming of the kingdom
> of Islam.

One of the leaders of the revolt proclaimed: 'We have extorted *swaraj*
from the white man and what we have secured we are not going to give up
so easily...We shall give Hindus the option of death or Islam...The Jews
and Christians, as believers in a revealed book, may be tolerated but the
idolatrous Hindus can only be allowed to live in a Muslim state on
sufferance.' The rebels murdered four Europeans but their real victims

were the Hindus. They ruthlessly murdered, converted people forcibly to Islam, raped women, desecrated temples, and pillaged and destroyed property. It was only strong and sustained military action that brought the situation under control at the end of the year. Unaware of the real situation, Gandhi said that the 'brave Moplahs [were] fighting for what they consider as religion, and in a manner which they consider as religious.' But the Moplahs had in fact dealt a heavy blow to Hindu-Muslim accord.

Just as the Moplah rebellion was nearing its close, serious rioting took place in Bombay when the Prince of Wales landed there in the forenoon of 17 November 1921.[1] There was a *hartal* in the city in response to the Congress decision to boycott the visit. This brought large crowds including mill-hands into the streets, and a free-for-all involving all communities started when the mob interfered with peaceful people using public transport, burnt tram cars and liquor shops, assaulted Europeans and generally dislocated the life of the citizens. The rioting continued for four or five days and it was officially estimated that 53 persons had been killed and 400 wounded. All this took place while Gandhi, the apostle of non-violence and communal harmony, was present in the city and had tried his best to restore calm. He undertook a fast for five days to restore order and as a penance for the excesses of the people. 'With non-violence on our lips,' he said in disgust, 'we have terrorised those who happened to differ from us. The *swaraj* that I have witnessed during the last two days has stunk in my nostrils.' The *hartal* was observed all over India and, at places other than Bombay, was generally peaceful.

In April 1921 Lord Reading had taken over as Viceroy from Lord Chelmsford. He had resigned his position as Lord Chief Justice of England to take up the Indian assignment, and before that had been a successful war-time Ambassador to the USA. Not wishing to let a tragedy like that at Jallianwala Bagh mar his regime, he started cautiously and let Congress go its own way for some months, but he was compelled to take action after the demonstration against the Prince of Wales. Various political associations were declared unlawful and altogether some 30,000 persons were arrested, including C. R. Das and his wife, Motilal and Jawaharlal Nehru, and Lajpat Rai. The Prince of Wales was due to spend Christmas at Calcutta, which was a hotbed of agitation, and a few days before that Lord Reading made an attempt to negotiate with Gandhi, but the effort came to nothing, chiefly because the latter put forward difficult conditions and dragged his feet. Das blamed Gandhi for having lost a golden chance.

[1] He was in India till 17 March 1922.

When Congress met at Ahmadabad at the end of December (1921), it was presided over by Hakim Ajmal Khan in the absence in jail of the President-Elect, C. R. Das. It re-affirmed the Calcutta and Nagpur resolutions and expressed its determination to continue non-co-operation 'till the Punjab and Khilafat wrongs are redressed and *swaraj* is established', and it appointed Gandhi as 'the sole executive authority of Congress' and also invested him with the power to appoint a successor in emergency'. Some excitement was caused during the session when Hasrat Mohani proposed that *swaraj* in the Congress creed should be clearly defined to mean 'complete independence, free from all foreign control.' The suggestion was rejected because Gandhi strongly opposed it on the ground that it showed 'lack of responsibility.' But the proposition was repeated year after year until it was finally adopted at the Lahore Congress in 1929 at the instance of none other than the Mahatma himself.

On 1 February 1922 Gandhi wrote to the Viceroy informing him that Bardoli, a *tehsil* in the Surat District of Gujarat with a population of 87,000, would embark on mass civil disobedience unless the demands listed by him were met within seven days. These demands were the freeing of all 'non-co-operating prisoners' convicted or under trial for non-violent activities; the declaration in clear terms of a policy of non-interference with all non-violent activities in the country, whether they be regarding the redress of Khilafat or Punjab wrongs or *swaraj* or any other purpose; and the freeing of the Press from all administrative control.

The Viceroy rejected these demands and Gandhi left for Bardoli to lead the movement personally. At this stage the Chauri Chaura tragedy happened. On 5 February twenty-two policemen were murdered by a mob. Gandhi immediately suspended the civil disobedience movement. This sudden retreat, ahead of the much-publicised trial of strength between the government and the non-co-operators, shocked all principal colleagues of Gandhi.

It specially affected the Muslims, who had never really subscribed to Gandhi's view of non-violence[1] and had accepted it only as a matter of tactics, because they were in no position to wage a violent struggle and needed Hindu support for the non-violent effort. The general bewilderment made the politics of the immediately following period comparatively

---

[1]Muhammad Ali, the foremost Khilafat leader, declared at the Cocanada Congress, 'When war is forced on a Muslim, and the party that does so has no other argument but this, then, as a Mussulman and the follower of the last of the Prophets, I may not shrink, but must give the enemy battle on his own ground and beat him with his own weapons. This is my own creed.'

barren. But the people had been roused and, not being able to vent their anger on the government, turned against their neighbours of the opposite community who presented the easier target. Hindu-Muslim rioting became a marked feature of the national scene. Gandhi's future non-co-operation movements were to be mainly Hindu efforts.

The calculating Viceroy, who so far had not touched the Mahatma, felt he could now safely deal with him too. Gandhi was arrested on 13 March 1922 and on 18 March was tried by an English judge, Broomfield, for sedition on the basis of three articles he had written in *Young India*. When he was brough into the courtroom clad only in a loin-cloth, everyone stood up to do him honour. He pleaded guilty and made a verbal statement explaining why 'from a staunch loyalist and co-operator' he had become 'an uncompromising disaffectionist and non-co-operator'. He accepted full responsbility for the outrages at Madras, Bombay and Chauri Chaura saying, 'I knew I was playing with fire. I ran the risk and if I was set free, I would still do the same,' and invited the full penalty of the law. 'I have no personal ill-will against any single administrator, much less can I have any disaffection towards the king's person. But I hold it to be a virtue to be disaffected towards a Government which, in its totality, has done more harm to India than any previous system. India is less manly under the British rule than she ever was before. Holding such a belief, I consider it to be a sin to have affection for the system. And it has been a precious privilege for me to be able to write what I have in the various articles tendered in evidence against me.'

The judge sentenced Gandhi to imprisonment for six years but prefaced the pronouncement of the sentence with these significant remarks: 'In the eyes of millions of your countrymen you are a great patriot and a great leader. Even those who differ from you in politics look upon you as a man of high ideals and of noble, and even saintly, life... But you have made it impossible for any government to leave you at liberty.' Gandhi's simple dignity and calm defiance touched the hearts of millions inside and outside India and in a large measure won back the affection and respect he had lost by not fulfilling his promise of *swaraj* within one year and suddenly calling off non-co-operation after Chauri Chaura. C. R. Das said, 'To read a story equal in pathos, dignity, and in sublimity you have to go back over two thousand years, when Jesus of Nazareth "as one that perverted the people" stood to take his trial before a foreign tribunal [presided over by Pontius Pilate]'. In the same vein, Muhammad Ali observed that 'it was reserved for a Christian government to treat as felon the most Christ-like man of our times and to penalize as a disturber of the public peace the one

man engaged in public affairs who comes nearest to the Prince of Peace.'
Though the government succeeded in concealing the Mahatma's person
behind prison bars, his presence in the form of portraits sprouted in
countless private homes and bazaar shops. The government never again
risked the spectacle of putting him on public trial.

Was the non-co-operation movement of 1920-21 a success or a failure?
It obviously was a failure so far as the achievement of concrete goals was
concerned. *Swaraj* was not achieved; the Punjab and Khilafat wrongs
were not redressed. But the campaign had woken the spirit of the people.
Though the subscribing members of Congress never exceeded six million,
its actual sympathisers began to number many times that figure. It had
proved itself to be a country-wide fighting machine. Government repression
had succeeded only in making prison and punishment more honourable.
There was a greater realization by the people of their rights, and more
consciousness that they must rely on their own efforts to win them. Their
faith in the *bona fides* of the foreign government was considerably
reduced. The country on the whole became more *swaraj*-conscious.

This political awakening cast an uncertainty over the future of the
British connection with India. Some British people began to ask whether
India could be held indefinitely and even whether keeping India was worth
the trouble. Lloyd George had to assure the House of Commons on 2
August 1922 that Britain would 'in no circumstances relinquish her
responsbility to India.' The apprehensions of British young men with
regard to service in India had already been roused by the Reforms Act of
1919, which had opened up the possibility of their having to work under
Indian ministers in charge of transferred subjects. The non-co-operation
agitation made them feel that things generally could only get worse for
them. Lloyd George described the Indian Civil Service as the steel frame
of the 'whole structure' of the Government of India and warned, 'if you
take the steel frame out the fabric will collapse.' He went on to hold out
the assurance that there was 'one institution we will not deprive of its
functions or of its privileges, and that is the institution which built up the
Raj…the British Civil Service in India.'

Some relief had been granted to the European members of the
services in 1919, in the form of an overseas allowance as a cushion
against the rising cost of living, but the substantial concessions,
including those relating to overseas pay and return passages to England for
officers and their families during service, came as the result of the
recommendations of the Lee Commission which submitted its report in

1924.[1] These measures steadied the 'steel frame' which had begun to wobble because of a spate of early retirements[2] and a paucity of candidates. But the self-confidence of the guardians of the Raj was shaken and never fully revived.

THE ABOLITION OF THE KHILAFAT

Lord Reading had seen for himself on his arrival in India how deeply concerned Muslims were about the Khilafat question. On 28 February 1922, he sent a telegram to London urging that the allies should evacuate Constantinople, give back to the Sultan his former sovereignty over the holy places and restore Thrace and Smyrna to Turkey. He also sought permission to publish the contents of the telegram to convince the Indian Muslims that the Government of India was doing its best for the Khalifa. Montagu, the Secretary of State, accorded this permission without obtaining the authority of the Cabinet to do so. He was a Jew, and he had angered many, including Prime Minister Lloyd George,[3] for his more sympathetic attitude toward Turkey and India. Lloyd George now forced him to resign and terminated his political career.

Meanwhile in Turkey, events were following their own course. The helpless government of the Sultan, dominated by an international force of occupation at Constantinople, had signed the Treaty of Sevres on 20 August 1920. But the treaty was not recognized by the Turkish nationalists, who under Mustafa Kemal Pasha's leadership built up a military force which in 1922 mounted an offensive against the Greeks and took Smyrna. On 1 November, Kemal proclaimed the abolition of the Sultanate and Muhammad VI fled from Constantinople on a British ship. Abdul Mejid,

---

[1] It is only fair to mention that the recommendations of the Commission also accelerated the rate of Indianisation of the civil services. The slowest rate of Indianisation was in the officer ranks of the armed forces. By the time of transfer of power in 1947, only two or three Indian officers had reached the rank of brigadier. The British Government was not above using this shortage as an argument for delaying independence, conveniently forgetting that it had been deliberately caused by its own policy.

[2] Under a scheme recently sanctioned by the Secretary of State in Council, officers were permitted to retire prematurely on pensions proportionate to their length of service. By 1922, 200 All-India Service officers had retired under this rule and by 1924 their number had risen to 345. This exodus happened when the ranks of All-India Services were already depleted on account of suspension of recruitment during the war.

[3] Lloyd George was strongly prejudiced against Turks. While decorating General Allenby with an order for the conquest of Palestine, for instance, he had referred to the campaign as a 'crusade' although two-thirds of Allenby's troops had been Muslims.

cousin of Muhammad VI, was declared Caliph. Kemal's successes enabled him to obtain greatly improved terms through the Treaty of Lausanne in July 1923. On 29 October, Turkey formally became a republic with Kemal Ataturk as President, and on 3 March 1924 the institution of the Khilafat...which had agitated the Indian Muslims so much, but whose incumbent had brought defeat and disaster to Turkey itself by getting involved in the world war...was abolished.

THE RISE OF HINDU-MUSLIM TENSION

By trying to build Hindu-Muslim unity by championing the cause of the Khilafat, Gandhi had committed a political blunder of significant magnitude. His aim was not to find common ground between Hinduism and Islam, as Nanak and Kabir had tried to do, nor to reach concord by political give-and-take, as the framers of the Lucknow Pact of 1916 had done. Gandhi's basic reason for supporting the cause of the Khilafat was frankly to preserve the differences between Hinduism and Islam.[1]

Whatever lofty notions the Mahatma might have harboured, to the common Hindu and Muslim the marriage was one of convenience. The Hindus needed Muslim support to present a united front to the British; the Muslims, not having a strong organization of their own nor a mass leader like Gandhi, needed Gandhi and Congress to give weight to their effort to preserve the temporal and spiritual status of the Sultan of Turkey. Khilafat was not an Indian issue, and the fact that the Muslims gave it more frenzied support than they had ever given to an Indian cause clearly showed that they were Muslims first and Indians afterwards. Gandhi accepted this as quite natural. In a statement published on 2 October 1921, he said 'the brave [Ali] brothers are staunch lovers of their country, but they are Mussalmans first and everything else after, and it must be so with every religiously-minded man.'[2]

Their passionate involvement in the Khilafat agitation, therefore, did not inspire in the Indian Muslims the feelings of Indian nationalism which would have strengthened Indian unity; it nourished instead the feelings of Muslim nationalism which in time developed into the demand for Pakistan. Two events made this clear even while the Khilafat movement was in full

[1] See, the quotation from *Young India* dated 20 October 1921 at p. 217.

[2] Jinnah, whom the Congress leadership later blamed for introducing religion into politics, on the other hand remained an Indian nationalist first and a Muslim afterwards till the 1930s. In 1931 he declared that he was 'an Indian first and a Muslim afterwards'. *See,* the section on 'Muslim Politics and the Rise of the Muslim League' in Chapter 16.

swing. In the summer of 1920, during the *hijrat* movement, several thousand Muslims tried to give up their homes in India and become citizens of the neighbouring Muslim state of Afghanistan, and in the following year the Moplahs rose in rebellion to found a Muslim kingdom on the Malabar coast of India. The Moplah outrages against the Hindus touched off a chain of unprecedented Hindu-Muslim clashes which became a regular feature of the Indian scene.

MUSLIM POLITICS IN THE DOLDRUMS

When the Khilafat movement died down the Muslims came out of the shadow of Gandhi but they were bewildered. They had been so wholly occupied with the fate of the Sultan of Turkey that there was now a void in their political life. The Muslim League had leaned so much on Congress that it found it hard to stand on its own feet. It was only the taste of Hindu Raj in 1937 that stirred them to unite on an all-India basis once more; but this time it was not Mahatma Gandhi whom they installed as their supreme commander but Quaid-e-Azam Mohammad Ali Jinnah.

On 19 September 1923, Jinnah issued a statement saying that he intended to stand for election to the Central Assembly and explained, 'I have no desire to seek any post or position or title from the government. My sole object is to serve the cause of the country as best as I can.' He was elected unopposed as an 'independent' Muslim candidate. In February 1924 the Assembly passed a resolution at his motion that the stores required by the central government should no longer be purchased by the Stores Department of the India Office in London but by a system of rupee tender in India (the amount spent on these stores was some 21 crores, i.e., 210 million rupees).

An effort to revive the Muslim League at the end of March 1923 failed; a session held at Lucknow under the chairmanship of Bhurgari had to be adjourned *sine die* because of a procedural wrangle about a quorum.[1] The next effort, a session presided over by Jinnah at Lahore in May 1924, however, was more successful.

Jinnah immediately renewed his plea for Hindu-Muslim unity based on a constitutional pact and stuck tirelessly to the theme for several years to come. He first mentioned the possibility that India might break up into

---

[1] During the Khilafat Movement the League was reduced to the status of an adjunct of Congress. The *Indian Quarterly Register* recorded that the League did not meet as a separate body between 1919 and 1924.

more than one state at the Sind Provincial Muslim League Conference in October 1938.

A few days before the Lahore session, he said that one of the objects of the League would be 'to bring about, in due course, through and by means of the All-India Muslim League organization, once more a complete settlement between the Hindus and the Muslims as was done at Lucknow in 1916.' He added that Muslim opinion was no less strong than that of Congress and other organizations, that the Government of India Act must be overhauled, and that immediate steps should be taken to establish Dominion status with responsible government for India. During his presidential address he stressed that 'one essential requisite condition to achieve *swaraj* is political unity between the Hindus and the Mohammedans; for the advent of foreign rule, and its continuance in India, is primarily due to the fact that the people of India, particularly the Hindus and the Mohammedans, are not united. *Swaraj* is an almost interchangeable term with Hindu-Muslim unity.'

The resolutions passed at Lahore reaffirmed that *swaraj* was one of the declared objects of the League, demanded that the provinces of India should be united under a common government on a federal basis with each province having 'full and complete' autonomy, and insisted that the representation of the Muslims should continue to be by means of separate electorates. The League urged that 'immediate steps be taken to establish *swaraj*, i.e., full responsible government'.

To emphasize its independence, the League gave up the practice of holding its meetings at the same time and place as Congress, which had made it look like an appendage to Congress. *The Civil and Military Gazette* reported on 20 November 1924: 'It appears that the majority of the newly-resuscitated Muslim League led by Mr M. A. Jinnah hold the view that if the League is to maintain its individuality it must meet at a place away from the venue of the Indian National Congress.' But the Muslims as a community had not yet found a sense of direction nor a leader of all-India authority. The League limped along as a lightweight party of upper-class members until it decided at the Lucknow session in April 1936 to become a mass party.

The presidential speech of Sir Abdur Rahim, who presided over the League session at Aligarh in December 1925, made it evident that the display of Hindu-Muslim cordiality of the Khilafat days was already a thing of the past. He lamented that the respective attitudes of the Hindus and the Muslims towards life and 'their distinctive culture, civilization and social habits, their traditions and history, no less than their religion, divide them so completely that the fact that they have lived in the same country for nearly a thousand years has contributed hardly anything to their fusion into a nation,' and he doubted 'that at any time in the history of India the relations between the two communities generally were so seriously strained as at present. In fact, some of the Hindu leaders have talked publicly of driving out the Muslims from India as the Spaniards expelled the Moors from Spain, that is, unless they perform *shuddhi* and become Hindus or submit to their full political programme.'

The disarray in the political ranks of the Muslims at that time was such that the League divided into 'groups'. In December 1927 one group (the 'Jinnah Group') met at Calcutta and another (the 'Shafi Group') met at Lahore; in October 1933 the 'Aziz Group' met at Howrah while in November of the same year the 'Hidayat Group' met at Delhi. Jinnah was so disgusted with the situation that in 1931 he decided to wash his hands of political life in India and settle down in London. In the meantime, power passed into the hands of local political barons, as the result of the 1937 elections in the Muslim majority provinces were to show.

The League began to shape up as an effective all-India party only after 1935, when Jinnah returned from England for good. During the years that the Muslims lacked solidarity, Congress made no serious effort to win them over by offering any meaningful political concessions. It claimed more vehemently than ever that it represented all the communities and that the communal problem had been artificially created by the British government to further its policy of divide and rule and would automatically disappear in the dawn of freedom. Therefore, all the situation demanded was that Britain should hand over power to Congress and leave India.

PART V

'I am authorized, on behalf of His Majesty's Government, to state clearly that, in their judgement, it is implicit in the declaration of 1917 that the natural issue of India's constitutional progress, as there contemplated, is the attainment of Dominion Status.'

Lord Irwin, 31 October 1929.

'This Congress...declares that the word *swaraj* in Article 1 of the Congress Constitution shall mean complete independence'.

Resolution passed at the Lahore session on 29 December 1929.

'We refuse to join Mr Gandhi, because his movement is not a movement for complete independence of India but for making the seventy millions of Indian Mussulmans dependents of the Hindu Mahasabha.'

Muhammad Ali, April 1930.

'Placed side by side with the frantic efforts made by Mr Gandhi to bring about Hindu-Muslim unity, the record (of the Hindu-Muslim relationship from 1920 to 1940) makes most painful and heart-rending reading. It would not be much exaggeration to say that it is a record of twenty years of civil war between the Hindus and the Muslims in India, interrupted by brief intervals of armed peace.'

Dr B. R. Ambedkar, the leader of the Untouchables.

CHAPTER 12

COMMUNAL ANTAGONISM

Indian nationalists are apt to overemphasize Britain's tardiness in transferring power to Indian hands and to underemphasize the continuous disagreement between Hindu and Muslim politicians over the shape of constitutional progress and the almost continuous Hindu-Muslim rioting that stifled the growth of healthy political institutions and practices.

Lord Irwin, who succeeded Reading as Viceroy in April 1926, was a true Christian and a good friend of India. He did his best to further the cause of constitutional advance but was frustrated by the die-hards in Britain, the bureaucracy in India, and above all, the communal differences in India. In a speech at the Chelmsford Club in Simla on 17 July 1926 he fervently appealed to Hindu and Muslim leaders to compose their differences for the good of their country:

> Let the leaders and thoughtful men in each community, the Hindu among the Hindus, and Moslem among the Moslems, throw themselves with ardour into a new form of communal work and into a nobler struggle, and fight for toleration. I do not believe that the task is beyond their powers.
>
> I see before me two ancient and highly organised societies with able and esteemed public men as their recognised leaders...In past centuries each community has made its great contribution to the annals of history and civilisation in India. The place that she has filled in the world in past ages has been largely of their creating.
>
> I refuse to believe that they can make no contribution now to rescue the good name of India from the hurt which their present discords inflict upon it...I appeal in the name of national life because communal tension is eating into it as a canker. It has suspended its activities. It has ranged its component parts into opposite and hostile camps.

On 29 August 1927, he repeated his appeal in his address to the Indian Legislature:

> I am not exaggerating when I say that, during the seventeen months that I have

been in India, the whole landscape has been overshadowed by the lowering clouds of communal tension, which have repeatedly discharged their thunderbolts, spreading far throughout the land their devastating havoc...United must be the effort if it is to gain success; and on the successful issue of such work depends the building of the Indian Nation. Yet the would-be builders must approach their task sorely handicapped and with heavy heart, so long as the forces to which they would appeal are distracted and torn by present animosities. For nothing wholesome can flourish in unwholesome soil, and no one may hope to build a house to stand against the wind and the rain and the storm of life upon foundations that are rotten and unsound.

We have already described the Moplah rebellion and the Bombay riots of 1921. During the Muslim festival of Muharram of 1922, large-scale Hindu-Muslim rioting took place in Multan, and in the words of the official publication *India, 1922-23*, 'the structure so painfully erected by Mr Gandhi had crumbled hopelessly.' The Muharram of 1923 was also the occasion for serious riots in Bengal and the Punjab. The riot in Calcutta in May lasted for several days and resulted in heavy casualties.

At this juncture, two Hindu and two Muslim communal movements sprang up. The Hindu movements were *sangathan* (binding together), for promoting physical culture so that the community could act effectively during communal trouble, and *shuddhi* (purification), founded by Shradhanand, for bringing back to the Hindu fold those Hindus who had embraced Islam. The rival Muslim movements were *tanzim* (organization) and *tabligh* (missionary effort).

On 12 January 1924, Gandhi suffered an attack of appendicitis in jail and was removed to Poona Hospital. He was operated upon by Colonel Maddock, a British surgeon, during a thunderstorm. The surgeon's electric torch fused during the operation, which had to be completed in the light of a hurricane lamp. Gandhi gradually recovered and became a good friend of the surgeon. The experience also toned down his prejudice against the Western system of medicine. He was released from jail on 5 February, four years early, on health grounds.

But Gandhi's freedom brought no improvement in Hindu-Muslim relations. The year 1924 was marked by communal riots in several places including Delhi, Gulbarga, Nagpur, Lucknow, Shahjahanpur, Allahabad, Jubbulpore and Kohat. The Muslims in Upper India were incensed by the publication of a blasphemous pamphlet about the life of the Prophet (PBUH) by a Hindu under the title *Rangila Rasul* (Playboy Prophet). The publisher of this work, Rajpal, was eventually murdered by a Muslim.

The outbreak at Kohat in the North-West Frontier Province which took place on 9 and 10 September was especially vicious. Its immediate cause was the publication of a virulently anti-Islamic poem by Jiwan Das, Secretary of the Sanatan Dharam Sabha. Since the population of the city was over-whelmingly Muslim, the Hindus suffered the most. Thirty-six were killed, a hundred and forty-five were wounded and four thousand had to be evacuated by a special train. Holding himself responsible for the shortcomings of his people, Gandhi imposed a three-week penitential fast upon himself. He started the ordeal at Delhi on 18 September under the roof of Muhammad Ali but was later moved to a house outside the city. The fast bore fruit in the form of an urgently summoned Unity Conference which met at Delhi from 26 September to 2 October. It was attended by some 300 leaders of different communities including Bishop Wescott, head of the Anglican Church in India. But the appeal for communal peace had no lasting effect.

Gandhi and his friend Shaukat Ali[1] were appointed by Congress to report on the Kohat riots but they could not agree on their findings. This difference of opinion marked the beginning of a rift between the Mahatma and his closest Muslim associates. Addressing a public gathering at Mirzapore Park in Calcutta on 1 May 1925, Gandhi dejectedly admitted his failure to bring about Hindu-Muslim accord. He said 'I have admitted my incompetence. I have admitted that I have been found wanting as a physician prescribing a cure for this malady. I do not find that either Hindus or Muslims are ready to accept my cure, and therefore I simply nowadays confine myself to a passing mention of this problem and content myself by saying that some day or other we Hindus and Muslims will have to come together, if we want the deliverance of our country.'

No less than sixteen communal riots took place in 1925 at different places, including Delhi, Aligarh, Arvi, and Solahpur. Calcutta was the scene of a series of serious communal clashes beginning in April 1926. The succeeding twelve months were marred by forty riots during which 197 persons were killed and nearly 1,600 were injured. There were riots also in the interior of Bengal, in Rawalpindi and in Allahabad; in Delhi there were five riots.

In the course of his address to the Legislature on 29 August 1927, Lord Irwin said, 'From April to July last year Calcutta seemed to be under the

---

[1] In November 1921 Gandhi had written, 'There are many stalwart and good Mussulmans I know. But no Mussulman knows me through and through as Shaukat Ali does'.

mastery of some evil spirit, which so gripped the minds of men that in their insanity they held themselves absolved from the most sacred restraints of human conduct. Since then we have seen the same sinister influences at work in Pabna, Rawalpindi, Lahore and many other places, and have been forced to look upon that abyss of unchained human passions that lies too often beneath the surface of habit and of law. In less than eighteen months, so far as numbers are available, the toll taken by this bloody strife has been between 250 and 300 killed, and over 2,500 injured.'

On 23 December 1926, Swami Shradhanand, who had preached in the Great Mosque at Delhi in 1919, was murdered in his sickbed by a Muslim fanatic named Abdur Rashid for his sponsorship of the *shuddhi* movement. In November 1927 Abdur Rashid was hanged in Delhi jail and his body was made over to his relatives for burial, but it was seized by a Muslim mob who broke past the police and rushed with it into the city before the authorities could recover it. Of the Hindu passers-by, two were killed and more than sixty injured.

The Indian Statutory Commission (popularly called the Simon Commission because it was presided over by Sir John Simon) summed up the situation as follows: 'Every year since 1923 has witnessed communal rioting on an extensive and, in fact, an increasing scale which has as yet shown no sign of abating. The attached list, which excludes minor occurences, records no less than 112 communal riots within the last five years, of which thirty-one occurred during 1927.' Besides loss of life, rioting always resulted in the large-scale destruction of property by arson and other means, and by looting of shops and houses.

From the beginning of April to the end of September 1927, twenty-seven riots took place...ten in the United Provinces, six in the Bombay Presidency, two each in the Punjab, the Central Provinces, Bengal and Bihar and Orissa and one in Delhi...resulting in about 103 killed and 1,084 wounded.

During the twelve months ending with 31 March 1929, there were twenty-two riots; 204 persons lost their lives and nearly a thousand were injured.

The year 1929-30 was comparatively quiet and witnessed only twelve riots, but 1930-31 was a bad year because Gandhi's non-co-operation movement resulted in clashes not only between Congress workers and the forces of law and order but also between Hindus and Muslims (the Muslims by and large had refused to take part in the non-co-operation agitation and resented the pressure of Congress volunteers to compel them to join the anti-government programme).

The most serious outbreak, covering over a hundred villages, took place in August in the Sukkur area of Sind. Riots also occurred in Kishorganj (Mymensingh District), Ballia (UP), Nagpur, Rawalpindi, Mirzapur District, Agra and Dhanbad (Bengal), Dehra Dun, Bulandshahr, Muttra, Azamgarh, Mainpuri and several other places.

In March 1931 Cawnpore suffered a particularly bloody and destructive riot. Murders, arson and large-scale looting went on for three days. Several temples and mosques were burnt down, destroyed and desecrated. The death toll was estimated to be between 300 and 500.

The year 1932-3 passed off comparatively peacefully but widespread violence returned in 1933-4. Riots broke out in Benares, Cawnpore, Lahore, Peshawar, Ayodhya, Bhagalpore, Cannanore (Madras), Agra and several places in the provinces of Bihar and Orissa, Bengal, Sind, Delhi, Punjab and the United Provinces.

A dispute between Muslims and Sikhs over a mosque standing in the precincts of a Sikh temple (Shahidganj Gurdwara) in Lahore led to prolonged tension between the two communities in 1934-5 and resulted in rioting in November.

In March 1935 Ilm Din, the Muslim who had killed Rajpal, the Hindu publisher of *Rangila Rasul,* was executed at Karachi for his crime. A crowd of abut 25,000 frenzied Muslims wished to take the body from the burial place to the city in a procession. All attempts to prevent the taking out of the provocative procession having failed, a platoon of the Royal Sussex Regiment was summoned to maintain peace. To save themselves from the fury of the mob, the soldiers fired 47 rounds resulting in 47 dead and 134 wounded. On 25 August, a communal riot broke out in Secunderabad.

The year 1936 was marred by four riots...in Firozabad (Agra District), Poona, Jamalpur (Monghyr District) and Bombay. 1937 was a bad year. Several riots took place in the Central Provinces and the Punjab. At Panipat fourteen persons were killed. British troops had to be called out to control a Muslim-Sikh riot in Amritsar. A riot in Madras left fifty injured. There were two communal riots in 1938 and six in 1938. The most serious during 1939 were those in Cawnpore in February (40 dead, 200 injured and 800 arrested) and in Sukkur in November (86 dead).

Of the cities, Bombay had the worst record. During the period February 1929 to April 1938, Hindus and Muslims rioted for 210 days and killed 550 persons and wounded 4,500 besides causing tremendous loss of property by arson and looting.

The immediate cause of trouble all over the country was usually the offence caused by one community to the other while celebrating its religious festivals. But there was also the rivalry for scraps of political power as hopes grew of the devolution of power from British to Indian hands. In the words of the Simon Commission:

This tension ... is a manifestation of the anxieties and ambitions aroused in both communities by the prospect of India's political future. So long as authority was firmly established in British hands, and self-government was not thought of, Hindu-Moslem rivalry was confined within a narrower field. This was not merely because the presence of a neutral bureaucracy discouraged strife. A further reason was that there was little for members of one community to fear from the predominance of the other. The comparative absence of communal strife in the Indian States to-day may be similarly explained. Many who are well acquainted with conditions in British India a generation ago would testify that at that epoch so much good feeling had been engendered between the two sides that communal tension as a threat to civil peace was at a minimum. But the coming of the Reforms and the anticipation of what may follow them have given new point to Hindu-Moslem competition...The one community naturally lays claim to the rights of a majority and relies upon its qualifications of better education and greater wealth; the other is all the more determined on those accounts to secure effective protection for its members, and does not forget that it represents the previous conquerors of the country. It wishes to be assured of adequate representation and of a full share of official posts.

After reviewing the harrowing record of Hindu-Muslim riots during the period 1920-40 Ambedkar concluded, 'placed side by side with the frantic efforts made by Mr Gandhi to bring about Hindu-Muslim unity, the record makes most painful and heart-rending reading. It would not be much exaggeration to say that it is a record of twenty years of civil war between the Hindus and the Muslims in India, interrupted by brief intervals of armed peace.'

CHAPTER 13

THE WORKING OF THE
REFORMS

The Duke of Connaught landed at Madras on 10 January 1921 to inaugurate the new constitution under the Act of 1919. Madras had evidently been selected as his landing place in preference to Bombay, which was the customary port of arrival for important visitors, because Bombay had acquired a reputation for civil turbulence and it was feared that the Congress call for the boycott of the Duke would result in disorderly demonstrations there. The Duke inaugurated the Chamber of Princes at Delhi on 8 February and the two imperial legislatures…The Council of State and the Legislative Assembly…in a joint session on the following day. At the latter ceremony he made the following appeal:

Since I landed I have felt around me bitterness and estrangement between those who have been and should be friends. The shadow of Amritsar has lengthened over the fair face of India...No one can deplore those events more intensely than I do myself...I appeal to you all, British and Indians, to bury along with the dead the mistakes and misunderstandings of the past, to forgive where you have to forgive, and to join hands and to work together to realise the hopes that arise from today.

But the non-co-operation movement was already in full swing and the estrangement between the mainstream of political India and the government had become unbridgable. The Hindus and the Muslims had their differences, but they were united in the view that the reforms offered too little and that a substantial immediate advance was necessary. When the elections for the Central and the Provincial legislatures were held in the autumn of 1920, they were boycotted by Congress as well as the Khilafat Conference. This enabled the Moderates under their new label of Liberals to capture most of the seats in the legislatures.

The Liberals desired the freedom of India no less than the non-co-operators. They differed from the latter only in tactics: they wished to attain their objectives by co-operation with the government.

The non-co-operation movement favourably affected the performance of the Liberals as legislators in two ways. In the first place, the Liberals were anxious to disprove the charge of being toadies of the government by displaying their patriotism. Secondly, the government wished their tenure to be successful to demonstrate the futility of non-co-operation. Though Congress tried to wreck the Act of 1919 by sometimes shunning the legislatures and at others by entering them, the constitution endured till 1937, when new legislatures came into being under the Act of 1935.

During the very first year of the new Central Assembly's life, the Liberals introduced a resolution asking for the establishment of full responsible government in the provinces and the transfer to popular control of all Central Departments except Defence and Foreign Affairs.

The government opposed the motion but agreed to convey the wishes of the Assembly to the Secretary of State. Pressure of public opinion, both inside and outside the Assembly, ultimately resulted in the appointment in 1924 of a mixed committee of officials and non-officials under Muddiman, the Home Member, but the terms of reference of the Committee limited its discretion to suggest ways and means of improving the working of the existing constitution by the use of the rule-making power granted under it. The Committee could not make recommendations for the amendment of the constitution itself.

The Assembly also compelled the Governor-General to resort to legislation by certification in regard to two unpopular measures.

The first was a Bill to prevent the distribution of books and newspapers which would excite disaffection against the rulers of the Indian states (1922) and the second doubled the salt tax (1923).

In its review of the achievements of the Assembly the Simon Commission observed that the Assembly 'had secured the repeal of legislation which Indian opinion regarded as "repressive", and the abolition of racial discrimination in criminal trials; it had brought effective pressure to bear on the Indianisation of the Army and on tariff policy; and its authority had been extended by the establishment of a practice by which the Executive submits such important taxes as income tax and salt duty for the approval of the Assembly in an annual Finance Bill.'

When the second elections to the legislatures took place in the autumn of 1923, members of Congress offered themselves for election under the name of the Swarajya Party. How this change took place is an important episode in the history of the Indian national movement because it meant the defeat of Gandhi and led to his self-imposed detachment from politics till the Calcutta Congress of December 1928 when, in the aftermath of the appointment of the Simon Commission, India once more had an important all-India issue to pursue and the Congress Party needed the weight of the masses to back up its demands.

Congress had appointed a Civil Disobedience Enquiry Committee in 1922 which had reported that the country was not prepared 'at present' to embark upon another round of Mass Civil Disobedience. But the question remained, what else could be done to keep the political spirit alive?

C. R. Das had always favoured entering the legislatures and vigorously propagated his viewpoint. His main supporter was Motilal Nehru. The 'no-changers', reflecting Gandhi's stand, were headed by Rajagopalachari of Madras. The issue came to the fore when the Congress met at Gaya in December 1922 under the presidentship of Das. Gandhi was still in jail.

In his presidential address, Das made a strong plea for council entry: 'The work of the councils for the last two years has made it necessary for non-co-operators to enter the Councils. The bureaucracy has received added strength from these reformed councils, and those who have entered the Councils speaking generally have practically helped the cause of the bureaucracy... These councils must, therefore, either be ended or mended. Hithereto we have been boycotting the councils from outside...But...these councils are still there. It should be the duty of Congress to boycott the councils more effectively from inside...An advancing army does not co-operate with the enemy when it marches into the enemy's territory.'

But the no-changers carried the day. In the words of the official history of Congress, Das was defeated because 'the spirit of Gandhi was all-pervading. Everyone took it to be an act of disloyalty to the master to turn his back on him, the moment he was found to be absent from Congress.' Das resigned his presidentship in protest and, along with Motilal Nehru, founded the Swaraj Party to contest the elections.

The pro-changers continued to gain strength as time passed and were able to reach a compromise with their opponents at the special session of Congress at Delhi in September 1923 where the following motion was carried:

While re-affirming its adherence to the principle of non-violent non-co-operation, this Congress declares that such Congressmen as have no religious or other conscientious objections against entering the legislatures are at liberty to stand as candidates and to exercise their right of voting at the forthcoming elections; and this Congress therefore suspends all propaganda against entering the councils.

When Gandhi was released from jail in the first week of February 1924, he at first stuck to the position that council entry was not compatible with non-co-operation. However, he ultimately bowed to the reality that the Swarajya Party had come to stay and made an agreement with Das and Motilal Nehru under which spinning and weaving, the removal of Untouchability and the promotion of Hindu-Muslim unity (the 'constructive' programme) would be the responsibility of all members of Congress, while work with regard to the legislatures would be carried on by the Swarajya Party as an integral part of Congress.

For the time being, the Mahatma was to concentrate on the 'constructive activities' and the Swarajists on political work. In August 1925 Gandhi wrote, 'I must no longer stand in the way of the Congress being developed and guided by educated Indians rather than by one like myself who has thrown in his lot entirely with the masses... The best way in which I can help...is by removing myself out of the way, and by concentrating myself solely upon constructive work.' He toured extensively in the rural areas and deepened his relationship with the masses.

Though the Swarajists did not have much time to prepare for the autumn 1923 elections, they met with striking success at the Centre. They captured forty-five seats, mostly at the cost of the Liberals who ceased to be an important factor in the politics of the country. The Independents also gave a good account of themselves and formed a group of twenty-four under Jinnah. With twenty-five official and fourteen nominated members, the government controlled a block of thirty-nine. Unable to act effectively by themselves, the Swarajists joined hands with the Independents to form the Nationalist Party. For this the Swarajists had to pay the price of modifying their purely wrecking tactics. Though the partnership worked fairly well on some occasions and caused embarrassment to the government, the gulf between the allies widened and with the passage of time the coalition practically ceased to exist.

Some Nationalist successes in the Assembly were the passing of an amendment which demanded the revision of the Government of India Act with a view to establishing full responsible government in India and for that purpose the convening of a Round Table Conference; the rejection of the demand under Customs in the budget; and the refusal of demands under Income Tax, Salt and Opium. The Assembly also carried an amendment which, among other things, rejected the recommendations of the Lee Commission and demanded the stoppage of recruitment in England for the civil services in India. This pressure resulted in the setting up of the Muddiman Committee which has already been mentioned. Of course, most of these successes amounted to no more than protest and pressure because the final power of legislation lay in the hands of the executive government, not in those of the legislature.

On 16 June 1925, C. R. Das suddenly passed away and, as stated by Subhas Bose, 'The Swaraj Party, which owed so much to him, was paralysed...and dissensions gradually arose within the party.'

Another factor which contributed to the proliferation of political parties was the continuing Hindu-Muslim antagonism. Muslims and Hindu Mahasabhites began to form their own groups.

In the third Assembly, for which elections were held in the autumn of 1926, the Swarajists could command the allegiance of only about one-third of the 105 elected members. The announcement of the appointment of the Statutory Commission (Simon Commission) in November 1927 diverted the attention of all parties to the larger question of India's constitutional future.

So far we have dealt with the working of the 1919 constitution at the Central level. But in fact it was only at the provincial level that an instalment of really responsible government had been introduced, in the form of ministers having charge of transferred subjects. This form of government requires a party system for its success; since this requirement was achieved only in Madras and the Punjab it was in these two provinces that the 1919 reforms worked best. In Madras the non-Brahmin majority banded together as the Justice Party to challenge the entrenched position of the brahmin minority.

In the Punjab, a combination of Muslims, Hindus and Sikhs representing rural interests formed the Unionist Party. One Punjab minister, Sir Fazl-i-Husain, greatly uplifted the Punjabi Muslims who were to form the backbone of the future state of Pakistan. As Education Minister he adopted special measures to encourage the education of backward classes and areas. These benefited all the communities, particularly the Muslims, who had been left far behind the Hindus in the field of education. Later, as Revenue Member (administering a reserved department), he was responsible for passing measures to safeguard the interest of rural debtors. These also benefited the Muslims relatively more, because most of the money-lenders and bankers who exploited the cultivators were non-Muslims. At the political level, Fazl-i Husain was mainly responsible for reviving the Punjab Muslim League and inviting the All-India Muslim League to hold its important session at Lahore in 1924. During the Round Table Conference in London, Fazl-i Husain was a member of the Viceroy's executive council, and by his behind-the-scenes efforts was able to influence the choice of Muslim delegates to the conference, and also the proper advocacy of Muslim interests during the deliberations.

Congress had boycotted the first legislatures, and in the second election the Swarajists did well only in Bengal and the Central Provinces and were at times able to obstruct the constitution in those two provinces by making it impossible for ministers to function.[1] Elsewhere the system simply limped along. The legislators were unable to form coherent and stable parties. The ministers, lacking a strong party of their own to back them up, therefore had to rely on the official bloc to keep them in office and became yes-men of the Governors.

In 1923 Surendranath Banerji, the Liberal minister for local self-government in Bengal, democratized the unpopular Calcutta Municipal Act which Curzon had enacted. This enabled the Swarajists under Das to capture the administration of India's largest municipality. Das was elected Mayor of Calcutta and Subhas Bose was appointed Chief Executive Officer of the corporation. The municipality discontinued the practice of giving receptions to the Viceroys and Governors and instead, began to extend that honour to national figures such as Gandhi and Motilal Nehru.

Indian politicians on the whole gave a good account of themselves. The level of debate in the Central Assembly was high and the ministers in the provinces got along surprisingly smoothly with the bureaucracy under them. Vithalbhai Patel, a Congressman like his more famous brother Vallabhbhai Patel, earned praise as the elected Speaker of the Central Assembly. All this added to the confidence of National leaders that India was fit for self-government.

The joint Select Committee in 1919 had recommended that India should have 'the same liberty to consider her interests as Great Britain, Australia, New Zealand, Canada and South Africa'. This recommendation resulted in the establishment of the 'Fiscal Convention', which meant that the Secretary of State would no longer interfere in fiscal matters on which the Government of India and the Indian Legislature were agreed.

---

[1] The reader's attention is invited to the fact that in the provinces the budget of the transferred departments could be thrown out by the legislature. The salaries of the ministers could also be refused and they could be subjected to a vote of no-confidence. These contingencies would compel the ministers to resign. The transferred departments would then have to be administered by the Governor in the same way as the reserved departments. But at the centre the Governor-General could override the Assembly by his powers of veto and certification. Moreover, the central departments were all headed by non-elected members and were under the full control of the Governor-General. The scope for making the constitution unworkable, therefore, really existed only at the provincial level.

Due to her war effort, India was also granted an 'international personality' by being represented in the Imperial War Cabinet and in the Imperial Conferences, by being invited to sign the Peace Treaty, and by admission to the League of Nations as an original member. But these honours were without real substance because India had no control over its external affairs and the representatives were either officials or nominees of the government.

THE HINDU MAHASABHA

The communal tension during the period under review encouraged the growth of the avowedly Hindu organization called the Hindu Mahasabha. Its roots go back to 1910 when leading Hindus, meeting at Allahabad, decided to found the All-India Hindu Mahasabha with headquarters at Allahabad. But it really came to life in 1923 when its session was reported in the *Indian Annual Register* for the first time.

Before long branches of the Mahasabha appeared all over the country and their activities contributed to the growth of communal tension.

THE AKALI MOVEMENT

From 1920 to 1925 the Punjab was disturbed by the Akali Movement. This arose from the demand by the Akalis, a reforming sect of Sikhs, that the Sikh *gurdwaras* (shrines) should be managed by committees elected under the aegis of the Shiromani Gurdwara Prabandhak Committee.

This was resisted by the *mahants*, the traditional administrators of the shrines. In one incident in 1921 about 130 Akalis, who entered the shrine at Nankana Sahib, the birthplace of Guru Nanak, were ambushed and slaughtered by gunmen who had been hired for the purpose by the *mahant*. Another famous incident took place at the Guru ka Bagh ('the garden of the *guru*'), a shrine near Amritsar where the Akalis adopted Gandhi's non-violent tactics. They approached the shrine in batches and refused to disperse when ordered by the police to do so. When the police assaulted them to prevent them from entering the precincts, they suffered the beating with remarkable patience. More than 5,000 were arrested and over 100 had to be taken to hospital. For a while a, a terrorist splinter group called Babar ('lion') Akalis caused alarm but was suppressed by the authorities. The agitation subsided after 1925 when the government conceded Akali demands. The agitation had caused the Sikhs to close ranks and excited Sikh nationalism, with important consequences for the future.

THE COMMUNIST PARTY OF INDIA

The Bolsheviks turned their attention to India soon after the success of their revolution. M. N. Roy, who appeared in Russia in 1920, became the spokesman for India and on his advice the Comintern in 1924 decided that the Communist Party of India should be established. Soon after that, however, the Communist International began to doubt Roy's capability and turned to R. Palme Dutt of the Communist Party of Great Britain for guidance. A series of British communists were dispatched to India and the Communist Party of India formally came into existence in 1925. Four Workers and Peasants parties in Bombay, Bengal, the Punjab and the United Provinces were also formed. They were given financial aid from Moscow and their policy was dictated by Moscow directly, and via England and the Continent.

Gandhi's ideology was considered inimical to communism. *The Programme of the Communist International* adopted by the First World Congress in September 1920 said:

> Tendencies like Gandhism in India, thoroughly imbued with religious conceptions, idealize the most backward and economically most reactionary forms of social life, see the solution of the social problem not in proletarian socialism, but in a reversion to these backward forms, preach passivity and repudiate the class struggle, and in the process of the development of the revolution become transformed into an openly reactionary force. Gandhism is more and more becoming an ideology directed against mass revolution. It must be strongly combated by Communism.

The communist effort in India was directed toward gaining control of the working classes by organizing them in unions and inciting them to strikes culminating in a general strike followed by revolution, and toward organizing the peasants in a similar fashion to effect an agrarian revolution.

But communist activity was suddenly interrupted on 20 March 1929, when the government arrested thirty-one of the most important communist leaders from various parts of the country and brought them to Meerut for trial in what is popularly known as the Meerut Conspiracy Case. It was not till 16 January 1933 that the trial court concluded its hearings and sentenced all but four of the accused to terms of imprisonment varying from life to three years. Philip Spratt and Benjamin Francis Bradley, who had come to India from England to advance the communist cause, were each sentenced to transportation for ten years. All the appeals were dismissed by the Chief Justice of the Allahabad High Court but the sentences were reduced and by the autumn of 1935 all the prisoners were released.

During the trial, the accused had been able to invoke considerable national sympathy by exploiting the liberal outlook and anti-British feelings of nationalist circles. A defence committee was formed of which the chairman was Motilal Nehru and the members included Jawaharlal Nehru. The accused took advantage of the opportunity provided by the trial for propagating communism. They 'took an inordinately long time in reading out well prepared statements', observed the Chief Justice, 'which the court had to take down word for word. In most cases they had nothing more than an exposition, on an elaborate scale, of the doctrines of communism, its tenets and its programme'. Though in visible terms the removal of the leading communists from the political scene had the effect of improving the industrial climate by a reduction in strikes, intellectually the country became more aware of the communist philosophy, and some young nationalists viewed the courage and secret methods of the communists with a certain amount of admiration. The statements of the accused during the trial, which were widely published, naturally painted communism in the best possible colours.

CHAPTER 14

APPOINTMENT OF THE SIMON COMMISSION AND ITS REPERCUSSIONS

Since the calling off of the non-co-operation movement after the Chauri Chaura incident, Indian politics had lacked a rallying theme, but this was unexpectedly provided by the British Government in November 1927. On the eighth day of that month Stanley Baldwin, the Prime Minister, announced in the House of Commons the appointment of a commission 'to inquire into the working of the Indian Constitution and to consider the desirability of establishing, extending, modifying or restricting the degree of responsible government'. Such a commission had been promised in the Reforms Act of 1919 at the end of ten years after the passing of that Act, but 'the Government have decided, for various reasons, which I need not now specify, that it is desirable to anticipate the date (December 1929) contemplated by the Act and to appoint this most important Royal Commission forthwith'.

The reason for advancing the date of the appointment of the commission, which Baldwin had chosen not to elaborate, was simply that the trend of the by-election results in the United Kingdom indicated that Baldwin's Conservative government was likely to be defeated by the Labour party in the elections which were due to take place in 1929. That party was considered in Conservative circles to be unduly sympathetic to Indian political aspirations. The Conservative government, therefore, decided to appoint a commission of its own choice while they had the chance to do so; in hastening the constitutional process, Baldwin was in fact trying to favour Britain, not India.

The chairman of the commission was to be Sir John Simon, a distinguished lawyer, and it had six other members including Clement Attlee, who was to preside over India's independence as Prime Minister in 1947. The total ommission of Indians from the commission was a psychological error of the first order and immediately raised a storm of protest in India. Government explanations that the members of the commission had all to be members of parliament, and assurances that the

Indian point of view would be given a full hearing and due consideration in various ways, fell on deaf ears. The Indians demanded complete equality with the British members of the commission; they said that they were not prepared to be treated merely as petitioners and witnesses.

Jinnah and Sir Tej Bahadur Sapru were both signatories to the All-India Leaders' Manifesto dated 16 November 1927 which declared that 'the exclusion of Indians from the commission is fundamentally wrong... Unless a commission on which British and Indian statesmen are invited to sit on equal terms is set up we cannot conscientiously take any part or share in the work of the Commission'. In his presidential address to the All-India Liberal Federation, Sapru said on 27 December 1927, 'Neither our self-respect nor our sense of duty to our country can permit us to go near the commission.'

Of the main parties, the Muslim League alone lacked unanimity on the issue of boycotting the Simon Commission. The [Sir Muhammad] 'Shafi Group', which met at Lahore (31 December 1927-1 January 1928), favoured co-operation while the 'Jinnah Group' which convened at Calcutta (30 December 1927-1 January 1928)[1], decided to boycott the Simon Commission. Jinnah declared:

A constitutional war has been declared on Great Britain. Negotiations for a settlement are not to come from our side. Let the Government sue for peace. We are denied equal partnership. We will resist the new doctrine to the best of our power. Jallianwalla Bagh was a physical butchery, the Simon Commission is a butchery of our souls. By appointing an exclusively white Commission, Lord Birkenhead has declared our unfitness for self-government. I welcome Pandit Malaviya and I welcome the hand of fellowship extended to us by Hindu leaders from the platform of the Congress and the Hindu Mahasabha. For, to me, this offer is more valuable than any concession which the British Government can make. Let us then grasp the hand of fellowship. This is indeed a bright day; and for acieving this unity, thanks are due to Lord Birkenhead.

At its session at Madras in December 1927, Congress resolved that 'the only self-respecting course for India to adopt' was to boycott the Simon Commission 'at every stage and in every form' and called upon the people of India to organize mass demonstrations all over India on the day it arrived in India and also in every city on the day it visited there. When the commission members landed at Bombay on 3 February 1928, they were greeted with a complete *hartal* in all the important cities of India. Altogether, the boycott was a complete success and the members of the commission everywhere were greeted with black flags and choruses of

[1] This session was attended by some Hindu leaders including Sarojini Naidu.

'Simon go back'. At the demonstration outside Lahore railway station on 30 October 1928, Lajpat Rai, who had a heart condition, received *lathi* blows on his chest at the hands of a European officer during a police charge. This, it was generally believed, precipitated his death, which took place on 17 November. When the commission visited Lucknow, Jawahrlal Nehru too had a taste of police *lathi* blows on two successive days (28 and 29 November 1928). 'Now that the excitement of the moment had passed', he recalled, 'I felt pains all over my body and great fatigue. Almost every part of me seemed to ache, and I was covered with contused wounds and marks of blows. But fortunately I was not injured in any vital spot.'

The Madras Congress was also memorable for the emergence into the front rank of the Congress leadership of Jawaharlal Nehru, who was destined to be the first Prime Minister of independent India. He was born in 1889 and had been educated at Harrow and Trinity College, Cambridge. He was also called to the bar but gave up his legal practice and joined Gandhi's non-co-operation movement in 1920.

That he had fallen under the Mahatma's spell is evident from the statement he made from the dock on 17 May 1922[1] : 'to serve India in the battle of freedom is honour enough. To serve her under a leader like the Mahatma is doubly fortunate.'

Nehru was an emotional intellectual. He differed from Gandhi's outlook and philosophy in a number of ways[2] but he was emotionally attracted by the Mahatma's affinity with the underpriviledged, his simple dignity, fearlessness and saintly charm. Gandhi 'dominates the Congress and the country not so much because of any opinions he holds and which are generally accepted', he explained, 'but because of his unique personality'. Subhas Bose correctly diagnosed that 'while his (Jawaharlal's) brain is with the left-wingers, his heart is with Mahatma Gandhi'. At the practical level, Nehru realized that Gandhi's leadership was indispensible for launching any mass movement.

For his part Gandhi was aware of Nehru's devotion to him and of his burning patriotism and his appeal to the young intellectuals of the country. For a while Nehru and the fiery Bose, idol of the Bengali youth, joined hands and campaigned for a total break with the British connection, which was at variance with Gandhi's own wish to retain the British connection on an equal footing with Britain and the other Dominions if possible, and

---

[1] He was on trial for criminal intimidation and abetment of extortion committed during the non-co-operation movement and was awarded eighteen months' rigorous imprisonment.

[2] *See*, the section on Mahatma Gandhi in Chapter 10.

to sever the ties with Britain only if necessary. Bose was the political heir to Das, who had differed from Gandhi on important issues, and did not revere Gandhi to the same extent as Jawaharlal. Eventually, Gandhi was able to undermine Bose[1] and elevate Jawaharlal so that in popularity and power, Jawaharlal became next only to Gandhi himself. In January 1942, Gandhi openly designated Nehru as 'my legal heir'.

Jawaharlal did not believe in council-entry and, like Gandhi, had been comparatively inactive while the *swarajists* had their way. In March 1926 he had gone to Europe with his father and some other members of the family and returned to India in time to attend the Madras Congress. While in Europe he had attended the Congress of Oppressed Nationalities at Brussels and visited Soviet Russia. He returned with renewed enthusiasm for freedom from foreign rule and 'with goodwill towards Communism, for, whatever its faults, it was at least not hypocritical and not imperialist... But Communists often irritated me by their dictatorial ways, their aggressive and rather vulgar methods, their habit of denouncing everybody who did not agree with them'.

At the Madras session Jawaharlal successfully proposed several resolutions. Some of these marked the commencement of his role as the foreign policy spokesman of the Congress. One welcomed the formation of the League Against Imperialism and promised Congress support in the struggle against imperialism; another demanded the recall of all Indian troops and police forces from China and from all foreign countries; a third condemned the war preparations of the British Government in India, in the Eastern Seas and specially in the North-West Frontier of India and declared that the people of India had no quarrel with their neighbours.

But Jawaharlal's most significant success was the passage of his resolution which read: 'This Congress declares the goal of the Indian people to be complete national independence.' Gandhi was still in semi-retirement from politics. He attended the Madras session but took no active part in the proceedings. Nevertheless, he afterwards expressed his displeasure in respect of the independence resolution: 'Congress stultifies itself by repeating year after year resolutions of this character, when it knows that it is not capable of carrying them into effect.'

Yet another notable resolution of the Madras Congress called for the setting up of an All-Parties Congress to draw up a constitution for India. This ultimately resulted in the production of what is known as the Nehru Report.

---

[1] *See*, p.189.

THE NEHRU REPORT

Indian pride had been stung by repeated taunts by Lord Birkenhead, the Secretary of State for India. Knowing that India was afflicted with communal disharmony, he had said in July 1925, 'Let them produce a constitution which carries behind it a fair measure of general agreement among the great peoples of India,' and he had reverted to the subject when the Simon Commission was nominated: 'I have twice invited our critics in India to put forward their own suggestion for a constitution. That offer is still open.'

As a result of invitations issued by the Working Committee of Congress 'to a large number of organizations', an All-Parties Conference met at Delhi in February and again in March 1928, but was unable to resolve certain differences between the Muslim League on the one hand and the Hindu Mahasabha and the Sikhs on the other.

When it met again at Bombay in May it was thought that a small committee might succeed in finding a way out. A committee was therefore appointed under the chairmanship of Motilal Nehru 'to consider and determine the principles of the Constitution for India'. Jawaharlal Nehru was General Secretary of Congress at that time. He was not a member of the Nehru Committee but attended the meetings of the Committee and assisted it generally.

The Nehru Report stated that 'there certainly are those who put their case on the higher plane of complete independence but we are not aware of any who would be satisfied with anything lower than Dominion Status'. It, therefore, opted for Dominion Status not 'as a remote stage of our evolution but as the next immediate step'. The 'Commonwealth of India' would have a House of Representatives consisting of 500 members, for the election of whom 'every person of either sex who has attained the age of twenty-one, and is not disqualified by law, shall be entitled to vote'. There would also be a Senate of 200 members elected by the Provincial Councils, a specific number of seats being alloted to each province on the basis of population. Clearly the central legislature as envisaged by the report was not based on the federal model, because the lower house was to be directly elected by general constituencies and in the upper house each province would not be given the same number of seats, like the Canadian, Australian, or American federations, but a number proportionate to its population. With regard to the Indian princely States, the 'Commonwealth of India' would discharge the same rights and obligations as the Government of India had done.

The committee recognized that 'the communal problem of India is primarily the Hindu-Muslim problem...[and] essentially the problem is how to adjust the differences between the Hindus and Muslims.' But it failed entirely to reconcile the claims of the two communities. It took shelter, instead, behind paper promises and unrealistic forecasts. At one place it wrote: 'If the fullest religious liberty is given, and cultural autonomy provided for, the communal problem is in effect solved, although people may not realise it. With this viewpoint before us we have provided several articles in the Declaration of Rights giving the fullest liberty of conscience and religion to each individual.' At another it prophesied: 'We are certain that as soon as India is free and can face her problems unhampered by alien authority and intervention, the minds of her people will turn to the vital problems of the day...parties will be formed in the country and in the legislature on entirely other grounds, chiefly economic we presume. We shall then find Hindus and Muslims and Sikhs in one party acting together and opposing another party which also consists of Hindus and Muslims and Sikhs. This is bound to happen if we once get going.'

A section of the Muslims at this juncture was prepared to accept joint electorates subject to certain conditions. They gathered at the Muslim Conference at Delhi on 20 March 1927 for which Jinnah, who presided, had issued invitations, and spelled out their position as follows:

After a protracted discussion, the Conference agreed to the institution of joint electorates under certain conditions. It was unanimously resolved that the Mohammedans should accept a settlement on the basis of the following proposals, so far as representation in the various legislatures in any future scheme of Constitution was concerned:

(1) Sind[1] should be separated from the Bombay Presidency and constituted into a separate province.

---

[1] The following facts may assist in understanding the constitutional debate:

In Sind the Muslims were 73.4 per cent, in the Punjab 55.3 per cent, in Bengal 54.0 per cent and in Baluchistan and NWFP they had an overwhelming majority. In India as a whole the Muslims were 24.1 per cent and the Sikhs 1.0 per cent. But the Sikhs pulled greater weight than their number because they were a militant people and were concentrated in the Punjab where they formed 14 per cent of the population. The Christians in India numbered fractionally more than the Sikhs (1.2 per cent) but they were thinly spread and were comparatively mild-tempered. The North-West Frontier Province was given the status of Governor's province in 1932 and Sind was separated from Bombay under the Act of 1935. Only Baluchistan continued to be centrally administered without an elected legislature of its own.

(2) Reforms should be introduced in the North-West Frontier Province and in Baluchistan on the same footing as in any other province in India

If this is agreed to, Mohammedans are prepared to accept a joint electorate in all provinces so constituted, and are further willing to make to Hindu minorities in Sind, Baluchistan and the North-West Frontier Province the same concessions that Hindu majorities in other provinces are prepared to make to Mohammedan minorities.

In the Punjab and Bengal, the proportion of representation should be in accordance with the population.

In the Central Legislature Mohammedan representation shall not be less than a third, and that also by a mixed electorate.

At its Calcutta session (30 December 1927-1 January 1928), the Jinnah Group of the Muslim League adopted a resolution on the lines of the 'Delhi Muslim Proposals'. During the debate Abul Kalam Azad supported the resolution on the ground that whatever treatment the Hindus accorded the Muslims in the Hindu-majority provinces, the Muslims would be in a position to accord the same treatment to the Hindus in the Muslim-majority provinces. But even Jinnah's conditional acceptance of joint electorates was unacceptable to the majority of Muslims. The Shafi Group positively distanced itself from 'the proposals formulated by some Muslims in their individual capacity at Delhi on 20 March 1927,' and in a statement to the Associated Press on 29 March 1927, explaining the Delhi Proposals, Jinnah himself acknowledged that though he was 'personally not wedded to separate electorates...the overwhelming majority of Mussulmans firmly and honestly believe that is the only method by which they can be secure'.

The provisions of the Nehru Report that the Muslims found most objectionable were the allocation of residuary powers to the centre (which negated provincial autonomy), the establishment of joint electorates, the refusal to reserve seats 'for any community in the Punjab and Bengal', and the repudiation of the principle of weightage on the ground that 'a minority must remain a minority whether any seats are reserved for it or not'. The report recognized that 'representation in excess of their proportion in the population fixed for Muslims in a number of provinces under the Lucknow Pact, as well as the Montagu-Chelmsford reforms, will disappear under our scheme'. It dismissed the principles of separate electorates and the reservation of seats because these devices were 'clumsy and objectionable methods' of giving a feeling of security to the minorities and it rejected the Muslim plea that their community should dominate in at least some parts of India because it was 'a novel suggestion' (another negation of provincial autonomy).

In unilaterally repudiating the Lucknow Pact, which had been in the nature of a Congress-Muslim League treaty of peace and fellowship, the authors of the report committed a colossal blunder. The Muslims never forgave Congress for it. It had given them a taste of the kind of constitution the Hindu majority would impose if they had the chance to do so. Prestigious Muslim politicians such as Jinnah and the Ali brothers, who had hitherto co-operated with Congress in various ways, were alienated and began to insist even more vehemently than before upon having constitutional safeguards.

At the All-Parties Convention, which opened at Calcutta on 22 December 1928 to consider the Nehru Report, Jinnah endeavoured to achieve an amicable settlement of the problem. He urged in vain that there should be no less than one-third Muslim representation at the centre, that the Muslims in the Punjab and Bengal should have seats reserved for them on a population basis and that the constitution should be federal, with residuary powers vested in the provinces. 'What we want,' he said, 'is that Hindus and Muslims should march together until our object is attained. Therefore it is essential that you must get not only the Muslim League but the Mussalmans of India and here I am not speaking as a Mussalman but as an Indian. And it is my desire to see that we get seven crores of Mussalmans to march along with us in the struggle for freedom. Would you be content with a few? Would you be content if I were to say, I am with you? Do you want or do you be not want the Muslim India to go along with you?' He left Calcutta a disappointed man and said to a friend, ' This is the parting of ways.'

During the proceedings of the convention Tej Bahadur Sapru, who was a member of the Nehru Committee and had drafted a part of the report, had tried to save the day by pleading, 'give him [Jinnah] what he wants and be finished with it. I am going to ask him to be reasonable but we must, as practical statesmen, try to solve the problem and not be misled by arithmetical figures,' but he was unable to carry the house.

The Nehru Report thus, instead of bringing Hindus and Muslims together, pushed them further apart. Jinnah so far had differed with Congress chiefly on Gandhi's programme of civil disobedience. He had continued to work for Hindu-Muslim unity and had striven shoulder to shoulder with Congress for the attainment of full responsible government. Henceforth he increasingly viewed Congress as a Hindu organization from which the Muslims could expect no justice. If the

Muslims wished to achieve their rightful place in India, they had to become a united community so that they could negotiate with Congress from a position of strength. It took time for these developments to grow and become visible, but the seed of Pakistan had been sown.[1]

Though the Nehru Report had angered the Muslims, it had also done them a good turn. They were at that time a divided community, but for the moment they forgot their differences and met in an All-Parties Muslim Conference at Delhi under the presidency of the Aga Khan. Prominent among those who attended were Jinnah, Shafi, and the Ali brothers. On 1 January 1929 the Conference unanimously adopted a manifesto of Muslim demands, of which the principle ones were that:

> In view of India's vast extent and its ethnological, linguistic, administrative and geographical or territorial divisions, the only form of government suitable to Indian conditions is a federal system with complete autonomy and residuary powers vested in the constituent States.

> The right of Moslems to elect their representatives on the various Indian legislatures through separate electorates is now the law of the land, and Muslims cannot be deprived of the right without their consent.

> In the provinces in which Mussalmans constitute a minority they shall have a representation in no case less than that enjoyed by them under the existing law [i.e. 'weightage'].

> It is essential that Mussalmans should have their due share in Central and Provincial cabinets.

That the Ali brothers subscribed to this manifesto meant that they too had openly parted company with their Congress friends on account of the Nehru Report. Muhammad Ali had been a party to the Delhi proposals and along with Jinnah had unsuccessfully tried at the All-Parties Convention at Calcutta to have the Nehru Report modified. In his view, 'the Nehru constitution is the legalised tyranny of numbers and is the way to rift and not peace. It recognises the rank communalism of the majority as nationalism. The safeguards proposed to limit the high-handedness of the majority are branded as communal.' Shaukat Ali was equally bitter: 'Motilal and the Nehru Committee have intentionally or unintentionally treated the Muslim point of view with undeserved contempt.'

---

[1] In the Central Assembly on 12 March 1929 Jinnah described the Nehru Report as 'nothing more than a Hindu counter-proposal to the Muslim demands which were made in 1927'.

But the unity of the Muslims at the Aga Khan's Conference was only apparent. With regard to the Nehru Report there were still some who desired its adoption, others who wanted it rejected, and yet others who favoured a compromise. At the Muslim League Council meeting at Delhi on 28 March, Jinnah presented fourteen points which were destined to become famous, but the meeting ended in disagreement. It was not till the late nineteen-thirties that Jinnah's Muslim League could claim to speak for all the Muslims of India. These fourteen points, nevertheless, are historically important because they represent Jinnah's considered response to the Nehru Report and inspired Muslim thinking in years to come. The draft resolution embodying the fourteen points ran as follows:

(1)   The form of the future constitution should be federal, with the residuary powers vested in the provinces.

(2)   A uniform measure of autonomy shall be granted to all provinces.

(3)   All legislatures in the country and other elected bodies shall be constituted on the definite principle of adequate and effective representation of minorities in every Province without reducing the majority in any Province to a minority or even equality.

(4)   In the Central Legislature, Mussalman representation shall not be less than one third.

(5)   Representation of communal groups shall continue to be by means of separate electorates as at present, provided it shall be open to any community, at any time, to abandon its separate electorate in favour of joint electorate.

(6)   Any territorial redistribution that might at any time be necessary shall not in any way affect the Muslim majority in the Punjab, Bengal and NWF Province.

(7)   Full religious liberty, i.e., liberty of belief, worship and observance, propaganda, association and education, shall be guaranteed to all communities.

(8)   No bill or resolution or any part thereof shall be passed in any legislature or any other elected body if three fourths of the members of any community in that particular body oppose such a bill, resolution or part thereof on the ground that it would be injurious to the interests of that community or in the alternative, such other method is devised as may be found feasible and practicable to deal with such cases.

(9) Sind should be separated from the Bombay Presidency.

(10) Reforms should be introduced in the NWF Province and Baluchistan on the same footing as in other provinces.

(11) Provision should be made in the constitution giving Moslems an adequate share along with other Indians in all the services of the State and in local self-governing bodies having due regard to the requirements of efficiency.

(12) The Constitution should embody adequate safeguards for the protection of Moslem culture and for the protection and promotion of Moslem education, language, religion, personal laws and Moslem charitable institutions and for their due share in the grants-in-aid given by the State and by local self-governing bodies.

(13) No cabinet, either Central or Provincial, should be formed without there being a proportion of at least one-third Moslem Ministers.

(14) No change shall be made in the constitution by the Central Legislature except with the concurrence of the States constituting the Indian Federation.

The draft resolution also mentions an alternative to the above provision in the following terms:

That, in the present circumstances, representation of Mussalmans in the different legislatures of the country and other elected bodies through the separate electorates is inevitable and further, the Government being pledged over and over again not to disturb this franchise so granted to the Moslem community since 1909 till such time as the Mussalmans chose to abandon it, the Mussalmans will not consent to joint electorates unless Sind is actually constituted into a separate province and reforms in fact are introduced in the NWF Province and Baluchistan on the same footing as in other provinces.

Further, it is provided that there shall be reservation of seats according to the Moslem population in the various provinces; but where Mussalmans are in a majority they shall not contest more seats than their population warrants.

The question of excess representation of Mussalmans over and above their population in provinces where they are in a minority is to be considered hereafter.

THE CALCUTTA CONGRESS

The Calcutta Congress commenced work after the All-Parties Convention had assembled to consider the Nehru Report in the same city. It lasted from 29 December 1928 till 1 January 1929. Its most important feature was the return of Gandhi to the centre of the political stage. The president-designate of the session, Motilal Nehru, was anxious to win the endorsement of Congress to the report over which he and his committee had laboured so much. He was aware that Bose and his own son Jawaharlal had a strong following which stood for 'complete independence', by which they meant severance of the British connection. Motilal needed Gandhi's support to win the approval of Congress for his own recommendation in favour of Dominion Status. Gandhi, fearing a split in Congress on the issue, agreed to strive for an acceptable compromise. He succeeded, but not without strenuous effort.

After negotiations between the two groups, which Jawaharlal found 'rather confusing and not very edifying', Gandhi believed he had obtained general agreement to the following resolution which he moved in the open session:

> Subject to exigencies of the political situation, this Congress will adopt the Constitution [recommended by the Nehru Committee] if it is accepted in its entirety by the British Parliament on or before the 31st December 1929, but in the event of its non-acceptance by that date or its earlier rejection, Congress will organise a campaign of non-violent non-co-operation by advising the country to refuse taxation and in such other manner as may be decided upon.

But the Mahatma was mistaken. Bose, supported by Jawaharlal, defiantly moved an amendment to the effect that the goal of the Indian people was 'complete independence' and there could be 'no true freedom till the British connection is severed'. The amendment was lost by 1,350 votes to 973 while 48 members remained neutral.

As no one really expected that the British Government would accept the Nehru constitution within a year, even Gandhi's resolution meant that the stage had been set for a confrontation with the government. And who but Gandhi could lead the movement effectively?

The Calcutta Congress also called upon the ruling Princes of the Indian States 'to introduce responsible government based on representative institutions in the States' and to 'enact laws guaranteeing elementary and fundamental rights of citizenship, such as rights of association, free speech, free Press, and security of person and property'.

LORD IRWIN'S STATEMENT OF 31 OCTOBER 1929

The years 1928 and 1929 were difficult for the British Government in

India. During the demonstrations against the Simon Commission there were assaults on the public by the police to prevent the demonstrators from getting out of hand. The death of Lajpat Rai following one of these incidents excited anger throughout the land.

Students all over Bengal, especially in Calcutta, had participated in the boycott of the Simon Commission and disciplinary action against a large number of them had been taken by the authorities. This caused the Students' Movement in Bengal to grow up under the encouragement of Bose and Jawaharlal. Soon, student organizations sprang up not only throughout Bengal, but also in other pars of the country.

Industrial labour was also in a state of agitation. A strike of 18,000 workers at the Tata Iron and Steel Works at Jamshedpur, less than 200 miles from Calcutta, lasted for some months. There were strikes near Calcutta, in the East India Railway Workshop and the Jute Mills. No less than 60,000 textile workers staged a strike in Bombay. There was also trouble in other places. The government eventually arrested thirty-one communist leaders on 20 March 1929 and put them on trial at Meerut, as already related. According to Jawaharlal some of the arrested persons were 'just trade unionists'.

In 1928, there was a successful demonstration of *satyagraha* by the peasants of Bardoli *tehsil* in Surat District where, in 1922, Gandhi had intended to start his Civil Disobedience Movement but had given up the idea because of the Chauri Chaura incident. The peasants of Bardoli at this time were angry at a recent enhancement of the land revenue by over twenty per cent. They appealed for guidance to Vallabhbhai Patel who, in consultation with Gandhi, advised them to refuse to pay the land revenue. The campaign of non-payment was well-organized and remained peaceful; coercive measures such as attachment and sale of land, seizure of buffaloes and imprisonment met with little success. The provincial government was considering action when Lord Irwin's government stepped in and ordered the local authorities to offer to hold an enquiry on the question of the assessment of land revenue, provided the peasants called off their campaign of non-payment. This offer was accepted. The enquiry having found in favour of the peasants, the land revenue demand was raised by a mere five per cent. The prisoners were set at liberty and the attached property was restored.

The Bardoli campaign was important for two things. First, it was demonstrated that Gandhi's method of peaceful civil disobedience could be successful provided it was undertaken for the redress of a concrete grievance and was carried out by dedicated and disciplined volunteers.

Secondly, it enhanced the status of Vallabhbhai Patel in the upper echelons of the Congress Party.

The year 1928 also witnessed a revival of terrorism. In December Bhagat Singh, who was accompanied by two other members of the Hindustan Socialist Army, shot dead a European police officer (J. P. Saunders) under the mistaken belief that he had delivered the *lathi* blows on Lajpat Rai's chest. On 8 April 1929, two members of the same association...Bhagat Singh and Batukeshwar Datta...each dropped a bomb on the official benches of the Central Assembly, killing no one but injuring some members. They were apprehended on the spot. Within a few weeks, the leaders and a large number of the members of the association were arrested. They were tried in what became known as the Lahore Conspiracy Case. During a hunger strike by prisoners in the jail, one of them, Jatindra Nath Das, died after sixty-four days of starvation. His death evoked much admiration in the country. On the morning of 23 December 1929, a bomb exploded under Lord Irwin's special train as it approached Delhi. The Viceroy was unhurt but some carriages were damaged and one servant was injured. On 23 March 1931, Bhagat Singh and his two companions were hanged for the murder of Saunders. Bhagat Singh is still remembered in India as a national hero.

Meanwhile, the Simon Commission had concluded its labours. It had paid two visits to India, the first from 3 February to 31 March 1928, the second from 11 October 1928 to 13 April 1929. The most influential leaders of the country had refused to have anything to do with the commission and Congress, which was the most influential political party in the country, was on the war-path. Its one-year ultimatum was due to expire at the end of December 1929. Clearly, some gesture of conciliation by the government was urgently needed.

The victory of the Labour Party in the May 1929 general election in England seemed to open the way for an initiative. Ramsay MacDonald replaced Stanley Baldwin as Prime Minister. The Labour Party had a tradition of friendliness toward India and some of its members had travelled to India to attend Congress sessions. In 1908 Dr Clark, MP, had not only attended the Madras Congress personally, but had also read a message from Keir Hardie, who had been mainly responsible for the foundation of the Labour Party. The famous Nagpur Congress session of 1920 was attended by three members of the Labour Party. Ramsay MacDonald himself had been invited to preside over the Congress session at Calcutta in 1911 but could not do so because of his wife's death.

In June, Lord Irwin went to England on four months' leave and had long consultations with the new government. He returned to India on 25 October 1929, and on 31 October made the following pronouncement:

> The Chairman of the [Simon] Commission...suggested that what might be required, after the Reports of the Statutory Commission and the India Central Committee have been made, considered and published, but before the stage is reached of the Joint Parliamentary Committee, would be the setting up of a [Round Table] Conference in which His Majesty's Government should meet representatives both of British India and of the States, for the purpose of seeking the greatest possible measure of agreement for the final proposals which it would later be the duty of His Majesty's Government to submit to Parliament... With these views I understand that His Majesty's Government are in complete accord... In view of the doubts which have been expressed both in Great Britain and India regarding the interpretation to be placed on the intentions of the British Government in enacting the Statute of 1919, I am authorised on behalf of His Majesty's Government to state clearly that in their judgment it is implicit in the declaration of 1917 that the natural issue of India's constitutional progress, as there contemplated, is the attainment of Dominion Status.

This was a twofold concession to Indian nationalism. In the first place it invited Indian leaders to sit as equals with their British counterparts to consider the future of India. The Indians thus got the Round Table Conference which they had desired. Secondly, India was being promised virtually complete independence because since 1926 that was what Dominion Status had come to means. But it was on the question of timing that the British Government and the Congress party eventually fell out. The former contemplated the grant of Dominion Status by stages; the latter wanted it in the immediate future.

A manifesto issued from Delhi early in November by Congress and Liberal leaders offered to attend the proposed Round Table Conference provided the British Government confirmed that the 'conference is to meet not to discuss when Dominion Status is to be established, but to frame a scheme of Dominion Constitution for India'. Because of his commitment to complete independence (i.e., independence without any British connection), Jawaharlal at first refused to sign the manifesto but he was persuaded to do so by Gandhi who said that, since Jawaharlal was due to preside at the Lahore Congress, the manifesto would lose much of its value if it did not bear his signature. Bose refused to sign the manifesto and, along with two others, issued a separate declaration opposing the acceptance of Dominion Status and participation in the Round Table Conference.

But Indian optimism was dampened when the prospect of Dominion Status for India came under fire in the British Parliament from powerful Conservatives such as Birkenhead and powerful Liberals such as Reading. The attitude of the Liberals was crucial because MacDonald's Labour Government was dependent for its survival on Liberal support.

On the eve of the Lahore Congress, Lord Irwin made one more effort to pacify Indian leaders. He invited them to meet him at Delhi on 23 December. Among those whom he saw that day were Gandhi, Motilal, Sapru and Jinnah. The meeting opened with expressions of horror at the explosion of the bomb under the Viceroy's train that morning and congratulations upon his escape, but it failed in its real purpose. Gandhi sought the assurance that the Round Table Conference would proceed on the basis of full Dominion Status. Lord Irwin was unable to provide this assurance.

THE LAHORE CONGRESS

In the provincial vote for the presidentship of the forthcoming Lahore Congress, ten provinces had voted for Gandhi, five for Vallabhbhai Patel and three for Jawaharlal Nehru. Gandhi was declared elected but he declined the honour and, when the All-India Congress Committee met at Lucknow on 28 September 1929 to elect a substitute, he proposed Jawaharlal's name. Patel thereupon stood aside and Jawaharlal was elected. Gandhi's reasoning, in the words of the official history of Congress, was that 'it is better that the engine should be in the charge of a young man full of enthusiasm, daring and confidence though the brakes should be in the charge of older and more seasoned and sedate politicians'.

Jawaharlal, just forty, was one of the youngest persons to preside over Congress. What made his selection unique was that he was immediately following his father in the highest office of the organization. In making Jawaharlal beholden to him the Mahatma had acted astutely. The older and conservative members of Congress had been worried at the growing strength of the left wing of the party under the combined efforts of Jawaharlal and Bose. After his election as president, Jawaharlal became a more compliant follower of the Mahatma. An early manifestation of this was Gandhi's success in prevailing upon Jawaharlal to sign the aforesaid Delhi manifesto in response to the Viceroy's statement of 31 October.

The Lahore Congress convened on the bank of the River Ravi on 29 December and concluded its deliberations on 31 December 1929. In his presidential address Jawaharlal said:

> Independence for us means complete freedom from British domination and British imperialism...India could never be an equal member of the Commonwealth unless imperialism and all it implies is discarded. So long as this is not done, India's position in the Empire must be one of subservience and her exploitation will continue...Out of imperialism and capitalism peace can never come. And it is because the British Empire stands for these and bases itself on the exploitation of the masses that we can find no willing place in it... I do not think that any form of Dominion Status applicable to India will give us real power. A test of this power would be the entire withdrawal of the alien army of occupation and economic control... I must frankly confess that I am a socialist and a republican and am no believer in kings of industry, who have greater power over the lives and fortunes of men than even kings of old, and whose methods are as predatory as those of the old feudal aristocracy... This Congress which claims self-determination cannot deny it to the people of the [princely] States. Meanwhile, Congress is perfectly willing to confer with such rulers as are prepared to do so and to devise means whereby the transition may not be too sudden. But in no event can the people of the States be ignored.

Gandhi personally moved the main resolution, which was passed with shouts of 'Mahatma Gandhi *ki jai*':

> This Congress is of opinion that nothing is to be gained in the existing circumstances by Congress being represented at the proposed Round Table Conference. This Congress, therefore, in pursuance of the resolution passed at its session at Calcutta last year, declares that the word *'Swaraj'* in Article I of the Congress Constitution shall mean complete independence, and further declares the entire scheme of the Nehru Committee's report to have lapsed, and hopes that all Congressmen will henceforth devote their exclusive attention to the attainment of complete independence for India. As a preliminary step towards organising a campaign for independence, and in order to make the Congress policy as consistent as possible with the change of creed, this Congress resolves upon complete boycott of the Central and provincial Legislatures and Committees constituted by the Government and calls upon the Congressmen and others taking part in the national movement to abstain from participating, directly or indirectly, in future elections, and directs the present Congress members of the Legislatures and Committees to resign their seats. This Congress appeals to the nation zealously to prosecute the constructive programme of Congress, and authorises the All-India Congress Committee, whenever it deems fit, to launch upon a programme of Civil Disobedience, including non-payment of taxes, whether in selected areas or otherwise, and under such safeguards as it may consider necessary.

At midnight of 31 December, Jawaharlal Nehru led a large crowd and hoisted the flag of independence.

The Lahore Congress witnessed the end of the Nehru constitution. Not only was it withdrawn as an olive branch to the British government, but its solution to the communal problem was also recognized to have been a failure. The relevant resolution read:

> As the Sikhs in particular, and the Muslims and the other minorities in general, had expressed dissatisfaction over the solution of communal questions proposed in the Nehru Report, this Congress assures the Sikhs, the Muslims and other minorities, that no solution thereof in any future constitution will be acceptable to Congress that does not given full satisfaction to the parties concerned.

Congress had learnt its lesson. It conveniently absolved itself from the difficult task of achieving communal agreement and stuck to the easier course of arguing that communal differences were the creation of foreign domination and would automatically disappear when British rule ended.

The Lahore Congress also resulted in the creation of a greater following for Congress in the North-West Frontier Province. Khan Abdul Ghaffar Khan...'The Frontier Gandhi'...had attended previous sessions along with individual delegates but Lahore, being near the frontier, enabled a large number of impressionable young Pakhtuns to attend the proceedings there. They went back full of enthusiasm and began to spread new ideas. From 1930 onward Ghaffar Khan's followers became vigorous supporters of the Congress movement.[1]

---

[1] Abdul Ghaffar Khan, elder brother of Khan Sahib, had started his Redshirt movement in 1920 because of Pathan resentment against the British Government for denying to their province the representative institutions given to other provinces in India under the new reforms. Congress being the only really effective political party in India at the time, the Redshirts joined forces with it against the British. They were popularly called *surkhposhan* (wearers of red clothes) because of the colour of the shirts they wore as a uniform. Their official designation was Khudai Khidmatgaran (Servants of God). In the course of a day-long discussion at his village in 1939, Khan Abdul Ghaffar Khan told one of the present authors (Burke) that he had affiliated his movement with the Congress Party mainly to ensure its survival. As a purely local organization the British Government could have easily crushed it without the knowledge of the outside world.

The Frontier Muslims wished to be ruled by nobody but to be left alone to practice their own form of traditional tribal democracy. They allied themselves with Congress at first not because they loved the Hindus more than the British but because Congress seemed the only means of getting rid of the British who were dominating them at the time. When Indian independence approached and the spectre of Hindu rule began to loom, they began to desert Congress. This will become apparent as the narrative proceeds.

CHAPTER 15

APPOINTMENT OF THE SIMON COMMISSION AND ITS REPERCUSSIONS (CONTINUED)

THE CIVIL DISOBEDIENCE MOVEMENT

Soon after the Lahore Congress, most Congress members walked out of the Central Assembly and the Provincial Councils. The All-India Congress Committee delegated to Gandhi its authority to launch the Civil Disobedience Movement and the country awaited the Mahatma's move with bated breath. 'In spite of the enthusiasm shown at the Congress session,' wrote Jawaharlal Nehru, 'no one knew what the response of the country would be to a programme of action...To give a start to our campaign, and partly also to judge the temper of the country, January 26 was fixed as Independence Day when a pledge of independence was to be taken all over the country'.

The pledge drafted by Gandhi was a long one. It said, in part, 'The British Government...has ruined India economically, politically, culturally and spiritually...We hold it to be a crime against man and God to submit any longer to a rule that has caused this four-fold disaster to our country.' Independence Day was observed with great enthusiasm in various parts of the country and, to quote Jawaharlal again, 'it revealed to us, as in a flash, the earnest and enthusiastic mood of the country...This celebration gave the necessary impetus to Gandhi, and he felt, with his sure touch on the pulse of the people, that the time was ripe for action.'

Even Gandhi's closest colleagues were taken aback when he decided to start the struggle by manufacturing salt, thus contravening the salt-law. 'We were bewildered,' recalled Jawaharlal Nehru 'and could not quite fit in a national struggle with common salt.' But the Mahatma had made a shrewd choice. The tax on salt was especially unpopular among the poor, who regarded salt as a bounty from nature. It affected

Hindus and Muslims alike and the making of salt was something in which everyone...old, young, man, woman, villager and city dweller...could participate. On 2 March 1930, Gandhi wrote to the Viceroy, 'I regard this tax [salt tax] to be the most iniquitous of all from the poor man's standpoint. As the independence movement is essentially for the poorest in the land, the beginning will be made with this evil.'

Equally ingenious was the programme for public salt-making. On 12 March, the Mahatma set out from Sabarmati *ashram*[1] on foot for Dandi on the sea-coast about 240 miles away, to manufacture salt by evaporating sea water. He was accompanied by seventy-nine volunteers from the *ashram* and was seen off by an estimated crowd of seventy-five thousand. He marched for twenty-four days, arriving at Dandi on 5 April, and manufactured salt on the following day, which was the anniversary of the inauguration of the non-co-operation movement, which on 13 April 1919 had suffered the Jallianwala massacre (6 to 13 April every year had been observed as National Week.)

Gandhi's march was a veritable pilgrim's progress. Villagers everywhere thronged to him and reverently listened to his message. More than 300 village headmen renounced their office. Gandhi's picturesque procession was a godsend to the national and international media, and illustrated accounts of mass devotion to Gandhi appeared in innumerable papers. 'As we saw the abounding enthusiasm of the people and the way salt-making was spreading like a prairie fire', observed Jawaharlal, 'we felt a little abashed and ashamed for having questioned the efficacy of this method when it was first proposed by Gandhi. And we marvelled at the amazing knack of the man to impress the multitude and make it act in an organised way.'

Originally, the Working Committee had authorized only Gandhi and his co-workers to start Civil Disobedience. However, while Gandhi was on the way to Dandi, the Working Committee met at Ahmadabad on 21 March and legitimized mass participation in the movement, as well as its expansion to cover activities other than salt making by permitting 'the Provincial Congress Committees to organize and undertake such Civil Disobedience as to them may seem proper and in the manner that may appear to them to be most suitable'. Civil Disobedience thus spread to old favourites such as the boycotting of foreign cloth, British goods, liquor, and drugs. Women came out of their seclusion in thousands and made effective pickets outside premises selling these items. Prominent among them were Jawaharlal's aged mother, sisters and wife. The last named was arrested on 1 January 1931. In many places, campaigns for non-payment of taxes and land

---

[1] On the banks of the River Sabarmati near Ahmadabad.

revenue were waged. Since at the time the world, and India with it, was in the grip of the great economic depression, these exhortations met with a ready response.

The government arrested Gandhi on 4 May 1930 after he had announced his intention to take possession of the salt works at Dharsana and Charsadda. His arrest was immediately followed by *hartals* all over the country. In Bombay there were strikes in cotton mills and railway workshops. At Sholapur six police posts were burnt down and several policemen were murdered; police firing killed 25 and wounded about 100. At Howrah too, the police had to open fire to disperse the crowd.

Salt depots at different places were raided. At most places Gandhi's followers remained non-violent under the rain of *lathi* blows which resulted in severe injuries. The most publicised raid was that at Dharsana on 21 May, in which 2500 volunteers took part. Webb Miller of the United Press USA witnessed the event personally and graphically described what he saw:

Mme Naidu called for prayer before the march started and the entire assemblage knelt. She exhorted them: 'Gandhi's body is in jail but his soul is with you. India's prestige is in your hands, you must not use any violence under any circumstances. You will be beaten but you must not resist; you must not even raise a hand to ward off blows'... A picked column advanced from the crowd... Police officials ordered the marchers to disperse under a recently imposed regulation which prohibited gathering of more than five persons in any one place. The column silently ignored the warning and slowly walked forward... Suddenly, at a word of command, scores of native police rushed upon the advancing marchers and rained blows on their heads with their steel-shod *lathis*. Not one of the marchers even raised an arm to fend off the blows. They went down like tenpins. From where I stood I heard the sickening whacks of the clubs on unprotected skulls. The waiting crowd of watchers groaned and sucked in their breaths in sympathetic pain at every blow...Then another column formed...They marched slowly towards the police. Although everyone knew that within a few minutes he would be beaten down, perhaps killed, I could detect no signs of wavering or fear. They marched steadily with heads up, without the encouragement of music or cheering or any possibility that they might escape serious injury or death. The police rushed out and methodically and mechanically beat down the second column. There was no fight, no struggle; the marchers simply walked forward until struck down.

Another eye-witness (F. W. Wilson, who wrote *The Indian Chaos*) noted that Congress volunteers were not above exaggerating the amount of beating to which they were subjected:

I have seen men who have not been within yards of a *lathi* fall on the ground and cry out that they had been hurt. I have seen them plastered indiscriminately with iodine, rushed on to a stretcher and driven away accompanied by roars of sympathetic cheers. I have actually seen a harmless spectator of a *lathi* charge seized by the over-zealous volunteer ambulance workers and held down on a stretcher kicking and struggling and protesting his innocence of hurt, while an eminent Parsi doctor bound up his head and arm.

A series of raids took place at Wadala near Bombay from 22 May onwards. On 1 June, 2500 volunteers figured in one of them. In one incident the principle of non-violence was breached. About 100 Congress volunteers led a mob of some 40,000 persons in a three-hour raid. The police used *lathis* and the mob used stones as missiles.

Some occurrences caused the government special concern. On the night of 18 April more than fifty terrorists raided the armouries at Chittagong in East Bengal, overpowered the guards and escaped with quantities of arms and ammunition.

Upon Abdul Ghaffar Khan's arrest in Peshawar on 23 April, disturbances broke out and fire was opened resulting in several deaths. Two platoons of Garhwal Rifles (Hindus) refused to fire at the unarmed public (mostly Muslims) and were court-martialled and punished. For some days control of Peshawar was lost. The tribesmen, ever spoiling for a fight and believing that British rule was on its last legs, made some raids into British territory.

The government had recourse to Press and other Ordinances. Congress organizations were outlawed and their property confiscated. Gandhi's arrest was followed by those of Jawaharlal and Motilal. Officially more than 60,000 persons were sent to prison but the actual number was larger because many political workers were charged with criminal offences such as intimidation and rioting and were not included in the count.

THE SIMON REPORT AND THE FIRST SESSION OF THE ROUND TABLE CONFERENCE

The Report of the Simon Commission was published in May 1930 but it had already been overtaken by Lord Irwin's announcement of 31 October 1929 promising the Round Table Conference. The Report's recommendations only served to alienate Indian nationalists further. It did not so much as mention Dominion Status, which had already been promised by the British Government as India's destination. The report declared that 'each province should be as far as possible mistress in her own house'. It recommended that dyarchy should lapse and the entire administration of the provinces be entrusted to ministers responsible to the legislature, except that the Governor would have overriding powers in certain matters such as the safety of the province or protection of the minorities. But no substantial change was recommended at the centre. The central government was to remain an official government not owing responsibility to the legislature. An all-India federation was envisaged which would include the princely States, but its achievement would have to be a lengthy process because 'a premature endeavour to introduce forms of responsible government at the Centre before the conditions for its actual practice have emerged would in the end result not in advance but in retrogression'.

In July 1930 Irwin made another effort to induce Congress to participate in the Round Table Conference by holding out the assurance that the Conference would approach its task unimpaired by the Simon Report. Sapru and Jayakar were permitted to visit Gandhi and the two Nehrus in jail, but in the end all efforts to obtain Congress co-operation failed.

The Round Table Conference in London held three sessions in all, the first from 12 November 1930 to 19 January 1931, the second from 7 September 1931 to 1 December 1931, and the last from 17 November 1932 to 24 December 1932.

The first session was inaugurated by the King and presided over by Prime Minister Ramsay MacDonald. It was attended by 89 members:16 from the three British political parties, 57 from British India and 16 from the Indian princely States. All the Indian interests except Congress were represented by well known figures. There were Muslims such as the Aga Khan, Jinnah, Shafi, and Muhammad Ali, and Hindu Liberals such as Sapru, Jayakar and Sastri. Sampuran Singh and Ujjal Singh represented the Sikhs, B. S. Moonje the Hindu Mahasabha, Ambedkar the depressed classes, Colonel Gidney the Anglo-Indians, K. T. Paul the Indian Christians, and Hubert Carr the British business community in India. The states were represented by the rulers of Bikaner, Kashmir, Bhopal and Patiala and by high officials from Hyderabad, Mysore and Gwalior.

The outlines of India's future constitution had already been sketched. Dominion Status, an all-India federation and provincial autonomy had been promised. Of the questions that still required determination, two stood out. The first was whether, and on what terms, the princely States would join the federation. There were 562 of them, ranging in size from Kashmir (84,471 square miles) to Vejononess (0.29 square miles). In the words of the Simon Report, 'they are ruled by hereditary Princes and chiefs who are in relations with the British Crown on terms which secure to them large powers of internal sovereignty, while their external relations are the responsibility of the Paramount Power.' The second important question facing the conference was the communal problem. The acceptance of provincial autonomy had partly resolved Muslim fears. In the Muslim majority provinces they could do to the Hindus what the Hindus did to the Muslims in the Hindu majority provinces. 'That gives us our safeguard,' said Muhammad Ali at the Round Table Conference, 'for we demand hostages as we have willingly given hostages to Hindus in other provinces where they form huge majorities.' But provincial autonomy was not the only safeguard which the Muslims demanded. Non-Muslim minorities also demanded safeguards. Thus the broad question remained: what electoral and constitutional safeguards should the constitution of independent India contain to protect the minorities?

With regard to the first problem the Round Table Conference scored an instantaneous breakthrough. Sapru, the very first speaker in the general discussion, made 'a very respectful appeal to some of my illustrious countrymen who are patriots first and princes afterwards,' and pleaded that 'the solution of the difficulty and the salvation of India' lay in the federal form of government. He invited the association of the States with British India mainly for three reasons:

> I say that they will furnish a stabilising factor in our constitution. I further say that the process of unification will begin at once. I lastly say that, in regard to matters of defence, they will furnish a practical experience which is yet wanting in British India.

The Maharaja of Bikaner, who immediately followed, agreed that 'an All-India Federation is likely to prove the only satisfactory solution of India's problem.' He went on to say that 'A Federation...has...no terrors for the Princes and governments of the Indian States. We, however, recognize that a period of transition will necessarily intervene before the Federal Government is fully constituted, and that federation cannot be achieved by coercion of the States in any form. The Indian Princes will only come into the Federation of their own free will, and on terms which will secure the just rights of their States and subjects.' Other speakers, princes as well as commoners, also welcomed a federation. Begum Shah Nawaz said that, 'for a big country like India, where different races and different interests exist, a government established on the basic principle of federation alone can be a success...The golden day for our country will be when the Indian India and the British India will link themselves for common purposes, thus forming themselves into one great nation.' With the achievement of unanimity with regard to the system of government at the centre, a major obstacle to an all-India responsible government had been overcome. MacDonald promised: 'With a legislature constituted on a federal basis, His Majesty's Government will be prepared to recognize the principle of the responsibility of the Executive to the Legislature'.

Why had the States decided to throw in their lot with British India? They were geographically, racially and culturally a part of greater India; their communications, trade and defence were inseparable from the rest of the subcontinent; their subjects could not remain unaffected by the growth of fundamental rights and democracy next door. The princes, moreover, were feeling dissatisfied with the definition of their constitutional status by the British government.

In 1926 Lord Reading had rebuffed the Nizam of Hyderabad's claim that in respect of the internal affairs of Hyderabad he stood on the same footing as the British government in India in respect of the internal affairs of India. 'The sovereignty of the British crown,' he was informed, 'is supreme in India, and therefore no ruler of an Indian State can justifiably claim to negotiate with the British Government on an equal footing...It is the right and duty of the British Government...to preserve peace and good order throughout India...The right of the British Government to intervene in the internal affairs of the Indian States is another instance of the consequences necessarily involved in the supremacy of the British Crown.' Hoping to retrieve the position, the princes had persuaded Lord Birkenhead to appoint in December 1927 a committee under Sir Harcourt Butler to report on the relationship between the Paramount Power and the Indian States but they fared no better. 'Paramountcy,' the committee reported, 'must remain paramount; it must fulfil its obligations.' The Paramount Power had the right to interfere with State sovereignty 'for the economic good of India as a whole,' and 'in case of widespread [popular] agitation for a change in the form and nature of Government, the Paramount Power would be bound to suggest such measures as would satisfy this demand.'

Although the Round Table Conference paved the way for a federation of princely India and British India, it was unable to solve the communal problem. In fact a further complication was added by Ambedkar's demand that for electoral purposes the Depressed Classes should be regarded as a community separate from the great Hindu family. The Depressed Classes as well as all the other minorities demanded separate electorates with weightage. The Muslim Delegation as a whole placed on record their position that 'no advance is possible or practicable, whether in the Provinces or in the Central Government, without adequate safeguards for the Muslims of India, and that no constitution will be acceptable to the Muslims of India without such safeguards.'

The British Government declared that 'it is the duty of the communities to come to an agreement among themselves.'

In his closing speech on 19 January 1931, the British Prime Minister stated that 'responsibility for the government of India should be placed upon Legislatures, Central and Provincial,' and held out the assurance that 'in such statutory safeguards as may be made for meeting the needs of the transitional period, it will be a primary concern of His Majesty's Government to see that the reserved powers are so framed and exercised as not to prejudice the advance of India through the new constitution to full responsibility for her own government.' Finally, he appealed to 'those engaged at present in civil disobedience' to co-operate in the future work of the Round Table Conference.

THE GANDHI-IRWIN PACT AND THE SECOND SESSION OF THE ROUND TABLE CONFERENCE

In order to give practical support to MacDonald's appeal Irwin announced on 25 January 1931 that, 'in order to provide opportunity for consideration of the statement made by the Prime Minister on the 19th January, my Government... have thought it right that members of the Working Committee of the All-India Congress should enjoy full liberty of discussion between themselves and with those who have acted as members of the Committee since January 1930.' The notification declaring the Working Committee to be an unlawful association was withdrawn and the release of the Congress leaders was handsomely timed to take place on 26 January, the anniversary of 'Independence Day'. On landing in India, the liberals Sapru and Sastri who had attended the Round Table Conference hastened to Allahabad where Gandhi and others had gathered round Motilal Nehru's sick-bed. They arrived too late to confer with Motilal, who passed away on 5 February, but were able to persuade Gandhi to write to the Viceroy for an interview.

The negotiations between Gandhi and Irwin began at Delhi on 17 February and continued intermittently till agreement was reached in the small hours of the morning of 5 March. The Gandhi-Irwin Pact stipulated, *inter alia*, that the Civil Disobedience Movement would be 'discontinued', (which signified that the agreement was a truce, not a permanent peace); that 'the boycott of British goods as a political weapon' would be given up; that picketing for the promotion of Indian goods or against the consumption of liquor and drugs would be carried out within the limits of ordinary law; that residents in villages immediately adjoining areas where salt could be made would be permitted to make it but not for sale; and that people imprisoned in connection with Civil Disobedience for offences which did not involve violence would be released. The Viceroy refused Gandhi's demand for a public enquiry into the conduct of the police.

The most important clause of the agreement was the following:

> As regards constitutional questions, the scope of future discussion is stated, with the assent of His Majesty's Government, to be with the object of considering further the scheme for the constitutional Government of India discussed at the Round Table Conference. Of the scheme there outlined, Federation is an essential part. So also are Indian responsibility and reservations or safeguards in the interests of India, for such matters as, for instance, Defence, External Affairs, the position of Minorities, the financial credit of India, and the discharge of obligations.

This part of the agreement came as a tremendous shock to those of Gandhi's colleagues who were thinking in terms of immediate independence. 'Were all our brave words and deeds to end in this?' mused Jawaharlal Nehru, 'The independence resolution of Congress, the pledge of 26 January, so often repeated?'

But the truth of the matter was that government as well as Congress desired a pause in their confrontation. Neither the Civil Disobedience Movement nor the boycott of the Round Table Conference decreed by Congress had been unqualified successes. Hindu-Muslim unity, which had given a national dimension to the non-co-operation movement of the Khilafat days, was lacking. The Muslims, except in the North-West Frontier Province, had largely shunned the Civil Disobedience Movement. At a meeting of the All-Indian Muslim Conference at Bombay in April 1930 Muhammad Ali declared, 'We refuse to join Mr Gandhi because his movement is not a movement for complete independence of India but for making the seventy millions of Indian Mussalmans dependent on the Hindu Mahasabha.' After the arrest of the Congress leaders the Civil Disobedience movement had lost its sense of direction and ceased to be a real threat. Congress workers were weary of strife and needed respite.

With regard to the Round Table Conference, Congress leaders had noted with dismay that apart from themselves everyone who was anybody in the politics of the country had attended the conference. 'One reality stood out,' wrote Nehru, 'that even in the hour of our country's sorest trial, and when our men and women had behaved so wonderfully, there were some of our countrymen who were prepared to ignore our struggle and give their moral support to the other side.' And of course those who had attended the conference could justifiably claim that the conference had made a real advance beyond the Simon recommendations.

For their part the forces of law and order...the magistrates, the police and the jail authorities...were not averse to a break in their exertions. And most of all there was the political reality that, though Congress was the only absentee from the London Conference, it was the best organized, most numerous and strongest political force in India and was recognized as such in America and elsewhere. No conference purporting to represent all the interested parties could be legitimate without it.

The inclusion of the States in the federation had pacified some of the conservative and liberal critics of the MacDonald government's Indian policy. It was thought that the conservative princes plus the Muslims would be able to balance the more radical Congress elements at the centre. But some conservatives, notably Winston Churchill, were still unreconciled and were incensed at the sight of the King Emperor's deputy in India negotiating as an equal with Gandhi, who in their eyes was a rebel. It was 'also alarming and also nauseating,' Churchill said in his address to the West Sussex Conservative Association on 23 February 1931, 'to see Mr Gandhi, a seditious Middle Temple lawyer, now posing as a *faqir* of a type well known in the East, striding half-naked up the steps of the Viceregal Palace, while he is still organizing and conducting a campaign of civil disobedience, to parley on equal terms with the representative of the King Emperor.'

Gandhi's next task was to have his pact with Irwin ratified by Congress, which was to commence a plenary session at Karachi on 29 March 1931. His tactics were superb and he got his way. It so happened that six days before Congress convened, Bhagat Singh and his two terrorist companions were executed, despite Gandhi's request to the Viceroy to have their capital punishment commuted. It was feared that this would strengthen the hand of those who were opposed to the pact. However, a tactful resolution on Bhagat Singh and his companions, while disassociating Congress from political violence, placed 'on record its admiration of the bravery and sacrifice' of the deceased. Kishan Singh, father of Bhagat Singh, was also persuaded to speak in support of the Congress leadership.

Gandhi asked Nehru, who was among those who were critical of the accord with Irwin, to move the resolution ratifying the pact. 'I hesitated,' recalled Nehru in his *Autobiography*, 'it went against the grain, and I refused at first... Almost at the last moment...I decided to sponsor it.' On an earlier page he had confessed: 'My father's death had brought him [Gandhi] particularly near to me.'

The resolution reiterated that 'the Congress goal of *Pura Swaraj* (complete independence) remains intact' but authorized Gandhi to represent it at the Round Table Conference 'with the addition of such other delegates as the Working Committee may appoint to act under his leadership.' Though the government was reported to be willing to invite a Congress delegation of between fifteen and twenty, the Working Committee in the end nominated Gandhi as the sole representative.

Two developments nearly caused Gandhi not to attend the Round Table Conference. One was the flaring up of a vicious communal riot at Cawnpore during the very week of the Congress session at Karachi...Gandhi was aware that his success at the London Conference depended upon his ability to achieve Hindu-Muslim agreement. The other was the growing tension between the Congress workers and the forces of law and order, with each party blaming the other for breaches of the Gandhi-Irwin truce.

The darkening of the political atmosphere had partly resulted from the fact that the conciliatory Lord Irwin had been succeeded as Viceroy by Lord Willingdon on 17 April 1931. Willingdon had been Governor of Bombay and Madras and Governor-General of Canada. His outlook was more bureaucratic than that of his predecessor and he believed in swift and stern measures to curb political agitation. He regarded Gandhi as 'the most Machiavellian, bargaining little political humbug I have ever come across'. Secretary of State Hoare rightly observed that unlike Irwin, Willingdon did not 'understand Gandhi's personality, and on that account underrated his power'.

But in the end, after some last-minute meetings with the Government of India representatives at Simla, Gandhi agreed to go to London and was provided with a special train to enable him to catch the boat from Bombay on 27 August. One of the concessions which had persuaded him to go was the promise that government would hold an enquiry into the allegation of police excesses in the collection of revenue in Bardoli. Shortly before the second session of the Round Table Conference began, there had been a change of government in the United Kingdom. The strain of the economic depression had resulted in the formation of a national government. Ramsay MacDonald remained Prime Minister but his government was predominantly Conservative. The Conservative Samuel Hoare had replaced the Labourite Wedgewood Benn as Secretary of State for India. There was bound to be greater emphasis on safeguards for minorities and less haste in the journey toward independence.

To some extent it was inevitable that the second session should have been an anticlimax. The first session had produced optimistic generalities. The task of filling in details raised difficulties. Ramsay MacDonald's closing speech reviewing the work of the second session was far less enthusiastic than the one he had made at the end of the previous meeting. 'It has not yet been possible for the States to settle among themselves their place in the Federation and their mutual relationship within it.' Furthermore there stood 'in the way of progress, whether for the Provinces or the Centre, that formidable obstacle, the communal deadlock...This Conference has twice essayed this task; twice it has failed.' Having come down to specific problems, the way ahead lay through 'bodies which are really committees and not unwieldy conferences'.

Gandhi was not the only newcomer to the second session. There were also Madan Mohan Malaviya, the poet-philosopher Muhammad Iqbal, Mrs Sarojini Naidu and some others. The last-named was a member of the Congress Working Committee but attended the session as a representative of Indian women. But Gandhi was the star attraction and all eyes were on him. His task was by no means an easy one. While his mandate was to demand independence forthwith, the British government were in no hurry to hand over power, and the princes and the minorities wished to have their rights clearly acknowledged beforehand and made a part of the constitution of independent India.

A larger delegation might have made matters even worse by generating greater heat. Jawaharlal Nehru and Bose would certainly have been more belligerent than the soft-spoken Mahatma. There really was not sufficient common ground between the various parties round the table for them to have arrived at an amicable settlement of the issues that divided them.

Gandhi caused resentment among other delegates by claiming that Congress alone represented 'all Indian interests and classes...Congress... does represent all the minorities which have lodged their claim here.' He was a member of the committee on minorities but failed in his endeavours to reconcile the different points of view and had to report, 'It is with deep sorrow and deeper humiliaton that I have to announce utter failure to secure an agreed solution of the communal question.' In the end MacDonald had to say that if the Indians could not reach a communal settlement amongst themselves, the British Government 'would be compelled to apply a provisional scheme' so that further progress in other respects was not barred. But he begged of them 'once more to take further opportunities to meet together and present us with an agreement'.

Gandhi was specially grieved at Ambedkar's demand for separate electorates for the Untouchables. Zafrulla Khan, who was a member of the Muslim delegation (and after independence was Pakistan's first Foreign Minister and later President of the International Court of Justice) has related how anxious Gandhi was to thwart Ambedkar. In his reminiscences, *Servant of God*, he states that several meetings between Gandhi and the Muslim delegation took place in the Aga Khan's suite in the Ritz Hotel at the instance of Mrs Naidu, but conversations ended when Gandhi insisted that the Muslim delegation must oppose the inclusion of separate representation for the Untouchables as this would disrupt Hindu society. The Muslims pointed out that it was for the Caste Hindus and Untouchables to come to an understanding with each other. Whatever agreement was reached between them would be supported by the Muslims, but they could not, while insisting upon separate electorates for themselves, oppose them for the Untouchables.

Gandhi also served on the committee on federal structure. On the subject of independence he said, 'I am here very respectfully to claim complete control over the army, over the defence forces and over external affairs.' Unlike Nehru, who wished to break off all constituitional ties with Britain, Gandhi asked for Dominion Status:[1] 'I still aspire to be a citizen, not in the Empire, but in a Commonwealth; in a partnership…if God wills it an indissoluble partnership…but not a partnership superimposed upon one nation by another. Hence you find here that Congress claims that either party should have the right to sever the connection, to dissolve the partnership.'

The second session of the Round Table Conference did take two important decisions. These were that the North-West Frontier Province

---

[1] In February 1937, Gandhi's close friend H. S. L. Polak asked him what he meant by the phrase 'Complete Independence', as it was one that lent itself to a number of interpretations. Gandhi replied: 'Your question is whether I retain the same opinion as I did at the RTC [Round Table Conference] of 1931. I said then and repeat now that so far as I am concerned, if Dominion Status were offered in terms of the Statute of Westminster, i.e., the right to secede at will, I would unhesitatingly accept it.'

would become a Governor's Province and that Sind would be given that status if it could be made financially viable .

Though Gandhi the politician had not been able to score many points round the conference table, Gandhi the ambassador-at-large of Congress performed admirably. Secretary of State Hoare, who had felt some trepidation before he had personally met the Mahatma, found Gandhi's manners 'superb' and soon settled down to an amicable relationship with him.

Gandhi declined official hospitality and stayed instead with his friends in the poor district of Bow in the East End of London. He talked and joked with the people during his daily walk and visited some of their homes. The children loved him and brought him toys on his birthday. He even proved to be a popular visitor in Lancashire, where the textile industry had suffered much because of the boycott of foreign cloth in India. He spoke at Eton, Cambridge and the London School of Economics and met notables such as Lloyd George, the Archbishop of Canterbury and other church dignitaries, Bernard Shaw and even Charlie Chaplin (Winston Churchill declined to see him). On the way home he met Mussolini in Italy but the Pope would not receive him.

In his book, *Nine Troubled Years*, Samuel Hoare has written an interesting account of Gandhi's meeting with King George V. At first the king demurred at inviting Gandhi, the 'rebel with no proper clothes on', to the garden party he was giving to the delegates, but in the end he agreed to include him in the guest list. 'It was arranged that at the party I was to fetch up Gandhi at a suitable moment for presentation to the King... When I presented him, there was a difficult moment. The King was obviously thinking of Gandhi's responsibility for civil disobedience. However, when they were once seated, the King's simple sincerity and Gandhi's beautiful manners combined to smooth the course of the conversation, though more than once I became nervous when the King looked resentfully at Gandhi's knees... As Gandhi was taking his leave, His Majesty could not refrain from uttering a grave warning: "Remember, Mr Gandhi, I won't have any attacks on my Empire." I held my breath in fear of an argument between the two. Gandhi's *savoir-faire* saved the situation with a grave and deferential reply. "I must not be drawn into a political argument in Your Majesty's Palace after receiving Your Majesty's hospitality." They then took leave of each other as friendly guest and host.'

THE RESUMPTION OF THE CIVIL DISOBEDIENCE
MOVEMENT AND ITS END

The Delhi truce between the government and Congress, which was already under strain before Gandhi left for London, had broken down completely by the time he returned to India on 28 December 1931. There were four main areas of conflict. Firstly, the conduct of the Bardoli enquiry into the excesses of the police had disappointed Congress, and on 13 November 1931 the Congress advocates...Vallabhbhai Patel and Bhulabhai Desai...withdrew from it on the ground that the trend of the enquiry was 'distinctly hostile and one-sided'. Secondly, terrorism in Bengal had intensified and the outrages included the murders of the Inspector General of Prisons and three successive Magistrates of Midnapore. Thirdly, a no-tax movement among the peasants of the United Provinces had been launched with Nehru's support. Fourthly, in the Frontier Province, the 'Redshirts' under Ghaffar Khan were propagating disaffection and had clashed with the police several times.

Lord Willingdon's government issued numerous Ordinances to suppress the disorder. In 1930 the Ordinances had been promulgated to meet the situation as it developed; now the government took the initiative and passed Ordinances in anticipation of things to come. 'Every conceivable power was given and taken under a batch of all-India and provincial Ordinances,' recalled Nehru, 'organizations were outlawed; buildings, property, automobiles, bank accounts were seized; public gatherings and processions forbidden and newspapers and printing presses fully controlled.' On 26 March 1932, Secretary of State Hoare stated in the House of Commons that drastic and severe Ordinances had been drawn up because 'the government, with the full knowledge at their disposal, sincerely believed that they were threatened with an attack on the whole basis of government and that Ordinances were essential if India was to be prevented from drifting into anarchy.'

Ghaffar Khan, his brother Khan Sahib and Nehru were already in prison when the Mahatma returned home. Gandhi's attempts to see the Viceroy came to nought after an exchange of telegrams, mainly because the latter declined to grant an interview under the threat of a formal resumption of the Civil Disobedience Movement. The fight was now openly on and Gandhi and Vallabhbhai Patel were arrested on 4 January 1932.

For about four months the Civil Disobedience Movement was prosecuted vigorously, but thereafter it began to flag. Pandit Malaviya reviewed the events of these four months in a public statement issued on 2 May 1932:

During these four months up to April 20th last, according to the reports published in the Press, 66,646 persons, among whom were included 5,325 women and many children, have been arrested, imprisoned and humiliated. This could not possibly include arrests in the far-off villages in the interior of the country and, therefore, Congress estimates the total arrests to be over 80,000 up to date. The jails are overcrowded and ordinary prisoners are being released before their time to make room for political prisoners. To this has to be added the number of arrests made during the last ten days, including those of the delegates to the Delhi Congress. According to the reports in the Press, firing has been resorted to in at least 29 cases with considerable loss of life. There have been *lathi* charges on unarmed crowds at 325 places. There have been 633 cases of house searches and 102 cases of confiscation of property. A general policy has been pursued of imposing extraordinarily heavy fines on persons who have been convicted in connection with the movement and property far in excess of what was necessary for realizing the amount of the fines has been attached and sold. The Press has been gagged as it has never been gagged before. 163 cases have been reported where the newspapers and public presses have been regulated by orders for confiscation, demands for security and consequent closing down of the presses, warnings, searches and arrests of editors, printers or keepers. Numerous public meetings and processions of non-violent men and women have been dispersed by *lathi* charges, and sometimes by firing.

Repression had its effect. In January and February, those convicted for political offences numbered 14,800 and 17,800 respectively. In March the figure dropped to 6,900 and continued to fall; in December it came to only 1,540.

To the utter bewilderment of even his own closest colleagues, the Mahatma suddenly diverted the attention of his followers from the Civil Disobedience Movement to the electoral rights of the Depressed Classes under Prime Minister MacDonald's communal award, and undertook his celebrated fast 'unto death' in September 1932, ending with the Poona Pact.[1] The news came to Nehru in gaol as a 'bombshell' and he felt annoyed with Gandhi 'for choosing a side-issue for his final sacrifice, just a question of electorate. What would be the result on our freedom movement? Would not the larger issues fade into the background, for the time being at least?...I felt angry with him at his religious and sentimental approach to a political question, and his frequent references to God in connection with it. He even seemed to suggest that God had indicated the very date of the fast. What a terrible example

---

[1] *See*, pp. 186-7.

to set.' Bose too lamented that the fast 'led to a complete side-tracking of the Civil Disobedience Movement in the country'. But more was to follow.

On 8 May 1933, Gandhi started a self-purification fast for twenty-one days which in his own words was 'a heart prayer for purification of myself and my associates for greater vigilance and watchfulness in connection with the Harijan cause'. The government released him on the same evening, declaring that it was doing so because of the nature of the object of the fast and the attitude of mind which it disclosed. At Gandhi's recommendation the Acting President of Congress (M. S. Aney) suspended the Civil Disobedience for six weeks. At the expiry of that period it was suspended for another like period. But these gestures had no effect on the Willingdon Government. An official communique of 9 May stated that there was 'no intention of negotiating with Congress for a withdrawal of the Civil Disobedience Movement'.

At an informal conference of Congressmen at Poona on 12 July 1933 which Gandhi attended, it was decided to suspend mass civil disobedience but to permit individual civil disobedience by persons who wished to offer it. This was a face-saving device. What chance of success did individual effort have when the mass effort had failed?

Gandhi was to inaugurate individual civil disobedience on 1 August but was arrested on the night before. He was released on 4 August and ordered to remain in Poona, but was re-arrested on the same day for disobeying the order and sentenced to imprisonment for one year. He commenced a fast on 16 August as a protest for not being allowed facilities to conduct an anti-Untouchability campaign. He became seriously ill and was released unconditionally on 23 August but decided to eschew political work and devote himself entirely to the cause of the Untouchables till the one-year sentence had expired.

'Ever since the Poona Conference of July 1933,' records the official *History of the Indian National Congress*, 'an increasing number of Congressmen were coming to form the view that, in the situation existing in the country as a result of Ordinance rule, a programme of entry into the Legislatures was necessary to find a way out of what was held to be a "stalemate".' At a conference at Delhi on 31 March under the presidentship of Dr Ansari it was decided to revive the Swaraj Party. Gandhi at that time was touring in the earthquake area of Bihar. Ansari went to Patna and held talks with him. On 7 April 1934, the Mahatma issued a statement advising 'all Congressmen to suspend civil resistence for *swaraj*...They should leave it to me alone.' At the same time Ansari also issued a statement with

Gandhi's approval that the political fight would now be conducted both within and outside the legislature. The curtain on the Civil Disobedience Movement was officially rung down by the All-India Congress Committee at Patna (18-19 May 1934). It confirmed the suspension of Civil Disobedience and endorsed the decision to enter the legislatures. In June the government ban on Congress bodies was removed and Congressmen contested the elections to the Assembly late in 1934.

As Nehru summed up: 'Apart from the severity of Government repression, the first severe blow to it [Civil Disobedience] came in September 1932 when Gandhiji fasted for the first time on the Harijan issue... Civil Disobedience was finally killed for all practical purposes by the suspension of it in May 1933. It continued after that more in theory than in practice... India was numbed by the violence and harshness of repression.'

Willingdon's government had thus triumphed physically, but emotionally the Congress leadership and the government had moved much further apart. Congress merely waited for a suitable opportunity to join battle once more.

Gandhi's personal saintliness was revered by his followers as deeply as ever but his political performance as the dictator of Congress came in for severe criticism. Already on 9 May 1933, a joint statement by Bose and Vithalbhai Patel had declared: 'We are clearly of the opinion that Mr Gandhi as a political leader has failed. The time has, therefore, come for a radical re-organization of Congress on a new principle with a new method, for which a new leader is essential as it is unfair to Mr Gandhi to work the programme not consistent with his life-long principles.' Gandhi resigned his membership of Congress at the Bombay session in October 1934. Though he held out the assurance that his advice and guidance would be available whenever necessary, he never again formally joined Congress. The official history of Congress contains this explanation of the Mahatma's formal withdrawal from the leading role on the political stage:

Gandhi had begun to feel that he [was] a big weight weighing down upon Congress and the more he had suppressed himself, the more had he added to that weight. Civil Disobedience had to be inaugurated by him, withdrawn by him, and regulated by him. Peace and war were his concern. He [was] the one person to whom Congress had been looking up for orders to halt or march, to advance or retreat. The withdrawal of such a mighty force could only make for the strength of the body on which it had been acting, even as the retirement of the father from the home would but strengthen the son, encourage him to take the initiative, fill him with a sense of responsibility and inspire him with hope and courage, the more so when the patriarch is prepared to make his advice and guidance available to the family or the Nation whenever necessary. Gandhi had given such an assurance. His object [was] to make the Indian National Congress a power in the land.

Freedom from the party label enabled Gandhi to assume the role of a political conciliator, which enabled him to tell the Viceroy and others in subsequent years that he was speaking only for himself and not as the representative of Congress. In this way he could find out, for the benefit of the Congress policy makers, how the other party's mind was working without committing Congress in any way.

THE THIRD SESSION OF THE ROUND TABLE CONFERENCE

The last session of the Round Table Conference turned out to be the least important of its three sessions. It was attended by only forty-six delegates. The British delegation contained members of the parties which supported the National Government but the Labour Party, now the opposition, refused to participate. Also missing was the Indian National Congress. Nor did any of the important princes appear personally; they sent ten officials as their representatives. The only prince who attended was the Raja of Sarila who represented the Small States. No startling decisions were expected and none emerged.

In opening the session the Prime Minister explained that 'its object was to supplement the work so far accomplished at the Round Table Conference, by filling in, in some detail, the more important gaps left by the discussions at the two previous sessions.' At the conclusion of the session Secretary of State Hoare claimed that 'we have clearly delimited the field upon which the future constitution is going to be built.' At the same time Lord Sankey, the Lord Chancellor, reflected the general feeling that the princes had lost their earlier enthusiasm for joining the federation. Addressing the Indian States' Representatives he said, 'I would beg you to convey to Their Highnesses this message, that they should endeavour to make up their minds as soon as possible about their entry into the Federation. You have excited the hopes of India. Hope deferred makes the heart sick'.

CHAPTER 16

THE ACT OF 1935

The British Government's proposals arising from the deliberations of the three sessions of the Round Table Conference were published as a White Paper in March 1933. After parliament had approved the White Paper, it set up a Joint Select Committee for making recommendations on which a Bill could be drafted. The Committee came into existence on 11 April 1933 and after 159 sittings produced its report on 22 November 1934. On 19 December a Bill was introduced on the basis of that report and eventually received Royal Assent on 4 August 1935, under the title of the Government of India Act 1935. The Act came into force on 1 April 1937.

Constitutionally, only members of parliament could be members of the Joint Select Committee and sixteen from each House were chosen to serve on it. They were assisted by twenty representatives from British India and seven from princely India. Their status was that of assessors but they were allowed to take part in general discussions and examine witnesses. The Committee was chaired by Lord Linlithgow, who had previously presided over the Royal Commission on Indian Agriculture and was appointed Viceroy of India in April 1936.[1] Die-hard Conservatives led by Winston Churchill in the Commons and Lord Salisbury in the Lords opposed the reforms at every stage and were largely blamed for retarding the legislative process.

The Act separated Burma from India and created two new provinces: Sind by separation from Bombay, and Orissa by separation from Bihar. Both the new provinces were given the same status as the older ones by making them Governors' Provinces.

Dyarchy was abolished in the provinces but it was introduced at the centre. In the provinces the ministers responsible to the legislature were to have control over all provincial subjects except that the Governor was to act 'in his discretion' in certain matters and 'exercise his individual judgement' mainly in the discharge of his special responsibilities, the more

---

[1] He was appointed Viceroy by Baldwin, who had succeeded MacDonald as Prime Minister in June 1935.

important of which were: the prevention of any grave menace to the peace and tranquility of the province; safeguarding the legitimate interests of the minorities; the protection of the rights of civil servants and those of the States and their rulers; and the prevention of discrimination against British commercial interests. The Governor was also authorized (under Section 93) to assume all powers of government in the event of a breakdown of the constitutional machinery. While discharging his 'discretionary' functions and 'special responsibilities', he could refuse assent to a bill, promulgate an ordinance which would be valid for six months or enact a Governor's Act which would have the same validity as an Act of the legislature.

The property qualification for the voters electing members of the provincial legislatures was lowered, giving the right to vote to 35 million persons. This was five times the number previously entitled to vote and about one-fourth of the number who would have been so entitled had adult suffrage been granted. The communal distribution of seats followed the 'Communal Award' as modified by the Poona Pact. The systems of separate electorates and weightage were retained.

Part II of the Act, providing for the establishment of a federal government at the centre, was to come into force only after princely States whose population would aggregate half the total population of all the States had acceded to the federation. A State was deemed to have acceded to the federation after its ruler had executed an Instrument of Accession. The federal government and legislature could exercise authority over the affairs of a State only within the limitations set out in the instrument of accession. Paramountcy or treaty relationship with the British Government was to be the concern of the Crown Representative (an additional title for the Governor-General). This was consonant with the Butler Committee's recommendation that: 'In view of the historical nature of the relationship between the Paramount Power and the Princes, the latter should not be transferred without their own agreement to a relationship with a new government in British India responsible to an Indian legislature.'

The Act provided for a bicameral legislature at the centre, and the princely States were given weightage in both. The upper house—the Council of State—was to have 156 members from the States; the lower house—the Federal Assembly—was to consist of 250 members from British India and not more than 125 from the States. The States' representatives were to be nominated by the rulers.

Ministers responsible to the legislature were to administer most subjects, but not defence and external affairs, which were to be administered by the Governor-General with the help of Counsellors responsible only to himself. The Governor-General had legislative powers similar to those of the Governors. His 'special responsibilities' were also similar to those of the Governors except that he had the additional responsibility to safeguard 'the financial stability and credit of the Federal Government'.

Since not even a single State had acceded to the federation by the time the Act of 1935 was superseded by the Indian Independence Act of 1947, the federation in fact never materialised; the centre continued to be administered under the Act of 1919. Both the British Government and Congress were responsible for this delay.

It was not till 1939 that the Viceroy could communicate to the rulers the terms on which the government would regard their accession as acceptable, and negotiations were suspended when World War II broke out. Congress made no secret of the fact that it regarded the princes as a reactionary element whom the British were using to buttress British imperialism; it saw no reason why the people in princely India should not demand the same freedom as the people in British India were striving for. When provincial autonomy under the new Act came into force in 1937, the contrast between the systems of government in the two Indias became even more marked than before, and propaganda against the princes both within their own territories and outside was stepped up. The princes feared that the Crown Representative, who would be the same person as the Governor-General, responsible to the federal legislature, would not be able to defend their rights effectively. They saw no point in joining such a federation.

The constitution under the Act of 1935 was a far cry from the promised goal of Dominion Status: the key portfolios of External Affairs and Defence remained under foreign control and the Governor-General and the Governors, in whose appointments and removals the legislatures had no hand and who were not responsible to the legislatures, could veto laws passed by the legislatures and, under certain circumstances, could themselves promulgate Ordinances or enact Acts.[1] Nor was it lost on anyone that the centre was so constructed that the conservative elements such as the princes, the Muslims and the Scheduled Castes[2] could thwart the Indian National Congress, which in organization and numbers was the most important political party in the country.

[1] The Governor-General could enact a 'Governor-General's Act' and the Governor a 'Governor's Act'.
[2] The Untouchables or the Depressed Classes were given the official name of 'Scheduled Castes'.

In his speech in the House of Commons on the bill on 4 June 1935, Attlee protested that 'this Bill...is deliberately framed so as to exclude as far as possible the Congress party from effective power in the new constitution. On many occasions provisions have been deliberately put forward with that end in view...the Government have yielded time after time to the States and time after time to the minority communities, but have always stood strongly up against any yielding to Congress or Nationalists... Is the Bill going to be worked by the people of India? I do not think so. The indications are that if it is going to be worked at all it will be in a grudging spirit and that it is only too likely that its provisions will be used not for seeing how far it can be made useful for self-government but as a means of getting something more.'

THE RESPONSE OF CONGRESS TO THE REFORMS OF 1935

At its Bombay session in October 1934, Congress endorsed the Working Committee condemnation of the White Paper in that it 'in no way expresses the will be the people of India,' and declared that 'the only satisfactory alternative to the White Paper is a constitution drawn up by a Constituent Assembly elected on the basis of adult suffrage or as near it as possible'.

Nehru, who presided over the Congress session at Lucknow in April 1936, made a wide-ranging address which was relevant not only to the issues then facing Congress, but also to some which were likely to arise in the near future: 'To this Act [Government of India Act 1935] our attitude can only be one of uncompromising hostility and a constant endeavour to end it...We should seek election on the basis of a detailed political and economic programme, with our demand for a Constituent Assembly in the forefront...One of the principal reasons for our seeking election will be to carry the message of Congress to the millions of voters and to the scores of millions of the disenfranchised...When we have survived the election, what then are we to do? Office or no office?...To accept office and ministry, under the conditions of the Act, is to negate our rejection of it and to stand self-condemned...So far as we are concerned we shall fight against it [federation] to our utmost strength, and the primary object of our creating deadlock in the provinces and making the new Act difficult of functioning, is to kill the federation. With the federation dead, the provincial end of the Act will also go and leave the slate clean for the people of India to write on. That writing, whatever it be, can never admit the right of the Indian States to continue as feudal and autocratic monarchies[1]...If we stand for any human, political, social or economic rights for ourselves, we stand for those identical rights for the people of the States...The world is filled with rumours and alarms of war[2]...and aggressive Facism or Nazism steps continuously on the brink of war...It must be our right to say whether we join a war or not, and without that consent there should be no co-operation from us...it becomes necessary for Congress to declare clearly now its opposition to India's participation in any imperialist war'. He said also that he was convinced that the only key to the solution of the world's problems and India's problems lay in socialism, which 'means the ending of private property except in a restricted sense'.

The resolutions passed at the Lucknow session reiterated the rejection by Congress of the new constitution 'in its entirety'; stressed the demand for a Constituent Assembly; decided that Congress should contest the elections under the new Act 'in accordance with the mandate of Congress'; considered it 'inadvisable' for Congress to commit itself at that stage to any decision with regard to acceptance or non-acceptance of office and left the question to be decided at the proper time by the All-India Congress Committee after consulting the provincial Congress Committees; and declared the opposition of Congress to the participation of India in the terrible war that threatened the world. The proceedings made it clear that opinion on the question of office acceptance was sharply divided, and the differences soon began to be publicly aired, threatening the unity of the party.

The next session of Congress, at Faizpur (27-8 December 1936), was also presided over by Nehru. It resolved that the matter of acceptance or non-acceptance of office would 'be decided by the All-India Congress Committee as soon after the provincial elections as is practicable'.

The election manifesto adopted by the All-India Congress Committee in August 1936 declared that 'the purpose of sending Congressmen to the legislatures under the new Act is not to co-operate in any way with the Act but to combat it and seek to end it'. The constructive programme of the

---

[1] In a statement at Calcutta on 3 May 1937 Nehru characterised the princes as 'the close allies of British imperialism' in the national struggle.

[2] On 21 October 1937, H. W. Emerson, Governor of the Punjab, reported to the Viceroy that, during a recent visit to his province, Nehru had stated that 'there was certain to be a big European war within a few years and the British Empire was likely to come to an end within fifteen years'.

Congress representatives would be 'to end various regulations, ordinances and Acts which oppress the Indian people' and to redeem its promises to reform the system of land tenure, revenue and rent.

Elections were held in the following winter and results became known in February 1937. Congress achieved a better result than was expected even by its own leadership. This was chiefly due to the fact that Congress possessed an efficient organization and most persons who gave their votes to the Congress candidates believed they were carrying out Mahatma Gandhi's wish. In five provinces...the United Provinces, Bihar, Orissa, Central Provinces, and Madras...Congress won clear majorities; in Bombay it could rely on some friendly groups to give it a majority; in Assam and the North-West Frontier Province it constituted the largest single party; in Bengal it captured only 60 out of 250 seats, in the Punjab only 18 out of 175 and in Sind only 8 out of 60. It was clear that Congress victories had been gained mainly in the Hindu-majority provinces. Congress had ventured to contest only 58 Muslim seats out of 482 in the eleven provinces. It won 26, but 15 of these were in the Frontier Province where Ghaffar Khan and his brother Khan Sahib enjoyed a special position; no less than 424 seats were taken by non-Congress Muslims.

After the elections Congress could not evade the issue of acceptance of office any longer. The unexpected scale of election successes only whetted the appetite for taking office; this was specially so in the provinces where Congressmen could form ministries. Jawaharlal Nehru and his followers, on the other hand, were still adamantly opposed to accepting office. On 18 March 1937 the All-India Congress Committee passed the following resolution which was a compromise between the two opposing viewpoints: 'The...Committee authorises and permits the acceptance of offices in provinces where Congress commands a majority in the legislature, provided the ministership shall not be accepted unless the leader of the Congress party in the legislature is satisfied and is able to state publicly that the Governor will not use his special powers of interference or set aside the advice of ministers in regard to constitutional activities.'

Who was the inventor of this formula? On 30 March Gandhi revealed in a statement to the Press that he was 'the sole author of the office-acceptance clause of the Congress resolution'. It transpired that he had been able to persuade Nehru before the Working Committee meeting not to oppose the proposition. This had ensured its smooth passage in the open meeting and prevented a split in the ranks of Congress.

The Governors refused to give the assurance demanded by Congress on the ground that it would be contrary to the responsibility imposed upon them by the Act and by their Instrument of Instructions. Congress thereupon declined to form ministries in the five provinces where it controlled the legislatures. Gandhi, who had already persuaded his own party to accept office if government provided a face-saving assurance, now turned his attention to the government.[1] In his statement of 30 March he also said that his desire in drafting the All-India Congress Committee resolution of 18 March 'was not to lay down any impossible conditions. On the contrary I wanted to devise a condition that would be easily accepted by the Governors. There was no intention whatsoever to lay down a condition whose acceptance would mean even the slightest abrogation of the constitution.' He indicated that he would be satisfied with 'a gentlemanly understanding' that the Governors 'would not exercise their special powers of interference as long as the ministers acted within the constitution'. But the government, aware of the difference of opinion within the Congress leadership, had no inclination, at that stage, to humour Congress.

In a letter dated 22 April 1937 to Lord Zetland, who had succeeded Sir Samuel Hoare as Secretary of State for India, Lord Linlithgow argued that 'it would be a capital error to yield anything material to Congress...the effect of any concessions to Congress would be most seriously to shake the Services.[2] I think too that any manifestation of power by Congress to compel His Majesty's Government and the Government of India to accept a substantial change in the scheme of constitution would alarm the princes...[and] the effect of any such concession to Congress upon public opinion in India would be immediately to raise the prestige of Congress to such a pitch that it would cease to be a political party and would be regarded by the country as a whole as master of India.'

Though both sides continued to put a brave face on the matter, both in fact were under pressure to seek a way out of the impasse. Upon the refusal of the Governors to furnish the assurance demanded by Congress, the Congress parties in the five 'Congress Provinces' had refused to form ministries and the Governors had been compelled to install interim ministries which did not command a majority in the legislatures. Under the Constitution the Governors were required to summon the legislatures

---

[1] He declared a few days later: 'My function is that of a mediator between Congress and the Government.' (*The Hindustan Times,* 16 April 1937.)

[2] In England, Zetland was reminded by Lord Willingdon that the Services had been demoralized after the Irwin-Gandhi conversations which had resulted in the Gandhi-Irwin Pact of 5 March 1931.

within six months, at which time the position of the interim ministries would have become impossible. In the Congress camp too, the office-acceptance group was gaining strength day by day.

The deadlock was resolved when the Congress Working Committee, meeting at Wardha from 5 to 8 July, decided to accept office. The resolution referred to statements made by Lord Zetland, Lord Stanley (Under-Secretary of State for India) and the Viceroy and stated that, though these declarations exhibited a desire to make an approach to Congress, they fell short of the assurances demanded by Congress. The Committee felt, however, that 'the situation created as the result of the circumstances and events that have since occurred, warrants the belief that it will not be easy for the Governors to use their special powers. The Committee has moreover considered the views of Congress members of the legislatures and of Congressmen generally. The Committee has, therefore, come to the conclusion and resolves that Congressmen be permitted to accept office.' The resolution made it clear that the purpose of accepting office was 'to further in every possible way the Congress policy of combating the new Act on the one hand and of prosecuting the constructive programme on the other.'

As the bias of the resolution itself makes clear, the main reason for accepting office was 'the views of Congress members of the legislatures and of Congressmen generally', and the statements of the three Lords were used as a face-saving device. These statements were conciliatory generalities and did not, as the Working Committee resolution itself conceded, amount to the assurance that Congress had demanded as a condition for accepting office. Congress had in fact climbed down, and the British Government had merely made it easier for it to do so. An examination of what Zetland, Stanley and Linlithgow had said will make this clear.

Zetland had stated in the House of Lords on 6 May 1937: 'The reserved powers of which so much has been made by Congress will not normally be in operation; indeed they only come into the picture if he [the Governor] considers that the carefully limited special responsibilities laid upon him by the Act and impressed upon him by the Instrument of Instructions are involved, but even if the question of their use does arise—here is emphasised the spirit in which it was intended that the Constitution should be worked—it would be altogether wrong to assume that a Governor would immediately set himself in open opposition to his Ministry. That is the last thing in the world that I should either expect or desire.'

In the same House, Stanley had said on 14 June that the British

Government was 'anxious that, where Congress has the majority in a province, its representatives should take office,' and it was 'more than ready' to meet Congress half way. It was the 'earnest desire' of every one of the Governors 'not to act as a watchdog over the constitution, not to try to find fault with their new ministers, but rather, whatever their party may be, to act towards them as friends and collaborators.'

Finally, on 21 June 1937 Lord Linlithgow had publicly held out the asurance that the mere fact that 'the Government of India Act covers contingenices such as the dismissal of ministers, breakdown of the Constitution, or the like, is not for one moment to be taken as involving an assumption that the framers of the Act, those concerned with its administration, or anyone, indeed, who is concerned for the constitutional progress and development of this great country, wishes to see those contingencies turned into realities.'

Interestingly, Jawaharlal Nehru and Sir Stafford Cripps, a leading member of the Labour Party in the United Kingdom who was to play a leading role in the final phase of India's progress toward freedom, had been in friendly touch with each other during this period. On 22 February 1937, Nehru wrote to Cripps on what he considered to be the significance of Congress successes at the polls: 'the really significant feature of the election campaign has been the shaking up of the masses'. Cripps responded on 3 March. He congratulated Congress on the 'splendid victories' it had won and said, 'we shall all await with the most profound interest...the attitude you propose to take as regards the operation of the India Act. I am certain that you will maintain the most rigid opposition to imperialism in all its forms and also against the many Fascist methods which are being adopted in India today.' Eleven days later Cripps followed up his letter with a cable to Nehru containing his advice on the question of office acceptance: 'We trust that the Indian people will not be led into any compromise over the new Constitution and that the elected representatives will use the power entrusted to them by the people to work for the establishment of freedom by refusing to partake of the empty fruits of office which can do nothing but poison the pure and free spirit of Congress. We salute you as brothers and sisters in the common cause of freedom.'

After Congress had decided to accept office, the interim ministries in the five Congress provinces resigned and were replaced by Congress ministries. Congress was also able to form ministries in Bombay and the North-West Frontier Province. In *India Wins Freedom*, Abul Kalam Azad has revealed that in two provinces the Congress Premiers were selected on communal considerations. In Bombay the acknowledged leader of the local Congress was Nariman, a Parsee, but thanks to the intervention of Vallabhbhai Patel, the chief ministership was allotted to B. G. Kher, a Hindu. In Bihar, the foremost Congress leader was Syed Mahmud, a Muslim, but Rajendra Prasad successfully manoeuvred to have Sri Krishna Sinha, a Hindu, installed as chief minister. 'One has to admit with regret', comments Azad, 'that the nationalism of Congress had not then reached a stage where it could ignore communal considerations and select leaders on the basis of merit without regard to majority or minority'.

At a Working Committee meeting at Wardha (14-17 August 1937) the working of Congress ministries was reviewed. The Congress premiers related their experience in office, which uniformly was that 'the Government was anxious to avoid conflict and the higher services were co-operating'. 'Indeed, it is becoming apparent, I think', wrote Zetland to Linlithgow on 18 September 1937, 'that the tendency on the part of the Governors generally will be not, as Congress feared, to meddle needlessly in the administration of their provinces, but rather to refrain from intervening too long where a case for legitimate interference on their part exists. I am wondering if we shall not come under fire when Parliament reassembles on the ground that the Governors have been guilty of offences not of commission but of omission.' The Muslims, as will be related in the section after next, certainly complained that the Governors in the Congress-run provinces failed to protect their rights under the constitution.

CONGRESS AND PROVINCIAL AUTONOMY UNDER THE ACT OF 1935

Provincial autonomy under the Act of 1935 meant that every provincial ministry would be able to formulate and carry out its own programme and it would be responsible to its own legislature. The Congress high command nullified this arrangement by imposing its own control over all the Congress governments. The Working Committee appointed a parliamentary sub-committee 'to be in close and constant touch with the work of the Congress parties in all the legislatures in the provinces, to advise them in all their activities, and to take necessary action in any case of emergency'. The members of the sub-committee were Abul Kalam Azad, Rajendra Prasad and Vallabhbhai Patel. Congress further showed its low regard for autonomy by not letting its most prestigious members take office.

The Muslims and the princes, who had accepted federation on the understanding that the provinces and the states would enjoy a large measure of freedom from the centre, were shocked that Congress had nullified the autonomy granted to the provinces under the constitution and began to wonder whether their interests would be safe under a Congress-dominated federation of free India. But Congress was not thinking of the short-term effects of this policy; it was more concerned with not letting anything blur its goal of complete independence or delay its attainment. The rationale for Congress policy was best explained by Nehru, who had become the political and constitutional exponent of the party (while Gandhi remained its moral preceptor and 'permanent super-president' ready to take the lead at crucial junctures).

Nehru feared that the exercise of provincial autonomy would fuel regional patriotism at the cost of national patriotism: 'First issues will sink into the background, independence itself will fade away and the narrowest provincialism raise its ugly head. Our policy must be uniform for the whole of India, and it must place first things first, and independence is the first thing of all.' There was, further, the danger that the trappings of high office might dazzle the incumbents: there was a 'grave risk of our getting involved in petty reformist activities and forgetting the main issue [achievement of independence]...We are apt to be misled by the illusion that we possess power.'

Ministers and legislators really owed responsibility not to the electorate but to Congress. 'That electorate', the Pandit argued, 'plumped for the Congress candidates, not because of their individual merits, but because they represented Congress and its programme. Nothing could be clearer than this. The vote was for Congress...It is to Congress as a whole that the electorate gave allegiance, and it is Congress that is responsible to the electorate. The Ministers and Congress Parties in the legislatures are responsible to Congress and only through it to the electorate.'

MUSLIM POLITICS AND THE RISE OF
THE MUSLIM LEAGUE

Until the second part of the nineteen-thirties, the Muslims had neither a father-figure like Gandhi to unite and lead them, nor a substantial and efficient party like Congress to further their causes. The Indian newspapers also were almost all owned by Hindus. Jinnah attended the first two sessions of the Round Table Conference in London but was not invited to the third session. It was the Aga Khan whom the Muslim delegates elected as their leader for the conference, and later the Hindus joined them and made him the spokesman of the entire Indian delegation. Secretary of State Samuel Hoare has written that it was Zafrulla Khan and the Aga Khan 'who contributed most to our discussions from the Moslem side of the table'. Zafrulla 'soon acquired an exceptional influence in the conference by his clear mind and grasp of complicated detail'. But neither the Aga Khan nor Zafrulla Khan represented any political party.

Hoare did not think much of Jinnah's role at the conference: 'Many of us could never follow the movement of his volatile mind. He never seemed to wish to work with anyone.' The reason why the Conservative Secretary of State found it difficult to follow Jinnah's thoughts must have been that he did not like what Jinnah said; ordinarily even those who did not agree with Jinnah had nothing but praise for his incisive mind.

What Jinnah told the 5th Plenary Meeting of the first session on 20 November 1930 was plain enough. He complained about the slow pace at which British promises of self-government for India were being implemented and reminded Prime Minister Ramsay MacDonald, who was chairing the meeting, that two years had already passed since he had expressed the hope at the British Labour Party Conference that 'within a period of months, rather than years, there will be a new Dominion added to the Commonwealth of our nations, a Dominion of another race, a Dominion that will find self-respect as an equal within the Common- wealth—I refer to India.'

Lord Peel had stated in the conference earlier that as the result of the non-co-operation movement by Congress, the Conservatives were 'harassed' by the anxiety that if they agreed to some constitution in the conference 'and if the representatives of India go back to work it, there is a party [Congress], a very strong party and an organised party, in India which will, as it were, wrest the opportunity from the hands of those who are here, and will merely use those powers that are granted, for furthering their own separatist and independent ends.'

Jinnah resented this as a ploy to delay political concessions to his country and made it clear that so far as the goal of self-government was concerned there was no difference between Congress and all the other interests in India: 'Now, Sir, let us understand the position in India. The position in India is this, and let me tell you here again, without mincing any words, that there is no section, whether they are Hindus or Muhammadans or whether they are Sikhs or Christians or Parsis or depressed classes, or even commercial classes, merchants or traders, there is not one section in India that has not emphatically declared that India must have a full measure of self-government.'

He pointed out that 'seventy millions of Musslamans—all, barring a few individuals here and there—have kept aloof from the non-co-operation movement. Thirty-five or forty millions of depressed classes have set their face against the non-co-operation movement. Sikhs and Christians have not joined it;' and he asked bluntly, 'Do you want every one of the parties who have still maintained that their proper place is to go to this Conference, and across the Table to negotiate and come to a settlement which will satisfy the aspirations of India, to go back and join the rest? Is that what you want?'

'The cardinal principle which will guide us throughout the deliberations of this Conference,' Jinnah observed, 'is that India wants to be mistress in her own house; and I cannot conceive of any constitution that you may frame which will not transfer responsibility in the Central Government to a Cabinet responsible to the Legislature...Whoever has used the phrase Dominion Status so far at this Table is concerned has always said, "with safeguards during the transitional period." Sir, that is going to be our cardinal principle.' Unlike Gandhi, who claimed that Congress represented everyone in India, thus implying that there were only two parties round the table—the British and Congress—Jinnah stressed that there were four main parties, namely the British, the Indian Princes, the Hindus and the Muslims.

Though he later criticised the federal constitution as framed by the Act of 1935, Jinnah at this stage welcomed the federal system in principle. 'There has arisen a new star in our midst today and that is the Indian Princes,' he said. 'We are now thinking of a dominion of All-India...I am very much moved by, and...I welcome warmly the noble attitude, the patriotic attitude, that the Indian Princes have shown.'

In 1931, Jinnah decided to take up residence in London and practice at the Bar of the Judicial Committee of the Privy Council. In a speech to the Aligarh Muslim University Union some years later, he explained:

I received the shock of my life at the meetings of the Round Table Conference... the Hindu sentiment, the Hindu mind, the Hindu attitude led me to the conclusion that there was no hope of unity...Whenever attempts were made to organise the Muslims, toadies and flunkeys on the one hand and traitors in the Congress camp on the other frustrated the efforts. I began to feel that neither could I help India, nor change the Hindu mentality, nor could I make the Mussalmans realise their precarious position. I felt so disappointed and so depressed that I decided to settle down in London. Not that I did not love India; but I felt utterly helpless. I kept in touch with India. At the end of four years I

found that the Mussalmans were in the greatest danger. I made up my mind to
come back to India, as I could not do any good from London.

But he still wished to continue his role as Ambassador of
Hindu-Muslim unity and bring about a constitutional settlement between
the two communities as he had done at Lucknow in 1916. During a visit
to India in 1931, before attending the second session of the Round Table
Conference, he said at Bombay, 'I am an Indian first and a Muslim
afterwards,' but that it was necessary for the Muslims to unite and become
strong so that they should not get 'tied hand and foot in a constitution
where a particular class of Hindus can possibly tyrannise over and deal
with them as they like'.

On 4 March 1934 he was elected Permanent President of the Muslim
League and presided over its Council meetings on that date and on 1-2
April. He was due to sail back to London on 23 April and some speakers
at the Council meeting said that he should stay in the country. He assured
them that he would be able to return home by air whenever needed. After
the Council meeting he told the Press, 'nothing will give me greater
happiness than to bring about complete co-operation between Hindus and
Muslims.' The crux of the matter was, 'can we completely assure Muslims
that the safeguards to which they attach vital importance will be embodied
in the future constitution of India?'

In October 1934, while still in London, Jinnah was elected to the
Central Assembly by the Muslims of Bombay City and attended the
Assembly session at New Delhi in February 1935. He sailed for England
on 23 April but returned on 24 October to participate in the political
developments in India, the Government of India Act 1935 having become
law in August that year. From now on, he had both feet in India.

Though Jinnah was the Permanent President of the Muslim League, he
invited Syed Wazir Hassan, the retired Chief Justice of the Lucknow High
Court, to preside over the League Session at Bombay on 11 and 12 April
1936.

At Jinnah's motion a resolution was passed protesting that the
Government of India Act of 1935 had been forced upon the people of India
against their will. It was decided to utilize the provincial scheme 'for what
it is worth' but the federal part was condemned outright because it was
'fundamentally bad...reactionary, retrograde, injurious and fatal to the
vital interests of British India *vis-a-vis* the Indian States and...calculated
to thwart and delay indefinitely the realization of India's most cherished
goal of complete independence'. Jinnah said there was only 2 per cent of

popular responsibility at the centre and 98 per cent of safeguards and special responsibilities for the Governor-General.

As to ways and means of putting pressure on the British Government to modify the Act, Jinnah said that armed revolution was an impossibility, while non-co-operation had been tried and found a failure. That left only constitutional agitation, which required all communities to stand shoulder to shoulder. Congress could never reach the goal until they approached the Muslims. If the Muslims organized themselves, Congress would be forced to accept them.

Another resolution declared that for the twin purposes of strengthening 'the solidarity of the Muslim community' and securing 'for the Muslims their proper and effective share in the provincial governments' it was essential that Muslims should organize themselves as one party with an advanced and progressive programme. Jinnah was appointed 'to form a Central Election Board under his presidentship, consisting of not less than thirty-five members, with powers to constitute and affiliate provincial Election Boards in various provinces'. This (12 April 1936) was the first time in its history that the League had undertaken a programme of mass contact.

The election manifesto of the League stated that it stood for the repeal of all repressive laws; for resisting economic exploitation of India; for reducing the heavy cost of administration and diverting funds to nation-building; for the nationalization of the army; and for the social, educational and economic uplift of the rural population. This programme was not far different from that outlined in the Congress manifesto and could have made it possible for the League and Congress to present a united front to the British Government; at least Jinnah thought so, but he was rebuffed by Congress.

Speaking at Nagpur on 1 January 1937, Jinnah said Hindus and Muslims should present a united front and stand and work together for the freedom of their motherland. It was the objective of the League to send out the best representatives to the new legislatures 'who would co-operate with other progressive groups for the uplift, progress and freedom of the motherland'. At about the same time, Nehru belittled the League by declaring that there were 'only two forces in the country, Congress and the Government'. In a speech at Calcutta on 3 January Jinnah retorted, 'there *is* a third party in this country and that is Muslim India.'

At Bombay on 9 February, Nehru publicly belittled Jinnah. He haughtily dismissed a Press report that Congress and Jinnah had concluded a secret pact: 'How on earth can I sign a pact with Mr Jinnah whom I have seen only once during the last five years and that too only for minutes at a students' meeting at Allahabad...After all, what does Mr Jinnah know of the national movement when he has not cared to take part in it even once? There are Muslims in Congress who can provide inspiration to a thousand Jinnahs.'

After the election, Nehru conceded (in his address to the All-India Convention of Congress Legislators on 19 March 1937) that Congress had 'lacked success' in regard to Muslim seats. The reason was that 'we have too long thought in terms of pacts and compromises between communal leaders and neglected the people behind them.' To talk of Muslims as a group dealing with Hindus and others as a group was 'a medieval conception'. 'We deal with economic groups today and the problems of poverty and unemployment and national freedom are common for the Hindu, the Muslim, the Sikh and the Christian. As soon as we leave the top fringe, which is continually talking of percentages of seats in the legislatures and state jobs, and reach the masses, we come up against these problems. This way lies the ending of what has long been known as the communal problem.' On the very next day Iqbal wrote to Jinnah asking him to hold an All-India Muslim Convention to rebut Nehru's speech and to state 'as clearly and as strongly as possible the political objective of the Indian Muslims as a distinct political unit in the country. From the Muslim point of view the cultural problem is of much greater consequence to most Indian Muslims. At any rate it is not less important than the economic problem.'

Nehru sent out a circular on 31 March urging Congress workers to make a special effort to enrol Muslims as members of Congress. Iqbal, who was watching the Congress efforts with some apprehension, again wrote to Jinnah (28 May 1937), and pointed out that if the League continued to 'remain a body representing the upper classes of Muslims' it would not be able to attract the masses. He argued that the future of the League depended on solving the problem of Muslim poverty. 'The atheistic socialism of Jawaharlal' was not likely to appeal to the Muslims, but 'happily there is a solution in the enforcement of the Law of Islam and its further development in the light of modern ideas. After a long and careful study of Islamic Law I have come to the conclusion that if this system of Law is properly understood and applied, at least the right to subsistence is secured to everybody. But the enforcement and development of the Shariat of Islam is impossible in this country without a free Muslim state or states.' The concluding words are highly significant: Muslim India's favourite poet-philosopher was beginning to think of an independent Muslims state or states in the subcontinent. He returned to the theme in his letter to Jinnah on 21 June: 'it is obvious that the only way to peaceful India is a redistribution of the country on the lines of racial, religious and linguistic affinities...Why should not the Muslims of north-west India and Bengal be considered as nations entitled to self-determination just as other nations in India and outside India are?' He pointed out that the Hindu Mahasabha, which he regarded as 'the real representative of the masses of the Hindus', had declared more than once that a united Hindu-Muslim nation was impossible in India.

But Jinnah, a man of determination who had striven so hard and for so long to bring about Hindu-Muslim unity, was not yet ready to admit defeat on that score. In a press interview at Bombay on 28 February 1937 he said that he was satisfied by the amount of success achieved by the League candidates despite not having a well-established organization. Overall, the League had captured 50 per cent of the Muslim seats. In the United Provinces 29 out of 35 League candidates had been elected and in Madras 10 out of 11. In Bombay two-thirds of Muslim seats had gone to the League. Nevertheless, 'we are free and ready to co-operate with any group or party if the basic principles are determined by common consent.' Clearly, he was still hoping Congress would invite the League to form coalition ministries to present a united front to the government. On 22 May 1937, he reiterated at a 'mammoth' Muslim meeting, 'we are prepared to fight for the country's freedom as equals with other parties, but never as camp followers.'

Unfortunately for the League, it was in the Muslim-majority provinces that it had fared the worst. These provinces, with a Muslim always at the head of the administration, felt less fearful of Hindu domination.

In the key province of the Punjab the Unionist Party, now under Sir Sikander Hayat Khan, had won 96 seats in a house of 175 and a stable Unionist ministry was installed. The League had secured only two seats and even the incumbent of one of these soon abandoned the League and joined the Unionist Party. Sikander formally became a member of the Muslim League in 1937 but his government remained Unionist and his relations with Jinnah never really became cordial. After Sikander's death in December 1942, his successor, Sir Khizar Hayat Khan Tiwana, and Jinnah became openly hostile. At the popular level, however, the League rapidly gained strength. (This was especially so after the Pakistan Resolution, as the result of the 1945 elections were to demonstrate; but it was only after the Punjab had been divided at the time of independence that a League ministry was established in the Pakistani part of the Punjab called West Punjab).

In the North-West Frontier Province (over 92 per cent Muslim), Dr Khan Sahib was able to form a Congress government.[1] In the remaining Muslim provinces of Bengal, Assam and Sind, only unstable coalitions could be formed because of a multiplicity of parties with shifting membership. In Bengal, Fazlul Haq, a dextrous and durable politician who was the leader of the Krishak Proja Samiti (Peasants and Tenants Party) formed a government, and in Assam a lawyer, Sir Muhammad Saadulla, formed a ministry, as did Sir Ghulam Hussain Hidayatullah, landowner and head of the Sind United Party, in Sind.

Thus while Congress had no difficulty in forming ministries in all the Hindu provinces as well as in the Muslim province of the North-West Frontier, the League was unable to form a ministry of its own in any Muslim province. It is no wonder that the Congress leadership thought they could give the League short shrift. They declined to invite the League to form a coalition with Congress in any province.

It is true that according to the Westminster parliamentary system Congress was entitled to form purely Congress ministries wherever it enjoyed an absolute majority in the legislature. But were conditions in India the same as in the United Kingdom? The parliamentary system pre-supposes that no single party holds the monopoly to govern. But Congress in India did not consider itself as merely one of the parties aspiring to hold office. It put itself forward as representing everyone in India and, therefore, the only organization entitled to govern. The implication of this was that it could rule indefinitely; others must join it or be branded as unpatriotic and unrepresentative.

Congress' claim to represent all classes and creeds in India was in fact manifestly unsustainable. It was overwhelmingly Hindu in composition and did not even represent all the Hindus, since the Hindu Mahasabha and the Untouchables denied its authority to speak for them. There were also the Muslim League and the Liberals who desired self-government as much as Congress but did not recognize its leadership.

'There is an essential difference between the body politic of this country and that of Great Britain,' pointed out Jinnah. 'The majority and

---

[1] By fighting the election under the banner of Congress, the 'Redshirts' had become a limb of the Congress Party. The title of 'Redshirt' fell into disuse but the Pathans maintained their individuality. They never took to wearing the Ganhi cap nor to hand-spinnng, which they looked down upon as women's work, and Gandhi's creed of non-violence was entirely alien to their culture which expected young boys to carry rifles on their backs. They managed to maintain greater freedom from the control of the Congress High Command than did the Congress parties of other provinces.

minority parties in Britain are alterable, tomorrow Liberal and the day after Labour. But such is not the case with India. Here we have a permanent Hindu majority and the rest are minorities which cannot within any conceivable period of time hope to become majorities. The majority can afford to assume a non-communal label, but it remains exclusively Hindu in its spirit and action.'

The British Government was conscious of the need for genuine minority representation in the provincial cabinets; the Governors were told in their Instructions to include in the ministries 'so far as practicable members of important minority communities'. But in a province where Congress enjoyed an absolute majority in the legislature the Governor had no means of compelling the premier-designate to include non-Congress members of minority communities in the cabinet. If the Governor did not accept the proposed team of ministers, the premier-designate could refuse to take office and leave the province with no ministry at all.

To Congress leaders it must have seemed more advantageous to set up purely Congress ministries in the Congress-dominated provinces than to invite the League to share power with them even though it was in these provinces that the League had achieved the best results in the election. With the prestige of office and the power to distribute favours including ministership, Congress seems to have thought that it was not the time to pamper and strengthen the League but an opportunity to teach it a lesson and eliminate it as a political force. In retrospect, however, this policy, as will be presently explained, proved to be a blunder, and the way in which the Congress ministries conducted themselves only made the position worse. Jinnah was able to rally the Muslims with the cry of 'Hindu Raj'.

It was in Bombay and the United Provinces that the Muslim League had scored its most notable successes and it was in these two provinces that initially there was the greatest hope that the League would be invited by Congress to form coalition ministries. In Bombay the League had won twenty out of 29 Muslim seats and in the United Provinces the 64 Muslim seats were shared as follows: Muslim League 26; Independent Muslims 28; National Agricultural Party 9; and Congress Muslim 1. B. G. Kher, who headed the Congress ministry in Bombay, was inclined to ask the League to join his administration but had to defer to the Congress ban on coalitions.

In the United Provinces a Congress-League coalition nearly came off. Abul Kalam Azad, a member of the Congress Parliamentary Sub-Committee, visited Lucknow to oversee the formation of a ministry. He was evidently in favour of inviting the League to form a coalition with

Congress. He discussed the question with Choudhry Khaliquzzaman and Nawab Ismail Khan, the leaders of the League in the province, and held out the hope that both of them would be appointed ministers. Thereupon they signed a note that the Muslim League party would work in co-operation with Congress and accept the Congress programme. But Azad's efforts were frustrated by Nehru, who was the president of Congress at the time. He wrote to Khaliquzzaman and Ismail Khan that only one of them could be taken into the ministry. This was not acceptable to them. In the end the League was told that the members elected on the League ticket could join the provincial government only on the following terms: 'The Muslim League Group in the United Provinces Assembly shall cease to function as a separate group. The existing members of the Muslim League Party in the United Provinces Assembly shall become part of the Congress Party... The Muslim League Parliamentary Board in the United Provinces will be dissolved, and no candidates will thereafter be set up by the said Board at any by-election.' Since this was tantamount to asking the League to sign its own death-warrant as a separate political party, the terms were naturally rejected and the proposal for a coalition government fell through. 'This was a most unfortunate development,' lamented Azad. 'If the UP League's offer of co-operation had been accepted, the Muslim League party would for all practical purposes have merged [with] Congress...Mr Jinnah took full advantage of the situation and started an offensive which ultimately led to Pakistan.'

The rebuff on the question of coalition ministries was followed by the galling experience of 'Hindu Rule'. Broadly, the Muslim complaints against Congress ministries, which held office from July 1937 to October 1939, were the hoisting of the Congress tricolour on buildings under the management of local authorities; the singing of *Bande Mataram* at the opening of the proceedings of the legislatures; the encouragement of Hindi at the cost of Urdu; the introduction of Gandhi's scheme of 'Basic Education' in villages; and the behaviour of the members of Congress— as if they were officials with executive powers and not merely members of a political party.

In the United Provinces the Congress ministry drafted a resolution that all government uniforms should be made of *khaddar* and that the police should be given caps of Gandhi pattern. The Governor discussed this resolution at a cabinet meeting before it was taken up in the Assembly. As a result, the resolution as actually passed was watered down to say that uniforms should be of *khaddar* 'so far as possible' and the proposal about Gandhi caps was eliminated.

On 5 October 1939, Rajendra Prasad, the then President of Congress, wrote to Jinnah that the charges of anti-Muslim policy by the Congress ministries were 'wholly unfounded' and offered to 'request the highest judicial authority in India, Sir M. Gwyer, Chief Justice of the Federal Court, to enquire into this matter'. Jinnah declined the proposal, stating that he had already placed the whole case before the Viceroy who, along with the Governors, had been entrusted under the constitution to protect the rights and interests of the minorities.

The League countered the flying of the Congress tricolour by hoisting its own Star and Crescent above it. In the end the practice of flying the Congress flag on public buildings was discontinued.

The singing of *Bande Mataram* was also finally dropped after it had been first curtailed by the Working Committee, which issued a statement on 28 October 1937 recognizing 'the validity of the objections raised by Muslim friends to certain parts of the song' and recommending that 'wherever the *Bande Mataram* is sung at national gatherings only the first two stanzas should be sung'.

Interestingly, the Government of India also viewed *Bande Mataram* with great disfavour. The Home Member (Sir Henry Craik) wrote to Lord Baden-Powell, the founder and head of the Boy Scouts movement, on 30 March 1937 to complain that *Bande Mataram* had been included in the national songs in the book *Scouting for Boys in India* and to request that it be dropped 'quietly' in the next edition. He gave two reasons for objecting to the song. First, though the song itself is 'generally' harmless, it originated as a 'hymn of hate' against the Muslims. (It appears in Chapter X of Bankim Chandra Chatterji's novel *Ananda Math* and is sung by Bhabananda who exclaims, 'The Hinduism of the Hindus cannot be maintained unless the "bearded drunkards" [the Muslims] are expelled'. Then there is the following exchange:-

Mahendra: 'How will you expel them?'

Bhabananda: 'By killing.')

Craik's second reason was that *Bande Mataram* had become the war cry of the terrorists in Bengal and, although the words simply meant 'Hail Mother', they were commonly shouted as a slogan by terrorists when committing outrages. Baden-Powell replied that he would arrange that the offending item was taken out of the next edition.

Gandhi's scheme of 'Basic Education' was introduced following a conference in October 1937 at Wardha chaired by him and attended by the Education Ministers of the Congress provinces and other interested persons. The 'Wardha Scheme' was introduced in the Congress provinces,

notably Bihar, the United Provinces and Bombay. It embodied Gandhi's favourite ideas of village uplift. The basic principle was that seven years' schooling 'should centre round some form of manual and productive work'. Hand-spinning was an important part of the curriculum; the medium of instruction was to be the mother tongue (which in effect meant Hindi); and there was to be no religious instruction (which to the Muslims is an essential part of education).[1] The Muslims were particularly angry that children were made to do reverence to Gandhi's portraits.

That Congress workers did in fact interfere in the administration undesirably was conceded by a resolution passed by the Working Committee in September 1938: 'It has come to the notice of Congress that Congress committees interfere with the ordinary administration...by seeking to influence officers and other members of the Services. Congress advises Congressmen not to interfere with the new course of administration.'

The broad impression created in the mind of the Muslims by Congress rule was well summed up by the Pirpur Report, a committee appointed by the All-India Muslim League to inquire into Muslim grievances in Congress provinces. In its report, published at the end of 1938, the committee observed:

The conduct of the Congress Governments seems to substantiate the theory that there is something like identity of purpose between Congress and the Hindu Mahasabha...We Muslims feel that, notwithstanding the non-communal professions of Congress and the desire of a few Congressmen to follow a truly national policy, a vast majority of the Congress members are Hindus who look forward, after many centuries of British and Muslim rule, to the re-establishment of a purely Hindu Raj.

At the twenty-fifth session of the Muslim League at Lucknow (15-18 October 1937) Jinnah complained that 'on the very threshold of what little power and responsibility is given, the majority community have clearly shown their hand: that Hindustan is for the Hindus'. He alleged that the responsibility of the British Government 'is no less in the disastrous consequences which may ensue. It has been clearly demonstrated that the Governor and the Governor-General, who have been given the powers and special responsibility to safeguard and protect the minorities under the Constitution which was made so much of by Lord Zetland, the Secretary of State for India, during the controversy of the assurances demanded by

---

[1] Gandhi explained that the teaching of religion had been left out 'because we are afraid that religions as they are taught and practiced today lead to conflict rather than unity'.

the Congress party, have failed to use them and have thereby been a party to the flagrant breach of the spirit of the Constitution and the Instrument of Instructions in the matter of the appointment of Muslim ministers.' His lips did not say so yet but his logical mind was unconsciously moving toward partition and Pakistan. If constitutional 'safeguards' had proved ineffective while supreme authority was still in the hands of the powerful British Government, what chance of success did they have when Congress as the majority party would be able to impose its will unhindered? The only course left was complete independence from Hindu majority rule.

Jinnah emphasised that the Muslims had to organize fully in order to 'acquire that power and strength which must come from the solidarity and the unity of the people'. The programme of mass contact had already borne good fruit. In every province where a League Parliamentary Board had been established, the League candidates carried away about 60 to 70 per cent of the seats they contested, and since the elections 'hundreds of District Leagues have been established in almost every province, from the farthest corner of Madras to the North-West Frontier Province'.

The Lucknow session was a landmark in many ways. Even the Muslim-majority provinces which previously had stood comparatively aloof from the League had woken up to the necessity for an all-India solidarity of their community. Sikander Hayat Khan, Fazlul Haq, and Muhammad Saadulla, premiers of the Punjab, Bengal and Assam respectively, all joined the League along with their followers in the provincial legislatures. This was a visible acknowledgement that the League was now the All-India party of the Muslims and Jinnah their All-India leader.

Other manifestations that the League was being transformed into a popular party were the hoisting of its green crescent-spangled flag at the site of the meeting; the lowering of the membership fee to a mere two annas; and the adoption of a wide-ranging economic, social and educational programme. The League also changed its creed. It was resolved that the League's object 'shall be the establishment in India of full independence in the form of a federation of free democratic states in which the rights and interests of the Mussalmans and other minorities are adequately and effectively safeguarded in the constitution'. That no complete break with Hindu India was contemplated at this point was further made clear in the resolution relating to the economic, social and educational programme. That resolution charged the Working Committee of the League not only to put the reform programme into effect but also 'to devise measures for the attainment of full independence and invite the co-operation of all political bodies working to that end'. Abdul Waheed, a delegate from

Peshawar, said during the debate that the Frontier Muslims had joined Congress because they could not understand the League creed which was not full independence. He hoped that they would now work with the League as it was changing its creed to what they desired.

As a concession to his new role as a mass leader, Jinnah, who hitherto had worn English suits, appeared at the Lucknow session in the national costume of an *achkan* (long coat buttoned to the neck) and *tang pyjamas*[1] (tight trousers). He also discarded his English hat in favour of a fur cap which immediately obtained the title of Jinnah Cap and soon acquired the same status among members of the Muslim League as the Gandhi Cap enjoyed among Congressmen.

Jinnah had always been respected in political circles for his integrity and ability and had been an eminent parliamentarian, but his personality was too westernized and aloof to attract a popular following. He had, moreover, incessantly talked of co-operation with the Hindu-dominated Congress Party, and his continuous denunciation of British imperialism was too revolutionary for most Muslims, who viewed the British presence in India with greater benevolence. It was his estrangement from Congress and his promise of saving the Muslims from 'Hindu Raj' that dramatically changed the situation. His constitutional brilliance had been beyond the common man, but his cry of 'Islam in danger' powerfully roused the emotions of all. He became a mass leader in a matter of months.

Presiding over the special session of the League at Calcutta in April 1938, Jinnah was able to report that in every province, District Leagues had been established and during the previous six months they had enrolled members 'not by hundreds, not by thousands but by lakhs'. There were also Muslim League parties functioning in seven out of the eleven provinces, and the large majority of Muslim Members in those provincial assemblies belonged to Muslim League parties. He also declared that the Muslim League claimed 'the status of complete equality with Congress'. He was still willing to 'live and let live' and said he would welcome an understanding on economic and political matters, 'but we cannot surrender, submerge or submit to the dictates or the ukase of the High Command of Congress, which is developing into a totalitarian and authoritative caucus, functioning under the name of the Working Committee, and aspiring to the position of a shadow cabinet in a future republic'.

---

[1] The Punjab under the Unionists and the Frontier Province under the Khan brothers remained difficult provinces for Jinnah. From 1943 he started to wear the baggy *shalwar* which was a part of the dress of the people of those parts. This was no doubt a gesture of greater affinity with the Punjabis and the Pathans.

TOWARD PAKISTAN

That India possessed a geographical, racial, cultural, linguistic and religious diversity of continental dimensions was obvious to everyone. It is not surprising that the idea of dividing it should have occurred to many persons before the Muslim League and Jinnah put forward their demand for Pakistan in 1940.

On the eve of the second battle of Tarain (AD 1192) Muhammad Ghori had offered to make peace with Prithvi Raj provided he himself could retain the north-western territories of Sirhind, the Punjab and Multan, while Prithvi Raj held sway over the rest of India.

Addressing the members of the Indian Association in the Town Hall of Manchester on 11 December 1877, John Bright had warned:

> And thus, if the time should come when the power of England, from some cause or other, is withdrawn from India, then each one of these States should be able to sustain itself as a compact, as a self-governing community. You would have five or six great States there, as you have five or six great States in Europe; but that would be a thousand times better than our being withdrawn from it now, when there is no coherence amongst those twenty nations, and when we should find the whole country, in all probability, lapse into chaos and anarchy and into sanguinary and interminable warfare.

Nor did orthodox Hindu leaders such as Lajpat Rai and Savarkar hesitate to proclaim that the Hindus in India constituted a nation of their own. In fact, Lajpat Rai advocated a partition of the country into a Muslim and a non-Muslim India. The Indian National Congress itself, at its twentieth session at Bombay in December 1904, had criticised the proposed partition of Bengal by Curzon on the ground that the measure would result in 'the division of the Bengali nation into separate units'. Though the bias of the British Government when it was contemplating the grant of independence to India was in favour of a united India, Prime Minister Attlee's statement of 20 February 1947 did contain the possibility that his Government might have to hand over power 'in some areas to the existing provincial Governments', which could have resulted in the setting up of even more than two independent states.

The first Muslim politician of stature to describe the Hindus and the Muslims as the two nations of India was Sir Syed Ahmed Khan. Most Pakistanis believe that the origin of the movement for the partition of India which culminated in the achievement of Pakistan can be directly

traced to the presidential address of the poet-philosopher Iqbal at the
Muslim League session at Allahabad in December 1930.

Iqbal (1877-1938) was born in Sialkot in the Punjab and took his MA
in Philosophy in 1899. He joined the staff of Government College, Lahore,
and in 1905 went for further studies to Europe for three years, in the course
of which he took a BA in Philosophy at Cambridge, and a Ph.D. in the
same subject at Munich. He was later called to the bar. In 1923, he was
knighted in recognition of his literary work.

His political development followed a course similar to some other
Muslim leaders, notably Jinnah and Muhammad Ali: they began as Indian
nationalists and ended up as Muslim nationalists.

The young Iqbal was a passionate advocate of Hindu-Muslim unity.
In his poem *Naya Shiwala* (The New Temple) he expresses equal
impatience with the Brahmin and the mullah and conceives a New
Temple where Love will prevail and the image of India will be adored.
His *Tiranah-yi Hind* (The Anthem of India) is entirely secular and
for that reason more suitable as the national song of India than *Bande
Mataram*, the fourth stanza of which invokes the Hindu godesses Durga
and Lakshmi. Iqbal's anthem runs:

> *Sare jahan se achcha Hindustan hamara*
> *Ham bulbulen hain iski yeh gulistan hamara*
> [Our Hindustan is the best country in the world.
> We are its nightingales: it is our garden.]

> *Mazhab nahin sikhata apas men ber rakhna*
> *Hindi hain ham vatan hai Hindustan hamara*
> [Religion does not teach us to bear malice toward one another.
> We are Hindis and our country is Hindustan.]

> *Kuchh bat hai kih hasti mit-ti nahain hamari*
> *Sadyon raha hai dushman daur-i-zaman hamara*
> [There must be some inherent strength in us because our individuality has
> endured though times have been adverse for many centuries.]

By 1930 he had developed into a Muslim nationalist and in his famous
address to the League that year said:

I would like to see the Punjab, North-West Frontier Province, Sind and
Baluchistan amalgamated into a single state. Self-government within the
British Empire, or the formation of a consolidated North-West Indian Muslim
state, appears to me to be the final destiny of the Muslims at least of north-west
India.

Read as a whole, the text makes it quite clear that what Iqbal was proposing at that stage was the grouping of the Muslim-majority provinces of north-west India into a single province within an India in which 'the Central Federal State' would exercise 'only those powers which are expressly vested in it by the free consent of the federal states'. He argued that: 'This centralization of the most living portion of the Muslims of India...will intensify their sense of responsibility and deepen their patriotic feeling. Thus, possessing full opportunity of development within the body politic of India, the north-west India Muslims will prove the best defenders of India against a foreign invasion, be that invasion one of ideas or of bayonets.' In fact a suitable 'redistribution' of provincial territories in the whole of India was desirable. 'It is clear that in view of India's infinite variety in climate, races, languages, creeds and social systems, the creation of autonomous states, based on the unity of language, race history, religion and identity of economic interests, is the only possible way to secure a stable   constitutional structure in India.' A 'proper redistribution [of territory] will make the question of joint and separate electorates automatically disappear from the constitutional controversy of India. It is the present structure of the Provinces that is largely responsible for this controversy...The Muslims of India can have no objection to purely territorial electorates if Provinces are demarcated so as to secure comparatively homogeneous communities possessing linguistic, racial, cultural and religious unity.'

Iqbal did not speak in terms of a 'free' Muslim state or states till May 1937.[1] In a letter to Edward Thompson dated 4 March 1934, he protested that Thompson, in his review of a book by Iqbal, had wrongly called him a 'protagonist of the scheme called "Pakistan"'; he emphasised that the scheme he had suggested in his Allahabad address was 'the creation of a Muslim province—i.e., a province having an overwhelming population of Muslims—in the north-west of India'. In his Allahabad speech Iqbal made no mention of a Muslim state in eastern India. Nor was his proposal of a large Muslim province in the north-west an original idea. A suggestion was made to the Nehru Committee that the Punjab, the North-West Frontier Province, Baluchistan and Sind should be amalgamated but the committee rejected it because 'it would mean the creation of an unwieldy province sprawling all over the north and north-west'. At Allahabad, Iqbal conceded that 'the exclusion of Ambala Division and perhaps of some districts where non-Muslims predominate will make it less extensive and more

---

[1] *See*, p. 312.

Muslim in population.' Iqbal's Allahabad discourse was a learned one and contained some striking ideas. It made a strong impact because it had been delivered by Muslim India's acknowledged national poet. There is no question but that Iqbal's poetry and ideas powerfully inspired Muslim nationalism which, in its own time, won Pakistan. His basic message was that the Muslims should derive inspiration from their great past for reviving their fortune. He was a tower of strength to Jinnah in the Punjab when the League there was overshadowed by the Unionists. He inspired the young intelligentsia of that province and they spread his message far and wide and made the Punjab a stronghold of the League and eventually brought down the Unionist Government. Iqbal had the political sense to recognize that it was Jinnah alone among the Muslim leaders who had the capacity to give them a strong lead. On 21 June 1937 he wrote to Jinnah that he was writing to him 'so often' because he was 'the only Muslim in India today to whom the community has a right to look up for safe guidance through the storm which is coming to north-west India, and perhaps to the whole of India'. Upon his death Jinnah said, 'his noble poetry interprets the true aspirations of the Muslims of India. It will remain an inspiration for us and for generations after us.'

It was Choudhary Rahmat Ali (1897-1951), a Punjabi studying at Emmanuel College, Cambridge, who invented and first used the expression 'Pakstan'[1] in a pamphlet in which he advocated the partition of India into independent Hindu and Muslim states. The title of the pamphlet was *Now or Never* and it was issued from Cambridge on 28 January 1933. It was principally aimed at the members of the Joint Select Committee which had been appointed to consider the future constitution of India and was due to commence its sittings in April 1933, but copies were distributed to other influential persons as well. The text had been drafted by Rahmat Ali, but in order to add weight to the representation, he had persuaded three other students to sign it along with himself.

In *Now or Never* Rahmat Ali expressed his profound disappointment that the Indian Muslim delegation to the Round Table Conference had agreed to the formation of an All-India federation, thereby 'signing the death-warrant of Islam and its future in India'. He claimed that his appeal was being issued 'on behalf of our thirty million Muslim brethren who live in Pakstan—by which we mean the five Northern units of India, viz.

---

[1] The letter i in the name Pakistan was added later. In an interview with Mountbatten on 17 May 1947, Jinnah explained the derivation of the word Pakistan as follows: 'P for Punjab; A for Afghan (i.e., Pathan or NWFP); K for Kashmir; I for nothing because this letter was not in the word in Urdu; S for Sind and TAN for the last syllable in Baluchistan'.

Punjab, North-West Frontier Province (Afghan Province), Kashmir, Sind
and Baluchistan'. He emphasised that the differences between the Hindus
and the Muslims in India:

> are not confined to the broad basic principles—far from it. They extend to the
> minutest details of our lives. We do not inter-dine; we do not inter-marry. Our
> national customs and calendars, even our diet and dress are different. It is
> preposterous to compare, as some superficial observers do, the differences
> between Muslims and Hindus with those between Roman Catholics and
> Protestants. Both the Catholics and Protestants are part and parcel of one
> religious system—Christianity; while the Hindus and Muslims are the followers
> of two essentially and fundamentally different religious systems.

The Muslims therefore deserved 'and must demand the recognition of
a separate national status by the grant of a separate Federal Constitution
from the rest of India'. He contended that constitutional safeguards 'can
never be a substitute for the loss of separate nationality' and asked, 'what
safeguards can be devised to prevent our minority of one in four in an All-
India Federation being sacrificed on every vital issue to the aims and
interests of the majority race, which differs from us in every essential of
individual and corporate life?'

How did he coin the name Pakistan?[1] In his book *Pakistan* (1947)
he explained that he had long agonized over finding a name which
would 'be charged with an irresistible eternal appeal to the heart and
head of all our people, and possessed of elemental power to seize
on our being and make us all go out crusading for the *Millat's*[2] mission.
I made it the be-all and end-all of my life, and devoted to it every
spark of the fire and fervour of my faith, and every particle of what
knowledge and enlightenment I possessed. I observed *chillahs*[3] and
prayed for Allah's guidance. I did everything that could help the
accomplishment of the task, and never lost faith in divine guidance.
I carried on till, at last, in His dispensation Allah showed me the
light, and led me to the name "Pakistan" and to the Pak Plan, both
of which are now animating the lives of our people.'

Rahmat Ali's scheme of Pakistan was discussed by the Joint Select
Committee. A British member of the Committee, Sir Reginald Craddock,
asked on 1 August 1933 whether any of the Delegates or witnesses were

[1] He now spelt the word with an i in it.
[2] *Millat*: nation.
[3] *Chillah*: a forty-day period of seclusion and prayer for the fulfilment of a wish.

aware that there was a scheme for federation of provinces under the name of Pakistan. The comments of three Indian Muslim politicians were: 'it is only a student's scheme'[1]; 'so far as we have considered it, we have considered it chimerical and impracticable'[2]; 'perhaps it will be enough to say that no such scheme has been considered by any representative gentlemen or association so far'.[3]

On 8 March 1940, Rahmat Ali made a statement at Karachi[4] in which he extended his original proposal for only one independent state in the north-west (Pakistan) to three independent Muslim nations in South Asia, the other two being '*Bang-i-Islam*' (the Muslim majority area of Bengal and Assam) and '*Usmanistan*' (the princely state of Hyderabad, because it was 'a part of our patrimony' and already enjoyed *de jure* sovereignty based on the Nizam's treaties with the British).

So far so good. He was not yet in conflict with the mainstream of Muslim politics. His original idea of Pakistan was largely founded on Iqbal's conception of a large and autonomous Muslim province in the same region. His new demand for three independent states also foreshadowed what actually transpired later. The Muslim League demanded a Pakistan composed of the north-western and north-eastern Muslim-majority areas of India and supported the Nizam's bid for independence. But driven by his sincere but fanatical notions Rahmat Ali lost his way, and in his book *Pakistan* advocated the preservation of 'the unity of the *millat*' by the integration of 'the 100 million Muslims in ten nations in the ten countries of Pakistan, Bangistan, Osmanistan, Siddiqistan, Faruqistan, Haidaristan, Muinistan, Maplistan, Safiistan and Nasaristan'.

If Rahmat Ali had confined himself to demanding only three Muslim states and had co-operated with Jinnah and the Muslim League in their struggle for Pakistan, his reputation would have stood much higher today than it does. However, towards the end of 1946 he bitterly castigated Jinnah, calling him 'Quisling-i-Azam' and blaming him for distorting the original conception of Pakistan. He also criticised the Muslim League for striving for a Pakistan which was perverse and puerile. When Jinnah accepted the plan of 3 June 1947, Rahmat Ali likened him to Judas for having 'betrayed, bartered and dismembered the *millat*'. The man who had the rare distinction of giving his motherland an inspiring name died

---

[1,2] The official transcript of the proceedings does not give the names of the persons who made these comments.

[3] This was stated by Khalifa Shujauddin.

[4] Afterwards issued in pamhlet form under the title, *The Millat of Islam and the Menace of 'Indianism'*.

of a chill in Cambridge on 20 February 1951, an exile in straitened circumstances.

In the Muslim League proceedings, the idea of the partition of India into two nations was first mooted at the provincial level. When Jinnah was invited to preside over the Sind Provincial Muslim League Conference which opened at Karachi on 8 October 1938, he said the greatest misfortune of India was that the Congress High Command had adopted 'a most brutal, oppressive and inimical attitude' towards the League. The average Congressman 'arrogates to himself the role of a ruler of this country,' but not possessing the educational qualifications, training, culture and traditions of the British bureaucrat, 'he behaves and acts towards the Mussalmans in a much worse manner than the British did towards Indians'. He went on ominously to warn that Congress was 'only tumbling into the hands of those who are looking forward to the creation of a serious situation which will break India vertically and horizontally'. He asked the Congress High Command 'to mark, learn and inwardly digest' the developments which were leading to a world war:

...the Sudeten Germans were forced under the heels of the majority of Czechoslovakia who oppressed them, suppressed them, maltreated them and showed a brutal and callous disregard for their rights and interests for two decades, hence the inevitable result that the Republic of Czechoslovakia is now broken up and a new map will have to be drawn.

The conference adopted the following resolution :

This conference considers it absolutely essential, in the interests of an abiding peace of the vast Indian continent and in the interests of unhampered cultural development, and the economic and social betterment and political self-determination of the two nations known as Hindus and Muslims, to recommend to the All-India Muslim League that they review and revise the entire conception of what should be the suitable constitution for India which would secure honourable and legitimate status to them.

At the national level, however, Jinnah and the Muslim League were not yet ready to make a formal bid for partition, although their bitterness was apparant and they were visibly edging towards it. At the All-India Muslim League session at Patna (December 1938), Jinnah complained that Congress had 'killed every hope of Hindu-Muslim settlement in right royal fashion of Fascism'. He alleged that 'Congress is nothing but a Hindu body...I say Congress does not even represent all Hindus. What about the Hindu

Mahasabha? What about the Liberal Federation?' He complained that
Congress was 'absolutely determined to crush all other communities and
cultures in this country, and to establish Hindu Raj'.

He recounted the objectionable actions of the Congress ministries and,
with regard to the Wardha Scheme of Education, said that the genius
behind it was Gandhi 'who is destroying the ideal with which Congress
was started. He is the one man responsible for turning Congress into an
instrument for the revival of Hinduism. His ideal is to revive the Hindu
religion and establish Hindu Raj in this country, and he is utilizing
Congress to further this object'.

A resolution referred to the 'atrocities' committed by the Congress
governments against the Muslims in Bihar, UP and CP and complained
that constitutional methods had failed to redress their grievances. It
authorized the Working Committee to resort to Direct Action 'if and when
necessary'.[1]

The wording of another resolution showed that the All-India Muslim
League did not yet claim that the Muslims in India were a nation by themselves:

> The All-India Muslim League reiterates its view that the scheme of federation
> embodied in the Government of India Act 1935 is not acceptable...it hereby
> authorizes the President of the All-India Muslim League to adopt such a course
> as may be necessary with a view to exploring the possibility of a suitable
> alternative which would safeguard the interests of the Mussalmans and other
> minorities in India.

That Jinnah had 'arrived' as the mass leader of the Muslims became
evident from the way he was greeted on arrival at Patna railway station.
The crowd for the first time greeted him with shouts of 'Quaid-e-Azam'
(the Great Leader). The seven-mile route to the site of the session was
thickly lined with people waving green flags, and the meeting itself was
so overcrowded that thousands had to stand outside. The League's
growing popularity was unmistakably demonstrated by its successes in the
by-elections relating to Muslim seats. During the period 1 January 1937
to 12 September 1947, it won 46 seats out of 56 as against 3 won by
Congress and 7 by independent candidates.

The League's increasingly militant pronouncements and its growing
popularity naturally roused the anxiety of the Congress leadership. On 19
October 1937 Gandhi wrote to Jinnah that the latter's presidential speech

---

[1] In fact this resolution was never implemented.

at the Lucknow session four days earlier was 'a declaration of war'. Jinnah, replying on 2 November, said that he had spoken 'purely in self-defence'. Further correspondence between Jinnah and Gandhi, between Jinnah and Nehru, and between Jinnah and Bose led to no settlement.

Bose was the president of Congress in 1938; his exchanges with Jinnah were significant in that they resulted in the definition of a stance which Jinnah henceforth consistently maintained in his negotiations with Congress as well as with the government. During its deliberations on 4 and 5 June, the Working Committee of the All-India Muslim League passed two important resolutions. The first declared that it was 'not possible for the All-India Muslim League to treat or negotiate with Congress the question of the Hindu-Muslim settlement except on the basis that the Muslim League is the [only] authoritative and representative organization of the Mussalmans of India'. The second said that it was 'not desirable to include any Muslim in the personnel of the proposed committee that may be appointed by Congress' to discuss the communal question with the League.

Bose wrote to Jinnah on 25 July 1938 that it was impossible for Congress to admit that the League alone represented all the Muslims of India. He argued:

There are Muslim organizations which have been functioning independently of the Muslim League. Some of them are staunch supporters of Congress. Moreover, there are individual Muslims who are Congressmen, some of whom exercise no inconsiderable influence in the country. Then there is the Frontier Province which is overwhelmingly Muslim and which is solidly with Congress.

He claimed that Congress was 'in no sense a communal organization' because, though the largest number of persons to be found among the Congress registers were Hindus, it had a 'fairly large number' of Muslims and members of other communities as its members.

Jinnah responded on 2 August:

The Council (of the League) is fully convinced that the Muslim League is the only authoritative and representative political organization of the Mussalmans of India. This position was accepted when the Congress-League Pact was arrived at in 1916 at Lucknow and ever since, till 1935 when Jinnah-Rajendra[1]

---

[1] The object of the Jinnah-Rajendra Prasad talks (23 January-1 March 1935), which ended in failure, was to find a basis of agreement to replace the Communal Award.

Prasad conversations took place, it has not been questioned...The Council are aware of the fact that there is a Congress coalition Government in the North-West Frontier Province and also that there are some Muslims in the Congress organization in other Provinces. But the Council is of opinion that these Muslims in the Congress do not and cannot represent the Mussalmans of India, for the simple reason that their number is very insignificant and that as members of Congress they have disabled themselves from representing or speaking on behalf of the Muslim community.

With the outbreak of World War II on 3 September 1939, world politics, and with it Indian politics, faced an unpredictable future.

Part VI

'...three dominations of long standing shackled the freedom of humanity. They were in the realms of class, sex and race...Some of the white races of Europe claimed superiority as a matter of inherent right over the coloured peoples of Asia and Africa...By an irony it was the Second World War, so hated by Gandhi, that finally sealed the doom of all these dominations...it was in the events during and arising out of the war that Asia secured her release from European domination'.

Lord Pethick-Lawrence

CHAPTER 17

WORLD WAR II

World War II broke out on 3 September 1939, when Britain and France declared war on Germany following the German attack on Poland. But the roots of the conflict go back much further.

Japan had started a prolonged unofficial war with China when it invaded Manchuria in September 1931 after withdrawing from the League of Nations. Nanking had fallen in December 1937. Italy had invaded Ethiopia in October 1935 without a declaration of war and annexed it on 5 May 1936. Though a member of the League of Nations, Ethiopia was abandoned to her fate by the international community.

In Europe, civil war broke out in Spain in July 1936. Italian and German volunteers joined the insurgents, while Russia supported the government with equipment and advisers. The war ended with the fall of Madrid in March 1939. General Franco, whom the Italians and the Germans had supported, came out victorious.

Germany announced its withdrawal from the League of Nations on 23 October 1933, and in March 1934 denounced the clauses of the Treaty of Versailles concerning German disarmament. In March 1936 it reoccupied the Rhineland which it had lost to France under the peace settlement following World War I, and a year latter annexed Austria. In 1938 Hitler demanded the annexation of German-speaking areas of Czechoslovakia. The British Prime Minister, Neville Chamberlain, thrice flew to Germany to confer with him. The third meeting at Munich on 29 September 1938, gave Hitler what he wanted. Czechoslovakia lost 5,000,000 inhabitants, (retaining 10,000,000) and 16,000 square miles (retaining 38,000) Chamberlain thought he had bought peace by appeasing the German Fuhrer, but he was mistaken. In March 1939, Hitler also took the rest of the country by force and annihilated the Czechoslovak state. This was clear notice that he was ready to extend his claims beyond German racial areas to fulfil the German requirement for *Lebensraum* (living space).

On 23 August 1939, the world was startled by the announcement that a German-Russian pact had been signed at Moscow. Under its terms, not only did each party promise to refrain from attacking the other, but also not to join any group of powers 'which is directly or indirectly aimed at the other party'. Having secured the neutrality of his big and erstwhile bitter enemy, Hitler invaded Poland on 1 September 1939. England and France, who had committed themselves to defend Polish independence, thereupon declard war on Germany. On 10 June 1940, Italy declard war on France and Great Britain. The hitherto European war developed into World War II when the Japanese made a surprise attack on the naval base at Pearl Harbour in Hawaii on 7 December 1941, and brought the United States of America into the conflict.

INDIAN REACTION TO INTERNATIONAL TENSION AND WORLD WAR II

The Indian National Congress, under the guidance of its international affairs mentor, Jawaharlal Nehru, had noted the gathering clouds of war with apprehension. Under his presidentship, the Lucknow session (April 1936) of Congress passed the following resolution on 'War Danger':

> Congress, at its sessions held in Madras in 1927, drew the attention of the country to the danger of imperialist war and the possibility of India being made a tool in such a conflict for imperialist purposes, and declared the right of the Indian people to refuse to participate in any such war without their express permission. That danger has become more evident and urgent since then with the growth of fascist dictatorships, the Italian attack on Abyssinia, the continuing Japanese aggression in North China and Mongolia, the rivalries and conflicts of the great imperialist powers, and the feverish growth of armaments, and vast and terrible war threatens the world. In such a war an attempt will inevitably be made to drag in and exploit India to her manifest disadvantage and for the benefit of British imperialism. Congress, therefore, reiterates its old resolve and warns the people of the country against the danger, and declares its opposition to the participation of India in any imperialist war.

In the course of his presidential address, Nehru feelingly referred to 'Italian imperialism bombing and killing the brave Ethiopians[1]; Japanese imperialism continuing its aggression in North China and Mongolia; British imperialism piously objecting to other countries misbehaving, yet carrying on in much the same way in India and the Frontier'.

---

[1] Nehru had recently returned from Europe where he had gone to visit his wife Kamla who was under treatment there. She died in Switzerland on 28 February 1936. A few days before his departure for India, Nehru received a message that Mussolini would like to meet him when he passed through Rome but he declined the invitation.

He spoke even more angrily when he presided over the next session of Congress at Faizpur (27-8 December 1936):

> How has this fascism grown so rapidly, so that now it threatens to dominate Europe and the world? To understand this one must seek a clue in British foreign policy. This policy, in spite of its outward variations and frequent hesitations, had been one of consistent support of Nazi Germany. The Anglo-German Naval Treaty threw France into the arms of Italy and led to the rape of Abyssinia. Behind all the talk of sanctions against Italy later on, there was the refusal by the British Government to impose any effective sanction. Even when the United States of America offered to co-operate in imposing the oil sanction, Britain refused, and was content to see the bombing of Ethiopians and the breaking up of the League of Nations system of collective security. True, the British Government always talked in terms of the League and in defence of collective security, but its actions belied its words and were meant to leave the field open to fascist aggression. Nazi Germany took step after step to humiliate the League and upset the European order, and even the British 'National' Government followed meekly in its trail and gave it its whispered blessing.
>
> Spain came then as an obvious and final test, a democratic government assailed by a fascist-military rebellion aided by mercenary foreign troops. Here again while fascist powers helped the rebels, the League powers proclaimed a futile policy of non-intervention, apparently designed to prevent the Spanish democratic government from combating effectively the rebel menace...I wish...that we would give some effective assistance to our comrades in Spain...yet I do not know what we can do in our helplessness when we are struggling ourselves against an imperialism that binds and crushes.

Resolutions on Spain and War Danger were passed. The former stated that Congress had followed with deep sympathy

> the struggle that is going on in Spain between the people of Spain and a military group aided by foreign mercenary troops and Fascist powers in Europe...Congress has noted with surprise that in this struggle the policy of non-intervention followed by the British Government has been such as to hamper in many ways the Spanish Government and people in fighting the Fascist rebels, and has thus in effect aided these rebels.

The War Danger resolution repeated that in the event of a world war taking place Congress must prepare the country to resist Indian manpower and resources from being utilised for the purposes of British imperialism.

Congress did not hold a regular session during 1937. In February 1938 it met at Haripura under the presidentship of Subhas Bose. Bose said,

'Great Britain seems to be caught in the meshes of her own political dualism resulting from her policy of divide and rule. Will she please the Muslim or the Hindu in India? Will she favour the Arabs or the Jews in Palestine?... In the case of Spain, British politicians are torn between such alternatives as Franco and the lawful government; and in the wider field of European politics between France and Germany.' He thought air power had revolutionized modern warfare and destroyed the insularity of Great Britain, and 'the clay feet of a gigantic empire now stand exposed'. The ultimate stage in India's progress would be the severance of the British connection, but once 'we have real self determination, there is no reason why we should not enter into the most cordial relations with the British people'.

A resolution of sympathy for China in her struggle for freedom was passed and the people of India were asked 'to refrain from purchasing Japanese goods'. The resolution on 'Foreign Policy and War Danger' repeated the accusation that British foreign policy had been 'consistently' supporting the fascist powers and reiterated the resolve of Congress to resist any attempt to involve India in a war 'without the express consent of her people'.

In June 1938, Jawaharlal Nehru went to Europe 'to freshen up' his 'tired and puzzled mind'. He flew straight to Barcelona and remained there 'for five days and watched the bombs fall nightly from the air'. He also went to England, Czechoslovakia and other places. It was a Europe with Chamberlain's 'appeasement in full swing'. He returned home in November 'sad at heart with many illusions shattered'.

Despite Gandhi's opposition, Bose was re-elected President and chaired the Tripuri session in March 1939. In his address, he said the Munich agreement had implied an abject surrender to Nazi Germany, as the result of which Germany had become the dominant power in Europe without a shot being fired. As a result of recent international developments, British and French imperialism had received a considerable setback. In India the time had come to give 'an ultimatum' to Britain for the grant of *swaraj* and if no reply was received within the stipulated time, resort should be had to mass Civil Disobedience and *satyagraha*. He believed that the British Government was 'not in a position to face a major conflict' like an All-India *satyagraha* for a long period.

It was decided to send a medical mission to China and once again, sympathy was expressed for China's struggle against 'inhuman imperialism'. The Foreign Policy resolution passed at Nehru's motion ran:

Congress dissociates itself entirely from British foreign policy which has consistently aided the Fascist Powers and helped in the destruction of democratic countries. Congress is opposed to imperialism and fascism alike and is convinced that world peace and progress require the ending of both of these. In the opinion of Congress, it is urgently necessary for India to direct her own foreign policy as an independent nation, thereby keeping aloof from both Imperialism and Fascism, and pursuing her path of peace and freedom.

In April 1939, the All-India Congress Committee condemned the despatch of a small body of troops to Aden 'as this can only mean their employment for British imperialist purposes'. On the eve of the outbreak of war, the Congress Working Committee met at Wardha (9-12 August 1939) and reiterated its opposition to 'all attempts to impose a war on India' and exploit Indian resources for imperialist ends. It also expressed its disapproval of the recent dispatch of Indian troops to Egypt and Singapore without the consent of the legislature. As a first step to giving effect to Congress policy, the Committee called upon all Congress members of the Central Legislative Assembly to refrain from attending the next session of the Assembly. The Committee reminded the provincial governments that they were not to assist the war preparations of the British Government in any way. If this policy were to lead to the resignation or removal of the Congress ministries, they must be prepared for this contingency.

In the event, India was brought into the war by a proclamation of the Viceroy on 3 September 1940. In all the member states of the British Commonwealth except Eire, war was declared on the advice of Ministers responsible to their respective legislatures.[1] Congress leaders deeply resented that neither they nor the Indian legislature had been consulted or even informed by the Viceroy before he made the declaration of war.

But what would have happened if Linlithgow had approached Congress for support in the war effort? Congress' goal since the Lahore Congress (1928) had been complete independence, and the recently passed Tripura resolution had repeated the demand not so that India could join the Allies in the war effort, but for the purpose of 'keeping aloof from both imperialism and fascism'.

For Britain to grant independence to India at this critical juncture was unthinkable. However, let us suppose for a moment that independence

---

[1] But India did not enjoy Dominion Status and the Viceroy's action was constitutionally correct.

was offered and Nehru out of his love for democracy and hatred for fascism had tried to persuade his colleagues to help in the war effort. There would still have remained the total opposition to any war by the Congress guru, Gandhi. Moreover, to whom was power to be handed over?[1] Congress claimed that it alone represented the Indian nation and was therefore entitled to receive power. This would certainly have been deeply resented by the Muslims, the princes, and the Scheduled Castes and would have set off an interminable controversy. By adopting the course he did, Linlithgow, while acting correctly under the then Indian constitution, managed to avoid endless debate and delay. He concentrated on the war effort and was able to obtain in India all the men and material that could be usefully utilized.

On 11 September, Linlithgow read out to both houses of the Central Legislature the King's message explaining that preparations for implementing the federal part of the Act of 1935 had been suspended because of the war. The provincial governments of the Punjab, Bengal and Sind continued to function normally throughout the war and their governments and legislatures decided to support the war effort. The attitude of the Punjab was specially important because by tradition it had furnished the finest and most numerous soldiers in the Indian Army. Sir Sikander Hayat Khan, Premier of the Punjab, had already declared, at the time of the Munich crisis in 1938, that his province would offer unconditional support to Britain in case of war just as it had done in World War I. On 25 August 1939 he announced: 'The manpower and resources of the Punjab will be unhesitatingly and ungrudgingly placed at the disposal of Great Britain and her allies, in the service of our motherland, and for the sacred cause of justice, righteousness and freedom.' The princes also, individually as well as collectively through their Chamber, pledged full support to the war effort, while the Liberals and the Hindu Mahasabha offered unconditional co-operation.

At the Viceroy's invitation, Gandhi met him on 5 September and stated afterwards:

I knew that I had no instructions from the Working Committee in the matter... Therefore there could be no question of any understanding or negotiation with me...If there is to be any, it would be between Congress and the Government. Having, therefore, made my position *vis-a-vis* Congress quite clear, I told His

---

[1] Power could have been transferred without immediate recourse to constitutional changes by a gentleman's agreement to treat the Viceroy's Executive Council as a Cabinet, but to which political party or parties could power be transferred?

Excellency that my own sympathies were with England and France from the
purely humanitarian standpoint. I told him that I could not contemplate without
being stirred to the very depth the destruction of London which had hitherto
been regarded as impregnable. And as I was picturing before him the Houses
of Parliament and Westminster Abbey and their possible destruction, I broke
down.

Nehru had flown to China on 20 August 1939, intending to stay
there for four weeks. At Chungking he met Marshal Chiang Kai-shek,
'that great man who has become the symbol of China's unity,' and
Madame Chiang several times. At the outbreak of war he rushed back
to India and on 8 September declared that Congress was not 'out to
bargain' with Britain and that 'in a conflict between democracy and
freedom on one side and Fascism and aggression on the other, our
sympathies must inevitably be on the side of democracy...I should
like India to play her full part and throw all her resources into the
struggle for a new order.'

However, Gandhi's support for Britain was only moral, not material,
and Nehru's was not as unconditional as it sounded. Abul Kalam Azad,
who was elected President of Congress toward the end of 1939, has written
in *India Wins Freedom* that Gandhi's view before and after the outbreak
of the war was that India must not participate in the war under any
circumstances even if such participation meant the achievement of India's
independence. For Gandhi, 'the issue was one of pacifism and not of
India's freedom'. His advice to the Czechs in October 1938 had been that
they should resist the Nazis with non-violent disobedience. To the Jews he
said they should suffer voluntarily, but refuse to be expelled or to submit
to discrimination. In July 1939 he had written to Hitler in an effort to
prevent a war.

For Nehru the choice was not so clear. On the one hand he wished to
side with the democracies against Nazism and Fascism which he hated so
intensely, and on the other he passionately desired India's freedom. The
dilemma could be resolved if India could become independent and then
join the war effort of its own free will on an equal footing with Britain, but
it never was resolved because, so far as the British Government was
concerned, any substantial constitutional changes in India during the war
were out of the question.

Congress' first official reaction to the war came in the form of a
resolution drafted by Nehru and passed on 15 September 1939 by the
Working Committee at Wardah, after a week's deliberations. It took the

'gravest view' of the facts that the British Government had declared India as a belligerent country and had passed ordinances and other legislation without the consent of the Indian people. It reiterated Congress' 'entire disapproval of the ideology and practice of Fascism and Nazism'. The Committee entirely agreed that democracy was in danger and must be defended, and its members were convinced that the interests of Indian democracy did not conflict with the interests of British democracy or of world democracy. But there was an inherent and ineradicable conflict between democracy for India or elsewhere, and imperialism and fascism. If Great Britain was fighting for the maintenance and extension of democracy, then she must necessarily end imperialism in her possessions, establish full democracy in India, and the Indian people must have the right of self-determination by framing their own constitution through a Constituent Assembly without external interference, and must guide their own policy. A free democratic India would gladly associate itself with other free nations for mutual defence against aggression and for economic co-operation.

'To allow for the full elucidation of the issues at stake,' the Committee refrained from taking any final decision at that stage but 'the decision cannot long be delayed'. The Committee, therefore, invited

...the British Government to declare in unequivocal terms what their aims are in regard to democracy and imperialism and the new order that is envisaged, in particular, how these aims are going to apply to India and to be given effect to in the present. Do they include the elimination of imperialism and the treatment of India as a free nation whose policy will be guided in accordance with the wishes of her people? A clear declaration about the future, pledging the government to the ending of Imperialism and Fascism alike, will be welcomed by the people of all countries, but it is far more important to give immediate effect to it, to the largest possible extent, for only this will convince the people that the declaration is meant to be honoured. The real test of any declaration is its application in the present, for it is the present that will govern action today and give shape to the future.

The Committee could not resist the temptation to ridicule the declaration of the rulers of the Indian States that they had offered their services and resources 'to support the cause of democracy in Europe...If they must make their professions in favour of democracy abroad, the Committee would suggest that their first concern should be the introduction of democracy within their own States in which today undiluted autocracy reigns supreme.'

Gandhi regretted that the Working Committee had rejected his view that whatever support was to be given to the British Government should be rendered unconditionally, but he reminded everyone that 'according to its constitution the Congress is a non-violent body: therefore its support would have been non-violent.'

The Muslim League did not possess a counterpart of Nehru to expound global issues, but consistently concerned itself with developments in the Islamic world. At first sight, the wider horizon of Congress seems much more impressive than the narrower one of the League. But the involvement of the League for the following reasons was emotionally far more intense.

With the decline of the Ottoman Empire, the Muslims of India had lost an overseas rallying point for universal Muslim resurgence and increasingly began to feel that, as the most substantial body of believers in the world, it was more incumbent upon themselves than upon others to strive for the solidarity of Islam. They began to take an even greater interest than before in the well-being of Muslims elsewhere. The poet Iqbal gave voice to these thoughts in 1933: 'Indian Muslims, who happen to be a more numerous people than the Muslims of all other Asiatic countries put together, ought to consider themselves the greatest asset of Islam.' In March 1937 he wrote to Jinnah, 'We must not ignore the fact that the whole future of Islam as a moral and political force in Asia rests very largely on a complete organization of the Indian Muslims.'

At the Delhi session in November 1933, the League had placed on record its 'emphatic protest' against the policy of the British Government of trying to make Palestine the national home of the Jews. Four years later, the League demanded the annulment of the British mandate in Palestine and warned the British government that if it failed to alter its present pro-Jewish policy in Palestine, 'the Mussalmans of India in consonance with the rest of the Islamic world will look upon the British as the enemy of Islam and shall be forced to adopt all necessary measures according to the dictates of their faith'. In December 1938 the Muslim League resolved that

the unjust Balfour Declaration, and the subsequent policy of repression adopted by the British Government in Palestine, aim at making their sympathy for the Jews a pretext for incorporating that country into the British empire with a view to strengthen British imperialism and to frustrate the idea of a federation of Arab states and its possible union with other Muslim states...This session of the League warns the British Government that if they persist in trying to give a practical shape to the idea prevalent among certain sections of the British and Americans that Palestine be made the national home of the Jews, it will lead to a state of perpetual unrest and conflict.

In the following year a Palestine Fund was opened.

After the outbreak of World War II, the League Council resolved that

> in view of the repeated reports that have reached India recently that there is a probability of war flames spreading and of aggression by foreign powers against the independence and sovereignty of the Muslim countries such as Egypt, Palestine, Syria and Turkey, the President is hereby authorized to fix a day for the purpose of expressing and demonstrating "[the] deep" sympathy and concern of Muslim India with Muslim countries and also conveying to those who have any such design that in the event of any attack upon Muslim countries, Muslim India will be forced to stand by them and give all the support it can.

The League also decided to organize a Red Crescent branch of the Muslim National Guard so that it could dispatch medical missions to Islamic countries should the ravages of war spread to them.

The Muslims of India regarded themselves, as well as the Muslims of other countries, as part of the world-wide brotherhood of Islam, but the Hindus did not have comparable ties with any foreigners. There were no Hindu countries in the world except India itself and Nepal, which geographically was a part of the South Asian subcontinent. To the Hindus it did not so much matter what happened to others; the important thing was how developments elsewhere affected the fate of India itself. Nehru summarised the extent of Congress interest in foreign affairs before independence in these words: 'In the nineteen-twenties [when he himself came to the fore] it...gradually developed a foreign policy which was based on the elimination of political and economic imperialism everywhere and the co-operation of free nations. This fitted in with the demand for Indian independence.'

Moreover, though the Congress foreign policy resolutions carried the party label, they were principally the result of the efforts of one man...Jawaharlal Nehru himself. Gandhi acknowledged that it was Nehru who had 'compelled India, through the Working Committee, to think not merely of her own freedom, but of the exploited nations of the world'. The Congress leadership on the whole was apathetic about foreign affairs[1] and

---

[1] Michael Brecher, in his *Nehru*, relates that Vallabhbhai Patel was asked by someone during the first Asian Relations Conference at Delhi in March 1947 whether the Conference would take any formal stand on the Indonesian demand for independence. His reply was 'Indonesia, Indonesia, let me see, where is Indonesia? You [had] better ask Jawaharlal about that.'

the Hindu masses cared even less to what happened to the peoples of other countries.

The Indian Muslims, on the other hand, were passionately involved in Muslim causes, the masses, being more orthodox, even more deeply than the leaders. During the Khilafat movement the most popular couplet among the Muslim masses was:

> *Boli amman Muhammad Ali ki*
> *Jan beta khilafat pe dedo*
> [So spoke the mother of Muhammad Ali:
> My son, lay down your life for the sake of Khilafat.]

Even a good friend of Britain like Sir Sikander Hayat declared at Karachi on 10 October 1938 that he would rather be 'shot down' than agree to Indian troops being sent to Palestine.

After seeing Gandhi on 5 September 1939, Linlithgow received Jinnah. British officialdom had up to that point been wary of Jinnah. They had regarded him as arrogant and unsociable and found his politics disagreeable. He had condemned British imperialism as intensely as any Congress leader. He had never tired of harping on the need for Hindu-Muslim unity, and the British could never forget that he had been the principal architect of the Congress-League Lucknow Pact of 1916. But in recent years, the picture had undergone a change. Congress had made no secret of their opposition to an 'imperialist war', thus forcing the government to lean more on the Muslim League. The League, moreover, had become a popular party. It had begun to claim equality with Congress and had acquired the position of being the sole representative body of the Muslims of India, and Jinnah had openly despaired of reconciliation with Congress. Henceforth, the Viceroy displayed no less respect for Jinnah than he did for Gandhi. In Jinnah's own words:

> After the war was declared, the Viceroy naturally wanted help from the Muslim League. It was only then that he realized that the Muslim League was a power. For it will be remembered that up to the time of the declaration of war, the Viceroy never thought of me, but of Gandhi and Gandhi alone... Therefore, when I got this invitation from the Viceroy along with Mr Gandhi, I wondered within myself why I was so suddenly promoted, and then I concluded that the answer was the 'All-India Muslim League', whose President I happen to be. I believe that was the worst shock that the Congress High Command received, because it challenged their sole authority to speak on behalf of India.

The Muslim League's official response to the situation created by the war was made by the Working Committee in a resolution passed on 18 September 1939. As a constitutional lawyer, Jinnah recognized that India did not have the same constitutional status as those members of the Commonwealth who enjoyed Dominion Status and were thus completely independent. Unlike Congress, the League therefore did not criticise the Viceroy for declaring war on India's behalf. The Working Committee resolution appreciated that the federal scheme had been suspended, but urged that it should be abandoned altogether, because the experience of the working of the provincial part of the 1935 constitution had 'resulted wholly in a permanent communal majority and the domination of the Hindus over the Muslim minorities'. Such a constitution was 'totally unsuited to the genius of the peoples of the country which is composed of various nationalities and does not constitute a national state'. The Committee expressed its deep sympathy for Poland, England, and France, but felt that 'real and solid' support to Great Britain could not be 'secured successfully' until the Governors were called upon to exercise their special powers to protect the rights of the Muslims in the Congress-governed provinces. It further urged the British Government that 'no declaration regarding the question of constitutional advance for India should be made without the consent and approval of the All-India Muslim League, nor any constitution be framed and finally adopted by His Majesty's Government and the British parliament without such consent and approval'. If the government desired full co-operation of the Muslims, 'it must create a sense of security and satisfaction amongst the Mussalmans and take into its confidence the Muslim League, which is the only organization that can speak on behalf of Muslim India.'

On 3 October 1939, Savarkar, President of the Hindu Mahasabha, Sir Chimanlal Setavald, the Liberal leader, Sir Cowasji Jehangir, a prominent Parsee, Kelkar and Mehta of the Democratic Swarajya Party and Ambedkar, leader of the Untouchables, wrote to the Viceroy not to regard Congress and the Muslim League as representing the whole or even the bulk of India and warned him that to concede the Congress claim to be the only party in India would be 'a death-blow to democracy'.

Lord Linlithgow made a public statement on 17 October 1939, setting out the government's position on war aims and war effort. It began with the assurance that the aim of British policy remained that India should attain Dominion Status. At the end of the war the British government would 'be prepared to regard the scheme of the 1935 Act as open to modification in the light of Indian views'. The minorities were assured that, during the discussion with regard to constitutional modifications, their views and interests would be given due weight as had always been done in the past. As to the immediate problem of securing 'the association of public opinion in India with the conduct of the war', the right solution would be 'the establishment of a consultative group, representing all major political parties in British India and the Indian princes, over which the Governor-General would himself preside'.

The Congress Working Committee considered the Viceroy's statement at a meeting held at Wardha on 22 and 23 October and called it 'an unequivocal reiteration of the old imperialist policy'. As a first step toward ending that policy, the Committee called upon 'the Congress ministries [in the provinces] to tender their resignation'. By 15 November, the ministries in all Congress-ruled provinces had resigned and were replaced by the direct rule of the Governors under Section 93 of the 1935 Act. Jinnah asked the Muslims to observe Friday 22 December as the 'Day of Deliverance'. He advised that all public meetings should be conducted in an orderly manner: 'Let there be no *hartals*, processions or any such demonstrations, but let a spirit of humility and mood of reflection prevail.'

The Working Committee of the Muslim League, which met on 22 October, neither accepted nor rejected the Viceroy's statement. It asked for further discussion and clarification. With regard to the Viceroy's promise that the federal scheme of the 1935 Act would be modified, the League insisted that the whole scheme must be scrapped and the entire constitutional problem be considered *de novo*. It commended the Viceroy's assurance to the minorities that their views and interests would be given due consideration when constitutional changes were discussed.

In the beginning of November the Viceroy discussed with Gandhi, Rajendra Prasad (the president of Congress) and Jinnah the question of expanding the Governor-General's Council as an *ad hoc* arrangement during the war, but the Indian leaders could not come up with such an agreement between themselves 'as would contribute to the harmonious working in the centre'. Rajendra Prasad had taken the position that it was 'impossible to co-operate with the government unless its policy was made clear in a declaration on the lines suggested by Congress'.

Meeting at Allahabad from 19 to 23 November 1939, the Congress Working Committee criticised the British Government for advancing the rights of minorities 'as a barrier to India's freedom' and declared again that 'the recognition of India's independence and of the right of her people to frame their constitution through a Constituent Assembly...is the only democratic method of determining the constitution of a free country...The

Constituent Assembly should be elected on the basis of adult suffrage, existing separate electorates being retained for such minorities as desire them. The number of members in the Assembly should reflect their numerical strength'. At its next meeting at Wardah (18-22 December 1939), the Working Committee returned to the favourite theme of Congress, that communal differences were caused by the imperial power and would disappear when that power was withdrawn: 'The communal question will never be satisfactorily solved so long as the different parties are to look to a third party, through whose favour they expect to gain special privileges...lasting unity will only come when foreign rule is completely withdrawn.' The Committee held out the assurance that differences with regard to minority rights would be 'referred to an impartial tribunal'.

Jinnah wrote to the Viceroy on 5 November 1939 seeking the assurance that no constitutional changes would be made without the approval of the two major communities of India, viz. the Muslims and the Hindus; that the entire problem of India's future constitution would be examined and reconsidered *de novo*; and that no Indian troops would be used outside India against any Muslim country. Lord Linlithgow replied on 23 December that the re-examination of India's constitutional status did 'not exclude examination of any part either of the Act of 1935 or of the policy and plans on which it is based'. He also said that the Government was 'not under any misapprehension as to the importance of the contentment of the Muslim community to the stability and success of any constitutional developments in India. You need, therefore, have no fear that the weight which your community's position in India necessarily gives their views will be underrated.' The question of Indian troops being used against a Muslim country, he pointed out, was hypothetical because the British government was not at war with any Muslim power.

When Congress convened for its regular session at Ramgarh under the presidentship of Abul Kalam Azad (19-20 March 1940), it largely reiterated its past pronouncements that Britain was 'carrying on the war fundamentally for imperialist ends...Congress therefore strongly disapproves of Indian troops being made to fight for Great Britain and of the drain from India of men and material for the purpose of the war... Congress hereby declares again that nothing short of complete independence can be accepted by the people of India...no permanent solution [of the communal problem] is possible except through a Contstituent Assembly...Congress cannot admit the right of the rulers of the Indian States...to come in the way of Indian freedom. Sovereignty in India must rest with the people, whether in the States or the provinces...the difficulty in regard to the States is of British creation and it will not be satisfactorily solved unless the declaration of the freedom of India from foreign rule is unequivocally made.'

Jinnah criticised the setting up of a Constituent Assembly on the lines suggested by Congress and also Congress' oft-proclaimed devotion to democracy. A Constituent Assembly elected by adult suffrage even with separate electorates would have a Hindu majority and thus be 'a second and larger edition of Congress'. It would be nothing but 'a packed body, manoeuvred and managed by a Congress caucus'. With regard to the promise by Congress that if the minorities differed from any majority decision the dispute would be referred to a tribunal, Jinnah said:

> Who will appoint the tribunal? And suppose an agreed tribunal is possible, and the awards made and the decision given, who will, may I know, be there to see that this award is implemented or carried out in accordance with the terms of that award? And who will see that it is honoured in practice, because, we are told, the British will have parted with their power, mainly or completely? Then what will be the sanction behind the award which will enforce it? We come back to the same answer; the Hindu majority would do it...and will it be with the help of the British bayonet or Mr Gandhi's *'Ahimsa'*? Can we trust them any more? Besides, ladies and gentlemen, can you imagine that a question of this character, of a social contract upon which the future Constitution of India would be based, affecting 90 millions of Mussalmans, can be decided by means of a judicial tribunal?

He caustically pointed out that Congress' dictatorial conduct belied its professions of democracy:

> I say what have these votaries, these champions of democracy done? They have kept sixty millions of people as Untouchables: they have set up a system which is nothing but a 'Grand Fascist Council'. Their dictator [Gandhi] is not even a four-anna member of Congress. They set up dummy ministries which were not responsible to the legislatures or the electorate but to a caucus of Mr Gandhi's choosing.

He said he had been criticised by the Congress Press that, in stating that the parliamentary system was unsuited to India, he was guilty of disservice to Islam, because Islam believes in democracy, and remarked, 'so far as I have understood Islam, it does not advocate a democracy which would allow the majority of non-Muslims to decide the fate of Muslims.'

THE PAKISTAN RESOLUTION

On 19 January 1940, *Time And Tide*, London, published an article by Jinnah on 'The Constitutional Maladies of India'. He argued in it that the 'root cause' of India's constitutional ills was the fact that 'democratic systems based on the concept of a homogeneous nation such as England's are very definitely not applicable to heterogeneous countries such as India.' He quoted the Report of the Joint Select Committee on Indian Constitutional Reform (Sessions 1933-4, Vol. 1, para. 1) that 'India is inhabited by many races...often as distinct from one another in origin, tradition and manner of life as are nations of Europe'[1]. He said Hindus and Muslims 'are in fact two nations representing two distinct and separate civilizations...both these religions are definite social codes which govern not so much man's relation with his God as man's relation with his neighbour.' While the Muslim League stood for a free India, it was 'irrevocably opposed to any federal objective which must necessarily result in a majority community rule under the guise of democracy and parliamentary system of government...a constitution must be evolved that recognises that there are in India two nations who both must share the governance of their common motherland. In evolving such a constitution, the Muslims are ready to co-operate with the British Government, Congress or any party so that the present enmities may cease and India may take its place amongst the great nations of the world.' By calling Hindus and

---

[1] The reader may be interested to find that the same Committee (Vol. 1, Report 1934, para. 20) wrote also:

'Parliamentary government as it is understood in the United Kingdom works by the interaction of four essential factors:

The principle of majority rule.

The willingness of the minority for the time being to accept the decisions of the majority.

The existence of great political parties divided by broad issues of policy rather than by sectional interests.

And finally, the existence of a mobile body of political opinion, owing no permanent allegiance to any party and therefore able, by its instinctive reaction against extravagant movements on one side or the other, to keep the vessel on an even keel.

In India, none of these factors can be said to exist today.

There are no parties, as we understand them, and there is no considerable body of political opinion which can be described as mobile.

In their place we are confronted with the age-old antagonism of Hindu and Muhammadan, representatives not only of two religions but of two civilizations; with numerous self-contained and exclusive minorities, all a prey to anxiety for their future, and profoundly suspicious of the majority and of one another; and with the rigid division of caste, itself inconsistent with democratic principle.'

Muslims two nations he was threatening partition, but his preference was still for a constitution under which the Hindus and the Muslims could live together contentedly and make their 'common motherland' a great nation.

It was on 24 March 1940 that the Muslim League finally put forward its demand for the partition of India. The League had convened at Lahore in regular session on 22 March. The political bombshell was embodied in a resolution moved on 23 March by Fazlul Haq, premier of Bengal, and seconded by Choudhry Khaliquzzaman. It was passed unanimously amid great enthusiasm on 24 March. The League circles first called it the Lahore Resolution but it later received the name Pakistan Resolution under circumstances which will be explained anon. Its most important part ran:

> Resolved: that it is the considered view of this Session of the All-India Muslim League that no constitutional plan would be workable in this country or acceptable to the Muslims unless it is designed on the following basic principles, viz. that geographically contiguous units are demarcated into regions which should be so constituted, with such territorial readjustments as may be necessary, that the areas in which the Muslims are numerically in a majority, as in the North-Western and Eastern zones of India, should be grouped to constitute Independent States in which the constituent units shall be autonomous and sovereign.

On the opening day, Jinnah had expounded the rationale of the resolution in his extempore presidential address lasting for a hundred minutes and frequently punctuated by thunderous applause. Though most of his audience of over 100,000 did not know English, he held their attention and visibly touched their emotions. He began by saying that since the last session at Patna fifteen months earlier, the League had established provincial Leagues in every province and 'there was not a single by-election in which our opponents won against Muslim League candidates'. He asserted that the Muslims were 'a nation by any definition':

> The Hindus and the Muslims belong to two different religious philosophies, social customs, and literature. They neither intermarry, nor interdine together, and indeed they belong to two different civilizations which are based mainly on conflicting ideas and conceptions. Their aspects on life are different. It is quite clear that Hindus and Mussalmans derive their inspiration from different sources of history. They have different epics, their heroes are different, and they have different episodes. Very often the hero of one is a foe of the other, and likewise, their victories and defeats overlap. To yoke together two such nations under a single State, one as a numerical minority and the other as a

majority, must lead to growing discontent and the final destruction of any fabric that may be so built up for the government of such a State.

The only course 'open to us all', he went on, 'is to allow the major nations separate homelands by dividing India into autonomous national states'. It was futile to expect that the nationalities which had remained as divergent as ever despite 1,000 years of close contact, would 'transform themselves into one nation merely by means of subjecting them to a democratic constitution and holding them forcibly together by unnatural and artificial methods of British parliamentary statutes'. The Lahore Resolution was loosely worded and was variously interpreted. It was only at the Muslim League Legislators' Convention in Delhi in April 1946 that Pakistan was clearly defined as a single sovereign state comprising six provinces, namely Bengal, Assam, the Punjab, North-West Frontier Province, Sind and Baluchistan.

The word Pakistan had not been used in the Lahore Resolution and the League hierarchy continued to use the description 'Lahore Resolution' until it was compelled to accept the word Pakistan because of its spontaneous adoption by the Muslim masses. To start with, however, it was the Hindus who derisively dubbed the resolution 'Pakistan'. But the move recoiled upon them.

Remembering how the Muslim leaders of the day themselves had rejected Rahmat Ali's Pakistan out of hand as chimerical, the Hindu Press and community by way of ridicule immediately nicknamed the Lahore Resolution 'the Pakistan Resolution'. Khaliquzzaman recalled:

The next morning the Hindu Press came out with big headlines: 'Pakistan Resolution Passed', although the word was not used by anyone in the speeches nor in the body of the Resolution. The Nationalist Press supplied to the Muslim masses a concentrated slogan which immediately conveyed to them the idea of a state. It would have taken long for the Muslim leaders to explain the Lahore Resolution and convey its real meaning and significance to them. Years of labour of the Muslim leaders to propagate its full import amongst the masses was shortened by the Hindu Press in naming the resolution the 'Pakistan Resolution'.

The League leaders would have been hard put to it to coin a more magical name for their goal than Pakistan, which every Muslim, literate or not, immediately interpreted as 'the Land of the Pure'. Carrying a clear meaning and an immediate appeal, the word itself became a factor in adding weight and vigour to the movement for a separate homeland for the

Muslims in the subcontinent. Thus in his own peculiar way Rahmat Ali, by conceiving the name Pakistan, had made a tangible contribution to the making of Pakistan.

The Muslims, at last, had found the key to the problem that had baffled them for so long. They had wanted India to be free but they did not wish to exchange British rule, which at least had the merit of being neutral between the Hindus and the Muslims, for Hindu rule, which they feared would inflict even greater humiliation upon them than British rule. They had ruled India for several hundred years before the British and could now revive Muslim glory at least in the parts in which they constituted a majority. No longer could the Congress leaders chide them that they merely had the negative policy of rejecting Congress proposals without formulating any worthwhile positive scheme of their own.

At first, the idea of Pakistan had but few friends. The Hindu reaction was predictably hostile. The British, whose attitude mattered the most, were also dismissive. Linlithgow wrote to Secretary of State Zetland on 25 March 1940 that he did not 'attach too much importance' to Jinnah's demand, which was as preposterous and incapable of acceptance as that which Congress were putting forward. In the House of Lords, Zetland said on 18 April 1940 that the acceptance of the Lahore Resolution 'would be equivalent to admitting the failure of the devoted efforts of Englishmen and Indians over a long period of concentrated effort: for those labours have been based upon the assumption that even in the admitted diversity of India, a measure of political unity could be achieved sufficient to enable India as a whole to take its place as an integral unit in the British Commonwealth of Nations'. Moreover, 'if separate Muslim States did indeed come into existence in India, as now contemplated by the All-India Muslim League, the day would come when they might find the temptation to join an Islamic Commonwealth of nations well nigh irresistible. More particularly would this be the case with the North-West of India, which would, in these circumstances, be a Muslim State coterminous with the vast block of territory dominated by Islam which runs from North Africa and Turkey in the West to Afghanistan in the East.'

THE GERMAN BLITZKRIEG AND ITS REPERCUSSIONS IN INDIA

The German invasion of Poland from the west on 1 September 1939 was followed by the Russian invasion on 17 September from the east. On 29 September, Germany and Russia divided Poland between them. There was then a lull in the fighting until 9 April 1940, when German forces occupied Denmark and invaded Norway. On 10 May they invaded Belgium, the Netherlands and Luxembourg, and on the same day Neville Chamberlain resigned as British Prime Minister and a coalition government including Conservatives and Labourites was formed under Winston Churchill; L. S. Amery replaced Zetland as Secretary of State for India. By heroic efforts, 215,000 British troops and 120,000 French troops were rescued from the beaches of France, chiefly from Dunkerque. After the Germans had occupied Paris on 13 June, France on 22 June concluded an armistice with Germany. On 24 June, Hitler declared that the war in the west was over.

After the collapse of the Netherlands, Belgium and France, the Germans occupied the Channel Islands and on 8 August opened the Battle of Britain by heavy air bombardment but failed to break British morale. On 16 September 1940 they lost 185 planes. The threat to Britain subsided when the Germans invaded Russia on 22 June 1941.

India was deeply affected by the German blitzkrieg of spring 1940 and many thought Britain might fall, which could bring the aggressive Germans to India through the Mediterranean and the Suez canal. Indians may have had their own differences with Britain but no one wanted Germany to win.

The Congress leadership was divided into two camps. Gandhi remained staunchly wedded to non-violence. On 6 July 1940 he addressed an appeal to 'every Briton' to accept the method of non-violence instead of war and let Hitler and Mussolini take possession of their 'beautiful island'. Some time later he not only repeated this advice to the British people but also called on Linlithgow and told him that the British should give up arms and oppose Hitler with spiritual force. The Viceroy was so taken aback that he forgot to show the normal courtesy of ringing for an ADC to escort the Mahatma to his car or even to bid a formal goodbye to him. In December 1940, Gandhi wrote to Hitler to stop the war (but the authorities did not foward the letter to the addressee).

Some members of the Congress Working Committee at first sided with Abul Kalam Azad, the President, who 'sought to take India into the camp of the democracies if only she was free'. These were Nehru, Patel, Rajagopalachari and Ghaffar Khan. Some others—Rajendra Prasad, Kripalani and Shanker Rao—were wholeheartedly with Gandhi.

When the Working Committee met at Wardha from 17 to 21 June 1940, it endorsed the stand of the party led by Azad. Its resolution noted that, true to his ideal of non-violence, Gandhi felt that 'at this critical phase in the history of man, Congress should enforce this ideal by itself declaring that it does not want that India should maintain armed forces to defend her freedom against external aggression or internal disorder'. The Committee, however, felt 'unable to go the full length with Gandhiji' and therefore absolved him from responsibility for the policy they wished to pursue. The Committee, while still adhering to the policy of non-violence 'in the national struggle for freedom', were unable to 'extend it to the region of national defence'. Meeting next at Delhi (3-7 July 1940), the Working Committee resolved that it was 'more than ever convinced that the acknowledgment by Great Britain of the complete independence of India' was 'the only solution of the problems facing both India and Great Britain'.

The Committee, therefore, demanded that a declaration to that effect 'should be immediately made and that as an immediate step in giving effect to it, a provisional National Government should be constituted at the Centre without delay'. The Committee declared that 'if these measures are adopted it will enable Congress to throw in its full weight in the efforts for the effective organization of the defence of the country'. The Wardha and Delhi resolutions of the Working Committee were confirmed by the All-India Congress Committee at Poona on 27 and 28 July.

The Working Committee of the All-India Muslim League resolved on 16 June 1940 that, in view of the grave world situation, a basis for co-operation should be found between the government and the Muslim League and such other parties as were willing to shoulder the defence of the country, and authorised Jinnah to get in touch with the Viceroy to explore the possibilities in that direction.

Jinnah interviewed the Viceroy on 27 June and on 1 July also submitted in writing the League's terms for co-operation. These were: that no pronouncement should be made by the government which would militate against the principle for the division of India laid down in the Lahore Resolution; that no interim or final scheme of constitution should be adopted without the previous consent of Muslim India; that to mobilize the full resources of the country for the war effort 'Muslim India leadership must be fully trusted as equals and have an equal share in the authority and control of the governments, central or provincial'; that the Executive Council of the Viceroy should be enlarged within the framework of the present constitution and Muslim representation must be equal to that of the Hindus if Congress came in, otherwise they should have the majority of the additional members; that in the provinces which were under the direct rule of the Governor under Section 93, non-official advisers should be appointed, the majority of whom should be Muslims, and where coalition ministries could be formed it would be for the parties concerned to come to an agreement amongst themselves; that there should be a War Council to be presided over by the Viceroy and which the Princes should be invited to join to advise the government with regard to matters connected with the prosecution of the war; and finally, that the representatives of the Muslims on the War Council, on the Executive Council and among the non-official advisers of the Governors in Section 93 provinces should be chosen by the Muslim League. Congress had invariably talked of 'democratic' constitutional solutions which meant that the Hindu majority in the country would always have the final say in policy matters. Jinnah, having claimed that the Muslims and the Hindus were each a nation, could now demand that the international practice of allowing every nation equal representation, irrespective of area and population, should be followed. During his presidential address at the March 1940 League session at Lahore, after asserting that the Muslims were a nation 'by any definition', he had said, 'the problem in India is not of an inter-communal but manifestly of an international character and it must be treated as such.'

Lord Linlithgow issued a statement on behalf of the British Government on 8 August 1940 which popularly became known as the 'August Offer'. It revived the offer to expand the Governor-General's Council by inviting representative Indians to join it and promised to establish a War Advisory Council consisting of representatives of Indian States and of other interests in the country. It also sought to placate both the Muslim League and Congress. It assured the minorities that the government 'could not contemplate the transfer of their present responsibilities for the peace and welfare of India to any system of government whose authority is directly denied by large and powerful elements in India's national life'. It stated that 'a moment when the Commonwealth is engaged in a struggle for existence is not one in which fundamental constitutional issues can be decisively resolved,' but promised that after the war a representative body would be set up 'in order to devise the framework of the new constitution'. The words 'Constituent Assembly' were not used, but in effect the Congress demand that it would be the Indians themselves who would frame their new constitution (and not the British parliament) was conceded.

In a meeting held at Bombay on 15-16 September 1940, the All-India Congress committee said that the Viceroy's statement showed that the British Government 'had no intention to recognize India's independence and would, if they could, continue to hold this country indefinitely in bondage for British exploitation'. The British Government had 'created an intolerable situation' and imposed upon Congress 'a struggle for the preservation of the honour and the elementary rights of the people'. Realizing that a 'struggle' with the government without Gandhi's magnetic leadership would be ineffective, the Committee proceeded to rehabilitate the Mahatma. It requested him to guide Congress in the action that should be taken, adding that the Delhi resolution confirmed by the All-India Congress Committee at Patna, which prevented him from so doing, had lapsed.

The reaction of the Working Committee of the All-India Muslim League to the August offer as described in its resolution of 2 September was non-committal. It called it unsatisfactory because several details were lacking and authorised Jinnah 'to seek further information and clarification'.

Linlithgow was an industrious and unflappable Scot. He was insensitive to Indian aspirations and believed that Britain could retain India for a long time to come. He was thus better equipped to hold his ground than to take sympathetic initiatives. Nehru characterized him as 'heavy of body and slow of mind, solid as a rock and with almost a rock's lack of awareness'. He has been criticised in some quarters for losing the chance to bring the Congress party into the war, but it must be remembered that the difficulties in the way of winning over Congress were well-nigh insurmountable.

The Viceroy was not a dictator who could impose his will on the numerous persons he had to deal with. He could only proceed with their consent and support. His masters, the British Government, were at this time under the control of Prime Minister Winston Churchill, and it is unthinkable that he would have permitted Linlithgow to make a declaration of Indian independence and form a 'national government' in which Congress was likely to be the dominant element. It was not until India seemed to be at the mercy of the advancing Japanese war machine that Churchill was persuaded to send out Sir Stafford Cripps to try to break the political impasse in India, as will be shown in the next chapter.

It was equally impossible for Linlithgow to form a truly national government in India in which Congress and the Muslim League would work together harmoniously. One has only to look at their perpetually discordant relationship to realize the truth of this sad conclusion. Already in an article in *Harijan* on 12 June 1940, Gandhi had reaffirmed the Congress position that it was the only 'democratic elected political organization' in India and that 'all the others' were 'self appointed or elected on a sectional basis'. Consequently, there were only two parties— those who sided with Congress and those who did not. Between the two there was no meeting ground. The League was equally uncompromising: Congress was a Hindu body, the League alone represented the Muslims and must have representation equal to that of Congress everywhere. There would have been endless wrangles too: about how much power was to be transferred to Indian leaders immediately; how the portfolios were to be distributed between the political parties; how the constitution of free India was to be framed and on what lines, and so on.

The princes, controlling a large part of the country and its resources and ever ready to assist the British Government, would also not have relished Congress supremacy. They were aware that Congress was no friend of theirs and was eager to take over parmaountcy from the British Government. Congress rule, which meant the rule of upper-caste Hindus, was also anathema to the Untouchable millions.

And what exactly did Congress mean by its promise to 'throw in its full weight in the efforts for the effective organization of the defence of the country'? The nimble-witted Congress spokesmen were notoriously hard to pin down. Were Indians simply to defend their own soil against external attack or were they willing to fight alongside the Allies world-wide? There was also no knowing when the Gandhian view of non-participation in the war under any circumstances would assert itself. We have already noted that the Working Committee was split from the very beginning into those who were in favour of fighting in support of the democracries if India was free, and those who sided with Gandhi in saying that Congress must not depart from its creed of non-violence under any circumstances. As a matter of fact Azad, in *India Wins Freedom*, has revealed that even before the Viceroy displeased Congress with his August Offer, the majority of the Working Committee had gone back on the resolutions recently passed by them at Wardha and Delhi, and had joined Gandhi. In July, all the members of the Working Committee except Nehru and Rajagopalachari jointly wrote to Azad that they agreed with Gandhi's views regarding the war and would resign from the Working Committee if the British Government accepted Congress' terms for participation in the war.

India's war effort was progressing quite well and the Viceroy was right in deciding that it would be highly risky to disturb the situation by creating political complications with unpredictable consequences. The princes, the Muslims and the other 'martial classes', the Hindu Mahasabha and the Liberals were all co-operating with the government to the desired extent. When the war broke out, the Indian army numbered 175,000. From the summer of 1940 it was rapidly expanded and totalled over 2,000,000 by the end of the war. An Eastern Group Supply Council was set up in India, whose activities gave an enormous fillip to Indian commerce and industry. The steel works were greatly expanded and the production of cement was increased. Indian businessmen, whether Hindus or Muslims or others, were glad to avail themselves of the opportunities provided. The educated Indians, often unable to find suitable employment, were glad to join the enlarged governmental machinery. Nor was there any shortage of eligible candidates to take up commissions in the army, navy and air force.

Jinnah made formal full-scale Muslim support conditional on certain political assurances and concessions but did not obstruct anyone wanting to help the government. He never said that Britain was engaged in an 'imperialist war'. He also agreed with the government view that the existing constitutional structure should be maintained for the duration of the war. In a statement to the correspondent of the *News Chronicle* on 27 December 1941, he said:

> The difference between the Muslim League and Congress is very vital as regards their respective attitudes towards this war. From the very beginning the Muslim League has offered the hand of fullest co-operation to the British Government provided a real share and voice in the authority and responsibility of Government at the Centre and the provinces was given, within the framework of the present constitution, without prejudice to the major issues involved with regard to the future constitution of India, whereas Congress have definitely and repeatedly declined to look at any proposal within the framework of the present constitution and the prevailing law. They insist upon the major issues being settled immediately, ignoring the Muslims, and that too in a manner detrimental to the vital interests of the Muslims.

At other times he explained that he 'could not play the role of a Recruiting Sergeant to collect money and materials without having any voice in their disposition', but the Muslim League was 'not non-co-operating'; 'our policy is of non-embarrassment, our policy is not to obstruct the war effort'. It was lost on no one that the purpose behind Jinnah's reservations was not to deter his community from assisting the government in the international struggle, but to maintain a strong bargaining position in the continual scramble for political power in India.

The Congress Party alone actively opposed the war effort. Its conciliation would have been of great moral value internationally but would have brought little additional material help in the prosecution of the war, and in fact would have unsettled those who were already co-operating with the authorities.

The units of the Indian army fought with their customary bravery wherever they were deployed. After Italy had joined the war, they fought under Lord Wavell in North Africa and Abyssinia and continued in North Africa under Auchinleck. They also participated in the fighting in Syria and Iraq. When Japan launched its onslaught on South-East Asia, Indian troops were diverted to that theatre of war. They gave a good account of themselves during the retreat from Malaya and Burma and when the tide of war turned, they figured prominently in the recapture of Burma.

In its Bombay resolution (15-16 September 1940), the All-India Congress Committee had requested Gandhi to guide Congress in the action that should be taken, but it indicated that Congress did not wish to take advantage of the difficult situation in which the British people found themselves at that time and wished Gandhi to formulate only a limited form of *satyagraha*. The resolution expressed admiration for the bravery of the British people and assured them that 'the spirit of *satyagraha* forbids Congress from doing anything with a view to embarrass them'. Congress, therefore, had 'no desire at the present moment to extend non-violent resistance, should this become necessary, beyond what is required for the preservation of the liberties of the people'.

In consonance with the spirit of the resolution, Gandhi did not raise the larger issue of independence in the *satyagraha* he launched on 17 October 1940, but only that of freedom of speech, by which he meant freedom to denounce war as a method of settling international disputes. Also, he did not start with a mass movement but only with individual *satyagraha*. The first person selected for action was his favourite disciple Vinod Bhave, who later became famous as his spiritual heir. He publicly read out the pledge: 'It is wrong to help the British war effort with men or money. The only remedy for war is to resist all wars by non-violent resistance'. After he had repeated this at different places, Bhave was arrested and sentenced to three months' imprisonment. Nehru was designated as the next *satyagrahi*. He was arrested and sentenced to sixteen months' imprisonment on the more serious charge of sedition for some speeches he had recently made. On 17 November, Gandhi escalated the movement by launching 'representative *satyagraha*', when persons were selected from groups such as the Congress Working Committee and members of the legislatures. Among those arrested during this phase were Rajagopalachari and Azad. On 5 January 1941, the number of protesters was further increased by asking the local Congress Committees to prepare lists of volunteers. Finally, in April, the ordinary members of Congress were invited to perform *satyagraha*.

The number of those convicted during this period reached over 20,000, but they constituted only a small part of the total membership of Congress. The movement raised no general enthusiasm and had no adverse effect on the war effort. The sentences awarded were of short duration, and those who came out of prison did not again offer themselves for imprisonment. Gandhi was not perturbed by the criticism that the movement had been a failure, explaining that the purpose was not 'to make an appreciable impression on the war effort' but to register 'a moral protest'.

In the August Offer, the Viceroy had stated that he would soon expand his Executive Council by inviting representative Indians to join it and would also establish a War Advisory Council. He had to postpone the idea because the major political parties were 'not prepared to take advantage of the opportunity offered to them'. Eventually he decided to proceed without the help of the political parties and in July 1941 enlarged his Executive Council to 12 besides himself, of which 8 were Indian and 4 British (in September 1939 , the Council had consisted of 7 members, apart from the Viceroy, of which 4 were British and 3 Indian). The non-official Indian members were not nominees of the political parties but were selected by the Viceroy on their personal merits. At the same time a National Defence Council was set up. It consisted of some 30 members chosen by the Viceroy to represent British India and the princely States. These changes, however, had little effect on nationalist opinion in India, which regarded the Viceroy's appointees as 'yes-men' of the government. It was noted that though the number of Indians in the Viceroy's Executive Council had been raised to eight, the portfolios of Defence, Finance, Home and Communications had been withheld from them. But the Indians in the Council were not lambs, They pressed the Viceroy to release the political prisoners, saying that this would have a beneficial effect on public opinion in India as well as in the USA. In the first week of December, Azad, Nehru and other *satyagrahis* were set free.

Of the eight Muslims who had agreed to serve on the National Defence Council, five were members of the Muslim League. These five were Sikander Hayat, Fazlul Haq and Saadullah—Premiers respectively, of the Punjab, Bengal and Assam—and the Nawab of Chhatari and Begum Shah Nawaz. Since they had accepted the Viceroy's invitation without consulting the Muslim League, Jinnah ordered them to resign. The three premiers obeyed. The Nawab of Chhatari had already resigned because he had been appointed as President of the Hyderabad Executive Council. Begum Shah

Nawaz refused to resign and was expelled from the League for five years. Sir Sultan Ahmed was similarly punished for joining the Executive Council. He was asked to resign and upon refusal to do so was expelled from the Muslim League for five years. This clearly demonstrated Jinnah's political ascendancy in Muslim India.

CHAPTER 18

THE CRIPPS MISSION

Sir Stafford Cripps' mission to India (23 March-12 April 1942) was the direct result of the spectacular Japanese victories that threatened India itself. After the German set-backs in the Battle of Britain and on the Russian front, the threat to India from the west had receded. But the rapid Japanese advance in the winter of 1941-2 made it seem that the Japanese could invade India from the east. After the disastrous fall of Singapore on 15 February 1942, the Japanese navy commanded the Bay of Bengal. Rangoon fell on 7 March and the gloom deepened while Cripps was in India. Colombo suffered an air raid on 5 April and on the next day Japanese bombs fell on Indian soil—at Vizagapatam and Cocanada. The Andaman islands were occupied and there was some panic in Calcutta and Madras.

Apart from the physical threat to India from Japan, Britain was under pressure from the USA and China to break the political deadlock and secure whole-hearted Indian participation in the war against Japan. In Churchill's War Cabinet itself, there was a demand from the Labour ministers, notably Attlee and Cripps,[1] that Indian good-will should be won by generous political concessions.

Generalissimo and Madame Chiang Kai-shek had visited India from 9 to 22 February 1942 as guests of the Viceroy and met not only the Commander-in-Chief and officials, but also the Indian leaders. The couple were already on friendly terms with Nehru and saw much of him during their visit. Chiang conferred with Gandhi, Azad and others and the Viceroy managed to arrange a meeting with Jinnah as well.

Before leaving India on 22 February, the Chinese leader broadcast a message to the Indian people from Calcutta. He said that China and India comprised one-half of the world's population and 'should freedom be denied to either China or India, there could be no real peace in the world'. He expressed the hope that Great Britain 'will as speedily as possible' give the people of India 'real political power'. Jinnah immediately issued a

---

[1] Clement Attlee was Lord Privy Seal till 19 February 1942. From that date he became Deputy Prime Minsiter and Stafford Cripps joined the War Cabinet as Lord Privy Seal and Leader of the House of Commons.

press statement complaining that Chiang Kai-shek was 'saturated with ideas of those who surrounded him most while in India' and stressing that Muslim India 'cannot accept the machinations of those who speak in the name of freedom for Hindu India only...both Hindu and Muslim nations should be free equally in their respective homelands'.

To emphasise the concern of the Government of India for China, at the end of March 1942 Linlithgow appointed Zafrulla Khan as the Agent-General for India in China, telling him 'how vastly important to the common war effort it is that during the coming critical months China should feel that in India she has an ally who can give effective help in turning the tables against Japan'. Zafrulla at that time was a puisne judge of the Federal Court and was given leave of absence from that position for six months for the stint in China.

Linlithgow was personally against breaking the deadlock with Congress by offering constitutional concessions. In an appreciation of the political position in India he telegraphed the Secretary of State for India, L. S. Amery, on 21 January 1942, saying that 'we should stand firm and make no further move' as such a course was not likely to improve India's contribution to the war. One the other hand, it was 'quite possible that further transfer of power might mean pressure on us for withdrawal of Indian troops and Indian supply'.

But Attlee wrote to Amery on 24 January that he found the Viceroy's dispatch 'distinctly disturbing' and added that it did not increase his confidence in the Viceroy's judgement. There was a lot of opinion in Britain which was not satisfied that there was nothing to be done but to sit tight on the declaration of August 1940. He returned to the subject more vigorously in a memorandum on 2 February. He argued that 'to mark time is to lose India,' and felt that 'a renewed effort must be made to get the leaders of the Indian political parties to unite. It is quite obvious from his telegram that the Viceroy is not the man to do this.' His conclusion was that a representative with power to negotiate within wide limits should be sent to India. Recalling that Lord Durham had saved Canada for the British Empire, he concluded that the situation called for 'a man to do in India what Durham did in Canada'.

On 11 March 1942, Prime Minister Winston Churchill announced in the House of Commons that the War Cabinet had 'agreed unitedly upon conclusions for present and future' action in respect of India but explained that a public statement on the subject forthwith might provoke a harmful constitutional and communal debate in India. Accordingly, it had been decided 'to send a member of the War Cabinet to India to satisfy himself upon the spot by personal consultation that the conclusions upon which we are agreed, and which we believe represent a just and final solution, will achieve their purpose. My Rt. Hon. and learned friend the Lord Privy Seal and Leader of the House has volunteered to undertake this task.' The purpose of the effort was to 'rally all the forces of Indian life to guard their land from the menace of the invader' and 'to aid India in the realization of full self-government'.

Cripps' friendship with the Congress leaders was well-known. In December 1939 he had visited India in his 'personal capacity' but with the informal assurance that if the Indians accepted his plan, the British Government would give it serious consideration. The core of his scheme was 'that the British Government should be prepared to assist in summoning a Constituent Assembly within one year of the termination of the war'. He had left for India on 30 November 1939. On the previous day he had written to his constituents, the Bristol East Labour Party, explaining the purpose of his visit:

> As you know, I have always taken a very great interest in the affairs of India and the struggle of the Indian people to attain their freedom, and their own democratic Governments. Owing to the action of the British Government and the War situation, matters have taken a very serious turn in India and it looks as if there is every prospect of a real clash occurring unless something can be done immediately to bring pressure upon the British Government to take a more enlightened view...I therefore decided to go to India entirely on my own, not of course in any sense as an agent or emissary for the Government, in order to get first-hand knowledge of the situation and do anything I can to assist in a solution.

At Allahabad Nehru and fifteen other Congressmen greeted Cripps 'with a most beautiful garland of flowers'. Nehru and Cripps, in the words of the latter's biographer, 'had so much in common that they felt toward each other like brothers'[1]. During his stay in India, Cripps also met Gandhi and Jinnah besides others. Jinnah told him that democracy in the British sense was impossible to apply to India because elections meant a communal division of the population and a permanent majority of the Hindus. Gandhi's view was that the British Government 'must make up its mind whether it trusted Congress and, if it did, must rely on Congress and the Constituent Assembly to safeguard the minorities'. When Cripps returned to Britain he summed up the Indian situation in these terms: 'There is an

---

[1] Eric Estorick, *Stafford Cripps, A Biography*, p. 195.

immediate danger of an outbreak of non-co-operation by the Indian people, as a result of the British Government's refusal to grant self-government to the Indian people and the right to decide their own future.'

On his 1942 mission on behalf of the British Government, Cripps arrived at Delhi by air on 23 March. At a press conference on the same afternoon he confessed that his association in the past had 'been more close with my friends in Congress,' but said that he was 'fully impressed with the need in any scheme for the future of India to meet the deep anxieties which undoubtedly exist among the Muslims and the other communities'. He made it clear that the offer he had brought might be altered on minor points, but 'no real, major, fundamental changes could be made'.

Before publishing the declaration embodying the proposals of the British Government, the visiting statesman disclosed the text to the Governors of the provinces and members of the Viceroy's Executive Council and then to the various political leaders and representatives of princely States as he met them on different dates.

It was on 29 March 1942 that Cripps first publicly disclosed the contents of the Declaration by reading it out at a press conference. The Declaration was formally published on the following day. It stated that the British Government had 'decided to lay down in precise and clear terms the steps which they propose shall be taken for the earliest possible realisation of self-government in India'.

The object was 'the creation of a new Indian Union which shall constitute a Dominion, associated with the United Kingdom and the other Dominions by a common allegiance to the Crown, but equal to them in every respect, in no way subordinate in any aspect of its domestic or external affairs,' and it would be achieved in the following manner:

(a) Immediately upon the cessation of hostilities, steps shall be taken to set up in India, in the manner described hereafter, an elected body charged with the task of framing a new Constitution for India.

(b) Provision shall be made, as set out below, for the participation of the Indian States in the constitution-making body.

(c) His Majesty's Government undertake to accept and implement forthwith the Constitution so framed subject only to:

(i) the right of any Province of British India that is not prepared to accept the new Constitution to retain its present constitutional position, provision being made for its subsequent accession if it so decides.

With such non-acceding Provinces, should they so desire, His Majesty's Government will be prepared to agree upon a new Constitution, giving them the same full status as the Indian Union, and arrived at by a procedure analogous to that here laid down.

(ii) the signing of a Treaty which shall be negotiated between His Majesty's Government and the constitution-making body. This Treaty will cover all necessary matters arising out of the complete transfer of matters from British to Indian hands; it will make provision, in accordance with the undertakings given by His Majesty's Government, for the protection of racial and religious minorities; but will not impose any restriction on the power of the Indian Union to decide in the future its relationship to the other Member States of the British Commonwealth. Whether or not an Indian State elects to adhere to the Constitution, it will be necessary to negotiate a revision of its Treaty arrangements, so far as this may be required in the new situation.

(d) the constitution-making body shall be composed as follows, unless the leaders of Indian opinion in the principal communities agree upon some other form before the end of hostilities:

Immediately upon the result being known of the provincial elections which will be necessary at the end of hostilities, the entire membership of the Lower Houses of the Provincial Legislatures shall, as a single electoral college, proceed to the election of the constitution-making body by the system of proportional representation. This new body shall be in number about one-tenth of the number of the electoral college.

Indian States shall be invited to appoint representatives in the same proportion to their total population as in the case of the representatives of British India as a whole, and with the same powers as the British Indian members.

(e) During the critical period which now faces India and until the new Constitution can be framed His Majesty's Government must inevitably bear the responsibility for and retain control and direction of the defence of India as part of their world war effort, but the task of organising to the full the military, moral and material resources of India must be the responsibility of the Government of India with the co-operation of the peoples of India. His Majesty's Government desire and invite the immediate and effective participation of the leaders of the principal sections of the Indian people in the counsels of their country, of the Commonwealth and of the United Nations.

Sir Stafford also commented on the terms of the Declaration in a broadcast on the same day. He defended the non-accession choice given to the provinces and the States by arguing that the following 'very simple fact' had to be recognized:

> If you want to persuade a number of people who are inclined to be antagonistic to enter the same room, it is unwise to tell them that once they go in there is no way out—they are to be for ever locked in together. It is much wiser to tell them they can go in and if they find that they cannot come to a common decision, then there is nothing to prevent those who wish from leaving again by another door. They are much more likely all to go in if they have knowledge that they can by their free will go out again if they cannot agree.

During his press conference on the previous day, Cripps had stated that Britain would leave India 'at the stage when the constitution-making body have decided upon the constitution,' and confirmed that the new Indian Union would be free to secede from the British Commonwealth. In a press conference on 31 March he said that there was nothing to prevent the Union from joining any contiguous foreign countries.

Though the Declaration had stated that non-acceding provinces would be granted the same status as the Indian Union, Cripps in his 31 March press conference said, 'there is no contemplation of any dominion being set up which consists solely of Indian States.' Abul Kalam Azad, reflecting on the Congress view, expressed satisfaction at Cripps' attitude toward the princes: 'He told the Maharaja of Kashmir that the future of the States was with India. No prince should for a moment think that the British Crown would come to his help if he decided to opt out. The princes must therefore look to the Indian Government and not the British Crown for their future. I remember that most of the representatives of the States looked crestfallen after their interview with Cripps.'

Cripps opened his negotiations with representative Indians by receiving the Congress President, Abul Kalam Azad, on the afternoon of 25 March. Congress had nominated Azad and Nehru as its spokesmen but the latter could not accompany Azad to the first meeting because of indisposition. Azad on this occasion was accompanied by Asaf Ali who assisted the former as interpreter. On 27 March Cripps also had a two and a quarter hour interview with Gandhi. Azad saw Cripps again on 28 March, and on the morning of 29 March Cripps invited Nehru to breakfast. Thereafter, Cripps met Azad either alone or along with Nehru several times. The Working Committee of Congress was called on 29 March and remained in session till 11 April. The negotiations broke down at the final meeting,

on the afternoon of 9 April, between Cripps and Azad, who was assisted
by Nehru. On 12 April Sir Stafford Cripps left Delhi for England via
Karachi. It was the implementation of paragraph (e) of the Declaration that
proved to be the insurmountable stumbling-block. Congress and Cripps
could not agree on the conditions under which Congress would be willing
to participate in the formation of an interim central government. We will
discuss this important question in some detail after describing the attitude
of the remaining principal parties who, despite their own respective
reservations with regard to the shape of the future constitution of India,
would have joined the provisional government if Congress had agreed to
do so.

Jinnah had been chosen by the Muslim League as its sole representative
and Cripps received him on 25 March, immediately after he had interviewed
Azad. He seemed to be surprised 'in the distance that it [the Declaration]
went to meet the Pakistan case'. As regards paragraph (e) he did not seem
to think that there would be much difficulty provided the Viceroy
consulted himself and Congress with regard to the composition of the
Executive Council, and treated it as a Cabinet rather than an Executive
Council as at present. At a later date Cripps was informed by Sikander
Hayat Khan that the Working Committee of the League had unanimously
decided to accept the scheme. Cripps had two further meetings with
Jinnah, the last being during the closing stages of the negotiations. He
asked Cripps to let him know the Congress decision confidentially in
advance as he was anxious not to give the Muslim League decision till he
knew what Congress was going to do.

The Hindu Mahasabha delegation headed by Savarkar expressed
themselves opposed to the non-accession part of the proposals.

The Sikhs were mainly interested in the possibility of some re-
alignment of the provincial boundaries which would result in the formation
of a province in which they would have a decisive voice as a large
balancing party between the Hindus and the Muslim.

For the Depressed Classes, Ambedkar and Rajah wrote to Cripps that
the proposals were unacceptable as they would place them under an
unmitigated system of Hindu rule. They said they would regard it as a
breach of faith on the part of the British Government if a constitution was
forced on them which did not safeguard their interests.

Cripps' conclusion was that 'the League would have been ready to
accept the proposals if Congress had been prepared to do so.'

The other minorities might have maintained their reservations with
regard to the other parts of the scheme but 'all of them would, I think, have

been willing to co-operate in interim arrangements under paragraph (e) if it had been possible, with the co-operation of Congress and the League, to proceed with the policy proposed in the draft Declaration'.

Before reviewing the course and contents of the Cripps-Congress talks, it would be helpful to recall the Indian background against which they were conducted. Perhaps the greatest obstacles with which Cripps had to contend were Congress mistrust of British promises, the feeling in India that Japan was likely to win the war, and Gandhi's creed of non-violence which demanded that under no circumstances should India participate in the war.

The Congress belief that British championship of democracy and freedom did not extend to India, which it wished to exploit for as long as possible, went back to World War I. In his presidential address to the Amritsar Congress in December 1919, Motilal Nehru had bitterly complained that 'in India the first fruits of the peace were the Rowlatt Bills and Martial Law. It was not for this that the war was fought.' In his account of the Cripps Mission, Azad subsequently wrote, 'I also remembered the course of events since the first World War. Britain had then declared that she was fighting German imperialism to protect the rights of the smaller nations. When the United States entered the War, President Wilson formulated his famous Fourteen Points and pleaded for the self-determination of all nations. Nevertheless the rights of India were not respected. Nor were the Fourteen Points ever applied to India's case. I therefore felt that all talk about the democratic camp was meaningless unless India's case was seriously considered.' Congress leaders claimed that Hindu-Muslim differences were fanned by the British to prolong their hold over India, and that the political concessions to the princes were also designed to serve the same end. British promises of self-government to India, they argued, were always loaded with the condition that Britain must honour its obligations to the minorities and the princes. To this rule, the Declaration which Cripps brought was no exception, for did it not give the option of non-accession to the Muslim-majority provinces and the princely states?

Churchill's statement in the House of Commons on 9 September 1941, that the provisions of the Atlantic Charter applied primarily to European countries, had served to further strengthen the already existing belief in British perfidy.[1] In the summer of the same year he had declared that he

---

[1] On 14 August 1941, President Roosevelt and Prime Minister Churchill had issued a Joint Declaration of Peace Aims, one of which was that they respected 'the right of all peoples

Continued on next page

had 'not become His Majesty's First Minister to preside over the liquidation of the British Empire'. If Britain did not grant freedom to subject peoples, Indians asked, what was the difference between western imperialism and fascism?

Among those who thought that the Allies could not win the war was no less a person than Mahatma Gandhi. Many in India asked themselves why they should give offence to the Japanese who were going to win the war anyway. Some argued that the Japanese wanted to attack India only because the British were there. These thoughts were reinforced by Japanese broadcasts promising deliverance from British Imperialism and by Subhas Chandra Bose's broadcasts from Radio Berlin to similar effect.[1]

Disbelief in British intentions and the prospect of a Japanese victory created the mood that India should help the Allies in the war only if it was granted independence immediately. As Azad put it, 'Who knew what would be the end of the war?...War had given India an opportunity for achieving her freedom. We must not lose it by depending upon a mere promise.'

Then there was Gandhi, the most influential figure in Congress. He was against India joining the war under any circumstances because it would violate his principle of non-violence. His resolve was further strengthened by the fact that he strongly disapproved of the offer Cripps had brought. During his meeting with the British emissary on 27 March 1942, Gandhi first explained that he was no longer officially connected with Congress and then gave his opinion that Congress would not accept the declaration, firstly because of the provisions relating to the States, and secondly,

---

to choose the form of government under which they will live' and wished 'to see sovereign rights and self-government restored to those who have been forcibly deprived of them'. This was enthusiastically greeted by Indian nationalists, but much to their chagrin Churchill told the House of Commons that, 'at the Atlantic meeting, we had in mind primarily the extension of the sovereignty, self-government and national life of the states and nations of Europe now under Nazi yoke and the principles which should govern any alterations in the territorial boundaries of countries which may have to be made. That is a quite separate problem from the progressive evolution of self-governing institutions in regions whose peoples owe allegiance to the British Crown'.

[1] After his resignation from the presidency of Congress in April 1939, Bose had organized a new party which he called the Forward Bloc. In August he was removed from the presidency of the Bengal Provincial Congress Committee and debarred from holding any elective office in Congress for three years. In July 1940 he was imprisoned by the Government for active opposition to the war effort but was released in December when he resorted to a hunger-strike. On January 26 ('Independence Day') he disappeared from his residence despite the vigil of the CID round his house. Eventually he surfaced in Berlin and, in January 1942 began regular broadcasts from there to India.

because of the non-accession option given to the provinces. Gandhi later related to his biographer, Louis Fisher, that after reading the Declaration he had told Cripps, 'if this is your entire proposal to India, I would advise you to take the next plane home,' and that Cripps had replied, 'I will consider that.' Cripps' own view, expressed after the unsuccessful termination of his mission, was that it was Gandhi's advice to the Congress Working Committee that had finally caused that body to reject the Declaration.

Gandhi is popularly believed to have called Cripps' offer 'a post-dated cheque on a failing bank', but Sitaramayya in his official *History of the Congress* informs us that in fact it was *Roy's Weekly* (Delhi) which had first used the description 'post-dated cheque on a crashing bank'.

After the negotiations had failed, Azad, on 10 April, wrote to Cripps blaming him for the result. Cripps replied on 11 April. Azad wrote back on the same day and at the same time released to the Press the text of the three letters as well as that of the resolution of the Congress Working Committee which he had privately handed over to Cripps on 2 April. Azad has also left behind an account of the day-to-day negotiations in his *India Wins Freedom*.

The Congress resolution of 2 April criticised the Declaration on three main grounds. It stated, firstly, that the fact that the representatives of the States would be nominated by the rulers and not chosen by the people might make the States 'barriers to the growth of Indian freedom'; secondly, 'the novel principle of non-accession for a Province is also a severe blow to the conception of Indian unity'; thirdly 'in today's grave crisis it is the present that counts,' and on this the proposals 'are vague and altogether incomplete and there would appear to be no vital changes in the present structure contemplated. It has been made clear that the defence of India will in any event remain under British control.'

Cripps had at first believed that a satisfactory solution to the defence question was the crux of the matter. At his suggestion, Azad and Nehru had a meeting with General Wavell, the Commander-in-Chief, on 3 April but nothing tangible resulted from it. With the permission of the British War Cabinet, Cripps on 7 April proposed that the Commander-in-Chief should remain a member of the Executive Council but should be entitled 'War Member', and that a new portfolio should be created, to be held by a representative Indian who would be called the Defence Co-ordination Member. An effort was made to hammer out an acceptable formula defining the respective functions of the two members. In this, Colonel Louis Johnson, Roosevelt's personal representative on supply matters, acted as an unofficial go-between. When Cripps received Azad and Nehru on 9 April, he hoped that the formula as finally composed would be acceptable to them. His version, as given in his report dated 6 July 1942 to the War Cabinet, is that the two Congress leaders raised no objection to the formula, 'it may be' because they had decided to break on another issue:

> The demand which they made was that the Viceroy should undertake to accept the majority decision of the Executive Council and should not do more than act as a constitutional monarch. I pointed out that this was not possible but that the degree of compromise towards such a position could only be determined if they would discuss it with the Viceroy on the basis of their general acceptance of the rest of the declaration.

> It seemed to me clear from the course of our conversation that they had come determined to find a reason for refusal and that, having discarded the earlier objections as valid causes, they had been driven to find this new reason.

Azad does not dispute the fact that the main cause of the breakdown was disagreement with regard to the status of the Viceroy's new council. In his letter to Cripps dated 10 April he wrote:

> While we cannot accept the proposals you have made, we want to inform you that we are yet prepared to assume responsibility provided a truly national government is formed. We are prepared to put aside for the present all questions about the future, though as we have indicated, we hold definite views about it. But in the present, the national Government must be a cabinet government with full power and must not merely be a continuation of the Viceroy's Executive Council.

But the then Congress President insists that the Congress demand that the new Council should function as a cabinet was not new and that in fact it was Cripps who had gone back on his earlier assurances. He states that when he saw Cripps for the first time on 25 March:

> I asked Sir Stafford what would be the position of the Viceroy in this Council. Sir Stafford replied that the Viceroy would function as a constitutional head like the King in the UK. In order to remove any room for doubt, I asked him to confirm that this would mean that the Viceroy, as a constitutional head, would be bound by the advice of the Council. Sir Stafford said that this was the intention. I asked again that the basic question was as to who would exercise power, the proposed Council or the Viceroy. Sir Stafford repeated that power would rest with the Council as it rests with the British Cabinet.

Azad alleges that when he called on Cripps again on 1 April, the latter's answers were quite different:

> He would not categorically state that the Viceroy would have the final say but the purport of what he said was that the Council would not have full and unfettered freedom of decision. He tried to explain this by saying that the position now enjoyed by the Viceroy could not be changed without a change in the law. He, however, stressed again and again that whatever maybe the position in law, in actual practice the Viceroy would behave like a constitutional head.

In his letter to Azad dated 11 April, Cripps rejected the suggestion that a 'truly national government' be formed which must be a 'cabinet government with full power' because:

> Without constitutional changes of a most complicated character and on a very large scale this would not be possible, as you realize. Were such a system to be introduced by convention under the existing circumstances, the nominated cabinet (nominated presumably by the major political organizations) would be responsible to no one but itself, could not be removed and would in fact constitute an absolute disctatorship of the majority.

> This suggestion would be rejected by all minorities in India, since it would subject all of them to a permanent and autocratic majority in the Cabinet. Nor would it be consistent with the pledges already given by His Majesty's Government to protect the rights of those minorities.

Cripps' reference to the pledges of the British Government to protect the rights of the minorities elicited the usual Congress position that the communal problem was a creation of the British.

'We are convinced', wrote Azad on 12 April, 'that if the British Government did not pursue a policy of encouraging disruption, all of us, to whatever party or group we belonged, would be able to come together and find a common line of action'.[1]

So, did Cripps in fact hold out the assurance at first that the new government would function as a cabinet and then back out of it? Let us first examine what he said on the subject at a press conference on 29 March:

---

[1] This oft-repeated wishful forecast did not prove correct. Ethnic and religious differences in India after independence did not decrease; in fact the, the removal of the neutral British administration has caused them to manifest themselves even more vigorously than before.

Question : What will be the position of the Central Legislature?

Answer : You cannot change the constitution. All you can do is to change the
conventions of the constitution. You can turn the Executive Council
into a Cabinet.

On 4 April Cripps telegraphed his estimate of the situation to Churchill,
which contained his assumption that under the new arrangement the
Executive Council 'will approximate to a cabinet'. On 6 April Amery
wired back the instruction of the War Cabinet: 'The position is and must
remain that the Viceroy in Council acts as a collective body responsible
to the Secretary of State and subject to the Viceroy's special powers and
duties under Sections 40 and 41 of Ninth Schedule of Act. There should
be no misunderstanding between you and Indian political leaders on this
point'.

Meanwhile, Linlithgow was pressing that his position in the proposed
government should be clearly defined. As already mentioned, he was from
the beginning against any change . On 2 March Amery, in a 'Private and
Personal' letter, had appealed to Churchill to support him 'against being
rushed by Cripps and Attlee on either the wording or the date of the
declaration'. He feared that Linlithgow might well feel that he was being
unfairly rushed and might talk of resigning, which Cripps and Attlee were
'very eager' to secure 'anyhow'. On 9 March Linlithgow actually threatened to resign and had to be soothed by Churchill, who explained that, 'It
would be impossible, owing to unfortunate rumours and publicity and the
general American outlook, to stand on a purely negative attitude, and the
Cripps Mission is indispensable to prove our honesty of purpose and to
gain time for necessary consultations.'

Before Cripps' final interview with the Congress leaders on 9 April,
Linlithgow forcefully reminded him of the stipulation of the War Cabinet
that the constitutional position of the Viceroy's Council cannot be altered
and asked him 'to make the position clear'. He could easily have spoken
to Cripps personally but evidently, to underline the importance he attached
to the subject, he resorted to the formal procedure of conveying his
message by letter.

Thus in his discussion with Azad and Nehru that afternoon, Cripps was
under strict orders from the War Cabinet to leave no doubt in the minds of
his hearers that his proposals in no way eroded the Viceroy's existing
supremacy over his Executive Council. It is no wonder that the Congress
dream of cabinet rule was shattered and the talks collapsed. It is true that
Cripps had stated in his press conference on 29 March that the constitution

could not be changed, but in his eagerness to sell his plan he seems to have painted an overly rosy picture of the possibilities it opened. That he tended to go beyond what his cabinet colleagues in Britain had in mind is shown also by another fact. He gave the Indian leaders to understand that, with the exception of the Commander-in-Chief, the Executive Council would be entirely Indian and consist of leaders of political parties. But in a letter to Linlithgow dated 11 April, Amery said that Cripps' ideas about the reconstitution of the Executive Council had 'frightened Winston and the Cabinet for our idea when Cripps left was certain[ly] not that of a completely clean sweep of the existing Executive, except for the Commander-in-Chief, but only of a substantial reconstitution which might possibly include Finance as well as part of Defence, but still leave you with some of your old Advisers, as well as with a balancing element, neither Hindu nor Muslim, which would get over Jinnah's otherwise not unreasonable demand for half the seats.' Amery also agreed with Linlithgow that a convention could not limit the powers which the Viceroy possessed under a written constitution. In Amery's view, 'when it came to suggesting that the new "National Government" should work under some sort of convention, Cripps was getting very near giving the whole case away'. The reality seems to lie in what Azad called a 'charitable' explanation for Cripps' attitude: 'As an Englishman, he was prone to place a greater emphasis on practice and convention than on written agreements. It is likely that he sincerely believed that once his proposals were accepted, conventions would develop in the way he had indicated in his first interview. Naturally however he could not give any formal assurances in this behalf and hence when we wanted a formal assurance he had to retreat from his earlier position.'

In his report of 6 July 1942 to the Cabinet, Cripps stated that the Congress decision to reject the proposals was a last minute change of front caused by the personal intervention of Gandhi during a two-hour telephone conversation between the Mahatma, who had returned to Wardah, and the Congress leaders at Delhi. Before this consultation the voting in the working Committee had been 7 to 5 in favour of acceptance but after it, it became 8 to 4 against. Cripps says that this conversation 'was reported by the Government of India to have taken place'. He does not say in so many words that the exchanges between the parties were monitored but, having regard to the ways of government secret services and Cripps' own implied admission, this is what must have actually happened, and Cripps' assertion that the decisive cause of his defeat was Gandhi's intervention must therefore be accepted as true.

Of the Working Committee, Nehru and Rajagopalachari had been in favour of accepting the Cripps offer. Rajagopalachari believed that the independence of India was being delayed because of differences between Congress and the Muslim League. On 23 April 1942 he had two resolutions passed by the Congress members of the Madras legislature for submission to the All-India Congress Committee. The first recommended the acceptance of Pakistan in principle and the second, the restoration of popular government in Madras. The second of these resolutions was withdrawn and the first was rejected by the All-India Congress Committee. He forestalled 'disciplinary action' for contravening the declared policy of Congress by resigning from the Working Committees, from his membership of Congress and from his seat in the Madras legislature. His purpose in releasing himself from these links was 'to be absolutely free to continue his campaign to convert Congress'.

Jinnah's first public reaction to the scheme sponsored by Cripps was expressed at the All-India Muslim League session at Allahabad on 3 April 1942. He said the Muslims felt 'deeply disappointed that the entity and integrity of the Muslim nation had not been expressly recognized'. The document showed that Pakistan was treated as 'a remote possibility' and that there was 'a definite preference for a new Indian Union'. The Muslim League formally rejected the Declaration directly after Congress had done so, but in a much milder tone. The Working Committee resolution expressed gratification that the possibility of Pakistan was recognized by implication[1] but regretted that the proposals were not open to any modification, which meant that no alternative proposals were invited. The main object of His Majesty's Government appeared to be to compel the two principal nations of India—the Hindus and the Muslims—to constitute one Indian Union. The creation of more than one Union had been relegated to the realm of remote possibility and was purely illusory. Since the Muslim League had finally decided that the only solution of India's constitutional problem was the partition of India into two independent zones, it would be unfair to compel them to enter a constitution-making body whose main function was to be the creation of a new Indian Union.

At a press conference on 13 April, Jinnah explained that the League had rejected the proposals because Pakistan was not conceded unequivocally, but added that the recognition given to the principle of partition 'was very much appreciated by Muslim India'. He stated that his party was prepared to come to any reasonable adjustment with regard to the present provided

---

[1] In Amery's words 'the nest contains the Pakistan cuckoo's egg'.

'all parties agree to the Muslim demand for Pakistan...details to be settled after the war'.

Roosevelt was deeply interested in the outcome of Cripps' visit to India. India had been the close preserve of the British, so the Americans had little direct knowledge of the extent of differences between Hindus and Muslims. Having themselves forged a single nation out of many diverse elements, they could not understand why the Muslim League wanted to break India up into two nations. It reminded them of the attempt made by the South in their own country to secede from the North by civil war. According to Churchill, the American president thought of the Indian freedom movement 'in terms of the thirteen colonies fighting George III'.

On 12 April 1942, Roosevelt telegraphed Churchill to postpone the departure of Cripps from India 'until one more effort has finally been made to prevent a break-down of the the negotiations'. He said, 'it is impossible for American public opinion to understand why, if there is willingness on the part of the British Government to permit the component parts of India to secede after the war from the British Empire, it is unwilling to permit them to enjoy during the war what is tantamount to self-government'. Churchill telegraphed back on the same day, 'I could not decide such a matter without convening the Cabinet, which was not physically possible till Monday. Meanwhile Cripps had already left... I do not propose to bring it [your telegram] before the Cabinet officially unless you tell me you wish this done. Anything like a serious difference between you and me would break my heart and would surely deeply injure both our countries at the height of this terrible struggle.'

The British Government and the Muslim League benefited from Cripps' failure the most. Churchill telegraphed Cripps on 11 April that he was 'very glad' that he was 'coming home at once' and assured him that the effect of his efforts 'throughout Britain and in the United States had been wholly beneficial'.

It was not impossible to modify the constitution quickly. In his letter dated 10 April, Azad reminded Cripps that the British Prime Minister had actually proposed a union of France and Britain on the eve of the fall of France. The truth of the matter was that Churchill and the other British diehards did not wish to hand over power to Indians during the war.

To form a government according to the wishes of Congress would have created all sorts of problems for the British. To start with, it would have been difficult to satisfy both Congress and the League with regard to their respective shares in the membership of the Executive Council and the distribution of portfolios between them. Once in office, there could be no

guarantee that they would work as a team on the lines of a British Cabinet.
Most of all, there was no knowing how the Congress element in the
government would have conducted itself having regard to the party's long
record of hostility towards the British Government and the presence of a
strong pacifist element in its leadership. The Viceroy could have dismissed
the Executive Council, but the ensuing crisis would then have been far
worse than the one resulting from not forming a new government in the
first place. India's contribution to the war effort was already as much as
could be satisfactorily utilized. Appeasing Congress may well have
affected the situation adversely by displeasing the Muslims and the
princes who were in the forefront of the war effort.

The Muslim League came out of the exercise well in many ways. Only
two years after passing the Pakistan Resolution it had glimpsed the
possibility of attaining its goal. Having to use the Muslims as a counterpoise
to the embittered Congress, the British now looked upon the Muslims even
more benignly than before. And by soon staging a revolt and courting
internment, Gandhi and his colleagues had left the field clear for Jinnah
to boost the already growing strength of the Pakistan movement.

The biggest loser was Congress. By failing to try to conciliate the
League, it lost the chance of keeping India united. Had the representatives
of Congress and the Muslim League had the opportunity of working side
by side in the common cause of rallying their motherland against the threat
of foreign invasion, they might have developed a feeling of comradeship
and so have softened the League's insistence upon partition. With
justification did Jinnah complain that Congress carried on negotiations
with Cripps 'over the head of all other parties whom it utterly ignored'.

The situation demanded that Congress should have taken the lead as the
strongest political party in the land and won over the lesser parties by
offering them gracious concessions and then presenting a united front to
the British. The initiative might have come to nothing, but the Congress
leaders did not even try. Instead, they maintained the arrogant position that
Congress represented the whole of India. In his letter to Cripps of 10 April
Azad wrote, 'We would point out to you that the suggestions we have put
forward are not ours only but may be considered to be the unanimous
demand of the Indian people'.

Congress also overplayed its hand by insisting upon a formal guarantee
that the Viceroy would treat his Executive Council as a cabinet. They
should have heeded Cripps' sound advice which, in Azad's words, was
that 'it was not necessary to insist on an expansion of the legal powers of
the Council or to lay it down in clear terms that it would have the final

decision. The force of circumstances would increasingly place the responsibility on the Indian leaders who formed the Executive Council.'

In July 1942 Linlithgow offered a concession to Indian public opinion by his second war-time expansion of the Executive Council. The membership now numbered fifteen in addition to the Viceroy and of these, eleven were Indian and four British. Defence was divided between a War Department under the Commander-in-Chief and a Defence Department under a Punjabi Muslim, Sir Feroze Khan Noon. The new members included a Sikh, a member of the Depressed Classes, and a representative of the British community in India. India was also given representation in the British War Cabinet and the Pacific War Council by the appointment of a member to each of the two bodies.

THE QUIT INDIA MOVEMENT

Churchill was quite content that Cripps had failed in his mission. Amery wrote to Linlithgow on 10 July 1942 that the Cripps mission 'has by now receded into the background of his [Churchill's] mind. For him the main thing about it has been the good effect in America; for the rest he is not interested'. But the reverse was the case with Gandhi. Azad noted, 'Gandhiji's mind was now moving from one extreme of complete inactivity to the other extreme of organized mass effort'. The Mahatma's writings and statements indicate how his mind was working. Writing in *Harijan* on 26 April 1942, he expressed his disquiet at the 'promise of a never-ending stream of soldiers from America and possibly China' and asked, 'Cannot a limitless number of soldiers be trained out of India's millions?' He said he looked upon the introduction of foreign soldiers in India as a 'positive danger'. He believed that American aid in the end amounted to American influence, if not American rule added to that of the British.

When the All-India Congress Committee met at Allahabad from 29 April to 2 May (1942), they had before them the draft of a resolution framed by Gandhi:

Japan's quarrel is not with India. She is warring against the British Empire... If India were freed her first step would probably be to negotiate with Japan... The Committee appeals to Britain, for the sake of her own safety, for the sake of India's safety and for the cause of world peace to let go her hold on India.

The Committee desires to assure the Japanese Government and people that India bears no enmity either towards Japan or any other nation... Therefore the Committee hopes that Japan will not have any designs on India. But if Japan attacks India...the Committee would expect all those who look to Congress for guidance to offer complete non-violent non-co-operation to the Japanese forces and not to render any assistance to them.

Gandhi's draft was modified by the committee because Nehru and some others were unhappy with it. Nehru argued that the withdrawal of the British would create an administrative vacuum, and that accepting Gandhi's draft would make India a passive partner of Japan, because if the British withdrew, Japan would insist upon certain facilities such as aerodromes, occupation of strategic points and passage for troops. He emphasised that the Japanese could not be stopped by non-violent non-co-operation and India would earn the hostility of everyone other than the Axis Powers. The resolution as finally passed retained Gandhi's main point, that Britain should withdraw and if the Japanese attacked, India would resist them non-violently, but Gandhi's conciliatory messages to Japan were omitted:

India's participation in the war was a purely British act... If India were free, she would have determined her own policy and might have kept out of the war, though her sympathies would in any event have been with the victims of aggression...Not only the interest of India, but also Britain's safety and world peace and freedom, demand that Britain must abandon her hold on India. It is on the basis of independence alone that India can deal with Britain or other nations. The Committee repudiates the idea that freedom can come to India through interference or invasion by any foreign nation, whatever the professions of that nation may be. In case an invasion takes place, it must be resisted. Such resistance can only take the form of non-co-operation as the British Government has prevented the organization of national defence by the people in any other way.

On 3 May Gandhi was asked whether, by asking the British to withdraw, he was not inviting the Japanese to attack India and replied 'I feel convinced that British presence is incentive for Japanese attack'. A week later he wrote in *Harijan:* '[The] presence of [the] British in India is [an] invitation to Japan to invade India. Their withdrawal removes the bait. Assume that it does not; free India will be better able to cope with invasion. Unadulterated non-co-operation will then have full sway.'

A representative of the *News Chronicle* (London) asked him on 14 May to whom the British would entrust the administration if they withdrew from India. Gandhi stated, 'they have to leave India in God's hands—but in modern parlance to anarchy'. The *Harijan* of 24 May reported him as saying that the beauty of withdrawal lay in its being immediate.

In his impatience to be rid of the British before the Japanese invaded India, he seemed even to have accepted the possibility of violence. The *Harijan* of 28 May quoted him as follows:

I waited and waited until the country should develop the non-violent strength necessary to throw off the foreign yoke. But my attitude has now undergone a change. I feel that it cannot afford to wait. If I continue to wait, I might have to wait till Doomsday. For the preparation that I have prayed for and worked for may never come and in the meantime I may be enveloped and overwhelmed by the flames that threaten all of us. That is why I have decided that even at certain risks, which are evidently involved, I must ask the people to resist the slavery.

But Nehru and others were able to make him realize that the withdrawal of Allied forces from India would make both India and China vulnerable. Answering the questions, would Indians form a national government if the British withdrew and would that government permit the United Nations to use Indian territory as a base of military operations, he now said that the first act of the national government would be to enter into a treaty with the United Nations for defensive operations. There would be no assistance beyond toleration of the United Nations on Indian soil under well-defined conditions. But there would be no prohibition against any Indian giving personal help by offering himself as a recruit or making a financial contribution. It should, however, be understood that the Indian Army would have been disbanded with the withdrawal of British power. Asked, further, what would 'free India' mean if Jinnah said that the Muslims would not accept Hindu rule, the Mahatma said, 'Then all parties will fight one another like dogs or will, when responsibility faces them, come to a reasonable agreement'. Gandhi also stated that the Allied cause lacked a moral basis while a great nation like India lay prostrate: 'I see no difference between Fascist or Nazi powers and Allies. All are exploiters, all resort to ruthlessness to some extent required to compass their end'.

On 5 July, Gandhi wrote a leading article in *Harijan* under the title 'Oh, the Troops' in which he explained why, after 'having drawn the entrancing picture of free India without a single British soldier,' he had now accepted the 'presence of British and even American troops'. He had changed his stand, he confessed, because 'it has been pointed out that not to consent to Allied troops remaining in India during the war is to hand over India and China to Japan, and to ensure the defeat of Allied Powers. This could never have been contemplated by me.'

At about the same time Gandhi wrote to Chiang Kai-shek at some length telling him that 'our mutual friend Jawaharlal Nehru, whose love of China is only excelled, if at all, by his love of his own country, has kept us in intimate touch with developments of the Chinese struggle'. He assured the Chinese leader that his appeal to the British to withdraw from India was in no way meant to weaken India's defence against the Japanese or to embarrass the Chinese in their struggle, but India could not play its rightful part while still 'in bondage'. India, he continued, did not wish to suffer the same fate as Malaya, Singapore and Burma, which the British had evacuated. India's proffered help had repeatedly been rejected by the British and the recent failure of the Cripps Mission had left a deep wound which was 'still running'. Out of that anguish had come 'the cry for immediate withdrawal of British power so that India can look after herself and help China to the best of her ability'. Unless independence and freedom of action were forthcoming, there was 'every likelihood of subterranean sympathy for Japan growing simply in order to weaken British authority in India'. He concluded, 'To make it perfectly clear that we want to prevent in every way Japanese aggression, I would personally agree, and I am sure the Government of free India would agree, that the Allied powers might, under treaty with us, keep their armed forces in India and use the country as a base for operations against the threatened Japanese attack.'

Early in July, Gandhi answered the question how he could think of a mass movement for liberation without a settlement with the Muslims:

For the moment I cannot reach the Muslim mind. Muslim League blocks my way...Therefore the only settlement with the British Government can be that their rule should end, leaving India to her fate. Thus assuming that the British leave, there is no government and no constitution, British or other. Therefore there is no Central Government. Militarily the most powerful party may set up its rule and impose it on India, if the people submit. Muslims may declare Pakistan and nobody may resist them. Hindus may do likewise, Sikhs may set up their rule in territories inhabited by them. There is no end to the possibilities. And to all this idle speculation let me suggest one more addition. Congress and the League being the best organised parties in the country, may come to terms and set up a provisional government acceptable to all. And this may be followed by a duly elected Constituent Assembly.

The Congress Working Committee convened at Wardha on 5 July 1942, and remained in session till it passed a resolution on 14 July which

Azad described as 'the first draft of the "Quit India Resolution".' During the discussion, Nehru said that what Gandhi had in view was in fact an open rebellion, even if the rebellion was non-violent. Gandhi liked the phrase and spoke of an open non-violent revolution several times. Azad tells us that the Mahatma had no clear programme of resistance. The only thing he said was that, unlike previous occasions, the people would not court imprisonment: they would resist arrest and submit to the government only if physically compelled to do so. Gandhi believed that with the Japanese at the door of India, the government would come to terms with Congress as soon as the movement was launched. Even if this did not happen, the British would hesitate to take any drastic steps and this would give Congress the time to organize an effective movement. Azad states, at the same time, that many people thought that Gandhi would win freedom for India by some magic or superhuman means and they would not have to make any personal effort.

The resolution passed and published on 14 July demanded that 'British rule in India must end immediately' because the freedom of India was necessary 'for the ending of Nazism, fascism, militarism and other forms of imperialism'. Ever since the outbreak of the war, Congress had 'steadily pursued a policy of non-embarrassment' but the 'abortive Cripps proposals showed that...the British hold on India was in no way to be relaxed'. The Congress representatives had 'tried their utmost to bring about a solution of the communal tangle. But this has been made impossible by the presence of the foreign power whose long record has been to pursue relentlessly the policy of divide and rule. Only after the ending of foreign domination and intervention can the present unreality give place to reality and the people of India, belonging to all groups and parties, face India's problems and solve them on a mutually agreed basis.' Congress had no desire to embarrass Great Britain or the Allied Powers and was 'therefore agreeable to the stationing of the armed forces of the Allies in India, should they so desire, in order to ward off and resist Japanese or other aggression, and to protect and help China'. Finally came the ultimatum:

> Should, however, this appeal fail, Congress cannot view without the gravest apprehension the continuation of the present state of affairs involving a progressive deteroration in the situation and the weakening of India's will and power to resist aggression. Congress will then be reluctantly compelled to utilise all the non-violent strength it might have gathered since 1920, when it adopted non-violence as part of its policy, for the vindication of political rights and liberty. Such a widespread struggle would inevitably be under the leadership of Mahatma Gandhi. As the issues raised are of the most vital and far-reaching

importance to the people of India, as well as to the peoples of the United Nations, the Working Committee refers them to the All-India Congress Committee for final decision. For this purpose the AICC will meet in Bombay on 7 August 1942.

After the resolution had been passed, Gandhi told the members of the Press, 'either they recognize India's independence or they don't. There is no question of one more chance. After all, it is an open rebellion.'

On 16 July, Miss Slade, daughter of the late British Admiral Sir Edmond Slade and a disciple of Gandhi known in India as Mira *Bahan*, wrote to the Viceroy asking for a meeting to 'interpret' Gandhi's mind to him. Linlithgow declined to grant an interview 'to a direct representative of Mr Gandhi' because of the contents of the recent Congress resolution and Gandhi's declaration of 'open rebellion', but arranged for her to call on his private secretary. However, she was given no hope that the Congress demands could be entertained.

Chiang Kai-shek, anxious that the British Government should come to terms with Congress before Gandhi actually launched his mass movement, addressed an appeal to Roosevelt. He expressed his fear that, following the Congress meeting in August, the situation could get 'out of control'. He believed that 'the wisest, the most enlightened policy for Britain to pursue would be to restore to India her complete freedom and thus to prevent Axis troops from setting foot on Indian soil'. He expressed his earnest hope 'that the United States would advise both Britain and India in the name of justice and righteousness to seek a reasonable and satisfactory solution, for this affects vitally the welfare of mankind and has a direct bearing on the good faith and good name of the United Nations'. The American President immediately (30 July) transmitted Chiang's message to Churchill and asked his advice as to the reply he should send.

Churchill promptly responded that the British Government did not agree with the Chinese leader's estimate of the Indian situation: 'The Congress party in no way represents India and is strongly opposed by over 90 million Mohammedans, 40 million Untouchables, and the Indian States comprising some 90 millions, to whom we are bound by Treaty. Congress represents mainly the intelligentsia of non-fighting Hindu elements, and can neither defend India nor raise a revolt. The military classes on whom everything depends are thoroughly loyal, in fact over a million have volunteered for the Army and the numbers recently volunteering greatly exceed all previous records...The Government of India have no doubt of their ability to maintain order to carry on government with efficiency and secure India's maximum contribution to the war effort whatever Congress may say or even do, provided of course that their authority is not undermined. His Majesty's Government have no intention of making any offer beyond the sweeping proposals which Sir Stafford Cripps carried to India... I earnestly hope therefore, Mr President, that you will do your best to dissuade Chiang Kai-shek from his completely misinformed activities, and will lend no countenance to putting pressure upon His Majesty's Government.'

In India, Rajagopalachari and three leading Madras Congressmen had the courage to write to Gandhi in the following terms a few days after the 14 July resolution had been passed:

It is not natural for any Government to withdraw without transferring their power to a successor by consent or without being forcibly replaced by another. The formation of a provisional Government, as well as the convening of a Constituent Assembly, is possible only if the continuity of the State is assured. We feel, therefore, that, however difficult the achievement of a Hindu-Muslim settlement may be while the British Government is here and functioning, it is essential before a demand for withdrawal can reasonably be made.

The major political organisations, namely the Congress Party and Muslim League, should evolve a joint plan with regard to a provisional Government which can take over power and preserve the continuity of the State. Even if we imagine that the British could ever, under moral compulsion, be made to withdraw unconditionally, we are convinced that the chaos which would follow under existing conditions would not permit within any reasonable time the formation of a provisional Government such as you contemplate.

The All-India Congress Committee met on 7 August and on the following day, passed the famous Quit India Resolution which confirmed the Working Committee resolution of 14 July and went on to state:

India, the classic land of modern imperialism, has become the crux of the question, for by the freedom of India will Britain and the United Nations be judged...The peril of today...necessitates the independence of India and the ending of British domination. No future promise or guarantees can affect the present situation or meet that peril...The AICC therefore repeats with all emphasis the demand for the withdrawal of the British Power from India. On the declaration of India's independence, a Provisional Government will be formed and Free India will become an ally of the United Nations...the Provisional Government can only be formed by the co-operation of the principal parties and groups in the country. It will thus be a composite government, representative of all important sections of the people of India. Its primary functions must be to defend India and resist aggression... The Provisional Government will evolve a scheme for a Constituent Assembly which will prepare a constitution for the Government of India acceptable to all sections of the people. This constitution, according to the Congress view, should be a federal one, with the largest measure of autonomy for the federating units, and with the residuary powers vesting in these units...The AICC would yet again, at this last moment, in the interest of world freedom, renew this appeal to Britain and the United Nations. But the Committee feels that it is no longer justified in holding the nation back from endeavouring to assert its will against an imperialist and authoritarian government which dominates over it and prevents it from functioning in its own interest and in the interest of humanity. The Committee resolves, therefore, to sanction, for the vindication of India's inalienable right to freedom and independence, the starting of a mass struggle on non-violent lines on the widest possible scale, so that the country might utilise all the non-violent strength it has gathered during the last twenty-two years of peaceful struggle. Such a struggle must inevitably be under the leadership of Gandhiji and the Committee request him to take the lead and to guide the nation in the steps to be taken.

The Committee asked the people to remember that non-violence was the basis of the movement but 'a time may come when it may not be possible to issue instructions or for instructions to reach our people, and when no Congress Committee can function. When this happens, every man and woman who is participating in this movement must function for himself or herself within the four corners of the general instructions issued.'

Accepting the responsibility of leading the movement as 'the chief servant of the nation', Gandhi said he could not wait any longer for India's freedom and called the proposed movement 'the last struggle' of his life. He also coined a short *mantra* (incantation) for his followers: 'We shall "do or die" in the attempt. We shall either free India or die in the attempt'. He stated further that, 'the real struggle does not commence today; I have yet to go through much ceremonial as I always do.' He said he would make every effort to see the Viceroy before starting the struggle.

But the Government of India struck immediately and arrested Gandhi, Nehru, Azad and others early in the morning of 9 August. The War Cabinet in London had at one time strongly favoured the idea that Gandhi should be deported to Aden and the Congress leaders to Nyasaland but, on the advice of the majority of the Governors and the members of his Executive Council, the Viceroy favoured internment in India, and the War Cabinet in the end accepted his recommendation. Gandhi was lodged in the Aga Khan's palace at Poona, and Azad, Nehru and other members of the Working Committee in the Ahmadnagar fort, under military control.

In his report to Amery on 11 August, Linlithgow reported that in taking swift and drastic action against Gandhi and the Working Committee, he had the unanimous support of his Executive Council, though at one time two or three members had displayed signs of doubt.

On 12 August Chiang Kai-shek sent a personal message to Gandhi, Nehru and Azad: 'I am deeply concerned over your arrest. Please take good care of yourself for your country's sake.' At the same time, Madame Chiang Kai-shek sent messages to Mrs Naidu and Mrs Pandit (sister of Jawaharlal Nehru).

One the same day, Chiang conveyed to Roosevelt his concern at the arrest of the Congress leaders and said that if matters were allowed to deteriorate further, 'the avowed object of the Allies in waging this war would no longer be taken seriously by the world and the professed principles of the United Nations would lose much of their spiritual significance'. He appealed to Roosevelt 'as the inspired author of the Atlantic Charter' to take measures to solve the problem facing India. Churchill told the American President that he took it amiss that Chiang 'should seek to make difficulties between us and should interfere in matters about which he has proved himself most ill-informed which affect our sovereign rights'.

Seymour, the British Ambassador, called on the Generalissimo on 11 August to explain the Indian situation to him. Chiang said he did not support the demand for an immediate withdrawal of the British but he desired a peaceful settlement of the problem in the interest of the Allied cause. In his opinion, the pivot of the Indian problem was the Congress Party and if that problem was solved, other aspects of the question could be solved without much difficulty. He said that in dealing with India, there was need for China to pursue a policy different from that of Britain because, if the people of India could not count upon the sympathy of some members of the United Nations, they would lose all hope and might turn to Japan for support. He suggested that America should play the role of mediator under a mandate from the United Nations.

Churchill strongly rejected the proposal that the American President should mediate between the British Government and Congress: 'I should like to place on record the fact that no British Government of which I am the head, or a member, will ever be prepared to accept such mediation on a matter affecting the sovereign rights of His Majesty the King Emperor.'

Meanwhile, the Government of India had not confined its attention to Gandhi and the members of the Congress Working Committee. It had also arrested all the other Congress leaders of any consequence and banned the All-India Congress Committee as well as all the Provincial Congress Committees except that of the North-West Frontier Province.[1] As has already been mentioned, Gandhi had not formulated any systematic plan of action for his non-violent rebellion. The prompt action of the government deprived it also of any recognizable leadership.

The Mahatma did state what in his view was permitted for disorganizing the government within the limits of non-violence, but he had omitted to explain how these acts of sabotage were to be perpetrated without provoking a violent confrontation with the forces of law and order:

> In my opinion looting or burning of offices, banks, granaries, etc. is not permissible. Dislocation of traffic communications is permissible in a non-violent manner—without endangering life. The organisation of strikes is the best, and if that can be accomplished it in itself will be effective and sufficient. It will be non-violence without blemish. Cutting wires, removing rails, destroying small bridges, cannot be objected to in a struggle like this provided ample precautions are taken to safeguard life. If the Japanese were invading us, there can be no doubt that even on principle of non-violent self-defence, these would have to be carried out. The non-violent revolutionaries have to regard the British Power in the same way as they (i.e., the revolutionaries) would the Axis Powers and carry out the same measures.

The disorders were sufficiently intense and destructive for Linlithgow to call them 'the most serious rebellion since that of 1857,' but their duration was short. Already on 1 September he could report that the situation was 'settling down very rapidly' and on 21 September that 'taken as a whole things are pretty comfortable'. By the end of the year the rebellion was virtually subdued.

Nor was the uprising national in terms of the numbers involved or the area affected. The participants were mainly the revolutionary elements, which had lurked underground all the time and now got their chance to act—students, riff-raff, and those sympathisers of Congress who did not share Gandhi's commitment to non-violence. No other political party responded to the Congress proclamation of rebellion.

---

[1] The Frontier Province appears to have been excluded because the Governor had reported to the Viceroy on 25 July 1942 that the morale of the police in his province was 'excellent' and there was no general sympathy on the part of the public with the aims of Congress, which had been losing ground steadily for some time.

Two or three days after the arrest of the Congress leaders, serious disorders erupted in parts of Bombay, Madras, the Central Provinces and Bengal, and very serious ones in Bihar and the eastern parts of the United Provinces, areas which had suffered the most also during the rebellion of 1857. Trouble broke out later in Orissa and Assam as well. The Punjab, North-West Frontier Province, Sind and the princely States remained relatively quiet.

The earliest targets were communications—railways, and the telegraph and telephone systems. By the middle of September, about 250 railway stations and 550 post offices had been attacked and destroyed or damaged. The railway system in Bihar and in adjoining parts of the United Provinces was disrupted, thus temporarily cutting off the forces which were deployed against the Japanese on the north-eastern frontier of India from their main bases of supply and reinforcements. At the same time, the war industries were deprived of fuel from the coal fields of Bihar. Tata's steel plant at Jamshedpur closed down completely and the men openly stated that they would not resume work until a 'national government' had been formed.

More than 155 police-stations and government building were set upon. Over 30 policemen were killed. At Chimur (less than 50 miles from Wardha) a magistrate, a police officer, a *naib-tahsildar* and a constable were murdered when they refused to resign their posts and join Congress.

The civil services, on the whole, gave an excellent account of themselves. Troops had to be used in support of the police specially in Bihar; 11 of them were killed and 7 wounded. By the end of the year over 1,000 rioters had been killed, 3,000 wounded and over 60,000 arrested.

The next episode in the drama was Gandhi's 'fast according to capacity', which he translated as twenty-one days. He started the ordeal on 10 February and ended it on 3 March. He had corresponded with Linlithgow but Linlithgow had not been able to convince him of his error, nor had he been able to convince Linlithgow that Congress was not to blame for the violence during the Quit India Movement. Linlithgow alleged that the proposed fast for a political purpose was a form of blackmail, but the Mahatma rejoined that it was 'an appeal to the Highest Tribunal for justice which I have failed to secure from you'.

The War Cabinet were against Gandhi's release during the fast, but accepted Linlithgow's contention that they should leave this matter to him as he was the man on the spot. The Viceroy and his Executive Council offered to set Gandhi free for the duration of the fast, but he turned down the overture, whereupon the Council decided by a majority that he should not be freed at all. The dissenting members were five Indians, three of whom subsequently resigned.[1]

At the time of the fast, Gandhi was seventy-three years and four months of age and in poor health. His survival confounded all medical prophets. The Governor of Bombay, within whose jurisdiction the Mahatma was interned, thought that the most likely explanation of the feat was 'first, that he knows more about fasting than any doctor and, secondly, that one or other of the non-official doctors gave him glucose to help him through and possibly more fruit juice than has been admitted'. The Surgeon-General of Bombay, who had closely followed Gandhi's condition during the fast, also suspected that something such as glucose had been added to his liquid diet, without his knowledge, by one of his private doctors, probably the lady doctor Sushila Nayar.

Gandhi achieved nothing by fasting. Linlithgow, on the other hand, won praise for having handled a delicate situation so resolutely. Amery telegraphed him on the very day Gandhi terminated his fast: 'Congratulations on your most successful deflation of Gandhi.' The succeeding months were so uneventful that Amery could state on 28 June 1943 that India had 'never been so quiet politically'. Near the end of his Viceroyalty[2] Linlithgow was able to write to the Secretary of State that he could feel that he was leaving the country 'in pretty good trim...The [political] deadlock itself causes no emotion in this country...The Working Committee are in jail and forgotten. One hardly sees a reference to them in the Press. Gandhi is equally out of the way of doing mischief.'

In the autumn and winter (1942-3), Bengal suffered a dreadful famine. The official estimate was that one and a half million died of starvation or its after-effects, but Nehru wrote feelingly, 'a million had died, or two million, or three; no one knows how many starved to death or died of disease during these months of horror. No one knows of the many millions of emaciated boys and girls and little children who just escaped death then, but are stunted and broken in body and spirit.'

The shortage of the rice crop was small and ordinarily would have been met by purchases from Burma and Thailand, but these sources were at this time under Japanese control. Prices had been rising sharply for some time because of panic-buying, but the provincial government was inefficient

---

[1] In a report to Amery on 1 September 1942, Linlithgow related that when he made clear to the Council that, 'I contemplated the old man dying, if he wanted to, one of them burst into tears at the table'.

[2] Linlithgow was succeeded by Wavell on 20 October 1943. Claude Auchinleck succeeded Wavell as Commander-in-Chief.

and imprudent and allowed the situation to get out of hand, while the central government under Linlithgow did not assert itself effectively. Relief efforts were also hampered by a lack of adequate transport facilities; the railway system was burdened by military supplies for the eastern front and boats had been requisitioned to deny them to the Japanese in case of invasion. It was not until Wavell arrived and took a vigorous interest in the tragedy that something worthwhile was done to alleviate the suffering. Within a week of assuming the Viceroyalty, he flew to Calcutta and went round the streets by night to see how the destitute were sleeping, and by day to see them fed. He also visited Contai district of Midnapore, one of the areas worst affected by the famine. He was able to induce the ministry to introduce systematic rationing and take other measures. He also directed the army to assist in the transport and distribution of supplies.

THE MUSLIM LEAGUE AND THE QUIT INDIA MOVEMENT

While Gandhi was incensed that Cripps had rejected the Congress demands, Jinnah was distinctly relieved at the outcome, as he promptly made clear at a press conference on 13 April 1942:

If the alternative proposals of Congress were accepted...it would have meant the setting up of a cabinet, irremovable and responsible to nobody but the majority, which would be at the command of Congress in cabinet. If such an adjustment had been arrived at, then it would have been a 'Fascist Grand Council' and the Muslims and other minorities would have been entirely at the mercy of the Congress raj.

Then to say that the future would be considered after war is to my mind absurd, because there would be nothing left of the future to discuss, except details...it would have been the death-knell to the Mussalmans of India.

In a statement to the Press on 22 June, Jinnah stated:

Now we are presented with a new formula, 'Quit India'. But after having said that Britain should withdraw he adds—he always keeps loopholes—'in an orderly manner'. Since his first pronouncement he has made explanation after explanation. It is clear to those who understand Gandhi's language that he wants the British Government to accept that Congress means India and Gandhi means Congress, and to come to terms with him as the spokesman of all India with regard to the transfer of power of government to the self-styled Indian National Congress, and to keep him in power by means of the British bayonet so that the Hindu Congress raj can dominate the Muslims and other minorities...

Independence and the freedom of all the peoples of this sub-continent should be thought of not only in negative terms of elimination of foreign authority resulting in anarchy, as Gandhi promises, but in a definite positive form of constitution and the setting up of a government to which the power and authority of the British can be transferred, and that could take the place of the foreign authority which Gandhi wants to end today. Such a government would command the confidence and allegiance of the different nationalities and interests in the sub-continent. So long as Congress maintains its present deception and false propaganda, India's progress will continue in jeopardy.

After the Congress Working Committee had passed its resolution of 14 July threatening to launch a mass movement, the Muslim League chief observed that it was the 'culminating point' in the programme of Gandhi and his Hindu Congress 'of blackmailing the British' and coercing them to transfer power to a government which would establish Hindu raj immediately. In a statement issued on 9 August on the Quit India resolution which Congress had passed the day before, Jinnah deeply regretted that 'Congress has finally declared war and has launched a most dangerous mass movement in spite of numerous warnings from various individuals, parties and organizations in this country'.

During a special interview with the *Daily Herald* of London on 14 August, he endorsed the action of the Government in arresting the Congress leaders and taking firm measures to quell the riots because it was 'faced with what is legally high treason'.

The Working Committee of the Muslim League met at Bombay from 16 to 20 August and passed a resolution which claimed that the Muslims were 'not a whit less insistent on freedom for the country,' but they were firmly convinced that the Congress movement was 'not directed for securing the independence of all the constituent elements in the life of the country, but for the establishment of a Hindu raj and to deal a death blow to the Muslim goal of Pakistan'.

The resolution called upon the Muslims to abstain from any participation in the Congress movement and to continue to pursue their normal life, and ended with a stern warning: 'The Working Committee hope that no attempt shall be made from any quarter to intimidate, coerce, molest or interfere in any manner with the normal life of the Muslims, otherwise the Muslims will be compelled to offer resistance and adopt all such measures as may be necessary for the protection of their life, honour and property'.

At a press conference on 13 September the Muslim League President reiterated that the Congress movement was 'unlawful and unconstitutional,' and added that an even greater objection was that it was a declaration of 'internecine civil war' because the movement had been launched to force demands which were strenuously opposed not only by the Muslim League but equally by the other minorities and interests in the country.

The warning of the Muslim League Working Committee was heeded. The Quit India insurgents left the Muslims strictly alone and there were no Hindu-Muslim disturbances during the upheaval.

CHAPTER 19

WAVELL'S INITIATIVES

THE INDIAN NATIONAL ARMY

Following the 1942-3 Russian winter and summer offensives, the Germans were disastrously defeated on the eastern front. In the first part of May 1943, the Axis resistance in North Africa also ended and the Allied forces landed in southern Italy on 2 September. Normandy was invaded by the Allied forces on 6 June 1944. On 28 April 1945, Mussolini was captured and executed, and on 2 May, Hitler was reported dead. The war in Europe ended with the surrender of Germany on 7 May.

In the Pacific, the tide of war turned against Japan in the summer of 1942, relieving the pressure on India. Japan suffered heavy losses in the battles of the Coral Sea (7 May), Midway Island (4-7 June) and the Solomon Islands (7 August). At the time of the Quit India rebellion, the Japanese navy and airforce were thus locked in a deadly struggle in the Pacific and were in no position to mount a sea-borne invasion of India.

During 1944, United States forces invaded the Marshall Islands, recaptured Guam, and began the re-conquest of the Philippines. With the capture of Okinawa in the summer of 1945, they obtained a strategic air-base. In the months that followed, United States land and carrier-based aircraft put the Japanese navy out of action and destroyed Japanese industry. An atomic bomb was dropped on Hiroshima on 6 August and another two days later on Nagasaki. The Japanese capitulated on 14 August and signed the formal terms of surrender on 2 September.

In the summer of 1943, however, the Japanese had still been entrenched in Thailand, Malaya and Burma and posed a threat to India. At this stage two things happened. To organize a campaign against the Japanese on the scale required, it was decided to relieve the Commander-in-Chief of India of the responsibility of conducting operations from India's frontiers eastwards, and Admiral Lord Mountbatten was appointed to the new command with the title Supreme Allied Commander South-East Asia. Secondly, Subhas Chandra Bose arrived at Singapore on 2 July. He was hailed as 'Netaji' ('the suprene leader'), took over the leadership of the

'Indian National Army' (INA) and formed a Provisional Government of Free India with the slogan *Chalo Delhi* (March to Delhi).

The INA had been founded by Captain Mohan Singh of the Indian army who had surrendered to the Japanese in Malaya. After the fall of Singapore, Mohan Singh raised a force of some 40,000 volunteers from Indian prisoners of war to fight alongside the Japanese and drive the British out of India. A number of Indian residents of South-East Asia, without any previous military training, also joined them.

A large number of the Indian prisoners of war had refused to join the INA and those who joined were not of one mind. The Japanese themselves preferred death to capture, and treated those who surrendered to them with cruelty and contempt. Many joined the INA to avoid the Japanese concentration camp; others volunteered intending to defect at the first opportunity and rejoin their old comrades. But a considerable number were genuine patriots who believed the Allies would lose the war, and that co-operation with the Japanese liberators would be to the advantage of their country. They had hoped that Indian soldiers still loyal to the British would flock to them when they confronted each other in battle, but this expectation was belied. Their former comrades shunned them as traitors and fought them as enemies.

The INA was not an efficient fighting machine; most of its officers were inexperienced, its training and equipment were not adequate and the Japanese had little real respect for it. Its political significance lay in the fact that the British could no longer place implicit faith in the loyalty of the Indian armed forces. The majority of the hurriedly-expanded war-time Indian army was non-Muslim[1] and the thousands[2] of Indians who had received permanent and war-time commissions belonged to the same stratum of society—educated Indians—as the politicians, and were as desirous of freedom as anybody else.

On 28 July 1942, Linlithgow reported to Amery that the Defence Member of his Council, Feroze Khan Noon, had told him that 'there was great and growing bitterness, now of long standing, among King's Indian Commission Officers' because of resentment that their British colleagues were better paid and given preferential treatment in matters such as acting rank, temporary command and the like. According to Feroze, who had 'wide family and personal connection with the Indian Army,' the task of finding really contented officers would not be an easy one. With regard to the 'general

---

[1] On the eve of independence the proportion of Muslims in the army was 29 per cent.

[2] By the end of World War II, the number of Indian officers in the Indian Army had risen to 15,740, though only two or three had reached the rank of Brigadier.

political reaction' of the officers 'at the moment', Feroze said quite frankly that, 'while they might not favour the Congress policy, they, Mohammedans alike with Hindus, were very much for Gandhi as the one man who could make the British sit up: and that he was not free from doubt as to the extent to which, if it came to firing, they would be anxious to fire on Congress supporters. He went so far [as] to affirm his doubts as to whether these officers would prove staunch in the event of a Japanese or German invasion of India.' To Feroze's opinion, Linlithgow added his own comment: 'Of course, what we are witnessing is, to some extent, the inevitable consequence of the growth of India towards full stature as a nation, and I fear that the ferment which Feroze reports will become more active and more pronounced as time goes on.' This lack of reliance on the Indian armed forces was one of the causes that contributed to the departure of the British from India.

To get back to the story of the war, the Japanese launched an offensive in Arakan in February 1944 and in March they threatened Imphal (in Manipur State, India). But they had stretched themselves too far and had had to divert their aeroplanes to the Pacific. They were forced to withdraw and this proved to be the turning point. By August they had been cleared from Indian soil and had retreated to Burma. The Allied forces mounted a counter-offensive and Rangoon was retaken in May 1945.

Having fought alongside the Japanese in the Imphal offensive, the INA had withdrawn in their company. When the Japanese evacuated Rangoon, they left it in the hands of the INA. The victorious allied forces disarmed the INA men and took them prisoner.

Bose had to flee from Rangoon. According to the official Japanese version, he died on 18 August 1945 when his plane caught fire on taking off from Taipei (Formosa). He is still revered in India as an indomitable fighter for freedom.

More than three years previously, just before Cripps' arrival in India, a news flash had reported that Bose had died in an aircrash. Gandhi was deeply moved and sent a message of condolence to Bose's mother in which he spoke of her son and his services to the motherland in glowing terms. The news proved to be false but Cripps complained to Azad that Gandhi, a believer in non-violence, should have heaped such praise on Bose, who had openly sided with the Axis powers and had been carrying on vigorous propaganda for the defeat of the Allies.

After the retreat from Imphal, the members of the INA were demoralized and had begun to desert and surrender in large numbers. They, along with those captured at Rangoon, were all sent to India. Prima facie they were guilty of having waged war against the King Emperor, a crime punishable with death. But the issue was not straightforward. Firstly, there were serious political considerations. India was striving for freedom and these men had fought in that cause. What could be the reaction of Indian public opinion and political leaders if these heroes were punished as traitors? Also, they were not all equally guilty. The authorities graded them as the 'Whites' (to be reinstated), the 'Greys' (to be cashiered), and the 'Blacks' (to be tried). In their eyes the real heroes were those Indian prisoners of war who had chosen to suffer Japanese torture and pressure rather than renounce their oath of loyalty.

WAVELL SUCCEEDS LINLITHGOW

On 15 June 1943, Prime Minister Churchill informed his colleagues in the War Cabinet that, at his recommendation, the King had approved the appointment of Sir Archibald Wavell[1] as Viceroy of India. He (Churchill) had learnt that Wavell had expressed the opinion that not enough had been done for social reform in India. He was in the 'fullest sympathy' that Wavell should strike 'this note' and 'there was the further consideration that our first duty at the present time was to defend India and that political reforms must wait until the military situation in the Far East had improved'.

Wavell was in England at that time. His appointment was announced on 19 June but he did not arrive in India till 18 October, to assume office two days later. He spent his time in London studying the problems that would face him in his new position and discussing them with Secretary of State Amery and the War Cabinet. Unlike Linlithgow, who had wished simply to hold his ground, the new Viceroy believed that the British Government must take the initiative and break the political deadlock in India. In a meeting with Amery on 10 September, he said that of the alternatives, whether an attempt should be made to secure a central government on the lines of the Cripps proposals or leave things as they were, he personally preferred the former course because, 'if such a government could be obtained there would be substantial advantages. Broadly, these would be a great relaxation of political and communal tension with the disappearance of the present sense of frustration, and a much more hopeful prospect of a reasonable settlement being achieved by agreement after the war.' In a memorandum he stated that his own

---

[1] Created a Viscount upon appointment as Viceroy and raised to an Earldom when he resigned that office in March 1947.

preference was against 'inaction and no change in the present government' and in favour of endeavouring 'to establish both in the provinces and at the Centre, coalition Governments committed to an acceptable war programme'.

At a farewell dinner in London held in his honour on 6 October, Wavell said that he was aware that 'some quarters' believed that political progress in India should not be attempted during the war. He agreed that the first aim must be to defeat the enemy but he did not think that that should necessarily bar political progress if progress was possible.

The question of the policy to be followed in India was discussed in the meetings of the Committee on India of the War Cabinet as well as in the War Cabinet itself. On 6 October, Churchill recorded a memorandum in which he stated that the fact that a new Viceroy was going to India afforded no reason for running risks. The Allies were preparing a very important offensive from India against Japan and there could hardly be a less suitable time for raising again the political agitation 'on its old and well-known lines, and for trying to form a responsible government based in the main on Gandhi'. If after six months or a year Wavell felt that he was 'unable to maintain conditions in India satisfactory to the military operations against Japan without negotiating with Mr Gandhi and Congress, a very grave issue would arise which we should have to consider on its merits. We shall certainly not be in a worse position to deal with the constitutional position in India after we have beaten Germany and Japan, and have revived the prestige of our arms in Burma and Malaya, than we are at the present time, when we ought to devote ourselves wholeheartedly to the prosecution of the war. Victory is the best foundation for great constitutional departures.'

The 'Directive to the Viceroy Designate' as finally drafted by Churchill was approved by the War Cabinet on 8 October. The directive re-affirmed that the declarations of the British Government in favour of the establishment of a self-governing India 'as an integral member of the British Empire and Commonwealth of Nations' remained the 'inflexible policy' of the British Government, but gave no scope to the Viceroy to take any initiative immediately. All he could do was to make proposals 'as occasion warrants'. He could do so even during the war, but he was to 'beware above all things lest the achievement of victory...should be retarded by undue concentration on political issues while the enemy is at the gate.'

The Viceroy was told that his first duty was the defence of India and that peace, order and a high condition of war-time well-being among the masses constituted 'the essential foundation of the forward thrust against the enemy'. The material and cultural conditions of the peoples of India would 'naturally' engage his earnest attention. He was asked further to make every effort to assuage the strife between Hindus and Muslims.

At the end of December, Wavell tried to offer a concession to Indian nationalism. He proposed to the Secretary of State that when the British incumbent of the Finance portfolio in his Executive Council left in April 1944, the position should be offered to an Indian and he recommended that Sir A. Ramaswami Mudaliar should fill it. But the Cabinet refused to appoint an Indian as Finance Member chiefly because Churchill and Sir John Anderson, the Chancellor of the Exchequer, had objected to such a course. However, in the summer of 1944, Wavell was able to create the portfolio of Planning and Development in his Executive Council and to appoint an Indian, Sir Ardeshir Dalal, to hold it.

GANDHI-WAVELL CORRESPONDENCE

On 17 February 1944, Gandhi wrote his first letter to Wavell from prison. He said he was staggered to read the speeches recently made in the Assembly on behalf of the government which denoted that the government was satisfied with things as they were going. Promises for the future, he went on, were valueless. He defended the Quit India demand because 'real war effort must mean satisfaction of India's demand'; the expression did not have 'the sinister and poisonous meaning' attributed to it by the Government of India. In fact 'the expression is charged with the friendliest feeling for Britain in terms of the whole of humanity'. Wavell acknowledged the letter on 25 February and enclosed a copy of the speech he had made in the Assembly on the same day as Gandhi had written his letter and explained that, as the said speech stated his point of view, he did not consider it necessary to say anything further.

The Mahatma wrote to Wavell again on 9 March and expressed his surprise that in his speech to the Assembly, Wavell had said that he saw no reason to release those responsible for the declaration of 8 August 1942 (the Quit India resolution) until he was convinced that the policy of non-co-operation and obstruction had been withdrawn 'not in sack-cloth and ashes, that helps no one, but in the recognition of a mistaken and unprofitable policy'. Gandhi argued that a resolution collectively arrived at could only be conscientiously withdrawn after joint discussion; is a prisoner ever free to exercise his conscience? He asked why the Viceroy was hesitating to put him in touch with the Working Committee of Congress so that he could find out their minds and reactions. He said he had already denied the government charge that Congress was responsible for the consequences of the Quit India movement.

Wavell responded on 28 March in forthright terms:

> I do not accuse you or the Congress party of any wish deliberately to aid the Japanese. But you are much too intelligent a man, Mr Gandhi, not to have realised that the effect of your resolution must be to hamper the prosecution of the war; and it is clear to me that you had lost confidence in our ability to defend India, and were prepared to take advantage of our supposed military straits to gain political advantage. I do not see how those responsible for the safety of India could have acted otherwise than they did and could have failed to arrest those who sponsored the resolution. As to general Congress responsibility for the disturbances which followed, I was, as you know, Commander-in-Chief at the time; my vital lines of communication to the Burma frontier were cut by Congress supporters, in the name of Congress, often using the Congress flag. I cannot therefore hold Congress guiltless of what occurred. I believe that the greatest contribution that the Congress party can make towards India's welfare is to abandon the policy of non-co-operation and to join whole-heartedly with the other Indian parties and with the British in helping India forward in economic and political progress.

Gandhi, writing on 9 April, denied Wavell's charge that Congress had tried to gain political advantage believing that Britain was unable to defend India. He said he was quite content to remain a prisoner unless there was 'a change of heart, view and policy' on the part of the government.

After a severe attack of malaria, there was a progressive deterioration in Gandhi's anaemia, blood pressure and kidney functions, and in the opinion of Surgeon General Candy and Dr B. C. Roy, an eminent Calcutta physician, there was a danger of coronary or cerebral thrombosis. Candy believed Gandhi was 'on the slippery slope'. On 4 May 1944, Wavell telegraphed Amery that Gandhi should be released on medical grounds. He stated that medical opinion, the Home Department (of the Government of India), and the Governors were overwhelmingly in favour of im-mediate release and that the Home Department believed that Gandhi was 'never likely to be an active factor in politics again'. He anticipated serious difficulties and resignations from his Executive Council if Gandhi died in custody. It was far better to set Gandhi free before public agitation became formidable and government might appear to be yielding to it.

Churchill recorded his own opinion on the same day (4 May) that Gandhi might be released as recommended by the Viceroy but added at the same time: 'We can always arrest him again if he commits new offences. It is of course understood that there will be no negotiations between him and the Viceroy'. Churchill's note was circulated to the members of the War Cabinet and they all concurred in Gandhi's release. On 6 May Gandhi was released.

The state of Gandhi's health was anxiously watched by everyone. In a dispatch to Wavell dated 11 May, Amery said:

> In one of his letters Byron said, 'My mother-in-law has been dangerously ill; she is now dangerously well.' I can only hope that that is not going to be true of our old friend Gandhi. Everybody is already reading into his release all sorts of ideas as to the beginnings of new consultations to 'break the deadlock'.

By 17 June, the Mahatma had picked up sufficient strength to make an attempt to break the political deadlock. He wrote to the Viceroy that he was being pressed 'to make some decisive contribution to the general good' but was unable to do anything unless he knew the mind of the Working Committee of Congress. He had pleaded as a prisoner for permission to meet the Working Committee; he was now repeating the request as a free man. If Wavell desired to see him before deciding the matter, he would gladly comply. Wavell wrote back on 22 June that a meeting between them at that time would be of no value. He also rejected Gandhi's requests to confer with the Working Committee on the ground that Gandhi had recently made public his adherence to the Quit India resolution. But he did not close the door to future negotiations: 'If after your convalescence and on further reflection you have a definite and constructive policy to propose for the furtherance of India's welfare, I shall be glad to consider it.'

Gandhi's renewal of political activity caused Churchill to ask the Viceroy, 'How does this square with the medical reports upon which his release on grounds of ill-health was agreed to by us?' Wavell stood his ground and replied that the Surgeon-General's report had been made in good faith and that Gandhi might have died if left in custody.

Having failed to secure a meeting with the Viceroy, the Mahatma gave a three-day (4-6 July) interview to Stuart Gelder of the *News Chronicle* (London) on the understanding that the contents of their conversation would not be published but conveyed to the Viceroy personally by Gelder. However, an account of the Gandhi-Gelder conversations was published prematurely, which caused Gandhi to issue two further statements on 12 July.

The main points made by Gandhi in the interview with Gelder and the two subsequent statement were:

a) that the world had moved on during the last two years and the whole situation had to be reviewed *de novo*;

b) that if he met the Viceroy he would tell him that his purpose was to help and not hinder the Allied war effort;

c) that he had no intention of offering civil disobedience;

d) that today he would be satisfied with a National Government with full control of the civil administration; the Viceroy would be like the King of England guided by responsible ministers; however, the Viceroy and the Commander-in-Chief would have complete control of military operations;

e) that he could do nothing without conferring with the Congress Working Committee.

Gandhi said that his proposals were quite different from the Cripps offer, which had contemplated 'almost perpetual vivisection of India'.

Clearly, by offering to assist in the prosecution of war the Mahatma had abandoned his much publicized commitment to non-violence under all circumstances, at least for the time being. His critics were not slow to observe that he had changed his tune because he had realized that it was the Allies who were going to win the war.

Hoping that his publicised proposals would soften Wavell's stand, Gandhi wrote to him on 15 July asking him 'to grant at least one of my requests contained in my letter of 17th June 1944', but Wavell refused to budge and repeated his suggestion that Gandhi should send him 'a definite and constructive' plan.

On 27 July, Gandhi wrote to Wavell:

Here is my concrete proposal. I am prepared to advise the Working Committee to declare that in view of changed conditions mass Civil Disobedience envisaged by the resolution of August 1942 cannot be offered and that full co-operation in the war effort should be given by Congress, if a declaration of immediate Indian Independence is made and a National Government responsible to the Central Assembly be formed subject to the proviso that, during the

pendency of the war, the military operations should continue as at present but
without involving any financial burden on India.

Wavell submitted to London the draft of the reply he intended to send
to Gandhi. It was debated in the India Committee as well as in the War
Cabinet. In the War Cabinet, Churchill 'expressed grave uneasiness as to
the position which has developed. It is most undesirable that the Viceroy
should find himself in correspondence with Mr Gandhi. It is surely
essential that a very firm line should be adopted and no risk run of our
giving the impression that we were truckling to Mr Gandhi.'

Wavell was quite upset at the alterations to his own draft ordered by the
War Cabinet but had no option but to comply, and on 15 August he wrote
to Gandhi rejecting his proposals, mainly on the ground that they were
'very similar to the proposals made by Maulana Abul Kalam Azad to Sir
Stafford Cripps in April 1942'.

The Cabinet's draft was much stiffer in tone than Wavell's. The
amendments that displeased the Viceroy the most were, firstly, that his
superiors had eliminated the following courteous sentence with which he
had wished to conclude his reply to Gandhi: 'You and Mr Jinnah have my
good wishes for your approaching discussion.'[1] Secondly, the War Cabinet
had inserted a paragraph of their own:

> No purpose would be served by discussion on the basis which you suggest. If
> however the leaders of the Hindus, the Muslims and the important minorities
> were willing to co-operate in a transitional government established and
> working within the present constitution, I believe good progress might be
> made. For such a transitional government to succeed there must, before it is
> formed, be agreement in principle between Hindus and Muslims and all
> important elements as to the method by which the new constitution should be
> framed. This agreement is a matter for Indians themselves. Until Indian leaders
> have come closer together than they are now I doubt if I myself can do anything
> to help.

The Indian Press called the Viceroy's letter 'rude' and 'arrogant' and
criticised it for dragging in the minorities to obstruct the progress toward
independence. Wavell recorded in his journal that all these criticisms had
resulted from the Cabinet's amendments and 'in fact Cabinet has destroyed
at one blow my reputation for fairness and good temper in my
correspondence with Gandhi, and has thus weakened my usefulness in any

---

[1] *See*, the next section for Gandhi-Jinnah negotiations.

eventual dealings with Congress. This was probably the PM's intention.'[1] Some weeks previously, he had written in the journal, 'I wonder if we shall ever have any chance of a solution till the three intransigent, obstinate, uncompromising principals are out of the way: Gandhi (just 75), Jinnah (68), Winston (nearing 70)'.

With Wavell's letter of 15 August to Gandhi, the latter's efforts to arrive at an agreement with the British Government reached a dead end. The impasse could now be resolved only in the following two ways: either the British Government would have to take the initiative and come up with a fresh proposal, or Congress and the Muslim League would have to accept the persistent challenge of the government and reach an understanding between themselves and confront the government with a joint demand.

GANDHI-JINNAH NEGOTIATIONS

Some commentators have stated that Gandhi turned to Jinnah only after he had been rebuffed by the British Government, but this view is not historically correct. It is true that Gandhi and Jinnah did not actually meet face to face until September 1944, but the origins of their negotiations go back much further.

The ball was set rolling by Rajagopalachari ('Rajaji') who, as already mentioned, had resigned from the Congress Party in July 1942 to be free to propagate his view that Congress should seek conciliation with the Muslim League on the basis of Pakistan. During Gandhi's fast in detention, Rajaji sent a telegraphic invitation to Jinnah on 12 February 1943 to attend a conference at Delhi on 18 February to consider the situation arising from Gandhi's fast. Jinnah replied that the matter was really one for the Hindu leaders to consider and he was unable to associate himself with the proposed conference. It was apparent, he went on to say, that there had been no change in Gandhi's attitude toward the Muslim League and now he had undertaken 'this dangerous fast' with a view to enforcing his demands, which, if conceded, would 'destroy the Muslim demand and involve a complete sacrifice of the vital and paramount interests of Muslim India'.

In March 1943, Rajaji was permitted to visit Gandhi in jail while the latter was still fasting, and was able to obtain his approval of a scheme for a settlement between Congress and the Muslim League. The main terms as spelled out in the 'Rajaji Formula' were:

---

[1] Wavell, *The Viceroy's Journal,* edited by Penderel Moon, p. 87.

Subject to the terms set out below as regards the constitution for Free India, the Muslim League endorses the Indian demand for Independence and will co-operate with Congress in the formation of a provisional interim Government for the transitional period.

After the termination of the war, a commission shall be appointed for demarcating contiguous districts in the north-west and east of India, wherein the Muslim population is in absolute majority. In the areas thus demarcated, a plebiscite of all the inhabitants held on the basis of adult suffrage or other practicable franchise shall ultimately decide the issue of separation from Hindustan. If the majority decide in favour of forming a sovereign State separate from Hindustan, such decision shall be given effect to, without prejudice to the right of districts on the border to choose to join either State.

These terms shall be binding only in case of transfer by Britain of full power and responsibility of the governance of India.

Jinnah at this stage had no inkling of the Rajaji formula, but in the course of his presidential address to the Muslim League session at Delhi on 24 April 1943 he said independently, 'Nobody would welcome it more than myself, if Mr Gandhi is even now really willing to come to a settlement with the Muslim League on the basis of Pakistan. Let me tell you that it will be the greatest day for both Hindus and Mussalmans. If he has made up his mind, what is there to prevent Mr Gandhi from writing direct to me? He is writing letters to the Viceroy. Why does he not write to me direct?' He added that the government would not 'have the daring to stop such a letter if it is sent to me'.

Gandhi, who was allowed newspapers during his internment, read an account of Jinnah's challenge in the Muslim League paper *Dawn* and wrote a letter to the Muslim leader on 4 May saying, 'I welcome your invitation. I suggest our meeting face to face rather than talking through correspondence ... I hope that this letter will be sent to you and, if you agree to my proposal, that the government will let you visit me'. It is not known on what basis Gandhi wished to negotiate with Jinnah. One possibility is that he wished to use the Rajaji formula as the starting point.

But the authorities detained Gandhi's letter and Linlithgow forwarded a copy to Amery, stating that he himself was in favour of sending it on to Jinnah and would have no objection to Jinnah seeing Gandhi in jail.

The issue of whether or not the letter should be delivered to Jinnah was anxiously considered by the members of the War Cabinet. Churchill, who was on a visit to Washington, telegraphed London on 14 May that 'a letter from an interned person seeking conference for the purpose of "uniting and driving the British out" should not be delivered', and warned that if the letter was delivered the government would 'certainly be dragged into endless conferences'. In a memorandum bearing the same date, Amery recommended that Gandhi and the Congress leaders should be kept 'entirely disconnected' unless they showed some sign of a change of heart or at least of a recognition that their own policy had failed. He warned that if Gandhi was allowed to see Jinnah it would be difficult to resist the further demand that the Congress Working Committee should also join in the discussion or, indeed, anyone else whom Gandhi might wish to see. Moreover, the delivery of the letter would be a concession to the 'truculent tone' of Jinnah's speech in which he had said that the government would not 'have the daring' to stop such a letter.

A new complication arose when Linlithgow informed Amery on 17 May that the fact that Gandhi had written to Jinnah was already known to the various members of Gandhi's entourage and there was a risk that the news might get out.

The War Cabinet eventually decided that the letter should not be forwarded but that Gandhi and Jinnah should be informed, after which the following communique should be issued :

> In accordance with their known policy in regard to correspondence or interviews with Mr Gandhi, the Government of India have decided that this letter cannot be forwarded and have so informed Mr Gandhi and Mr Jinnah. They are not prepared to give facilities for political correspondence or contact to a person detained for promoting an illegal mass-movement, which he has not disavowed, and thus gravely embarrassing India's war effort at a critical time. It rests with Mr Gandhi to satisfy the Government of India that he can safely be allowed once more to participate in the public affairs of the country, and until he does so the disabilities from which he suffers are of his own choice.

The communique was duly issued on 27 May and on the following day Jinnah, whom the government had furnished with the substance of Gandhi's letter, told Reuters that Gandhi's letter could only be construed as a move to embroil the Muslim League with the British Government as a means of helping his release. He reiterated that if Gandhi was prepared to write a letter and was willing to settle on the basis of Pakistan, the Muslim League were prepared to bury the past. He still believed the British Government would not stop such a letter.

It was on 8 April 1944 that Rajaji at last revealed the contents of his formula to Jinnah. He personally handed over a copy of the text to Jinnah, together with a covering letter explaining that he was doing so on Gandhi's behalf because Gandhi himself was unable to negotiate any settlement personally on account of the restrictions imposed on him by the government. During their oral exchanges at the time, Jinnah expressed his willingness to place the formula before the Muslim League Working Committee, but Rajaji somehow got the impression that Jinnah had rejected it. After Gandhi's release from detention, Rajaji resumed his efforts and on 30 June (1944) telegraphed Jinnah, with Gandhi's approval, urging him to reconsider the matter, otherwise he would publish the formula together with 'your rejection'. Jinnah protested at Rajaji's assertion that he had rejected the plan and offered once more to submit it to the Working Committee provided Gandhi 'now sends me direct his proposal'. The negotiations were terminated on 8 July by Rajaji's letter stating that no purpose would be served by placing the proposal before the League Council so long as it did not have Jinnah's own support, and that he was releasing the correspondence to 'take the public into confidence'.

The position in the middle of July 1944, therefore, was that the Mahatma was getting nowhere with Wavell or Jinnah. He now pursued his quest for settlement with both with renewed vigour. He wrote to Jinnah on 17 July, 'I have not written to you since my release. Today my heart says that I should write to you. We will meet whenever you choose. Do not disappoint me.' Jinnah, who at the time was in Kashmir, replied that he would be glad to receive Gandhi at his residence in Bombay on his return. In the meanwhile, Gandhi's postal overtures to Wavell had ended in failure with the latter's communication of 15 August, and this put extra pressure on Gandhi to reach an accord with Jinnah. They met at Jinnah's house in Bombay on 9 September and thereafter corresponded at some length. They also personally conferred together a number of times up to 27 September, but without arriving at an agreement. They did not keep any minutes of their verbal discussions but the texts of their letters are available.

The first letter in the series was written by Jinnah to Gandhi on 10 September, and we learn from it that during their meeting on the previous day Jinnah had tried to persuade Gandhi to accept the Pakistan Resolution of March 1940, while Gandhi had put forward the Rajaji formula. The main points that emerged during the debate were the following.

Jinnah complained that Gandhi's claim that he had come to discuss Hindu-Muslim settlement in his individual capacity raised 'great difficulty' in his way because he himself could speak only in his capacity as President of the Muslim League. Gandhi characteristically claimed, 'Though I represent nobody but myself, I aspire to represent all the inhabitants of

India', to which Jinnah replied, 'I cannot accept that statement of yours. It is quite clear that you represent nobody else but Hindus, and as long as you do not realize your true position and the realities, it is very difficult for me to argue with you.'

For his part, Gandhi questioned the right of the Indian Muslims to call themselves a nation. 'I find no parallel in history', he wrote in one of his letters, 'for a body of converts and their descendants claiming to be a nation apart from the parent stock', to which Jinnah rejoined:

> We maintain and hold that Muslims and Hindus are two major nations by any definition or test of a nation. We are a nation of a hundred million, and, what is more, we are a nation with our own distinctive culture and civilization, language and literature, art and architecture, names and nomenclature, sense of value and proportion, legal laws and moral codes, customs and calendar, history and traditions, aptitudes and ambitions. In short, we have our own distinctive outlook on life and of life. By all canons of international law we are a nation.

The two leaders also differed with regard to the boundaries of Pakistan and how the issue of whether India should be divided at all was to be determined. Gandhi said his assumption was that 'the Muslims living in the north-west zones, i.e., Baluchistan, Sind, North-West Frontier Province and that part of the Punjab where they are in absolute majority over all the other elements, and in parts of Bengal and Assam where they are in absolute majority, desire to live in separation from India.' Jinnah protested that if this proposal was 'given effect to, the present boundaries of these provinces would be maimed and mutilated beyond redemption and leave us only with the husk'. His position was that Pakistan would comprise the whole of six provinces, viz. Sind, Baluchistan, North-West Frontier Province, the Punjab, Bengal and Assam.

Gandhi also said that the issue of partition should be decided by a vote of the entire adult population of the six provinces concerned. Jinnah, on the other hand, maintained that only Muslims should vote on the question because 'we claim the right of self-determination as a nation, and not as a territorial unit'.[1]

---

[1] Jinnah's insistence that only the Muslims in the Muslim-majority provinces should be asked to vote on the issue of Pakistan was understandable. In the two biggest provinces, Bengal and the Punjab, the Muslims were only in a small numerical majority which the non-Muslims—who were more affluent, better organized and who controlled most of the Press—might have overturned.

But the immediate reasons why the talks broke down were, firstly, that Gandhi stated, 'we reach by joint effort independence for India as it stands. India, become free, will proceed to demarcation, plebiscite and partition if the people concerned vote for partition.' This to Jinnah meant that Congress wanted to get rid of the British first so that they could then be in a position to deny Pakistan to the Muslims. He therefore insisted that 'we come to a settlement of our own immediately'. Second, Gandhi said that he could be 'no willing party to a division which does not provide for the simultaneous safeguarding of common interests such as defence, foreign affairs and the like'. Denial of complete control over these vital subjects clearly meant denial of sovereignty to Pakistan. It is no wonder that a frustrated Jinnah told Gandhi that, 'as a result of our correspondence and discussions I find that the question of the division of India as Pakistan and Hindustan is only on your lips and it does not come from your heart.'

In his replies to a questionnaire posed by the Sapru Committee regarding his talks with Jinnah, Gandhi conceded that 'the breakdown took place because we would not come to agreement on the "two-nations" theory of the Quaid-i-Azam. I accepted the concrete suggestion of division of India as between members of the same family and, therefore, reserving for partnership things of common interest.'

During a press conference on 4 October (1944), Jinnah said:

My attention has been drawn to Mr Gandhi's press statement which was published on 29 September. It is a pity that he thinks that the presence of a third party hinders a solution, and it was very painful to me when he said, a mind enslaved cannot act as if it was free. No power can enslave the mind and soul of man, and I am sure Mr Gandhi is the last person to allow his mind to be enslaved. I do hope that he will get over this depression from which he is perpetually suffering. We have to reach an agreement of our own and find a solution in spite of that third party.

The Muslim League president also expressed his amazement that Gandhi 'should repeat *ad nauseam* that he has by his offer satisfied the essence of the Lahore Resolution. It would be difficult to conceive of a more disingenuous, tortuous and crooked assertion which he keeps on repeating naively.' To the question whether there was any possibility of his meeting Gandhi again in the near future, Jinnah replied, 'Mr Gandhi says that it depends on the inner voice. I have no admission to that place. I cannot say.'

Though the Gandhi-Jinnah negotiations failed to achieve the avowed goal of Hindu-Muslim unity, they brought to Jinnah and the Muslim League two important political gains. Firstly, the supreme leader of Congress had now offered to discuss the question of Pakistan seriously— hitherto Congress and the Mahatma had kept the door to that subject uncompromisingly shut.

Secondly, Congress could no longer justifiably claim that it stood for all the communities in India including the Muslims. That he thought it necessary to approach the President of the Muslim League for a Hindu-Muslim settlement was tacit admission on Gandhi's part that it was the Muslim League that really represented the Muslims and that Jinnah was as much a personification of the League as he himself was of Congress.

Not surprisingly, Jinnah's personal prestige moved up several notches. This made it easier for him to deal with those Muslim leaders who still dared to challenge his authority. One such leader was Sir Khizar Hayat Khan, premier of the Punjab.

THE JINNAH-KHIZAR RIFT

Khizar had succeeded Sikander as head of the Unionist Ministry in the Punjab in 1942. During the Lucknow session of the Muslim League in October 1937, Sikander had announced that he would advise all the Muslim members of the Unionist party in the Punjab to join the Muslim League. He had however, not dissolved the Unionist Party and had maintained the label Unionist for his ministry. It was not till April 1944 that Jinnah felt confident enough to challenge that position. He personally visited the Punjab for several days for a show-down with Khizar.

Jinnah said no one could owe allegiance to two political parties, and demanded that the name 'Unionist Party' should be discarded and be replaced by the 'Muslim League Coalition Party'. Khizar claimed that under the 'Sikander-Jinnah pact' it had been agreed that, while the Punjab Muslims would support the Muslim League on all-India issues, the description of the ministry as Unionist would be retained and Jinnah would not interfere in provincial matters. Jinnah denied that there had been any 'pact' between him and Sikander. 'How could there be a pact between a leader and a follower?' he asked.

Though some of his followers had begun to waver, Khizar himself insisted that he was entitled to be both a Unionist and a Muslim Leaguer.

When Jinnah, in a two-and-a-half hour meeting on 20 April, argued that for a Muslim to adhere to the Unionist party as well as to the Muslim League was like keeping a mistress in addition to a wife, Khizar responded wittily that being a Muslim himself, he was entitled to have two wives.

Not long afterwards, Khizar was expelled from the Muslim League. His defiance of Jinnah cost him dear in the long run. His followers began to desert him in increasing numbers as Jinnah's domination over Muslim politicians continued to grow with his performances in episodes such as the Gandhi-Jinnah debate and the Simla conference in the following year, which he managed to frustrate single-handedly.

THE SIMLA CONFERENCE

As the fortunes of war began to turn in favour of the Allies, Wavell felt that the time had come for him to make proposals for a resolution of the political deadlock in India.

During an informal discussion of the political situation in the Governors' conference on 31 August 1944, Wavell gave it as his view that in the short-term, India could be kept quiet, but the long-term view was 'less comfortable' because 'as soon as the war with Japan ended, His Majesty's government's cheque would be presented and would have to be honoured'. The Defence of India Rules would lapse and the political prisoners would have to be released. There would be economic and other problems such as large numbers of demobilized Indian soldiers, some of them discontented, and a strong Indian Army, still under arms and perhaps open to political influence. Discontent was inevitable. It would be wise to provide educated Indians with some outlet for their administrative and political energy. On 20 September the Viceroy sent his proposals to the Secretary of State and on 24 October he followed these up with a letter to Churchill on the same lines.

His objective, as stated in the letter to Churchill, was to form 'a provisional government, of the type suggested in the Cripps declaration, within the present constitution, coupled with an earnest but not necessarily simultaneous attempt to devise a means to reach a constitutional settlement'. He complained that the 'vital problems of India are being treated by HMG with neglect, even sometimes with hostility and contempt. If the aim of the British Government is to retain India as a willing member of the British Commonwealth it must make some imaginative and constructive move without delay. A move made generously and honestly, even if it failed, would do good.'

Wavell had told Amery that he attached much importance to his proposals and was prepared to visit London to urge their acceptance, but it was not till 11 January 1945 that he was informed that that he could come in late March. He eventually arrived on 23 March.

Churchill had not been happy at the prospect of seeing the Viceroy. On 1 January he had minuted, 'I expect he is going to make trouble and stage a scene for resignation'. On 25 March the Prime Minister also turned down Amery's recommendation for a small dinner party at 10 Downing Street to mark the arrival of Lord and Lady Wavell, with the observation that his meeting with the Viceroy 'had better be purely official'.

During his conferences with his superiors, Wavell stoutly defended his proposals. Two meetings[1] soon after his arrival in London made him aware that it would not be easy for him to obtain an early and sympathetic decision from the cabinet. The first was a discussion in the India Committee on 27 March which showed that none of the members liked his proposals though none of them had an alternative. When Attlee called his proposals undemocratic, Wavell rejoined that the body he was proposing was certainly more democratic than the present Executive Council.

The second was a one-and-a-quarter hour meeting with Churchill on 29 March. The Prime Minister thought that the problem of India 'could be kept on ice,' but Wavell told him quite firmly that the question of India was very urgent and very important. Wavell's impression was that Churchill seemed 'to favour partition into Pakistan, Hindustan, Princestan, etc.'

Exasperated by the long delay in obtaining a decision he wrote to Churchill on 24 May that he had submitted his proposals six months before his arrival in London, and that a further eight weeks had now passed without any result. He had had five meetings with the India Committee, but for more than a month he had had no communication with either the India Committee or the Cabinet.

During May, while Wavell was still in England, the war in Europe came to an end, the coalition government in England broke up and a Conservative 'caretaker' Government under Churchill took office, with Amery continuing as Secretary of State for India. It was on 31 May that the visiting Viceroy at last got a go-ahead from the cabinet largely on the lines he had desired.[2] He left London on 1 June and landed at Karachi on 4 June.

---

[1] The account of these meetings given here is based on the relevant entries in Wavell's journal.

[2] Wavell recorded in his journal that, on 31 August 1945, Churchill revealed to him that the only reason he had agreed to Wavell's political move was that the India Committee had all told him that it was bound to fail.

The British Government's new proposals were publicly disclosed on 14 June, on which date the Viceroy made a broadcast at New Delhi and the Secretary of State made a statement in the House of Commons.

In his broadcast, Wavell said that the proposals he was making were not an attempt to impose a constitutional settlement, but the hope that the Indian parties would agree among themselves on a settlement of the communal issue had not been fulfilled, and in the meantime great problems had to be solved. He therefore invited the Indian leaders to take counsel with him :

> ...with a view to the formation of a new Executive Council more representative of organised political opinion. The proposed new Council would represent the main communities and would include equal proportions of Caste Hindus and Muslims. It would work, if formed, under the existing constitution. But it would be an entirely Indian council except for the Viceroy and the Commander-in-Chief, who would retain his position as War Member. It is also proposed that the portfolio of External Affairs, which has hitherto been held by the Viceroy, should be placed in charge of an Indian Member of Council, so far as the interests of British India are concerned. Such a new Executive Council will be almost entirely Indian, and the Finance and Home Members will for the first time be Indians, while an Indian will also be charged with the management of India's Foreign Affairs. Moreover, Members will now be selected by the Governor-General after consultation with political leaders. The Council will work within the framework of the present constitution; and there can be no question of the Governor-General agreeing not to exercise his constitutional power of control; but it will of course not be exercised unreasonably. I should make it clear that the formation of this interim Government will in no way prejudice the final constitutional settlement.

One of the main tasks of this new Executive Council, he stipulated, would be to prosecute the war against Japan with the utmost energy. He claimed that the proposals were intended to make an agreement on a new constitution easier.

He stated further that he had invited the following persons to a conference in Simla on 25 June to advise him in regard to the formation of the new Executive Council :

> Those now holding office as Premier in a provincial Government; or, for provinces now under Section 93 Government, those who last held the office of Premier; the Leader of the Congress Party and the Deputy Leader of the Muslim

League in the Central Assembly; the leader of the Congress Party and the Muslim League in the Council of State; also the leaders of the Nationalist Party and the European Group in the Assembly; Mr Gandhi and Mr Jinnah as the recognised leaders of the two main political parties; Rao Bahadur N. Siva Raj to represent the Scheduled Classes; Master Tara Singh to represent the Sikhs.

He expressed the hope that an agreement on the formation of the new Executive Council would thus be reached and also that coalition ministries would be formed in provinces which at the moment were being administered by their Governors (under Section 93 of the Act of 1935).

The Viceroy concluded the broadcast with the announcement that orders had been given for the immediate release of the members of the Congress Working Committee who were still in detention.

The Congress Working Committee met at Bombay on 21 and 22 June and decided that Congress 'as an organization should participate in the Simla Conference,' and authorised the President of the Congress, Abul Kalam Azad, to represent the party. After his usual protestation that he represented 'no institution' and could not attend the conference as a representative of Congress, Gandhi agreed to come to Simla.

On 24 June Wavell separately interviewed Azad, Gandhi and Jinnah.

Azad appeared to accept the main principles underlying the proposals, including whole-hearted support for the war effort. He said Congress would accept equality of Caste Hindus and Muslims but would not compromise on the method of selection. Congress must have a voice in the selection of non-Hindus; the Muslims in particular must not be selected by an exclusively communal body.

Gandhi said he would attend the conference if the Viceroy insisted but would simply 'sit in a corner'. He gave a 'general blessing on the proposals' and added that he had recommended them to the Working Committee. In the end he did not attend the formal meetings but remained available at Simla for the duration.

Jinnah expressed the anxiety that the Muslims would be in a minority in the new Executive Council because the other minorities such as the Sikhs and the Scheduled Castes would always vote with the Hindus, and that the Viceroy would be most reluctant to exercise his veto. He claimed that the Muslim League had the right to nominate all Muslim members to the Council. Wavell said he could not accept this. Jinnah argued that the League had won all the by-elections in the preceding two years and therefore represented all the Muslims of India. He suggested that the Viceroy was thinking of the nomination of Muslims by Congress, to which the latter replied that he also had in mind the nomination of a Muslim by the Punjab Unionist Party.[1] Jinnah protested that the Unionist Party had betrayed Muslim interests.

The Congress leaders had begun to see things in a new light. Evidently they had realised that they had made a mistake in rejecting the Cripps offer and had wasted three years in jail by launching the Quit India rebellion. When Azad and Nehru had visited Commander-in-Chief Wavell during Cripps' visit he had appeared to Azad to speak like a politician rather than like a soldier, but now Azad was impressed by the frankness and sincerity of the Viceroy'...I saw that his attitude was not that of a politician but a soldier'. On the same afternoon (24 June) Azad gave a brief report of his meeting with Wavell to the Congress Working Committee and expressed the opinion that, though Wavell's offer was no different from that of Cripps, it should be accepted. Circumstances had changed. The war in Europe was now over and even Japan could not last long. Once the war was over, the British would have no special reason to seek Congress co-operation. Congress should participate in the conference and accept the terms if these were at all suitable.

Azad also says that Gandhi was present at the meeting but did 'not on this occasion raise the question that participation in the war meant that Congress was giving up non-violence'.

On the very first day of the conference (25 June), it became clear that the crux was the composition of the Executive Council; all parties would accept the proposal if they could reach agreement on the method of selection. Jinnah refused to see Azad but agreed to meet Pant[2] as the Congress spokesman, but their talks failed because Congress would not accept the League's demand for the exclusion of Congress Muslims. By

---

[1] The Viceroy was anxious to buttress Khizar and the Unionist Party against Jinnah's onslaughts. During the April-May crisis of 1944, when Jinnah demanded that the name 'Unionist Party' should be given up in favour of the title 'Muslim League Coalition Party', the Governor of the Punjab and the Viceroy had encouraged Khizar to stand up to Jinnah.

Khizar was an anglophile who did not relish the prospect of the British leaving India. He did not favour Pakistan. A princely landlord and a straightforward gentleman, he ran a clean administration and was well content with things as they were. If the Muslim League were to get into power at the centre, it would have created all sorts of problems for him.

The British government did not wish to do anything that would disturb the political set-up in the Punjab, which was the richest source of fighting men in India and a surplus food-producing area. Khizar and his Unionist colleagues were enthusiastic supporters of the war effort.

[2] Premier of the United Provinces 1937-9 and member of the Congress Working Committee.

29 June it became clear that the parties would not be able to come up with an agreed list of Executive Councillors and the conference was adjourned to 14 July to enable them to file separate lists. In the following days all the parties except the Muslim League sent their respective lists to the Viceroy.

At the same time Wavell confidentially prepared a list of his own for the membership of the Executive Council. This consisted of five Caste Hindus (two of whom were not members of Congress); five Muslims (four of whom were members of the Muslim League[1] and the fifth a nominee of Khizar Hayat Khan, leader of the Unionist party of the Punjab); one Sikh; two Scheduled Castes; and one Indian Christian. Including the Viceroy himself and the Commander-in-Chief, this would make an Executive council of sixteen.

In a meeting with the Viceroy on 27 June, Jinnah had said that he wanted a council of fourteen, with five Hindus, five Muslims, one Sikh and one Scheduled Caste. He said this was the only council in which the Muslims would stand a chance of not being out-voted on every issue. It was after seeing Jinnah on 11 July that the Viceroy accepted that the conference had failed because he had been unable to accede to Jinnah's demands. He gave Jinnah the names of the four Muslim League members and of the non-League Muslim member from the Punjab on his own list.[2] But Jinnah said that it was impossible for him to co-operate unless (a) all Muslim members were drawn from the League, and (b) no decision objected to by the Muslims should be taken in council except by a clear two-thirds majority or some similar provision.

Jinnah had also explained his point of view by statements to the Press. On 29 June he said, 'I know the Viceroy's veto is there and I know that Mr Amery says that the veto will be exercised to protect minorities, but also I know that the Governor-General and Viceroy will be placed in a very invidious position if he were to exercise the veto constantly and as a normal business. Therefore, there is no adequate provision against Congress forcing their decisions by a majority vote against the Muslim bloc. Therefore, we will have to consider how to provide against this position'.

He explained also why the Muslim League and nobody else was entitled to give names for the entire Muslim bloc to the Viceroy:

---

[1] Jinnah's own name was not on the list because he had made it known that he had no desire to hold office personally.

[2] Obviously to win Jinnah's approval, Wavell had refrained from choosing any Nationalist [Congress] Muslim.

I am told that in the Central Legislature, there is not a single Congressite Muslim from a Muslim electorate. There are two Muslims who have been returned by joint electorate. There cannot be unanimity in this world. I do not think you will find it anywhere in the world. There are a handful of Muslims who are outside the League, and there are Muslims who are in Congress. But how many?

After the failure of the conference he said that, 'if we accept this arrangement the Pakistan issue will be shelved and put into cold storage indefinitely, whereas Congress will have secured under this arrangement what they want, namely, a clear road for their advance towards securing Hindu national independence of India, because the future Executive will work as a unitary Government of India, and we know that this interim or provisional arrangement will have a way of settling down for an unlimited period, and all the forces in the proposed Executive, plus the known policy of the British Government and Lord Wavell's strong inclination for a united India, would completely jeopardise us.'

When the conference met on 14 July, Wavell formally announced its failure and sportingly blamed himself for the result: 'I wish to make it clear that the responsibility for the failure is mine. The main idea underlying the conference was mine. If it had succeeded, its success would have been attributed to me, and I cannot place the blame for its failure upon any of the parties.' In fact the Viceroy deserved the greatest praise. With resolution and persistence he had succeeded in winning the consent of Churchill and others to opening the Indian question and giving the Indian leaders another chance to install a national government.

It was the two principal political parties, Congress and the Muslim League, that were really responsible for the failure. They had taken up positions which admitted of no compromise. If Congress had allowed the Muslim League to have a monopoly of Muslims, it would have been tantamount to accepting that it was purely a Hindu body. And if the League had permitted Congress to nominate Muslims, it would have thereby accepted the Congress claim that it represented all the communities in India. In his final report to Amery on the Simla Conference, Wavell correctly diagnosed that:

The immediate cause of the failure of the conference was Jinnah's intransigence about Muslim representation and Muslim safeguards. The deeper cause was the real distrust of the Muslims, other than Nationalist Muslims, for Congress and the Hindus. Their fear that Congress, by parading its national character and using Muslim dummies, will permeate the entire administration of any united

India is real, and cannot be dismissed as an obsession of Jinnah and his immediate entourage.

Congress leaders blamed Jinnah for the lost opportunity and said that the Viceroy should have gone ahead without the League. But in fact the entire plan had been based on the idea that the Executive Council would be an all-party body. During Wavell's discussion with the India Committee on 26 March 1945, Attlee had raised the possibility that the members of the proposed Executive Council might walk out if they were overriden by a viceregal veto, to which the Viceroy had replied that the real safeguard was the communal balance; unless Hindus and Muslims were united, they could not out-vote him. And in his broadcast of 15 June, Wavell had clearly warned that, if the conference failed, the existing Executive Council would continue. While the conference was still in session, Azad had protested to Wavell (12 July) that one party should not be allowed to block progress, at which the Viceroy had reminded the Congress President that 'the attitude and mistakes of Congress had blocked progress on more than one occassion.'

It was unthinkable for a government presided over by Churchill to hand over power to the erstwhile rebellious Congress party. In a letter to Wavell the day after the collapse of the conference, Gandhi wrote, 'I must not hide from you the suspicion that the deeper cause is perhaps the reluctance of the official world to part with power, which the passing of the virtual control into the hands of their erstwhile prisoners would have meant.'

Jinnah was under great stress during the Simla Conference. Wavell recorded in his journal: 'I had one and a half hours with Jinnah yesterday (8 July). He was obviously in a high state of nervous tension, and said to me more than once, "I am at the end of my tether"; he also said, "I ask you not to wreck the (Muslim) League".' After the failure of the conference the impression gained ground that Jinnah would be able to veto any constitutional advance of which he did not approve, and that it was necessary to win his favour if one aspired to be accepted as a representative Muslim. On 12 July 1945, Amery wrote to Wavell that Congress 'must now either acquiesce in Pakistan, or realise that they have somehow or other to win over Muslim support against Jinnah, and that a mere facade of tame Congress Muslims does not help them.'

To complicate matters further, Tara Singh, the Sikh leader, had ominously declared on the last day of the conference that the Sikhs could accept Pakistan only if the Muslims agreed to a separate Sikh state.

CHAPTER 20

THE LABOUR PARTY TAKES OFFICE IN THE UNITED KINGDOM

Two important events, not long after the Simla Conference, further enlivened the political scene in India. On 26 July 1945 the results of the national election in the United Kingdom were announced. Labour under Attlee won a sweeping victory by winning 388 seats out of 640. Pethick-Lawrence[1] replaced Amery as Secretary of State for India. And on 14 August Japan, under the impact of the two atom bombs, surrendered earlier than had been expected.

Congress circles, counting on the traditional sympathy of the Labour Party with Indian aspirations for freedom, expected some quick new moves. The *Hindustan Times* hailed the defeat of the Conservatives as the 'downfall of India's oppressors' and the Congress President and his colleagues sent messages of congratulations to the Labour Prime Minister. For the Muslim League, however, the change of government in Britain created fresh worries.

Inside India the end of the war brought new problems. There were food and cloth shortages, a reduction of employment opportunities, the prospect of large-scale demobilisation, and rising Hindu-Muslim tension.

On 21 August it was announced in New Delhi that central and provincial elections would be held in the coming winter, and on 24 August Wavell, in response to a summons from the new government, left for London for consultations. There he found that, unlike the Churchill government whom he had to prod for action, the Attlee Cabinet were all for quick action irrespective of the problems that had to be faced. Wavell told the India and Burma Committee on 29 August that the scheme represented by the Cripps offer was no longer acceptable in India. If a constituent assembly as contemplated by that offer were set up, it would

---

[1] Created Baron on 16 August 1945.

be boycotted by one or other or possibly by both the major communities. The Muslims would boycott it unless the Pakistan issue was conceded, and to concede that would certainly lead to a boycott by the Hindus. He thought it most unlikely that Jinnah would now enter into discussions without a prior guarantee of acceptance in principle of Pakistan. His own judgement was that Jinnah spoke for 99 per cent of the Muslim population of India in their apprehension about Hindu domination. Before further progress could be made, the problem of Pakistan had to be faced, perhaps by a declaration by the British Government that an examination of the Pakistan issue was necessary. After his return to India, Wavell made the following authorised announcement on 19 September:

> It is the intention of His Majesty's Government to convene as soon as possible a Constitution-making Body, and as a preliminary step they have authorised me to undertake, immediately after the elections, discussions with representatives of the Legislative Assemblies in the Provinces, to ascertain whether the proposals contained in the 1942 Declaration are acceptable or whether some alternative or modified scheme is preferable. His Majesty's Government have further authorised me, as soon as the results of the Provincial elections are published, to take steps to bring into being an Executive Council which will have the support of the main Indian parties.

In a letter to the provincial Governors, the Viceroy explained that the proposals represented 'a compromise between the conviction that there can be no real settlement except by agreement, and the determination to solve the Indian problem whether the Indians like the solution or not'.

Commenting on Wavell's statement, Jinnah said that no attempt to solve the Indian problems would succeed except on the basis of the acceptance of Pakistan.

THE TRIAL OF THE INDIAN NATIONAL ARMY OFFICERS

The announcement in October that three officers of the Indian National Army, a Hindu, a Muslim, and a Sikh, would be tried by court-martial during the following month in the Mughal Red Fort in Delhi immediately raised a storm of protest. The All-India Congress Committee had already declared in the third week of September that 'it would be a tragedy' if the officers of the INA 'were punished for the offence of having laboured, however mistakenly, for the freedom of India'. Gandhi wrote to Sir Evan Jenkins (Private Secretary to the Viceroy) on 29 October, 'Can the government afford to ignore the almost, if not the wholly, unanimous opinion of the Indians of all shades of opinion? India adores these men who are on their trial'. As Nehru put it later: 'Behind the law there was something deeper and more vital, something that stirred the subconscious depths of the Indian mind. The trial dramatized the old contest: England versus India.' A strong defence committee was formed. It included Nehru, who had given up legal practice long ago but donned his barrister's gown for this special occasion, and the legal luminaries Tej Bahadur Sapru and Bhulabhai Desai. During the trial, which commenced on 5 November, Desai argued that the INA was the military force of a properly constituted government which the accused had joined as true patriots. Jinnah did not figure personally in the proceedings, but the Muslim League associated itself with the defence.

It soon became clear that the public trial of the three INA officers and the choice of the historic Red Fort as its stage had been a political blunder. In Bose's home town of Calcutta, a students' procession in favour of the INA developed into a serious riot which raged from 21 to 23 November. It resulted in substantial casualties and damage: 33 (including an American) killed; nearly 200 police, fire brigade and soldiers (70 British and 37 American) and about 200 civilians injured; 150 military or police vehicles and a large number of civilian cars destroyed or damaged.

On 26 November General Auchinleck[1], the Commander-in-Chief, wrote to Wavell that he felt that there was a growing feeling of sympathy for the INA among the 'Indian ranks' of the army, and on the following day the Governor of the North-West Frontier Province recommended that the Commander-in-Chief 'should at once announce that, as Indian opinion is opposed to the trial of these persons, he wipes the whole thing out and takes no further proceedings against anyone'. The Government of India decided that in future only those cases would be proceeded with in which there were allegations of brutality.

The trial of the three officers already in the dock concluded on 31 December. Each one of them was sentenced to transportation for life, cashiering and forfeiture of pay and allowances. The Commander-in-Chief confirmed the finding of the court but remitted the sentences of transportation for life while confirming the sentences of cashiering and forfeiture of pay and allowances.

Fifteen other officers and men of the INA were tried and sentenced

---

[1] Promoted to the rank of Field-Marshal with effect from 1 June 1946.

before Auchinleck decided, at the end of April 1946, to discontinue all further proceedings.

Azad has written that there was no longer anything secret about the upsurge for freedom. All sections of the services—civil and military—were moved by the same spirit. Men and officers of the defence forces declared openly that they had poured out their blood during the war on the assurance that India would be free. They demanded that this assurance must now be honoured. 'Wherever I went during this period', he relates, 'young men of the defence forces came out to welcome me and expressed their sympathy and admiration without any regard for the reaction of their European officers.'

The unrest among the Indian armed forces manifested itself in minor incidents in the army and the air force, and on 18 February 1946 the ratings of the Royal Indian Navy mutinied at Bombay, the principal naval base in the country. Officers were thrown out of the ships, British soldiers were attacked in the streets and the mutineers roamed the city in naval lorries. Congress and Muslim League flags were hoisted to give a political slant to the uprising. On 21 February there was fighting between the mutineers and the soldiers who tried to control them. On 22 February the mutineers, who had seized the majority of the ships in the harbour, trained their guns on the city and ignored the demand that they should surrender. More than 200 persons were killed during the disturbances.

The rioting and violence alarmed the Congress leadership. Azad thought that it was not the appropriate time for direct action: 'we must now watch the course of events and carry on negotiations with the British Government'. Nehru said, 'what has happened clearly demonstrates how anti-social elements in a vast city like Bombay exploit a situation. Our freedom is near at hand today. We have all the virtues for winning our freedom but I confess that we lack discipline, which is essential in a free country.'

Azad found Auchinleck 'friendly' and was able to obtain the assurances that there would be no victimization if the mutineers returned to duty unconditionally and that their grievances would be sympathetically considered. Through the personal efforts of Patel, who had the support of Jinnah and Nehru, the mutineers surrendered on 23 February 1946.

There had been, at the same time, minor outbreaks in Calcutta and Madras and a serious uprising at Karachi which was suppressed with considerable loss of life and casualties among the mutineers.

POLITICAL FERMENT IN INDIA

Both the principal political parties, Congress and the Muslim League, stood for independence, but their time-tables were different. The League wanted Pakistan to be promised before other issues were discussed. For the time being it was content to prepare for the forthcoming elections which would demonstrate that the Muslims of India were overwhelmingly for Pakistan. Congress reverted to the 'Quit India' mood, demanding power without unnecessary delay. The Viceroy believed that Congress was paving the way for a mass struggle.

In an interview with the Viceroy on 3 November 1945, Nehru said that Congress could make no terms with the Muslim League under the League's present leadership and policy. He practically admitted that he was preaching violence, but did not see how violence could be avoided if legitimate aims could not be attained otherwise. The impression left behind on Wavell's mind was that Nehru seemed to have 'reached the state of mind of a fanatic'. On 12 November, Reuters reported from New Delhi that Nehru had said at a public meeting, 'India must not wait for the next move of the Labour Government. She must depend on her own people and prepare herself for a mass battle for freedom, which may come sooner than people expect.'

Pant and Patel were equally threatening in their pronouncements. At a mass meeting on 21 October, Pant declared that the 'Quit India' resolution of 1942 was a signal for rebellion in the country and that that signal was still their lode-star. On 1 November Patel said that Congress 'was not going to sit quiet after the elections and wait on the convenience and pleasure of the British Government. Congress would demand an immediate and final solution of the Indian problem.'

During an interview with Gandhi on 10 December, Wavell impressed on him the harm which the violent speeches of the Congress leaders were doing. Gandhi admitted the danger of violence and indicated that he was trying to reduce the temperature. But things continued much as before. It seemed the ageing Mahatma was losing his grip on his intransigent followers.

THE PARLIAMENTARY DELEGATION

On 4 December it was announced in London that His Majesty's Government would send a Parliamentary Delegation to India. The move had resulted from Pethick-Lawrence's feeling that there was an unfortunate lack of first-hand knowledge of Indian conditions among the back-benchers in parliament. A ten-member all-party Parliamentary Delegation arrived in India on 5 January 1946 under the leadership of Professor Robert Richards, a member of the Labour Party, and stayed in the country for about a month. Wavell found that their knowledge of India was 'not very comprehensive' but they were 'keen and interested'. They toured India and met the various leaders. They were politely received but aroused little enthusiasm because they had brought no new political proposals and had no negotiating powers.

The delegates conveyed their individual impressions orally to Attlee on 13 February 1946. Mrs Nichol said that she had begun her visit to India impressed by the strong necessity of maintaining the unity of India but as time went on she began to feel that some form of Pakistan must be conceded. R.W. Sorensen regarded Pakistan as wholly irrational but, in his view, necessary. In his individual written report of 13 March to the Secretary of State for India, Sorensen said that all the members were agreed that the Indian situation was one of 'almost explosive urgency'.

WAVELL'S APPRECIATION OF THE POLITICAL SITUATION

On 27 December, Wavell sent an 'appreciation of the political situation' to the Secretary of State which contained the following 'general conclusions':

(a) That Congress commands the support of practically the whole of articulate Hindu opinion; and could undoubtedly bring about a very serious revolt against British rule;

(b) That we could still probably suppress such a revolt, after a considerable amount of bloodshed;

(c) That if we do have to suppress Congress we have nothing to put in its place, and should be driven to an almost entirely official rule, for which the necessary numbers of efficient officials do not exist.

In other words, we shall be placed in a quite untenable position, unless we find a solution, and we must do so by some means or other. Our chief problem is to find some bridge between Hindu and Muslim.

His view was that the British Government must take the initiative immediately, because after the Indian elections Congress would undoubtedly present its demands with the threat of a mass movement.

He also proposed a 'programme for political action' with the basic purpose of forming 'a new central Executive as early as possible'. If Congress and the Muslim League were unable to come to an agreement, the British Government should not permit another deadlock but must be ready to make its own award. His 'breakdown plan' would be based on two points of principle :

A. If the Muslims insist on self-determination in genuinely Muslim areas this must be conceded.

B. On the other hand there can be no question of compelling large non-Muslim population to remain in Pakistan against their will.

If these principles were followed, the effect would be 'that at least two divisions of the Punjab and almost the whole of western Bengal including Calcutta would have to be allowed to join the Union. The attractiveness of Pakistan to the Muslims would largely disappear. Only "the husk", in Jinnah's own words, would remain.' Wavell believed that, faced with the situation thus created, 'there would be at least a chance' that Jinnah would forgo Pakistan and 'set to work to secure the best possible terms for the Muslims inside the Union of India'.

Since in the end it was only a reduced Pakistan that Jinnah was able to secure, it seems that it would have been wise on the part of all concerned to have taken Wavell's plan of partition seriously. The amount of resulting bloodshed and chaos at this stage would have been less than that accompanying the same arrangement in 1947, by which time the law and order situation had deteriorated beyond control.

In his interviews with Casey[1] and Wavell, Gandhi shrewdly summed up the dilemma facing the British Government with regard to Pakistan. It must make up its mind between those who had always opposed it (Congress) but who now wanted the right thing, a united India, and those who had helped it (the Muslims) but now wanted the wrong thing, a divided India. Nehru on the other hand had begun to think on the same lines as Wavell. In a letter to Stafford Cripps on 27 January 1946 he seemed to accept that partition might have to be conceded, provided certain conditions were satisfied: 'Even if the Muslims as a whole support the League and Pakistan, that can only mean a division of both Punjab and Bengal. Jinnah has indignantly rejected this. What then? Compulsion of other areas to join

---

[1] Richard Gardiner Casey, Governor of Bengal January 1944-February 1946.

Pakistan? That is inconceivable and impossible. Thus the crux of the Pakistan issue is this : A Pakistan consisting of only part of Punjab and part of Bengal, or no separation at all.'[1]

THE CABINET MISSION'S NEGOTIATIONS WITH THE INDIAN LEADERS

The British Government side-stepped Wavell's programme of action, and on 22 January 1946 Pethick-Lawrence telegraphed the Viceroy that it had been decided to send a Mission of three Ministers to conduct negotiations with Indian leaders 'in association with yourself'. Wavell's first reaction was not happy. He feared that in the end he may be 'left with all the loose and awkward ends to tie up'. He also felt concerned as to his own status in the negotiations, but was assured by the Secretary of State that the negotiations would be undertaken by the visiting Ministers and the Viceroy acting together 'as a team'.[2] On 19 February, Pethick-Lawrence announced in the House of Lords that it had been decided to send out to India a special mission of Cabinet Ministers consisting of the Secretary of State for India (Pethick-Lawrence), the President of the Board of Trade (Stafford Cripps) and the First Lord of the Admiralty (A.V. Alexander).

Speaking at Jhansi on 2 March, Nehru threatened that, 'if the British Cabinet Mission fails to solve the pressing problems which clamour for solution, a political earthquake of devastating intensity will sweep the entire country. The truth is the people are tired of foreign domination and want to end it immediately.'

Jinnah said he hoped to make the Cabinet Mission realize the true situation and satisfy them that the division of India into Pakistan and Hindustan was the only solution for India's constitutional problem. Prime Minister Attlee's statement in the House of Commons on 15 March, that while the British Government was mindful of the rights of the minorities, it could not allow a minority to place their veto on the advance of the majority, caused Jinnah to reiterate that the Muslims of India were not a minority but a nation and that self-determination was their birthright.

---

[1] This is an important letter because it shows that Nehru was willing to concede Pakistan as early as in January 1946 provided the Muslim League accepted the partition of the Punjab and Bengal. For text of the letter, *see, The Transfer of Power*, Volume VI, p. 851.

[2] During the Cripps Mission, Linlithgow had not been invited to partake in the negotiations with the Indian leaders.

The Mission reached Karachi on 23 March and arrived in New Delhi on the following day. Wavell's entry in his journal for 24 March reads: 'The three Magi have arrived. They are pleasant and friendly but I am still doubtful whether they have got any definite plan in their heads.' In fact their brief from the British Cabinet was:

> to secure agreement amongst the Indian leaders as to the method of arriving at the new constitutional structure for India and the setting up of an interim executive. You should discuss and explore all possible alternatives without proceeding upon any fixed or rigid pre-conceived plan. You have liberty to say that His Majesty's Government will be prepared to recommend to Parliament any constitutional arrangement for the granting of independence and self-government to India, provided that it incorporates the following cardinal points:
>
> (a) Some form of protection must be included either by constitutional or treaty provision for the protection of religious and racial minorities.
>
> (b) Satisfactory provision must be made for the defence of India and the India Ocean area.
>
> (c) [The Crown's] paramountcy [over the Indian Princely States] must not be handed over to an Indian Government.
>
> (d) A satisfactory means must be devised for winding up the financial position of India and Great Britain arising out of the present regime...
>
> Negotiations for a treaty of friendship will follow upon the institution of the new constitutional structure.

In his speech in the House of Commons on 15 March 1946, Prime Minister Attlee had said, 'My colleagues are going to India with the intention of using their utmost endeavours to help her to attain her freedom as speedily and fully as possible. What form of Government is to replace the present regime is for India to decide; but our desire is to help her to set up forthwith the machinery for making that decision.' In answer to a question from a pressman at Karachi on 23 March, Cripps said that the purposes of the delegation's 'present mission could be fulfilled without legislation. These purposes are to get machinery set up for framing the constitutional structure in which Indians will have full control of their own destiny and the formation of a new interim government.'

In Pethick-Lawrence's words, 'Cripps was, of course, well acquainted with Gandhi and other leaders. My friendship with Gandhi was of long standing. Some thirty years previously he had lunched with my wife and myself in my flat in London... In the cold weather of 1926-27 my wife and I had met him again in India, when we attended the annual meeting of Congress in Gauhati. In 1931 I had sat with him on the Round Table Conference ... Since then we had had some personal correspondence, and he had had my good wishes on his birthday, which happened to be the same day of the year as my wedding day...Alexander...had not hitherto had any direct contact with Indian problems or personalities, but was no doubt selected by the Prime Minister as a man of sound broad judgement in touch with British public opinion generally.'

Among the Indian officials who assisted the delegation were two competent Hindus—Sir Bengal Rau, on special duty in the Governor-General's Secretariat (Reforms), and V. P. Menon, Reforms Commissioner (constitutional adviser to the Viceroy). The bias of the team was thus heavily in favour of the Congress Party. Wavell tried to keep the balance even between Congress and the Muslim League and was often backed up by Alexander.

Cripps possessed the sharpest brain in the delegation and acted as the chief draftsman. That he and Pethick-Lawrence maintained continuous private contacts with Congress leaders was a source of much annoyance to the orderly mind of Field Marshal Wavell.

The results of the elections to the Central Legislative Assembly had been declared towards the end of December 1945 and the outcome of the elections to the Provincial legislatures became known in the early part of 1946. The Muslim League had fought these elections on the issue of Pakistan versus United India, and its claim had been amply vindicated.

In the Central Assembly the Muslim League won every Muslim seat; the nationalist (Congress) Muslims forfeited their deposits in many cases. Congress achieved overwhelming success in the general constituencies; the Hindu Mahasabha and other candidates in most cases had withdrawn their candidature to avoid the ignominy of defeat. The Muslim League polled 86.6 per cent of the votes cast in Muslim constituencies. In a total of 102 seats the breakdown was: Congress 36, Muslim League 25, Independents 21, Nationalist Party 10 and Europeans 8.

The results of the provincial elections further emphasized that Congress and the Muslim League were the two main parties in the country. Congress won an absolute majority in eight provinces and formed ministries there.

Of the five provinces which the Muslim League wished to include in Pakistan, the key provinces were the Punjab and Bengal. Out of the total of eighty-six Muslim seats in the Punjab, the Muslim League captured seventy-five. Congress won fifty-one seats, the Akali Sikhs twenty-two, the Unionists twenty, and the Independents seven. After political manoeuvring the position became: Muslim League seventy-nine, Congress fifty-one, Akali Sikhs twenty-two, Unionists ten and Independents ten. The League was the largest single party but did not enjoy an overall majority. Premier Khizar Hayat's Unionist Party, which was anti-Muslim League, had fared miserably in the elections but Khizar was able to continue as Premier in the new ministry because Congress and the Akalis joined hands with him.

The Bengal Assembly consisted of 250 members. The Muslim League took 113 (out of a total of 119 Muslim seats). Congress captured eighty-seven. A League ministry under H. S. Suhrawardy was formed.

In Sind, the League won twenty-seven seats; one independent Muslim joined the party later. Nationalist Muslims secured three seats, the Syed group four and Congress twenty-one. A League ministry under G. H. Hidayatullah was installed by the Governor. In Assam Congress had a clear majority and formed a ministry under Gopinath Bardoloi which included one Nationalist Muslim.

The League fared badly in the North-West Frontier Province, where it captured seventeen seats as compared to thirty (including nineteen Muslim seats) won by Congress. Other Muslims secured two seats and Akali Sikhs one. Congress formed a ministry under Khan Sahib.

Not long after the complete election results became known, Jinnah called the All-India Muslim League Legislators' Convention at Delhi (7-9 April), which was attended by nearly 500 members of the Provincial and Central Legislatures who had recently been elected on the Muslim League ticket. It was the first gathering of its kind in the history of Indian politics and was called by some 'the Muslim Constituent Assembly'. In his presidential address, Jinnah said that the Convention would lay down 'once and for all in unequivocal terms what we stand for'. He said that Congress desired that the British Government should first grant independence and then hand over the government to Congress by setting up a national government of Congress' conception. When Congress was saddled in power it would proceed to form a constitution-making body with sovereign authority to decide the fate of the 400 million inhabitants of the subcontinent. The League must not accept a single constitution-making body which would only register the decree of Congress, because the Muslims would be in a hopeless minority in it. If any interim constitution was forced on the Muslims they must resist it in every possible way.

A resolution passed unanimously by the Convention (the 'Delhi Resolution') stated that no formula devised by the British Government for transferring power to the peoples of India would be acceptable to the Muslim nation unless it conformed to the following principles:

That the zones comprising Bengal and Assam in the North-East and the Punjab, North-West Frontier Province, Sind and Baluchistan in the North-West of India, namely Pakistan zones where the Muslims are in a dominant majority, be constituted into a sovereign independent State and that an unequivocal undertaking be given to implement the establishment of Pakistan without delay;

That two separate constitution-making bodies be set up by the people of Pakistan and Hindustan for the purpose of framing their respective constitutions;

That the acceptance of the Muslim League demand of Pakistan and its implementation without delay are the *sine qua non* for Muslim League co-operation and participation in the formation of an Interim Government at the Centre;

That any attempt to impose a constitution on a united-India basis or to force any interim arrangement at the Centre contrary to the Muslim League demand will leave the Muslims no alternative but to resist such imposition by all possible means for their survival and national existence.

The Cabinet Mission's task, of getting the Indian politicians to agree to political arrangements within the scope of the Mission's brief, was easier stated than achieved. They laboured for more than three months, the last two of which in Delhi were unbearably hot. The only relief the visitors could manage was a short holiday in Kashmir and some working days at Simla. They made plans to leave Delhi on 20 May, 31 May, 10 June and 19/20 June but could not actually leave till 29 June 1946.

In the course of an account of the Mission's endeavours which he sent to the King on 8 July, Wavell observed, 'It is not really questionable which is the more trying to the temper and patience, the climate of Delhi in the hot weather, or the quibblings, hagglings, tergiversations, and small-mindedness of political leaders, specially of Congress—the latter have it by a distance; but to have suffered the combination of the two over a long period without loss of courtesy or hope was a fine tribute to the Mission.'

The Mission began by bringing themselves 'up to date with the situation' and conferring with the Viceroy, the Governors of the provinces, and the Executive Council. They started interviewing the leaders representing different interests on 1 April. It will suffice for our purpose to describe the more important of these meetings.

Azad, the Congress President, conferred with the Mission on 3 April and stated that the picture that his party had of the future of India was that of a Federal Government with fully autonomous provinces with residuary powers vested in the units. The compulsory federal subjects might be Defence, Communications, Foreign Affairs and such others as might be absolutely necessary for the administration of the country as a whole.

Gandhi saw the Mission on 3 April and said, 'Pakistan is a sin'. A stage would arrive when the British Government must declare that there must be only one constitution-making body. In the interim period let Jinnah form the first government and 'choose its personnel from elected representatives in the country'.

When Jinnah appeared before the Mission on 4 April he explained at some length why he thought it better for the future of India that there should be a Pakistan. The core of his argument was that 'India is really many and is held by the British as one'. He agreed that common railways, customs and so forth were convenient. As soon as the fundamentals of Pakistan were agreed to, these things could be settled. He certainly contemplated treaties and agreements governing such matters. As regards defence, he thought some arrangement should be made but this could only be on the basis of two sovereign states with treaty relations. With respect to the boundaries of Pakistan, Jinnah said he was quite willing to consider adjustments. He did not wish to keep Hindus in Pakistan against their will and they could migrate, but he could not reduce the area of Pakistan below the point on which the state could live. He said, specifically, that 'Pakistan without Calcutta would be like asking a man to live without his heart.'

All the four Sikh representatives, whom the Mission received on 5 April, asked for a Sikh state if India were partitioned. Gyani Kartar Singh said the Sikh state should include the whole of the Lahore and Jullundur divisions as well as the districts of Hissar, Karnal, Ambala, Simla, Montgomery and Lyallpur. Sardar Baldev Singh said that Khalistan (the Sikh state) would be the Punjab excluding only the Multan and Rawalpindi divisions with an approximate boundary along the Chenab river.

On 11 April, the Mission issued a statement saying that since their arrival they had heard the opinions of the most important political elements in India and now proposed to enter the next phase of their negotiations, which was to arrive at a solution acceptable to all sides.

In a statement made on 15 April, Azad outlined the Congress position, following four days' discussion by the working committee, as: (i) complete independence; (ii) a united India; (iii) a single Federation composed of fully autonomous units which would have residuary powers in their hands; (iv) two lists of central subjects, one compulsory, the other optional. Maulana Azad felt that the Congress formula ought to meet all legitimate Muslim fears while avoiding the inherent defects of the Pakistan demand.

During an interview between the Mission and Jinnah on 16 April, the Secretary of State told the Muslim League President that the delegation had concluded that the full and complete demand for Pakistan had little chance of acceptance but that progress might be made in one of two ways. First, agreement might be reached on a separate state of Pakistan consisting of Sind, North-West Frontier Province, Baluchistan, the Muslim-majority districts of the Punjab except perhaps Gurdaspur, Eastern Bengal, and the Sylhet district of Assam.

The inclusion of Calcutta in Pakistan could not be justified on any principle of self-determination. Pakistan on this basis would need to contract a defensive alliance with Hindustan and enter into special treaty relations with it.

The alternative suggestion was that Congress and the Muslim League should together evolve an agreed scheme for an Indian Union. If the League accepted the principle of central control for the essential subjects, say Defence, Foreign Affairs and Communications, it might then be possible to include in one Federation the whole provinces of Sind, Baluchistan, North-West Frontier Province, the Punjab and Bengal, plus perhaps the Sylhet district of Assam. In such a Union the two parts might have equal representation.

Jinnah said he did not think that the domination of the Muslims by the Hindus could be prevented in any scheme in which they were kept together. He went on to say that once the principle of Pakistan was conceded, the question of the territory of Pakistan could be discussed, but he could not in any event accept the exclusion of Calcutta. He claimed six provinces, and if Congress considered that was too much, they should say what they considered he ought to have. He was not prepared to say what he was willing to give up.

The delegation informed Attlee on 18 April that there was no prospect of settling the Pakistan issue by agreement and that they themselves would have to propound a basis for settlement. They were working on it and would finalize it after their return from Kashmir (the delegation took an Easter break in Kashmir from 19 to 24 April).

On 27 April they wrote identical letters to Azad and Jinnah inviting each of them to nominate four negotiators with a view to discussing with the Mission the possibility of agreement upon a scheme based upon the following fundamental principles:

The future constitutional structure of British India to be as follows:-

A Union Government dealing with the following subjects:- Foreign Affairs, Defence and Communications. There will be two groups of Provinces, the one of the predominantly Hindu Provinces and the other of the predominantly Muslim Provinces, dealing with all other subjects which the Provinces in the respective groups desire to be dealt with in common. The Provincial Governments will deal with all other subjects and will have all the residuary sovereign rights.

It is contemplated that the Indian States will take their appropriate place in this structure on terms to be negotiated with them.

Azad nominated, besides himself, Nehru, Patel and Abdul Ghaffar Khan. Jinnah chose, besides himself, Nawab Muhammad Ismail Khan, Liaquat Ali Khan and Abdur Rab Nishtar. The Mission went up to Simla on 1 May and the tripartite conference ('the Second Simla Conference') held seven sessions there from 5 to 12 May. Gandhi did not attend the Conference but went to Simla and was in touch daily with the Congress leaders and also had some private discussions with the members of the Mission. At the opening meeting, Jinnah refused to shake hands with Azad, to the latter's obvious annoyance, but, as Wavell noted in his journal, 'Congress have been very provocative in bringing up here two Muslims out of four, when they are almost entirely a Hindu organization.'

After the Conference had been in session for only two days, the Mission began to despair of agreement and telegraphed Attlee that the parleys might end on 11 or 12 May or even sooner, and that they were aiming at issuing their own statement, suggesting the future line of action, on 16 May.

Outside the full Conference, Jinnah and Nehru also met to consider Nehru's proposal that Congress and League differences be submitted to an umpire whose decision would be final, but they reached no agreement. Jinnah said the first question which would arise was the question of the partition of India. The Muslim League regarded this as settled by the verdict of the Muslims in the election. It was inconceivable that a matter of this sort should ever be the subject of arbitration. There would be no means of enforcing the arbitrator's decisions, and difficulties would arise over the selection of a single person to arbitrate.

The opposing parties summarized their differences in their respective communications of 12 May to the Mission.[1] The Muslim League enunciated ten 'principles' as their 'minimum demands by way of an offer'. The more important of these were (the numbers given here are as in the original):

1. The six Muslim Provinces (Punjab, NWFP, Baluchistan, Sind, Bengal and Assam) shall be grouped together as one group and will deal with all other subjects and matters except Foreign Affairs, Defence and Communications necessary for Defence,[2] which may be dealt with by the Constitution-making bodies of the two groups of Provinces—Muslim Provinces (hereinafter named Pakistan Group) and Hindu Provinces—sitting together.

2. There shall be a separate Constitution-making body for the six Muslim Provinces named above, which will frame Constitutions for the Group, and the Provinces in the Group will determine the list of subjects that shall be Provincial and Central (of the Pakistan Federation) with residuary sovereign powers vesting in the Provinces.

4. After the Constitutions of the Pakistan Federal Government and the Provinces are finally framed by the Constitution-making body, it will be open to any Province of the Group to decide to opt out of its Group.

6. There should be parity of representation between the two Groups of Provinces in the Union Executive and the Legislature, if any.

7. No major points in the Union Constitution which affect the communal issue shall be deemed to be passed in the joint Constitution-making body, unless the majority of the members of the Constitution-making body of the Hindu Provinces and the majority of the members of the Constitution-making body of the Pakistan Group, present and voting, are separately in its favour.

8. No decision, legislative, executive or administrative, shall be taken by the Union in regard to any matter of controversial nature, except by a majority of three-fourths.

---

[1] These submissions by the Muslim League and Congress are important and interesting because they express the standpoints which the Mission tried to reconcile in its own Statement of 16 May 1946.

[2] This of course meant that the Muslim League at this stage was willing to forgo the demand for a fully independent Pakistan and accept a federal relationship between Pakistan and India.

10. The Constitution of the Union shall contain a provision whereby any Province can, by a majority vote of its Legislative Assembly, call for reconsideration of the terms of the Constitution, and will have the liberty to secede from the Union at any time after an initial period of ten years.

The chief 'points suggested on behalf of Congress as a basis of agreement' were (numbers as in the original) :

2. The Constituent Assembly shall draw up a constitution for the Federal Union. This shall consist of an All- India Federal Government and Legislature dealing with Foreign Affairs, Defence, Communications, Fundamental Rights, Currency, Customs and Planning, as well as such other subjects as, on closer scrutiny, may be found to be intimately allied to them.

3. All the remaining powers shall vest in the Provinces or Units.

4. Groups of Provinces may be formed and such groups may determine the Provincial subjects which they desire to take in common.

5. After the Constituent Assembly has decided the constitution for the All-India Federal Union as laid down in paragraph 2 above, the representatives of the Provinces may form groups to decide the Provincial constitution for their group and, if they wish, a group constitution.

6. No major point in the All-India Federal Constitution which affects the communal issue shall be deemed to be passed by the Constituent Assembly unless a majority of the members of the community or communities concerned present in Assembly and voting are separately in its favour...

Congress also sent a note to the Mission containing its comments seriatim on the 'principles' formulated by the League. The more significant ones related to numbers 1, 4, 6, 7, and 10 :

1. The proper procedure is for one constitution-making body or Constituent Assembly to meet for the whole of India and later for groups to be formed if so desired by the Provinces concerned...

4. There is no necessity for opting out of a Province from its group as the previous consent of the Provinces is necessary for joining the group.

5. We consider it essential that the Federal Union should have a Legislature. We also consider it essential that the Union should have power to raise its own revenue.

6 and 7. We are entirely opposed to parity of representation as between groups of Provinces in the Union executive or legislature....

10. The constitution of the Union will inevitably contain provisions for its revision. It may also contain a provision for its full reconsideration at the end of ten years. The matter will be open then for a complete reconsideration. Though it is implied, we would avoid reference to secession as we do not wish to encourage this idea.

Following the final session of the Conference on 12 May the Mission issued two communiques. The first read: 'After considering the views put forward by the two parties, the Conference has come to the conclusion that no use would be served by further discussions, and that therefore the Conference should be brought to a conclusion'. The second stated that it was the intention of the Mission to issue a statement expressing their views as to the next steps to be taken.

While the Conference was dealing with the long-term issue of constitution-making, the Viceroy had opened discussions also on the more immediate question of setting up an interim government. On 5 May the delegation informed Attlee that Wavell hoped soon to form 'an Executive Council in which all the portfolios, including that of War Minister, will be held by Indian leaders'. In an interview on 13 May, Jinnah told Wavell that whether or not the Muslim League came into the interim government would depend on whether the statement which the Mission intended to issue seemed likely to offer a solution to the long-term issue. His fear was that Congress planned to get control of the central government, shelve the fundamental long-term issue and concentrate on getting control in the provinces.

THE CABINET MISSION'S PROPOSALS OF 16 MAY 1946

The Mission returned to Delhi from Simla on 14 May and on 16 May issued their statement. The statement explained that, despite the joint efforts of the Mission and the Indian political parties, it had not been found possible for the Indian people themselves to agree upon the method of framing the new constitution under which they would live. The Mission were therefore putting forward 'proposals', which they believed would enable the Indians to attain independence 'in the shortest time and with the least danger of internal disturbance and conflict'.

Being 'greatly impressed by the very genuine and acute anxiety of the Muslims lest they should find themselves subjected to a perpetual Hindu-majority rule', the Mission in the first instance had examined the question of a sovereign state of Pakistan consisting of the six provinces claimed by the Muslim League, and had rejected it mainly on the ground that it would not solve the communal minority problem, because the size of the non-Muslim minorities in such a Pakistan would be 'very considerable': 37.93 per cent in the North-Western Area and 48.31 per cent in the North-Eastern Area. Also, there would be Muslim minorities numbering some 20 million in the remainder of British India, dispersed among a total population of 188 million. Every argument that could be used in favour of Pakistan could also be used in favour of the exclusion of the non-Muslim areas from Pakistan.

The statement also rejected the idea of a smaller Pakistan confined to the Muslim-majority areas, because such a Pakistan was regarded by the Muslim League as quite impracticable. The Mission themselves also felt convinced that any solution which involved a partition of Bengal and the Punjab would be contrary to the wishes and interests of a very large portion of the inhabitants of these provinces, each of which had its own common language and a long history and tradition. Moreover, a division of the Punjab would leave substantial bodies of Sikhs on both sides of the boundary.

The Mission then indicated the nature of a solution which in their view 'would be just to the essential claims of all parties, and would at the same time be more likely to bring about a stable and practical form of constitution for All-India'. The outline sketched by them envisaged three tiers.

At the top would be the Union of India, comprising both British India and the princely States. The bottom tier would comprise provinces and states. The provinces would be free to unite together in groups, and such groups, if formed, would constitute the middle tier.

To bring the contemplated constitution into being, a Constituent Assembly would be set up. Its numbers would be elected by the members of the provincial legislatures, each province contributing numbers proportionate to its population. The voting would be by communities, Muslims, Sikhs and 'general'—'general' would include everyone who was not either Muslim or Sikh. For each one million of the population there would be one representative. The States would contribute members to the constitution-making body proportionate to their total population.

After a preliminary meeting of the Constituent Assembly, the provincial representatives would divide themselves into three sections: Section A would consist of Madras, Bombay, United Provinces, Bihar, Central Provinces and Orissa; B of the Punjab, North-West Frontier Province and Sind; and C of Bengal and Assam (sections B and C would have had Muslim majorities). Each section would frame the constitutions of the provinces belonging to it and would also decide whether a group should be formed and with what subjects it should deal. Lastly, the Constituent Assembly would reassemble to decide the constitution of the Union. The Mission recommended that this constitution for All-India should take the following basic form:

1. There should be a Union of India, embracing both British India and the States, which should deal with the following subjects: Foreign Affairs, Defence, and Communications; and should have the powers necessary to raise the finances required for the above subjects.

2. The Union should have an Executive and a Legislature constituted from British Indian and States' representatives. Any question raising a major communal issue in the Legislature should require for its decision a majority of the representatives present and voting of each of the two major communities as well as a majority of all the members present and voting.

3. All subjects other than the Union subjects and all residuary powers should vest in the Provinces.

4. The States will retain all subjects and powers other than those ceded to the Union.

5. Provinces should be free to form groups with Executives and Legislatures, and each group could determine the provincial subjects to be taken in common.

6. The Constitution of the Union and of the groups should contain a provision whereby any Province could by a majority vote of its Legislative Assembly call for a reconsideration of the terms of the Constitution after an initial period of ten years and at ten-yearly intervals thereafter.

The statement also made further recommendations to allay the fears of the Muslims and other minorities: (1) Resolutions altering the basic form of the constitution as recommended by the Mission or involving a major communal issue should not be passed by the constitution-making body unless accepted by each of the major communities. (2) After the inauguration of the constitution, it should be open to any province to elect to come out of the group in which it had been placed. Such a decision should be taken by the new legislature of the province after the first general election under the new constitution. (3) An Advisory Committee would be set up at the preliminary meeting of the Constituent Assembly to report on the rights of citizens, minorities and tribal and excluded areas.

The statement declared that it would be necessary to negotiate a treaty between the Union Constituent Assembly and the United Kingdom to provide for certain matters arising out of the transfer of power.

Finally, the statement emphasised that, while the constitution-making proceeded, it was of the 'greatest importance' to set up 'at once' an interim government in which all the portfolios, including that of War Member, would be held by Indian leaders having the confidence of the people.

At a press conference on the same day, Cripps made it clear that a departure from the basic form of the constitution as recommended in the statement could only be made if a majority of both communities agreed to it. With regard to the princely States, the Mission had already spelled out the position in a Memorandum addressed to the Chancellor of the Chamber of Princes on 12 May 1946. Its last paragraph ran:

When a new fully self-governing or independent Government or Governments come into being in British India, His Majesty's Government's influence with these Governments will not be such as to enable them to carry out the obligations of paramountcy. Moreover, they cannot contemplate that British troops would be retained in India for this purpose. Thus, as a logical sequence and in view of the desires expressed to them on behalf of the Indian States, His Majesty's Government will cease to exercise the powers of paramountcy. This means that the rights of the States which flow from their relationship to the Crown will no longer exist and that all the rights surrendered by the States to the Paramount Power will return to the States. Political arrangements between the States on the one side and the British Crown and British India on the other will thus be brought to an end. The void will have to be filled either by successor Government or Governments in British India, or failing this, entering into particular political arrangements with it or them.

The Memorandum asserted that 'the British Government could not and would not in any circumstances transfer paramountcy to an Indian Government', and the Secretary of State explained to Azad that when paramountcy ceased to exist, the States would achieve a position of independence at the same time as British India. But the Memorandum did not fail to point out that the letter of the law was one thing and the demands of practical politics were something else. 'In the meanwhile', it stated, 'the Indian States are in a position to play an important part in the formulation of the new constitutional structure for India, and His Majesty's Government have been informed by the Indian States that they desire, in their own interests and in the interests of India as a whole, both to make their contribution to the framing of the structure, and to take their due place in it when it is completed.'

Throughout their Statement of 16 May, the Mission had used the expressions 'we propose' or 'we recommend', which meant that their scheme was not immutable. Gandhi and other Congress leaders took full advantage of this and adopted positions which suited their own purposes and practically rejected the Mission's scheme. And who was responsible for creating this useful opening? The answer is provided by Pethick-Lawrence himself:

> Gandhi had foreseen that some document would ultimately be issued, and had expressed his urgent hope that it would not be couched in the language of an award, but would take the form of a proposal to Indian parties. This was, in fact, in accordance with the realities of the situation, for it was impossible for the British Government, in the process of withdrawing its authority completely from India, to enfore conditions as to how subsequent authority there should be exercised. The statement, therefore, met Gandhi's wishes in this respect.

Azad and Nehru were interviewed by Wavell and Alexander in the afternoon of 17 May. It turned out that Nehru was thinking about immediate independence; 'in fact,' noted Wavell in his journal, 'he disclosed almost nakedly the real Congress objective—immediate control of the Centre, so that they can deal with Muslims and Princes and then make at leisure a Constitution to suit themselves'.

Gandhi lost no time in publicly interpreting the implications of the Mission's statement in his own way. Speaking after his prayer meeting on 17 May, he said the document was not an award but a recommendation. It was, therefore, open to the Constituent Assembly to vary the recommendation or improve upon it. There was no 'take it or leave it'. If there were restrictions, the Constituent Assembly would not be a sovereign body free to frame a constitution of independence for India. Similarly, the provinces were free to reject the very idea of grouping. In a letter to the Secretary of State dated 20 May, he asserted that there could be 'no question of parity, whether the Government is allowed to be formed by Congress or the Muslim League'. On the same day he sent to Cripps the draft of an article which he had prepared for the next issue of the *Harijan*. He started by calling the Mission's statement 'the best document the British Government could have produced'. He had come to the conclusion that 'there is nothing in it binding in law...What is binding is that part of it which commits the British Government.'

The perturbed delegation immediately telegraphed Attlee that Congress proposed to attack the grouping proposal and also objected to parity in the interim government, both of which points might be crucial in securing Muslim co-operation. If the delegation did not give way to these demands the authorities might be faced before long with direct action by Congress.

Jinnah gave his initial reaction to the Mission's proposals in a statement issued on 22 May. He expressed his regret that the demand for a sovereign state of Pakistan, which was the only solution to the communal problem of India, should have been denied by the Mission on the basis of 'commonplace and exploded arguments', and that the League's proposal for separate constitution-making bodies for Pakistan and Hindustan should have been turned down. He warned that Muslim India would resist any attempt to impose a federal constitution on a united-India basis, or to force any interim arrangement at the centre contrary to the League's wishes. He concluded by stating that the final decision would be made by the Working Committee and the Council of the Muslim League.

After the Congress Working Committee had met on 24 May, Azad forwarded a copy of its resolution to the Secretary of State. Its main points were the following: that independent India 'must necessarily have a strong central authority capable of representing the Nation with power and dignity in the councils of the world'; that the Governor-General might continue as the head of the government during the interim period but the government should function as a cabinet responsible to the central legislature; that the continued presence of a foreign army of occupation was a negation of independence; that Congress read the statement to mean that the respective provinces would make their choice whether or not to belong to the section in which they were placed; that in laying down the procedure for the election of the Constituent Assembly, the basis of representation in the ratio of one to a million had been overlooked in the case of European members of Assemblies in Assam and Bengal[1]; that the manner of appointing States' representatives for the Constituent Assembly must approximate the method adopted in the provinces; and that the Constituent Assembly must be considered as a sovereign body with final authority for the purpose of drawing up a constitution and giving effect to it. The resolution

---

[1] Congress objected to the presence of Europeans in the Constituent Assembly because they were foreigners and non-nationals and enjoyed such 'fantastic weightage' that with a population of only 21,000 in Bengal and Assam they would have returned seven members. Congress feared that the Europeans would side with the Muslims in important matters and further tilt the balance in their favour in Section C.

ended with the intimation that 'in the absence of a full picture' Congress was unable to give a final opinion at that stage.

The Cabinet Delegation responded to Jinnah's statement of 22 May as well as to the Congress Working Committee's resolution of 24 May in a press statement released on 25 May. They explained that their recommendations were the nearest approach to reconciling the views of the two main parties and that the scheme stood 'as a whole'; that there was no intention of interfering with the discretion of the Constituent Assembly once it was formed and started its work on the basis of the delegation's plan; that when the Constituent Assembly had completed its labours, His Majesty's Government would recommend to Parliament such action as might be necessary for the cession of sovereignty to the Indian people subject only to two matters which were mentioned in the Statement, namely adequate provision for the protection of the minorities and willingness to conclude a treaty with His Majesty's Government to cover matters arising out of the transfer of power; that the Congress view, that provinces could in the first instance make the choice whether or not to belong to the section in which they were placed, did not accord with the Delegation's intention because the grouping of provinces was an essential feature of the scheme; that the question of how the States' representative should be appointed to the Constituent Assembly was one which must be discussed with the States; that the existing constitution must continue during the interim period and the interim government could not therefore be made responsible to the central legislature; that during the interim period the British Parliament had the ultimate responsibility for the security of India and it was necessary that British troops should remain; and that it was for the Europeans to decide whether they wished to exercise the right given to them to seek election to the Constituent Assembly.

Azad next (25 May) asked Wavell for a formal assurance that the interim government would in practice function like a Dominion Cabinet.[1] He expressed confidence that the other questions would present no difficulty. Wavell replied on 30 May that 'the spirit in which the Government is worked will be of much greater importance than any formal document and guarantees. I have no doubt that, if you are prepared to trust me, we shall be able to co-operate in a manner which will give India a sense of freedom from external control and will prepare for complete freedom as soon as the new Constitution is made.' This assurance was accepted by

---

[1] The Muslim League made no attempt to reduce the veto power of the Governor-General because it believed that this provision protected it against Congress arbitrariness.

Congress because of 'the friendly tone' of the Viceroy's letter and the desire of Congress 'to find some way out'.

When Jinnah saw Wavell on 3 June, he told the Viceroy that the absence of parity at the centre was a very difficult point for the Muslim League to accept. Jinnah also asked what would happen if Congress rejected the proposals and the Muslim League accepted them. Wavell said that, 'speaking personally', he thought that if the Muslim League accepted the proposals they would not lose by it and that His Majesty's Government would go on with constitution-making on the lines they had proposed. Jinnah then enquired whether the Muslim League would in these circumstances be invited to join the interim government and be given their due proportion of the portfolios. The Viceroy said that he thought that he could guarantee that the Muslim League would have a share in it. Jinnah requested this assurance in writing as it would help him with his Working Committee.

After consulting the members of the delegation, Wavell sent for Jinnah in the afternoon and told him that he could give him, on behalf of the delegation, his personal assurance that they would go ahead with the plan laid down in their statement so far as circumstances permitted if either party accepted. On the following day, Wavell confirmed the assurance in a letter to Jinnah.

At its meeting on 6 June, the Working Committee of the Muslim League passed a resolution stating its views on the statement of the Cabinet Mission. The resolution criticised the statement for rejecting the demand for Pakistan and reiterated that 'the attainment of the goal of a complete sovereign Pakistan still remains the unalterable objective of the Muslims in India, for the achievement of which they will, if necessary, employ every means in their power, and consider no sacrifice or suffering too great'. The Muslim League expressed its willingness to co-operate with the proposed constitution-making body because 'the basis and the foundation of Pakistan are inherent in the Mission's plan by virtue of the compulsory grouping of the six Muslim provinces in Sections B and C.' With regard to the proposed interim government, the Council authorized the President to negotiate with the Viceroy and take such decisions as he deemed proper.

Jinnah told the Viceroy on 7 June that the Muslim League would not join the interim government except on the ratio of five Congress, five League and two others. As regards portfolios, the League was interested in Defence, External Affairs, and Planning and Development, with the last of which Commerce would go. The only portfolio he would consider taking personally was Defence. (This was the first and only time that Jinnah expressed an interest in holding any office during British rule.) On the next day Jinnah returned to the subject of Congress-League parity by letter because a very sinister agitation had been set afoot by the Congress Press against 'your formula' of twelve portfolios—five League, five Congress, one Sikh and one Christian or Anglo-Indian. He said that, but for the Viceroy's assurance of parity, the Muslim League would not have approved the Mission's scheme. Any departure from the formula would not secure the co-operation of the League. Wavell wrote back that he had not given any assurance on the 5: 5: 2 ratio, but that this was what he had in mind and what he had also told Congress. He hoped that agreement could be reached on that basis.

Azad and Nehru had an important meeting with the Mission on 10 June. Azad said that the composition of the interim government was a vital matter; numerous statements had been made in League circles that parity was essential but Congress was entirely opposed to parity. The intention of the Muslim League was to create deadlock in order to bring about Pakistan. The Viceroy argued that the interim government had to meet an abnormal situation in which the great difficulty was the conflict between the two main parties. The government would have to be a coalition of these two parties, and it must work in harmony. To get the government formed it would be necessary to make certain concessions to the minorities. He had, therefore, always worked on the basis of 5:5:2 proportions. He would not regard this as in any way a precedent establishing a claim to parity, but simply as an expedient for the interim period. He thought this was the only way to get together an interim government of both parties. It was no doubt a concession from the Congress point of view, but he hoped that Congress would accept it for the common good of India.[1]

Nehru threatened that Congress would work for a strong centre and against the group system, and that it would succeed. Congress did not think that Jinnah had any real place in the country. With regard to parity, Nehru said it was beyond the power of Congress to agree to it because its supporters would not accept it.

Azad said that to include Scheduled Caste representation in the Congress quota would mean that Caste Hindus, who were the largest element in the population of India, would get a very small share of

---

[1] In an interview with Gandhi on 11 June, Wavell said that if both parties were determined to work for the common good of India, parity had no real meaning, but 'if one party was out to dominate the government, then obviously the government would do no good'.

representation. Congress would like a larger Executive Council of fifteen including Nationalist Muslims, a Sikh, a Parsee and an Indian Christian.

Two days later, Nehru handed over to Wavell a list of 15 names for the interim government: 5 Congress (all Hindus), 4 Muslim League, 1 non-League Muslim, 1 non-Congress Hindu, 1 Congress Scheduled Caste, 1 Indian Christian, 1 Sikh, 1 Congress woman. Wavell told him at once that the list would be quite unacceptable to Jinnah.

The Mission reported to Attlee on 14 June that the Viceroy had induced Jinnah to say that if Congress would accept a government of 13 composed of 5 Congress, 5 Muslim League, 1 Scheduled Caste representative who would be Congress, and 2 other minority representatives, he would put that to his Working Committee.

Later on the same day Wavell received a letter from Azad which in his view 'practically amounted to turning down both the Statement of 16 May and the interim government'. Azad repeated Congress' objection to the grouping of the provinces and the representation of the Europeans in the Constituent Assembly[1], turned down Wavell's list of thirteen for the interim government and emphatically rejected any idea of parity in its membership. He informed the Viceroy that Congress would not be able to assist him 'in the difficult tasks ahead'.

At this point the Mission concluded that no useful purpose would be served by prolonging the discussions and informed Azad and Jinnah that they would issue a statement on the action they proposed to take.

The Cabinet Mission's statement of 16 June announced that the Viceroy was issuing invitations to fourteen persons named in it to serve as members of the interim government. The invitees consisted of six Hindu members of Congress, including a member of the Scheduled Castes, five members of the Muslim League, and three representing the minority communities of Sikhs, Indian Christians and Parsees. Clause 8 of the statement, which was later to cause trouble with Jinnah, ran:

> In the event of the two major parties or either of them proving unwilling to join in the setting up of a coalition Government on the above lines, it is the intention of the Viceroy to proceed with the formation of an interim Government which will be as representative as possible of those willing to accept the Statement of May 16th.

---

[1] On 15 June the European Party in the Bengal Legislative Assembly, under the Mission's pressure behind the scenes, announced that they would not nominate anyone for election to the Constituent Assembly, but this answered only one of the Congress objections to the Cabinet Mission's plan.

The list of fourteen mentioned above did not contain any non-League Muslims, and this question once again became the subject of a heated controversy between Congress and the Muslim League and, for the time being, wrecked Wavell's efforts to instal a coalition interim government representing the two main parties. When Azad and Nehru saw Wavell on 18 June they complained about not having any non-League Muslim in his list and indicated that they might wish to substitute Zakir Husain, a non-League Muslim, for one of the Congress Hindus. But later on the same day, Jinnah told the Viceroy that Zakir Husain was a 'quisling' and his nomination instead of a Congress Hindu was absolutely unacceptable. Before the day was out, Jinnah wrote to Wavell that he had placed the matter before the League Working Committee and they had unanimously confirmed the principle that the Muslim League would never accept the nomination of any Muslim to the interim government other than a Muslim Leaguer.

The Secretary of State informed his colleagues in the Mission on 19 June that he had been informed that Gandhi, at the Congress Working Committee meeting on the previous day, had thrown his weight behind the inclusion of a Nationalist Muslim in the interim government. Next day the delegation learnt that at a further meeting of the Congress Working Committee held on 19 June, Gandhi had again put forward his case for the inclusion of a Congress Muslim in the government.

On 23 June the Cabinet Mission pleaded hard with a strong Congress delegation consisting of Azad, Nehru, Patel and Rajendra Prassad not to press the inclusion of a Muslim among the Congress representatives in the interim government. The Secretary of State warned that if Congress did so 'they would thereby jeopardise the whole future of India'. He reiterated that this would not be taken to create a precedent or approve a principle. The delegation had not given Jinnah any assurance that they accepted the view that the Muslim League represented all Muslim political opinion, and that no other party except the Muslim League had any right to nominate a Muslim for a political post. He thought the greatest obstacle to India going forward towards independence was the inability to get started. The value of getting a start made was so great as to be worth, not the sacrifice of a principle, but abstinence from enforcing it for the time being. If the delegation insisted upon the inclusion of a Congress Muslim, Jinnah would not accept it and there would be no coalition government. Wavell urged that on occasions of this sort the stronger party was in a position to make a concession and it might very well pay them to do so.

But the Congress leaders refused to budge. Azad said the matter of

appointment of a Nationalist Muslim was one on which Congress had
expressed themselves clearly throughout. Nehru said that Congress
disagreed with the presumption that progress could only be made with the
co-operation of the Muslim League. Patel believed that if they gave up
their stand it would 'force all the Muslims out of Congress'.

The Working Committee of Congress passed a resolution on 25 June,
a copy of which Azad promptly sent to the Viceroy. It rejected the
proposals for the formation of an interim government. With regard to the
long-term recommendations for the constitution-making body contained
in the statement of 16 May, the Committee decided that 'Congress should
join the proposed Constituent Assembly'. The resolution made it clear that
Congress disapproved of 'the limitations of the Central Authority as
contained in the proposals' as well as of the system of grouping of
provinces, but had agreed to participate in the Constituent Assembly
because it felt that there was sufficient scope for remedying these defects.

In his letter forwarding the text of the resolution, Azad reminded
Wavell that the Congress leaders had, in the course of their meetings and
correspondence with the Mission, already pointed out the defects in the
proposals of 16 May and given their own interpretation of the plan. He
made it clear that Congress still adhered to those views and had decided
to work the proposals 'with a view to achieve our objective'.

The Mission decided that, 'although cleverly worded', the Congress
President's reply must be regarded as an acceptance of the long-term
proposals[1] and invited Jinnah on the same afternoon to confer with them.
The Secretary of State told the Muslim League President that the delegation
were satisfied that the Congress letter constituted an acceptance. It was not
in any way a provisional acceptance. The Muslim League, in accepting the
statement, had also adhered to their own point of view and had made
statements maintaining their goal of complete sovereign Pakistan, and
others which went quite as far as any reservations made by the Congress.
Jinnah complained that the reservations made by Congress were most vital
and undermined the whole thing.

The Viceroy said that the point now reached was that the delegation
proposed to go ahead with the Constituent Assembly and constitution-
making, treating both parties as having accepted the statement of 16 May

---

[1] In a note prepared for the Mission, Wavell had written, 'Congress manoeuvres have now
put us into a very difficult position, both with Mr Jinnah and as to the formation of an Interim
Government'. He said he could not see how he could ask Jinnah to form a government 'since
both sides have now accepted the 16 May statement; unless we decided that the Congress's
[sic] is a dishonest one, as it in fact is, and refuse to regard it as an acceptance'.

with reservations. As Congress had refused the proposals about the interim government, the statement of 16 June fell to the ground. In accordance with paragraph 8 of that statement he would make an attempt to get a representative coalition government of those who had accepted the May statement. He thought Mr Jinnah would agree that it was no use making a further attempt immediately, and he proposed that there should now be an interval during which a caretaker government would be appointed. After a short interval he would try again to from a coalition government, which he believed was the right solution. Jinnah protested that he had understood that if one party rejected the offer of 16 May they would go ahead with the other. His view was they should proceed now to form an interim government on the basis of the statement of 16 June with the Muslim League.

In their final statement on 26 June, the Cabinet Mission expressed their satisfaction that constitution-making could now proceed with the consent of the two major parties but regretted that it had not so far proved possible to form an interim government. They were determined that the effort to form an interim government should be renewed. Owing, however, to the very heavy burden which had been cast upon the Viceroy and the party leaders during the previous months, it was proposed that further negotiations should be adjourned for a short interval while the elections for the Constituent Assembly would take place. Until a new interim government could be formed the Viceroy would set up a caretaker government of officials. It was also announced that it was not possible for the Delegation to remain longer in India and they would leave for England on 29 June.

Jinnah issued an angry statement on 27 June criticizing the decision to postpone the setting up of an interim government and saying that it was very difficult to see what were the mysterious causes behind it...Clause 8 of the statement of 16 June had made it quite clear that the delegation and the Viceroy were 'in honour bound to go ahead with the formation of the interim government immediately with those who were willing to come into the interim government'. Any attempt to whittle down the assurances given to the Muslim League would be 'regarded by Muslim India as a going back on the part of the Cabinet Delegation and the Viceroy on their pledged word in writing and as a breach of faith'.

Wavell believed that Congress had accepted the long-term proposals under Cripps' and Pethick-Lawrence's private advice. In the summary of the Cabinet Mission's work recorded in his journal on the day following the Delegation's departure, he wrote: 'It was, I think, definitely sharp practice on his [Cripps'] part, after having several times assured me, when

I raised the point, that there was no possible chance of Congress accepting the May 16 Statement unless they came into the interim government, to point out to Congress, as I am sure he did, the tactical advantage they would gain by accepting the May 16 Statement, even with reservations, and thus preventing Paragraph 8 of June 16 being operated in Jinnah's favour. And the S. of S. did so too.' He also thought, 'Gandhi ran to form and was the real wrecker.'[1]

As already stated, not long after the publication of their Statement of 16 May, the Mission began to fear that Congress might turn down their proposals. The Secretary of State telegraphed Attlee on 26 May that if that happened, the government were 'likely then to be faced with open rebellion'. He recommended that, in that case, the British 'should affect a partial and orderly withdrawal from certain provinces of Hindustan, remaining for a time in the ports, in the larger [princely] States, in Jinnah's territory [the areas claimed for Pakistan] and possibly elsewhere'. On the day of the Cabinet Delegation's departure from India (29 June), Wavell prepared a note 'On Present Position in India' in which he warned that a crisis might suddenly arise in India. He said there were doubts whether the Indian Army would respond if asked to suppress a Congress mass movement, or to deal with widespread communal trouble. Another problem was that the strength of the British element in the Indian Civil Service and the Indian Police Service had been reduced because of the stoppage of recruitment during the war. In his letter to the King on 8 July, Wavell plainly stated that the British had neither the power nor the will to remain in control of India 'for more than an extremely limited period'. The British must try to leave India united and must secure the co-operation of Congress, which represented the great majority of Indian political opinion 'whatever our views on the past record of that party'. At the same time he wrote to Sir Alan Lascelles, Private Secretary to the King: 'The depressing thing is that one should have to hand over the control of India to such small men; the mentality of most of them is that of the small lawyer and *bania*.'

Jinnah was feeling despondent at the outcome of the Cabinet delegation's visit but he was soon rescued from his predicament by the Congress leaders, especially by Jawaharlal Nehru, who had just succeeded Azad as the President of the Congress.[2] When the All-India Congress Committee

---

[1] *See*, p. 445. Gandhi influenced the Working Committee to insist upon the inclusion of a Nationalist [Congress] Muslim in the Interim Government.

[2] Patel was a strong candidate to follow Azad but Gandhi's support for Nehru caused Patel to step down. As the Mahatma said at a later date, 'Jawaharlal... a Harrow boy, a Cambridge graduate and a barrister, is wanted to carry on the negotiations with Englishmen.'

met at Bombay on 7 July 1946 to ratify the decision of the Working
Committee accepting the long-term plan of the Cabinet Mission, Nehru
took the chair. Though the decision of the Working Committee was
endorsed, it was emphatically stated that Congress would participate in the
Constituent Assembly entirely on their own terms. Azad, who introduced
the resolution, said that the Working Committee had made it clear that
there should be no compulsion in the matter of grouping; provinces should
be free to decide whether they wished to join a particular group or not.
Nehru went even further and declared that they were not bound by a single
thing except that they had decided for the moment to go into the
Constituent Assembly. Patel asserted that Congress had made it clear that
representatives of provinces should have the right to decide at the initial
stage whether they would join the group to which they had been allotted.

At his press conference on 10 July, Nehru repeated that they had agreed
to go into the Constituent Assembly but had agreed to nothing else; 'what
we do there, we are entirely and absolutely free to determine. We have
committed ourselves on no single matter to anyone.' With regard to a
treaty with Great Britain he said, 'If the British government presume to tell
us that they are going to hold anything in India because they do not agree
either in regard to the minorities or in regard to the treaty, we shall not
accept that position.' Referring to grouping, he said that the big probability
was that there would be no grouping. He also visualized a much stronger
Centre than the one outlined by the Cabinet Mission: among other matters,
there must be some overall power to intervene in a grave crisis such as
breakdown of the administration or economic upheaval and famine. The
scope of the Centre, even though limited, inevitably grows, he argued.
Azad has frankly admitted that Nehru's claim that Congress would be free
to modify the Cabinet Mission plan reopened the whole question of
political and communal settlement, and Jinnah took full advantage of this
'mistake'. Louis Fisher, who attended the press conference, said to Nehru,
'You have changed the entire basis of the agreement with England.' Nehru
smiled and replied, 'I am fully aware of that.'[1]

Since Nehru's rewriting of the Cabinet Mission scheme served as the
immediate excuse for the Muslim League to withdraw its own acceptance
of that scheme, Azad calls it 'one of those unfortunate events which
change the course of history'. He thinks 'the acceptance of the Cabinet

---

[1] Louis Fischer in his Introduction to Azad's *India Wins Freedom,* p. xvii. This
Introduction is found in the edition published in New York by Longmans Green but not in
the Indian editions.

Mission Plan by both Congress and the Muslim League was a glorious event in the history of the freedom movement in India. It meant that the difficult question of Indian freedom had been settled by negotiation and agreement and not by methods of violence and conflict. It also seemed that the communal difficulties had been finally left behind.' But his rosy premise and his conclusion are both highly unrealistic.

In their respective terms of acceptance, Congress as well as the Muslim League had made it unmistakably clear that neither of them was prepared to work harmoniously for the achievement of a common goal. Each was determined to gain its own ends despite the bitter opposition of the other party. The division of the constitution-making body into sections, and the final structure into three tiers (Centre, Groups, Provinces), provided endless opportunities for wrangling and obstruction. The Sikhs, who had been placed in the predominantly Muslim section B, were furious and would have demanded Khalistan, and the Scheduled Castes would have played off the Muslims against the Caste Hindus. And to induce the princely States to join the Union would have posed problems of its own. Wavell assessed that the Constituent Assembly 'may not survive even the first meeting'.

Even in the almost impossible event of a constitution emerging from the discordant Assembly, there could never have been any finality because every province was entitled to call for a reconsideration of the constitution after an initial period of ten years and at ten-yearly intervals thereafter. This was an everlasting invitation to disruption.

Pethick-Lawrence and Cripps tried to reassure the Muslim League in the wake of Nehru's press statement of 10 July. Both their speeches on 18 July, in the House of Lords and House of Commons respectively, contained the following passage:

> ...they [the Indian political parties] can put forward their views as to how the Constituent Assembly should conduct its business. But having agreed to the Statement of May 16, and the Constituent Assembly elected in accordance with that statement, they cannot, of course, go outside the terms of what has been agreed. To do so would not be fair to other parties who come in, and it is on the basis of that agreed procedure that His Majesty's Government have said they will accept the decisions of the Constituent Assembly.

CHAPTER 21

TOWARD TRANSFER OF POWER

THE INTERIM GOVERNMENT

On 22 July 1946, the Viceroy addressed identical letters to Nehru and Jinnah asking them whether Congress and the Muslim League would be prepared to enter an Interim Coalition Government on the following basis:

(a) The Interim Government will consist of fourteen members.

(b) Six members (to include one Scheduled Caste representative) will be nominated by the Congress; Five members will be nominated by the Muslim League. Three representatives of minorities will be nominated by the Viceroy. One of these places will be kept for a Sikh.

It will not be open to either Congress or the Muslim League to object to the names submitted by the other Party, provided they are accepted by the Viceroy.

(c) The Congress and the Muslim League will each have an equitable share of the most important portfolios.

(d) The assurances about the status of the Interim Government which I gave in my letter dated 30th May to Maulana Azad will stand.

When the All-India Muslim League Council met at Bombay (27-29 July 1946), Jinnah dismissed the assurances given by Pethick-Lawrence and Cripps in Parliament on 18 July as no more than a 'pious expression', because they provided no effective check or remedy 'in the event of Congress, which happens to have a brute majority in the Constituent Assembly, taking any decision which is *ultra vires* and incompetent of that Assembly'. He stressed that the essential part of the scheme from the Muslim League point of view was grouping B and C[1] and noted that it was that part which had been unequivocally repudiated by Congress. He said that the League Council had been summoned because a new situation had been created by the position

---

[1] The B and C grouping of provinces in the north-west and north-east of India with their Muslim majorities contained the embryo of Pakistan.

which Congress had taken and which in a nutshell was: 'We are committed to nothing, and we are going to the Constituent Assembly to achieve our objective, and according to our sweet will, we will do what we like on the basis of the interpretations which have already been announced to the world'. He felt that the Muslim League had exhausted all appeals to reason. The only tribunal to which they could now go was the Muslim nation.

The Council passed two resolutions. The first stated that the participation of the Muslims in the proposed constitution-making machinery was fraught with danger and that the Council, therefore, withdrew its acceptance of the Cabinet Mission's proposals. The second declared that the time had come for the the Muslim nation to resort to direct action to achieve Pakistan and to get rid of British slavery and the contemplated future Caste Hindu domination. It directed the Working Committee to prepare a programme of direct action and called upon the Muslims to renounce the titles conferred by the alien government forthwith. A number of top-ranking Muslim Leaguers and others attending the session renounced their titles immediately to the accompaniment of 'frenzied cheers'.

In his concluding remarks, Jinnah said, 'We have taken a most historic decision. Never before in the whole life-history of the Muslim League did we do anything except by constitutional methods and constitutional talks. We are today forced into this position by a move in which both Congress and Britain have participated. We have been attacked on two fronts—the British front and the Hindu front. Today we have said good-bye to constitutions and constitutional methods. Throughout the painful negotiations, the two parties with whom we bargained held a pistol at us; one with power and machine-guns behind it, and the other with non-co-operation and the threat to launch mass civil disobedience. This situation must be met. We also have a pistol.' He claimed that the Muslim League had been moved by higher considerations than the rest of India. To secure freedom for all and to prevent bloodshed and civil war, the League had sacrificed the full sovereignty of Pakistan and voluntarily delegated three subjects to the Union 'to work for ten years'.

On 31 July, Jinnah informed Wavell that the Muslim League was unable to accept the proposals made by him on 22 July. He complained that these proposals destroyed the principle of parity as well as of representation according to communities and gave a clear majority to Congress as against the Muslim League.[1] Wavell thereupon decided to form an interim

---

[1] The Muslim League feared that some of the minority members in the proposed Interim Goverment, specially the Sikhs, would side with Congress.

government with the help of Congress and expressed the hope that the Muslim League would join it later and make it a coalition.

In an apparent attempt to induce the Muslim League to reverse its decision rejecting the long-term part of the Cabinet Mission Statement of 16 May, the Working Committee of Congress met at Wardha and on 10 August passed a resolution which stated that it stood by the resolution passed by itself on 26 June and ratified by the All-India Congress Committee on 7 July. But the new resolution nullified any good that the move might have done by stating in the same breath that, 'provincial autonomy is a basic provision and each province has the right to decide whether to form or join a group or not,' and emphasizing 'the sovereign character of the Constitution for India without the interference of any external power or authority'.

Not surprisingly Jinnah, in a statement issued on 13 August, said that the resolution was only a repetition of the Congress stand taken from the very beginning, only put into different language. Congress had reiterated its repudiation of the grouping and emphasized once more the sovereign character of the Constituent Assembly, which connoted that it would not be bound by anything laid down in the Statement of 16 May and would be free to decide every question by [its Hindu] majority.

At Nehru's invitation he and Jinnah conferred together on 15 August, but could not come to an agreement on the question of the League joining Congress in the Interim Government. The stumbling block was the insistence by Congress on its right to nominate a Nationalist Muslim as part of its quota in the Interim Government.

The Working Committee of the Muslim League decided that Friday 16 August should be observed as Direct Action Day. It passed off quietly except in Calcutta. At Calcutta the Muslim League Ministry under H. S. Suhrawardy declared 16 August as a holiday[1] and it was later alleged that there would have been no trouble if there had not been a holiday, 'for Satan finds some mischief still, for idle hands to do'. But Governor Burrows, with whose 'full knowledge and approval' the decision had been taken, did not agree with this view, arguing that many of the mischief-makers were people who would have been idle hands anyhow. If shops and markets had been open, there would have been even more looting and murder than there was. The European shops were closed and none was damaged. The trouble seemed generally

---

[1] The account given here is based mainly on the report sent by Sir Frederick Burrows, Governor of Bengal, to Lord Wavell on 22 August 1946.

to have started when Hindu-owned shops refused to close. The confrontation did not involve foreigners; it was a straight Hindu-Muslim affair.

The Muslims from early on 16 August were in an aggressive mood and their processions were well-armed with lathis, iron rods or missiles. Their efforts to force Hindu shops to close were greeted with showers of brickbats from the roofs above—indicating that the Hindus were also not unprepared for trouble—and from this sort of exchange of missiles matters soon degenerated into arson, looting and murder.

A Muslim League meeting held on the same afternoon was attended by 30,000 -50,000 persons. The Chief Minister (Suhrawardy), made a speech 'of which his audience naturally remembered the hot passages more clearly than the cold', and many of the listeners started looting Hindu shops as soon as they left the meeting.

The scale of rioting was unprecedented. 'I can honestly say', continued Burrows, that parts of the city on Saturday [17 August] morning were as bad as anything I saw when I was with the Guards on the Somme'.[1] The situation did not ease up until 20 August. The attitude of the police was unsatisfactory but it was the natural result 'of the constant vituperation levelled in the Legislature and the Press against any police officer who resorts to firing however fully the circumstances justified his action'. The army was called in on the afternoon of 16 August and 'the only thing which prevented a complete collapse of the administration was the three battalions of British troops'. Even the corpses had to be removed by British troops as no one else was willing to undertake that task. The volunteers were paid five rupees per body. Luckily there was no trouble elsewhere in Bengal, except some rioting and looting in Sylhet on 16 and 17 August.

According to a Written Answer to a Parliamentary Question in the British Parliament on 18 November, the casualty figures for Calcutta for the period 16-19 August were 4,000 dead and 10,000 injured. In his letter of 21 August to Pethick-Lawrence, Wavell had reported that appreciably more Muslims than Hindus had been killed.

The 'Great Calcutta Killing' marked the start of the bloodiest phase of the 'war of succession' between Hindus and Muslims and it became increasingly difficult for the British to control India. Previously they had to cope with Congress civil disobedience movements. Now, furious Muslims had also come out in the streets in their thousands.

---

[1] The Battle of the Somme (July-November 1916) during World War I.

A communique issued on 24 August announced that the existing members of the Governor-General's Executive Council had resigned and that in their places the following persons had been appointed: Pandit Jawaharlal Nehru, Sardar Vallabhbhai Patel, Dr Rajendra Prasad, M. Asaf Ali, C. Rajagopalachari, Sarat Chandra Bose, Dr John Matthai, Sardar Baldev Singh, Sir Shafaat Ahmad Khan,[1] Jagjivan Ram, Syed Ali Zaheer and Cooverji Hormusji Bhabha. Two more Muslim members were to be appointed later. It was stated that the Interim Government would be installed on 2 September.

The communique was supplemented by a broadcast by Wavell on the same day. He said no one was sorrier than he was that it had not been possible to secure a coalition by including the Muslim League in the Interim Government and no one could be more sure that it was a coalition government that was needed in the interests of all the communities in India. He stated that it was still open to the Muslim League to propose five names for places in a government of fourteen, of which six would be nominees of Congress and three would be representatives of the minorities.

Two days later, Jinnah declared that the Viceroy had struck a severe blow to Muslim India and had added insult to injury by nominating three Muslims who did not command the confidence of Muslim India. He reiterated that the only solution to India's problems was the division of India into Pakistan and Hindustan.

Wavell paid a one-day visit to Calcutta, returning to Delhi on the night of 26 August. While in Calcutta, he had a series of interviews with officials as well as politicians. He also toured the scenes of the recent rioting as well as the relief centres. On 27 August he invited Gandhi and Nehru to see him. He described to them what he had seen in Calcutta, and told them that the only way to avoid similar trouble all over India was to achieve Hindu-Muslim settlement. He stressed the importance of coalition governments both in Bengal and at the centre, and that the crux of the whole matter lay in the doubt about the Congress interpretation of the grouping in the Constituent Assembly. He said he could not take the responsibility of calling together the Constituent Assembly until this point was settled and asked Gandhi and Nehru to make a statement in the following terms:

Congress are prepared in the interests of communal harmony to accept the intention of the Statement of 16 May that Provinces cannot exercise any option affecting their membership of the Section or of the Groups if formed until the

---

[1] Some days later Shafaat Ahmad Khan was stabbed and wounded by two Muslims in Simla.

decision contemplated in paragraph 19 (viii) of the Statement of the 16th May[1] is taken by the new Legislature after the new constitutional arrangements have come into operation and the first general elections have been held.

When Gandhi resorted to 'long legalistic arguments', Wavell told him that he, Wavell, 'was a plain man and not a lawyer' but he knew perfectly well that compulsory grouping was the whole crux of the Cabinet Mission plan.

On the following day, Gandhi wrote an uncharacteristically angry letter to Wavell: 'Your language last night was minatory. As representative of the King you cannot afford to be a military man only...You should be assisted, if necessary, by a legal mind...Congress claims to know both the Hindu and Muslim mind more than you or any Britisher can do. Unless, therefore, you can wholly trust the Congress Government which you have announced, you should reconsider your decision, as I have already suggested...You will please convey the whole of this letter to the British Cabinet.'

In demanding that Wavell should communicate the contents of his letter to the British Government, Gandhi had shrewdly calculated that Wavell's superiors would not approve of his having displeased Gandhi and Nehru. Pethick-Lawrence immediately consulted Attlee and wired back: 'We must ask you not to take any steps which are likely to result in a breach with Congress...If we had had time...we should have asked you not to say that you would not convene the Constituent Assembly until the point about grouping was settled, but only that you would have to postpone it further.'

Of course, the difference in approach to the political problems of India between the British Cabinet ministers and Wavell was nothing new. We have already mentioned Wavell's criticism of the way the Secretary of State and Cripps had conducted their Mission to India. He had repeated his view in his letter to the King on 8 July: 'It was a mistake that the Mission should have had, outside the official discussions, such a continuous and close touch with one of the two main parties, Congress; this naturally aroused the deep suspicion of the Muslim League.' That the Labour Government in England, for its part, had increasingly begun to think poorly of Wavell's capacity to cope with the intricacies of the task facing

---

[1] Paragraph 19 (viii) read: 'As soon as the new constitutional arrangements have come into operation it shall be open to any Province to elect to come out of any group in which it has been placed. Such a decision shall be taken by the Legislature of the Province after the first general election under the new Constitution'.

him was amply brought home to him by a letter which Attlee had sent him on 22 July: 'You as a soldier without political advisers must be somewhat in the same position as a Prime Minister would be without the advice of the Chiefs of Staff on military matters... Your hand would be strengthened if you had with you someone...who could act as an intermediary for you with the politicians.' Attlee thought Sir Maurice Gwyer[1] would make a suitable adviser for the purpose. Wavell heatedly wrote back on 1 August that he would sooner trust his own judgement than Gwyer's and added, 'I appreciate, however, that you and HMG may feel that you would rather have a politician than a soldier at the head of India at present; and if you wish to recommend to His Majesty to make a change, I shall of course accept your decision without any question. I took up my present position as a war appointment, since the then Prime Minister judged, rightly or wrongly, that it was where I could best serve the war effort.'

With the British Cabinet as well as Gandhi alienated from him, Wavell's days as Viceroy were now clearly numbered.

That the Viceroy had formed an Interim Government consisting only of the Congress nominees added further fuel to the communal fire. On 31 August, Jenkins (Governor of the Punjab), reported to Wavell that the Muslims were frightened and angry. They thought that the refusal of the British Government to put the Muslim League in power when Congress was non-co-operating, and the apparent eagerness to bring in Congress as soon as the party positions were reversed, could be explained only as a deep-laid plot between the British and Congress. The Muslims regarded the formation of the Interim Government as an unconditional surrender of power to the Hindus, and feared that the Governor-General would be unable to prevent the Hindus from using their newly-acquired power for the suppression of the Muslims all over India.

The Interim Government duly took office on 2 September. The important portfolios of External Affairs, Home, Defence and Finance were held by Nehru, Patel, Baldev Singh and Matthai (an Indian Christian) respectively. Nehru was appointed Vice-President of the Council, which meant that he could preside at Council meetings in the absence of the Viceroy.

On 8 September Wavell forwarded to the Secretary of State a note entitled 'A Policy for India' in which he said that it was 'essential' for the British Government to have 'at once a definite plan' for the withdrawal of its control from India. He believed that in India the British must rule either

[1] Chief Justice of India 1937-43; Vice-Chancellor of Delhi University 1938-50.

firmly or not at all. He assumed that the British government would not be prepared to change its policy and announce a decision to rule India for another fifteen or twenty years[1], and therefore estimated that the maximum time for which they could hold India under existing circumstances was a year and a half, or until the spring of 1948. He proposed a planned withdrawal by stages, most of the Congress provinces being vacated first.[2] An announcement of British intentions must be made at the latest by 1 March 1947. A programme of withdrawal would confront the princely States as well as the provinces of British India with the 'realities of the situation'.

At a meeting held under the chairmanship of Attlee at 10 Downing Street on 23 September, Cripps said that the moment British withdrawal was announced, everyone in India would start scrambling for position; civil war would erupt at once. On 28 September, the Secretary of State informed Wavell that the government view was that if a withdrawal became unavoidable, it should be done from India as a whole as quickly as possible and without a long period of notice. The decision as to when a situation had arisen which compelled such a withdrawal could only be taken in the light of circumstances as they developed.

In the meantime, the elections to the Constituent Assembly[3] had been completed in July. Congress won 201 seats out of 210 allotted to the general constituencies. The Congress members included 25 representatives of the depressed classes, 7 Christians, 3 Anglo-Indians and 12 women. Of the 78 Muslim seats, the Muslim League won 73. The Sikhs had left the four seats earmarked for them vacant but were persuaded to fill them later. Their fear was that under the proposed grouping they would not be able to opt out of the predominantly Muslim Group B.

After Congress had taken the reins at the centre on 2 September, Jinnah faced a desperate situation. The armed forces were predominantly Hindu and Sikh and the Indian members of the other services were predominantly Hindu. The British were preparing to concede independence to India and if they withdrew leaving Congress in undisputed control, Congress would

---

[1] 'An announcement of this kind', Wavell believed, 'would change the whole position because it would rally support to our side and would involve the immediate reinforcement of the Services.'

[2] This would have permitted a concentration of British power in northern India, where the greatest trouble was expected in the final stages of the transfer of power.

[3] The Assembly was designed to consist of 385 members including 93 representatives of the princely States.

be free to deal with the Muslims as it wished. Wavell too felt unhappy at the purely Congress Interim Government. He genuinely desired a Hindu-Muslim settlement and a united India, and had worked hard to that end. More immediately, he needed the Muslim League in the government to act as a counterpoise to Congress.

Congress alone was reluctant to admit the Muslim League into the Interim Government. At his prayer meeting on the day Congress took office Gandhi said, 'the door to *purna* [complete] *swaraj* has opened,' and told his listeners that full freedom would be achieved only when their 'uncrowned king, Jawaharlal,' and his colleagues had rendered true service. On 26 September, Wavell pleaded with Nehru and Gandhi, in separate interviews, that it would help him to persuade Jinnah to co-operate if he could give him an assurance that Congress would not insist on nominating a Nationalist Muslim. Nehru replied that Congress could not give way on that issue. Gandhi said if it had been merely a Congress 'right' they could have made concessions on it but since it was a 'duty', it was a different matter.

Two days later, Wavell informed Jinnah that he had not succeeded in persuading the Congress leaders to make a gesture by not appointing a Nationalist Muslim. The Muslim League President realized that Congress would not give up the right to nominate a Nationalist Muslim and that he would have to accept that position if he did not wish to leave the Interim Government solely in the hands of Congress. When he saw Wavell on 2 October he therefore said nothing at all on the issue of a Nationalist Muslim. Wavell rightly inferred from this that the Muslim League wanted to come into the Interim Government. On 13 October Jinnah wrote to Wavell that, though the Muslim League did not agree with much that had happened, 'in the interests of the Mussalmans and other communities it will be fatal to leave the entire field of administration of the Central Government in the hands of Congress', and the League had therefore decided to nominate five members for the Interim Government. On 15 October he gave the Viceroy the following five names: Liaquat Ali Khan, I. I. Chundrigar, Abdur Rab Nishtar, Ghazanfar Ali Khan and Jogindar Nath Mandal. The last named was a Scheduled Caste Hindu and was obviously a tit-for-tat for the Congress insistence upon including a Nationalist Muslim in its own quota. To accommodate the five League nominees, Congress obtained the resignations of Sarat Chandra Bose, Shafaat Ahmad Khan and Syed Ali Zaheer (there were already two vacancies).

Addressing the students of Islamic College, Lahore, on 19 October, Ghazanfar Ali Khan declared, 'We are going into the Interim Government to get a foothold [in the] fight for our cherished goal of Pakistan.' Liaquat Ali Khan was reported as having said at Karachi on 20 October that the League took its decision to enter the Interim Government because 'Congress in its heart was adverse to the League entry'. He added that this was in no way inconsistent with the League's Bombay resolution on direct action, and that the Muslims must not relax in their preparation for the final struggle for winning Pakistan.

At a later date (15 November 1946) Jinnah said that the Muslim League members of the Interim Government were there 'as sentinels who would watch Muslim interests in the day-to-day administration of Government'.

The division of portfolios between the Congress and League members of the Interim Government was not easily achieved. Of the important portfolios, the League wished to secure either External Affairs or Defence. Wavell believed the League should have one portfolio from Defence, Home or External Affairs, but Nehru informed him that a change in any of them was not acceptable to Congress, though the League could have Finance, 'should they so desire it'. Wavell then told Nehru, 'I must allot the Home portfolio to the Muslim League,' to which Nehru bluntly replied that Patel had said he would resign from the Interim Government if the portfolio of Home was taken away from him, and 'we cannot continue in government without him'. The problem was finally solved by the acceptance of Finance by the Muslim League.

The reconstituted Interim Government as installed on 26 October consisted of the following:

External Affairs and Commonwealth Relations :	Jawaharlal Nehru
Defence :	Baldev Singh
Home (including Information and Broadcasting) :	Vallabhbhai Patel
Finance :	Liaquat Ali Khan
Posts and Air :	Adbur Rab Nishtar
Food and Agriculture :	Rajendra Prasad
Labour :	Jagjivan Ram
Transport and Railways :	M. Asaf Ali
Industries and Supplies :	John Matthai
Education and Arts :	C. Rajagopalachari

Works, Mines and Power	:	C. H. Bhabha
Commerce	:	I. I. Chundrigar
Law	:	Jogindar Nath Mandal
Health	:	Ghazanfar Ali Khan

Azad has revealed that Congress had offered Finance to the League at the suggestion of Rafi Ahmad Kidwai, a Nationalist Muslim of the United Provinces. Kidwai argued that Finance was a highly technical subject and the League had no member who could handle it effectively. His view was that the League would therefore refuse it. If this happened Congress would lose nothing. If on the other hand a League nominee accepted the Finance portfolio he would soon make a fool of himself. Either way Congress would stand to gain. Patel jumped at the proposal and gave it his strongest support.

The Muslim League side of the story is related by Chaudhri Muhammad Ali.[1] He states that he had advised Jinnah in June 1946, when the formation of an Interim Government was first under consideration, that if the League wished to influence the policies of government in every department it should take charge of Finance. He had not been able to convince Jinnah of the strategic importance of Finance at that time but now that events had 'practically forced the Finance portfolio upon the League' he was sent for again and repeated his advice even more forcefully. His recommendation was accepted and he became an unofficial adviser to the Muslim League bloc in the government. This was nothing unusual 'since many of the senior Hindu officials were acting in a similar capacity for the Congress bloc'.

Azad states that Patel soon 'realized that he had played into the hands of the League by offering it Finance. Whatever proposal he made was either rejected or modified beyond recognition by Liaquat Ali. His persistent interference made it difficult for any Congress Member to function effectively. Internal dissensions broke out within the Government and went on increasing.'

In an interview on 14 October, Wavell had made it quite clear to Jinnah that the presence of the Muslim League in the Interim Government was conditional on its acceptance of the Cabinet Mission Statement of 16 May relating to the Constituent Assembly (which would involve a reconsideration of the League's Bombay resolution by which it had

---

[1] Muhammad Ali at that time was Financial Adviser, War and Supply, in the Governemt of India. After independence he become Secretary-General of the Government of Pakistan and was Prime Minister from 1955 to 1956. This account is taken from his book, *The Emergence of Pakistan*.

withdrawn its earlier acceptance). Jinnah said he realized this but it would be necessary to secure certain guarantees from Congress first. In an interview with George Abell[1] on 16 November, Liaquat said that the League could not enter the Constituent Assembly without a guarantee by the British Government in respect of grouping and of provincial constitutions being framed by sections. Gandhi, however, had already (23 October 1946) declared that the Cabinet Mission had no authority to interpret its own proposals in respect of the Constituent Assembly because 'No lawgiver can give an authoritative interpretation of his own law...if...there is a dispute...a duly constituted court of law must decide it.'[2]

Congress' position, as spelled out by Nehru in a letter to Wavell dated 23 October, was that it stuck to its own interpretation of the Statement of 16 May and did not accept that of the Cabinet Mission. Congress, however, would abide by the decision of the Federal Court 'in all such matters of interpretation'. But on 30 September he had already publicly admitted that he had written to Gopinath Bardoloi, Prime Minister of Assam, assuring him that: 'Provincial autonomy must be maintained and a province must decide both about grouping and about its own constitution. It is true that we have accepted the Federal Court's decision with regard to the interpretation and we must abide by that decision of ours. But in no event are we going to agree to a province like Assam being forced against its will to do anything.'[3]

On 21 November the Viceroy issued invitations for the meeting of the Constituent Assembly on 9 December. Jinnah issued a statement on 22 November that the summoning of the Constituent Assembly was 'one more blunder of very grave and serious character' and that no representative of the Muslim League would participate in it.

In an equally outspoken speech on the same day, Nehru complained that the Muslim League had been endeavouring to establish itself as the King's Party in the Interim Government, and the British Government for its part had been exploiting that position for its own purposes. He alleged that there was a mental alliance between the League and senior British

---

[1] Private Secretary to the Viceroy.

[2] Jinnah on the other hand argued that the authors themselves (the British Cabinet Mission and the government) ought to know what the proposals were: a mediator making a proposal should know what it means.

[3] The Congress leaders in Assam feared that if Bengal and Assam were grouped together, the whole region would be dominated by Muslims, and Bardoloi had submitted a memorandum to the Congress Working Committee on the subject. The Assam Assembly had elected representatives to the Constituent Assembly but the Provincial Congress Party had instructed its members not to take part in Section C.

officials. He felt that Congress should remain in the Interim Government, but for how long that would be he could not say. What form their struggle should take would have to be considered when the occasion arose. He warned the Viceroy that their patience was 'fast reaching the limit'.

These threats from both the major parties, together with the deteriorating law and order situation[1] and the Viceroy's warnings that the growing crisis called for a 'definite policy' on the part of the British Government, caused the British Government to invite the Indian leaders for discussions to find a way of preventing a breakdown.

The Conference met in London from 3 to 6 December. Nehru represented Congress, Jinnah and Liaquat the League, and Baldev Singh the Sikhs. The last meeting, attended by all of those who had taken part in the discussions, took place on 6 December under the chairmanship of Prime Minister Attlee, who said that the British Government had asked the Indian leaders to come to London in the hope that they might be able to assist in settling the differences which had arisen between the parties in regard to the Constituent Assembly. The British Government had done their part but they had been unable to get acceptance by either side of the view held by the other. He then read out the statement which was to be issued by the British Government that night:

> The Cabinet Mission have throughout maintained the view that the decisions of the sections should, in the absence of agreements to the contrary, be taken by simple majority vote of the representatives in the sections. This view has been accepted by the Muslim League, but Congress have put forward a different view. They have asserted that the true meaning of the Statement, read as a whole, is that the provinces have a right to decide both as to grouping and as to their own constitutions. His Majesty's Government have had legal advice[2] which confirms that the Statement of 16th May means what the Cabinet Mission have always stated was their intention... On the matter immediately in dispute, His Majesty's Government urge Congress to accept the view of the Cabinet Mission in order that the way maybe open for the Muslim League to reconsider their attitude.

As an obvious warning to Congress if it remained intransigent, the statement concluded as follows:

---

[1] To be discussed presently.

[2] The crucial part of the Lord Chancellor's opinion had been that 'it is for the majority of the representatives in each section taken as a whole [not for individual provinces] to decide how provincial constitutions shall be framed and to what extent, if any, they shall be grouped'.

There has never been any prospect of success for the Constituent Assembly, except upon the basis of an agreed procedure. Should a Constitution come to be framed by a Constituent Assembly in which a large section of the Indian population had not be represented, His Majesty's Government could not of course contemplate—as the Congress have stated they would not contemplate—forcing such a Constitution upon any unwilling parts of the country.

Nehru and Baldev Singh left London on the following morning to attend the opening meeting of the Constituent Assembly. When the Constituent Assembly convened on 9 December, all the Muslim League seats remained vacant.

On 13 December, Nehru moved the 'Objectives Resolution' in the Constituent Assembly which declared, *inter alia*, that India would be 'an independent sovereign republic'.[1] This was criticised by Sir John Colville[2] in a letter he wrote to the Secretary of State on 18 December on the grounds that only one political party (Congress) at that time was represented in the Assembly.

While the Hindu and Muslim politicians were exchanging hot words, their ordinary followers had been exchanging hard blows. On the eve of the installation of the Congress Interim Government at Delhi in September, a communal riot erupted in Bombay. After a four-day visit to the riot-torn city, Wavell noted in his journal on 20 October that since 1 September there had been 1,500 casualties, of which more than 360 had been fatal, almost equally divided between Hindus and Muslims. There were certain quarters in which no Muslim could go without an escort, and vice-versa.

Ever since the 'Great Calcutta Killing' of August, the authorities in East Bengal had felt apprehensive that communal rioting might break out again in their own area. This actually happened in the second week of October in the districts of Noakhali and Tippera. The Muslim leader Ghulam Sarwar, who was suspected of having fomented the trouble, was promptly arrested and the situation was brought under control by the end of the month. General Tuker[3] estimated that the total killed was 'well under three hundred'. Many Hindus had been forcibly converted to Islam. The Hindu population had panicked and a large number had fled and

---

[1] The 'Objectives Resolution' was passed by the Constituent Assembly during a six-day session which commenced on 20 January 1947.

[2] The Governor of Bombay who at this time was acting as Viceroy in the absence of Wavell, who was still in London.

[3] Lieutenant-General Sir Francis Tuker, G.O.C.-in-C. Eastern Command, who wrote, 'A tale of the last two years of British rule in India by one who watched events from the Headquarters of Eastern Command' in *While Memory Serves*.

become refugees. What made matters infinitely worse was that 'terrible and deliberately false stories were blown all over the world by a hysterical Hindu Press, and these stories did infinite harm in India by kindling in Bihar and the United Provinces the Hindu desire for revenge. This in turn, after the Bihar and United Provinces outbreak, kindled the indignant and violent emotion which flung the Muslims of the Punjab into their civil war of reprisal.'

In the second half of October Nehru paid an official visit to the North-West Frontier Province in his capacity as the Member for External Affairs[1] in the Interim Government. He intended to be escorted during his tour by Khan Sahib, the Congress Premier, and his brother, Abdul Ghaffar Khan, who had acquired the title of 'the Frontier Gandhi'. Sir Olaf Caroe, the Governor, had made a special trip to Delhi and advised him that a visit at that time, when a coalition was on the *tapis,* would be exceedingly ill-timed but, if he was determined to carry it out, he must make the approach on non-party lines and on no account travel with the frontier leaders of a single party. The Muslim League and its demand for Pakistan had been gathering strength for some time and there were reports that a large number of persons who previously had supported the Khan brothers had gone over to the Muslim League. Azad, supported by Gandhi, had tried to dissuade Nehru from visiting the Frontier Province so soon after assuming office. In Azad's view, Nehru had 'not yet consolidated his position. His tour in the Frontier at this stage would give the dissident elements an opportunity of organizing their opposition to Congress'. Azad states that the Khan brothers had 'exaggerated the extent of their influence...In fact, however, there was quite a powerful group against the Khan brothers'. Azad also feared that since a majority of the officials were against Congress they would sympathize with those opposition elements.

On learning of Nehru's impending visit, the Muslim League intensified its propaganda and the Pir of Manki Sharif undertook a tour for that purpose. When Nehru landed at Peshawar airport, he found thousands of Pakhtuns massed there with black flags and shouting hostile slogans. Khan Sahib and others who had come to receive him were helpless and themselves needed police protection.

On the next day, Nehru left on a tour of the tribal area and encountered hostile demonstrations everywhere. It was a great shock to the tribesmen

[1] Which included Tribal Affairs. The Governor of the North-West Frontier Province was also the Agent for Tribal Affairs, and for that part of his duties was responsible to Nehru as the member for External Affairs.

to see a Hindu coming down to talk to them from a position of real
authority. The ugliest incident took place as Nehru's party was leaving
Malakand. It was described by Nehru himself in his official note on the
tour in these words: '[The demonstrators] surrounded our car. Smashed all
the glass and made a dangerous and murderous attack upon us...Ultimately
we got through when Dr Khan Sahib took a revolver from the orderly in
the car and brandished it about without firing it.' Nehru was not badly hurt
but suffered bruises on the ear and chin. Khan Sahib and Ghaffar Khan
were also injured. Nehru complained in his note that he was reminded at
every step that he had come against the wishes of the hierarchy and that
he himself would be responsible for any consequences. He displayed
admirable fearlessness throughout the tour. But politically the visit was a
mistake: the Muslim League gained further ground at the cost of the
Congress Party.

Early in November the Hindus in Bihar avenged themselves for the
happenings in East Bengal by massacring Muslims. That the provincial
Congress Ministry had declared 28 October as Noakhali Day to mourn the
deaths of Hindus in East Bengal greatly added to the frenzy of the
miscreants. Tuker writes:

Of all the terrible doings of 1946 this fearful carnage was the most shocking.
Its most dastardly side was that great mobs of Hindus turned suddenly, but with
every preparation for the deed, upon the few Muslims who had lived and whose
forefathers had lived in amity and trust all their lives among these very Hindu
neighbours. It has never been ascertained who was the organising brain of this
well-laid, widely-planned plot of extirpation. All that we do know is that it went
to a fixed plan and schedule...The number of Muslim dead, men, women and
children, in this short, savage killing was about seven thousand to eight
thousand. The Muslim League tried to put the figure at between twenty and
thirty thousand. Our reports show this to be a considerable exaggeration.

On 15 November Jinnah said at a press conference that 'the exchange
of population will have to be considered seriously as far as possible
especially after this Bihar tragedy'. Shortly after the slaughter in Bihar a
dreadful massacre of Muslims took place at Garhmuktesar in the United
Provinces during a Hindu festival attended by two or three hundred
thousand Hindus. According to Tuker:

Practically every Muslim man, woman and child was murdered with appalling
cruelty. Either here or later even pregnant women were ripped [open], their
unborn babies torn out and the infants' brains bashed out on walls and on the

ground. There was rape, and women and children were seized by the legs by burly fiends and torn apart... The murderers' women stood about, laughing with glee at the burning booths, egging on their menfolk...Unfortunately there was not a single British police officer in control of the area of the trouble. The Senior Superintendent of Police, the District Magistrate and the Superintendent of Police were all Hindus.

Liaquat told Abell on 18 November that the state of the country was one of civil war. In a letter he wrote to the Secretary of State on 22 November, Wavell said that the recent disorders had not been sudden outbreaks of excitable people as had often occurred in the past, but were deliberately planned by the worst political elements, and they showed that neither the police nor the Indian officials could now be relied on to act impartially.

Wavell had stayed on in London after the meetings between the Indian leaders and the British Government had ended on 6 December. But his hope that he would obtain from the Attlee Cabinet a clear definition of its policy toward India was not realized. On the eve of his departure for India he wrote to the British Prime Minister on 20 December:

If I am to return to India on Sunday to undertake the very serious responsibilities there, with no settled policy after nearly three weeks at home, I feel I should have your personal assurance on certain points, i.e.:

(a) That HMG does recognise that we must make arrangements with a view to the transfer of power in India not later than 31 March 1948.

(b) That you accept in principle my general plan of withdrawal by stages, subject to further examination in the next few weeks, here and in India...

In his reply dated 8 January 1947, Attlee said:

While it would be desirable to announce a time limit for the continuance of British rule in India, it was considered that it would not be advisable to fix a day...The Cabinet did not approve of the approach to the problem on the basis of a military evacuation. It was considered that a different approach was required—viz. that of close co-operation with the Indian Governments at the Centre and in the Provinces in order to work out with them plans for handing over the Government in India, as a going concern. There was a feeling that withdrawal by stages was an encouragement to fragmentation.

MOUNTBATTEN'S APPOINTMENT AND ATTLEE'S STATEMENT OF 20 FEBRUARY 1947

Unbeknown to Wavell, Attlee on 18 December (1946), while Wavell was still in London, had invited Rear-Admiral Viscount Mountbatten to see him and had offered him the Viceroyalty of India. Mountbatten had first toured India in 1921 as a member of the entourage of David, Prince of Wales (afterwards King Edward VIII), and later, as Supreme Allied Commander, South-East Asia, he had earned praise for his handling of military co-ordination as well as for his liberal attitude toward the post-surrender nationalist movements there. Since the headquarters of the Command were initially at New Delhi, he had met Wavell frequently and discussed the questions of the day with him. As a second cousin of King George VI he enjoyed an aura which was expected to impress all Indians, specially the princes. The unconcealed eagerness of the Attlee Government to send Mountbatten as Viceroy gave him a strong bargaining position and he used it to ask for special terms before accepting the assignment on 11 February.

The conditions which he succeeded in getting accepted were that his career in the navy would not be prejudiced by the interlude in India; that he would be able to take out additional staff of his own choice to supplement the staff he would take over from Wavell[1] ; and that he would be given a clear directive setting out what he was expected to achieve. He insisted on being consulted with regard to the wording of the directive as

---

[1] Among the additional staff Mountbatten brought out with him from the United Kingdom were his Chief of Staff, Lord Ismay, his Principal Secretary, Sir Eric Mieville, and his Press Attache, Alan Campbell-Johnson. Ismay and Mieville had been Viceroy Willingdon's Military and Private Secretary respectively and Campbell-Johnson had served under Mountbatten in London, when Mountbatten was Chief of Combined Operations, and in South-East Asia when Mountbatten was Supreme Allied Commander. Ismay had been Churchill's Chief of Staff during World War II. Campbell-Johnson published his journal as *Mission with Mountbatten* in 1951. Cripps, instigated by Nehru and Krishna Menon, suggested that George Abell should be moved from the post of Private Secretary to the Viceroy but Mountbatten decided to retain him. Krishna Menon was Secretary, India League London (1929-47), and a good friend of Nehru. Mountbatten conferred with Krishna Menon twice before going out to India.

Krishna Menon came to India after Mountbatten's appointment as Viceroy and according to Mountbatten proved 'invaluable as a link' with Nehru. Menon, furthermore, kept Mountbatten informed of the background of what was going on in Congress circles generally. 'I [Mountbatten] would recruit his assistance to "put over" any points which I found too delicate to handle myself, or at all events to prepare the ground for me.' In August 1947 Menon was appointed High Commissioner for India in the UK.

well as of the statement of policy which Attlee proposed to make in the
House of Commons on 20 February.

At first he had stipulated that he could only be of use in India if he were
'to go out at the open invitation of the Indian parties, in a capacity which
they would themselves define,' but this was dropped when Attlee explained
that it was impracticable. He claimed later that he had obtained
'plenipotentiary powers in handling complex and decisive discussions
with the Indian leaders,' but there is no record of this anywhere. On the
other hand the directive given to him clearly enjoined: 'If by 1 October
you consider that there is no prospect of reaching a settlement on the basis
of a unitary government for British India, either with or without the co-
operation of the Indian States, you should report to His Majesty's
Government on the steps which you consider should be taken for the
handing over of power on the due date.' He duly submitted to London his
'Plan Balkan' for the transfer of power and flew there personally to plead
for its revision afterwards, as discusssed in the next chapter.

Like Wavell before him, Mountbatten insisted that an announcement
'terminating the British Raj on a definite and specified date' must be made
otherwise the Indians might not believe that he had come to end the
'Viceregal system'. However Attlee thought that naming 'an exact day
of the month' would not be wise but agreed to make 'a clear statement
of timing'. In the end a compromise was reached that it would suffice to
name 'an actual month'.

To the Viceroy-Designate's consternation, Cripps offered to accompany
him to India. Mountbatten got out of the difficulty by representing to
Attlee that the presence of a man of Cripps' 'prestige and experience could
not fail to reduce me to a mere figure-head in the eyes of the people he
would be negotiating with'. In his letter to the King he expressed himself
more openly:

Sir Stafford 'bouleversed' me by offering to come out himself on my staff if
I'd accept and the PM agreed! That was a swift one because if I do have to go
I don't want to be hamstrung by bringing out a third version of the Cripps
offer!!!... the next day Stafford came round to see me and again assured me of
his desire to place his services at my disposal—so I had a brain-wave and said
'I'll accept your offer on one condition and that is that you take the appointment
which I consider would help me most'—he fell for that and agreed—then I said
'I'd like [you] to go to the India Office and thus be my rear-link with HMG'.

The salient parts of Attlee's statement on Indian Policy in the House of
Commons on 20 February ran as follows:

His Majesty's Government desire to hand over their responsibility to authorities established by a constitution approved by all parties in India in accordance with the Cabinet Mission's plan, but unfortunately there is at present no clear prospect that such a constitution and such authorities will emerge. The present state of uncertainty is fraught with danger and cannot be indefinitely prolonged. His Majesty's Government wish to make it clear that it is their definite intention to take the necessary steps to effect the transference of power into responsible Indian hands by a date not later than June 1948...if it should appear that such a constitution will not have been worked out by a fully representative Assembly before the time mentioned.[above], His Majesty's Government will have to consider to whom the powers of the Central Government in British India should be handed over, on the due date, whether as a whole to some form of Central Government for British India or in some areas to the existing Provincial Governments, or in such other way as may seem most reasonable and in the best interests of the Indian people.

In regard to the Indian States, as was explicitly stated by the Cabinet Mission, His Majesty's Government do not intend to hand over their powers and obligations under paramountcy to any government of British India. It is not intended to bring paramountcy, as a system, to a conclusion earlier than the date of the final transfer of power, but it is contemplated that for the intervening period the relations of the Crown with individual States may be adjusted by agreement.

It was announced at the same time that Mountbatten would succeed Wavell as Viceroy in March.

The directive to Mountbatten took the form of a letter to him from Attlee dated 18 March 1947 which read:

...It is the definite objective of His Majesty's Government to obtain a unitary Government for British India and the Indian States, if possible within the British Commonwealth, through the medium of a Constituent Assembly, set up and run in accordance with the Cabinet Mission's plan, and you should do the utmost in your power to persuade all parties to work together to this end, and advise His Majesty's Government, in the light of developments, as to the steps that will have to be taken.

Since, however, this plan can only become operative in respect of British India by agreement between the major parties, there can be no question of compelling either major party to accept it...

It is, of course, important that the Indian States should adjust their relations with the authorities to whom it is intended to hand over power in British India; but as was explicitly stated by the Cabinet Mission, His Majesty's Government do not intend to hand over their powers and obligations under paramountcy to any successor government. It is not intended to bring paramountcy as a system to a conclusion earlier than the date of the final transfer of power, but you are authorised, at such time as you think appropriate, to enter into negotiations with individual States for adjusting their relations with the Crown.

You will do your best to persuade the rulers of any Indian States in which political progress had been slow to progress rapidly towards some form of more democratic government in their States. You will also aid and assist the States in coming to fair and just arrangements with the leaders of British India as to their future relationships.

The date fixed for the transfer of power is a flexible one to within one month; but you should aim at 1 June 1948 as the effective date for the transfer of power...

You should take every opportunity of stressing the importance of ensuring that the transfer of power is effected with full regard to the defence requirements of India. In the first place you will impress upon the Indian leaders the great importance of avoiding any breach in the continuity of the Indian Army and of maintaining the organisation of defence on an all-Indian basis. Secondly you will point out the need for continued collaboration in the security of the Indian Ocean area for which provision might be made in an agreement between the two countries...

It was not till Attlee wrote to him on 31 January (1947) that Wavell came to know that he would soon be relieved of his position as Viceroy. Attlee made two main points: first, 'You were, I understand, informed that your appointment was a war appointment and that while the usual term for a Viceroy is five years, this might not apply. I think that three years was mentioned. This has now expired', and second, [in view of the fact that] 'it is specially necessary that the Viceroy should be in full agreement with the policy of His Majesty's Government, I think that you may agree that the time has come to make a change in the Viceroyalty.' The Prime Minister ended the letter by stating that he would recommend his, Wavell's, name for the dignity of an Earldom in recognition of the 'self-sacrificing and loyal service' which he had rendered in India.

Wavell wrote back on 5 February agreeing that his appointment was a war one and that no fixed term of office was given, but said Attlee was 'in error about a term of three years having been mentioned'.[1]

---

[1] Here Wavell's memory was at fault, because in narrating 'the history' of his appointment as Viceroy in his journal he had written (on 24 June 1943) that Prime Minister Churchill had

Continued on next page

He also protested that 'so summary a dismissal of His Majesty's representative in India is hardly in keeping with the dignity of the appointment. It has been usual to give a retiring Viceroy six months' notice of his replacement'.

Wavell still had no inkling who his successor was likely to be. That Mountbatten would be the next Viceroy was telegraphed to him by Attlee on 12 February, the day after Mountbatten had definitely agreed to accept the post. On 13 February Wavell recorded in his journal: 'An unexpected appointment but a clever one from their point of view; and Dickie's personality may perhaps accomplish what I have failed to do'. He promptly sent a message to Mountbatten: 'I am delighted that since we are going we are handing over to you and Edwina [Lady Mountbatten]; it couldn't be better.' He also expressed his regrets to Attlee that the termination of his appointment should have become a subject of party controversy in the Press, and assured him that he would do or say nothing that would embarrass his successor and would do his best to assure him welcome.

No one had ever questioned Wavell's integrity. His grasp of Indian politics was sound and realistic and the Attlee Government accepted two of his main recommendations—that the date of Indian independence must be announced, and that Britain must leave the country within eighteen months. His proposal for a phased withdrawal was rejected but no alternative plan was put in its place.

He had a poor opinion of both Indian and British politicians and by training and temperament was not fitted to negotiate with them. He looked for straightforward dealings and tidy solutions in politics, a game in which these decencies are scarce.

He wished India well and worked doggedly to achieve a Hindu-Muslim settlement and leave behind a peaceful and united India. Congress and the Muslim League each owed him a debt of gratitude. When he took over as Viceroy the Congress leaders were still under detention after the failure of the Quit India rebellion. Their political fortunes were at a low ebb and the Churchill Government was in no mood to revive a dialogue with them. It was entirely due to Wavell's persistent pleading that the British Government agreed to take the initiative, release the Congress leaders and let Wavell

---

invited him to dinner on 14 June and offered him the post saying that it would probably be a war appointment only and that he would make a political appointment after the war; 'he indicated three years as the limit of my tenure'. At a meeting of the War Cabinet on 15 June, at which Attlee was present, Churchill had also informed his colleagues that it was proposed to offer Wavell the appointment of Viceroy 'for a period of three years'.

hold the Simla Conference to try to form a Congress-Muslim League coalition at the centre. Azad, who was the president of Congress at the time, paid this handsome tribute to him:

> After the failure of the Cripps Mission Churchill's Government had made up their mind to put the Indian question in cold storage for the duration of the war. Indian opinion could also find no way out and the events after 1942 had further increased the bitterness. To Lord Wavell must belong the credit for opening the closed door. In spite of initial opposition from the Coalition Government, he was able to persuade them to agree to make a new offer to India. The result was the Simla Conference. It did not succeed but everything that has followed since then has been a logical development of the courageous step which he took.

> I am confident that India will never forget this service of Lord Wavell, and when the time comes for the historian of independent India to appraise the relations of England and India, he will give Lord Wavell the credit for opening a new chapter in these relations.

Believing, as he did, that India's political salvation lay in Hindu-Muslim accord, Wavell endeavoured to hold a balance between Congress and the Muslim League, disregarding Gandhi's warning that he would never succeed in riding two horses at the same time. This earned him Gandhi's and Nehru's displeasure in the latter part of his term. Azad has written that Nehru and his 'other colleagues' were against Wavell but that he himself had been won over by the Viceroy at their very first meeting: 'I found him a rugged, straightforward soldier void of verbiage and direct both in approach and statement. He was not devious like the politician but came straight to the point and created in the mind an impression of great sincerity which touched my heart.'

Though Wavell was personally against the division of India, his fair-mindedness did not permit him to let Congress take advantage of the fact that the Muslim League was the weaker party.[1] This enabled the League to gather strength and fight for Pakistan more effectively.

From the British point of view, Attlee's substitution of Mountbatten for Wavell at the crucial time when the British were about to hand over power to the Indians, was wise. By the end of 1946 Wavell, on his own admission,

---

[1] That he favoured a united India and desired a good understanding with Congress is evident from the following quotation from his letter dated 8 July 1946 to the King: 'We must try to leave India united; and we must secure the co-operation of Congress, which represents the great majority of Indian political opinion, whatever our views on the past record of that party.'

was a disappointed and depressed person. Reviewing the past year in his journal on 31 December 1946 he wrote, 'Continual hard work and almost continual failure. No rest, no success', and modestly concluded, 'It is a great strain on a small man to do a job which is too big for him, if he feels it too big.' Mountbatten on the other hand was believed to be capable of meeting the politicians on their own ground and outsmarting them. Attlee told Mountbatten that fundamentally it was not Wavell's general policy in the past that was in question but its implementation 'today'; urgent action was needed to break the deadlock, and the principal members of the cabinet had reached the conclusion that a new personal approach was perhaps the only hope. The British Prime Minister evidently hoped that Mountbatten would be able to extricate Britain from the shambles in India with the least possible damage to its reputation and material interests.

Attlee's statement of 20 February was debated in both Houses of Parliament in the United Kingdom. In the House of Lords, Lord Templewood (the former Secretary of State for India, Sir Samuel Hoare) moved a censure motion but withdrew it for lack of sufficient support. The decisive contribution to the discussion was that of Lord Halifax (who as Lord Irwin had been Viceroy of India). He argued that there was no solution for India that was not fraught with the gravest objection and he was not prepared to condemn what the government of the day was doing unless he could honestly and confidently recommend a better solution. In the House of Commons, Cripps defended the policy of the government by practically repeating what Wavell had been saying in his dispatches:

> [The] alternatives [are] fundamentally two...first, we could attempt to strengthen British control in India...to maintain for as long as might be necessary our administrative responsibility while awaiting an agreement amongst the Indian communities. Such a policy would [mean]...we should remain in India for at least fifteen to twenty years, because for any substantially shorter period we should not be able to reorganise the Services on a stable and sound basis...The second alternative [is]... to persuade the Indians to come together, while at the same time warning them that there was a limit of time during which we were prepared to maintain our responsibility while awaiting their agreement...We [rule] out the first alternative as both undesirable and impracticable.

Cripps also explained that if it was not found possible to transfer power to a central government, 'We shall be forced to choose the most appropriate government or governments to which to hand over power. It might be the then existing provincial governments or some form of combined government for parts of India...We could not accept the forcing of unwilling provinces into a United Indian Government if they have not been represented in the making of the constitution.'

Since Congress was represented in the Constituent Assembly while the Muslim League had shunned it, Cripps' statement clearly envisaged the division of India into Congress provinces and Muslim League Provinces.[1]

Winston Churchill, in the course of a scathing attack, said, 'In handing over the Government of India to these so-called political classes we are handing over to men of straw of whom in a few years no trace will remain.'

After a two-day debate the government won by 337 votes to 185.

In India, the Attlee statement had a calming effect at the leadership level. Congress had been increasingly pressing Wavell to expel the Muslim League from the Interim Government on the ground that the League had not withdrawn its rejection of the Cabinet Mission plan relating to the Constituent Assembly, while the Muslim League had been pointing out that Congress too had never accepted the plan in accordance with the authoritative interpretation of the British Government. The Working Committee of the Muslim League had passed a resolution at Karachi, on 31 January 1947, stating that: 'Congress as a major contracting party has not accepted the statement of 16th May 1946, as clarified by the Statement of the 6th December 1946,' and demanding that the Constituent Assembly should be dissolved forthwith because:

the elections to, and thereafter the summoning of, the Constituent Assembly, in spite of strong protests and most emphatic objections on the part of the Muslim League, was *ab initio* void, invalid and illegal as not only the major parties had not accepted the statement but even the Sikhs and the Scheduled Castes had also not done so; and that the continuation of the Constituent Assembly and its proceedings and decisions are *ultra vires,* invalid and illegal.

On 5 February the Viceroy had received a formal demand from the Congress nominees in the Interim Government for the expulsion of the Muslim League members of the Government and on 13 February Nehru had threatened that delay in taking the necessary action would 'necessarily lead us to reconsider our position in the Interim Government'. Two days later Patel announced at a press interview that Congress would withdraw from the Interim Government if the Muslim League were allowed to

---

[1] Of course, Cripps was only elucidating the basic policy which Attlee had laid down in his statement of 20 February 1947.

remain in it without abandoning their boycott of the Constituent Assembly.

Attlee's declaration of the new policy on 20 February, however, saved the Interim Government. In an interview with Wavell two days later Nehru described the declaration as a courageous document which would have far-reaching effects, and said that Congress would not press for an immediate answer to the demand that the Muslim League should not remain in the central government.

At street level in India, however, the prospect of the British leaving India in the near future intensified the communal war of succession, especially in the Punjab.

In the Punjab an unnatural situation prevailed. The Muslim League had won 79 out of 86 Muslim seats in the 1946 elections but had been denied office because the rump of Muslim Unionists under Khizar Hayat Khan had formed an alliance with Congress Hindus and Akali Sikhs. The League leaders were feeling frustrated and wished to overthrow Khizar's coalition government. Both sides were preparing for a showdown. Hindu and Muslim 'private armies' in the form of the RSSS[1] and Muslim League National Guards were being trained for fighting.

Matters came to a head on 24 January 1947, when both were declared unlawful bodies. Searches of premises of both the organizations at various places were carried out without incident except at Lahore, where some League leaders obstructed the search and were arrested. On the following day, fifteen Muslim League members of the Legislative Assembly were arrested for defying the ban on processions and meetings. Women also demonstrated on their own and some were arrested. About 1,000 steel helmets were recovered form the Lahore office of the National Guards. In his report to the Viceroy, Sir Evan Jenkins, Governor of the Punjab, reported that 'tear smoke was freely used' on 25 January for dispersing the crowds.

On 27 January the Governor reported that agitation was reported from a dozen districts outside Lahore but did not amount to much except at Amritsar and Jullundur. At Amritsar the Superintendent of Police had been seriously injured by a stone or brick.

The ban on the RSSS and National Guards was withdrawn on 26 January but the agitation continued and all important Muslim League leaders were arrested. On 4 February, Wavell reported to the Secretary of State that it seemed 'more than likely that' Khizar's days as Premier were numbered.

---

[1] Rashtriya Swayam Sewak Sangh.

Jenkins called Attlee's statement of 20 February, that the British would pull out of India by a stated date, 'a very dangerous decision, amounting to an invitation to the warring parties to make real war upon one another'. Khizar told the Governor that the announcement was 'the work of lunatics' and became increasingly gloomy and no longer willing to resort to strong action.

On 25 February the Governor reported that there was violence in several districts. At Amritsar the Additional District Magistrate (a Muslim) sustained a fractured skull, police casualties numbered about 55, including one dead, and casualties among demonstrators numbered about 110.

On 26 February the Khizar Government tried to conciliate the Muslim League. The ban on meetings was withdrawn and the arrested leaders were released. The League, for its part, called off the movement. On 2 March Khizar resigned, saying, 'It is now incumbent on me to leave the field clear for the Muslim League to come to such arrangements *vis-a-vis* the other parties as it might consider in the best interests of the Muslims and the province.' The Governor invited the Khan of Mamdot, leader of the Muslim League in the Punjab, to form the government, but the League could not immediately muster a majority, so on 5 March the Governor took over direct charge of the administration under Section 93.

On 1 April, the private secretary to the Viceroy brought to the notice of the private secretary to the Governor of the Punjab that Ghazanfar Ali Khan, one of the Muslim League members of the Interim Government, kept saying that if there was a general election in the Punjab it would be possible for the Muslim League to obtain a stable majority, and asked what was the maximum number of seats that the League could win in the Punjab. The Governor's private secretary sent him an analysis of the probable result, to which the Governor personally appended a note of his own which read: 'There is little doubt that if a General Election were held now, the Muslim League would win 90 seats or thereabouts [in a house of 175] and would thus have a clear (though hardly stable) majority. But in the present situation this result would have no significance. The Hindus and Sikhs would positively refuse to let a Muslim Ministry (with or without Christian or Scheduled Caste support) function at all. The Sikhs in particular would rebel and would use force; and the Ministry would be unable to hold a Session of the Assembly...A Muslim Ministry now would mean instant civil war.'

When the Governor went to New Delhi to attend the Governors' Conference he reported verbally to Mountbatten (on 14 April) that Khizar, in order to save all the turmoil of elections, had offered to lead his Unionist

Muslims into the League and so enable them to form a Government. But the Viceroy and the Governor agreed that a communal government would only make matters worse and that Section 93 administration must continue.

The Punjab thus remained under the direct administration of the Governor until the transfer of power despite periodic representations by the Muslim League that it had acquired the allegiance of a majority of the members of the provincial assembly.

In the meantime, the continual denial of office increasingly frustrated the Muslims, and communal tension and the number of casualties began to mount apace. On 4 March, Master Tara Singh, the Sikh leader, shouted 'Pakistan murdabad'[1] and, brandishing a sword, proclaimed 'raj karega Khalsa, agey rahe na koi'.[2] Two police officers who interviewed Tara Singh at Amritsar on 10 March reported that he was extremely excited, asserting that civil war had already begun and threatening attacks on police stations and a mass Sikh rising.

On 4 March large-scale rioting broke out in Lahore and on 5 and 6 March also in Multan, Rawalpindi, Amritsar and Jullundur, with smaller disturbances elsewhere. The worst affected parts were the predominantly Muslim districts of Attock, Rawalpindi and Jhelum in the north-west and Multan in the south-west, where trouble rapidly spread to rural areas. General Frank Messervy, G.O.C.-in-C. Northern Command wrote:

> In the rural areas attacks were launched by large mobs of Muslim peasants who banded together from several hamlets and villages to destroy and loot Sikh and Hindu shops and houses in their area. In some areas arson and loot were the main objects, and casualties inflicted on the Hindu-Sikh community were not great. In others savagery was carried to an extreme degree and men, women and children were hacked or beaten to death, if not burned in their houses. There were also quite a number of cases of forcible conversion of males and abduction of females. Having served for 34 years, mostly in the Punjab and with Punjab troops, I would never have believed that agitation could have aroused the normally chivalrous and decent PM [Punjabi Muslim] peasant to such frenzied savagery as was widely prevalent. Much of this savagery was undoubtedly deliberately intensified by the wildest rumours, the commonest of which was an impending attack by a large Sikh Army.

---

[1] 'Death to Pakistan'

[2] 'The Sikhs will rule; no resister will remain.' Penderel Moon, *Divide and Quit*, p.77. Moon, a member of the Indian Civil Service, was in India at the time of partition.

The events in the Punjab had their repercussion in the adjoining North-West Frontier Province, where the Muslim Leaguers organized demonstrations against the Congress Ministry of Dr Khan Sahib. On 21 February a procession in Peshawar broke the police cordons and came right up the road in front of the Governor's house and into Khan Sahib's garden besieging his house on all sides. Tear gas was used but when the police were ordered to fire they quietly disobeyed orders. The mob broke all the windows of Khan Sahib's house. Eventually the Deputy Commissioner was able to get the crowd to move on. There was also trouble in Mardan and elsewhere and League leaders, including members of the provincial legislature, were arrested. The arrest of the Pir of Manki Sharif angered his followers in the tribal areas. On 5 March, Wavell reported to the Secretary of State that the Congress ministry in North-West Frontier Province 'may not last very long'. At a Muslim League demonstration at the Assembly Hall in Peshawar on 10 March, troops had to open fire, resulting in fifteen casualties, two of whom subsequently died.

Nehru had wished to visit the Frontier Province but gave up the idea at Wavell's request. On 19 March he wrote to Wavell that he had been 'hurt by this development,' and said that he presumed that the Viceroy had advised him against the visit because Governor Caroe had again objected to it. He went on to say that it was clear that there was no co-operation between the Governor and the Prime Minister of the province and recommended that the Governor should be asked to retire. Wavell replied that in asking him not to go to the Frontier Province he had acted on his own because the troops and the police already had their hands full of trouble and were in no position to provide special protection to anyone. He tactfully kept silent on the subject of Caroe's retirement.

CONGRESS ACCEPTS PARTITION OF INDIA

The disturbances in the Punjab finally persuaded the non-Muslim minorities that their safety lay in the partition of the province, which in effect meant partition of India into Muslim and non-Muslim majority areas. One of the resolutions passed by the Working Committee of Congress at New Delhi on 8 March 1947 stated that the tragic events in the Punjab had 'demonstrated that there can be no settlement of the problem in the Punjab by violence and coercion, and that no arrangement based on coercion can last. Therefore, it is necessary to find a way out which involves the least amount of compulsion. This would necessitate a division of the Punjab into two

Provinces, so that the predominantly Muslim part may be separated from the predminantly non-Muslim part. The Working Committee commend this resolution, which should work to the advantage of all the communities concerned, and lessen friction and fear and suspicion of each other.'[1]

In his letter forwarding the resolutions to Wavell, Nehru wrote that the principle underlying the Congress suggestion for the partition of the Punjab applied to Bengal also. In an interview with Wavell on 10 March, he suggested that there might as a temporary measure be two ministries under the Governor, one for the eastern part of the Punjab and one for the western. Governor Burrows reported to the Viceroy on 19 March that the movement for partitioning Bengal was 'gathering momentum'.

In a speech to the All-India States Conference on 18 April, Nehru said, 'The Congress...have recently on practical considerations passed a resolution accepting the division of the country.' A few days later he plainly stated, 'The Muslim League can have Pakistan if they want it but on the condition that they do not take away other parts of India which do not wish to join Pakistan.'

The Working Committee resolution of 8 March about partitioning the Punjab had been passed without consulting Gandhi. He was at the time in Bihar on a mission to restore communal harmony there, but as Pyarelal[2] has pointed out, 'such a thing would have been inconceivable in olden days. Even when he was ranging over the length and breadth of India, they did not fail to consult him before taking any vital decisions.' Pyarelal thinks Gandhi's colleagues who were now in the Interim Government began to consult him less and less because they did not wish to go back 'into the wilderness and begin the non-violent way afresh...not an easy change-over after getting accustomed to the ways of power.'

Gandhi wrote to Nehru on 20 March asking him the reason behind the resolution of 8 March and saying that his own view was against any partition based on communal grounds. He wrote to Patel also on the same day: 'Try to explain to me your Punjab resolution if you can. I cannot understand it.'

_____

[1] On 11 March Baldev Singh wrote to Wavell confirming that the Congress resolution recommending the partition of the Punjab was fully supported by the Sikhs: 'The only solution is a division of the Punjab and the creation of a new Province embracing the contiguous area where non-Muslims form a clear majority as a whole and have large property interests.'

[2] Pyarelal had been Gandhi's secretary for a long time. The quotation that follows is from his book, *Mahatma Gandhi, The Last Phase*.

Patel replied on 24 March that the resolution had been adopted 'after the deepest deliberation...You have expressed your views against it. But you are, of course, entitled to say what you feel right.' Nehru in his letter of 25 March argued that the resolution had been passed 'so that reality might be brought into the picture'. At his prayer meeting on 1 April, Gandhi said, 'My writ runs no more...No one listens to me any more...I am crying in the wilderness.'

Nehru had entertained the possibility of partition as early as on 27 January 1946 provided the Punjab and Bengal were divided.[1] Patel was a comparatively recent convert. V.P. Menon in his *Transfer of Power in India* has stated that he had obtained Patel's agreement to partition 'late in December 1946 or early in January 1947' provided 'power could be transferred at once on the basis of Dominion Status'.

Of course, neither Nehru nor Patel was happy to see India divided after they had stood for a united India for so many years. Azad has written that Nehru believed that partition was 'by nature' wrong but that there was no alternative to it. Patel had disclosed his inner thoughts to a friend in Bombay in a letter dated 4 March 1947:

> I do not think that the British Government will agree to division. In the end, they will see the wisdom of handing over the reins of Government to the strongest party. Even if they do not...a strong Centre of the whole of India—except Eastern Bengal and a part of the Punjab, Sind and Baluchistan—enjoying full autonomy under the centre will be so powerful that the remaining portions will eventually come in.

Some Pakistani critics of Jinnah have blamed him for accepting a 'moth-eaten' Pakistan, but his ultimate consent to the division of the Punjab and Bengal was not a sudden about-turn.

The Muslim League leaders had not been oblivious of the fact that the arguments they used in favour of Pakistan could equally be used in favour of the exclusion from Pakistan of those non-Muslim areas in the Punjab and Bengal which were contiguous to India. In his 1930 Allahabad address, Iqbal had conceded the rationale for the omission of Ambala Division and some other non-Muslim majority districts from the Muslim province of his conception.[2] The authors of the original Pakistan Resolution of 24 March 1940 had also recognized that some 'territorial re-adjustments' may be necessary for the demarcation of the Muslim majority areas for

---

[1] *See*, pp. 424-5 (Nehru's letter of 27 January 1946 to Cripps).

[2] *See*, p. 323.

which they were demanding sovereign status.[1] Jinnah personally told the Cabinet Mission on 4 April 1946 that he was willing to consider boundary adjustments.[2] On 16 April he again said to the Mission that the question of the territory of Pakistan could be discussed.[3] In their own Statement of 16 May 1946, the Mission accordingly noted that, 'The Muslim League were prepared to consider the adjustment of boundaries at a later stage, but insisted that the principle of Pakistan should first be acknowledged.' The Mission pointed out that not only parts of the Punjab and Bengal but 'the whole of Assam except the district of Sylhet' would also have to be excluded from Pakistan.

Congress had acquiesced in the partition of India, and the League in the partition of the provinces in question, as unhappy compromises. At heart, Congress still longed for a united India and the League for six whole provinces for Pakistan, and neither party abandoned its manoeuvres to achieve its basic objective until the plan of 3 June 1947 decided the terms of transfer of power once and for all. The British government preferred to leave behind a united India along the lines of the Cabinet Mission proposals and stated that it would continue to seek the agreement of the Indian parties to such a solution, but made it clear at the same time that, if it failed in its efforts, it would consider other alternatives. In other words, if the Muslim League could stay the course until June 1948, partition was a certainty.

The position in India at the time of Mountbatten's arrival thus was that Gandhi was the only outstanding leader[4] who was still against partition under any circumstances.

LIAQUAT'S BUDGET

On 28 February 1947, Liaquat Ali Khan presented to the Central Assembly the budget for the coming fiscal year (April to March). He claimed that his proposals had been made in the interests of 'social justice and development'.[5] To assist the poor he abolished the salt tax and raised the minimum exemption limit for income tax from 2,000 rupees to 2,500.

[1] See, p. 349.
[2] See, p. 430.
[3] See, p. 431.
[4] Azad also was against partition, but being a Muslim in an overwhelmingly Hindu party, he was in no position to prevail against Nehru and Patel.
[5] Liaquat was the first Indian to hold the portfolio of Finance in the Governor-General's Executive Council.

To catch the tax-evaders and squeeze the profiteers he proposed to set up a Commission to investigate the accumulation of wealth by tax evasion, and to levy a special income tax of 25 per cent on business profits exceeding 100,000 rupees and a graduated tax on capital gains exceeding 5,000 rupees.

These proposals were economically sound. C. N. Vakil, a Hindu economics professor of Bombay University, commented on them in the following terms:

> The poor man was made to pay for the war in the form of continuously rising prices by inflationary methods...a process which, incidentally, helped the rich to become richer. Not only [that], but a class of new rich also came into existence...Some of the methods of evasion of the payment of taxes and encouragement of black markets became so common that they were considered as almost natural...The poorer sections of the community and, particularly, the middle classes were being gradually squeezed out.

Liaquat's budget was also in tune with the professions of the Congress party. Azad admitted that:

> It was the declared policy of Congress that economic inequalities must be removed and capitalist society replaced by one of a socialist pattern. This was the stand also in the Congress election manifesto. In addition, both Jawaharlal and I had issued statements regarding the profits earned by businessmen and industrialists during the war years. It was open knowledge that some of this income had gone underground and escaped the income tax. This had meant that large resources were denied to the Government and we felt that the Government of India should take strong action to recover taxes which were due but had remained unpaid.

But the fact remained that it was the rich Hindus who were the hardest hit because it was they who formed the majority of rich capitalists. Liaquat's critics alleged that he had deliberately hurt Hindu big businessmen who financed the Congress party and had profitted from the Congress policy of boycotting foreign goods. The loudest critics of the budget were the orthodox Hindus Rajagopalachari and Patel[1] because (in Azad's words) 'they thought that his [Liaquat's] main motive was to harm the business community as the majority of them were Hindus'. Azad himself pointed out to his colleagues that 'the proposals were in conformity with declared Congress principles' and should be examined on their merits. It

---

[1] Patel was the Congress party's principal fund collector and had friendly links with Hindu big business houses.

was also alleged that Liaquat had tried to drive a wedge between the right and the left wings of the Congress party (led respectively by Patel and Nehru).

By abolishing the salt tax Liaquat fulfilled a long-standing wish of Mahatma Gandhi. Gandhi's famous anti-salt tax campaign of 1930 had yielded only marginal success: the inhabitants of coastal areas, a fraction of India's vast population, were permitted to manufacture salt freely for their own consumption. In his very first meeting with the Cabinet Mission on 3 April 1946, Gandhi urged that the salt tax should be abolished for everyone. On the day Congress formed the Interim Government he said at his prayer meeting that 'one of the first acts of the new Government should be to remove all vestige of the salt tax'. On 22 October 1946 (i.e., four days before the Muslim League entered the Interim Government and Liaquat took office as Finance Member), Wavell wrote to Pethick-Lawrence, 'The Interim Government decided at the last meeting of the Cabinet[1] to abolish the Salt Tax.' By ending the salt tax in his budget Liaquat stole Congress' thunder.

---

[1] The Interim Government had been installed without any change in the constitution. Legally, therefore, it was no more than the Governor-General's Executive Council. At a press conference on 26 November 1946, Jinnah's attention was drawn to the fact that the Viceroy himself called it a cabinet. Jinnah said that Nehru was very keen on this word 'cabinet' and the Viceroy went along to please Nehru; 'little things please little minds and you cannot turn a donkey into an elephant by calling it an elephant'.

CHAPTER 22

TOWARD TRANSFER OF
POWER (CONTINUED)

MOUNTBATTEN: THE OPENING PHASE

Lord and Lady Mountbatten arrived in New Delhi on 22 March 1947, accompanied by their daughter Pamela, who had been taken away from school to team up with her parents in the 'social diplomacy' which was to be a marked feature of her father's Viceroyalty. The Wavells having left on 23 March, Mountbatten was sworn in on 24 March and broke with precedent by making a short speech at the ceremony. He said his was not a normal Viceroyalty because the British Government was resolved to transfer power by June 1948 and so much needed to be done before that. He paid a handsome tribute to Lord Wavell who had 'done so much to take India along the path to self-government'.

Mountbatten was a highly gifted person. He was a youthful forty-six, possessed a fine presence, an intelligent mind, the faculty of quick decision, and the resilience to take set-backs in his stride. He was also a hard and methodical worker and kept himself well-informed by incessant discussions with interested parties and his own advisers. At the same time he was inordinately vain and ambitious, and had a burning desire to succeed and project himself in the best possible light. The author of his official biography sums up:

> A picture of Mountbatten without his warts would indeed be unconvincing, for, like everything else about him, his faults were on the grandest scale. His vanity, though child-like, was monstrous, his ambition unbridled. The truth, in his hands, was swiftly converted from what it was to what it should have been. He sought to rewrite history with a cavalier indifference to the facts to magnify his own achievements. There was a time when I became so enraged by what I began to feel was his determination to hoodwink me that I found it necessary to place on my desk a notice saying: REMEMBER, IN SPITE OF EVERYTHING, HE WAS A GREAT MAN.[1]

---

[1] Philip Ziegler, *Mountbatten, The Official Biography*, pp. 701-2

The new Viceroy was ably assisted in his task by his charming wife, Edwina. Like her husband, and unlike many other British people in India, she never exhibited any colour prejudice. She was not only a gracious hostess within the precincts of the viceregal palace but was also a keen and courageous social worker, often venturing into riot-stricken areas to visit improvised hospitals and destitute refugees. She became a close personal friend of Jawaharlal Nehru[1]. Nehru's biographer diagnoses:

> As for Lady Mountbatten, it can only be surmised that she helped to fill a void in Nehru's life. He had always suffered from a sense of loneliness. His wife's death at an early age had accentuated this feeling. Especially during the Partition days, when he was more prone to moods of despair, Lady Mountbatten's sympathy was a source of comfort. She, too, was a cultivated Westerner, and a woman of great charm who could understand him as most Indian women whom he knew could not.[2]

Nehru was in fact no stranger to the Mountbattens when they arrived in India. A year earlier (18-26 March 1946), Nehru had visited Singapore, at the instance of Lord Wavell[3], to investigate the condition of the Indian community there as a representative of the Indian National Congress. Mountbatten at that time was in Singapore as the Supreme Allied Commander. Nehru's visit was frowned upon by the local British administration because he had been concerned with sabotaging the war effort under Gandhi's 'Quit India' movement and because Singapore had been the headquarters of the INA. Indeed, the British Military Administration had signalled to New Delhi that they could not provide any transport for the Indian leader.

Nehru had not long before come out of prison, and the effects of imprisonment on his mind and general outlook had not entirely worn off. Wavell had sent a message to Mountbatten that Singapore presented 'a magnificent opportunity to begin the cure,' and had added that Nehru personally was a man of great culture and sincerity and 'very probably' the future prime minister of India, and should be treated accordingly.

---

[1] According to Pyarelal, Lady Mountbatten was 'a "secret weapon" of no small value in Mountbatten's arsenal'.

[2] Michael Brecher, *Nehru*, p. 412.

[3] That Nehru had visited Singapore at the suggestion of Wavell is stated by Campbell-Johnson in *Mission With Mountbatten* on p. 30. The account of the visit given here is taken principally from Ziegler's *Mountbatten*, pp. 326-8 and *The Transfer of Power* VII, pp. 134-6.

The Supreme Allied Commander accordingly placed his own car at Nehru's disposal and he was driven in it from the airport to Government House, where he was welcomed by Mountbatten and given tea. Thereafter Mountbatten and Nehru, seated side by side, drove off to the YMCA. This display of cordiality by Mountbatten transformed the temper of the crowds lining the route. Instead of staging an anti-British demonstration, they staged one of Anglo-Indian unity. At the YMCA they were warmly greeted by Lady Mountbatten and lustily cheered by a huge disorderly crowd.

In deference to Mountbatten's wish, Nehru abandoned his plan to ceremoniously lay a wreath on the INA monument and contented himself with quietly depositing a personal wreath. But he could not refrain from having a dig at Jinnah during his very first press conference. 'Jinnah', he said, 'rather reminds me of the man who was charged with the murder of his mother and father and begged the clemency of the court on the ground that he was an orphan.'

So far as Nehru and the Mountbattens personally were concerned, the visit was an unqualified success. When Nehru landed at Rangoon on his way back to India he told Aung San[1] that Mountbatten was 'a very noble specimen of British imperialism'. Nehru and Krishna Menon had told Cripps that Mountbatten's nomination as Viceroy would be 'most acceptable' to the Congress leaders. After the announcement of the appointment, Ismay said that 'there was a danger of an issue being made of Mountbatten's selection as a pro-Hindu and anti-Muslim League appointment'. And indeed, the mutual liking between the Mountbattens and Nehru, born at Singapore, quickly developed into a genuine friendship. This was of immense political advantage to the Viceroy as well as to the Congress leader. In Mountbatten's view[2] Nehru was 'indispensable' for the handing over of power to take place in the most peaceful and dignified manner possible.

If Mountbatten's talents were formidable, the task awaiting him in India was daunting. In his very first Personal Report to London (dated 2 April 1947) he wrote:

The scene here is one of unrelieved gloom...I can see little common ground on which to build any agreed solution for the future of India. The Cabinet is fiercely

[1] A General in the Burmese National Army which had been set up by the Japanese to assist in the war against the Allies.
[2] Expressed at the Staff Meeting on 4 April 1947.

divided on communal lines; each party has its own solution and does not at present show any sign of being prepared to consider any other.

In addition, the whole country is in a most unsettled state. There are communal riots and troubles in the Punjab, NWFP, Bihar, Calcutta, Bombay, UP, and even here in Delhi. In the Punjab all parties are seriously preparing for civil war, and of these by far the most businesslike and serious are the Sikhs, who already have a plan to seize the main irrigation centres in order to exercise physical control over the whole of the Punjab.

The end of the war and civil strife had brought the economy to the brink of collapse. There was shortage of food and widespread industrial unrest.

The definite promise that India would be given independence by a fixed date made it much easier for Mountbatten to work toward a friendlier relationship with the Congress Party. The Muslims, the princes and the Untouchables, who hitherto had served British interests by acting as a counterbalance to the rebellious Congress, lost their special position. In post- independent India, it was the Congress Party which was expected to rule the country. It was therefore Congress which now had to be cultivated. That Mountbatten's own view of the Indian problem was markedly similar to that of Congress enabled him to court the leaders of that party without any qualms. He was so strongly opposed to the demand for Pakistan that he called it 'this mad Pakistan'.[1]

No sooner was the new Viceroy sworn in than he got down to work. He had long meetings with Nehru and Liaquat on the same afternoon. He preferred direct contact to writing letters and held innumerable interviews during his term of office. No notes were taken at the time, but during a fifteen-minute interval before the next engagement, Mountbatten dictated the gist of what had just been said.

---

[1] After summarizing a rambling interview with Liaquat on 19 April 1947, Mountbatten surmised, 'I have an impression that Mr Liaquat Ali Khan intends to help me find a more reasonable solution than this mad Pakistan'. Even when he was working on 'Plan Balkan', which involved partition, he wrote to the Secretary of State (on 1 May 1947), 'The more I look at the problems in India the more I realise that all this partition business is sheer madness and is going to reduce the economic efficiency of the whole country immeasurably.'

At an earlier interview (on 3 April) Liaquat had complained to Mountbatten that he found his Congress colleagues in the Interim Government 'utterly impossible people to work with' and the position had become so intolerable that, 'if Your Excellency was only prepared to let the Muslim League have the Sind Desert, I would still prefer to accept that and have a separate Muslim State in those conditions than to continue in bondage to Congress with apparently more generous concessions'.

He also held staff meetings almost daily at which recent developments were reviewed and the future course of action was considered. Minutes of these discussions were kept.

He was aware that the key personalities in Congress were Gandhi, Nehru and Patel. Nehru, the popular idol, and Patel, the realist, were in the prime of their political life and were in a position to deliver the goods on behalf of the organization. Gandhi was no longer active in mundane party affairs but he was still of immense importance as 'the spiritual factor behind Congress'. In the Muslim League the dominant figure was indisputably Jinnah.

Socially the Viceroy and his consort opened the doors of the viceregal palace to a category of Indians—members of Congress and others—who had never been admitted there before. The guest list of the garden party they gave for the delegates to the Asian Relations Conference on 28 March ran to nearly 700. During their stay of fifteen months in India, they entertained 7605 guests to luncheon, 8313 to dinner and 25,287 to garden parties and receptions. They made it a rule that no less than 50 per cent of those present must be Indians. Pamela Mountbatten, sitting with two English ladies to whom she had not been introduced, heard one say to the other, 'It makes me absolutely sick to see this house full of dirty Indians.' Mountbatten recounted this story at the Governors' conference and asked them to send home anybody who expressed sentiments of that type. Mountbatten also appointed three Indian ADCs.

Mountbatten's first interview with Nehru lasted for three hours. When asked about Jinnah, Nehru said that Jinnah's success among Muslims had been due to his 'negative qualities' and it was not, therefore, 'to be hoped that logic would prevail'. Mountbatten felt that Congress were 'beginning to see that they cannot go out of the Commonwealth; but they cannot afford to say that they will stay in; they are groping for a formula'. As Nehru prepared to take leave, Mountbatten said to him, 'I want you to regard me not as the last Viceroy winding up the British Raj, but as the first to lead the way to new India.' Nehru seemed immensely moved and said, 'Now I know what they mean when they speak of your charm being so dangerous.'

Liaquat's interview lasted for two hours and started with a discussion of the budget. Mountbatten recorded that, 'Liaquat gave me his version of how the Coalition Government has been formed—a totally different version to that rendered by Nehru—and quite untrue.'

Patel's first interview with Mountbatten took place on 25 March. He told the Viceroy that he ought to dismiss the Muslim League members of the government 'because they represented an organisation which, as a result of their "direct action" resolution, had the avowed intention of attacking the central organisation'.

A short-lived crisis erupted on 1 April when Nehru informed Mountbatten that an already much-postponed resolution demanding the release of the twelve INA men[1] was coming up in the Legislative Assembly on the day after next, and was expected to be passed.[2] When Mountbatten consulted Auchinleck on the same day, the Commander-in-Chief told him that if he gave in on the issue, he would lose the confidence of the army and he and most of his officers would have to resign.

In the end Mountbatten was able to obtain the agreement of the two sides to the following formula. The Commander-in-Chief would request the available judges of the Federal Court to 'examine the proceedings of various courts-martial and give their opinion as to the desirability of reviewing the findings and sentences in each case, and make a report to the Commander-in-Chief whether in their opinion the findings and sentences should be altered or modified in any manner'. When the motion was taken in the Central Assembly on 3 April, Nehru said that the government would resign[3] if the compromise was not accepted. Thereupon the resolution was withdrawn.

Nehru, Liaquat and Patel, being members of the government, were, of course, in constant communication with the Viceroy. By 11 April, Mountbatten had reached sufficient rapport with Nehru to have been able to write after an interview on that day that, 'Pandit Nehru was obviously pleased to find that my independent and impartial conclusions were very much on the same lines as he would like to have seen them adopted, namely a unified India with a strong centre.'

On the following day Mountbatten told Patel that in his own view, 'the very best for India would be a firm Union with a strong Central Government' and that the one solution he did not wish to be forced into was Pakistan, but that if it were Pakistan, it would have to be a truncated Pakistan.

Patel had the reputation of being a tough party boss but Mountbatten was able to establish a smooth relationship with him directly as well as

---

[1] See, pp. 420-1. Fifteen men had been tried and convicted before the Commander-in-Chief decided to discontinue all proceedings. Three of them had already been released after serving their sentences; twelve were still in prison.

[2] It had the support of both Congress and the Muslim League and was expected to be passed unanimously.

[3] Liaquat had promised to give Nehru full support if things became difficult.

through V. P. Menon, who was the trusted adviser of both of them. After their first meeting Mountbatten wrote that Patel had been 'most charming for the first hour of this interview'. Azad states that Mountbatten always referred to Patel as a walnut—'a very hard crust outside but soft pulp once the crust was cracked'. Sometimes Mountbatten, in a jocular mood, would tell Azad that he had spoken to Walnut, and Walnut had agreed with him on every question.

Gandhi's first meeting with the new Viceroy took place on 31 March and lasted for two and a quarter hours. 'Gandhi showed no inclination for getting down to business' and just reminisced. Pyarelal noted that, 'Gandhi returned from the meeting greatly impressed by the Viceroy's sincerity, gentlemanliness and nobility of character'. Mountbatten for his part recorded, 'We parted... feeling that we had progressed along the path of friendship'.

To his second meeting with Mountbatten (on 1 April), Gandhi brought his honorary grand-daughter, Manu, with him. Mountbatten said to Manu,

'You are a lucky girl. My daughter tells me she feels jealous of you on seeing your photographs with Mr Gandhi. I shall be sending her to attend your prayer meeting.' Gandhi asked the Viceroy if Manu could roam about the garden so that they could proceed with their talk uninterrupted.

'Certainly', replied the Viceroy. Then addressing Manu, he added: 'All this is yours; we are only trustees. We have come to make it over to you.'

'You can search her person for any hidden arms,' Gandhi put in laughing.

'I am perfectly satisfied there can be no need for that in a disciple of yours,' replied the Viceroy with a smile.

After some preliminary conversation, Gandhi gave Mountbatten 'the first brief summary of the solution' which he wished him to adopt: 'Jinnah should forthwith be invited to form the Central Interim Government with members of the Muslim League. This Government to operate under the Viceroy in the way the present Interim Government is operating. Any difficulty experienced through Congress having a majority in the Assembly to be overcome by their able advocacy of the measures they wished to introduce.' Mountbatten mentioned Gandhi's plan to Nehru later on the same day. Nehru was not surprised to hear of it since it was the same one Gandhi had put up to the Cabinet Mission[1] which had been turned down

---

[1] Gandhi had told the Cabinet Mission on 3 April 1946, 'Let Mr Jinnah form the first Government and choose its personnel from elected representatives in the country'.

as being impracticable. Nehru also said that he was anxious for Gandhi to stay a few days longer in Delhi as he had been away for four months and was rapidly getting out of touch with events at the centre. Nehru also 'aptly pointed out' (Mountbatten's words) that Gandhi was going round with ointment trying to heal one sore spot after another on the body of India, instead of diagnosing the cause of this eruption of sores and participating in the treatment of the body as a whole.

During the Gandhi-Mountbatten meeting on 2 April, the Mahatma 'came down firmly for his great plan'. If Jinnah should refuse the offer, Gandhi pointed out, the offer would have to be made to the only other great party in India—Congress. When Mountbatten 'twitted him' that he really desired that a government run by Congress should be formed, the Mahatma assured the Viceroy 'with burning sincerity' that this was far from being the case.

In a frank note on Gandhi's plan, V. P. Menon wrote:

> He [Gandhi] is not being quite fair to HE when he puts forward his proposal that the selection of the Cabinet for an Interim Government should be left entirely to Jinnah. He knows full well that similar offers have been made by him in the past and that Jinnah never took them seriously... There is no reason to suppose that Jinnah will now accept an offer which he has rejected previously. If he forms a Government composed entirely of Muslim League nominees, that Government will find itself facing a predominant Congress majority in the Central Legislature from which Jinnah has to get his essential legislation and supply. On the other hand, if there is a coalition, it will have to be formed on conditions more acceptable to Congress than to the League. In either event, the assurance of co-operation by Congress is more a wishful thinking and would certainly place Jinnah in the position of having to adjust his views to those of Congress...
>
> It is suggested that if Jinnah rejects the offer, the same offer is to be made *mutatis mutandis* to Congress. It should be borne in mind that all the factors which have been mentioned as working to the disadvantage of Jinnah will for the same reason work to the advantage of Congress. HE's main task is to find a solution to the present deadlock between the League and Congress. It is no solution to suggest that power should be transferred to Congress to the exclusion of the Muslim League. If the proposition were as simple as that, it would have been solved long ago.

There can be but little doubt that Gandhi was asking Mountbatten to stop seeking agreement between Congress and the Muslim League and to hand over power to Congress, but instead of saying so straightforwardly, he gave it the moral wrapping of mentioning the Muslim League first. Mountbatten told his Staff Meeting on 5 April that Gandhi 'had insisted on the inclusion of the clause that if Mr Jinnah rejected the offer it must thereafter be made to Congress,' and he called Gandhi's scheme 'undoubtedly wild'.[1]

The problem was finally solved on 11 April, when Gandhi wrote to Mountbatten that he had discussed the formula with Nehru and several members of the Working Committee but had failed to carry any of them with him except Abdul Ghaffar Khan. He asked the Viceroy to omit him from his 'consideration', and added that so far as the Congress point of view was concerned, the Congress members of the Interim Government 'will be complete advisers'.

On 12 April, Gandhi advised Mountbatten to go on strengthening the Interim Government and make it function correctly for the next fourteen months, after which power should be handed over to the Interim Government. 'This,' recorded Mountbatten, 'staggered Ismay and myself, and we both pointed out that that meant handing over power to one party, to the great disadvantage of the other party, the Muslim League, which would not fail to produce strife, possibly leading to civil war.'

That the Mahatma had decided to take a back seat and let Nehru and Patel carry on the negotiations was a blessing in disguise. There was no telling what other mind-boggling ideas he might have come up with.

Mountbatten did not have his first encounter with Jinnah until 5 April, twelve days after his first meeting with Nehru. Secretary of State Pethick-Lawrence, who as head of the Cabinet Mission had considerable personal experience of negotiating with Jinnah, had warned the Viceroy on 3 April, 'You still have the toughest customer to come in Mr Jinnah'. And indeed their first meeting immediately showed that they were miles apart, not only in politics but also in temperament. 'When Mr Jinnah first arrived,' recorded the Viceroy, 'he was in a most frigid, haughty and disdainful frame of mind'. When Jinnah said that he had come to tell Mountbatten exactly what he was prepared to accept, the latter replied that the object of the first interview was that they should make each other's acquaintance. After Jinnah had left, Mountbatten said, 'My God, he was cold. It took most of the interview to unfreeze him.' A dinner for Jinnah and his sister fixed for that night was postponed till the following day. The reason, as recorded by Campbell-Johnson, was 'simply that Mountbatten felt he

---

[1]Ziegler in *Mountbatten* has revealed that in fact Mountbatten had called it 'undoubtedly mad' but that in the final record the word 'mad' was watered down to 'wild'.

could not sustain another session with Jinnah today'. Jinnah stayed one
hour past midnight when they came to dinner and Mountbatten felt that
'the ice was really broken'. Jinnah claimed that there was only one
solution—a 'surgical operation' on India, otherwise India would perish
altogether. Mountbatten said he had not yet made up his mind and pointed
out that an 'anaesthetic' must precede any 'surgical operation'.

After only two meetings Mountbatten realized that his celebrated
charm and powers of persuasion would not be able to deflect the Quaid-
i-Azam from his chosen path. On 7 April, the Viceroy confessed at the
Staff Meeting that, 'he felt positively certain that the only way to obtain
Mr Jinnah's co-operation would be to tell him that the British accepted
Pakistan (a truncated version if necessary) as the ultimate goal from the
Muslim point of view; but that we did not intend to create chaos by turning
it over to him more quickly than was possible; nor was it for us to tell
Indians exactly how to set it up.'

During his interview with Jinnah later on the same day, Mountbatten
'tried by every means' to make him accept the Cabinet Mission Plan and
enter the Constituent Assembly, but Jinnah protested that it was quite
valueless trying to go back to the Cabinet Mission Plan because 'it was
clear that in no circumstances did Congress intend to work the Plan either
in accordance with the spirit or the letter,' and stated that India had passed
beyond the stage at which any such compromise solution could possibly
work.

On the following day, Mountbatten pointed out that if he accepted
Jinnah's arguments for the partition of India he would have to apply them
also to the partition of the Punjab and Bengal. While admitting the logic
of what Mountbatten said, Jinnah was most upset at Mountbatten giving
him a 'moth-eaten' Pakistan. Mountbatten said that he regarded it as a very
great tragedy that Jinnah was forcing him to give up the idea of a united
India, and painted a picture of the greatness which a united India of 400
million people could achieve. Jinnah replied that nothing would have
given him greater pleasure than to have seen such unity, and 'he entirely
agreed that it was indeed tragic that the behaviour of the Hindus made it
impossible to share in this.' On 10 April, Jinnah again asked Mountbatten
to make Pakistan 'viable'.

Jinnah however accepted Mountbatten's proposal to subscribe to an
appeal for communal peace. Congress, supported by Mountbatten, desired
that it should be issued over the signatures of Gandhi, Jinnah and Acharya
B. Kripalani, who had succeeded Nehru as President of Congress in
October 1946. Jinnah successfully insisted that Gandhi alone should be his

co-signatory. The appeal was issued on 15 April. It had little effect on the communal situation, but Mountbatten's press attaché claimed it as 'the first victory for his [Mountbatten's] open diplomacy'. When Kripalani called on Mountbatten on 17 April, Mountbatten expressed his regret that he had been unable to get Jinnah to agree to accept Kripalani as a co-signatory to the peace appeal. Kripalani said, 'Let us face it, you have been heavily defeated by Mr Jinnah in your first round with him.' Kripalani also told the Viceroy, 'The point has now been reached at which Congress must reluctantly accept the fact that the Muslim League will never voluntarily come into a Union of India. Rather than have a battle we shall let them have their Pakistan, provided you will allow the Punjab and Bengal to be partitioned in a fair manner.'

The Jinnah-Mountbatten meeting on 10 April, which lasted for three hours, was the sixth of their gruelling sessions in a row. Mountbatten's utter failure to budge the Muslim leader had bruised the most vulnerable traits in his character—his pride and his vanity. In the Staff Meeting on 11 April he gave vent to his frustration: 'It seemed that appeals to his [Jinnah's] reason did not prevail'; 'he gave the impression that he was not listening'; 'he was impossible to argue with'; 'Mr Jinnah was a psychopathic case'.

'PLAN BALKAN'

Jinnah's stonewalling had the desired effect of making Mountbatten realize that he stood no chance of achieving Jinnah's consent to an undivided India. At the very Staff Meeting on 11 April at which he had expressed himself in strong terms against Jinnah, the Viceroy ordered Ismay to start work on the details of a plan which assumed that it had been impossible to reach agreement on the Cabinet Mission Plan for a unified India, but he stressed that:

> when and if the time came for this plan to be announced, he wanted a most careful preamble to be written making it clear that his view had all along been completely impartial; that it was only when it became apparent that the retention of any form of an united India would start civil war that he had regretfully been obliged to give up this ideal; and that he had therefore chosen a means which gave the choice of their future, as well as the somewhat primitive democratic machinery could allow, to the Indian people themselves.

The plan which had lost ground was called 'Plan Union' and the new plan was called 'Plan Balkan'. Broadly speaking, 'Plan Balkan' meant demission of power to the provinces or to such confederations as the provinces may be able to form by grouping themselves together before the transfer of power.

At the two-day Governors' Conference which opened on 15 April, 'Plan Balkan' was discussed and the draft was afterwards revised in the light of the consensus reached at the meetings. Mountbatten told the Governors that the dominating impression which he had gathered since arrival in India was the necessity for a very early decision on how power was to be transferred. This need had not been fully appreciated before he left London. He thought 'a quick decision would also give Pakistan a greater chance to fail on its demerits'.

In his Personal Report to London on 1 May, Mountbatten wrote that he would be sending Ismay on the following day with the final draft of 'Plan Balkan' and requested that Ismay be 'released' after a week carrying the necessary authority for him to go ahead because it was 'impossible to exaggerate the need for speed'. 'The essence of the plan,' he explained, 'is to make it apparent to the people of India and to the world in general that we are allowing, so far as possible, Indians themselves to choose how they wish us to transfer power. Provinces will have the right to decide whether they will all work with the present Constituent Assembly; whether only some will adhere to it; and whether others will wish to set up a new Constituent Assembly. In the case of the three Provinces, Punjab, Bengal and Assam, in which partition has been asked for if Pakistan takes place, I am proposing machinery to allow the Provinces themselves to decide if they want partition. There is a reluctance to accept any formula, which I believe to be due to the desire of the Indians to force the British to make a decision how they will transfer powers, so that we may get the blame if things ultimately go wrong.'

V. P. Menon, the Reforms Commissioner, has recorded that he had 'always' been opposed to the plan which Ismay took to London, but his protests in discussions with the other advisers to the Viceroy had been in vain. In his own words, 'The theory that provinces should become initially independent was particularly abhorrent to me...[if] there was no strong central government to which...power could be transferred, the whole country would inevitably drift into chaos and civil war.'[1] Menon told

---

[1] V.P. Menon, *The Transfer of Power in India*, p. 357. These observations of Menon show that H.V. Hodson (*The Great Divide* p. 300) is not right in assuming that Menon had never

Continued on next page

Mountbatten later that he had broken down and wept when Ismay took 'Plan Balkan' to London and not the plan which Menon himself had been sponsoring.[1] But Menon was to have the last word in the argument; this will become evident as we proceed.

DEVELOPMENTS IN THE NORTH-WEST FRONTIER PROVINCE

During the second part of April 1947 developments in the North-West Frontier Province and Bengal came to the fore. During the Governors' Conference, Caroe said that his province was liable to 'drop to bits' at any moment and that the only way of relieving tension was to announce a general election straight away. The question was discussed on 16 April in a meeting at which Mountbatten presided and which was attended by Nehru and Caroe among others. Caroe said there had been a swing against Khan Sahib's Congress government in the preceding twelve months. Nehru believed that elections, if held immediately, would probably cause some disturbances but conceded that it was desirable to obtain the views of the people before the final hand-over of power was effected. In a letter to Mountbatten on 17 April, Nehru said that, 'to announce now that an election will be held would undoubtedly be looked upon as a triumph for the policy pursued by the Muslim League and as an open rebuff to the present Ministry...No proposal should be such as to make people think that it is a surrender to the violent methods and encouragement of the Muslim League.'

A further meeting convened by the Viceroy on 18 April, for which Khan Sahib had flown in, produced only an acrimonious debate between the Governor and his Premier. Mountbatten thereupon decided to visit the province personally and assess the situation on the spot.

The Viceroy, accompanied by Lady Mountbatten and their daughter, touched down at Peshawar soon after midday on 28 April and drove to Government House. There he learnt that a crowd of Muslim League

---

been shown the text of the draft plan which Ismay took to London. In fact Ismay had enlisted Menon's help in composing it suitably (*see*, p. 500 for Ismay's request to Menon to put 'some flesh' upon the draft).

[1] For the history and main features of Menon's plan, *see*, the section 'Formulation of the New Plan'.

demonstrators estimated at 50,000 had gathered less than a mile away and would angrily march on Government House unless he showed himself to them. After consulting the Governor and the Premier, Mountbatten decided to show himself to the crowd from the top of a nearby railway embankment. Lady Mountbatten accompanied him as it was reported there were many women in the gathering. The crowd was good-humoured and greeted the Viceroy with shouts and flag-waving. He stood for a few minutes in company with the Governor and other officials and then withdrew after saluting, but without making any address.

On the same afternoon Mountbatten conferred with Khan Sahib and his cabinet of four ministers. He said his instructions from the British Government were that India should be handed over in accordance with the will of the people so far as that could be found out. Though he would be telling the Muslim League that he would not yield to violence, he told them 'privately' that he thought elections were necessary. Khan Sahib told Mountbatten that Jinnah had no control over the Muslim League in the Frontier and the the League was run by the Governor and his officials 'with the object of throwing my government out of power'. Commenting on these allegations in his Personal Report to London on 1 May,[1] Mountbatten wrote, 'I could not suppress my laughter at such a fantastic suggestion.'

The meeting with the ministers on 28 April was followed by one with local Hindu representatives, who complained of a lack of adequate police protection.

Mountbatten next received the Muslim League leaders, who had been released from gaol for the occasion. He ordered that they should all be lodged in the same gaol so that they could consult each other; also that they should be permitted to go to Delhi on parole to see Jinnah.

All the sixteen senior officials, Indian and British, with whom Mountbatten talked during the same day 'were absolutely convinced that fresh elections at the earliest possible moment were absolutely necessary if a great disaster was to be avoided'.

On the following day the Viceregal party made a tour of the Khyber and attended a couple of *jirgas* (tribal meetings) in which the tribesmen made clear their bitter opposition to Hindu Raj; they said they would rather make terms with Afghanistan. Some pressed hard for Pakistan. After lunch Mountbatten and his entourage left the Frontier Province.

---

[1] On 23 April 1947, the Earl of Listowel had succeeded Lord Pethick-Lawrence as Secretary of State for India.

PROPOSAL FOR A UNITED INDEPENDENT BENGAL

With regard to Bengal an interesting situation was created when Suhrawardy, the Muslim League Premier, told Mountbatten on 26 April that he was confident that he could get Bengal to remain united and independent and could obtain Jinnah's agreement to such a course. Mountbatten replied that this was very good news, for he was against splitting India up into many units and considered it far better to keep Bengal as one economic unit than to have it partitioned. When Mountbatten mentioned the idea to Jinnah later on the same day, he replied without hesitation, 'I should be delighted. What is the use of Bengal without Calcutta? They had much better remain united and independent. I am sure they would be on friendly terms with us'.

The chances of a communal settlement were greater in Bengal than in the Punjab, where racial, cultural, and linguistic differences were deeper. In Bengal, one language was spoken and written by all, and most Muslims were converts from Hinduism and had retained elements of their ancestral culture. Sarat Chandra Bose, brother of the late Subhas Bose, also advocated a united independent Bengal.

FORMULATION OF THE NEW PLAN

Pending the British Government's approval of the plan which Ismay had taken to London, Mountbatten went up to Simla on 7 May for a change of air. He took with him V. P. Menon and Mieville. Nehru and Krishna Menon followed as his guests on 8 May.

At Mountbatten's suggestion, V. P. Menon discussed with Nehru on 8 and 9 May his own plan for the transfer of power. This plan eventually formed the basis of Statement of the British Government of 3 June 1947, under which power was finally transferred to India and Pakistan. Its broad outlines, in V. P. Menon's own words, were:

> ...that the Muslim majority areas should be separated from India and that the transfer of power should be to two central Governments, India and Pakistan, on the basis of Dominion Status, each having its own Governor-General. Pending the drafting of a constitution by the respective Constituent Assemblies, the interim constitution for each of the two Dominions would be based on the Government of India Act of 1935, suitably adapted for the purpose. The existing Indian Legislature would be dissolved and its place taken by the

respective Constituent Assemblies, to which the central Government in each case would be responsible.

Menon, who outshone all the other advisers of the British Government at this critical juncture, was a remarkable person. He had started in government service as a lowly clerk, and by sheer merit had reached the top echelon, which normally was the preserve of the Indian Civil Service. He first visited England in 1931 as a member of the staff for the Round Table Conference. He possessed to a high degree the skill of a draftsman and the insight of a politician, and was appointed Reforms Commissioner in 1942. Lord Wavell held him in high esteem and took him to London on his visits for consultations with His Majesty's Government. Being a Hindu and a known confidant of Patel, Menon was at first kept in the background by Mountbatten. In a note dated 26 March 1947, Abell wrote that Menon 'now is genuinely convinced of the rightness of the Congress view' and that it was therefore 'not possible to take him into confidence as fully as has been done in the past'. But Mountbatten's appreciation of Menon's worth grew as he got to know him better. Even Menon's friendship with Patel turned out to be a useful asset, because it smoothed the Viceroy's relations with Patel. When Mountbatten directed Ismay on 11 April 1947 to work out the details of 'Plan Balkan', it was to Menon that Ismay had turned with the request to 'amend the draft in any way you think proper and put some flesh upon it'.[1]

Shortly after the war had ended, Menon had written a paper which envisaged the modification of the 1935 Act to allow Dominion Status within its purview. He had forwarded the paper to the India Office with Lord Wavell's permission, but without result. Late in December 1946, or early in January 1947, he had a long discussion with Patel in which he argued that it was better that the country should be divided than that it should gravitate towards civil war. It would be best to transfer power to two central governments on the basis of Dominion Status. He dictated the outlines of his plan in Patel's presence and later sent it to the Secretary of State. Patel had assured him that if power could be transferred at once on the basis of Dominion Status, he would use his influence to have it accepted by Congress. Menon had naturally not mentioned to the Secretary of State that the proposals were acceptable to Patel, though he did say that he had reason to believe that Congress would accept transfer of power on the basis of Dominion Status.

---

[1] *Transfer of Power* X, p. 193.

No action was taken in London on Menon's proposals because it was believed there that Congress would not accept Dominion Status. Since the Lahore Resolution of December 1929, the creed of Congress had been 'complete independence', and Nehru in his presidential address there had ruled out Dominion Status because, 'I do not think that any form of Dominion Status applicable to India will give us real power'. More recently, in January 1947, the Constituent Assembly (which the Muslim League had boycotted) had passed a resolution to proclaim India an independent sovereign republic. This had further barred India's inclusion in the Commonwealth, the members of which at that time were 'united by a common allegiance to the Crown'.[1]

As the result of his discussions with Nehru on 8 and 9 May 1947, Menon reported to the Viceroy that Nehru was not averse to the transfer of power on the basis of Dominion Status. At a conference called by Mountbatten on 10 May and attended by Nehru, Mieville and Menon, the last named repeated what he had already explained to Nehru.

On the same day Mountbatten received back from London the plan he had sent through Ismay finalized and approved by the British Government. He immediately invited the following five leaders to meet him round the table at Delhi on 17 May for a 'final talk' before announcing how the government proposed to transfer power in India: Nehru, Patel, Jinnah, Liaquat and Baldev Singh. Following a 'hunch', Mountbatten gave Nehru the text of the plan as the latter was going to bed on the evening of 10 May. On the following morning Nehru wrote to him that the proposals had 'produced a devastating effect' upon him. They presented 'an entirely new picture—a picture of fragmentation and conflict and disorder and, unhappily, also of a worsening of relations between India and Britain'. He promised to follow up the letter with a note on the proposals.

Mountbatten immediately convened a meeting which was attended by Nehru, V. P. Menon, Mieville and two other members of the Viceroy's staff. Nehru handed over to Mountbatten the note he had promised. In the

---

[1] Jinnah, on the other hand, had consistently stated that Pakistan would remain within the Commonwealth. Mountbatten's view on the question 'as to what line was to be taken with any such parts [of divided India] as might apply independently to remain within the Commonwealth' was that 'it would be disastrous to allow only, for example, Pakistan to remain in' because it might mean backing Pakistan in a war against India. But he was given a lesson in Commonwealth constitution by Jinnah, who pointed out that it was not a question of Pakistan applying for admission to the Commonwealth, but on the contrary a question of whether the Commonwealth was in a position to expel Pakistan against its wish. He said Churchill had assured him that the British people would never stand for Pakistan being expelled.

note he complained that the assertion in the proposals that they had taken shape after full consultation with political leaders in India was 'completely wrong'. He wrote that hitherto they had proceeded on the basis of the Cabinet Mission's plan. They had accepted that certain Muslim majority areas might go out of the Union if they so willed, but the Union was still the basic factor. The proposals, however, started with the rejection of the Indian Union and invited the claims of large numbers of successor states who would be permitted to unite if they so wished into two or more states. At the meeting Nehru complained that the final draft would encourage the belief that India was being 'Balkanised'. The procedure now appeared to be: first separation, then a request to join up again. The previous process had been the opposite—first a request for unity and then the option to secede. He claimed that he had been shown only a one-and-a-half page long 'rough' draft by Mieville before the proposals were sent to London. Mieville, however, 'made it absolutely clear that the draft which he had shown Pandit Nehru was the full draft of the whole plan'.[1]

In his letter of 11 May to Mountbatten, Nehru also blamed the British Government for having so altered the original proposals as to make them unacceptable. 'The relatively simple proposals that we had previously discussed now appeared in the garb that HMG had provided for them, in an entirely new context which gave them an onimous meaning.' Attlee protested later that all London had done was 'to try to clarify the presentation of the case'; the only alteration of substance had been that, instead of an election in the North-West Frontier Province, it had been decided to hold a referendum there, and this had been done at Mountbatten's own suggestion to meet Nehru's objection to a general election. Mountbatten himself thought, 'the new draft appeared better than ours'. Indeed, if Mountbatten had felt that the proposals had been altered for the worse by the British Government, he would hardly have issued invitations to the Indian leaders to receive the finalized version on 17 May. The truth seems to be that his two-day session with Menon had caused Nehru to view the constitutional problem in a different light. As Nehru had not been allowed to retain a copy of the original draft of the plan to study in his own time, its full implications evidently had not registered with him at that time.

---

[1] In a message to Ismay dated 12 May, Mieville called Nehru's attitude a volte face. Mountbatten's version as given at the Staff Meeting on 3 May was that 'the only Indian leaders who had seen the full draft of the plan were Mr Jinnah and Pandit Nehru...and they had not been allowed to retain any documents. Apart from them, the outline of the plan had been discussed with Mr Liaquat Ali Khan, Sardar Patel and Sardar Baldev Singh.'

In his letter of 11 May to the Viceroy, Nehru made it clear that the announcement of 'this new policy and proposals by HMG' would provoke wide and deep resentment all over the country, and no responsible leader outside the Muslim League would be able to persuade the country to accept them. A revolt by Nehru and Congress was unthinkable for Mountbatten, who had done so much to cultivate them. He thanked his 'hunch' for having shown the plan to Nehru before it was made public with disastrous results. Without that hunch, he told his staff, 'Dickie Mountbatten would have been finished and could have packed his bag. We would have looked complete fools with the Government at home, having led them up the garden [path] to believe that Nehru would accept the Plan.'

Mountbatten telegraphed Ismay to stay on in London to 'pilot through' his new proposals 'on Dominion Status'. He characterized Nehru's unexpected change of attitude as a 'bombshell'. Ismay replied that the situation was so confused that Attlee and his colleagues thought that either a cabinet mission should fly to India or Mountbatten should come to London, and that he had taken it upon himself to say that Mountbatten would be opposed to any ministers proceeding to India and would rather come himself. Ismay's message was followed by a formal invitation from Attlee asking Mountbatten to come to London for consultations. A communique issued on 11 May announced that the Viceroy's meeting with the Indian leaders fixed for 17 May had been postponed until 2 June. At a Staff Meeting on 12 May, Mountbatten decided that the plan should be redrafted on the basis of no option for independence being given to Bengal or any other province. This was obviously done to meet Nehru's strongly-expressed wish that India should not be 'balkanized'.

At Mountbatten's request V. P. Menon had already prepared a draft of the new plan on 11 May. Mountbatten showed it to Nehru, who said that it would not be unacceptable to Congress. Menon also kept Patel informed of developments by telephone, and obtained his assurance that there would be no difficulty in Congress accepting Dominion Status.

The Viceroy returned to Delhi from Simla on 14 May. Being anxious to avoid further 'bombshells', he was determined to obtain the clear agreement of the leaders of the political parties to the new plan before leaving for England. He asked Menon to draw up a 'Heads of Agreement', which Menon took to Nehru, Patel and Baldev Singh and Mieville took to Jinnah and Liaquat. Thereafter Mountbatten conferred in turn with Nehru and Patel, with Jinnah and Liaquat and with Baldev Singh, and the plan was finalized in the light of those discussions. The more important items of the Heads of Agreement were: that the basis of power should be the

Government of India Act 1935, modified to conform to the Dominion Status position; that in the event of the decision being taken that there should be two sovereign states, the executive of each area should be responsible to its respective constituent assembly; and that the Governor-General should be common to both the states (it was 'suggested' that the present Governor-General should be re-appointed).

Nehru sent a note on 16 May that Congress accepted the plan generally but 'strictly subject to other parties agreeing to it as a final settlement'. On the following day he sent some further comments to Mountbatten in the form of a letter in which he agreed that the Governor-General should be common to both the states, if there were to be two states, and that for their part Congress would be happy if he could continue in this office.

At a Staff Meeting on 16 May, Mountbatten said that Jinnah and Liaquat had accepted the plan as outlined in the Heads of Agreement but had declined to state this in writing. Mountbatten informed the meeting that 'he had already cautiously tried threatening Mr Jinnah that, unless he met requirements adequately, power would be demitted to the Interim Government on a Dominion Status basis. Mr Jinnah had taken this very calmly and said that he could not stop such a step in any event. His Excellency the Viceroy said that this abnormal reaction, which was typical of Mr Jinnah, was rather disturbing. If Mr Jinnah saw himself betrayed he might derive great satisfaction by going down in history as a martyr for his cause, butchered by the British on the Congress altar.'[1]

When, on 15 May, Mountbatten discussed with Liaquat the question of Dominion Status for Pakistan and Hindustan under one Governor-General, he found Liaquat 'surprisingly receptive to this idea'. But when the Viceroy raised the question of a joint Governor-General in a meeting with Jinnah and Liaquat on 17 May, Jinnah said he felt that it would be better to have two Governors-General. Jinnah said further that there should be a representative of the Crown to be responsible for the division of assets between the two states and he expressed

---

[1] In a press interview on 9 May, Patel had declared that the current British policy of 'remaining neutral but holding power is a way of propagating civil war' and asserted that the political impasse would be broken at once if power were transferred to the Interim Government as a dominion government 'with the Viceroy standing out', but that 'it would be neither practicable nor justifiable to grant Dominion Status to the Interim Government'.

While Mountbatten was away in England seeking the approval of the British Government for the new plan for the transfer of power, Jinnah caused a sensation (on 22 May) by demanding an eight-hundred-mile 'corridor' to link West and East Pakistan. Nehru called the demand 'fantastic and absurd' and on his return Mountbatten prevailed upon Jinnah not to pursue it.

his keenness that Mountbatten should fill that post. Mountbatten said he could not consider taking on the post suggested by Jinnah because 'it would be an impossible position if the so-called "Arbitrator" was junior in rank to the Governors-General, who would be the King's representatives'. Mountbatten suggested that Jinnah should send him a letter giving a full description of his suggestion of a supreme arbitrator. He asked Jinnah to state clearly in the letter that if his scheme was deemed by the government to be unpractical he would accept, as an interim measure, the appointment of a common Governor-General between the two countries. The requested letter never arrived, presumably because Jinnah did not wish to state that he would accept a common Governor-General if his plan for an arbitrator was turned down.

Mountbatten, accompanied by V. P. Menon, left for London on 18 May and returned to New Delhi on 30 May. The new plan—that power would be transferred to India and Pakistan as Dominions, with the Act of 1935 basically serving as their respective constitutions for the time being—had a number of obvious advantages: power could be transferred quickly without waiting for the newly independent countries to complete their new constitutions; India would remain within the Commonwealth, at least to start with;[1] British civil and military officers already in India would readily volunteer to assist the new administrations for the desired period; and above all it was a plan which was being sponsored by the Viceroy with the consent of the principal Indian parties. Mountbatten, therefore, had no difficulty in obtaining the approval of the British Government to the new proposals.

He was also able to win Churchill's enthusiastic support and a promise that the opposition would help to rush the necessary legislation through. Churchill authorized him to give Jinnah a curt message: 'This is a matter

---

[1] It was hoped that if transitional Dominion Status worked well, it might continue as a permanent arrangement.

Republican India was ultimately accommodated within the Commonwealth by modifying the basis of Commonwealth membership. According to a declaration made by the prime ministers of all the Commonwealth countries, including India and Pakistan, on 27 April 1949, the basic bond between the member states was no longer to be 'common allegiance to the Crown' but the acceptance of the King [not the Crown] as a '[mere] symbol' of the free association of the members 'and as such the Head of the Commonwealth'. In his book, *The Commonwealth*, Patrick Gordon Walker, Secretary of State for Commonwealth Relations at the time, has revealed that this formula had been first suggested by Foreign Minister Zafrulla Khan of Pakistan.

When Pakistan framed a republican constitution in 1956, it too continued its membership of the Commonwealth.

of life and death for Pakistan, if you do not accept this offer with both hands.'

In India the *Times of India* of 30 May, in a report dated 29 May, stated that 'since his return to New Delhi five days ago, Mr Gandhi has, every evening, at his prayer meeting, preached against "vivisection of the motherland" in terms disquietingly militant'. But at the Viceroy's Staff Meeting in New Delhi on 31 May, V. P. Menon said that it was Patel's opinion that not too much account should be taken of the recent utterances of Mr Gandhi in favour of a united India.

As already arranged, Mountbatten presented the new plan to the Indian leaders for their acceptance on 2 June. Those invited were Nehru, Patel and Kripalani as representatives of Congress; Jinnah, Liaquat and Nishtar as representatives of the Muslim League; and Baldev Singh as the representative of the Sikhs. In his introductory remarks, Mountbatten specially drew the attention of the Indian leaders to paragraph 20, under the heading of 'Immediate Transfer of Power', and reminded them that they had always impressed upon him that the transfer of power should take place with the utmost speed. It would be advantageous if transfer took place 'not only before June 1948, but also as long before that date as possible'. Prime Minister Attlee had given orders that the necessary legislation should be given top priority and the law officers of the Crown had set to work at once. He went on to explain that the statement which His Majesty's Government would issue was the same as had been seen by the Indian leaders except for small drafting alterations for clarification, and he distributed copies of the statement to those present. He asked the leaders to take the copies to their Working Committees and to let him know by midnight that night what those Committees thought of it.

The Congress leaders prophesied that their Working Committee would be in favour of acceptance and promised to let Mountbatten have their views in writing that night. Jinnah said that the Muslim League Working Committee would not be able to commit themselves without prior reference to the All-India Muslim League Council. He undertook to convene the Council in a week's time but when pressed, promised verbally to give Mountbatten the reaction of the Working Committee that night. Mountbatten informed the meeting that he intended to make a broadcast over All-India Radio on the following evening and persuaded Nehru, Jinnah and Baldev Singh to do the same after him.

Jinnah called on the Viceroy at 11 p.m. on 2 June and said he would support the proposals personally and do his utmost to have them accepted. His Working Committee was hopeful that the plan would be accepted by the All-India Council of the Muslim League. To Mountbatten's question whether he would be justified in advising Attlee to go ahead and make the statement, Jinnah firmly replied 'yes'. But, still apprehensive of what Jinnah might say at the leader's meeting on the following day, Mountbatten requested him simply to nod his head in assent when he (Mountbatten) declared that he felt satisfied with the assurances given. Jinnah agreed to do so and duly nodded his head at the proper moment.

The Congress President's letter was received by the Viceroy at 0015 hours on 3 June. It stated that the Congress Working Committee was prepared to accept the plan and recommend it to the All-India Congress Committee for acceptance 'in order to achieve a final settlement'. At the same time, it was made clear that Congress believed in a united India as fully as ever and hoped that 'when present passions subsided' a 'willing union of all parts of India will take place'. With regard to the proposed referendum in the North-West Frontier Province, the Congress President requested that the choice should include 'independence'.

Baldev Singh's letter arrived on the morning of 3 June. He accepted the principle of division as laid down in the plan but hoped that the Boundary Commission would be instructed to take note not only of the factor of Muslim-majority and non-Muslim-majority geographical areas, but also of 'other factors' such as the amount of property owned by non-Muslims and the amount of land revenue paid by them, and the location of Sikh cultural institutions.

When Mountbatten's meeting with the Indian leaders re-convened on 3 June, he said he had been happy on receiving the reports from the party leaders and concluded with the observation that the plan represented 'as near 100% agreement as it was possible to get'. He asked those present at the meeting to request their subordinate leaders to refrain from speeches which might produce violent reactions. Liaquat said there should be a request for restraint on the part of 'super-leaders' as well. He complained that many of Gandhi's speeches at his prayer meetings could be taken as an inducement to violence. Kripalani and Patel sprang to Gandhi's defence. Sensing trouble, Mountbatten diverted everyone's attention by throwing on the table copies of a lengthy paper prepared by his staff entitled, 'The Administrative Consequences of Partition'. 'The severe shock that this gave to everyone present,' he recounted in his Personal Report, 'would have been amusing if it was not rather tragic'. Evidently the political leaders had not until then realized the enormity of the administrative problems awaiting them in the wake of the decision to partition the country.

THE PLAN OF 3 JUNE 1947

The statement of the British Government was made by Attlee in the House of Commons and by the Earl of Listowel in the House of Lords at 3.30 p.m. Double British Summer Time on 3 June 1947. It stated that the British Government had always desired to transfer power in accordance with the wishes of the Indian people themselves but the Indian political parties had not been able to agree how this could be done. 'In the absence of such an agreement the task of devising a method by which the wishes of the Indian people can be ascertained has devolved on His Majesty's Government'; hence the plan set out in the statement.

The existing Constituent Assembly would continue to function but any constitution framed by it could not apply to those parts of the country which were unwilling to accept it. The procedure outlined in the statement was designed to ascertain the wishes of such unwilling parts on the question whether their constitution was to be framed by the existing Constituent Assembly or by a new and separate Constituent Assembly.[1] After this had been done, it would be possible to determine the authority or authorities to whom power should be transferred.

The Provincial Legislative Assemblies of Bengal and the Punjab (excluding the European members) will therefore each be asked to meet in two parts, one representing the Muslim majority districts and the other the rest of the Province.

The members of the two parts of each Legislative Assembly sitting separately will be empowered to vote whether or not the Province should be partitioned. If a simple majority of either part decides in favour of partition, division will take place and arrangements will be made accordingly.

For the immediate purpose of deciding on the issue of partition, the members of the Legislative Assemblies of Bengal and the Punjab will sit in two parts according to Muslim majority districts (as laid down in the Appendix) and non-Muslim majority districts. This is only a preliminary step of a purely temporary nature as it is evident that for the purposes of final partition of these Provinces a detailed investigation of boundary questions will be needed; and, as soon as a decision involving partition has been taken for either Province, a Boundary Commission will be set up by the Governor-General, the membership and terms of reference of which will be settled in consultation with those concerned.

---

[1] This in effect meant that they were to choose whether they wished to join India or Pakistan.

It will be instructed to demarcate the boundaries of the two parts of the Punjab on the basis of ascertaining the contiguous majority areas of Muslims and non-Muslims. It will also be instructed to take into account other factors. Similar instructions will be given to the Bengal Boundary Commission. Until the report of a Boundary Commission has been put into effect, the provisional boundaries indicated in the Appendix will be used.

The Legislative Assembly of Sind was similarly authorised to decide at a special meeting whether that province wished to participate in the existing Constituent Assembly or to join a new one. If it was decided to partition the Punjab, a referendum would be held in the North-West Frontier Province 'of the electors of the present [provincial] Legislative Assembly' to choose which Constituent Assembly they wished to join. The referendum would be held 'under the aegis of the Governor-General and in consultation with the provincial Government'.

Baluchistan would also be given an opportunity to reconsider its position and the Governor-General was examining how this could most appropriately be done.

Though Assam is predominantly a non-Muslim Province, the district of Sylhet which is contiguous to Bengal is predominately Muslim. There has been a demand that, in the event of the partition of Bengal, Sylhet should be amalgamated with the Muslim part of Bengal. Accordingly, if it is decided that Bengal should be partitioned, a referendum will be held in the Sylhet district, under the aegis of the Governor-General and in consultation with the Assam Provincial Government, to decide whether the district of Sylhet should continue to form part of the Assam Province or should be amalgamated with the new Province of Eastern Bengal, if that Province agrees. If the referendum results in favour of amalgamation with Eastern Bengal, a Boundary Commission with terms of reference similar to those for the Punjab and Bengal will be set up to demarcate the Muslim majority areas of Sylhet District and contiguous Muslim majority areas of adjoining districts, which will then be transferred to Eastern Bengal.

Agreements with tribes of the North-West Frontier of India will have to be negotiated by the appropriate successor authority.[1]

With regard to the princely States the statement made it clear that the policy 'contained in the Cabinet Mission Memorandum of 12th May 1946 remains unchanged'.

---

[1] Since the North-West Frontier Province in due course decided to join Pakistan, the 'appropriate successor authority' turned out to be Pakistan.

Paragraph 20 of the statement, under the heading, 'Immediate Transfer of Power', stated that His Majesty's Government agreed with the major political parties that there should be the earliest possible transfer of power in India and proposed 'to introduce legislation during the current session [of parliament] for the transfer of power this year [1947] on a Dominion Status basis to one or two successor authorities'.

Mountbatten made his broadcast on All-India Radio on 3 June precisely when Attlee and Listowel were presenting the plan to Parliament at Westminster (7 p.m. Indian Standard Time). He said that nothing he had seen or heard had shaken his 'firm' opinion that, with a reasonable measure of goodwill between the communities, a unified India would be 'by far' the best solution of the problem, but there could be no question of coercing any large areas in which one community had a majority to live against their will under a government in which another community had a majority. The only alternative to coercion was partition. He ended with the prayer: 'May your decisions be wisely guided and may they be carried out in the peaceful and friendly spirit of the Gandhi-Jinnah appeal.'[1]

The Viceroy's broadcast was followed by a reading of the Government Statement, and finally the leaders of the three principal Indian political parties came to the microphone and conveyed their acceptance of the plan in the following words:

NEHRU: ...It is with no joy in my heart that I commend these proposals to you, though I have no doubt in my mind that this is the right course. For generations we have dreamt and struggled for a free and independent united India. The proposals to allow certain parts to secede, if they so will, is painful for any of us to contemplate. Nevertheless, I am convinced that our present decision is the right one even from the larger viewpoint.

The united India that we have laboured for was not one of compulsion and coercion, but a free and willing association of a free people. It may be that in this way we shall reach that united India sooner than otherwise and that she will have a stronger and more secure foundation. We are little men serving great causes, but because the cause is great, something of that greatness falls upon us also...

JINNAH: ...It is for us to consider whether the plan as presented to us by His Majesty's Government should be accepted by us as a compromise or a settlement. On this point I do not wish to prejudge. The decision of the

[1] The reference was to the Gandhi-Jinnah appeal for communal peace made on 15 April 1947. See, pp. 494-5.

Council of the All India Muslim League which has been summoned to meet on Monday, 9th June, and its final decisions can only be taken by the conference according to our constitution precedents and practice.

But so far as I have been able to gather, on the whole, reaction in the Muslim League circles in Delhi has been hopeful...

BALDEV SINGH: ...It [the plan] does not please everybody, not the Sikh community, anyway. But it is certainly worthwhile. Let us take it...

In his broadcast Jinnah also called upon the Provincial Muslim League of the North-West Frontier Province to cease its campaign of civil disobedience because it had been decided to seek the mandate of the people there by a referendum. On the morning of 4 June, the Viceroy addressed a press conference attended by some 3000 representatives of the Indian and world's Press. After making an opening address he fielded nearly a hundred questions. By all accounts it was a brilliant performance, showing his mastery of the subject and quick-wittedness.

In his opening remarks he said that he had been 'astounded' to discover that it was mainly at the request of the Sikhs themselves that Congress had passed the resolution asking for the partition of the Punjab[1] which would divide their community into two almost equal parts. He had spent a great deal of time in seeing whether there was any solution which would 'keep the Sikh community more together' but, not being a 'a miracle worker', had had not been able to find a solution to the problem.

With regard to the princely States, Mountbatten said, in answer to a question, that it would be his duty to hand back paramountcy to each of the States. After that they would be free agents to either enter the Constituent Assembly or make other arrangements as they deemed necessary, but they would not be able to 'enter the Commonwealth separately as Dominions'.

It was during the press conference that Mountbatten publicly stated that the transfer of power could take place on 'about 15 August' 1947. He had in fact realized within a few days of his arrival in India that the explosive situation demanded that power should be transferred as early as possible. At a Miscellaneous Meeting on 10 May 1947, at which Nehru and V. P. Menon were present, he had expressed the hope that the target date of June 1948 could be brought forward 'by almost a year'. In the paper on 'The Administrative Consequences of Partition' which he had distributed at his meeting with the Indian leaders on 3 June, it had been stated that it was his intention that

---

[1] *See*, pp.479-80 for the Congress Working Committee resolution of 8 March.

the Act setting up the two Dominions of India and Pakistan should be 'brought into operation at the earliest possible date after its enactment, in any case not later than 15 August 1947'. At his meeting with the Members of the States on the same day he again mentioned 15 August as the date on which power should be demitted. But the last word on the subject was had by Indian astrologers, whom nobody dared to contradict. They ruled that 15 August would be inauspicious but conceded that 14 August would be lucky and a compromise was worked out. The Indian Constituent Assembly was summoned to meet late on the evening of 14 August so that it could take over power as the parliament of independent India at the stroke of midnight.

After the press conference Mountbatten learnt that Gandhi was proposing to criticise the plan for the transfer of power at his prayer meeting that evening. He immediately sent a message to the Mahatma to come and see him at any time before the prayer meeting. Gandhi arrived at 6 p.m. with the prayer meeting due at 7 p.m. Mountbatten told him that he shared his upset feelings that India would be divided and reminded him that he had worked hard to avoid that decision, but when no agreement could be reached he had followed the Gandhi principle of avoiding coercion or violence. Gandhi was mollified and at the prayer meeting declared: 'The British Government is not responsible for partition. The Viceroy has no hand in it. In fact he is as opposed to division as Congress itself but, if both of us...Hindus and Muslims...cannot agree on anything else, then the Viceroy is left with no choice.'

The Council of the All-India Muslim League met at Delhi on 10 June and stated in its resolution that, although it could not agree to the partition of Bengal and the Punjab or give its consent to such partition, it had to consider the plan for the transfer of power as a whole. It gave full authority to Jinnah 'to accept the fundamental principles of the plan as a compromise' and left it to him to work out the details.

The All-India Congress Committee convened in Delhi on 14 June and endorsed the 3 June plan. However, it expressed the hope that India would be reunited one day: 'The AICC earnestly trusts that when the present passions have subsided, India's problems will be viewed in their proper perspective and the false doctrine of two nations in India will be discredited and discarded by all.' Gandhi urged the Committee to accept the plan. If at that stage the AICC rejected it, what would the world think, he argued; all the parties had accepted it and it would not be proper for Congress to go back on its word.

All the main political parties had thus accepted the plan, 'but acceptance was one thing; its implementation was a different matter altogether,' commented V. P. Menon. 'Here was a task which normally should have taken years to accomplish but which had to be compressed into the short space of a few weeks! It was a task before which anybody would have quailed, for it was one which seemed verily to tempt the Gods.'

THE CONSTITUTIONAL AND LEGAL FORMALITIES OF PARTITION AND INDEPENDENCE

When Mountbatten and Jinnah welcomed Suhrawardy's conception of a united and independent Bengal on 26 April 1947, Mountbatten was hopeful of obtaining London's approval to 'Plan Balkan', which permitted the provinces to decide their own fate. But after the Viceroy, Congress and the Muslim League had all accepted that British India should be divided into only two dominions, the independence of Bengal or of any other province was no longer a feasible aspiration.

When Mieville had asked Nehru on 27 May how he viewed the proposal of an independent Bengal, 'he reacted strongly and said there was no chance of Hindus there agreeing to put themselves under permanent' Muslim domination'.

Gandhi, on the other hand, told Shyamprasad Mukerjee, the Hindu Mahasabha leader, on 13 May that he favoured an independent undivided Bengal because 'repudiation of the two-nation theory in action by the Muslim League, with Jinnah's concurrence as consent, would leave nothing of the Pakistan plan based on that theory'. But after Jinnah had agreed to the revised plan, that British India be divided into only the two Dominions of India and Pakistan, the Bengal Provincial Muslim League adopted a resolution on 28 May stating that it 'stood firmly with the Muslim League's demand for Pakistan'. On the same day, the General Secretary of the All-India Congress Committee also issued a statement repudiating the formula for a united sovereign Bengal.

On 8 June Gandhi wrote to Sarat Bose that he had discussed the matter with Nehru and Patel and had found both of them 'dead against the proposal'. The dream of a united Bengal thus faded away.

The Bengal Legislative Assembly met on 20 June and voted in accordance with the procedure laid down in the 3 June 1947 plan. As a result, the province was divided into West Bengal, which would join India, and East Bengal, which would join Pakistan. The proceedings in the Punjab Assembly on 23 June similarly resulted in the partition of that province into East Punjab and West Punjab, which would join India and Pakistan respectively. On 26 June the Sind Legislative assembly too, opted for Pakistan.

In the case of Baluchistan, the Viceroy decided that the future of the province should be decided by the *Shahi Jirga*, excluding the Sardars of Kalat State but including, for this purpose, the non-official members of Quetta Municipality; they voted to join Pakistan.

In Sylhet, the referendum went in favour of Pakistan : 239,619 persons voted in favour of joining Pakistan and 184,914 against.

The referendum in the North-West Frontier Province had a complicated background. Mountbatten was at first in favour of holding a fresh election to ascertain the will of the people, and said so in his meeting with Khan Sahib and his cabinet colleagues at Peshawar on 28 April. But because of the recent growth in the popularity of the Muslim League, Khan Sahib feared that he might lose the election, and with it his premiership, if the issue before the voters was simply whether they wished to join India or Pakistan. He therefore came out with the alternative that the Frontier Province should have the choice of becoming independent under the name Pathanistan. In this he had Gandhi's support. Campbell-Johnson, who was present at the meeting on 28 April, has recorded that Khan Sahib raised the question of Pathanistan, a concept in which 'Gandhi has for some time been actively interested'. But the examination of the subject did not proceed far because 'the discussion became somewhat disjointed and explosive'.

The available evidence, however, makes it clear that the cry for independence was a ploy ultimately to secure the adherence of the province to India. In a letter to the Secretary of State on 3 June, Mountbatten wrote: 'There has been a growing demand in the Province for independence and subsequent decision on their relation with the rest of India... Nehru spoke about Khan Sahib wishing to join the Union of India at a subsequent stage'. And Abdul Ghaffar Khan wrote to Gandhi on 8 June: 'We are also against Pakistan and would like to have a free Pathan State within India'.

Congress had supported Khan Sahib in his opposition to fresh elections. In a letter dated 1 May, Mountbatten informed the Secretary of State that Nehru had made it clear that 'Congress will refuse to take part in the election as a strong gesture of their disapproval'. And, as already stated, the only amendment of substance which the Attlee government had made to 'Plan Balkan' was to substitute a referendum for fresh elections in the

Frontier Province.'[1] The 3 June plan had retained this provision and limited the choice to joining India or Pakistan, as was the case everywhere else.

Strangely enough, the acceptance of the 3 June plan did not deter Congress from supporting the Khan brothers in their agitation for a referendum in their province which would include independence as a third choice. As already mentioned, the very letter of the Congress President accepting the 3 June plan contained this request.[2] Mountbatten had to remind Nehru in an interview on 5 June that it had been at Nehru's own request that the choice of independence for the provinces had been removed to avoid 'Balkanisation' and 'expressed surprise that he should have been a party to such a manoeuvre'. Mountbatten's remostration had its effect. Soon afterwards, in his correspondence with Gandhi, Nehru stoutly defended the decision to hold a referendum in the Frontier Province. The facts of that episode were as follows.

In a letter to the Viceroy on 8 May, Gandhi had protested that a 'referendum at this stage in the Frontier (or any province for that matter) is a dangerous thing'. On 7 June he similarly protested to Nehru about his agreeing to the holding of a referendum. Nehru wrote back that the question of referendum was a settled fact and to boycott it would be a 'a very dangerous procedure to follow,' because 'to give up without a struggle means a certain lack of integrity through fear of consequences and leads to the collapse of the organisation which was unable to face the issue.'

Abdul Ghaffar Khan, however, persisted in his attitude that unless the choice included the option of independence, his party would not participate in the referendum[3]. In a statement issued on 24 June he declared that limiting the choice to the two alternatives of India or Pakistan 'makes it a communal question, and people will be confused by this communal approach. We do not want to encourage communalism in our province.' Gandhi offered him the following consolation in a letter on 5 July: 'Boycott would certainly result in a legal victory for Pakistanis but it

---

[1] Jinnah had originally favoured fresh elections but agreed to a referendum when Mountbatten pointed out that a referendum would abolish the heavy weightage (12 seats in a house of 50) which the small Hindu-Sikh minority enjoyed in the Assembly of the North-West Frontier Province.

[2] See, p. 507.

[3] Interestingly, the Afghan Minister in London in a note dated 13 June had also protested that 'the referendum which is being arranged for the North-West Frontier Province is not compatible with justice as it debars the province from choosing either to form a separate free State or join its motherland Afghanistan'.

would be a moral defeat, if without the slightest fear of violence from your side, the bulk of the Pathans refrained in a dignified manner from participating in the referendum.'

When the referendum was conducted, from 6 to 17 July, 289,244 votes were cast for Pakistan and 2,874 for India. The total electorate entitled to vote in the referendum was 572,798; the vote for Pakistan, therefore, was 50.49%. In his Personal Report dated 25 July 1947, Mountbatten commented:

> It is particularly satisfactory that over 50% of the total electorate voted for joining Pakistan (and the total votes cast were only 15% less than last time without a boycott), as that disposes of any possible argument on the Congress side that, in spite of the boycott, the Province was not really in favour of joining Pakistan.

In deference to Congress wishes, Caroe had been replaced as Governor by General Rob Lockhart, and the referendum had been conducted by Brigadier J. B. Booth as Referendum Commissioner, assisted by British officers of the Indian Army. Liaquat had represented to Mountbatten on 11 June that the Khan Sahib ministry should also be dismissed because there was 'a much greater likelihood of the Ministers abusing their powers than the Governor', but the Congress ministry was allowed to function until it was finally dismissed on 21 August 1947 by Jinnah as Governor-General of Pakistan.

Thus each of the territories which were to comprise Pakistan—East Bengal, Sylhet, West Punjab, Sind, Baluchistan and the North-West Frontier Province—had positively signified its wish to form a part of Pakistan.

His Majesty's Government lost no time in providing the legal framework for giving effect to the political decision that power should be transferred to two independent countries. The draft bill, which later became the Indian Independence Act, 1947, was shown to the Indian leaders by Mountbatten, and their comments were taken into account before Attlee presented it to the House of Commons on 4 July. It was passed by that House on 15 July and by the House of Lords on the following day. It received the Royal Assent on 18 July.

The Act ordained that as from the fifteenth day of August 1947 'two independent Dominions shall be set up in India, to be known respectively as India and Pakistan'. The words 'India Imperator' and 'Emperor of India' were to be omitted from the Royal Style and Titles of the King of

England. Each of the new Dominions was to have a Governor-General and the same person could be the Governor-General of both the new Dominions.

The Constituent Assembly of each Dominion was to function as the legislature as well as the constitution-making body of the Dominion. The legislature of each of the new Dominions would have full authority to make laws for that Dominion and no law passed by it would be void on the ground that it was repugnant to the laws of England or the provisions of any existing or future Act of Parliament of the United Kingdom. The Government of India Act, 1935, suitably modified and adapted, would remain in force in the two Dominions until superseded by the new constitutions.

The Governor-General was to make provision for the division of the Indian armed forces between the new Dominions and for the command of those forces until the division was completed.

The districts which were 'provisionally' included in the new provinces of East Bengal and West Pakistan were named but the actual demarcation of the boundaries was to conform to the 'Award' of the boundary commissions 'appointed or to be appointed' by the Governor-General. The 'Award' was defined as the 'decisions of the chairman contained in his report to the Governor-General'.

The suzerainty of His Majesty over the Indian States was to lapse on 15 August 1947.

During the debate on the Indian Independence Bill in parliament, both the Government and the opposition spokesmen expressed their unhappiness that India had to be divided. Prime Minister Attlee declared, 'For myself, I earnestly hope that this severance may not endure and that the two new Dominions which we now propose to set up may, in course of time, come together again to form one great member State of the British Commonwealth of Nations.' Opposition leader Harold Macmillan echoed these sentiments: 'We must hope with the Prime Minister that in this partition are also the seeds of some form of future unity.'

CHAPTER 23

THE TRANSFER OF POWER

THE PROCESS OF PARTITION

The period between 3 June 1947, when the plan for the transfer of power was announced, and 15 August, when the two new Dominions were to receive power, was only 72 days. As a dramatic daily reminder to the officials engaged in partition work, Mountbatten caused to be placed on the desk of each one of them a tear-off calender displaying the number of days left till 15 August.

For Pakistan, the process and consequences of partition posed far more serious problems than for India. The Government of India would continue to function at Delhi much as before, while Pakistan would have to start *ab initio* at a new capital; India was better off in terms of the number of officers and staff at its disposal; having been designated the successor state to the outgoing administration,[1] India took over all the existing diplomatic and trade missions abroad; the systems of currency and banking, and of railways and other communications, had been organized on an all-India basis and were controlled from Delhi, which was also the headquarters of the army, navy and air force; all ordnance factories and most military store depots, and almost all the commercial and industrial centres, were located in India; and the Central Government records and archives were stored in Delhi.

THE PARTITION COMMITTEE

After the announcement of the 3 June plan, a Partition Committee of the Cabinet was set up. It consisted of Patel and Rajendra Prasad representing Congress, and Liaquat and Abdur Rab Nishtar representing the Muslim League, with Mountbatten as the chairman. The Committee was only a fact-finding body; it could make proposals but could not take final decisions. Its first meeting took place on 13 June and it was agreed to set

---

[1] As will be discussed later.

up a Steering Committee as well as ten expert Sub-Committees consisting of officials.

H. M. Patel, a member of the Indian Civil Service, represented India, and Chaudhri Muhammad Ali, a member of the Indian Audit and Accounts Service, represented Pakistan on the Steering Committee which made recommendations to the Partition Committee. The expert Sub-Committees were assisted by Departmental Committees (for example, the sub-Committee for Assets and Liabilities had twenty-one Departmental Committees).

Patel and Muhammad Ali won universal praise for their business-like give-and-take, but at the political level, the negotiations sometimes got heated.

A meeting of the Partition Committee on 26 June illustrates the difficulty of reaching a decision on the division of even ordinary assets, as well as Mountbatten's resourcefulness in preventing a dispute from getting out of hand. Liaquat Ali Khan requested that one of the six printing presses belonging to the Government of India should be allotted to Pakistan and moved to Pakistan's proposed capital, Karachi. Patel immediately flared up and said none of the six presses could be spared by India. When Mountbatten appealed to him to release at least one press to Pakistan he replied 'no one asked Pakistan to secede'. Mountbatten later discussed the matter with Patel privately and was able to obtain his agreement that Pakistan could have the use of a press forthwith provided it was not moved and was used by Pakistan only until a new press had been set up at Karachi. Mountbatten undertook to send a telegram to London urging that the highest priority should be given to the transport of a press to Karachi. He sent the promised telegram on 27 June; Listowel replied on 4 July that the government had no power to direct manufacturers to give priority to such a demand but promised to use 'pressure and persuasion to accelerate manufacture and shipment [of the press]'.

THE PARTITION COUNCIL

After a decision on partition became known (i.e., immediately any one province had voted in favour of partition[1]), the Partition Committee was raised to the status of Partition Council which had the power to reach final decisions. To enable Jinnah to participate, its membership was no longer restricted to members of the Interim Government. Congress continued to be represented by Patel and Prasad with Rajagopalachari as alternate

[1] This happened on 20 June 1947, when the Legislative Assembly of Bengal so voted.

member, while the Muslim League was represented by Jinnah and Liaquat with Nishtar as alternate member. Mountbatten, of course, continued as chairman. The Council held its first meeting on 27 June.

Perhaps two of the most remarkable meetings of the Partition Council were those which took place on 30 June and 22 July 1947. At the meeting on 30 June, the scheme for the partition of the armed forces was agreed to by everyone without a hitch. This was chiefly due to the efforts of C. M. Trivedi, Governor of Orissa, who had been called to Delhi to help in formulating the plans for the reconstitution of the armed forces. He had been Secretary of the Defence Department during the war and was the only Indian who had any experience of high-level defence organization. Fortunately, he not only enjoyed the confidence of the Congress leaders but was also a personal friend of Liaquat Ali Khan. 'In eight days' hard work,' wrote a much relieved Mountbatten in his Personal Report dated 4 July, 'he [Trivedi] was able to obtain concessions from the leaders and lobby the final paper so successfully that the Partition Council meeting itself went off more smoothly than any meeting I have ever seen.'

Those present at the Partition Council Meeting on 22 July were: Mountbatten (in the chair); for the future government of India, Patel and Rajendra Prasad; for the future government of Pakistan, Jinnah and Liaquat; and for the Sikhs, Baldev Singh.[1]

The Council issued a declaration that both the future governments were determined to establish peaceful conditions for the completion of partition; that after partition the minorities would be fairly and equitably treated; that the legitimate interests of all citizens would be safeguarded; and that there would be no discrimination against those who, before 15 August, might have been political opponents. Both governments also 'pledged themselves to accept the awards of the Boundary Commissions, whatever these may be'.

To safeguard the peace in the Punjab during the period of change-over to the new conditions, both governments agreed on the setting up of a Special Military Command[2] under Major-General T.W. Rees, with Brigadier D. S. Brar (India) and Colonel Ayub Khan[3] (Pakistan) as his

---

[1] Baldev Singh was not a regular member of the Partition Council and attended this meeting by special invitation because of the nature of the questions discussed. For the threat of disorder from the Sikhs, *see,* the section on Law and Order.

[2] Which generally came to be called The Punjab Boundary Force. For a further account of the Boundary Force, *see,* the section on Law and Order.

[3] Ayub Khan became Commander-in-Chief of the Pakistan army in 1951 and was President of Pakistan from 1958 to 1969.

advisers. The Command would cover twelve civil districts of the Punjab[1]. After 15 August, Rees would 'control operationally the forces of both the new States in this area and...be responsible through the Supreme Commander and the Joint Defence Council to the two Governments'. It was added that a similar force would be set up in Bengal should it be considered necessary.

The assurances held out by the leaders of all the three important communities in their joint declaration meant that they contemplated no transfer of population and wished the minorities to stay on in their traditional homelands.

THE ARBITRAL TRIBUNAL

The need for a machinery for giving decisions on those matters relating to the division of assets and liabilities on which the two governments could not agree was felt by both sides. Accordingly, an Arbitral Tribunal was set up with effect from 14 August 1947, and the end of March was fixed as the target date for the completion of its work. The Tribunal consisted of one representative each of India and Pakistan, with Sir Patrick Spens as chairman. Sir Patrick resigned from his office as Chief Justice of India to take up the new position and undertook to accept no other appointment in India afterwards.

DIVISION OF THE ARMED FORCES

Attlee's directive to Mountbatten had been to impress upon the Indian leaders the importance of avoiding any breach in the continuity of the Indian Army and of maintaining the organization of defence on an all-India basis.[2] Moreover, British officers like Ismay, who had served in the Indian Army in the past, and like Auchinleck, who were still serving in it, were emotionally averse to the division of the Indian armed forces. In his Memoirs, Ismay recalled that he had done his 'utmost' to persuade Jinnah to reconsider the decision to divide the Indian Army: 'I asked him to remember that an army was not merely a collection of men with rifles and bayonets and guns and tanks; it was a living entity, with one brain, one heart and one set of organs.'

But to Jinnah the concept of one army for two sovereign states was

---

[1] These districts which were named in the statement of the Council were twelve of the total of fourteen districts which one or other party claimed to be 'disputed'.

[2] See, p. 471.

totally unacceptable, especially when it was predominantly non-Muslim.[1] In his meeting with Mountbatten on 7 April 1947, he demanded that the defence forces must be separated. Mountbatten drew Jinnah's attention to a recent statement by some Indian officers that it would be a minimum of five years before the Indian Army could stand on its own feet without the help of British officers, and asked him whether he seriously considered that 'the miracle of cutting the army into half' could be performed by June 1948. Jinnah 'smiled in a cryptic way' and said, 'How then do you propose to leave in June 1948; is it then your intention to turn this country over to chaos and bloodshed and civil war?'

Jinnah's oral representation about the division of the armed forces was followed on the same day by a formal letter from Liaquat to Mountbatten. 'The division of India', Liaquat argued, 'implies the division of the armed forces to serve Pakistan and Hindustan. Without its own armed forces Pakistan would be like a house of cards.'

Mountbatten wrote back on 9 April that the issue of the partition of India had yet to be decided and, 'in any case, so long as I am Viceroy, I consider it my duty to ensure that no steps are taken which will weaken the Indian Army as the ultimate resource on which the country depends for maintaining internal security as well as external defence. I could not agree to splitting up the Army while Parliament is responsible for India.'

Auchinleck presented his views in an *aide-memoire* to the Defence Minister on 20 April:

> The Armed Forces of India, as they now stand, cannot be split up into two parts each of which will form a self-contained Armed Force...The formation of two separated Armed Forces is not just a matter of redistributing certain classes of men. It is a matter of the greatest complexity and difficulty, not only in the preliminary planning stages but also, and more particularly, in the practical means of bringing any such plan into being.

> Any such drastic reorganization would have to be carried out in stages over a period of several years, and during this period there would be no cohesive Armed Force capable of dealing with any serious defensive operations on the North-West Frontier.

---

[1] By the end of the war the strength of the Indian armed forces had risen to over two million, making it the greatest voluntary force in the world, and the number of Indian army officers had risen to 15,740, though only two or three of them had reached the rank of brigadier. Auchinleck informed Mountbatten in an interview on 14 April 1947 that the proportion of Muslims in the army was 29% and that 'most of the senior officers were Hindus, as the Muslim senior officers had, for one reason or another, faded out'.

But at a meeting of the 'Defence Committee India' on 25 April 1947, Liaquat, while conceding that the final decision to partition the armed forces had to await the political decision to partition the country, insisted that there must be a plan in readiness to go ahead if Pakistan was accepted. Mountbatten conceded that 'there must be a plan because when Pakistan was announced it would be imperative at once to let the armed forces know where they stood, and to reassure them that preparations for their separation were in a hand'. The Committee directed the Commander-in-Chief 'to think out (a) the personnel of the small high level committee he should set up, and (b) the broad outline of the problems it will have to tackle if the decision taken involves separation...' The division of the army was thus accepted in principle, though planning at that stage was to be in broad outline only.

Once the partition of the country had been decided, it was no longer possible to delay the actual reconstruction of the armed forces, and after the usual spadework, a plan was approved by the Partition Council in its meeting of 30 June, as already mentioned.

An Armed Forces Reconstitution Committee of officials was immediately set up, with Auchinleck as chairman, to work out the details of the division of the armed forces.

It was recognized that, from 15 August 1947, India and Pakistan should each have under its control forces predominantly non-Muslim and Muslim, respectively. The process of reconstitution would be in two stages. First there would be a 'rough and ready division of the armed forces on a communal basis...The next stage would be to comb out the units themselves on the basis of voluntary transfer [i.e., each man was to be given the right of choosing whether he will serve India or Pakistan].

For the time being, the Indian Armed Forces as a whole would remain under the control of the existing Commander-in-Chief in India, but with effect from 15 August 1947, a Joint Defence Council for India and Pakistan was to be set up to remain in existence till 1 April 1948, unless its existence was extended by the Governors-General of India and Pakistan[1] acting jointly. The Council was to consist of the Governor-General of

---

[1] *See*, the section on the Governor-Generalships of Indian and Pakistan. On 2 July 1947, Jinnah told Mountbatten that he himself would be the first Governor-General of Pakistan, which meant that Mountbatten from 15 August would be Governor-General of India only. The order setting up the Joint Defence Council was promulgated on 11 August, by which time it was known that with effect from 15 August 1947, Mountbatten would be Governor-General of India and Jinnah of Pakistan.

India (i.e.Mountbatten)[1], the Defence Ministers of India and Pakistan and the Supreme Commander (Auchinleck was designated Supreme Commander from 15 August). The Joint Defence Council was to be 'in exclusive control' of the division of the armed forces and their equipment and stores. The Supreme Commander was to have operational control only over units in transit from one Dominion to the other.

Once the decision to reconstitute the forces had been taken, Auchinleck, Ismay, and other British officers who had been unahappy at the thought of the division, exerted themselves loyally to accomplish the task. Both India and Pakistan appointed British officers as heads of their respective armies, navies and air forces. For the post of Commander-in-Chief they selected General Sir Rob Lockhart and General Sir Frank Messervy, respectively.

Though the separation of the personnel of the armed forces was completed satisfactorily, Pakistan suffered badly in the matter of the division of equipment and stores, because the Indians managed to get rid of the Supreme Commander prematurely.

On 26 September, Mountbatten wrote to Auchinleck 'probably the most difficult letter that I have even written':

...Scarcely had the new set-up come into force, when a volume of criticism started, not only in the papers (which I managed to get stopped) but in the Cabinet itself...One of the most balanced and level-headed Ministers complained recently that you seemed to regard yourself as the champion of Pakistan's interests; such is the reward of strict impartiality![2]

The only 'way out of the dilemma' which Mountbatten could see was for Auchinleck himself to write a letter to Mountbatten proposing the winding up of the Supreme Headquarters. He concluded the letter by saying that at his recommendation the Prime Minister had agreed to recommend his [Auchinleck's] name for a barony.

Auchinleck decided not to accept the peerage but saw no alternative to writing the required letter and did so on 6 October, recommending that the Supreme Commander and his headquarters should disappear on 30 November 1947 instead of closing on the original date of 1 April 1948.

In a report written on 28 September for the Prime Minister and other authorities in London, Auchinleck said:

[1] Jinnah had agreed that Mountbatten should be the chairman of the Joint Defence Council.

[2] John Connell, *Auchinleck*, p. 916.

I have no hesitation whatever in affirming that the present India Cabinet are implacably determined to do all in their power to prevent the establishment of the Dominion of Pakistan on a firm basis... If we are removed, there is no hope at all of any just division of assets in the shape of movable stores belonging to the former Indian Army.

The attitude of Pakistan, on the other hand, has been reasonable and co-operative throughout. This is natural in the circumstances, as Pakistan has practically nothing of her own and must obtain most of what she wants from the reserves of stores, etc., now lying in India.[1]

Auchinleck's proposal to shut down his Headquarters on 30 November came up before the meeting of the Joint Defence Council at Lahore on 16 October. Mountbatten was in the chair. India was represented by Baldev Singh and Gopalaswami Ayyenger, and Pakistan by Liaquat Ali Khan. When the Indians 'smoothly hinted that the division of stores and equipment was a routine matter to be settled between the two dominions themselves,' Liaquat said, 'the division of stores is not a minor but a major matter. An army without equipment is as much use as tin soldiers.' But with Auchinleck himself no longer willing to stay on, Liaquat's efforts to save the Supreme Commander's headquarters were of no avail; it had to close down on 30 November 1947.

RECONSTITUTION OF THE INTERIM GOVERNMENT

The reconstruction of the Interim Government was one of the most difficult problems which Mountbatten had to solve. In his Personal Report dated 27 June 1947 he wrote:

As there are only seven weeks left before partition I had hoped that all parties would be content to continue working with the present Interim Government under the standstill arrangements to which all parties had agreed. But it appears that Nehru, who is becoming more and more temperamental through overwork, protested that this would be a breach of faith in that I had agreed to obtain His Majesty's Government's consent to giving the Congress Party complete control over their own area whilst giving the League adequate safeguards for Pakistan areas. He apparently informed his Working Committee that he would resign forthwith unless this arrangement were honoured, and there was a danger of other Congress leaders following his example and my being left without a responsible Congress Government.

[1] John Connell, op. cit., pp. 920-2.

When Mountbatten told Jinnah that he planned to call for the resignations of all members of the central government, and ask the leaders of each of the two parties to nominate their own future governments, Jinnah said that the Governor-General had no authority to do so, and later (29 June) sent a note arguing that the proposed action would be illegal under the Act of 1935 which was still in force. He insisted that the question be referred to His Majesty's Government for decision.

Mountbatten, having forwarded Jinnah's views to London, received a telegram from Attlee on 3 July which conceded that the Viceroy's plan 'could be challenged', and promised that Clause 9 of the Independence Bill would be amended to give the Governor-General the necessary authority to proceed as he desired. Clause 9 (1) (e) of the Indian Independence Act accordingly read:

> The Governor-General shall by order make such provision as appears to him to be necessary or expedient for authorising the carrying on of the business of the Governor-General in Council between the passing of this Act and the appointed day [15 August] otherwise than in accordance with the provisions in that behalf of the Ninth Schedule to the Government of India Act, 1935.

Thus armed, Mountbatten was able to issue the following communique on 19 July 1947:

1. In order to facilitate the setting up of the new administration of Pakistan His Excellency the Viceroy has decided with the concurrence of the party leaders that the Interim Government should be reconstituted on the following lines:

2. The Government will consist of two groups representing the two successor Governments of India and Pakistan.

3. The two groups will meet separately to consider matters concerning their own territories, and jointly under the chairmanship of the Governor-General to consider matters of common concern.

4. The existing Departments will be manned by the staff who have elected to remain in India, and will be in charge of the Members representing India. The personnel who have chosen to serve in Pakistan will be withdrawn from the existing Departments, and will staff Departments which will be organized at once in Delhi, and will be in charge of the Pakistan Members of the Cabinet.

5. There will thus be what amounts to two provisional Governments, one for

India and one for Pakistan, each dealing with its own business and consulting the other on matters of common concern.

On 7 August, Jinnah left India for good and flew to Karachi, where the Constituent Assembly of Pakistan commenced its existence on 11 August.

COMPENSATION TO THE SERVICES

The question of payment of compensation to members of the Secretary of State's Services for the premature termination of their service due to the transfer of power had been under consideration before Mountbatten took office in India. On 30 April 1947, the Viceroy was able to announce the terms of the grant of compensation to members of the Civil Services appointed by the Secretary of State, and to Regular officers and British Warrant Officers of the Indian Naval and Military Forces.

A distinction was made between Europeans and Indian members of the Secretary of State's Services. The former would no longer be serving under the ultimate control of the British parliament while the latter would continue to serve their own country on the same terms as before. The entitlement to compensation of the Indian officers, therefore, was limited to such as :

1. are not invited to continue to serve under the Government of India after transfer of power; or

2. can satisfy the Governor-General that their actions in the course of duty during their service prior to the transfer of power have damaged their prospects, or that the appointments offered to them are such as cannot be regarded as satisfactory in the altered circumstances; or

3. can show to the satisfaction of the Governor-General that they have legitimate cause for anxiety about their future in the Province where they are now serving, and that no suitable transfer can be arranged.

The Government of India agreed to pay the pensions due under the normal conditions of service; compensation was paid by the British Government.

Though the Government of India offered the same pay and terms of service to those officers who continued to serve under it, most European officers preferred to take compensation[1] and retire.

THE INTERNATIONAL STATUS OF
THE TWO NEW DOMINIONS

Nehru argued that Hindustan would automatically succeed to the position of India as an international entity. The seceding parts constituting Pakistan would have to build up their own government. Jinnah insisted that it was not a question of secession, but of division—two new states were being created, neither of which could claim to be the successor of India in the international sphere and each of which would therefore have to secure recognition separately as a member of the family of nations.

The British Government upheld Nehru's contention and set out their views in a telegram which Listowel sent to Mountbatten on 5 July 1947:

> The question of international status of the two new Dominions is not one which will be finally determined by terms of this Bill. It is a matter for members of UNO and other foreign States as much as for HMG in the UK. Our own view is that the new Dominion of India continues the international personality of existing India and that she will succeed as a matter of international law to the membership of UNO which the existing India enjoys as an original signatory of the San Francisco Charter. Similarly, representatives of the Dominion of India will, in our view, be entitled to membership of existing international organisations and specialised agencies in which India has hitherto participated.

This opinion was endorsed by Dr Ivan Kerno, Assistant Secretary-General of the United Nations, who prepared a memorandum on the subject on 12 August 1947, with the approval of the Secretary-General of the United Nations.

This enabled Mountbatten to promulgate the Indian Independence (International Arrangements) Order, 1947, of 14 August 1947 which read as follows:

1.   The international rights and obligations to which India is entitled and subject immediately before the 15th day of August, 1947, will devolve in accordance with the provisions of this agreement.

2.(1) Membership of all international organisations together with the rights and obligations attaching to such membership, will devolve solely upon

---

[1] The lump sum granted as compensation was in addition to the regular pension earned by service.

the Dominion of India...

(2) The Dominion of Pakistan will take such steps as may be necessary to apply for membership of such international organisations as it chooses to join.

3. (1) Rights and obligations under international agreements having an exclusive territorial application to an area comprised in the Dominion of India will devolve upon that Dominion.

(2) Rights and obligations under international agreements having an exclusive territorial application to an area comprised in the Dominion of Pakistan [for example the tribal area of the North-West Frontier] will devolve upon that Dominion.

4. Subject to Articles 2 and 3 of this agreement, rights and obligations under all international agreements to which India is a party immediately before the appointed day will devolve both upon the Dominion of India and upon the Dominion of Pakistan, and will, if necessary, be apportioned between the two Dominions.

As a matter of fact Nehru, who had held the portfolio of External Affairs since the inauguration of the Interim Government in September 1946, had begun to advance the interests of India long before it was even decided whether there would be such a country as Pakistan. He had been permitted by the British Government to function virtually as if he were the Foreign Minister of an independent country. 'We shall take full part in international conferences,' he had said, 'as a free nation with our own policy and not merely as a satellite of another nation.'

Nehru sent an Indian delegation to the autumn 1946 session of the General Assembly under the leadership of his sister, Vijaya Lakshmi Pandit. Pakistan could not show up in the United Nations arena till a year afterwards.

At a staff meeting on 9 May 1947, Mountbatten said that he had agreed with Nehru that the latter 'should now go ahead with appointing representatives to foreign countries without consulting the Muslim League. Pakistan, when formed, could either appoint their own, share his, or share the British representatives.'

Indian ambassadors to the more important countries were accredited even before India legally became independent. The Indian High Commissioner in the United Kingdom, hitherto principally concerned with trade and administrative matters, assumed full diplomatic functions in September 1946; Asaf Ali presented his letter of credence to Truman in

Washington on 1 March 1947, and Mrs Pandit to Shvernik in Moscow on 13 August 1947. For Pakistan, Habib Rahimtoola did not arrive in London as High Commissioner till the middle of August 1947; M. A. H. Ispahani presented his credentials in Washington on 8 October 1947, and Shoaib Qureshi in Moscow on 13 December 1949.

When the date of the constitutional independence of India and Pakistan (15 August 1947) arrived, the Indian Ministry for External Affairs simply continued to function as it had already done for nearly a year. Nehru literally kept sitting in the same chair as Foreign Minister which he had occupied as vice-president of the Viceroy's Council. It was not until August 1947 that the Pakistani Foreign Office at Karachi was set up amid utter turmoil with practically no available resources in men and material. 'I shall never forget', recalls Vincent Sheean, 'that when I first visited the new establishment...there was only one typewriter in the whole Foreign Office.'[1]

THE GOVERNOR-GENERALSHIPS OF INDIA AND PAKISTAN

We have already mentioned that it was on 17 May that Mountbatten first raised with Jinnah the question of a common Governor-General between Pakistan and India and that Jinnah had said that he would prefer separate Governors-General for the two countries and would like Mountbatten to occupy the position of a Crown Representative for the division of assets between the two new dominions.[2]

Mountbatten left for London on 18 May to obtain the approval of the British Government for his revised plan for the transfer of power, and returned from there on 30 May. Thereafter he tried to get an answer from Jinnah on the matter of the Governor-Generalship, but the latter always put off giving an answer. Finally, Jinnah said he could not let Mountbatten know until he had seen the Indian Independence Bill. After he had seen the Bill, he still did not wish to answer till he had consulted two of his colleagues who were away at the referendums in the North-West Frontier Province and Sylhet.

Nevertheless, Mountbatten and his advisers had convinced themselves that in the end Jinnah would accept a common Governor-General. At the staff meeting on 9 June Mountbatten had said, 'Pakistan would be the Dominion which would gain most advantages if he [Mountbatten] stayed behind as Governor-General of both Dominions. In fact, if he has

---

[1] Vincent Sheean, *Nehru*, p. 93.
[2] *See,* pp. 504-5.

his own separate Governor-General, Mr Jinnah might well wreck his prospects'. During an interview with Mountbatten on 23 June, Jinnah had said that whatever decision he reached would not be taken on grounds of not wanting the Viceroy, in whom he had implicit trust and confidence, but the rule of his life was that he must always consider the interests of his people; at various times of his career he had had to pass over those nearest and dearest to him. But Mountbatten's optimistic conviction that Jinnah ultimately would have to accept him as Governor-General of Pakistan was not shaken.

For Mountbatten personally, of course, a request from both Dominions to become their Governor-General would have been the crowning glory. His name would have been enshrined in history for all time, as the statesman with the magic touch who had not only achieved the impossible, by solving the dreaded India-Pakistan problem with the consent of Congress and the Muslim League, but who, at the same time, had attained the unthinkable by winning in equal measure the trust of both these historical foes.

Mountbatten was utterly taken aback when Jinnah at last told him on 2 July that he himself would be Pakistan's Governor-General.[1] The Muslim League leader explained that he wished to have British Governors in every province of Pakistan except Sind which, since it would be under his personal supervision in Karachi, could have a Muslim Governor. He pointed out, further, that he had also agreed to the three heads of the Pakistani Defence Services being British, and concluded by saying that the only way in which he could sell the idea of all these British officials would be to become the Governor-General of Pakistan himself. He pressed Mountbatten to remain as Governor-General of India.

All Mountbatten's efforts to move the Quaid-e-Azam from his resolve to become Governor-General of Pakistan were in vain. When Mountbatten threatened, 'Do you realise what this will cost you?' Jinnah said sadly, 'It may cost me several crores of rupees in assets,' to which Mountbatten replied, 'It may well cost you the whole of your assets and the future of Pakistan,' and left the room.

---

[1] At an interview with Jinnah on 24 July 1947, Ismay complained that the 'eleventh hour announcement' by Jinnah that he himself would assume the Governor-Generalship of Pakistan had 'put the Viceroy in an extremely awakward position'. But Jinnah 'kept on reiterating that he had never given the Viceroy the slightest grounds for believing that he would agree to a common Governor-General and that there seemed to be no object in pursuing the argument'.

In his telegram to Attlee on the following day, Mountbatten reported that he had spent another four hours trying to make Jinnah realize the advantages that Pakistan would gain from having the same Governor-General as India until partition was complete, and the Viceroy's Conference Paper, VCP 115, dated 5 July recorded: 'During the next twenty-four hours [after Jinnah had stated that he himself would be Governor-General of Pakistan] the Viceroy spent much time in pointing out to both Mr Jinnah and Mr Liaquat Ali Khan, and on one occasion to a meeting consisting of Mr Jinnah, Mr Liaquat Ali Khan, Mr Rahman and Mr Muhammad Ali, the enormous advantages that Pakistan would gain from sharing, for a short initial period, the same Governor-General as Hindustan.'

Having totally failed to convert Jinnah to his point of view, Mountbatten decided to send Ismay to London to seek 'higher guidance'.

Mountbatten not only felt greatly disappointed, but also deeply embarrassed at what for him was an entirely unexpected development. At the staff meeting on 9 June he had observed that 'it was essential for the legislation which was going to be introduced, amending the Government of India Act to confer Dominion Status upon Hindustan and Pakistan, to include provision for the two Dominions to have the same man as Governor-General', and the Indian Independence Bill had been drafted on the assumption that there would be one Governor-General during a transitional period.[1] In his letter to Attlee dated 5 July, Mountbatten described Jinnah's announcement that he himself would be the Governor-General of Pakistan as a 'bombshell', and confessed that he considered 'the whole of this situation to be my fault. I should have foreseen it, and have cleared the position with both Jinnah and Congress one way or the other three or four weeks ago'. In a letter to his daughter Patricia on the same day he expressed himself even more dejectedly:

Your poor old Daddy has finally and irretrievably 'boobed' and I've now landed myself in a position from which I cannot conceivably extricate myself with honour. Either I accept to stay with the Dominion of India and be for ever accused of taking sides... or I let down the Congress leaders...Mummy feels I should preserve my reputation for impartiality and go on 15th August. The others feel I cannot let down Nehru and must stay. In both cases I'm in the wrong. In fact I've at last made a mess of things through over-confidence and over-tiredness. I'm just whacked and worn out and would really like to go.

I'm so depressed darling, because until this stupid mishandling of the Jinnah

---

[1] The Indian Independence Act had provided that 'the same person may be the Governor-General of both the new Dominions'.

situation I'd done so well. It has certainly taken me down many pegs.[1]

Ismay reached London on 7 July and saw Attlee for an hour on the same afternoon. A meeting of the India and Burma Committee of the Cabinet was convened in the evening and sat until nearly midnight. Early next morning , Attlee and Ismay met the principal opposition leaders and then Ismay went to see Churchill. In the afternoon, Ismay was received by the King. Everyone in London thought Mountbatten must remain as the Governor-General of the new India. On 8 July, Attlee telegraphed Mountbatten: 'I would ask you most earnestly to accept Governor-Generalship of India during the transition period. I believe this to be essential if transition is to go through smoothly.' Mountbatten replied on 9 July that under 'these special circumstances' he could not but agree to become Governor-General of India.

Those who wished Mountbatten to stay on as Governor-General of India had advanced the following arguments. First, if Mountbatten at this stage was to refuse India's invitation to be its Governor-General, the Congress leaders would feel that Jinnah had scored another triumph over them.[2] The Indians would feel 'as a lover scorned' and relations between Britain and India, which had improved so dramatically, would deteriorate. Secondly, Mountbatten's presence in India would mean that relations between India and Pakistan would stand a good chance of being friendly and the division of assets would proceed more smoothly. Thirdly, the British civil and military officers who had opted to serve India might have second thoughts if Mountbatten and his team left.[3] Fourthly, the princes would feel that without Mountbatten's help, they would not be able to get a square deal from Congress. It would appear that Jinnah's proposal for separate Governors-General for India and Pakistan and, in addition, a Crown Representative with arbitral jurisdiction over both countries, was never given the consideration it deserved. The common Governor-General would have been a constitutional functionary who would have been bound to follow the advice of each one of the two cabinets. What would he have done when these cabinets made diametrically opposite recommendations? He could have only mediated between them; he could not have overruled

---

[1] Philip Ziegler, *Mountbatten*, p. 398.

[2] In Ismay's colourful language, 'Congress would have been livid with Jinnah for having once more cooked their goose'.

[3] In Campbell-Johnson's words: 'From the point of view of British prestige it is a tremendous thing that Congress, at the moment of victory in its seventy years' struggle with the British, should go out of its way to invite Englishmen to stay on in this way.'

the party he believed to be in the wrong. The arbitrator on the other hand would have had all the opportunity to mediate that the joint Governor-General could have had, plus the authority in reserve to impose his decision on the recalcitrant party.

It is stated that 'Jinnah's idea of an "arbitrator" or "stake-holder" was put up verbally to representatives of the India Office for their opinion' and that 'they were unanimous that such a system would be unconstitutional and unworkable'.[1] But Jinnah was not alone in feeling that the situation called for the appointment of some person other than a constitutional Governor-General to help India and Pakistan resolve their differences. When Mountbatten saw Churchill during his visit to London in May, the latter suggested that if Mountbatten 'were appointed Governor-General of Hindustan and Governor-General of Pakistan...[he] might adopt the title of "Moderator".'[2] During his visit to London in July, Ismay reported to Mountbatten that at a meeting at which Attlee met the opposition leaders, the Liberal leader Lord Samuel 'was anxious to revive the idea of a Viceroy presiding over the two Governors-General, but the rest of the meeting turned this down as impracticable, probably unacceptable to Congress and too late'.[3]

The real reason why Jinnah's proposal was rejected seems to be that Mountbatten personally was averse to taking on the unpleasant task of trying to arbitrate between India and Pakistan. There was only one person at that time who could have dared to act as umpire between the two countries and that person was Mountbatten. Once he had indicated that he was unwilling to volunteer for the role, the matter so far as his Majesty's Government was concerned was at an end. We have Mountbatten's own words showing how thankless the position of an arbitrator seemed to him. In his Personal Report No. 8 dated 5 June 1947 he had written:

Both sides were still very anxious to obtain my services as arbitrator in all matters of dispute in working out the partition. But I pointed out that since both sides were already approaching the problem from such widely divergent points of view it was clear that I should have to give a decision which one side or the other side would dislike practically every day, and however much they now professed to believe in my impartiality, such a procedure could not fail to undermine their confidence in me within a very short time.[4]

---

[1] *Transfer of Power* XI, p. 916.
[2] *Transfer of Power* X, p. 946.
[3] *Transfer of Power* XII, p. 24.
[4] *Transfer of Power* XI, p. 164.

Pakistanis believe that Jinnah's decision against having a common
Governor-General 'had far-reaching effects. The loss that Pakistan would
incur in material assets was easy to foresee. But there were other intangible
factors, such as the accession of the States, the Kashmir question, and the
award of the Boundary Commission, in which the balance was tilted
against Pakistan with far more momentous consequences'.[1]

But what Jinnah's followers at that time needed most was a sense of
security, and their own Quaid-e-Azam's decision personally to become
the head of state of the country which he had done so much to create for
them provided just that. Even Mountbatten conceded that 'Jinnah had
scored an undoubted victory from the psychological point of view over
Congress in not having a "foreigner" as the first Governor-General of
Pakistan'.[2] Chaudhri Muhammad Ali correctly assessed that 'in the
struggle for survival that lay ahead, moral factors would count far more
than material losses'.

Jinnah's action may well have saved the infant state of Pakistan from
an early demise. India and other prophets of doom were predicting that
Pakistan was a mistake which history would soon rectify by returning it
to Greater India. During the debate on the Indian Independence Act, Attlee
as well as the Leader of the Opposition had expressed the hope that
partition would not endure.[3] Mountbatten himself had never made any
secret of his belief that the division of the subcontinent into two separate
states was a tragic ending to British rule there. In fact, he had devised a
strategy by which he hoped to recapture lost ground.

His instruments for turning defeat into victory were to be the common
Governor-Generalship and the joint Defence Council. This is clear from
what H. V. Hodson has written in his book, *The Great Divide*:

> ...it was still Lord Mountbatten's hope and resolve that a rudimentary Centre
> would survive partition, for defence and all that went with it. Two means were
> thought to assure this—a common Governor-Generalship for the initial period,
> an intention frustrated by Mr Jinnah, and the Joint Defence Council, which
> though operative for six months after the transfer of power was undermined in
> its general and long-term purpose by the enmity between the two Dominions
> after the Punjab troubles and the Kashmir conflict.[4]

---

[1] Chaudhri Muhammad Ali, *The Emergence of Pakistan*, p. 178.
[2] Mountbatten's *Report on the Last Viceroyalty* (submitted to His Majesty's Government in September 1948), IOR:L/P and J/5/396, p. 123.
[3] *See*, p. 517.
[4] H. V. Hodson, *The Great Divide*, p. 535. Hodson had been entrusted with 'all the papers'
Continued on next page

With regard to the Defence Council, Hodson has quoted from a letter which Mountbatten himself wrote to the King:

> My original idea had been that the Council should continue in its existing form for at least another year—and I secretly hoped for ever. It could carry on under my chairmanship (if both sides so wished) until I left, and then under the chairmanship of the Prime Minister of the Dominion in which each successive meeting took place. It was in my mind that its scope might indeed expand, to cover financial and economic matters also, and eventually External Affairs and Communications, which would mean the 'virtual accession' of the two Dominions to one another, on the same basis as the States.[1]

It needs little imagination to realize that such an 'accession' by unequals to each other would have spelled the end of Pakistan as a sovereign state and assured its absorption by India. This became precisely the fate of all the princely States, which had been persuaded to surrender only the three specified subjects of Defence, External Affairs and Communications, with unequivocal assurances that the terms of the Instrument of Accession would not be varied without the ruler's consent, and that his sovereignty in all other matters would remain intact.

THE RADCLIFFE BOUNDARY AWARDS[2]

Under the 3 June Plan, the Governor-General had been authorised in the event of partition to set up boundary commissions, the membership and terms of reference of which were to be settled 'in consultation with those concerned'. As a result of the Viceroy's discussions with the Indian leaders the following agreed steps were taken.

On 13 June it was decided:

    (i)   that each Boundary Commission should consist of an independent chairman and four other persons, of whom two should be nominated by Congress and two by the Muslim League;

Mountbatten had brought back from India, and Mountbatten also assisted him in writing the book by talking with him and finally reading the manuscript.

[1] Ibid., p. 512. At a meeting of the Joint Defence Council on 19 March 1948, Nehru and Liaquat decided that the Council should be closed down after that session.

[2] The difference between the provisional (alsod called notional) boundaries of Bengal and the Punjab as laid down in the First and Second Schedules of the Indian Independence Act 1947 and the boundaries as finally demarcated by Radcliffe is displayed in two maps at the end of Vol. XII of the *Transfer of Power* series.

(ii) that all these persons should, if possible, be of high judicial standing;

(iii) that Congress would include a Sikh in the two persons nominated by them for the Punjab Boundary Commission...

And on 30 June the Viceroy was able to issue the following Announcement :

(1)   There shall be two Boundary Commissions, one for Bengal and the other for the Punjab, consisting of the following [High Court judges]:-

For Bengal:-

Chairman ... To be appointed later.
Members ..... Mr Justice Bijan Kuman Mukherjee.   ) Nominees of
              Mr Justice C. C. Biswas.   ) Congress
              Mr Justice Abu Saleh
                  Mohammed Akram.   ) Nominees of the
              Mr Justice S. A. Rahman.   ) Muslim League

For the Punjab:-

Chairman ... To be appointed later.
Members ..... Mr Justice Din Muhammad.   ) Nominees of the
              Mr Justice Muhammad Munir.   ) Muslim League
              Mr Justice Mehr Chand Mahajan.   ) Nominees of
              Mr Justice Teja Singh.   ) Congress

(Note :- it is intended to appoint the same person as Chairman of both the Boundary Commissions.)

(2)   The two Boundary Commissions shall be summoned to meet as early as possible by the Governors of the respective Provinces, and shall submit their reports at the earliest possible date.

(3)   The terms of reference for the two Commissions shall be as follows:-

For Bengal:-

The Boundary Commission is instructed to demarcate the boundaries of the two parts of Bengal on the basis of ascertaining the contiguous majority areas of Muslims and non-Muslims. In doing so, it will also take into account other factors.

In the event of the referendum in the District of Sylhet resulting in favour of amalgamation with Eastern Bengal, the Boundary Commission will also demarcate the Muslim majority areas of Sylhet District and the contiguous Muslim Majority areas of the adjoining districts of Assam.

For the Punjab:-

The Boundary commission is instructed to demarcate the boundaries of
the two parts of the Punjab on the basis of ascertaining the contiguous
majority areas of Muslims and non-Muslims. In doing so it will also take
into account other factors.[1]

It will be noticed that the Boundary Commission of Sylhet was asked
simply to demarcate Muslim majority areas, while the Punjab and Bengal
Commissions were required not only to ascertain the contiguous majority
areas of Muslims and non-Muslims, but also to take into account 'other
factors'. In the event, Radcliffe and his colleagues on the Sylhet Commission
unanimously decided that it had been intended that they should take into
account other factors in respect of Sylhet as well.[2] 'Other factors' was an
elastic criterion and the manner of its application by Radcliffe in dividing
Bengal and the Punjab pleased none of the Indian parties.

Sir Cyril (later Viscount) Radcliffe, a leading member of the English
Bar, was appointed chairman of both the Commissions and he arrived in
India on 8 July. That Congress and Muslim League nominees on the
Commissions would not reach an agreed solution to any of the boundary
problems was a foregone conclusion. The Indian Independence Act,
therefore, laid down that 'award' in relation to a Boundary Commission
would mean the 'decisions' of the chairman contained in his report to the
Governor-General. Thus, in the end, the precise boundaries of the two new
dominions were determined solely by Radcliffe.

Since Pakistanis later alleged that Mountbatten was able to influence
Radcliffe to make awards which were partial to India, it is relevant to
examine the circumstances that led to Radcliffe's appointment as chairman
of both Boundary Commissions. A careful reading of the available
material on the subject reveals that the leading part in securing Radcliffe's
selection for that crucial position was played by Mountbatten himself,
who had known him during the war. To what extent, if any, that rendered
Radcliffe amenable to Mountbatten's persuasion can only be conjectured.

The story begins on 7 June 1947 when Mountbatten telegraphed
Secretary of State Listowel that he might have to ask him for a member of
the Judicial Committee of the Privy Council as chairman of the Arbitral
Tribunal.[3] After consulting the Lord Chancellor, Listowel replied that
members of the Judicial Committee of the Privy Council must be ruled out

---

[1] The terms of reference of both Commissions had been proposed by Congress.
[2] *Transfer of Power* XII, p. 755 (paragraph 7 of Radcliffe Report relating to Sylhet).
[3] *Transfer of Power* XI, p. 259, f.n. 1.

because of their age, and that the possibility of a High Court judge being made available had also to be ruled out because of pressure of work. An approach was, however, being made to Sir Cyril Radcliffe, who would 'fill the bill admirably.'[1]

Jinnah's interview with Mountbatten on 23 June is important for our purpose and it would be best to give Mountbatten's own version of what was said:[2]

> He [Jinnah] then said that he felt it would be impossible for both parties to agree upon the two Chairmen and he therefore suggested that a distinguished member of the Bar from England might come out as an independent Chairman for both Commissions and that his decision should be final. He should, in fact, act as an Umpire. It was suggested that in view of the fact that the Arbitral Tribunal in Mr Jinnah's opinion would not be functioning seriously for some time to come, whoever was appointed Chairman of that Tribunal (and the composition of the Tribunal has not yet been agreed to by Congress) might come out from England in the near future and act as Chairman of the two Boundary Commissions before taking over his duties with the Tribunal. He did not anticipate that the work of the Boundary Commission would last very long. The Viceroy told Mr Jinnah, in confidence, that the man who had been suggested as Chairman of the Arbitral Tribunal was Sir Cyril Radcliffe. Mr Jinnah, while saying that he would like a day or two to consider whether he thought Sir Cyril to be a suitable Chairman, knew of him and of the high reputation which he held at the Bar.[3]

It is not quite clear who 'suggested' that whoever was appointed chairman of the Arbitral Tribunal could first act as chairman of the two Boundary Commissions, but it seems that the suggestion was made by Mountbatten, basing it on Jinnah's view that the Arbitral Tribunal would not be functioning for some time to come. Be that as it may, two points are clear. First, that Radcliffe's name was first brought into the conversation by Mountbatten, not by Jinnah, and that Listowel had recommended Radcliffe as chairman of the Arbitral Tribunal only. But when the question was discussed at the Special Committee of the cabinet[4] on 26 June, Mountbatten stated that he had asked Listowel to propose suitable persons for appointment as chairmen of the Boundary Commissions and that the

---

[1] Ibid., p. 336.

[2] Mountbatten personally dictated the gist of what had been said at such interviews. *See,* p. 488.

[3] *Transfer of Power,* XI, p. 581.

[4] At which Jinnah was not present because he was not a member of the Interim Government.

540 THE BRITISH RAJ IN INDIA

Secretary of State had recommended Radcliffe.[1] He went on to say that if it proved difficult to find any other person he would suggest that Radcliffe might be considered for the chairmanship of both the Boundary Commissions. 'The idea generally appealed to the members and they agreed to consider it further' after Mountbatten had formally written to Patel and Liaquat setting out details of Radcliffe's experience and the terms on which he might be invited to come to India.[2]

On 27 June, Mountbatten wrote to Listowel that he was glad to hear from him of the possible appointment of Radcliffe [as chairman of the Arbitral Tribunal] and added, 'I saw a certain amount of him when he was Director-General at the Ministry of Information during the war and formed a high opinion of him.' He went on to inform the Secretary of State that Jinnah had 'suggested that Radcliffe, if he proves acceptable, might perhaps serve in the first instance as chairman of both Boundary Commissions'.[3]

On the same day he wrote in his Personal Report, 'At the first meeting of the Partition Council held today, Jinnah's proposal was accepted by Congress, namely that Sir Cyril Radcliffe should be appointed as the Chairman of both Boundary Commissions with a final casting vote.'[4] In the afternoon, he also sent a telegram to Listowel by name, and reported that at a meeting of the Partition Council that morning, 'it was agreed that one Englishman should be appointed Chairman of both [the Boundary] Commissions and the man whom they wanted was Radcliffe'.[5]

Upon arrival in New Delhi, Radcliffe stayed with Mountbatten for two days 'to get into the picture'. He was allotted the Comptroller's House in the viceregal estate where, in Campbell-Johnson's words, 'he could work in isolation'. H. C. Beaumont, a member of the Indian Civil Service, was appointed to serve him as secretary.

The Bengal Boundary Commission considered the question relating to the division of the province of Bengal separately from that relating to the future of Sylhet District and consequently produced two separate reports.[6]

---

[1] *Transfer of Power* XI, p. 655. Footnote 1 correctly points out that in fact in the Mountbatten-Listowel correspondence Radcliffe so far had been mentioned only as a possible chairman of the Arbitral Tribunal.

[2] No record is available of any such letters.

[3] *Transfer of Power*, XI, p. 678.

[4] Ibid., p. 682.

[5] Ibid., p. 708.

[6] Including the report of the Punjab Boundary Comission there were thus three reports in

___*Continued on next page*

The public sittings of the Commission relating to the Province of Bengal took place at Calcutta from 16 to 24 July, and those of the Punjab Boundary Commission at Lahore from 21 July to 31 July. Radcliffe visited Calcutta and Lahore, but in view of the fact that he was chairman of both commissions, whose proceedings were taking place simultaneously, he did not attend the public sittings but made arrangements to study daily the record of the proceedings and of all material submitted. After the close of the public sittings, Radcliffe held discussions with his colleagues on the Bengal Commission in Calcutta and with his colleagues on the Punjab Commission in Simla.

The open sittings of the Bengal Boundary Commission relating to Sylhet District and the areas adjoining took place at Calcutta from 4 to 6 August. Radcliffe did not attend the open sittings but kept himself informed daily and afterwards held discussions with his colleagues in New Delhi.

Since Mountbatten was later criticised for having increased the Indian death toll by deliberately delaying the disclosure of the Boundary Awards until 16 August, it is pertinent to note that when the question first arose, he displayed as much anxiety as Indian leaders that the awards should be made known as soon as possible. In his Personal Report on 27 June, Mountbatten wrote that Jinnah's proposal that Radcliffe should preside over both the Commissions was accepted by the Congress as it 'was considered to be the only way in which the boundaries could be definitely settled before the 15th August'.[1] Radcliffe was invited to the Viceroy's staff meeting on the very day of his arrival in New Delhi and Mountbatten 'emphasised the desirability of the work of the Boundary Commission being finished by 14th August'.[2]

On 10 July, Mountbatten informed the Partition Council that he 'had been assured by Sir Cyril Radcliffe that he will be able to submit his reports by the 14th August'.[3]

In his Personal Report to London dated 11 July, the Viceroy wrote:

Nehru, Jinnah and the Boundary Commissions have all agreed that the work should be completed by the 15th August and Sir Cyril Radcliffe has concurred. All are very pleased that the Bill will make the findings of the Boundary

---

all. Though they purported to be reports of the Boundary Commissions, they were in fact 'awards' by Radcliffe, as already explained.

[1] *The Transfer of Power* [henceforth TOP] XI, p. 682.
[2] TOP XII, p. 12.
[3] Ibid., p. 66.

Commissions an Award, since no party could contemplate with equanimity the riots which would break out if the boundaries remained indefinite on the day of the transfer of power.

Jenkins, Governor of the troubled province of the Punjab, was specially anxious to receive the report of the Boundary Commission as early as possible, so that the legitimate successor authorities could take charge of the disputed areas, deploy their own forces of law and order suitably, and also alert the Boundary Force. S. E. Abbott, his private secretary, wrote to the Viceroy's private secretary (Abell) on 16 July that the Governor had asked him 'to make a special request for as much advance intimation not only of the date of the award but also of its contents as can be given. Whatever the date and whatever Government will be in power when the award is announced, it will be necessary to take precautions, especially in those districts which are likely to be affected, particularly those in the Central Punjab.'

After a visit to Lahore, Mountbatten wrote to Radcliffe on 22 July that all parties there had 'emphasised that the risk of disorder would be greatly increased if the award had to be announced at the very last moment before the 15th August... I know that you fully appreciate this, but I promised tha I would mention it again to you, and say that we should all be grateful fo every extra day earlier that you could manage to get the award announced I wonder if there is any chance of getting it out by the 10th.'[1] Radclifft replied on the next day, 'I do not think that I could manage the 10th: bt I think that I can promise the 12th, and that I will do the earlier date if I possibly can.'[2] On 6 August, Mountbatten wrote to Jenkins, 'I have not forgotten your request that you should be given advance warning of the nature of the Boundary Commission's award, and I will try to secure this.'[3]

However, when at the Viceroy's staff meeting on 9 August it was stated that Radcliffe would be ready that evening to announce the award of the Punjab Boundary Commission, Mountbatten made an about-turn. He admitted that he had asked for the award to be ready by 10 August but said 'it was now for reconsideration whether it would in fact be desirable to publish it straight away. Without question, the earlier it was published the more the British would have to bear the responsibility for the disturbances which would undoubtedly result'. He emphasized the necessity for maintaining secrecy not only on the terms of the award but also on the fact

---

[1] Ibid., p. 290.
[2] Ibid., p. 305.
[3] Ibid., p. 557.

that it was ready that day.[1] It would appear that his prime consideration no longer was the saving of Indian lives; it now was the preservation of Britain's good name.

Altogether, the ninth of August was an eventful day. It was also on that day that Nehru had sent to Mountbatten a note by A. N. Khosla, a Hindu irrigation engineer, with the request that the same be forwarded to Radcliffe. In the note Khosla had written:

> The first headworks of this system [Sutlej valley canals] is at Ferozepore from which irrigation water is taken to Bikaner. The second headworks is at Sulaimanki, which is also in Ferozepore district. According to notional division both these headworks would fall in East Punjab. It however appears that Sir Cyril Radcliffe's mind may be working in the direction of giving Ferozepore and Zira *tahsils,* having a small Muslim majority east of the Sutlej, to Pakistan, in return for giving Gurdaspur and part of Lahore district to East Punjab. That will be disastrous from the point of view of East Punjab and Bikaner State from the irrigation point of view and disastrous to India as a whole from the strategic point of view, because the only line of defence, that is the Sutlej, will have been pierced by the bridge at Ferozepore and between this and Delhi there is no natural barrier.[2]

On the following day, Mountbatten wrote to Nehru that since he did not wish to do anything to prejudice the independence of the Boundary Commission, it would be wrong for him to forward any memorandum. But Pakistanis allege that Mountbatten did influence Radcliffe at Nehru's request. We will have more to say on this subject later. For the present we wish to mention two pieces of evidence.

The first is the following entry under 9 August in the diary of W. H. J. Christie, joint private secretary to the Viceroy:

> George [Abell] tells me HE is in a tired flap & is having to be strenuously dissuaded from asking Radcliffe to alter his award.[3]

The second is Hodson's statement that:

> At about the same time Lord Mountbatten had a private meeting with Sir Cyril

---

[1] Ibid., p. 611.
[2] Ibid., p. 619.
[3] MSS EUR. D 718/3.

Radcliffe to discuss the date on which the awards were to be announced...It took place in Lord Ismay's house on the viceregal estate in Delhi over an evening drink on or about 9 August.[1]

Given Mountbatten's state of mind as described by Christie, we leave it to the reader to judge whether, at the meeting with Radcliffe, he was content simply to discuss the timing of the disclosure of the awards and restrained himself from supporting the important request which had just been made by Nehru, who was not only his close personal friend, but was also the politician upon whose goodwill he depended the most for the success of his difficult mission in India.

On 10 August Mountbatten received a frantic message from Burrows, Governor of Bengal, which read: 'It is essential that we should have at least 24 hours' notice [of the award] for putting on the ground effectively our internal security arrangements in Calcutta on publication of awards.'[2]

On 11 August Ismay received a verbal protest from Liaquat to the effect that Gurdaspur or a large part of it had been given to East Punjab; that reportedly it was a political decision, not a judicial one; and that if true it was a grave injustice amounting to a breach of the faith on the part of the British. Ismay promptly wrote back that the Viceroy was determined to keep clear of the whole business and that he (Ismay) had been told that Radcliffe's report was not yet ready.

The twelfth of August was another eventful day. We possess three versions of the staff meeting and other developments on that day:

1. V. P. [Menon] showed a quite unexpected flare-up of communal bias when he heard about the C[hittagong] H[ill] T[racts]. HE most anxious to postpone publication till after 15th. Pug [Lord Ismay] against this for administrative reasons. HE adamant: sent Alan [Campbell-Johnson] and me [John Christie] to Sir CR[adcliffe] to arrange the dates. CR refused flat—too many people know it's ready. Stretched a point to redate 13th; will arrive complete after HE has gone to Karachi. Back to HE who had a couple. Didn't like it, but swallowed it.[3]

2. Mountbatten agreed...that John Christie and I [Campbell-Johnson] should call on Radcliffe immediately to find out when we might expect the Awards to be in the Viceroy's hands... He [Radcliffe] explained that both the Punjab

---

[1] H. V. Hodson, *The Great Divide*, pp. 351, 354.
[2] TOP XII, p. 646.
[3] Entry in Christie's diary under 12 August 1947, MSS EUR. D718/3.

and Bengal Awards were complete and ready, but that the Sylhet Award was not.

It seemed, therefore, that unless Mountbatten was to make a major issue of the matter, it would be physically very difficult for all three Awards to come into his possession before his return to Delhi on the evening of 14th August, or for the texts to be printed and available before the 16th—Independence Day itself being a national holiday. We returned at once to Viceroy's House and advised Mountbatten of the position, who was greatly relieved to have this ready-made solution at his disposal.[1]

3. The matter came to a head at the meeting which I held with members of my staff on the evening of 12th August. An advance copy of the Bengal Award had been seen by my staff, but I had deliberately refrained from reading it. I was told, however, that it allotted the Chittagong Hill Tracts to Pakistan. My Reforms Commissioner, Mr V. P. Menon, was present at the meeting and was able to warn us of the disastrous effect that this was likely to have on the Congress leaders.[2]

The Punjab and Bengal Awards bear the date 12 August and the Sylhet Award 13 August, but in view of the entry in Christie's diary quoted above, it must be taken that Radcliffe kept his promise and delivered all the three Awards on 13 August.

At the staff meeting on 12 August, Menon had warned that the allotment to Pakistan of the Chittagong Hill Tracts was certain to cause Nehru and Patel to 'blow up'. If the details of the award were given to them before 15 August, he went on to say, they might well refuse to attend the meeting of the Constituent Assembly which Mountbatten was to address, and if given to them later in the day they would refuse to come to the state banquet and the evening party. Mountbatten thereupon decided that 'somehow', the leaders must be prevented from knowing the details of the

---

[1] Campbell-Johnson, *Mission with Mountbatten,* p. 153. Mountbatten left for Karachi on the afternoon of 13 August to preside over the ceremony of the transfer of power to Pakistan and returned to Delhi on the afternoon of 14 August.

[2] *Report on the Last Viceroyalty*, submitted to HMG by Mountbatten in September 1948, IOR:L/P and J/5/396, p. 162, para 159. There seems to be no reason why the proposed Punjab Award also had not been seen by Mountbatten's staff; it had obviously been ready because Radcliffe had wished to announce it on 9 August. Nevertheless, Menon would have us believe that 'no one, not even Lord Mountbatten, had seen or read the Award' until copies were handed over to the leaders. Menon states that the Award was disclosed to the leaders on 17 August. (V. P. Menon, *The Transfer of Power in India,* p. 402.) In fact this was done on 16 August, as will be described anon.

awards until after 15 August; 'all our work and the hope of good Indo-
British relations on the day of the transfer of power would risk being
destroyed if we could not do this.'[1]

On 13 August Mountbatten therefore wrote to Nehru and Jinnah: 'I am
advised that Sir Cyril Radcliffe is sending me the Award of the Boundary
Commission in the course of today, but that it cannot arrive before I leave
for Karachi. At present, therefore, I have no idea of its contents.' He
proposed that there should be a meeting at Delhi on 16 August to decide
the timing and publication.[2] At the same time he directed the Governors
of the Punjab and Bengal that on 15 August the successor governments
should be given charge up to the 'notional' boundaries.[3] He claimed
afterwards that he had examined the awards only on his return from
Karachi on 14 August.[4]

Before leaving for Karachi on 13 August, Mountbatten received an
angry letter from Patel in which he stated that a deputation of the
Chittagong Hill Tribes had seen him that morning and expressed their
grave apprehension that their area was going to be included in East Bengal
under the Boundary Commission Award. He had told them that the
proposition was so monstrous that if that should happen they would be
justified in resisting it to the utmost of their power and could 'count on our
maximum support to such resistance'. No fair reading of the terms of
reference of the Boundary Commission, he argued, could make a ninety-
seven per cent non-Muslim area a part of Pakistani Bengal.[5] Mountbatten's
comments show how upset he was at Patel's outburst:

> From this [Patel's letter] it will be seen that the one man I had regarded as a real
> statesman with both feet firmly on the ground, and a man of honour whose word
> was his bond, had turned out to be as hysterical as the rest. Here he was
> suggesting that if indeed the Chittagong Hill Tracts were put into East Bengal
> the people would be justified in resisting this award by force and that the
> Central Government would be bound to support them! So much for his
> undertaking on behalf of India to accept and implement the awards whatever
> they might be.

---

[1] Viceroy's Personal Report dated 16 August 1947, TOP XII, p. 760. In this connection
he seems to have been unconcerned about the effect on Anglo-Pakistani relations.

[2] Ibid., p. 693.

[3] That is to say boundaries as had been provisionally laid down in the Indian Independence
Act.

[4] *Report on the Last Viceroyalty*, p. 163, para 164.

[5] TOP XII, p. 691.

The crazy part about all this is that Burrows [Governor of Bengal] had explained to me that the whole economic life of the people of the Hill Tracts depends upon East Bengal, that there are only one or two indifferent tracks through the jungle into Assam, and that it would be disastrous for the people themselves to be cut off from East Bengal. The population consists of less than a quarter of a million, nearly all tribesmen who, if they have any religion at all, are Buddhists (and so are technically non-Muslims, under the terms of the Boundary Commission). In a sense Chittagong, the only port of East Bengal, also depends upon the Hill Tracts; for if the jungles of the latter were subjected to unrestricted felling, I am told that Chittagong port would silt up. Candidly I was amazed that such a terrific crisis should have blown up over so small a matter. However, I have been long enough in India to realise that major crises are by no means confined to big matters.[1]

The meeting to consider the Awards duly convened at the Governor-General's house on the afternoon of 16 August (copies had been made available to the ministers three hours earlier). Besides Mountbatten, it was attended by Nehru, Patel, Baldev Singh, Liaquat and Fazlur Rahman.[2] Nehru protested against the allocation of the Chittagong Hill Tracts to East Bengal. Nehru and Baldev Singh said the Punjab Award would have a bad effect on the Sikh mind and Liaquat said that it would produce an equally unfavourable reaction among the Muslims. Patel expressed the view that the only solution to the Punjab Award was a transfer of population on a large scale.

'If', wrote Mountbatten in his Personal Report on the same day, 'it had not been so serious and rather tragic, their mutual indignation would have been amusing...It was only after they had been complaining loudly for some time they appeared to realise that there must be some advantages to them if the other parties were equally dissatisfied; and so after some two hours of very delicate handling, we arrived at the conclusion that the awards must be announced and implemented loyally forthwith...It is quite clear to me that if we had not brought the leaders together to hear each other's indignation and thus regain their sense of of porportion, we might have had as serious a blow-up as V. P. Menon feared.'

That Mountbatten's decision to delay the disclosure of the Punjab Boundary Award, which had been ready since the evening of 9 August, cost extra Punjabi lives, cannot be doubted, and Mountbatten's own earlier requests to Radcliffe to expedite his task and the urgent pleas of the

[1] Ibid., p. 761.
[2] Fazlur Rahman was an East Pakistani Muslim League leader who was a member of the Pakistani Cabinet.

Punjabi authorities for an early intimation of the contents of the Award make it evident that they all knew beforehand that that would be the case.

After the Awards had been published, Mountbatten conceded in his Personal Report that:

> From the purely administrative point of view, there were considerable advantages in immediate publication so that the new boundaries could take effect from 15th August, and the officials of the right Dominion could be in their places to look after the districts which had been allotted to their side before that date.

But he added: 'However, it had been clear all along that, the later we postponed publication, the less would the inevitable odium react upon the British'.[1]

It is not easy to defend Mountbatten's willingness to sacrifice Indian lives to reduce the amount of blame which was expected to attach to his own country. But his second reason for postponing the disclosure of the contents of the Boundary Awards until after the transfer of power—to avoid a political blow-up—made sense. The Congress as well as the Muslim League leaders were furious when copies of the Awards were provided to them on 16 August, but by then power had already been amicably transferred to them and Britain was cleanly out of the game. Had the information been revealed earlier, the Congress leaders may well have blown up, as predicted by Menon, and the Muslim League leaders could hardly have done less. The laboriously-contrived constitutional process for the orderly transfer of power would have been suddenly thrown out of gear just as it was on the point of fruition.

Congress criticism of the contents of the Radcliffe Awards in Bengal chiefly related to the allotment to Pakistan of the Chittagong Hill Tracts which we have already discussed. With regard to the Punjab Award, Congress echoed the Sikh feelings of disappointment. The Muslim League catalogue of grievances against the boundary decisions, however, was longer and more serious and calls for a fuller examination.

In Bengal, Pakistan had lost some Muslim-majority areas but had also gained some non-Muslim ones. The chief Pakistani criticism was the allotment of Calcutta to India. As an important industrial and commercial centre, Calcutta would have strengthened the economy of East Pakistan, and as a major seaport it would have provided an important sea-link between the two wings of Pakistan.

---

[1] TOP XII, p. 760.

In the Punjab 'other factors' had worked wholly to Pakistan's detriment. Some Muslim-majority areas, though contiguous to Pakistan, were given to India while no non-Muslim-majority territory was made over to Pakistan.

Pakistanis allege that the real culprit was not Radcliffe, but Mountbatten, who was basically anti-Pakistan and was especially incensed because Jinnah had frustrated his ambition to be the Governor-General of both India and Pakistan. It was Mountbatten, they say, who went to the extent of making Radcliffe change in India's favour the Awards he had already decided to announce.

That Radcliffe should have consulted Mountbatten and his staff was but natural. He had never visited India before and there is no suggestion anywhere that he knew much about Indian history, geography and politics, and he was required to complete his intricate assignment hurriedly at the height of the gruelling Indian summer.[1] After their appointment as members of the Boundary Commissions, his colleagues were judges in name only. In fact, they had become advocates of the respective parties who had nominated them. Where could Radcliffe turn to for enlightenment except to the Viceroy and his staff? We can cite two instances in which members of Mountbatten's secretariat did discuss boundary questions with Radcliffe.

The first is Menon's own admission at the staff meeting on 28 July, the minutes of which read: 'Menon said that he had suggested to Sir Cyril Radcliffe the possibility that Nankana Sahib might be made a sort of Vatican.'[2] The second is an entry in Christie's diary under 25 July: 'Dined with Ismay. Cyril Radcliffe and Christopher Beaumont were there... I gave C.R. [Cyril Radcliffe] a thumbnail sketch of the CHT [Chittagong Hill Tracts], which is going to be a problem (with map).'[3]

We have already mentioned Mountbatten's meeting with Radcliffe over an evening drink at Ismay's house on 9 August. There must have been numerous other such social occasions at which Mountbatten and his staff met Radcliffe and talked shop as officials are wont to do.

---

[1] In a conversation with Mosley, Radcliffe recalled later, 'After a few days of it [the Punjab summer heat], I seriously began to wonder whether I would come out of it alive. I have thought ever since that the greatest achievement which I made as Chairman of the Boundary Commission was a physical one, in surviving.' Leonard Mosley, *The Last Days of the British Raj*, p. 197.

[2] TOP XII, p. 377. Nankana Sahib is the birth-place of Guru Nanak, the founder of the Sikh religion. It is located in the territory which Radcliffe later awarded to Pakistani Punjab.

[3] MSS. EUR.D 718/3.

Had Mountbatten and all his staff been impartial, no one could have justifiably criticised Radcliffe for having consulted them. They would have been regarded as his only reliable source of information and advice in India. The trouble arose from the fact that Mountbatten was decidedly pro-Congress, and the adviser on his staff who influenced him the most was V. P. Menon, a Hindu close to Patel.

Radcliffe's final reports were bound to dissatisfy the Congress as well as the Muslim League leaders. He could hardly afford to alienate the Viceroy as well. Even prudence demanded that he should show his drafts to those who were more familiar with the highly controversial subject than he was.

We have already noted Mountbatten's own admission that 'an advance copy of the Bengal Award had been seen by my staff'.[1] Then we have the following note which Philip Noel-Baker, Secretary of State for Commonwealth Relations, addressed to Prime Minister Attlee on 26 February 1948, when the Kashmir dispute was being discussed in the United Nations and it was feared that Zafrulla Khan might allege that Mountbatten had caused Radcliffe to make his award in terms which would facilitate Kashmir's accession to India:

> Mr Henderson[2] states that Sir Cyril Radcliffe told him that he showed the first draft of the proposed Award to the authorities in Delhi, and that on further consideration he made the Award in terms which departed from the first draft, but he did not attempt to elicit from Sir Cyril Radcliffe at the time whether the departure from the first draft had been suggested to him from any quarter.[3]

Specifically, Pakistanis allege that Calcutta was made over to India as a part of a deal which Mountbatten had made with Congress behind the Muslim League's back. They draw attention to a public speech by Patel at Calcutta on 15 January 1950 in the course of which he said, 'We made a condition that we would only agree to partition if we did not lose Calcutta'[4], and conclude that such a condition could have been made only with Mountbatten.

Chaudhri Muhammad Ali puts Pakistan's claim to Calcutta as follows:

> In the city of Calcutta itself, Muslims formed only a quarter of the population,

---

[1] *See*, version 3 at p. 545. If Radcliffe had shown an advance copy of the Bengal Award to Mountbatten's staff, why would he not also show them the Punjab Award?
[2] Parliamentary Under-Secretary of State for India at the relevant time.
[3] PREM 8/821.
[4] *The Hindu*, 16 January 1950.

but the hinterland, on which the life of Calcutta as a city and port depended and of which it formed an integral part, was a Muslim majority area. Calcutta had been built mainly by the resources of East Bengal, which also provided the bulk of its seamen and port workers. Pakistan had, therefore, a strong claim upon Calcutta and its environs, even on a demographic basis. There was also another important factor working in favour of the Muslim claim to Calcutta. A large section of Calcutta's population consisted of Scheduled Castes who were allied with the Muslim League both in provincial and all-India politics... If a free plebiscite to determine whether Calcutta should go to India or Pakistan had been held in Calcutta, it was likely that the result would have been a victory for Pakistan.[1]

The forecast that a plebiscite in Calcutta could have gone in favour of Pakistan was not without foundation. At the staff meeting on 25 April 1947, Mountbatten

...considered it highly probable that the Muslims would demand a plebiscite for Calcutta and the areas immediately surrounding that city. He understood that the population thereof was composed of a quarter Muslim, a quarter Caste Hindus and the remaining half Scheduled Caste Hindus and other minorities. He believed that both Mr Jinnah and Mr Liaquat Ali Khan thought that the Muslim League would win a plebiscite in the Calcutta area...the avowed intention of referring the choice of their future to the Indian people themselves was that a completely fair answer should be obtained. It would be most undesirable to lay down a procedure of self-determination which would give the wrong answer.[2]

But the British view that Calcutta would have to be allotted to India did not originate with Mountbatten. During his interview with the Cabinet Mission on 16 April 1946, Jinnah demanded to know the reason why Calcutta could not be given to Pakistan and was told by Secretary of State Pethick-Lawrence that 'what the delegation were doing was seeking for a basis of agreement. They did not think that agreement could be reached on the basis that Calcutta was included in Pakistan.'[3]

At the end of May 1947, Suhrawardy pleaded with Mountbatten that Calcutta be put under the joint control of Congress and the Muslim League during the period while partition was actually taking place. Mountbatten sent Menon to obtain Patel's agreement to six months'

[1] Chaudhri Muhammad Ali, *The Emergence of Pakistan*, p. 207.
[2] TOP X, p. 415.
[3] TOP VII, p. 283.

joint control of Calcutta. Patel's reply was very firm: 'Not even for six hours'.[1]

Thus, although Mountbatten's opportunities and capacity to influence Radcliffe are not in doubt, in the particular case of Calcutta it was not because of him that that important city became a part of India; it happened because the British Government had been aware since the time of the Cabinet Mission that Congress would angrily reject the partition plan altogether if Calcutta was given to Pakistan.

However, Pakistani grievances with regard to the Punjab Boundary Award have real substance. The most bitter criticism is directed against the grant to India of those important areas in Gurdaspur and Ferozepore districts which had Muslim majorities and were contiguous to Pakistan.

Chaudhri Muhammad Ali explains how Pakistan suffered from the way in which Radcliffe divided the district of Gurdaspur:

> The district had four *tahsils* of which only one, Pathankot, had a non-Muslim majority; the other three, Gurdaspur, Batala, and Shakargarh, had Muslim majorities. The district as a whole had a bare Muslim majority, but that was largely because of the high percentage of Hindus in Pathankot *tahsil*. Gurdaspur district was contiguous to the state of Jammu and Kashmir. For the Indian Union, rail and road communication with the state was only possible through the plains of this district that was flanked by high mountains in Indian territory to the east. If Radcliffe had awarded India only the non-Muslim-majority *tahsil*, Pathankot, India would still not have gained access to Jammu and Kashmir, since the Muslim-majority *tahsils*, Batala and Gurdaspur, to the south would have blocked the way. By assigning these two Muslim-majority *tahsils* also to India, Radcliffe provided India with a link to the state of Jammu and Kashmir and paved the way for the bitterest dispute between India and Pakistan.[2]

Indian manoeuvres to deprive Pakistan of Gurdaspur also go back to the Cabinet Mission days. The initiators were two Hindus in key positions in the Government of India: the ubiquitous V. P. Menon, and Sir B. N. Rau, a former judge of the Bengal High Court and Prime Minister of Kashmir and at this time on special duty in the Governor-General's secretariat. In response to a request from the Viceroy's private secretary, Menon on 23 January 1946 forwarded his own and Rau's joint 'suggestions for demarcation of the Pakistan areas'. The part relating to Gurdaspur read:

[1] *Report on the Last Viceroyalty*, p. 80, para. 28.
[2] Chaudhri Muhammad Ali, *The Emergence of Pakistan*, p. 215.

The Sikh objection in the Western Zone can be met, to some extent, by excluding the districts of Amritsar and Gurdaspur from 'Pakistan'. These two form a compact block, whose total population is a little over 2.5 millions, of which a little under 1.25 millions—i.e., a little under 50 per cent, are Muslims. This form of partition will cut across existing Divisional boundaries, but has the advantage of meeting the most serious of the Sikh objections, though not all of them; for, wherever the line may be drawn, there will still be some Sikhs left on the wrong side. If the existing Lahore, Rawalpindi, and Multan Divisions are included in 'Pakistan', the number of Punjab Sikhs in 'Pakistan' would be about 2.2 millions and in 'Hindustan' about 1.5 millions; with the exclusion of the districts of Amritsar and Gurdaspur, the corresponding figures would be 1.5 millions and 2.2 millions, so that the majority of them would now fall in 'Hindustan', although a substantial minority would still be left in 'Pakistan'. On the whole the best plan would be to exclude these two districts from the Western Zone...[1]

British officialdom in India as well as in the UK readily fell for the cunning argument that the recommendation would help pacify the Sikhs. The Sikhs were the favourite 'martial race' of the British; they had rendered valuable services during the Great Rebellion of 1857 and the two world wars and had always formed a valuable part of the Indian army. And they were the ones who were going to suffer the most as the result of partition. The Hindus got Hindustan and the Muslims Pakistan. The Sikhs dreamed of Sikhistan but instead their community was going to be cut into two parts. Anything that would alleviate their plight was welcome and it was hoped that the proposed concession might even soothe their fury to some extent and reduce the amount of communal bloodshed.

That Amritsar should go to India because it is the sacred city of the Sikhs was understandable, but the assertion that Gurdaspur was inseparable from Amritsar because the two of them formed a 'compact bloc' was far-fetched. Nevertheless, it too, was swallowed.

On 29 January the Secretary of State for India, who was preparing to lead the Cabinet Mission to India, urgently telegraphed the Viceroy to let him have recommendations 'as regards definition of genuine Muslim areas if we are compelled to give a decision on this'.[2]

The Viceroy replied on 6 February:

In the Punjab the only Muslim-majority district that would not go into Pakistan under this demarcation is Gurdaspur (51% Muslim). Gurdaspur must go with Amritsar if the Sikhs must stay out of Pakistan. But for this special importance

---

[1] R/3/1/105.
[2] Ibid.

of Amritsar, demarcation in the Punjab could have been on divisional boundaries.[1]

When the Cabinet Mission interviewed Jinnah on 16 April 1946, he was told that 'agreement might perhaps be reached on a separate state of Pakistan consisting of, say, Sind, North-West Frontier Province, Baluchistan and the Muslim-majority districts of the Punjab except perhaps Gurdaspur'.[2]

It is not surprising that Mountbatten, who was pre-disposed to favour India, should have accepted the existing official position with regard to Gurdaspur with alacrity. During his press conference on 4 June 1947 he declared without hesitation that the Boundary Commission was unlikely to 'throw' the whole of Gurdaspur district 'into the Muslim majority areas' because the population of that district was 50.4 per cent Muslim and 49.6 per cent non-Muslim.[3]

In pressing this view upon Radcliffe, he was on strong ground—it was not his own opinion, it was a question already carefully considered and settled by the Governments of India and the United Kingdom.

Secretary of State Noel-Baker conceded in a note he sent to Prime Minister Attlee on 25 February 1948 that:

There is some reason for thinking that Sir Cyril Radcliffe at the last moment altered his boundary award so as to assign to the E. Punjab a salient in the original demarcation of the W. Punjab boundary which included Gurdaspur. But we have no knowledge that this was done on the advice of Lord Mountbatten.[4]

In refuting the allegation that Mountbatten persuaded Radcliffe to divide Gurdaspur in such a manner that India would obtain a land route to Kashmir, Hodson writes that the Kashmir frontier 'was not in anybody's mind at the time'.[5] But in fact it definitely was in the minds of three very important persons—V. P. Menon, Mountbatten and the Maharaja of Kashmir—all of them decidedly partial to India.

Menon prepared a brief for Mountbatten on 17 July for his talk with Abdur Rab Nishtar[6] and wrote in it:

[1] Ibid.
[2] TOP VII, p. 281.
[3] Nicholas Kaye, *Time Only to Look Forward*, p. 30.
[4] PREM 8/821.
[5] H. V. Hodson, *The Great Divide*, p. 355.
[6] TOP XII, p. 213. The newly created States Department had two ministers—Patel representing Congress and Nishtar representing Pakistan.

Kashmir presents some difficulty. It is claimed by both the Dominions, and at the present moment my feeling is that the issue should not be forced by either party. It is possible that a predominantly Muslim State like Kashmir cannot be kept away from Pakistan for long and we may leave this matter to find its natural solution. Unlike Hyderabad, it does not lie in the bosom of Pakistan and it can claim an exit to India, especially if a portion of the Gurdaspur district goes to East Punjab.

Mountbatten told the Nawab of Bhopal and the Maharaja of Indore, in an interview on 4 August 1947, that Kashmir 'was so placed geographically that it could join either Dominion, provided part of Gurdaspur were put into East Punjab by the Boundary Commission'.[1]

The Maharaja's wish for a land link with India is mentioned in Mountbatten's Personal Report of 16 August: 'He [the Maharaja of Kashmir] now talks of holding a referendum to decide whether to join Pakistan or India, provided that the Boundary Commission give him land communications between Kashmir and India.'[2]

Is it not possible that it was very much in Jawaharlal Nehru's mind as well?

Ziegler's defence that Mountbatten 'at the time was still engaged in trying to ensure that the Maharaja of Kashmir acceded to Pakistan'[3] and could not, therefore, have been interested in providing India with land communications with it, does not hold water when the two important items in Mountbatten's conversations with the Maharaja and Prime Minister Kak during his visit to Kashmir from 18 to 23 June 1947 are scrutinized. They have the appearance of a recommendation to join Pakistan. We will examine their true worth in the section on Kashmir in Chapter 24.

With regard to Ferozepore district, Pakistanis point out that the Ferozepore Headworks, except for the Bikaner Canal, irrigated mostly Muslim-majority areas in and contiguous to Pakistani Punjab, and they allege that in fact the Muslim-majority *tahsils* of Ferozepore and Zira, contiguous to Pakistan, were at first allotted by Radcliffe to Pakistan and were made over to India as the result of a last-minute intervention by Mountbatten.

The main evidence they rely upon is a letter and map which Abell, Private Secretary to the Viceroy, sent on 8 August to Abbott, Private Secretary to the Governor of the Punjab. Abell's letter runs:

---

[1] Ibid., p. 509.
[2] Ibid., p. 769.
[3] Philip Ziegler, *Mountbatten*, p. 420.

I enclose a map showing roughly the boundary which Sir Cyril Radcliffe proposes to demarcate in his award, and a note by Christopher Beaumont describing it. There will not be any great changes from this boundary, but it will have to be accurately defined with reference to village and *zilla* boundaries in Lahore district...The award itself is expected within the next forty-eight hours.[1]

According to the map the *tahsils* of Ferozepore and Zira formed a part of Pakistan but in Radcliffe's final award of 12 August they were included in India.[2]

It is important to note that while Abell had warned that some changes might have to be made in defining the village and *zilla* boundaries in Lahore district in the interests of greater accuracy, he had envisaged no change in the Ferozepore part of the award.

Hodson has belittled the significance of Abell's communication by stating that 'the exchange of information was entirely at private secretary level. Sir Cyril was aware that such correspondence was proceeding but did not see either the letter or the map.'[3] But this is not the way in which responsible members of the Indian Civil Service discharged their duties. It is inconceivable that Beaumont should have acted in such an important matter without consulting Radcliffe and obtaining his precise instructions. Radcliffe proposed to announce the Punjab Award on 9 August, as we have already stated; the Award must have been almost ready on 8 August.

At any rate, we have Radcliffe' own confirmation that the source of Abell's information was none other than Radcliffe himself, and that he did change his Award afterwards. Let us explain.

Sir Archibald Carter, Permanent Under-Secretary of State, Commonwealth Relations Office, invited Radcliffe to his office on 9 August 1948 to assist in the formulation of an answer to a possible parliamentary question on the subject of 'influence' in demarcating the boundaries at the time of partition. Afterwards, Carter prepared a draft and forwarded it to Radcliffe for his comment and advice. The draft was amended by Radcliffe. The following version shows the words excluded by Radcliffe in brackets and the words added by him in italics.

[1] TOP XII, p. 579.

[2] A copy of this map has been reproduced (between pp. 246-7) in *The Partition of the Punjab 1947, A Compilation of Official Documents,* Vol. I, by Mian Muhammad Sadullah, published by the National Documentation Centre, Lahore, in 1983. The Award relating to Gurdaspur district as shown in it is the same as finally announced, which means that the Mountbatten-Radcliffe collusion respecting Gurdaspur must have taken place prior to 8 August 1947.

[3] H. V. Hodson, *The Great Divide,* p. 353.

Sir George Abell's letter of the 8th August 1947, which has been made public by the Pakistan authorities, communicated to Sir Evan Jenkins, the then Governor of the Punjab, [a provisional] *the rough statement of a proposed boundary* between East and West Punjab. The information contained in it was derived from Sir Cyril Radcliffe, Chairman of the Boundary Commission, as the result of a very proper enquiry from Sir Evan Jenkins whether he could have advance information about the boundary so that the best dispositions might be made of military force and police.

The boundary indicated by this communication of the 8th August differed from that contained in [Sir Cyril's final] *the* award of the 13th August as *ultimately made by Sir Cyril in its treatment of an* [in respect of a small] area in the Ferozepore District. I understand from Sir Cyril that he found the treatment of this area a question of considerable difficulty and on this point he reached a final conclusion differing from that which he was disposed to adopt at [a slightly earlier stage] *the time when Sir George Abell asked him for advance information.*

Sir Cyril has informed me that his award of the 13th August was the result of his own unfettered judgement and that at no stage was any attempt [of any kind] made by the Governor-General to influence his decision. That this is so I have no doubt at all.[1]

That Radcliffe had originally awarded the Ferozepore and Zira *tahsils* to Pakistan and later gave them to India is confirmed by Sir Evan Jenkins, Governor of the Punjab at the time of partition:

Sir E. Jenkins, in a letter dated April 1948 to Lord Mountbatten in which he too discussed points of controversy which had arisen over the Punjab Award, described the two documents in question as follows: 'The enclosures were a schedule (I think typed) and a section of a printed map with a line drawn thereon, together showing a Boundary which included in Pakistan a sharp salient in the Ferozepore District. This salient enclosed the whole of the Ferozepore and Zira *tahsils*'. Jenkins also stated that: 'About the 10th or 11th August, when we were still expecting the award on 13th August at latest, I received a secra-phone message from Viceroy's House containing the words "Eliminate Salient"... The change caused some surprise, not because the Ferozepore salient had been regarded as inevitable or even probable, but because it seemed odd that any advance information had been given by the Commission if the award was not substantially complete'.[2]

---

[1] Hugh Tinker, 'Pressure, Persuasion, Decision: Factors in the Partition of the Punjab, August 1947', *Journal of Asian Studies,* Vol. XXXVI, No. 4, August 1977, pp. 703-4.
[2] TOP XII p. 579 (Footnote).

On the question of whether or not Radcliffe changed the Ferozepore award under pressure from Mountbatten, we have already described the Indian representation forwarded to Mountbatten by Nehru on 9 August, and his meeting with Radcliffe in the evening of, or about, the same day. Interestingly, an important Indian source not only concedes, but positively claims, that Radcliffe altered the Ferozepore award as the result of Mountbatten's intervention on India's behalf. This source is a book entitled *Reminiscences of an Engineer* written by Kanwar Sain, a canal engineer who was in the service of Bikaner state at the time of partition. The book contains a chapter under the heading 'Mountbatten Alters Punjab Boundary (at Eleventh Hour)'. Sain relates that Sarup Singh, an Indian irrigation engineer, was told on the evening of 8 August that he should select his headquarters outside the three *tahsils* of Ferozepore district—Ferozepore, Zira and Fazilka—because instructions had been received from the Governor of the Punjab that these *tahsils* were likely to be allocated to Pakistan. As this meant the transfer to Pakistan of the Ferozepore Headworks and the head-reach of the Gang Canal which served Bikaner State, Sarup Singh reported the situation to Sain by special messenger. Sain received the message on the morning of 10 August and, accompanied by Sardar Panikkar, the Prime Minister of the State, saw the Maharaja of Bikaner on the same day. The Maharaja having placed his own plane at their disposal, Sain and Panikkar arrived in Delhi before the day was out and with some difficulty secured an interview with Mountbatten on the following morning.

At first Mountbatten's attitude was stern but:

I [Sain] picked up the courage to say to His Excellency, 'Our Master has asked us to convey that if the Ferozepore Headworks and the Gang Canal go to Pakistan, His Highness, in the interest of his subjects, would have no option left but to opt for Pakistan'. As I said this, I could see a change in the colour of the face of Lord Mountbatten. He said nothing and we left His Excellency's room.

In the evening, we heard on the radio that the announcement of the Radcliffe Award would be delayed by a few days. Sardar Panikkar and myself wondered whether this had something to do with our interview with His Excellency that morning. When the Award was announced on the night of 17 August, we were happy to find that the Ferozepore Headworks and the entire area on the left bank of the river in which Gang Canal was located, were left with India.[1]

As 'positive proof' that Mountbatten had intervened as the result of his

---

[1] Kanwar Sain, *Reminiscences of an Engineer*, p. 122.

representation on the morning of 11 August, Sain quotes with evident approval two disclosures made on 22 April 1960, by Justice Munir, Chief Justice of Pakistan, at a function of the High Court Bar Association in Lahore[1]. Munir stated, firstly, that he had been told by Radcliffe 'in the most unequivocal terms that the three *tahsils* of Ferozepore, probably Ferozepore, Zira and Fazilka, were coming to Pakistan', but when the award finally came out, these *tahsils* went to India. Munir said, secondly, that during a lunch hosted by Radcliffe at the Service Club before the Commission dispersed, 'we decided to ask him whether he himself had taken a decision after reading the reports and discussing the matter with the other members. The reply was that he had to see the Governor-General (Lord Mountbatten) before he could say anything.'[2]

Finally, Ziegler, who had interviewed Sir Ian Scott, writes, 'Ian Scott, Deputy Private Secretary [to Mountbatten at the time of partition], believes that it is possible that Mountbatten might have gone along with a suggestion from Nehru over Ferozepore.'[3]

Mountbatten himself, in a letter to Jenkins dated 19 March 1948, wrote:

I am, of course, unable to say whether any adjustments were made to the previous boundary line between 8th and 12th August. But the assumption that can be drawn is that the line indicated in the documents attached to Abell's letter was only a tentative one, and that it was amended subsequently to 'balance' the Bengal boundary line.[4]

The evidence in support of the allegation that Mountbatten had colluded with Radcliffe is necessarily circumstantial, and it is for the reader to judge for herself or himself to what extent the accusation stands proved. In trying to arrive at a fair conclusion, special attention must be paid to the following matters.

After showing the first draft of the Award to 'the authorities in Delhi', why did Radcliffe make the changes only in India's favour? There is nothing to suggest that Radcliffe was personally prejudiced against Pakistan. On the other hand, there is ample evidence that Mountbatten was deeply anxious to cultivate India's goodwill.

Mountbatten admits that an advance copy of the Bengal Award had

---

[1] It will be recalled that Munir was a member of the Punjab Boundary Commission. At that time he was a judge of the Punjab High Court.

[2] Kanwar Sain, op.cit., p. 123

[3] Philip Ziegler, *Mountbatten*, p. 421.

[4] Hugh Tinker, op. cit., p. 703.

been seen by his staff.[1] Nevertheless, he wished us to believe that he himself had deliberately refrained from reading it.[2]

But what is the meaning of Radcliffe's statement to Henderson that he had shown the first draft of the award to the 'authorities in Delhi'? The Indian Independence Act required him to report to the Governor-General, not to his staff. Is it conceivable that Radcliffe showed the draft to Mountbatten's staff but not to Mountbatten himself? On 12 August, Radcliffe told Christie and Campbell-Johnson that he could not withhold publication longer than 13 August, because 'too many people' knew that the Award was ready. Indeed, the protests against the forthcoming Awards by Liaquat, Menon, Patel and the Indian canal engineers, all of them consistent with the actual contents of Abell's communication to Abbott and of the Awards as formally revealed afterwards, indicate that the details of the draft were an open secret. Yet Mountbatten wrote to Nehru and Jinnah on 13 August that he had 'no idea' of the contents of Radcliffe's Award. Considering all the evidence discussed above, including Mountbatten's own words and conduct, one is constrained to say, in Shakespeare's words, that, 'the lady doth protest too much, methinks'. Even Ziegler, who on the whole is sympathetic to Mountbatten, concedes that 'a nugget of uncertainty remains', and Noel-Baker 'hardly gave the Viceroy an unequivocal acquittal'.[3]

In a broadcast speech Jinnah could do no more than to console his countrymen thus:

> We have been squeezed in as much as was possible and the last blow that we have received was the Award of the Boundary Commission. It is an unjust, incomprehensible and even perverse Award. It may be wrong, unjust and perverse; and it may not be a judicial but a political award, but we have agreed to abide by it and it is binding upon us. As honourable people we must abide by it. It may be our misfortune but we must bear this one more blow with fortitude, courage and hope.

POSTSCRIPT

After the above section on the Radcliffe Boundary Awards had been completed, the Daily Telegraph of 24 February 1992 featured a statement by

---

[1] He had to admit this to explain how Menon knew that the Chittagong Hill Tracts were being allotted to Pakistan.

[2] *See,* version 3 at p. 545 and its footnote.

[3] Philip Ziegler, *Mountbatten*, p. 421.

H. C. Beaumont, who had been Radcliffe's secretary. The article bore the caption, 'How Mountbatten bent the rules and the Indian border'. One of the present authors, who in his younger years had been Beaumont's colleague in the Indian Civil Service, got in touch with him. Beaumont responded generously and in the course of the exchanges that followed made the following main points:

1. The Muslim-majority *tahsils* of Ferozepore and Zira were at first allotted by Radcliffe to Pakistan but were subsequently awarded by him to India. The change was made 'under pressure from Mountbatten, in turn under pressure from Nehru, and also almost certainly from Bikaner...Mountbatten interfered and Radcliffe allowed himself to be overborne. Grave discredit to both.'

It was at a lunch hosted by Ismay that Mountbatten succeeded in changing Radcliffe's mind. Radcliffe told Beaumont that Ismay had asked him not to bring Beaumont with him. The pretext was that there would not be enough room at the table for the extra guest. Beaumont knew this to be untrue because he has lived in the house occupied by Ismay for six months. This was the first time that Radcliffe and Beaumont 'had been separated at any sort of function'. That evening the line was changed. George Abell, private secretary to Mountbatten at the relevant time, told Beaumont some years later in England that Ismay and Mountbatten had told Radcliffe that if he did not agree to the change it would result in 'civil war [between India and Pakistan] or at least something like it'.

Beaumont did not keep a diary but thinks Ismay's lunch must have taken place on 11 or 12 August 1947.

2. The award relating to Gurdaspur district was entirely Radcliffe's own; there was no outside influence at all.

3. Beaumont has 'not the slightest doubt' that V. D. Ayer, assistant secretary to the Boundary Commission, kept Nehru and V. P. Menon informed as to where the boundary lines were going. 'It was a mistake to appoint a Hindu (the same would have been true for a Muslim) to the confidential post...An assistant secretary to the Commission should have been brought from the UK'.

THE ANDAMAN AND NICOBAR ISLANDS

When the question of the future of the Andaman and Nicobar Islands was discussed in the India and Burma Committee of the British cabinet on 17 June 1947, the Secretary of State for India informed them that in the opinion of the Viceroy, any attempt by His Majesty's Government to separate the islands from India would probably provoke violent opposition from all parts of India, and that such a proposal would seriously undermine the Viceroy's own position.[1] Mountbatten had also warned that any

[1] TOP XI, p. 482.

attempt by the British Government to claim the Islands as colonies 'might go a long way toward nullifying the recent improvement in Indo-British relations'.

It was, therefore, 'with distress' that, when the first draft of the Indian Independence Bill arrived, Mountbatten found that provision had been made that the Andaman and Nicobar Islands should cease to be a part of India after 15 August 1947. He 'decided' that the best course would be to omit all reference to the said islands in the Bill, 'so that they would automatically become part of the future Dominion of India'. The British government supported him in this decision; 'the only person who did not like it was Mr Jinnah, who sent a message to Mr Attlee and Mr Churchill saying that he thought they should be part of Pakistan'.[1]

---

[1] *Report on the Last Viceroyalty,* p. 115, paras. 137, 138, 139. The message sent by Jinnah to Attlee and Churchill was that India had no claim to the Islands because the people living there were not connected with the peoples of India by ethical, religious or cultural ties. Pakistan's claim to the Islands was very strong since the only channel of communication between eastern and western Pakistan was by sea and those islands occupied the sea route and provided fuelling bases. India had no such claim. TOP XI, p. 938.

APPENDICES

The attached documents relating to the Radcliffe Boundary Award were recently discovered by the authors in the archives of the India Office Library and Records and the Public Records Office. Appendices A, B, C, D and E throw new light on the manner in which the Gurdaspur award was manipulated in India's favour and Appendix F provides authoritative confirmation that Radcliffe had shown the first draft of his award to the 'authorities in Delhi' and had subsequently altered it.

LETTER OF 23 JANUARY 1946 FROM V.P. MENON TO GEORGE ABELL, PRIVATE SECRETARY TO THE VICEROY

182/AS
23/1/46

No. R. 205/46

<u>Most Secret</u>

New Delhi, 23rd January '46.

r S/S l. lttr.
at p 137

My dear Abell,

When Rau and I discussed the 'breakdown' provisions with you, you wanted suggestions for demarcation of the Pakistan areas. The accompanying note embodies our suggestions on the question of demarcation. What sort of Constitution the demarcated areas are to have is a different matter upon which Sir Stafford Cripps did not commit himself very definitely. His statements on this subject, when put together, amount to this:- "Two contiguous Provinces may form a separate Union": "A new Dominion may be formed out of two or three non-acceding Provinces provided it is physically possible": "We propose to respond to the request of the non-acceding Provinces, which may be that they want separate Dominions or may be that they want one". What kind of Constitution Sir Stafford Cripps would have been prepared to consider for the areas that we have suggested for Pakistan is therefore difficult to gather, and until there is a properly co-ordinated scheme, it might be wiser not to commit oneself to the grant of any particular form of Constitution for the demarcated areas. In this connection I would invite attention to paragraphs 28 to 31 of the Secretary of State's memorandum No.1.B.(45)13 dated 9.9.45 and the minutes of the discussion thereon at the fifth meeting of the India and Burma Committee dated 11.9.45.

Yours sincerely,

G.E.B. Abell, Esq., CIE., OBE.

ENCLOSURE TO V.P. MENON'S LETTER TO GEORGE ABELL OF 23 JANUARY 1946

<u>MOST SECRET</u>

Demarcation of "Pakistan" areas.
—————

The total population of British India is about 296 millions, of which Muslims form about 79 millions or about 27 per cent.

The Muslim League claims that the Western Zone consisting of the Punjab, Sind, the North-West Frontier Province, and British Baluchistan, and the Eastern Zone consisting of Bengal and Assam are predominantly Muslim and should therefore be formed with a separate independent State, "Pakistan". The total population of the Western Zone is about 36 millions, of which about 22 millions are Muslims and 14 millions non-Muslims. The latter thus form about 38 per cent. of the total population. The Eastern Zone has a total population of about 70 millions, of which about 34 millions or 49 per cent. are non-Muslims. The non-Muslims in both Zones are thus a substantial minority; moreover, there are considerable blocks of territory in each Zone where they form the majority of the population. If Muslims, who form about 27 per cent. of the total population of British India, can validly claim separation of the predominantly Muslim Zones from British India, it is difficult to deny the counter-claim of the Sikhs and Hindus, who form a much larger percentage of the population of these Zones for separation from "Pakistan" of the blocks of territory in which they predominate. In fact, "Pakistan" will have to satisfy at least two tests:-

(1) Each Zone must form a continuous block of territory in which the Muslims predominate.

(2) The non-Muslim population in each Zone (who may be assumed to be hostile to "Pakistan") should not be much more than 27 per cent. of the total population.

The extreme form of "Pakistan" claimed by the Muslim League does not satisfy the second condition. Even the exclusio

exclusion of Assam from the Eastern Zone would not materially alter the case, for this would bring down the non-
Muslim population of that Zone to about 45 per cent,
while the percentage in the Western Zone would still be
38.   Thus even a "Pakistan" consisting of the predominantly Muslim Provinces with their existing boundaries
cannot be defended.

The next suggestion is that the Western Zone should
consist of Sind, the North-West Frontier Province, British Baluchistan, and the Lahore, Rawalpindi, and Multan
Divisions of the Punjab, and the Eastern Zone of the
Rajshahi, Dacca, and Chittagong Divisions of Bengal.
This obviously satisfies the first of the above two conditions; we have to see if it satisfies the second.   The
total population of the Western Zone on this basis works
out to about 26 millions of which about 7 millions or a
little over 26 per cent. are non-Muslims.   The corresponding figures for the Eastern Zone are 37 millions,
11 millions, and 30 per cent.   The second condition also
is therefore almost satisfied.   Two objections may be
urged against this proposal, from opposite quarters: in
the West it includes in "Pakistan" the district of
Amritsar which is not only predominantly non-Muslim (of
a total population of 1.4 millions the Muslims number
.66 million and non-Muslims .74 million) but is also
particularly sacred to the Sikhs; and in the East, it
excludes from "Pakistan" the vital port of Calcutta.

It is not possible to meet the latter objection
even by a district-wise partition, for the Calcutta "district", even considered by itself, is largely non-Muslim;
of a total population of 2.1 millions, only about .5
million, or under 25 per cent, are Muslims.   The only
result of a district-wise partition in Bengal would be
to exclude the districts of Darjeeling and Jalpaiguri
from "Pakistan" and to include therein the districts

of

- 3 -

Nadia, Murshidabad and Jessore, which would merely cut
across the existing Divisional boundaries without any
compensating advantage.

The Sikh objection in the Western Zone can be met,
to some extent, by excluding the districts of Amritsar
and Gurdaspur from "Pakistan".   These two form a compact block, whose total population is a little over 2.5
millions of which a little under 1.25 millions - i.e., a
little under 50 per cent. are Muslims.   This form of
partition will cut across existing Divisional boundaries,
but has the advantage of meeting the most serious of the
Sikh objections, though not all of them;   for, whenever
the line may be drawn, there will still be some Sikhs
left on the wrong side.   If the existing Lahore, Rawalpindi, and Multan Divisions are included in "Pakistan",
the number of Punjab Sikhs in "Pakistan" would be about 2.2
millions and in "Hindustan" about 1.5 millions;   with the
exclusion of the districts of Amritsar and Gurdaspur, the
corresponding figures would be 1.5 millions and 2.2
millions, so that the majority of them would now fall in
"Hindustan", although a substantial minority would still
be left in "Pakistan".   On the whole, the best plan may
be to exclude these two districts from the Western Zone,
so that the net result would be to include in "Pakistan"

    (a) Sind, the North-West Frontier Province, British
        Baluchistan, and the Lahore, Rawalpindi, and
        Multan Divisions of the Punjab minus the dis-
        tricts of Amritsar and Gurdaspur.

    (b) The Rajshahi, Dacca, and Chittagong Divisions
        of Bengal.

Appendix C

TELEGRAM FROM THE SECRETARY OF STATE FOR INDIA TO THE VICEROY

Telegram XX

TOP SECRET.
248-S

From - Secretary of State.

To   - Viceroy.

2030. Dt 29th Jan. recd. 30th Jan. 1946 (100-2256) (TOR-0345).

Important.

SUPERINTENDENT SERIES.   TOP SECRET.

It would help me to know when I may expect
to receive your recommendations as regards definition
of genuine Moslem areas if we are compelled to give
a decision on this and also your proposals as regards
the treaty on which I understand your officials have
been at work.   Time is getting very short and if
*proposed Mission is to have as much freedom of nego-
tiation as I should*like*It will be desirable for them
to have discussed these issues particularly with others
here before leaving.   I hope therefore that you can
let us have your views on both these matters, within a fortnight.

. . . .

ECS
DEW

LSMy sent to R.R. Menon with 20/p/46

Appendix D

REPLY FROM THE VICEROY TO THE
SECRETARY OF STATE

Telegram X..   Secret.
                                23-SC.
From :- Viceroy.
To :-   Secretary of State. (R.'d. H.o. /~ H. M. & R.c)
23- SC.
Dated 6th February 1946. (T00-2100)

Immediate.

Top Secret. Superintendent Series. Your 2090 of 29th
January.
    If compelled to indicate demarcation of genuinely Muslim
areas I recommend that we should include:
    (a) Sind, N.W.F.P., British Baluchistan and the Rawalpindi
Multan and Lahore divisions of the Punjab less Amritsar and
Gurdaspur districts.
    (b) In Bengal, the Chittagong and Dacca divisions, the
Rajshahi division (less Jalpaiguri and Darjeeling), the Nadia,
Murshidabad and Jessore districts of the Presidency division;
and in Assam the Sylhet district.

2. In the Punjab the only Muslim majority district that would
not go into Pakistan under this demarcation is Gurdaspur (51%
Muslim). Gurdaspur must go with Amritsar for geographical
reasons and Amritsar being the sacred city of the Sikhs must
stay out of Pakistan. But for this special importance of
Amritsar, demarcation in the Punjab could have been on divisional boundaries. Fact that much of Lahore district is irrigated
from Upper Bari Doab Canal with headworks in Gurdaspur district
is awkward but there is no solution that avoids all such
difficulties.

3. Greatest difficulty is position of the Sikhs with their
homelands and sacred places on both sides of the border. This
problem is one which no version of Pakistan can solve.

4. The population figures that follow are in thousands. The
Punjab including Punjab States has a Sikh population of 5,116.
Of these under proposed scheme 1,461 will be in Pakistan and
the rest in Hindustan. Of those in Pakistan xxx a substantial
number are in districts which under any arrangement are bound
to be in Pakistan e.g. Rawalpindi (64) and colony districts of
Lyallpur (265) and Montgomery (175).

5. We should make it clear in any announcement that this is
only an indication of areas to which in H. .G's view the Muslims
can advance a reasonable claim; modifications in the boundary
might be negotiated and no doubt the interests of the Sikhs in
particular would be carefully considered in such negotiation.
Some such saving clause is indicated by the importance of
preventing immediate violence by the Sikhs.

7. In Bengal the three Muslim majority districts of the
Presidency division must I think be included in Pakistan, though
this brings the frontier across the Ganges. The demarcation
includes in Pakistan all Muslim majority districts and no Hindu
majority districts.

8. There is no case, consistently with the principle suggested
in the breakdown plan, for including Calcutta in Pakistan. The
Muslims will probably try to negotiate for its being made a
free port. If the negotiations fail Eastern Bengal's prospects
as a separate autonomous State will be seriously affected. But
the Muslims if they insist on Pakistan, must face up to this
problem like that of the Sikhs, and they may have to agree to
some sort of a centre in exchange for making Calcutta a free
port. This would be a welcome development.

9. The population figures of Pakistan on this demarcation

2.

ould be (in thousands):

East zone: Muslims - ~~30,602~~   30,603   *Corrected*
      Non-Muslims - ~~14,482~~   13,480   *by*
      Total - ~~45,084~~   44,083   *Telegram*
         6,187   *No. 3785*

West zone: Muslims - 18,210   *dated.*
      Non-Muslims - ~~5,633~~   5,583   *18.7.46*
      Total - 23,843   23,793

10. Treaty. Rau's first draft on Defence, External Affairs
rotection of Crown servants and relations with Indian
States is being sent by the next fast air mail bag.
ections on Minorities and Finance will follow shortly.

A 7 752/28/47

Appendix E

NOTE OF 25 FEBRUARY 1948 FROM PHILIP NOEL-BAKER, SECRETARY OF STATE FOR COMMONWEALTH RELATIONS, TO CLEMENT ATTLEE, PRIME MINISTER OF THE UNITED KINGDOM

SERIAL NO. 3/48

PRIME MINISTER

You have asked for a draft reply to Lord Mountbatten's personal telegram to you No. 458 of 24th February in which he asks for copies of the evidence alleged by Begum Liaquat Ali Khan to have been sent to you that he was implicated in the Punjab troubles by failure to arrest Sikh leaders and by having tampered with the Radcliffe Award.

There is documentary evidence of the first allegation in paragraph 3 of the message to you from the Prime Minister of Pakistan dated 10th September (item 1 in the print attached). This message was communicated to the Government of India on 21st September.

This accusation was repeated with a reference to "an unfortunate change in the Radcliffe Award at Pakistan's expense" in a conversation at New York between Sir M. Zafrullah and myself on 19th January recorded in New York telegram No. 139 of 20th January. This telegram was repeated to the U.K.H.C. New Delhi (No. 234).

We have no precise knowledge here of the basis of these allegations. The question whether Tara Singh should or should not be arrested before the transfer of power was clearly one of policy for decision by the Governor-General, since at the time the Province was under Section 91 Government. after the resignation of Sir Khizar Hayat Khan's Ministry. There is some reason for thinking that Sir Cyril Radcliffe at the last moment altered his boundary award so as to assign to the E. Punjab a salient in the original demarcation of the W. Punjab boundary which included Gurdaspur. But we have no knowledge that this was done on the advice of Lord Mountbatten.

P.N.B.

25th February, 1948

COMMONWEALTH RELATIONS OFFICE

Appendix F

NOTE OF 26 FEBRUARY 1948 FROM NOEL-BAKER
TO ATTLEE

SECRET

COMMONWEALTH RELATIONS OFFICE,
DOWNING ST., S.W.1.

SERIAL NO. 4/48

PRIME MINISTER,

I have asked the Secretary of State for Air
whether he can shed any light on the circumstances
in which an alteration was made at the last minute
in the Radcliffe Award.

Mr. Henderson states that Sir Cyril Radcliffe
told him that he showed the first draft of the proposed
Award to the authorities in Delhi, and that on further
consideration he made the Award in terms which departed
from the first draft, but he did not attempt to elicit
from Sir Cyril Radliffe at the time whether the
departure from the first draft had been suggested to
him from any quarter.

To obtain information on the latter point it
would, therefore, be necessary to refer further to
Sir Cyril Radliffe.   This does not seem very desirable,
at all events at this stage.

In the circumstances, I suggest that I should send
a strictly personal message to Zafrullah in the terms
that I showed to you last night, and of which I attach
a copy. *This would, as you pointed out, not expressly
deny it in terms what Zafrullah said; but it would
warn him off in strong terms, I would, therefore, be
much better than nothing. Shall I so proceed?* PJNB.

26th February, 1948

Form sent
B.C.
26.2.48

CHAPTER 24

THE INTEGRATION OF THE PRINCELY STATES

The Indian States, which at the time of the transfer of power numbered about 565,[1] varied in size from 84,471 square miles (Kashmir) to 0.29 square miles (Vejononess). In terms of population, the largest was Hyderabad with some 16 million people. While some of the larger States had visions of complete independence, the smaller ones could think only in terms of either acceding to one of the new Dominions or of becoming viable by forming a union with other States.

The communal composition of the population of the States followed the general pattern of the rest of the subcontinent. The States in the north-west had a Muslim majority, the rest, a Hindu majority. If Congress and the Muslim league, having accepted partition on the basis of Muslim-majority and non-Muslim-majority areas, had followed the same principle with respect to the accession of the States, they could have avoided much trouble, but in those tense days, it seemed impossible for them to come to a mutual understanding on any major issue. The situation was further complicated by the fact that in some cases Muslim rulers ruled over Hindu-majority areas and vice versa. The two largest states—Hyderabad and Kashmir—created the largest amount of ill-feeling between the two newly-independent neighbours.

But let us first sketch the historical background of the problem. The princes had played a major role in the consolidation and maintenance of British power in India. In 1825 Sir John Malcolm[2] had written:

> I am decidedly of the opinion that the tranquillity, not to say security, of our vast oriental possessions is involved in the preservation of native principalities which are dependent on us for protection. These are also so obviously at our mercy, so entirely within our grasp, that besides other and great benefits we

---

[1] The Report of the Indian Statutory Comission, II, p. 193 gave the number of States as 'nearly 600' but Mountbatten put the number at about 565.

[2] John Malcolm (1769-1833) was a civil servant who rose to be Governor of Bombay.

derive from their alliance, their co-existence with our rule is of itself a source of political strength, the value of which will never be known till it is lost.

However, the usefulness of the princes was not generally appreciated till the revolt of 1857 during which, in Lord Canning's words, they had played the role of 'breakwaters in the storm which would have swept over us in one great wave'. They were rewarded with the promise in Queen Victoria's Proclamation that, 'We shall respect the rights, dignity and honour of native Princes as our own.' During the two World Wars, the Indian princes rendered whole-hearted assistance to the paramount power.

At the same time, the people of the States were influenced by the rise of nationalism in India. In December 1927, the All-India States' People's Conference had been founded with the object of attaining 'responsible government for the people in the Indian States through representative institutions under the aegis of their rulers'. It was, in effect, the States' arm of the British Indian Congress Party.

Congress leaders also began to ponder over the status of the States in the future body politic of India. The Nehru Report (1928), while conceding that there was an 'Indian India' consisting of the States, went on to prophesy that:

It would be very poor statesmanship and short-sighted policy to ignore those obvious historical, religious, sociological and economic affinities which exist between the people of British India and the people of these States. Nor do we think that it is possible to erect artificial geographical barriers between the two. Ideas and opinion travel from one part of India to another much more rapidly than was the case sixty or seventy years ago, and it would be absurd to deal with the problem of Indian States on the assumption that the dynamic forces now in operation in British India can for a very long period of time be expected to spend themselves on the borders of British India. It is inconceivable that the people of the States, who are fired by the same ambitions and aspirations as the people of British India, will quietly submit to existing conditions forever, or that the people of British India, bound by the closest ties of family, race and religion to their brethren on the other side of an imaginary line, will never make common cause with them.

The Report recommended that:

The Commonwealth [of India] shall exercise the same rights in relation to, and discharge the same obligations towards, the Indian States, arising out of treaties or otherwise, as the Government of India has hitherto exercised and discharged.

In case of any difference between the Commonwealth and any Indian State on any matter arising out of treaties, engagements, *sanads* or any other documents, the Governor-General-in-Council may, with the consent of the State concerned, refer the said matter to the Supreme Court for its decision.

Encouraged by Congress's remarkable success in the provincial elections of 1937, the people of the States began to agitate for responsible government with renewed vigour. There was unrest in several States which the rulers tried to suppress with strong measures. Gandhi, who at first had favoured non-interference in the internal affairs of the States, could no longer maintain his neutrality, and on 3 December 1938 he declared that there was no half-way house between total extinction of the States and full responsible government. He advised the princes to cultivate friendly relations 'with an organization [Congress] which bids fair in the future, not very distant, to replace the paramount power'.[1] In 1939 Nehru was elected president of the States People's Conference, emphasizing the fact that the Conference was but the States' wing of the British Indian Congress Party. On the eve of the Quit India rebellion of 1942, Gandhi advised the princes to come to terms with him: 'When I am gone Pandit Jawaharlal Nehru will have no patience with you'.

The relations between the princes and the British Government remained sympathetic while Congress was their common adversary. But a change became discernible as soon as Britain began to think in terms of granting freedom to India in a way which would assure friendly relations with the successor government, in which Congress was expected to be the predominant, if not the sole, participant. It was not the containment but the conciliation of Congress that now became the prime objective of British policy.

Cripps' Declaration (29 March 1942) primarily related to British India; it desired the Indian political leaders to join the existing constitutional set-up in which the princes played no part. The States would be invited to appoint representatives to the constitution-making body after it had been elected by the provincial legislatures. In his press conference on 31 March, Cripps made it clear that there was 'no contemplation' of any dominion being set up which consisted solely of Indian States.[2] However, this did not deter the Indian States' Delegation from representing to him that 'the

---

[1] V. P. Menon, *Integration of the Indian States*, p. 43. Gandhi had once described the Indian princes as 'British officers in Indian dress'. (H.S.L. Polak, H.N. Brailsford, Lord Pethick-Lawrence, *Gandhi*, p. 194.)

[2] TOP I, p. 575.

States should be assured...that in the event of a number of States not finding it feasible to adhere, the non-adhering States or groups of States, so desiring, would have the right to form a Union of their own with full sovereign status in accordance with a suitable and agreed procedure devised for the purpose'.[1]

By talking with the princes Corfield[2] gathered that the impression they had got from Cripps was that His Majesty's Government was only interested in a settlement with British India, and the States would have to do their best to fit into whatever settlement was made.

We have already quoted Azad's statement that Cripps had told the Maharaja of Kashmir that the future of the states lay with India, and no prince should harbour the illusion that the British Crown would come to his help if he decided to opt out.[3] Menon has also recorded that 'the Cripps Mission brought home to the rulers the discomforting realization that if the interests of British India and the States come into conflict His Majesty's Government would almost certainly let down the States'.[4]

With regard to the States, the 3 June 1947 plan for the transfer of power simply stated that his Majesty's Government's 'policy towards the Indian States contained in the Cabinet Mission Memorandum of 12 May 1946 remains unchanged,' and the Indian Independence Act declared that the suzerainty of His Majesty over the Indian States would lapse on 15 August 1947.

We have already described the Cabinet Mission's Memorandum on the princely States and the Secretary of State's statement to Azad that when paramountcy ceased to exist, the States would achieve a position of independence at the same time as British India. We also pointed out that this reference to independence was academic. There was no suggestion that even the large States could aspire to an international status. The only path indicated was for all of them to enter into a federal relationship with the government or governments to which power would be transferred in British India or to enter into 'particular political arrangements' with it or them.[5]

---

[1] Ibid., p. 734. Churchill was sympathetic to the aspiration of the princes to form a sovereign state of their own. *See*, p. 411 for his reference to 'Princestan' during a meeting with Wavell on 29 March 1945.

[2] Conrad Corfield, *The Princely India I Knew*, p. 126. Corfield, a member of the Indian Political Service, retired after rising to the post of Political Adviser to the Crown Representative.

[3] *See*, p. 366.

[4] V. P. Menon, *Integration of the Indian States*, p. 52.

[5] *See*, p. 438.

Paramountcy had never been formally defined:

> Broadly, it meant that the Crown was obliged to protect the Rulers and their dynasties from external aggression or internal revolt, while the Rulers recognised the right of the Crown to conduct their foreign relations, regulate disputed successions, conduct minority administrations, intervene in their internal affairs in case of gross misrule, lease territories or receive financial subventions in return for military protection, and co-ordinate their defence arrangements.[1]

The Viceroy wore two hats. He was Governor-General of British India, deriving his powers from the Government of India Act 1935, and he was Crown Representative for the conduct of relations with the princely States, deriving his authority from the paramountcy of the Crown over the States. As Crown Representative he had under him a political adviser who was the head of the political service.

Cripps had already made clear in March 1942 that it was not contemplated to set up any Dominion consisting only of the princely States. This was confirmed by Mountbatten during his press conference on 4 June 1947, when he said that the States could not enter the Commonwealth separately as Dominions.

Behind the scenes, Mountbatten had already warned the British Government in May that 'if we admit that the Indian States or even some of them can be admitted as separate Dominions into the Commonwealth we shall be charged with disintegrating India and Congress is likely to withdraw its application for Dominion Status. The solution seems to be to take the line that we cannot accept as members of the Commonwealth any of the Indian States unless they first associate themselves with one of the two Dominions of British India. In that case their relation with the Crown could be through one of the Governors-General...'[2]

On 20 June Listowel wrote to Mountbatten:

> We have scrupulously avoided, and must continue to avoid, doing anything which might be taken by individual States as an encouragement to them to stand out of the new Indian set-up—this, I am sure you will agree, applies particularly to Hyderabad, Travancore and any other States which are reported to have declared their intention to assert independence—and we must clearly give any assistance in our power towards the working out of satisfactory new arrangements between the States and the successor authorities.[3]

---

[1] *Report on the Last Viceroyalty*, p. 12, para. 72.

[2] TOP X, p. 970.

[3] TOP XI p. 540.

Then on 16 July 1947, during the debate on the Indian Independence
Bill in the House of Lords, Listowel said, 'We do not, of course, propose
to recognize any States as separate international entities'.[1] This authoritative
declaration by the Secretary of State for India virtually shut the door to
independence for every State in India for it gave them notice that, since the
British Government would not recognize their independence, no other
government in the world was likely to do so and thus they would have to
opt for either India or Pakistan.

Meanwhile, Congress leaders had made plain what their own policy
toward the States was. In an address on 18 April 1947 to the All-India
States' People's Conference at Gwalior, Nehru was reported to have said
that any State which did not come into the Constituent Assembly then
would be regarded as hostile, and would have to bear the consequences of
being so regarded. The aim of Congress was to liberate as much of India
as it could and then deal with the question of independence for the rest.
When Mountbatten protested that it was highly reprehensible for a
member of the Interim Government to make a statement like that without
prior reference to the Cabinet, Nehru pleaded that he had been speaking
only in his capacity as the President of the States' People's Conference.

After the acceptance of the 3 June 1947 plan, the Standing Committee
of the States' People's Conference, meeting on 11 and 12 June, resolved
that the conception that any State was free to go out of the Union of India
would reduce India to anarchy. None of the States was completely
independent at the time of the advent of British power—in some way or
other they had all recognized and submitted to the suzerainty of the
Mughal Empire, the Maratha Supremacy, the Sikh Kingdom or, later, the
British Power. It had to be recognized that on the lapse of paramountcy,
sovereignty would reside in the people of the States. If any State refused
to join the Constituent Assembly of India, the Constituent Assembly
should allow the people of that State to elect their own representatives.[2]

At a meeting of the All-India Congress Committee on 14 and 15 June,
Gandhi said, 'They [the princes] must recognize the paramountcy of the
Indian people as they had accepted the paramountcy of the British
power.'[3] And Nehru asserted that, 'there is a certain inherent paramountcy
in the Government of India which cannot lapse...which must remain

[1] Parliamentary Debates, House of Lords, Sessions 1946-1947 (10 and 11 Geo VI),
p. 814.
[2] TOP XI, p. 283.
[3] Pyarelal, *Mahatma Gandhi*, Vol. II, *The Last Phase*, p. 341.

because of the very reasons of Geography, History, Defence etc...'[1]

Jinnah's view was legalistic. In a statement on 17 June 1947 he said that the choice of the States was not limited to joining one or other Constituent Assembly; they were free to remain independent if they so desired.[2]

The pace of Indian constitutional change had always been set by British India. In his speech to the Conference of Rulers on 25 July 1947, Mountbatten explained that he had to deal with the problem of India first because, 'until that problem was solved it was quite useless to try to start on a solution of the problem of the States'. There had been 'a universal acceptance' among the States of the Cabinet Mission's Memorandum of 12 May 1946, but it was only when the parties accepted the 3 June 1947 plan and it was realized that 'withdrawal of paramountcy would enable the States to regain complete sovereignty' that he got 'a starting point from which to try and deal fairly with the States'.[3]

Mountbatten convened a meeting of party leaders including Jinnah, Nehru, and Baldev Singh on 13 June, at which it was agreed that a States Department should be set up to deal with questions of common interest between the States and the successor governments in British India. The new department would consist of two sections, ready for the partition of the country. During the proceedings Nehru and Jinnah had sharply differed on the constitutional status of the States. Jinnah averred that 'every Indian State was a sovereign State...for every purpose except in so far as they had entered into treaties with the Crown'. Nehru said he 'differed altogether'. What were the tests of sovereignty, he asked. One was the capacity for international relations. The States had no such capacity. Another was the capacity for declaring war. The States had no such capacity.

The proposal to create a States Department was formally approved by the Interim Government and Mountbatten was much relieved when Nehru asked Patel to take charge of the new department. 'I am glad,' he wrote in his Personal Report on 27 June, 'that Nehru has not been put in charge of the new States Department. Patel...is essentially a realist and very sensible... Even better news is that V. P. Menon is to be the Secretary'.[4] Abdur Rab Nishtar was nominated to look after the interests of the Muslim League, assisted by M. Ikramullah, who would have the rank of joint secretary.

---

[1] Michael Brecher, *Nehru*, p. 345.
[2] TOP XI, p. 438.
[3] TOP XII, p. 347.
[4] Menon's Secretaryship of the States Department was in addition to his duties as Reforms Commissioner.

Menon realized that the prospect of some States striving for an independent existence would balkanise India and the situation had to be carefully handled. Even before he took charge of the secretaryship of the States Department on 5 July, he had persuaded Patel that Mountbatten's co-operation should be enlisted to solve the problem because, 'apart from his position, his grace and his gifts, his relationship to the Royal Family was bound to influence the rulers'. Accordingly, Menon asked Mountbatten for his help in getting the States to accede on three subjects.[1] 'I felt,' Menon recorded, 'that he was deeply touched by my remark that the wounds of partition might to some extent be healed by the States entering into relationship with the Government of India and that he would be earning the gratitude of generations of Indians if he could assist in achieving the basic unity of the country'. After thinking the matter over, Mountbatten accepted, to Menon's 'relief and joy'.[2] Mountbatten already possessed Attlee's directive that he should 'aid and assist the States in coming to fair and just arrangements with the leaders of British India as to their future relationships'.[3]

Of the 565 States, only 14, including Kashmir, were contiguous with Pakistan. The problem, therefore, was of far greater magnitude for India than it was for Pakistan. Jinnah was prepared to negotiate with each State separately, but such a course was not practicable for India. Instead of bargaining with individual States, Menon drew up two standard documents—an Instrument of Accession for Defence, External Affairs and Communications, and a Standstill Agreement to continue arrangements in matters of common concern such as customs, currency, railways, irrigation, electric power and national highways during the interim period.[4] Some rulers were willing to execute the Standstill Agreements, but wished to mark time with regard to the Instrument of Accession.

On 5 July, Patel issued a conciliatory statement which had been drafted for him by Menon:

The States have already accepted the basic principle that for defence, foreign affairs and communications they would come into an Indian Union. We ask no more of them than accession on these three subjects, in which the common

---

[1] The three subjects were those on which the Cabinet Mission had suggested the States should accede to the Union of India—Defence, External Affairs, and Communications.

[2] Menon, op. cit., pp. 97-8.

[3] *See*, p. 471.

[4] For forms of these two documents *see*, TOP XII, pp. 468-73. The Standstill Agreements had also been envisaged in paragraph 4 of the Cabinet Mission Memorandum of 12 May 1946.

interests of the country are involved. In other matters, we would scrupulously respect their autonomous existence...I should like to make it clear that it is not the desire of the Congress to interfere in any manner whatever with the domestic affairs of the States. They are not enemies of the Princely Order but, on the other hand, wish them and their people, under their aegis, all prosperity, contentment and happiness. Nor would it be my policy to conduct the relations of the new Department with the States in any manner which savours of domination of one over the other...I hope the Indian States will bear in mind that the alternative to co-operation in the general interest is anarchy and chaos which will overwhelm great and small in common ruin if we are unable to act together in the minimum of common tasks.[1]

Once Mountbatten had agreed to help, he plunged into the task with his customary vigour. On 25 July he addressed the Chamber of Princes with the object of persuading as many States as possible to accede to one Dominion or the other before 15 August. The speech, which was made without notes, pleased Menon so much that he called it 'the apogee of persuasion'.[2] Mountbatten pointed out that:

...there has grown up during the period of British administration, owing to the fact that the Crown Representative and the Viceroy are one and the same person, a system of co-ordinated administration on all matters of common concern which meant that the sub-continent of India acted as an economic entity. That link is now to be broken. If nothing can be put in its place, only chaos can result, and that chaos, I submit, will hurt the States first—the bigger the State the less the hurt and the longer it will take to feel it—but even the biggest of the States will feel herself hurt just the same as any small State.

He urged the States to accede on Defence, External Affairs and Communications: Defence was 'a matter that a State could not conduct for itself' and 'if you do not link up with one or the other of the Dominions, you will be cut off from any source of supplies of up-to-date arms or weapons'; 'External Affairs is inextricably linked up with Defence'; and 'Communications is really a means of maintaining the life-blood of the whole sub-continent'.

He held out the assurance that the States were being invited to accede on three subjects only and drew attention to the fact that the Instrument of Accession contained 'an explicit provision that in no other matters has the Central Government any authority to encroach on the internal autonomy

---

[1] TOP XI, p. 929.
[2] For text of address *see*, TOP XII, pp. 347-52.

or sovereignty of the States'. This would be 'a tremendous achievement for the States. But I must make it clear that I have still to persuade the Government of India to accept it.[1] If all of you would co-operate with me and are ready to accede, I am confident that I can succeed in my efforts...if you are prepared to come, you must come before 15th August'. Finally, he warned them that they could not 'run away' from the Dominion which was their neighbour any more than they could from the subjects for whose welfare they were responsible.

After the States Department had been established on 5 July, Conrad Corfield ceased to be the Political Adviser for all practical purposes. He felt that the princes would have been in a stronger position to negotiate if they could do so after paramountcy had been remitted to them on 15 August; Mountbatten, as the representative of the paramount power, was holding out promises which could not be guaranteed after independence. He dutifully arranged Mountbatten's conference with the Chamber of Princes on 25 July, but excused himself from attending it, and flew to England on 23 July, retiring from service on the same date.

More importantly, Mountbatten's tactics as expressed in his address to the Chamber of Princes caused Listowel to send him a critical message on 1 August. After making the general observation that the British authorities must not add to the pressure under which the States were already labouring, the Secretary of State raised two objections to the contents of the address. He said, first, that he was doubtful about Mountbatten's statement that if the States did not link up with one or the other dominion, they would be cut off from any source of supplies of up-to-date arms. Secondly, he said he was not clear why the States should be given the time limit of joining before 15 August. It seemed to him that the States were entitled to say that, before deciding the question of accession finally, they wished to see the constitutions as they emerged from the Constituent Assemblies, so that they could judge as to what sort of structure they were joining.[2]

Mountbatten replied on 8 August. He wrote testily that he could not help feeling that things were moving so fast in India that 'the India Office have been unable to keep abreast of them'. He argued that the promise of independence to the States based on the Cabinet Mission's memorandum read with the 3 June plan 'would not be worth a moment's purchase' unless they had the support of one of the two new dominions, principally

---

[1] This was not in fact true because Patel in his statement of 5 July had already promised that, but for Accession on three subjects, the States would have complete autonomy.
[2] TOP XII, p. 459.

'because of the wide gap that prevails between the rulers and the ruled'. Barring a few States, the rest had no real military forces of their own and such police as they possessed were hardly adequate to deal with internal trouble.

In his 25 July address, he went on, he had advised the princes to accede while he as Crown Representative was 'still in a position to safeguard their interests'. All that the States were asked to surrender were powers which they never exercised during their association with the British government and which by virtue of their limited resources they were not in a position to discharge effectively. Accession was for 'a temporary period'. When the constitution was framed, 'the States will have another opportunity of judging...whether they would like to adhere to the new constitution'.

He reiterated his already well-tried admonition that it was of paramount importance to secure the good-will of independent India:

> The Indian Dominion, consisting nearly of three fourths of India, and with its immense resources and its important strategic position in the Indian Ocean, is a Dominion which we cannot afford to estrange for the sake of the so-called independence of the States. I have no doubt that you will agree with me that we should leave no stone unturned to convince the Indian Dominion that although we had to agree to the plan of partition, we had no intention to leave it balkanised or to weaken it both internally and externally.

Finally, he emphasized that he was acting in the interests of the princes because, 'once the present chance is missed the terms which the princes will receive will not anywhere be as generous as the terms which I can secure for them now'.[1]

On the evening of 28 July, Mountbatten held a reception for over fifty ruling princes and a hundred States Representatives, which Menon said was 'in the nature of a last-minute canvassing of voters near the polling booth'.[2] 'Those of Their Highnesses,' wrote Campbell-Johnson, 'who had not already signified their intention of signing the Instrument of Accession were duly shepherded by the ADCs one by one for a friendly talk with Mountbatten. He in his turn passed them on in the full view of the company to V. P., who conducted them across the room to see Patel. There were Maharajas three deep in a semicircle watching this process. One veteran Prince was heard to remark, "Who's HE getting to work on now"?'[3] The

---

[1] For the text of Mountbatten's letter *see,* TOP XII, p. 584.

[2] V. P. Menon, *Integration of the Indian States*, p. 113.

[3] Campbell-Johnson, *Mission with Mountbatten*, p. 144.

Viceroy also gave a luncheon to several of the leading princes for the same purpose on 1 August. 'After paying their bread-and-butter respects to Their Excellencies, they [the guests] ran the gauntlet of ADCs, who helped to form virtual "Aye" and "No" lobbies on their attitude to Accession'.[1]

A Foreign Office circular of 6 August 1947 providing guidance to chiefs of British diplomatic missions pointed out that since His Majesty's Government did not propose to recognize any Indian State as a separate international entity, 'it would be most unfortunate if any other power gave such recognition to any State at this stage as this would prejudice the negotiations now in progress between the Indian States and the new Dominions'. It was understood that the United States Government had received reports that certain Arab States may be contemplating diplomatic recognition of certain Indian States after 15 August. The State Department had accordingly instructed posts in Egypt and the Middle East to inform the governments to which they were accredited that the United States shared the desire of the British Government that Indian States should associate themselves with one or other of the new Dominions, and that the United States had no intention of according any Indian State diplomatic recognition.

The position of the princes was inherently weak. By guaranteeing them protection against external aggression as well as internal subversion, the British Government had secured their dependence on itself, but the policy had weakened the sense of responsibility and moral fibre of the rulers. Barring some honourable exceptions, they were a decadent class more interested in a life of luxury for themselves than in the welfare of their subjects. The standard of civil liberties in the States was low and the people of the States could not remain unaffected by the wind of change blowing in British India.

During the debate on the Indian Independence Bill in the House of Commons on 10 July, two members made perceptive references to the Indian States. Lester Hutchinson said they were 'remarkable examples of the survival of the unfittest. They would not have existed without the might of the paramount power behind them.' And Woodrow Wyatt thought 'the worst thing' which the British Government ever did in India was to take away from the people of the States the ultimate sanction that a people always have against a bad ruler—the sanction of revolt and rebellion. Before the States Department was set up, Patel had told Mountbatten not to bother about the States because after the transfer of

---

[2] Ibid., p. 147

power the people of the States would rise, depose their rulers and throw in their lot with Congress.[1]

The princes, moreover, had no unity of purpose. Some had joined the Constituent Assembly [of India][2] while others had stood aside. Their reaction to the 3 June plan was also discordant. On 1 June, Mountbatten had disclosed the outline of the plan privately to the Nawab of Bhopal and the Maharaja of Bikaner in separate meetings. The Nawab was highly critical of the plan and complained that his Majesty's Government had once more let the States down. The Cabinet Mission Plan would have produced a weak centre[3] he pointed out, but the new plan would set up two strong centres; the States would be destroyed whichever Dominion they joined. The Maharaja of Bikaner, on the other hand, said that Congress had extended a 'great welcome' to those States which had sent representatives to the Constituent Assembly; the rulers of the States which had not sent representatives 'had been activated purely by selfish reasons'.[4]

Copies of the plan of 3 June 1947 were first made available to the princes when Mountbatten met the members of the States Negotiating Committee earlier that day. His advice to those who were doubtful about whether or not to join either Constituent Assembly was to cast their minds forward ten years and consider what the situation in the country and in the world as a whole was likely to be at that time.

By 15 August, apart from the States which clearly had to accede to Pakistan, all but three had succumbed to Mountbatten's pressure and joined India.[5] The three in question were Junagarh, Hyderabad and Kashmir. Before discussing the cases of these three, let us refer to Bhopal, Travancore,

---

[1] H. V. Hodson, *The Great Divide*, p. 367.

[2] It will be remembered that the Constituent Assembly of Pakistan did not come into existence until 11 August 1947, at Karachi.

[3] He explained this at greater length in a letter to Mountbatten on 22 July 1947: 'The States' acceptance of the Cabinet Mission's plan was only accorded under the belief that there would be one United India in which the States, the Muslim League and other minorities would be able to combine, and by their combined voting power would be able to hold their proper position in the future constitutional structure of India. The position under the present plan is vastly different, for any State or group of States acceding to the "India Dominion" would be relegated to the position of a permanent powerless minority at the mercy of the Congress party, whose avowed intention it is to wipe out the Princely Order from the political map of India'. TOP XII, p. 292.

[4] TOP XI, p. 32. Hodson, op. cit. p. 361.

[5] In the interests of accuracy it should be mentioned that two small Hindu-majority States under Muslim rulers in Kathiawar had also not yet acceded to India, but this proved to be inconsequential.

Dholpur, Rampur and Jodhpur, all of which gave Mountbatten trouble before they came to terms with him.

BHOPAL

The Nawab of Bhopal resigned as Chancellor of the Chamber of Princes and at first wished to remain independent. On 22 July he wrote to Mountbatten that, though Congress made no secret of its intentions to destroy the princes, 'We, the independent states, are still prepared to negotiate with both Dominions on a basis of complete equality and reciprocity'. He said that Bhopal State was not prepared to attend the meeting on 25 July, when Mountbatten was to address the Chamber of Princes, because the rulers were being invited 'like the Oysters to attend the tea party with the Walrus and the Carpenter'.[1]

In his Personal Report on 8 August, Mountbatten wrote that the Nawab of Bhopal had informed him that he wished to adbicate in favour of his twenty-three-year-old daughter, and that he was thinking of serving Pakistan 'presumably as a Governor-General'.

The Nawab finally asked for ten days' extension [beyond 15 August] before signing the Instrument of Accession and the Standstill Agreement, but accepted Mountbatten's proposed compromise and signed and dated his Instrument of Accession and Standstill Agreement before the midnight of 14 August, and delivered them to Mountbatten in a sealed envelope on the understanding that they would not be handed over to the States Department until the evening of 25 August.

TRAVANCORE

The Dewan (chief minister) of Travancore, Sir C. P. Ramaswami Aiyar, had started in June to send telegrams to Mountbatten and to issue statements to the Press saying that Travancore would become completely independent on 15 August 1947. On 6 July, the Dewan said in a telegram to Attlee that the independence of Travancore was essential 'for its existence and for the maintenance of those high standards of life, education and public health which are more easily realisable in this State than elsewhere in India'. Attlee referred the Dewan to his speech in the House of Commons on 10 July, in which he had expressed the hope that all States would in due course find their appropriate place within one or other of the new dominions within the British Commonwealth.

---

[1] TOP XII , pp. 291-7.

During an interview with Mountbatten on 22 July, the Dewan declared that Travancore would never accede to the Dominion of India and that he had already made preliminary terms with Jinnah, including a trade agreement. After Mountbatten had 'worked on him for two hours' he came round as far as to say that he might consider a treaty with India.

When he came back on the following day, Mountbatten informed him that Patel was not prepared to accept a treaty; Travancore could either accede to India or stay right out. Mountbatten also told him that Dalmia[1] had that morning paid 5 lakhs of rupees into the Travancore Congress Party funds to start internal trouble after 15 August, and that there was more to follow, and advised him that his only escape from internal trouble lay in accession to India. The Dewan recognized that this was a serious matter and asked Mountbatten to write to the Maharaja putting his proposals before him. Mountbatten immediately gave him a letter for the Maharaja containing the assurance that accession on the three subjects of Defence, External Affairs and Communications 'would not detract from the independence of Travancore'.[2] On 25 July a murderous attack with a billhook was made on the Dewan at Trivandrum, the capital of Travancore. He escaped with facial injuries. At the same time, Congress threatened direct action, including the burning of buildings and toddy shops, from 1 August. Not surprisingly, the Maharaja acceded to India on 30 July.

In a letter to Mountbatten dated 9 August, Listowel wrote with evident satisfaction 'I am sorry to hear that C. P. Ramaswami Aiyar should have been so severely mauled on his return to Travancore, but no doubt his going out of business at any rate temporarily has had the valuable effect of deciding the Maharaja to call off his bid for independence.'[3]

DHOLPUR

The Maharaja of Dholpur believed so deeply in the divine right of kings that Mountbatten feared that it might not be possible to make him see the need for accession to a future republic. Mountbatten had several interviews and exchanges of letters with him and also got as many other rulers to speak to him as he could. A letter which Mountbatten wrote to the Maharaja on 29 July shows the extent to which he could go to secure the accession of a prince:

---

[1] A rich industrialist sympathetic to the Congress Party.
[2] TOP XII, p.298.
[3] Ibid., p. 633.

I have never been able to understand Your Highness's point of view that you are afraid that if you sign the Instrument of Accession you will find yourself linked against your will to an independent Government without a monarchical head. If you accede now you will be joining a Dominion with the King as head. If they change the constitution to a republic and leave the British Empire, the Instrument of Accession does not bind you in any way to remain with the republic. It would appear to me that that would be the moment for Your Highness to decide if you wish to remain with India or reclaim full sovereign independence.

I know that His Majesty would personally be grieved if you elected to sever your connection with him whilst he was still King of India now that it has been made clear that this would not involve you in accepting to remain within a republic if this was inacceptable to you when the time came. I too will be grieved if I find that Your Highness refuses to accede before the 14th August.[1]

It was not untill the evening of 14 August that the Maharaja personally told Mountbatten that he had finally decided to sign the Instrument of Accession to India. He bade farewell to the Viceroy with tears in his eyes, saying, 'this breaks an alliance between my ancestors and your King's ancestors which has existed since 1765'

RAMPUR

Rampur was a small state in the United Provinces. It had a Hindu majority but a Muslim ruler. The Nawab of Rampur accompanied by his Chief Minister, Bashir Husain Zaidi, came to see Mountbatten on 5 August. The Nawab complained that Jinnah had been bringing every possible pressure to stop him from acceding to India. Zaidi said Liaquat and other Muslim leaders had threatened him with dire consequences if the Nawab deserted Pakistan and joined India. Zaidi had replied that Rampur would gladly join Pakistan if the Muslim League could transfer it to a position of contiguity with Pakistan. Zaidi asked Liaquat specifically how Pakistan could help Rampur against India. Liaquat replied, 'by moral support'. Zaidi had therefore advised the Nawab to accede to India. The Muslim League thereupon organized riots in Rampur in which several government buildings were set on fire and the servant of an inspector of police was burnt alive. The riots were put down under Mountbatten's orders by 300 of the Crown Representative's Police[2] and half a battalion of troops.

[1] TOP XII, p. 392.
[2] The Viceroy had at his disposal 1,500 men called the Crown Representative's Police for use at his discretion to maintain law and order in the States.

JODHPUR

Jodhpur was a Hindu-majority state with a Hindu ruler. It bordered on Pakistan and by acceding to Pakistan would have provided indirect contiguity to Pakistan for some other Rajput states. On 8 August, Mountbatten received a letter from the Prime Minister of Jodhpur telling him that the young Maharaja of Jodhpur had been taken to see Jinnah in the presence of the Nawab of Bhopal. Jinnah had offered Jodhpur the use of Karachi as a free port; the free import of arms; jurisdiction over the Jodhpur-Hyderabad (Sind) railway; and a supply of grain to famine-threatened districts on condition that Jodhpur would declare its independence on 15 August and then join Pakistan.[1]

The Maharaja's visit to Jinnah alarmed Mountbatten and Patel and he was promptly summoned to appear before the Viceroy. The States Department had 'really got the wind up' about the possibility of Jodhpur acceding to Pakistan and opening the way for some others to do the same, and 'Patel was prepared to go to almost any lengths to prevent it happening'. He promised that the Maharaja could continue to allow his Rajputs to carry and import arms without restriction; that India would supply food for Jodhpur's famine stricken districts; and that he would give the highest priority for the building of a railway from Jodhpur to Cutch to open up a port for Jodhpur.[2] The Maharaja, evidently satisfied, acceded to India.

However, when the Nawab of Bhopal saw Mountbatten on 11 August, he related quite a different version of the Maharaja's interview with Jinnah and assured Mountbatten 'on his word of honour' that what he was telling was the exact truth. He said that he had taken the Maharaja of Jodhpur to see Jinnah because the Maharaja was 'particularly anxious' to see the Muslim League chief 'as quickly as possible' to find out what terms he would offer. At the interview, the Maharaja asked Jinnah what terms he was offering to the States which wished to establish a relationship with Pakistan. Jinnah replied, 'We are ready to come to treaty relations with the States and we shall give them very good terms, and we shall treat them as independent States'. The Nawab stated that, 'The question of whether he should or should not sign an Instrument of Accession never arose.'[3]

---

[1] TOP XII p. 603.
[2] TOP XII, p. 767.
[3] TOP XII, p. 660.

JUNAGARH

The three States which had not acceded to either Dominion by 15 August 1947—Junagarh, Hyderabad and Kashmir—were all ruled by princes whose own religion was different from that of the majority of their subjects. If the principle which had governed the partition of India and the provinces of the Punjab and Bengal had been followed, Junagarh and Hyderabad, which had Hindu majorities and were contiguous with India, should have joined India, and Kashmir, which had a Muslim majority and for the most part was contiguous to Pakistan, should have opted for Pakistan. But, true to form, Congress and the Muslim League managed to quarrel over all three of them.

Junagarh, a State on the Kathiawar coast, had an area of 3,337 square miles and a population of about 700,000, of whom over 80 per cent were Hindus. Its ruler was a Muslim. By land it was entirely contiguous to India but it could maintain communication with Pakistan by sea through its port, Veraval, which is about 300 miles south of Karachi.

Congress had assumed that Junagarh would accede to India and was taken by surprise when newspapers reported on 17 August that the State had acceded to Pakistan on 15 August. The accession was accepted by Pakistan on 5 September and on 13 September Pakistan informed India of its decision. Mountbatten, now Governor-General of India only, protested to Governor-General Jinnah that Pakistan's acceptance of Junagarh's accession was 'in utter violation of the principles on which the partition of India was agreed upon and effected'.

A meeting of the Indian Cabinet had been summoned for the afternoon of 17 September. Having come to know that the members of the Cabinet had decided amongst themselves to take military action against Junagarh, Mountbatten sent for Nehru and Patel before the meeting and was able to persuade them to take no action which would put India in the wrong and Pakistan in the right. He urged them to stand by the principle of a referendum to discover the people's will. At the cabinet meeting, Nehru and Patel were able to dissuade their colleagues from demanding an outright military invasion of Junagarh. It was decided instead that 'Indian and local troops of acceding States should be disposed round Junagarh but should not occupy it'.[1]

At a public meeting at Bombay on 25 September the Kathiawar Congress leaders announced the formation of an *Arzi Hukumat* (Provisional

---

[1] H. V. Hodson, *The Great Divide*, p. 431. Campbell-Johnson, *Mission with Mountbatten*, p. 194.

Government) of Junagarh, and a press communique issued by the Government of India on 6 October declared that any decision involving the fate of large numbers of people must necessarily depend on the wishes of those people and that the issues regarding Junagarh should, therefore, be decided by a referendum or plebiscite of the people of the State.

Finding his position increasingly hopeless, the Nawab of Junagarh fled to Karachi toward the end of October. On 2 November Junagarh was occupied by the *Arzi Hukumat,* and on 9 November Indian troops marched into the State and the administration was taken over by the Indian Regional Commissioner. Finally, a referendum conducted by the Indian authorities in February 1948 resulted in India's farour.

HYDERABAD

Hyderabad was the premier State in India. Its population was about sixteen million, its area was over 82,000 square miles, and its revenue was 26 crores of rupees (260 million) per annum. It had its own coinage, paper currency and stamps. Not surprisingly, it felt it was entitled to assume sovereign status after the British had relinquished power in India. Its population was over 85 per cent Hindu but its ruler, the Nizam, was a Muslim. His pre-eminence among the Indian princes was underscored by the appellation 'His Exalted Highness'. He was also permitted to call himself 'Faithful Ally of the British Government'.

The Nizam's dynasty had been founded early in the eighteenth century by Nizamul Mulk, a grandee of the Mughal Empire. Because of its size and resources the Muslims of India were emotionally interested in its future. Chaudhri Muhammad Ali, who was a confidant of Jinnah, has written that Jinnah's pronouncements that with the lapse of paramountcy the States would regain their full sovereignty were not made merely because of 'the Quaid-i-Azam's penchant for constitutionalism...They were also intended to safeguard Hyderabad's independence. By the same token they might jeopardize Kashmir's accession to Pakistan but that was not considered a great risk'.[1] But Hyderabad occupied the heartland of south India and was surrounded on all sides by Indian territory.

Nine days after the 3 June 1947 partition plan had been announced, the Nizam issued a *firman* (proclamation) that he had decided not to send representatives to either of the two Constituent Assemblies; that upon the departure of the paramount power he would be entitled to 'resume' the

---

[1] Chaudhri Muhammad Ali, *The Emergence of Pakistan*, p. 230.

status of an independent sovereign; and that 'the question of the nature and extent of the association or relationship between my State and the units in British India remains for decision at a later stage.'

On 11 July, Mountbatten received a delegation from Hyderabad headed by the Nawab of Chhatari[1] and including Sir Walter Monckton, a member of the English bar who was the Nizam's Constitutional Adviser. Mountbatten conceded that legally the States would be 'absolutely free' after 15 August, but with regard to the requests which had been made by the Nizam of Hyderabad for Dominion Status, pointed out that the British Government had decided that it could not agree to the grant of Dominion Status to individual States. Although Hyderabad was a country of the size of France with a population bigger than any existing Dominion, it was completely enclosed by the territories of British India and His Majesty's Government did not feel that they could commit themselves to the responsibility of coming to the aid of a country which was thus surrounded.[2]

When Mountbatten informed Jinnah on the following day of his interview with the Hyderabad delegation, Jinnah said, 'If Congress attempted to exert any pressure on Hyderabad, every Muslim throughout the whole of India, yes, all the hundred million Muslims, would rise as one man to defend the oldest Muslim dynasty in India.'[3] When a delegation from Hyderabad went to see Jinnah, he said he could not agree to the Nizam's joining India even if he inserted a clause that his forces must never be used to fight Pakistan; 'I require Hyderabad as an active ally and not as a neutral in any such war', he declared.[4]

The negotiations between the Nizam and Mountbatten continued through correspondence and through Hyderabad's delegations to Delhi. Mountbatten, who had great confidence in his powers of persuasion in face-to-face talks, regretted that he never was able to meet the Nizam personally.

We have Monckton's note[5] on a meeting of the Hyderabad delgation with Mountbatten on 3 August. It states that Mountbatten said 'repeatedly and emphatically that if HEH [His Exalted Highness] did not join the [Indian] Dominion, his State would be ruined and he would lose his throne'. During Mountbatten's temporary absence from the meeting, V.P.

---

[1] The Nawab of Chhatari was President of the Nizam's Executive Council, i.e., the Prime Minister.

[2] TOP XII, pp. 81, 85.

[3] Ibid., p. 121.

[4] Ibid., p. 337.

[5] Ibid., p. 495.

Menon elaborated on the consequences if Hyderabad did not join India: 'There wouldn't be any overt act but there would be refusal of grain levy and of taxes and other payments. Disorders would arise and if they became serious, as they would, India would not stand by and see that state of affairs to continue. Their propaganda was not only for accession but for responsible government. If responsible government were conceded, he had no doubt that Hyderabad would join the Dominion.'

On 8 August the Nizam wrote to Mountbatten that he could not contemplate bringing his State 'into organic union with either of the two new Dominions' but was willing to see it play 'its proper part in the defence of the Indian sub-continent' and to conduct its foreign policy 'in general conformity with the Foreign Affairs of the whole sub-continent'. He was prepared to enter into a treaty with India which would provide that Hyderabad would remain neutral if the two Dominions pursued a mutually hostile foreign policy.[1]

After consultations with Patel, Mountbatten made it clear to Monckton and Chhatari that India would not accept a treaty with Hyderabad but would insist on accession. However, hoping that given more time the Nizam might accept accession, Mountbatten was able to induce the Indian Cabinet to grant an extension of two months beyond 15 August, after which Hyderabad must accede to India. At a Staff Meeting on 7 August, he explained that the main reason why the Nizam had not yet decided to accede to India was that although the Muslims in his State represented only 15 per cent of the population, they filled almost all the government, police and military posts. Therefore, it was against a revolt by them rather than a revolt by the non-Muslims that he had to guard. The Nizam felt that it would take time to educate 'the all-powerful minority to the step of accession'. Although Mountbatten became a constitutional Governor-General on 15 August, he continued to conduct negotiations with the Nizam at the request of the Indian cabinet.

In the meantime the *Razakars,* the extreme Muslim organization in Hyderabad under the command of Kasim Razvi, were gaining strength[2], and at the end of November installed Laik Ali, a local industrialist, as President of the Executive Council.

Though India normally refused to sign a Standstill Agreement with a State which did not at the same time execute the Instrument of Accession, in the case of Hyderabad it accepted a Standstill Agreement on 29 November 1947.

---

[1] Ibid., p. 575.

[2] Every *Razakar* had to take an oath that he would fight to the last to maintain the supremacy of Muslim power in the Deccan.

On 21 June 1948, Mountbatten left India without securing Hyderabad's accession to India. The pressure against Hyderabad mounted as Menon had threatened. There were charges of raids and breaches of the Standstill Agreement by both sides. On 24 August Hyderabad filed a complaint before the Security Council of the United Nations. Indian forces invaded Hyderabad on 13 September, two days after Jinnah's death, and subdued all resistance within a week. 'Operation Polo' cost about 800 lives, mostly among the less well-equipped Hyderabad forces.

KASHMIR

The Kashmir problem dates back to the days of the transfer of power and remains unresolved to this day. India and Pakistan have already fought three times over Kashmir and could go to war over it again. At the present time, the State stands divided between the two countries and each side alleges that the other is in unlawful possession of the territory under its control. Because of its importance in the history of Indo-Pakistani relations, the dispute needs to be discussed in some detail.

The State of Jammu and Kashmir, with an area of 84,471 square miles, was the largest princely State in India. Because of its mountainous terrain it was sparsely populated. On the eve of the transfer of power its population was as follows:[1]

Jammu
Muslims	1,208,675	61%
Hindus	772,760	39%
Kashmir		
Muslims	1,589,488	92%
Hindus	139,217	7.8%
Total Muslims in the State	3,101,247	77.11%
Total Hindus in the State	809,165	21%
Total Sikhs in the State	65,903	
Total Buddhists in the State	40,696	
Others	4,605	
Total population	4,021,616	

The State occupied a strategic position because it had borders with Tibet, China and Afghanistan, and was parted from the Soviet Union only

---

[1] TOP, XI, p. 442.

by a strip of under fifty miles. In the subcontinent, Kashmir bordered largely, though not wholly, on Pakistan. Before the Radcliffe Boundary Award which was made on 16 August, it had no road connection with what was to be the territory of independent India. Its only access to the outside world by road was along the Jhelum Valley via Rawalpindi; its only rail link was also with the future Pakistan at Sialkot. Pakistan's three vital rivers—the Indus, the Jhelum and the Chenab—all originate in Kashmir, and down their waters floated the timber which was Kashmir's most valuable export. Fruit, another important product, was also transported via Rawalpindi. In the reverse direction, Kashmir's necessities of life, including salt, sugar, and petroleum as well as the tourists with their spending money, had all to pass through Pakistan. Thus the two principles of accession—communal majority and geographical contiguity—both demanded that Kashmir should accede to Pakistan. But its ruler was a Dogra Hindu, Sir Hari Singh, who had ascended the throne on 23 September 1925.

We have already related how a Dogra chieftain named Gulab Singh became the ruler of Jammu and Kashmir in 1846. During the century that followed, the Hindu Dogras ruled their hapless Muslim subjects with the greatest cruelty and callousness. Until 1934, for example, the slaughter of a cow, even if useless, was a capital offence.

However, not even the placid politics of Kashmir could remain forever unaffected by the agitation launched in India by Gandhi from 1920 onwards. Spearheaded by Sheikh Abdullah, a young man recently returned from Aligarh Muslim University, the movement in Kashmir at first took the form of demands by Muslims for a better life in their own country. By 1931, the agitation had become serious enough for the Maharaja to order Abdullah's arrest and declare martial law. Upon his release in the following year, Abdullah resumed his political activity and founded a political party called the All-Jammu and Kashmir Muslim Conference.

Broadly, politics inside Kashmir in the ensuing years followed the same course as politics next door in the North-West Frontier Province. Just as, in their efforts to win autonomy from the British, the Khan brothers had turned for help to the Indian National Congress as the only effective political party in India at the time, Abdullah, too, turned to Congress for assistance in his fight for liberation from the oppressive rule of the Maharaja. In 1939, he converted the Muslim Conference into the National Conference, opening its doors to both Muslims and non-Muslims. In 1940, the Muslim League passed the Pakistan Resolution. This caused one of Abdullah's right-hand men, Ghulam Abbas, to separate from his chief and revive the Muslim Conference (1941). Kashmiri politics thus assumed virtually the same shape as Indian politics. The National Conference was already an appendage of the Congress Party of India; the Muslim Conference now became that of the Muslim League. During this period, Abdullah also formed a close personal friendship with Jawaharlal Nehru.

As the movement for Pakistan gathered momentum, Abdullah's popularity correspondingly diminished among his Muslim compatriots, just as that of the Khan brothers had slipped in the adjoining territory. 'As Muslims in British India became more and more pronounced in their support for an independent Pakistan', writes Korbel, 'the Muslims in Jammu and Kashmir began to return to the Muslim Conference led by Ghulam Abbas, abandoning the ranks of the National Conference of Sheikh Abdullah.'[1]

Though Abdullah and Abbas were pursuing different ends, the Maharaja, as the sole repository of power, was their common target. In his eyes, therefore, they were both equally reprehensible. On 20 May 1946, Abdullah was arrested and sentenced to nine years' imprisonment for treason. In September, Abbas was apprehended for launching a 'direct action' campaign against the ruler. Thus, when the Congress and League leaders accepted the partition plan in India on 3 June 1947, both of Kashmir's foremost political leaders were prisoners of the Maharaja.

The origins of the Kashmir dispute between India and Pakistan are less well-known than they deserve to be in the interests of accurate history. Even writers of the calibre of Menon, who had access to official documents and was also close to Congress circles, and Hodson, who had seen all the Mountbatten papers relating to India, have averred that Indian leaders at first took no interest in the accession of Kashmir, but were forced to get involved when the tribesmen, backed by Pakistan, invaded Kashmir in the fourth week of October 1947. Menon asserts:

If the invasion by the raiders had not taken place, I can say in the face of any contradiction that the Government of India would have left Kashmir alone.[2]

And Hodson writes:

In the light of later events, it is hard to credit that at this stage the Indian leaders

[1] Josef Korbel, *Danger in Kashmir*, p. 22. Korbel had served as a member of the United Nations Commission on India and Pakistan and in that capacity had visited India, Pakistan and Kashmir, conferred with their leaders and met their people.
[2] V. P. Menon, *Integration of the Indian States*, p. 413.

seemed indifferent to the accession or non-accession of Kashmir and Jammu[1]...The fanatical concern which developed in India after the State's accession, and especially after this event had brought India and Pakistan into open conflict, are in sharp contrast to the comparative detachment with which the State's future was viewed in Delhi before the end of October 1947.[2]

First a word about Menon himself. At a staff meeting on 30 June 1947, he had stated that 'to depart from the "Muslim-majority" principle at this stage' in respect of the Chittagong Hill Tracts 'would be extremely dangerous and lead to endless complications'.[3] But when it came to overwhelmingly Muslim-majority Kashmir, he wrote in a brief for Mountbatten on 17 July 1947 that it 'presents some difficulty' and 'the issue should not be forced by either party...Unlike Hyderabad, it does not lie in the bosom of Pakistan and it can claim an exit to India, especially if a portion of the Gurdaspur district goes to East [i.e. Indian] Punjab'.[4] Evidently, he was hoping that time and the Radcliffe Award would solve the 'difficulty' in the way of Kashmir joining India.[5]

With regard to the earnest desire of the two Indian leaders, Gandhi and Nehru, that Kashmir should affiliate itself with India, Mountbatten recorded in his Personal Report of 27 June 1947 that, 'On the subject of the States, Nehru and Gandhi are pathological... They were both very anxious that he [the Maharaja of Kashmir] should make no declaration of independence, and should, in fact, indicate a willingness to join the constituent Assembly [of India].'[6]

Jawaharlal Nehru's deep sentimental attachment to his beautiful ancestral homeland, Kashmir, is well known and, indeed, no one has expressed this love in more lyrical terms than Nehru himself. Writing of a visit he made there in 1940, he said that he had been repeatedly invited to go there by Sheikh Abdullah and other friends 'and everyone who was of Kashmir reminded me that I, too, was a son of this noble land and owed a duty to it. I smiled at their insistence, for the urge within was far greater than any that they could have placed before me.' And on getting there, 'my

---

[1] H. V. Hodson, *The Great Divide*, p. 383.

[2] Ibid., p. 441.

[3] TOP XI, 798.

[4] TOP XI, p. 213.

[5] *See,* pp. 552-5, showing that Mountbatten and the Maharaja of Kashmir were equally aware that Kashmir's accession to India would become feasible if the Boundary Comission awarded the desired part of Gurdaspur district to India, and examining the Pakistanis' allegation that Mountbatten influenced Radcliffe to do just that.

[6] TOP XI, p. 687. In June 1947 there existed only the Constituent Assembly of India.

mind was filled with excitement of my return, and it pleased me to be welcomed everywhere as a brother and a comrade, who, in spite of long absence, was still of Kashmir, and was coming back to his old homeland... Wherever I went these women of Kashmir came to welcome me and treat me as a brother or a son. It was a joy to meet them and see the affection in their eyes. At Mutton, old Kashmiri ladies came to bless me and kiss me on the forehead, as a mother does to her son.' Kashmir herself was 'like some supremely beautiful woman, whose beauty is almost impersonal and above human desire...As I gazed at it, it seemed to me dream-like and unreal, like the hopes and desires that fill us and so seldom find fulfilment. It was like the face of the beloved that one sees in a dream and that fades away on awakening.' The visit was over, 'but Kashmir calls back, its pull is stronger than ever, it whispers its fairy magic to the ears, and its memory disturbs the mind. How can they who have fallen under its spell release themselves from this enchantment?'[1] With remarkable premonition of what happened after independence, he wrote at another time, 'My partiality for it [Kashmir] occasionally leads me astray.'[2] 'May I take the House into my confidence?' he said, in a speech to the Constituent Assembly on 7 September 1948, when the dispute with Pakistan was in full swing. 'In the early stages, towards the end of October and in November, and indeed subsequently, I was so exercised over Kashmir, and if anything had happened or was likely to have happened to Kashmir, which, according to me, might have been disastrous for Kashmir, I would have been heartbroken. I was intensely interested, apart from the larger reasons which the government have, for emotional personal reasons: I do not want to hide this: I am interested in Kashmir.'[3]

On the other hand Patel, though no friend of Pakistan, was willing to see Kashmir go to Pakistan. As a realist he foresaw that Kashmir with its Muslim majority would contribute to India's instability.[4]

Congress's visible efforts to get Kashmir in fact commenced several months before the first tribesman was seen inside Kashmir. In May 1947 Acharya Kripalani, President of the Indian Congress Party, visited Kashmir but 'failed to persuade the Maharaja to join the Constituent

---

[1] Jawaharlal Nehru, *The Unity of India*, pp. 221-40.
[2] Nehru, *The Discovery of India*, p. 571. This book was written by Nehru in 1944, during imprisonment in Ahmadnagar Fort.
[3] Nehru, *Speeches*, I, pp. 194-5.
[4] *See*, p. 607.

Assembly [of India]'.[1] In commenting on Kripalani's visit, a leading Congress newspaper revealed Congress strategy: 'If the Maharaja evolves a new democratic constitution and holds fresh elections under it, enabling Sheikh Abdullah's party to have its legitimate share in the administration, the co-operation of Kashmir with the Constituent Assembly and its marriage with the Indian Union will be facilitated.'[2]

Kripalani was followed into Kashmir by the Maharajas of Patiala, Kapurthala and Faridkot and by the rulers of the Punjab Hill States, all of whom were intent upon discharging the 'noble mission'—to use the *Tribune's* phrase—of persuading the Maharaja of Kashmir to follow their own example and join India.

At the beginning of June, Nehru told Mountbatten that he must go to Kashmir immediately to secure the release from prison of Sheikh Abdullah. A few days later Gandhi saw Mountbatten and suggested that he should go to Kashmir to prepare the way for Nehru. Mountbatten was able to persuade them to let him go instead and made a visit to the State from 18 to 23 June. At his request Nehru on 17 June sent him a note on Kashmir. This note reveals Nehru's scheme for overcoming the hurdle of the Muslim majority in Kashmir. That it had Gandhi's support will become evident when we describe the Mahatma's own visit to Kashmir in early August and his report on it to Nehru.

In his note Nehru sketched the recent political developments in Kashmir and went on:

Sheikh Abdullah's organization, the Kashmir National Conference, has demonstrated its hold on the masses and there is no doubt that Sheikh Abdullah himself is by far the most outstanding leader in Kashmir...The National Conference has stood for and still stands for Kashmir joining the Constituent Assembly of India. From the Maharaja's point of view this is obviously desirable and preferable to joining the other Assembly. Mr Kak[3], however, comes in the way and it has been reported that he has told the Maharaja that the Viceroy favours Kashmir joining the Pakistan Assembly because of the geographical situation of the State. Mr Kak has also tried to convince the Maharaja that as soon as he joins the Indian Union, there will be communal riots in the State and that possibly hostile people from the surrounding territory of Pakistan might enter Kashmir and give trouble. The Maharaja is timid and is in a fix. There is no doubt that if Mr Kak remains in control, he will himself see to it that there are communal riots.

---

[1] Sisir Gupta, *Kashmir*, p. 95.
[2] *The Tribune*, 29 May 1947.
[3] Ram Chandra Kak, a Kashmiri, had been Prime Minister of Kashmir since 1945.

Nehru recommended two immediate steps. First, Kak 'must be removed from his position of authority'. Secondly, Sheikh Abdullah and other political prisoners must be released. And he concluded with the following observations:

> If any attempt is made to push Kashmir into the Pakistan Constituent Assembly, there is likely to be much trouble because the National Conference is not in favour of it and the Maharaja's position would also become very difficult. The normal and obvious course appears to be for Kashmir to join the Constituent Assembly of India. This will satisfy both the popular demand and the Maharaja's wishes. It is absurd to think that Pakistan would create trouble if this happens.[1]

Upon arrival in Kashmir, Mountbatten found the Maharaja 'politically very elusive', and the only conversations that took place were during car drives. Mountbatten urged the Maharaja and Kak not to make any declaration of independence but to find out, one way or another, the will of the people of Kashmir and to announce their intention by 14 August and send representatives accordingly to one Constituent Assembly or the other. He told them that the newly created States Department was prepared to give an assurance that if Kashmir went to Pakistan this would not be regarded as an unfriendly act by the Government of India. He stressed the dangerous situation in which Kashmir would find itself if it lacked the support of one of the two Dominions by the date of the transfer of power. His intention was to give this advice privately to the Maharaja alone, and then to repeat it in the presence of Kak with George Abell and the Resident, Colonel Webb, present, when minutes could be kept. The Maharaja suggested that the meeting should take place on the last day of the visit, but when the time came the Maharaja sent a message that he was confined to bed with colic and unable to attend the meeting. It seemed that this was his usual excuse to avoid a difficult discussion.[2]

When Mountbatten returned to Delhi, Nehru was disappointed to learn that the Viceroy had not been able to obtain Abdullah's release, and renewed his urgent request to go to Kashmir personally. The Maharaja as well as Mountbatten were both against any political leaders visiting Kashmir. In the case of Nehru, in particular, they were apprehensive that an ugly incident similar to the one in May 1946 might take place. At that time, Nehru had rushed to Kashmir in the middle of important discussions with the Cabinet Mission to assist in the defence of Abdullah, who was on

---

[1] For the full text of Nehru's note *see*, TOP XI, pp. 442-8.

[2] Campbell-Johnson, *Mission with Mountbatten*, p. 120.

trial for treason. He was prohibited from entering the State and was arrested at Uri for defying the ban. With Wavell's help, Azad was able to speak to Nehru on the telephone and persuade him to return on the promise 'that the Congress would make his cause in Kashmir their own'. Wavell then arranged for an aeroplane to bring Nehru back to Delhi.

By 27 July, Nehru's patience had run out and he wrote to Mountbatten that he had 'decided' to go to Kashmir on about 4 August. On the next day, Mountbatten appealed to Gandhi to suggest to Nehru that his own visit at that time would be better than a visit from Nehru, 'for I really do not know how the future Prime Minister [of India] can be spared from Delhi with only 18 days left for him to take over'. Nehru, having seen Mountbatten's letter, wrote to the Mahatma immediately that he would go ahead with his plans because 'as between visiting Kashmir when my people need me there and being Prime Minister, I prefer the former'.[1]

Mountbatten summoned an urgent meeting with Gandhi, Nehru and Patel on 29 July at which Patel said that between the 'two evils' of a visit by Gandhi or one by Nehru, 'Gandhiji's visit would be the lesser evil'. Finally, it was agreed that Gandhi should go.[2] Mountbatten was privately informed that when Patel had tried to reason with Nehru the night before the meeting, Nehru 'had broken down and wept, explaining that Kashmir meant more to him than anything else'.[3]

Gandhi reached Srinagar on the afternoon of 1 August and kept his promise to Mountbatten that he would refrain from making any political speeches, but he saw the Maharaja, Kak and the National Conference workers. On returning to Delhi, he sent 'a report' to Nehru, in the course of which he wrote reassuringly: 'Bakshi [Ghulam Muhammad, Abdullah's deputy in the National Conference] was most sanguine that the result of the free vote of the people, whether on the adult franchise or on the existing register, would be in favour of Kashmir joining the [Indian] Union provided of course that Sheikh Abdullah and his co-prisoners are released, all bans were removed and the present Prime Minister was not in power.' In a letter to Patel he said, 'He (the Maharaja) wishes to remove Kak...the only question is how...In my opinion the Kashmir problem can be solved'.[4]

Prem Nath Bazaz, the well-known Kashmiri Hindu writer, sums up the 'real nature' of Gandhi's visit in these words: 'The Congress leaders were ready to help the Maharaja but on two conditions. First, Ram Chandra

---

[1] Pyarelal, op. cit., p. 354.
[2] TOP XII, p. 397.
[3] *Report on the Last Viceroyalty*, p. 147, para. 59.
[4] Pyarelal, op. cit., p. 357-8.

Kak, who was for his own reasons in favour of the State remaining independent, was to be replaced by a new Prime Minister acceptable to the Congress leaders and secondly, the State was to accede to the Indian Union.'[1]

Gandhi's optimistic assessment, that a majority in favour of India in Kashmir could be secured provided the power structure in the State was suitably manipulated, obviously heartened the Maharaja. Mountbatten in his Personal Report of 16 August 1947 wrote, 'He [the Maharaja] now talks of holding a referendum to decide whether to join Pakistan or India, provided that the Boundary Commission give him land communications with India.'[2]

Within a week of Gandhi's visit to the State, Kak was replaced as Prime Minister by Janak Singh, a Dogra, and on 29 September Abdullah was released and conferred with the Congress leaders in Delhi.

Five years later, Nehru revealed the advice given to Abdullah and his colleagues: 'This matter [accession to India] must not be hurried and it was our idea that a Constituent Assembly should be elected in Kashmir quickly and as soon as possible decide these and other questions.'[3]

So, what about the contention of Mountbatten's defenders that during his visit to Kashmir he endeavoured to make the Maharaja join Pakistan? His advice, that the decision to join either India or Pakistan should be announced after ascertaining the will of the people, has been taken to mean that he was in effect, asking the Maharaja to accede to Pakistan because the majority of the Kashmiris, being Muslim, would have voted for Pakistan. But, as we have pointed out above, the Viceroy's favourite friend, Nehru, had already indicated to him how the political situation inside Kashmir could be manipulated to make it seem that popular opinion was in favour of uniting with India. And Gandhi, after an on-the-spot assessment of the situation in the beginning of August, had confirmed that the scheme sketched out by Nehru would indeed do the trick.

Mountbatten's intimation to the Maharaja that the Indian States Department (of which Patel was the Minister in charge), was prepared to give an assurance that if Kashmir went to Pakistan this would not be regarded as an unfriendly act by the Government of India, also lacked substance. It is true that Patel at that stage believed that the inclusion of Muslim-majority Kashmir in India would lead to instability, and it seems

---

[1] Prem Nath Bazaz, *The History of the Struggle for Freedom in Kashmir*, p. 318.

[2] TOP XII, p. 769. The Maharaja's wish for land communications with India was granted, as already discussed in the section on the Radcliffe boundary awards in a previous chapter.

[3] *Lok Sabha Debates*, 26 June 1952, Col. 2587.

that it was no more than Patel's personal assurance that Mountbatten was armed with. The assurance most certainly did not have the endorsement of Nehru, who was Patel's chief in the Interim Government, nor that of Gandhi, who was the most prestigious figure in the political party to which Patel belonged. It did not even have the backing of Menon, who was Patel's own right-hand man and Mountbatten's favourite counsellor. Far from being willing to let Kashmir go to Pakistan, these three very important persons were actively engaged in getting Kashmir for India.

In the middle of October 1947, the pro-Indian forces inside Kashmir were further augmented by the appointment as Prime Minister of Kashmir of Mehr Chand Mahajan, a judge of the Punjab High Court, who in Sardar Patel's words, 'was released for Kashmir for strategic and tactical reasons'.[1] This can only mean that he was to secure Kashmir's accession to India. Mahajan, who subsequently became India's Chief Justice, has revealed that upon appointment to the Kashmiri post he had been assured by the Indian authorities that he would be given 'military aid whenever I wanted it'.[2] Quite obviously, the Indians were determined to take Kashmir even if they had to use military force to do so.

In the meantime, the members of the Muslim Conference had been pressing the Maharaja to join Pakistan and, on 19 July, passed a resolution to that effect. Trouble started towards the end of July when the Maharaja ordered his Muslim subjects to surrender their arms to the police. The Muslims responded by organizing themselves as guerrillas in the hills of Poonch, an area abounding with demobilized ex-servicemen who had fought in the Second World War in the ranks of the British Indian Army. While the tough warriors of Poonch held their own against the Maharaja's forces, the Muslims in Jammu Province, where Hindus formed a considerable portion of the population and where Sikhs and other militants from India had infiltrated, were slaughtered by the thousands.

At a press conference on 15 October, Mahajan alleged that raids from West Pakistan into Kashmir were being organized, and that Pakistan was preventing essential supplies such as petrol, cloth, and food from reaching the State. However, the state administration backed down from their own proposal for an impartial inquiry when it was accepted by Pakistan.[3]

---

[1] N. C. Mahajan, *Looking Back*, p. 188. Mahajan left Kashmir in the first week of March 1948, vacating the position of Prime Minister for Abdullah. He published his autobiography, *Looking Back,* in 1963.

[2] Ibid., p. 150.

[3] K. Sarwar Hasan (ed.), *Documents on the Foreign Relations of Pakistan, The Kashmir Question*, p. 68.

By this time the tribesmen of the Frontier, whose feelings had long been inflamed by the atrocities in East Punjab and the massacre of fellow Muslims next door to them in Kashmir, lost their patience. On 22 October a large band of tribesmen crossed the border into Kashmir to wage a holy war (jihad) against the Dogra forces.

'There are sound reasons to believe,' observes Bazaz, 'that if the Congress leaders had not made repeated and vigorous attempts to influence the Maharaja to function in a partisan spirit and take the fatal step of making preparations for joining India, there would have been no incursion of tribesmen into Kashmir'.[1]

Advancing rapidly, the forward units of the tribesmen captured the power station near Srinagar on 24 October. They could have taken the capital and its airport had their main body not lingered behind for pillage. Everyone is agreed that early in the morning of 27 October, a battalion of Sikhs was flown to Srinagar from India and saved the city, but whether this happened after the Maharaja had acceded to India or before he had done so is not clear. If V. P. Menon is to be trusted, the Maharaja signed the Instrument of Accession as well as the accompanying letter to the Governor-General (Mountbatten) on 26 October, making the state a part of Indian territory and thus legally justifying its defence thereafter by Indian soldiers. On the other hand if the then Prime Minister of Kashmir, M. C. Mahajan, is to be believed, the formalities of accession actually took place on 27 October, after the Indian troops had gone into action in Kashmir earlier that day. The Instrument of Accession and the accompanying letter of the Maharaja both bear the date 26 October. The implication of Mahajan's evidence, therefore, is that these documents were fraudulently antedated by a day to confer legitimacy upon the Indian military intervention in Kashmir that had already taken place.

Let us first note the facts which are not in dispute. On 24 October, when Srinagar was threatened, the Maharaja appealed to India for help. In response, the Government of India on 25 October sent V. P. Menon by air to Srinagar to study the situation. Menon found the Maharaja totally unnerved. During the night the Maharaja collected his family and valuables and fled to Jammu. Early in the morning of 26 October Menon accompanied by Mahajan flew back to Delhi. But Menon and Mahajan give different versions of what subsequently transpired on 26 and 27 October.

Menon says that immediately on his arrival in Delhi on 26 October, he went to a meeting of the Defence Committee and reported his impressions.

[1] P. N. Bazaz, *The History of* the *Struggle for Freedom in Kashmir*, p. 338.

Mountbatten, who was the president of the Committee, said that it would be improper to move Indian troops into what was at that time an independent country, but if it were true that the Maharaja was 'now anxious to accede to India, then Jammu and Kashmir would become part of Indian territory. This was the only basis on which Indian troops could be sent...He further expressed the strong opinion that in view of the composition of the population,[1] accession should be conditional on the will of the people being ascertained by a plebiscite...This was readily agreed to by Nehru and other ministers...Soon after the meeting of the Defence Committee I flew to Jammu accompanied by Mahajan...He [the Maharaja] was ready to accede at once.' The Maharaja signed the Instrument of Accessions in the standard form and also addressed an explanatory letter to the Governor-General, and Menon took these documents to Delhi on the same day (26 October). At a meeting of the Defence Committee that evening, the Maharaja's offer of accession was accepted 'subject to the proviso that a plebiscite would be held in the State when the law and order situation allowed', and it was decided that an infantry battalion should be flown to Srinagar the next day.[2]

Mahajan narrates that on arrival at Delhi on 26 October, he immediately drove from the airport to the residence of Prime Minister Nehru where Patel was also present and 'requested immediate military aid on any terms'. Nehru was at first hesitant, but Mahajan insisted that 'the army must fly to save Srinagar this evening or else I will go to Lahore and negotiate terms with Mr Jinnah'. Abdullah, who was staying with Nehru, had been listening to the exchanges from an adjoining room. He supported Mahajan's request that 'military aid must be sent immediately'. Nehru's attitude thereupon changed and he said he would call a meeting of the Defence Council at 10 a.m. to discuss the matter. He asked Mahajan to go to the house of Defence Minister Baldev Singh, where Mahajan intended to stay, and promised to convey the decision of the committee to him through Baldev Singh before lunch. At 12.45 p.m. Baldev Singh came home and told him that it had been decided to send two companies of Indian troops to Srinagar. The cabinet meeting that evening affirmed the decision of the Defence Committee and, at about dinner time, Nehru sent a message to Mahajan that he should fly to Jammu with Menon 'to inform the Maharaja of this decision and also to get his signature on certain supplementary documents about the accession'. Mahajan 'frankly informed

---

[1] This obviously refers to the fact that the majority of the population of Kashmir was Muslim while the Maharaja who was being asked to accede to India was a Hindu.

[2] For Menon's version see his *The Integration of the Indian States*, pp. 397-401.

him [Nehru] that I was not prepared to go to Jammu till I get news from my aerodrome officer at Srinagar that the Indian forces had landed there. Panditji [Nehru] did not insist and said, "You can fly to Jammu next morning"...In the early hours of the morning of the 27th I could hear the noise of the planes flying over Sardar Baldev Singh's house and carrying military personnel to Srinagar. At about 9 a.m. I got a message from the aerodrome officer of Srinagar that troops had landed there and had gone into action. On receipt of this I flew to Jammu with Mr V. P. Menon...Mr Menon and myself met His Highness [the Maharaja] at the palace...After some discussion, formal documents were signed which Menon took back to Delhi. I stayed at Jammu.'

It will be noticed that Mahajan clearly states that he went to Jammu with Menon on 27 October after he had received definite confirmation from the aerodrome officer at Srinagar that Indian troops had actually arrived there and started to fight. Further, that 'formal documents' which Menon took back to Delhi were signed by the Maharaja later on that day.[1]

There seems to be no good reason why Menon's word should be preferred to Mahajan's. It was natural for Menon to twist the truth to present his country's conduct in a more favourable light, but what possible reason could Mahajan have for making up a version which damaged the case for his motherland and conflicted with the formal position adopted by his government?

Mahajan fudges the description of the documents which Menon carried back from Jammu to Delhi. He refers to them as 'certain supplementary documents about the accession' at one place and as 'formal documents' at another. However, all the available evidence is unanimous that the official documents signed by the Maharaja which Menon brought back were none other than the Instrument of Accession and the covering letter from the Maharaja to Mountbatten.

The Maharaja's letter had two notable features. It did not accuse the Government of Pakistan of giving direct assistance to the tribesmen, as India was to allege later, but simply mentioned that the infiltration of the tribesmen into Kashmir could not have taken place without the 'knowledge' of the Pakistani authorities. Secondly, it granted India's standing wish that Abdullah should be installed in a place of power in the state government. 'It is my intention,' the letter ran, 'at once to set up an Interim Government and to ask Sheikh Abdullah to carry the responsibilities in this emergency [jointly] with the Prime Minister.'[2] Mountbatten's reply (27 October)

---

[1] For Mahajan's version see his *Looking Back*, pp. 150-5.
[2] For the text of the Maharaja's letter *see*, J. Korbel, *Danger in Kashmir*, p. 80.

stated that India had decided to accept accession 'in the special circumstances' described by the Maharaja and that,

> in consistence with their policy that in the case of any State where the issue of accession has been the subject of dispute, the question of accession should be decided in accordance with the wishes of the people of the State, it is my Government's wish that, as soon as law and order have been restored in Kashmir and its soil cleared of the invader, the question of the State's accession should be settled by a reference to the people.[1]

Joseph Korbel has this to say on India's haste in securing the accession of Kashmir:

> Why...did he [Mountbatten] advise that Indian military assistance to the Maharaja must be covered by the legal technicality of accession? How could he have reasoned that it would be illegal for Kashmir (which was at the time of invasion technically an independent country) to ask for military help from India without preceding the request by accession?...Why was there at this point no appeal made to the United Nations?...Finally, it is most difficult to understand why no one, particularly Mountbatten, advanced the most obvious idea—that of immediately getting into contact with the Karachi government for consultation.[2]

Though India made much of Pakistan's alleged complicity in the tribal invasion, the truth seems to be that the Government of Pakistan at that time was tottering under the weight of millions of refugees and other partition problems and was in no position to organize intervention in the conflict. Sir William Barton assessed the situation in these terms:

> If an attempt had been made to drive them [the tribesmen] back, the whole border from Chitral south to Quetta would have burst into flame, and at that time Pakistan forces were still disorganized and largely unequipped, thanks to India's refusal to hand over Pakistan's share of the military supplies left by the British. They could not have held down a tribal rising and might have been driven across the Indus. This would have given the Afghans an opportunity of taking territory as far as the Indus, which they look on as Afghanistan irredenta. In such an event Pakistan would either have been absorbed in India, or have become a satellite of that country.[3]

---

[1] Ibid., p. 83.

[2] Ibid., p. 79.

[3] Sir William Barton, 'Pakistan's Claim to Kashmir', *Foreign Affairs*, January 1950. George Cunningham, Governor of the Frontier Province at the time, told Kingsley Martin that once the holy war concept spread among the tribes, neither he himself nor anyone else could have stopped them. Campbell-Johnson, *Mission with Mountbatten*, p. 292.

At a popular level, of course, there was much sympathy and support in Pakistan for the Kashmiris, and many West Pakistanis crossed the border as volunteers to help fellow Muslims in distress. Furthermore, many Poonchis from among those serving in the ranks of the Pakistani regiments left their posts to fight beside their kinsmen.

In another development, the Muslim Conference, which had already passed a resolution on 19 July 1947 that Kashmir should accede to Pakistan, on 24 October set up its own government in areas already liberated from the Maharaja, and assumed the name 'Azad [Free] Kashmir'.

On the night of 27 October, General Douglas Gracey[1] telephoned Auchinleck that he had received orders from Jinnah which, if he obeyed, would activate the 'Stand Down' order (i.e., the withdrawal of all British officers). Auchinleck flew to Lahore on the following day and met Gracey and Jinnah. Gracey said that the orders which he had not obeyed were to send troops into Kashmir. Auchinleck pointed out to Jinnah the 'incalculable consequences of military violation of what now is territory of the Indian Union in consequence of Kashmir's sudden accession'.[2] Gracey emphasized the military weakness of Pakistan. Jinnah withdrew the orders but was very angry. He accepted Auchinleck's suggestion that he should meet Mountbatten and Nehru to find a way out of the dangerous situation and Auchinleck conveyed the proposal to Mountbatten.

Mountbatten was in favour of a meeting between the Indian and Pakistani leaders at Lahore on 1 November to resolve the problem amicably but Nehru 'fell suddenly ill'[3] and Mountbatten had to go alone. Jinnah proposed that the two Governors-General should jointly conduct a plebiscite in Kashmir, while Mountbatten said a plebiscite should be held by the United Nations, and the meeting ended inconclusively. Campbell-Johnson has explained that, 'Jinnah's objection, which he made quite clear at the Lahore meeting, is not to the idea of a plebiscite as such, but to the presence of Indian troops in Kashmir while it is being held, which he claims likely to prejudice any chance of its being impartial'.[4]

In the meantime, the Maharaja had installed Abdullah as the head of an

---

[1] Gracey was acting as commander-in-chief of the Pakistani army in the absence of General Messervy.

[2] 'The British Commander-in-Chief, Lockhart, on the instructions of India's Defence Committee [of which Mountbatten was the chairman], had ordered Indian troops to fly into Kashmir; this was a perfectly proper and legal step, since Kashmir had acceded to India.' John Connell, *Auchinleck*, p. 931.

[3] Ibid.

[4] Alan Campbell-Johnson, *Mission with Mountbatten*, p. 233

Emergency Government in Kashmir. Bazaz comments:

> On the day the Maharaja was forced to establish the Emergency Administration in the State, many leaders in India believed that Pakistan could not exist for long. The war in Kashmir was considered as a godsend. It was thought that the Indian armies would push the tribesmen and Azad Kashmir forces back beyond the boundaries of the State. The Red Shirts of [the] Khan brothers were expected to rise in rebellion in the NWFP against the League Government. Dr Khan Sahib had come to Kashmir soon after the release of Abdullah and had long talks with the Nationalist leader in Srinagar.[1]

The respective positions taken up by Prime Ministers Nehru and Liaquat in the ensuing months have some interesting features.

In striking contrast with India's later assertion that Kashmir was strictly a domestic matter for India, Nehru's telegram to Liaquat dated 30 October made this bold promise: 'Our assurance that we shall withdraw our troops from Kashmir as soon as peace and order are restored and leave the decision about the future of the State to the people of the State is not merely a pledge to your Government but also to the people of Kashmir and to the world.'[2]

Another telegram from the Indian Prime Minister belied India's future contention that the Maharaja's signature on the Instrument of Accession had legally concluded the question and that Mountbatten's letter of 27 October to the Maharaja was of no consequence: 'here let me make clear that it has been our policy all along that, where there is a dispute about the accession of a State to either Dominion, the decision must be made by the people of that State. It was in accordance with this policy that we added a proviso to the Instrument of Accession of Kashmir.'[3]

Nehru also clearly held out the promise that the referendum in Kashmir would be 'held under international auspices like the United Nations'.[4] However, when Liaquat proposed that an impartial administration be set up in Kashmir to ensure freedom of voting, Nehru barefacedly claimed that 'Sheikh Abdullah's administration...is impartial'.[5]

With regard to the Maharaja's accession to India, Liaquat emphatically

---

[1] Prem Nath Bazaz, op. cit., p. 404.

[2] K. Sarwar Hasan (ed.), *Documents on the Foreign Relations of Pakistan, The Kashmir Question,* p. 67.

[3] Ibid., p. 74. The 'proviso' was in fact contained in Mountbatten's letter to the Maharaja dated 27 October, *see*, p. 597.

[4] Ibid., p. 75.

[5] Ibid., p. 93.

stated that Pakistan could never accept it because

> ...'accession' was fraudulent inasmuch as it was achieved by deliberately creating certain conditions, with the object of finding an excuse to stage the 'accession'. It was based on violence because it furthered the plan of the Kashmir Government to liquidate the Muslim population of the State. The accession was against the well-known will of an overwhelming majority of the population and could not be justified on any grounds whether moral or constitutional, geographical or economic, cultural or religious.[1]

Pakistan pointed out, further, that the Maharaja had no authority left to execute the Instrument of Accession because his subjects had overthrown his government by a successful revolt and forced him to flee from the capital.[2]

Under Mountbatten's pressure, India ultimately decided to refer the question to the United Nations and, on 1 January 1948, filed a formal complaint against Pakistan in the Security Council.

It is noteworthy that India, which was later to place the utmost emphasis on the allegation that Pakistan was the 'aggressor' in Kashmir, filed the petition in the Security Council under Section 35 of Chapter VI, which relates to 'Pacific Settlement of Disputes', and not under chapter VII, which deals with acts of aggression. India prayed that Pakistan be called upon immediately to cease assisting the raiders as otherwise India might be 'compelled' to enter Pakistani territory to take action against the invaders. Accession to India was defended because the request had come not only from the Maharaja, but also 'from the largest popular organization in Kashmir, the National Conference, headed by Sheikh Muhammad Abdullah ...on behalf of the people of Kashmir'. It was promised once more that, after the raiders had been expelled, the people of Kashmir 'would be free to decide their future by the recognized democratic method of a plebiscite or referendum...under international auspices'.

Pakistan denied giving assistance to the raiders and, in turn, accused India of the genocide of Muslims and of forcible possession of Junagarh, which had joined Pakistan, and prayed that the Security Council appoint a commission to assist in the solution of the 'various problems' between India and Pakistan, because friendly relations were possible only by the elimination of 'all differences'.

---

[1] Ibid., p. 100.

[2] *Security Council, Official Records, Fourth Year, Special Supplement No. 7, UNCIP Third Report, S/1430,* 9 December 1949.

Opening for India in the UN Security Council on 15 January 1948, Gopalaswami Ayyenger emphasized that the expulsion of the invaders and the stoppage of the fighting were the 'only tasks' to which the Council should address itself. He reiterated the Indian promise that: 'The question of the future status of Kashmir *vis-a-vis* her neighbours and the world at large, and a further question, namely, whether she should withdraw from her accession to India, and either accede to Pakistan or remain independent, with a right to claim admission as a Member of the United Nations—all this we have recognized to be a matter for unfettered decision by the people of Kashmir, after normal life is restored to them.'

On behalf of Pakistan, Zafrulla Khan asked for more time than until the following afternoon to prepare a reply because the issues were not as simple as the representative of India had tried to make out, but Ayyenger vehemently opposed the request because 'the situation does not brook delay'. Some members of the Security Council were later to twit Ayyenger about this when, finding that India was not getting her own way, Ayyenger himself insisted upon a long adjournment.

Zafrulla said Pakistan was woefully short of military supplies and in no condition to help anyone. Nor did the tribesmen, who were well known for their fighting prowess and their capacity to acquire or manufacture guns and rifles, or the Poonchis, 70,000 of whom were ex-servicemen, need any help. He said the situation demanded that 'everyone' who had gone into Kashmir from outside should be made to leave and the Kashmiris should then freely 'express the way in which they want to go'.

While the lengthy debate was in progress the Security Council passed two resolutions. That of 17 January asked the parties not to aggravate the situation but to do everything in their power to improve it. It also requested both governments to inform the Council immediately of any 'material change' in the situation. The resolution of 20 January established a mediatory commission, which eventually came to have five members and was called the United Nations Commission on India and Pakistan (UNCIP).

Matters came to a head on 6 February when the President of the Council for that month, General McNaughton of Canada, tabled a resolution which evidently reflected the views of the majority at the time. It called for a withdrawal of all irregular forces from Kashmir; the establishment of law and order jointly by Indian and Pakistani forces followed by the withdrawal of regular forces; the setting up of an interim administration commanding the confidence of the people of Kashmir; and the holding of a plebiscite, under the 'authority' of the Security Council.[1]

---

[1] Text in K. Sarwar Hasan (ed.) *Documents on the Foreign Relations of Pakistan, The Kashmir Question*, p. 162.

Ayyenger found the suggestion relating to the replacement of Abdullah's administration by a neutral one and the withdrawal of the Indian armed forces unacceptable. He insisted that the plebiscite must be organized and conducted by the existing administration in Kashmir with the role of the Council limited to sending observers 'to see how that plebiscite is conducted'. While the debate was in progress, Ayyenger suddenly asked for an adjournment until a date between 15 and 20 March. Several members reminded him of his earlier opposition to the short adjournment requested by Zafrulla, and one of them, the representative of Colombia, turning Ayyenger's own words round, said that if the proceedings were interrupted the Indian delegation would be travelling 'while Jammu and Kashmir burn'.[1] The Indian delegate angrily complained that the 'great country' which he represented had not elicited at the hands of the Security Council the consideration to which it was entitled.[2] The Council had to give way and the hearing was adjourned. Ayyenger left New York on 12 February and it was not till 16 March that the Council took up the Kashmir question again.

Zafrulla explains the reason for Ayyenger's request for an adjournment:

> Britain was, for the purpose of the Kashmir case, represented by the Minister for Commonwealth Affairs, Mr Philip (later Lord) Noel-Baker...Mr Noel-Baker talked to Sir Gopalaswami Ayenger and Sir Girja Shankar Bajpai and asked them to try to persuade Prime Minister Nehru to agree to go along with the resolution. He was given some hope that the Prime Minister might be brought round, when Mr Noel-Baker received a telegram from Prime Minister Attlee to desist. After the six sponsors of the resolution had spoken and the resolution was about to be put to the vote, Sir Gopalaswami announced that his delegation had been called to Delhi for consultations. and requested an adjournment of the debate till their return.[3]

In his unpublished *Reminiscences* Zafrulla says more plainly that Noel-Baker personally told him that just when he, Noel-Baker, was feeling hopeful that India might accept the Security Council proposals, the 'disastrous telegram' arrived from Attlee and 'upset the whole business'.[4]

Once more it was Mountbatten who was pulling wires on behalf of India. In his Personal Report to the British Government dated 3 February 1948, he wrote, 'In my own view—and I have discussed this with

---

[1] Security Council Official Records, 243rd Meeting, 10 February 1948.

[2] Ibid., 245th Meeting, 11 February 1948.

[3] Muhammad Zafrulla Khan, *Servant of God, a Personal Narrative*, pp. 152-3.

[4] *Reminiscences of Sir Muhammad Zafrulla Khan*, pp. 338-9.

Gordon Walker [Parliamentary Under-Secretary of State for Commonealth Relations] who stayed with me from 29th January to 1st February—the time has now come when, in order to break the deadlock in the Security Council, some concession must be made to India to meet their original application that measures should be taken at once to stop the fighting.'[1] And on 17 February Campbell-Johnson recorded in his journal, 'Mountbatten is worried because he feels that Attlee and Noel-Baker do not seem to be showing themselves sufficiently alive to the psychological influences of this dispute and that their attempt to deal out even-handed justice is producing heavy-handed diplomacy.'[2] On 23 February the same author noted that after his visit to Ceylon, Gordon Walker was 'back in Delhi at a crucial moment in the Kashmir dispute...He has, I think, been able to see for himself that Mountbatten is not exaggerating the bad impression caused here by the British attitude at the United Nations.' Mountbatten was 'frankly' saying that the policy adopted towards Kashmir by the British Delegation at the Security Council was weakening the attitude of the Indian Government toward continuing the Commonwealth connection.[3]

Britain's change of front had far-reaching consequences and greatly reduced the chances of a Kashmir settlement on a reasonable basis. As the United States and most other member states in the Council in the early years had little experience of Indo-Pakistan questions, they held Britain's views in special respect.

Instead of the proposed resolution of 6 February which India had found so objectionable, the Security Council, after another debate, passed a watered-down resolution permitting India to retain her forces in Kashmir in the 'minimum strength required for the support of civil power' and stating that the Secretary-General of the United Nations would appoint a Plebiscite Administrator who would act 'as an officer of the State of Jammu and Kashmir'.[4]

The UNCIP arrived in the subcontinent on 7 July, landing at Karachi on that day.

Meanwhile, with the advent of spring and the melting of mountain snows, the Indian army had mounted an offensive in Kashmir. On 13 April

[1] *Governor-General's Personal Report, No. 8* dated 3rd February 1948, MSS EUR D 714/86, p.6.
[2] Alan Campbell-Johnson, *Mission With Mountbatten*, p. 287.
[3] Ibid., pp. 289-91.
[4] K. Sarwar Hasan (ed.), *Documents on the Foreign Relations of Pakistan, The Kashmir Question*, p. 162.

1948 *The Times'* correspondent cabled from Srinagar that 'the long-awaited spring offensive in Jammu and Kashmir has begun'.[1] A week later General Douglas Gracey, Commander-in-Chief of the Pakistani army, reported to the Pakistani Government the grave consequences for Pakistan if the Indian army pursued its objective unhindered. On crossing the Ravi and the Chenab, the Indian forces would come right up to the Pakistani border, 'thereby sitting on our doorsteps, threatening the Jhelum bridge, controlling the Mangla canal headworks, and having the irrigation in Jhelum and other districts at their mercy. The occupation of Poonch by the Indians would adversely affect the morale of the Pakistani troops, many of whom were Poonchis. The loss of Muzaffarabad or Kohala would 'enable the Indian Army to secure the rear gateway to Pakistan through which it can march in at any time'. It would also encourage Afghanistan[2] and the subversive elements within Pakistan. Gracey stated that, if disastrous consequences to Pakistan were to be avoided, it was 'imperative that the Indian army is not allowed to advance beyond the general line Uri-Poonch-Nawshera'.[3]

In the circumstances described by Gracey, the Pakistani Government had no option but to order units of the Pakistani army to move into Kashmir and hold defensive positions. As Zafrulla put it later, 'anyone responsible for the security of Pakistan who did not at least do that should have [been] impeached and executed'. On 8 July, as soon as Zafrulla met the members of the UNCIP, he informed them that Pakistan had been compelled to deploy her forces inside Kashmir. To the Indian charge that the participation of the Pakistani army in the Kashmir fighting constituted a 'material change' in the situation which Pakistan was bound immediately to convey to the Security Council under the terms of its resolution of 17 January, Zafrulla replied that the 'material change in the situation' had first been caused by India, who mounted a big offensive in Kashmir. 'Did the Government of India, in mounting their offensive, notify the Commission?' he asked.[4]

After talking to leaders on both sides and studying the situation, the Commission passed a resolution on 13 August 1948 which had three parts. Part I asked India and Pakistan to order a ceasefire and Part III called upon

---

[1] *The Times*, 14 April 1948.

[2] Afghanistan was at that time agitating for the setting up of an independent state under the title of 'Pakhtunistan' in the north-western frontier areas of Paksitan.

[3] K. Sarwar Hasan (ed.), *Documents on the Foreign Relations of Pakistan, The Kashmir Question*, p. 174.

[4] Ibid., p. 136.

them to reaffirm that Kashmir's future status would be determined by the Kashmiris themselves.

Part II proposed that both governments accept these principles as a basis for a truce agreement: (1) As the presence of Pakistani troops in Kashmir constituted a material change in the situation, Pakistan should withdraw her troops. (2) The tribesmen and Pakistani nationals not normally resident in the state should also withdraw. (3) Pending a final settlement, the territory vacated by the Pakistani troops would be administered by the local authorities under the surveillance of the Commission. (4) When the Commission notified the Government of India that the tribesmen and the Pakistani nationals had withdrawn and the Pakistani forces were being withdrawn, the Government of India would begin to withdraw the bulk of her forces. (5) Pending the acceptance of the conditions for a final settlement, the Indian Government would maintain, within the lines existing at the moment of the cease-fire, the minimum forces necessary to assist the local authorities in the observance of law and order.[1]

India accepted the resolution, but Pakistan objected that it did not contain detailed guarantees for a free plebiscite.[2]

After another round of negotiations, the Commission was able to get the two governments to agree to a cease-fire from 1 January 1949, and also to certain proposals which were embodied in the Commission's resolution of 5 January. By spelling out the arrangements for a plebiscite, this resolution was meant to supplement that of 13 August 1948 which Pakistan had deemed inadequate. A plebiscite would be held after the Commission had found that the ceasefire and truce agreement set forth in the resolution of 13 August had been carried out. The Secretary-General of the United Nations would, in agreement with the Commission, nominate a Plebiscite Administrator who, though formally appointed to office by the government of the State, would be given 'the powers he considers necessary' for ensuring the impartiality of the plebiscite. After the requirements of the truce agreement had been fulfilled, the Commission and the Plebiscite Administrator would determine the final disposal of Indian and State armed forces as well as the forces in Azad Kashmir. Provision was made for the expulsion of persons who had entered the State since 15 August 1947 and also for the return of citizens who had left the State on account of disturbances.[3]

---

[1] Ibid., p. 180.

[2] Josef Korbel, *Danger in Kashmir*, p. 144.

[3] K. Sarwar Hasan op. cit., p. 212.

The resolutions of 13 August 1948 and 5 January 1949 form the basic resolutions for the settlement of the Kashmir dispute, but there has been no movement towards their implementation all these years, except that a cease-fire line was established by mutual agreement on 27 July 1949.

Each side has blamed the other for the impasse, but India has consistently refused to have recourse to arbitration or adjudication to determine which side is to blame and what can be done to move forward.

In an article, 'Nehru in Retrospect' Attlee, on the whole an admirer of Nehru, wrote:

> I can recall many long discussions with Mr Nehru on the vexed question of Kashmir, sometimes between the two of us, sometimes with other prime ministers, but they proved fruitless. Although we proposed every possible variant in order to have fair plebiscite, to which he had already agreed in principle, we could not get acceptance from Mr Nehru. I have always considered this the blind spot of a great statesman.[1]

According to the principles governing the partition of British India, Kashmir belonged to Pakistan, and the letter K in the name of the country stands for Kashmir. Pakistanis are grieved that India possesses the better part of the former State, including the valley which is its heartland. The cards were heavily stacked against Pakistan, and the position Pakistan had taken on the rights of the princes and its response to the problems as they arose did not make the situation any easier. Autocratic states were as out of date in the middle of the twentieth century as British imperialism, which was on the way out: the strong wind of change which was blowing across the country was bound to sweep them away sooner or later. Jinnah's view that a State could remain independent or join either Dominion irrespective of its geographical location, and the fact that the ruler belonged to a religion different from the majority of his subjects, would have caused untold complications. Islands of independent States would have balkanised the subcontinent, and the disregard for the principles of contiguity and religion would have led to trouble between the ruler and his subjects and between India and Pakistan.

The Pakistani contention that the Muslim Nawab of Junagarh could accede to Pakistan even though the majority of his subjects were Hindus and his State was contiguous to India, made available to India the plea that the Maharaja of Kashmir could do the same. Campbell-Johnson wrote

---

[1] *Illustrated Weekly of India*, Sunday 22 November 1964, p. 31.

with obvious relish, 'On this particular issue [accession of Kashmir to India] Jinnah has been hoist with his own petard.'[1]

A major concern for Jinnah was that Hyderabad should become a sovereign state, friendly to Pakistan and an ally in case of a conflict with India.[2] Chaudhri Muhammad Ali has conceded that one reason why Jinnah took the stand that a State could remain independent was 'to safeguard Hyderabad's independence'.[3] There was some chance while the Hyderabad problem was unsolved that India might have let Kashmir go to Pakistan if Pakistan stopped encouraging Hyderabad to bid for independence.

The Hyderabad-Kashmir *quid pro quo* was discussed by Patel and Liaquat at a meeting toward the end of 1947 at which Chaudhri Muhammad Ali was personally present. Ali has written that when Liaquat dwelt on the inconsistency of the Indian stand with regard to Junagarh and Kashmir, Patel 'could not contain himself and burst out: "Why do you compare Junagarh with Kashmir? Talk of Hyderabad and Kashmir, and we could reach an agreement". Patel's view at this time and even later was that India's effort to retain Muslim majority areas against the will of the people was a source not of strength but of weakness to India.[4] He felt that if India and Pakistan agreed to let Kashmir go to Pakistan and Hyderabad to India, the problems of Kashmir and Hyderabad could be solved peacefully and to the mutual advantage of India and Pakistan.'[5] But Jinnah was over-confident about Kashmir and believed that it would come to Pakistan anyway. 'Kashmir', he would say, 'will fall into our lap like a ripe fruit'.[6] This was a surprising miscalculation.

It should not have been difficult to foresee that the Maharaja, being a Hindu, would, if compelled by circumstances to make a choice, accede to India, and Pakistan had no equivalent of Mountbatten to further its interests. The Maharaja was against any political leaders coming into his State. He and Mountbatten managed to keep Jinnah out[7] but Mountbatten was able to persuade the Maharaja to accept a visit from Gandhi. Mountbatten's wit and military experience were well suited to dealing

[1] Campbell-Johnson, op. cit., p. 225.
[2] *See*, p. 582.
[3] *See*, p. 581.
[4] Campbell-Johnson also noted in his journal on 1 December 1947, 'Those in Congress who want a Hindu State do not want Kashmir, but the Government's action in Kashmir has temporarily silenced them'. *Mission with Mountbatten*, p. 246.
[5] Chaudhri Muhammad Ali, op. cit., p. 299.
[6] Ibid., p. 297.
[7] Ibid., p. 290. Ali states that Jinnah wanted to go to Kashmir in September 1947 but the Maharaja did not wish him to come.

with the crisis as it developed. Campbell-Johnson wrote in his diary on 28 October, 'It was a sudden emergency calling at once for restraint and quick decision. Mountbatten's extraordinary vitality and canniness were well adapted to the demands of the hour.'[1]

It is only because of the much-criticised tribal invasion and the subsequent intervention of the Pakistani army to slow the Indian advance that Pakistan happens to be in possession of a part of Kashmir. But for those developments, the entire State today would have been under Indian rule.

Though the manner in which Mountbatten hustled the princes into accession can be questioned, the political benefit of promptly integrating the States into the body politic of independent India cannot be doubted.

---

[1] Campbell- Johnson, op. cit., p. 223.

Chapter 25

THE DAWN OF FREEDOM

At its inaugural session on 11 August 1947, the Pakistani Constituent Assembly elected Jinnah as its President, and on the following day it gave formal recognition to Jinnah's position by resolving that, as from 15 August, he should be addressed as 'Quaid-i-Azam Mohammad Ali Jinnah, Governor-General of Pakistan' in all official documents. On the afternoon of 13 August, Lord and Lady Mountbatten flew from Delhi to Karachi. Intelligence sources had warned of a plot to throw a bomb at Jinnah during the state procession on the following day, but Jinnah had stated that if Mountbatten was prepared to go through with the drive, then so was he. It was, therefore, agreed to leave the arrangements unchanged.

That evening, Mountbatten presided over a meeting of the Pakistani cabinet. Thereafter, he and his wife attended a state banquet which was followed by a reception attended by some 1500 of the leading citizens of Pakistan.

The state procession on 14 August took place in open cars with Jinnah and Mountbatten in the leading car, and Miss Fatima Jinnah and Lady Mountbatten in the next car. The route was thickly lined with enthusiastic crowds. Mountbatten addressed the Pakistani Constituent Assembly. On the return journey, when the procession turned in at the gates of Government House, Jinnah said, 'Thank God I have brought you back alive.' Mountbatten commented how much more serious it would have been if he, Jinnah, had been 'bumped off'.[1]

Pakistan became constitutionally independent on the midnight between 14 and 15 August. Jinnah assumed the office of Governor-General on 15 August and the Pakistani cabinet, with Liaquat Ali Khan as Prime Minister was sworn in on the same day.

The Mountbattens returned to Delhi on the afternoon of 14 August. At twenty minutes past midnight that night Rajendra Prasad, President of the Constituent Assembly, and Nehru, the Prime Minister, went to Mountbatten and informed him that they had taken over power at the

---

[1] TOP XII, pp. 769-71.

midnight session of the Constituent Assembly which had endorsed the decision of the leaders that Mountbatten should become their first Governor-General. Nehru ceremoniously handed over an envelope and said, 'May I submit to you the portfolios of the new cabinet?' When Mountbatten opened the envelope later he found that by oversight it was empty.

The activities on the fifteenth of August, which in Mountbatten's own words was 'the most remarkable and inspiring' day of his life, started at 8.30 a.m. with the swearing in of the Governor-General and the members of the cabinet in the Durbar Hall of what had previously been the Viceroy's house and now became Government House. A state procession from Government House then left for the Council Chamber where Mountbatten addressed the Indian Constituent Assembly. After the ceremonies at the Council Chamber, the procession returned to Government House. 'Never have such crowds been seen within memory of anyone I [Mountbatten] have spoken to...Apart from the usual cries of *"Jai Hind"* and "Mahatma Gandhi *ki jai"*, a surprising number shouted out "Mountbatten *ki jai"*, and "Lady Mountbatten *ki jai"* and more than once "Pandit Mountbatten *ki jai".'*[1]

In the afternoon the Mountbattens attended a children's party, and at 6 p.m. the flag-hoisting ceremony took place. At Mountbatten's request, Nehru had agreed that the ceremony would not include the lowering of the Union Jack. Finally came the state banquet, followed by an evening party attended by nearly 3,000 persons which lasted till the early hours of the morning.[2]

But the most famous Indian was missing from the Independence Day celebrations in India's capital. Gandhi had gone to Calcutta a few days previously on his way to the Noakhali district of Bengal where riots had taken place in the previous year. Mountbatten noted that the Mahatma's absence was 'intentional' and offered this explanation for it: 'He had never given the 3rd June Plan his unqualified blessing, and he realised that his position might be difficult. He also realised that it would be difficult to fit him into the programme in the way in which not only he himself but the people generally would feel that he was entitled'.[3]

Mountbatten's addresses to the Constituent Assemblies of Pakistan and India both began with a message of greeting and goodwill from

---

[1] This contrasted sharply with Mountbatten's experience in India in 1921 when he was on the staff of the Prince of Wales during the Prince's visit to India which was boycotted.

[2] TOP XII, pp. 771-4.

[3] *Report on the Last Viceroyalty*, p. 148, para. 64.

the King, but the speech itself was more cordial to the Indian than to the Pakistani audience in three respects.

Firstly, to the Pakistanis he said, 'Be assured always of my sympathy and support as I watch your continuing efforts to advance the cause of humanity', while to the Indians he was able to state, 'From today I am your constitutional Governor-General and I would ask you to regard me as one of yourselves, devoted wholly to the furtherance of India's interests'.

Secondly, he was non-committal with regard to the rationale for the creation of Pakistan and its future place in the world: 'The birth of Pakistan is an event in history. We, who are a part of history, and are helping to make it, are not well-placed, even if we wished, to moralise on the event,' but 'what is happening in India is of far more than purely national interest. The emergence of a stable and prosperous state will be a factor of the greatest international importance for the peace of the world'.

Thirdly, his tribute to Jinnah, the only Pakistani leader named in the address, was merely correct and friendly: 'Our close personal contact, and the mutual trust and understanding that have grown out of it, are, I feel, the best omens for future relations. He has my sincere good wishes as your Governor-General.' His references to Patel, Gandhi and Nehru on the other hand were fulsome. Patel was a 'far-sighted statesman'; Gandhi was the 'architect' of India's 'freedom through non-violence'; and Nehru was 'a world-renowned leader of courage and wisdom' whose 'trust and friendship have helped me beyond measure in my task'.[1]

Unfortunately, the dawn of freedom in the subcontinent did not witness only jubilation and festivity as manifested in the streets and palaces of the Governors-General in Karachi and New Delhi. We will deal with the subject of law and order during the transfer of power in the next section. But the picture of 15 August 1947 would remain incomplete if we did not illustrate what was happening elsewhere by referring to two horrible occurrences which took place on that day in Amritsar and Lahore, the two principal cities of the Punjab.

During the afternoon of 15 August 'a Sikh mob paraded a number of Muslim women naked through the streets of Amritsar, raped them and then hacked some of them to pieces with *kirpans* and burned the others alive...The same night in Lahore a Muslim mob set fire

[1] For the full texts of Mountbatten's addresses to the Contituent Assemblies of Pakistan and India *see*, *Report on the Last Viceroyalty*, appendices XI and XII.

to a Sikh *gurdwara*; nobody knows how many were killed in this attack, since in the rubble and ashes next morning it was impossible to count the corpses.'[1]

LAW AND ORDER

Some of the battles in the war of succession to fill the power vacuum which the British were expected to leave behind in India before long had already been fought before Mountbatten arrived in India. The massacre of Muslims in Bihar in November 1946[2] and of non-Muslims, among whom the Sikhs were the main target, in the north-western districts of the Punjab and in Multan in the first part of March 1947,[3] had brought home to the Indian leaders the truth that the partition of India was unavoidable. About Bihar Pyarelal, Gandhi's secretary and biographer wrote, 'the Bihar disturbances of 1946 finally shattered the dream of an undivided India'.[4] And the March 1947 Punjab happenings had actually caused the Working Committee of Congress to pass their famous resolution of 8 March recommending the partition of the Punjab.[5]

In his very first Personal Report, dated 2 April 1947, Mountbatten had noted that the whole country was in an unsettled state and that in the Punjab, all parties were seriously preparing for civil war, and of them 'by far the most businesslike and serious' were the Sikhs.

In May, there was serious Hindu-Muslim trouble in Gurgaon district. Some 140 villages were burnt with heavy casualties. Mountbatten noted on 31 May, 'We are very thin on the ground with troops all over India, considering the number of disturbances with which we have to contend.'

In an interview with Sir Evan Jenkins, Governor of the Punjab, on 19 May, Master Tara Singh, the Sikh leader, 'intimated that in Pakistan the Muslims would massacre all the Sikhs and Hindus and that in the other part of the Punjab the Sikhs and Hindus would massacre all the Muslims'.[6] On 31 May, Jenkins reported to Mountbatten that,

---

[1] John Connell, *Auchinleck*, p. 906. Rees, commander of the Punjab Boundary Force, happened to be present in Amritsar on the day of the tragedy but reached the scene too late to save the victims. *Kirpan* : a sword, sometimes worn symbolically in miniature, one of the five emblems of the Sikh faith; *gurdwara* : a Sikh temple.

[2] *See*, p. 466.

[3] *See*, p. 478.

[4] Pyarelal, op. cit. p. 641.

[5] *See*, p. 479-80.

[6] TOP X, p. 893

'communal tension throughout the Punjab is extremely high, and amounts to mass hysteria...in many districts there have been incidents including bomb explosions, cases of arson and communal murders'.[1]

The announcement of the plan of 3 June 1947 eased the situation for a while, but the communities soon were at each other's throats again. The Deputy Commissioner of Lahore reported that, up to 28 July, of 20,256 houses within the walled city, 1,120 had been destroyed.

The Punjab Boundary Force under Major-General Rees became operative on 1 August. It consisted of about two divisions of mixed composition, Muslim and non-Muslim. The twelve districts in which it was to act in aid of the civil authorities had an area of 37,500 square miles, larger than Ireland, and a population of about fourteen and a half million tough and pugnacious Punjabis. The civil authorities whom the PBF were meant to assit had been declining in prestige and strength for some years past and 'from the beginning of August the final decline set in; the reshuffle of personnel (officers, clerks, police—everybody) of records, files, and office furniture etc. was under way'.[2]

The Punjab police had been about 70 to 80 per cent Muslim. Muslim policemen in East Punjab refused to continue to serve there and non-Muslim policemen in West Punjab all wanted to go east. On 15 August, the Jullundhar Division in East Punjab alone was short of 7,000 police-men due to the departure of Muslim members of the force. There was thus 'little effective civil government machinery to work with, other than the two new governors and their new ministers and a certain number of willing senior officials'.[3] Most British civil and police officers retired on 15 August. The machinery of government after 15 August in West Punjab 'almost ceased to function and in East Punjab to all intents and purposes it did cease to function'.

The Boundary Force had been the only worthwhile machinery to prevent the situation from getting even worse, but a Joint Defence Council meeting at Lahore decided to disband it with effect from the midnight of 31 August. In a report to the King on 2 September 1947 Mountbatten explained: 'It had gradually become apparent that the political leaders of both Dominions felt that their hands were tied until this step was taken; moreover, as the communal virus had started to

[1] TOP XI, p. 23.
[2] *Report of the Punjab Boundary Force (The PBF) 1 August-Midnight 1-2 September 1947*, by Major-General T.W. Rees, p. 4. Henceforth referred to as the *Rees Report*.
[3] Ibid.

infect the troops themselves, and as increasingly serious reports were spread exaggerating this infection, some such measure became inevitable.'[1]

Ferocity had 'reached its first peak' in the first week of August in the key Sikh area, the Manjha, where Sikh *jathas* (organized groups) resorted to mass violence against Muslims in the rural areas, which caused retaliation by Muslims on non-Muslims in West Punjab. 'Throughout, the killing was pre-mediaeval in its ferocity—neither age nor sex was spared; mothers with babies in their arms were cut down, speared or shot; and Sikhs cried "Rawalpindi" as they struck home. Both sides were equally merciless.'[2] In the third week after the transfer of power on 15 August the fighting became really widespread and reached its highest point; large-scale migration abated only in November.

When Auchinleck flew to Lahore on 14 August he saw 'smoke rising from every village, to the limits of that vast horizon, and along the dusty roads the endless streams of refugees trudging east and west'. A decade later he recalled that it was 'a terrible and never-to-be-forgotten sight'. On 21 September, the Mountbattens, accompanied by Ismay, Campbell-Johnson and others, made a round tour by air of some four hundred miles over the routes of the 'great refugee migrations between the East and West Punjab'. Campbell-Johnson noted, 'as we approached the Ravi we had our first aerial vision of the scale of this desperate exodus. We were looking down on one of the greatest movements of population in recorded history, and then only a small segment of it...We flew, in fact, for over fifty miles against this stream of refugees without reaching its source'. He estimated that another column of refugees over which they flew 'must have been at least forty-five miles long'. Even their 'brief bird's-eye view must have revealed nearly half a million refugees on the roads' that day.[3]

> The tactics and armament of the Muslims and non-Muslims varied from furtive killings in city lanes or lonely country places to planned attacks by large armed bands on villages, trains, or convoys. The armament varied from primitive axe, spear, and club to the most modern tommy-gun and light machine-gun. Training in the use of weapons had been going on for many months.[4]

It is impossible to compile accurate statistics of casualties and refugees

---

[1] H. V. Hodson, op. cit. p. 409.
[2] *The Rees Report*, p.7.
[3] Campbell-Johnson, op. cit. pp.200-1
[4] *The Rees Report*, p. 21.

in a civil war involving guerilla fighting between such large numbers, over such a large area and lasting so long. Some estimates follow:

R. C. Majumdar: 'India had to pay a heavy price for freedom. According to an estimate, not probably much exaggerated, "600,000 Indians died and 14,000,000 lost their homes".'[1]

Campbell-Johnson: 'In this communal irruption twelve million Hindu Sikhs and Moslems were involved, and migration of some nine million people began overnight in an area the size of Wales.'[2]

H. V. Hodson puts the number of deaths of men, women and children at 'around' 200,000 and the number of migrants at 'some five million'.[3]

Chaudhri Muhammad Ali: 'Within a matter of weeks over twelve million people had left their homes'[4] and 'the number of refugees West Pakistan had to accommodate exceeded by some 1.7 million the number of evacuees who had left.'[5]

The Hindus achieved Hindustan and the Muslims Pakistan, but for the Sikhs Khalistan remained an empty dream. The Sikhs blamed the Muslims for bringing about the division of their community and vented their anger on them. 'Once the mass killings by Sikhs started in the Amritsar district early in August, the conflict became a fight mainly between Sikhs and Muslims, with Hindus involved only to a minor degree.'[6]

The Sikhs made no secret of their resolve to resort to violence. On 8 July, Reuters reported from New Delhi, 'India's 5,700,000 Sikhs, most of whom live in the Punjab, wore black armbands as they prayed in their *gurdwaras* today in protest against the threat to split their community under the British plan for India'. Amar Singh Dosanj, Acting President, and Amar Singh Ambalvi, General Secretary of the Shiromani Akali Dal, declared that 'a boundary on the Chenab river was their minimum demand'.[7] On 10 July Giani Kartar Singh told Jenkins that 'there must be an exchange of population on a large scale'[8] and on the following day, Jathedar Mohan Singh told him that 'the only solution was a very substantial exchange of population. If this did not occur, the Sikhs would be driven to facilitate it by a massacre of Muslims in the Eastern Punjab.'[9]

[1] R. C. Majumdar (ed.), *Struggle for Freedom*, p. 792.

[2] Campbell-Johnson, op. cit. p. 355.

[3] H. V. Hodson, op. cit. p. 418.

[4] Chaudhri Muhammad Ali, *The Emergence of Pakistan*, p. 261.

[5] Ibid., p. 261.

[6] The *Rees Report*, p.21.

[7] TOP XII, p. 17.

[8] Ibid., p. 72.

[9] Ibid., p. 103.

The Sikhs had three distinct advantages over their opponents. Firstly, they had a remarkable ability to organize themselves into *jathas* for common action:

> Their information system and use of their considerable number of horsemen were also very skilfully organized. In the main, the *jathas* were armed with swords and spears (the Sikhs being allowed to carry their *kirpan* (Sword) by law); and there was normally a nucleus or hard-core armed and skilled in the use of the modern lethal weapons mentioned. The Muslims, certainly in the early stages, never reached the state of organization achieved by their opponents.[1]

Ismay, who had flown over central Punjab with Mountbatten on 21 September, noted:

> The contrast between the two columns was striking. The movement of the Sikhs had been carefully planned and was being executed with military precision. There was little or no interval between the bullock carts, in which the women and young children and goods and chattels were loaded, and all the men who were capable of bearing arms moved in front and on the flanks of the column. The Muslim migration had evidently been unpremeditated, and their column straggled hopelessly over fifty miles of road. From the air it looked like a pathetic stream of ants.[2]

Secondly, the Sikhs were better armed than the Muslims: every one of them carried a *kirpan* or sword and they also 'often carried shields and armour'.[3] In an interview with Mountbatten on 19 April 1947, Liaquat, while agreeing that on religious grounds the *kirpan* could not be banned, urged that Muslims should also be allowed to carry swords to defend themselves. Mountbatten argued that two wrongs did not make a right; two men each with a sword were more likely to start a fight than two men with one sword between them.[4] Auchinleck was also convinced that 'the solution to the problem was to take stronger measures against the Sikhs; he was particularly incensed when the government withdrew its ban on the wearing of *kirpans*, or ceremonial swords. This measure proved, he said, that the authorities were afraid to deal with the Sikhs as they should be dealt with.'[5]

---

[1] The *Rees Report*, p. 7.
[2] *The Memoirs of General the Lord Ismay*, p. 441.
[3] The *Rees Report*, p. 22.
[4] TOP X, p. 331 *Report on the Last Viceroyalty*, p. 59, para. 85.
[5] Ziegler, *Mountbatten*, p. 435.

The third factor which gave the Sikhs the upper hand was the role played by the Sikh States of East Punjab who maintained armed forces and police of their own. In the first week of May 1947, the Maharaja of Patiala came to see Mountbatten and told him that the Sikh leaders were perturbed because he was ruining the idea of 'Sikhistan', since the partition line which was reported to have been chosen would divide the Sikhs into two almost equal parts. The Maharaja appealed to Mountbatten to make the partition line on the basis of Sikh landed property, Sikh sacred buildings and Sikh interests. Mountbatten explained this was a matter for the Boundary Commission. The Maharaja said, 'In that case I greatly fear the Sikhs will fight.' Mountbatten replied, 'If they do, Maharaja Sahib, they will have to fight the Central Government, for I and my Government are determined to put down any attempts at communal war with a ruthless iron hand; they will be opposed not only by tanks and armoured cars and artillery, but any concentrations may be bombed and machine-gunned from the air. You can tell your Sikhs that if they start a war they will not be fighting the Muslim League, but the whole might of the armed forces of India.' Mountbatten gave the same warning on different occasions to other Sikh rulers such as the Maharaja of Nabha and the Raja of Faridkot.[1]

On 21 May, S. E. Abbott, Private Secretary to the Governor of the Punjab, sent to R. V. Borckman, Personal Secretary to the Viceroy, an intelligence report compiled by himself from various sources saying that the Sikhs 'are determined on an offensive against the Muslims where they are in a majority in the area which the Sikhs are demanding' and that:

> most of the Sikh States and some others are also involved. Patiala is said to have agreed to supply arms and ammunition as well as explosives. He is supposed to have sent some of his soldiers, armed and in mufti, already to Amritsar. Faridkot held back but gave way on being promised Ferozepore district. Nabha is not in the business himself but his Dewan is and some of the Nabha Sirdars. Alwar, Dholpur, Bikaner and Bharatpur have all promised arms and ammunition. Kapurthala has given money and shelter to Sikh refugees but is not prepared to go further at the moment.[2]

Governor Jenkins reported to Mountbatten ten days later that two armed parties from Faridkot and Nabha States had arrived in Lahore during the preceding fortnight and had caused 'two scares'.[3]

---

[1] *Report on the Last Viceroyalty*, p. 60 paras. 94-7.
[2] TOP X, p. 942.
[3] TOP XI, p. 24.

An officer who had served in the Punjab Boundary Force recorded, 'The States of Kapurthala and Patiala have provided sanctuary for raiding Sikh *jathas*, and also safe bases for them to operate from.'[1]

In the concluding part of the *Report on the Last Viceroyalty*, Mountbatten confessed, 'My threats to the Sikh rulers and leaders may now appear to have been empty: it is doubtful, however, if any other approach to them would have been more successful.'[2]

The Sikh solidarity against the Muslims gave a fillip to the feelings of Sikh nationalism and the movement for Khalistan (sometimes also called Sikhistan). They regarded getting rid of the Muslims from East Punjab as the first step toward the goal of a Sikh homeland and thereafter getting rid of the Hindus as the second and final step.

In his interview with Jenkins on 10 July 1947, Giani Kartar Singh said that he had never trusted and did not 'now' trust Congress. He saw the final Sikh State as a kind of buffer-state between Pakistan and India.[3]

Jenkins noted that on the following day 'strong distrust of Congress' was also apparent when Jathedar Mohan Singh stated the Sikh case.[4]

After Giani Kartar Singh had seen Jenkins again on 30 July the Governor recorded:

The Giani Sahib gave me some interesting information on the future of East Punjab. He said that the Sikhs favoured the amalgamation of the non-Punjabi speaking districts with the UP or with another new Province. They would then try to organize what remained of East Punjab as a Sikh-majority Province. The Sikh States would come in with them on this—they had not of course given the Hindus any idea of their intentions yet, as they wanted Hindu help over the boundary question.[5]

At Mountbatten's request, Jenkins prepared a memorandum on 4 August 1947[6] answering the main criticisms against the Punjab Government for its handling of the disturbances. He said:

The critics are themselves participants in the events which they profess to deplore. During the disturbances Nehru, Patel, and Baldev Singh have visited various parts of the Punjab. They have done so nominally as members of the

---

[1] Lieutenant-General Sir Francis Tuker, *While Memory Serves*, p. 449.
[2] *Report on the Last Viceroyalty*, p. 170, para. 9.
[3] TOP XII, p. 74,
[4] Ibid., p. 103.
[5] Ibid., p. 431.
[6] For text of this memorandum *see*, TOP XII, pp. 511-27.

Central Government, but in fact as communal leaders. To the best of my belief not one of them made during these visits any contact of importance with any Muslim... Conversely when Liaquat Ali Khan or Ghazanfar Ali Khan visited the Punjab, they did so not to assist the administration, but to assist the Muslims. When a Hindu leader talks about 'utter ruthlessness, or 'martial law' he means that he wants as many Muslims as possible shot out of hand; Muslim, Hindu, and Sikh persist in regarding themselves as blameless. Moreover, there is very little doubt that the disturbances have in some degree been organized and paid for by persons or bodies directly or indirectly under the control of the Muslim League, Congress, and the Akali party. The evidence of this is to be found in the daily intelligence summaries, and in the solicitude with which prominent men—particularly   among the Hindus—take up the cases of suspects belonging to their own community.

To the charge that the British were able to crush, without difficulty, the disturbances of 1942 but failed to deal in the same way with the disturbances of 1947, Jenkins answered that the critics were not comparing like with like. In 1942, the attacks were concentrated on government property and government servants, in other words, on points that were largely known. In 1947 the 'two nations' fought one another in the streets, in the markets, in the fields, and in the villages.

It was asserted also that Congress Governments had no difficulty in suppressing disturbances and that the worst province of all was the Punjab which was still 'under British rule'. Jenkins pointed out that:

During 1946 and/or 1947 very serious disturbances occurred in: Bombay under a Congress Government; Calcutta and Noakali under a Muslim League Government, Bihar under a Congress Government, the NWFP under a Congress Government, the United Provinces under a Congress Government.

To the demand that Martial Law should have been declared at least in Lahore and possibly elsewhere, Jenkins replied that in the conditions prevailing at the time this would have been an inappropriate step, an opinion in which the senior military commanders concurred with him; 'cloak and dagger' activities were not a situation in which troops could act decisively.

Mountbatten had made some bold promises to put down the expected disturbances. At a meeting of the Defence Committee India on 25 April 1947, 'he pointed out that he bore personal responsibility for law and order which he must carry until such time as he could hand it over to one or more responsible authorities. While he bore that responsibility he had in the last resort the use of British troops to fall back on.'[1]

When Azad warned him on 14 May that rivers of blood would flow during the partition of the country, Mountbatten replied:

> At least on this one question I shall give you complete assurance. I shall see to it that there is no bloodshed and riot. I am a soldier, not a civilian. Once partition is accepted in principle, I shall issue orders to see that there are no communal disturbances anywhere in the country. If there should be the slightest agitation, I shall adopt measures to nip the trouble in the bud. I shall not use even the armed police. I shall order the Army and the Air Force to act and use tanks and aeroplanes to suppress anybody who wants to create trouble.[2]

The only effective answer to the problem would have been large-scale deployment of British troops, who alone could be trusted to act impartially, but after 14 August it was unthinkable to authorize the use of British troops in a situation over which the British cabinet and parliament exercised no control. And had they become involved in the communal fighting earlier, could they be asked abruptly to disengage themselves at the stroke of midnight on 14 August, just when the civil war was expected to escalate sharply?

Penderel Moon comments that, 'In defence of themselves and their own Raj the British had used unlimited force, but in defence of one Indian community against another they had appeared content to stand aside and do nothing.'[3] This criticism is unfair because the use of British troops was equally unacceptable to both Congress and Muslim League leaders. They could hardly invite the assistance of British troops at the very time when they were in the process of getting rid of British domination. There is no reliable evidence to indicate that the Indian leaders urged the use of British troops, while on the other hand Mountbatten has recorded that the services of British troops had not been asked for by 'either Dominion Government'.[4]

---

[1] TOP X, p. 436.

[2] Maulana Abul Kalam Azad, *India Wins Freedom*, p. 207.

[3] Penderel Moon, *Divide and Quit*, p. 81.

[4] *Report on the Last Viceroyalty*, p. 169, para. 4. After considering the recommendation of Mountbatten, who had consulted the Commander-in-Chief, the British Government decided that after 14 August 1947 British troops could be used only to save British lives (TOP XII, p. 395). British troops began to leave India on 17 August 1947 and the withdrawal was completed on 28 February 1948.

Nor was Mountbatten's promise to use aeroplanes redeemed. 'The offensive use of aircraft was discussed at the highest political and military levels' but the proposal was abandoned because it was difficult enough to recognize ground personnel from the air even in regular warfare; in civil strife the difficulty of distinguishing raider from refugee was even greater.[1]

Mountbatten has also been criticised for not ordering the arrest of Sikh leaders. This question was seriously considered on 5 August, at a meeting at which G. R. Savage, a police officer employed in the Punjab CID, reported to Mountbatten, Jinnah, Liaquat and Patel. Savage said the Sikh leaders had lost control of their people and Tara Singh, in particular, was determined to take revenge on Muslims. Mountbatten was in favour of having the Sikh leader arrested 'at about the time of the Boundary Commission's Award' but gave up the idea because Jenkins, Mudie (Governor-Designate of West Punjab) and Trivedi (Governor-Designate of East Punjab) 'unanimously decided that arrests should not be made until after the Boundary Commission's Award was announced, and the new governments were responsible for law and order'.[2] In arriving at this decision these officials were no doubt influenced by the fact that the Award of the Boundary Commission was expected to be announced any day. It was not until 13 August that Mountbatten informed Jenkins that the Award would be announced one day after the transfer of power. Since the inflammatory intentions of the Sikh leaders had been known to the authorities long before the Savage report, Pakistanis justifiably blame Mountbatten for not ordering the arrest of the militants at a much earlier stage.

The truth of the matter is that neither Mountbatten nor the Congress and Muslim League leaders had anticipated the massive scale which the Punjab disturbances would reach.

At his press conference on 4 June 1947, Mountbatten was asked whether he foresaw any mass transfer of population. He replied, 'Personally I do not—I am speaking as a prophet—because of the physical difficulties involved which you can visualise...But I equally think that a measure of transfer of population will come about in a natural way, that is to say people will just cross the boundary, or the government may take steps to transfer population.'

The declaration issued by the Partition Council on 22 July 1947 showed

[1] *The Rees Report*, p. 27. *Report on the Last Viceroyalty*, p. 169, para. 3.
[2] TOP XII, pp. 537-9, 389, 765.

that the Congress and Muslim League leaders also hoped that partition would be completed without too much dislocation of population and disturbance of the peace.[1] The Sikh leaders seemed to be in favour of making preparations for the transfer of population in the Punjab, but Nehru and Jinnah and their followers turned down the suggestion.[2]

In the last part of August, Nehru and Liaquat made a joint tour of the affected areas to restore peace. Afterwards, at a conference in Lahore on 3 September, the two Prime Ministers reiterated 'the determination of the two Central and the two Provincial Governments that law and order should be immediately established and all lawlessness suppressed and punished', but this threat had no practical effect. Their flocks were utterly out of control.

The situation went out of control because of the manner in which partition was effected; the civil services, the police and the army were all in a state of temporary disintegration. Here again, the national leaders were as much to blame as Mountbatten. Congress as well as the Muslim League had agreed to all the steps which were taken to transfer power. If the Indians, who had been inveterate critics of British rule, had believed that Mountbatten was to blame for the massacres, they would scarcely have shouted, 'Pandit Mountbatten *ki jai*' on Independence Day. In fact he held their complete trust up to his final departure in June 1948.

Mountbatten has also been blamed for advancing the date of independence from June 1948 to 15 August 1947. But before him, Wavell had already recognized that the British had neither the power nor the will to remain in India for more than an extremely limited period[3] and he had asked His Majesty's Government to make arrangements for the transfer of power not later than 31 March 1948.[4] The date of 15 August, though publicly announced by Mountbatten for the first time in his press conference of 4 June, was a decision which he had reached after a deliberate assessment of the situation.[5] Had independence been delayed for any length of time beyond 15 August, the disorders might very well have spread to other places in India instead of remaining largely confined to the Punjab. As Rajagopalachari said to Mountbatten in March 1948, 'If you had not transferred power when you did, there would have been no power to transfer.'

---

[1] *See*, pp. 520-1.
[2] *Report on the Last Viceroyalty*, p. 102, para. 55 and p. 171, para. 14.
[3] *See*, p. 458.
[4] *See*, p. 467.
[5] *See*, p. 511-12.

However, while we consider that circumstances, rather than individuals, were to blame for the tragic events of 1947, we are unable to endorse H. V. Hodson's view that the British 'transmitted power in peace and order'.[1] In fact, the transfer of power was accompanied by a horrific civil war in the Punjab. Perhaps what Hodson means is that the Indians were killing only one another and not the British.

But is a civil war preferable to a war of independence against a foreign occupying power? Though all fighting is inherently evil, a war of liberation has some redeeming features—it inspires heroic action and feelings of national solidarity and pride. A civil war on the other hand is an unmitigated calamity—it debases character and leaves behind abiding feelings of bitterness and shame.

At the same time we do not subscribe to the extreme verdict that the final chapter was 'one of the most discreditable' in the history of Britain's connection with India[2] because the British did not kill the Indians; the Indians themselves were murdering each other and, therefore, must primarily carry the guilt. As a matter of fact the British displayed considerable political ingenuity and maturity in the manner in which they handed over power to the people of the Indian subcontinent.[3]

Luckily, the greater part of India remained relatively calm, but Delhi and the western districts of the United Provinces were too close to the Punjab to remain unaffected by the upheaval next door. Refugees in their millions poured out of the Punjab bent on revenge, and in Delhi the situation became so desperate that Mountbatten, who had gone to Simla for a rest, was urgently summoned back to the capital by a frantic telephone call from Menon on 4 September.

When the Governor-General and his party arrived at Government House in New Delhi on the afternoon of 6 September 'we found V. P. [Menon] awaiting Mountbatten with a message from Patel hoping that he [would] grip the situation firmly without delay. Nehru came round immediately to enlist his [Mountbatten's] active and overriding authority to deal with the emergency, followed by Patel.'[4]

---

[1] H. V. Hodson, op. cit. p. 396.

[2] Viscount Templewood, 'Some Reflections on Indian Constitutional History', *Asiatic Review*, October 1952.

[3] *See*, Epilogues.

[4] Campbell-Johnson, op. cit. p. 178. Campbell-Johnson comments that 'to recall Mountbatten in this way is a great tribute to the quality of their [Nehru and Patel's] character and leadership'. By shifting the responsibility for controlling their people to the shoulders of Mountbatten, who was not only their 'constitutional' Governor-General but also

Continued on next page

Mountbatten proposed that an Emergency Committee should be set up. This was 'at once' agreed to by Nehru and Patel, and at their insistence Mountbatten agreed to be the chairman. Mountbatten 'by his vigour, decision and leadership, and Pandit Nehru and Sardar Patel by their wise abnegation, may well have saved Delhi from disaster, the Government of India from collapse, and the nation from being rent apart.'[1] The question may well be asked: How did Pakistan—with a proportionately greater refugee problem, with a proportionately smaller number of senior officials still in the process of settling down in their new capital, with the ailing Jinnah[2] as the only outstanding leader, and having no Mountbatten to save it—manage to survive?

It was generally feared that, like Lahore and Amritsar, Calcutta too would suffer death and destruction, but it was saved by Gandhi's presence. On 11 August the provincial premier, Suhrawardy, called on the Mahatma and persuaded him not to proceed to Noakhali until peace was assured in Calcutta.[3] Suhrawardy shared Gandhi's lodging among the Untouchables and assisted him in pacifying the people.

When at the end of August

news of the atrocities in the north brought about a threatening recrudescence of communal trouble, Gandhiji immediately began a fast 'to end only if and when sanity returns to Calcutta'. The entire police force of north Calcutta undertook a 24-hour fast in sympathy, while continuing on duty. Within four days there was complete peace. After one of Gandhiji's prayer meetings on the Calcutta *maidan*, thousands of Hindus and Muslims mingled and embraced one another. No word of Government could have given so much confidence and assurance as this one man alone had inspired in the minorities on either side. Perhaps the best description of Gandhiji's part in maintaining communal peace in Bengal was made by Lord Mountbatten when, in a broadcast, he referred to Gandhiji as 'the one-man boundary force who kept the peace while a 50,000 strong force was swamped by riots'.[4]

a foreigner, the Indian leaders in fact exposed their limitations. Other occasions on which they made use of their constitutional Governor-General's superior capacity were the organization of the airlift to repel the tribal invasion of Kashmir in October 1947, and the negotiations beyond 15 August 1947 to obtain Hyderabad's accession to India. Mountbatten was chairman of the Indian Defence Committee. 'At this body, by request of Pandit Nehru and his other Ministers, the Governor-General presided, thus acting in some sense as Prime Minister in matters of defence...'. H. V. Hodson, op. cit. p. 448.

[1] H. V. Hodson, op. cit. p. 415.

[2] Jinnah had been in poor health for some years past and died of tuberculosis on 11 September 1948.

[3] Pyarelal, op. cit. *The Last Phase* II, p. 364.

[4] V. P. Menon, *The Transfer of Power in India*, p. 434.

At the end of September, Gandhi returned to Delhi and tried to restore peace there. From 13 January 1948 he undertook a fast, and ended it five days later when a Peace Committee representing the various communities in Delhi signed a pact promising amity and the protection of the Muslim minority.

Gandhi's efforts to save the Muslims angered militant Hindus, and on the afternoon of 30 January 1948 one of them, Nathuram Godse, fired three shots at him at close range as he was walking to his prayer meeting. One shot hit his abdomen and two his chest. He fell chanting '*Ram, Ram*' ('Oh God, Oh God') and died shortly afterwards.

Godse belonged to Sivaji's and Tilak's Maratha country. Like Tilak, Godse came from Poona; like Tilak he was a Chitpavan Brahmin; and like Tilak he published a right-wing Hindu paper. At his trial, Godse stated, 'I sat brooding intensely on the atrocities perpetrated on Hinduism and its dark and deadly future if left to face Islam outside and Gandhi inside, and...I decided all of a sudden to take the extreme step against Gandhi.'[1]

MOUNTBATTEN APPRAISED[2]

During his Viceroyalty, Mountbatten served his country well. Attlee rightly complimented him thus:

> I am conscious that I put you in to bat on a very sticky wicket to pull the game out of the fire. Few people would have taken it on and few, if any, could have pulled the game round as you have.[3]

The last Viceroy certainly deserves unqualified praise for his management of the Congress and Muslim League leaders. The situation was highly explosive, and the danger of a breakdown of the process of transfer of power by agreement was ever present. Wavell had complained to George VI that to induce Congress and the Muslim League to co-operate 'reminds me of one of my childhood puzzles—a little glass-covered box with three or four different coloured marbles which one had to manipulate into their respective pens by very gentle oscillations; just as the last one seemed on the point of moving in, some or all of the others invariably ran out.'[4]

---

[1] Louis Fischer, *The Life of Mahatma Gandhi*, p. 540.
[2] *See also*, the section on the Radcliffe Boundary Awards, the chapter on Integration of the Princely States and the section on Law and Order.
[3] TOP XII, p. 213.
[4] Philip Ziegler, op. cit. p. 352.

Mountbatten was a superb chairman, always able to prevent a meeting from disintegrating. A meeting of the pre-partition cabinet in the first part of June is a case in point. Nehru wished to announce a number of diplomatic appointments and hoped that Mountbatten would rule that they did not concern Pakistan. Liaquat objected and hinted that Pakistan would not wish to have an ambassador appointed to Moscow. This caused Nehru to flare up, since his own sister, Mrs Pandit, had been proposed for the post. Liaquat responded equally violently and pandemonium broke loose and everyone talked at once. After calling the offenders to order, Mountbatten remonstrated, 'Gentlemen, what hopes have we of getting a peaceable partition if the very first discussion leads to such a disgraceful scene as this?' and deferred the matter, saying he would give a ruling later. He then surveyed the faces round the table and said, 'I am not going on with the next item until I see a row of smiling faces in front of me.' This broke the tension and everybody laughed.[1]

However, his personal achievements have been exaggerated as a result of his zeal for projecting himself in a favourable light even if it entailed departure from the truth.[2] Two instances may be cited.

It will be recalled how chagrined Mountbatten was when Jinnah denied him the Governor-Generalship of Pakistan.[3] But in an article, 'Jinnah: a Retrospect', which he contributed to a book sponsored by the Government of Pakistan to celebrate the centenary of Jinnah's birth, he wrote, 'it was a surprise when he [Jinnah] suddenly announced that he intended to be Governor-General of Pakistan...But I did not personally resent this decision, as has been the common opinion, for it saved me from the daunting task of having to try to ride two separate horses simultaneously.'[4]

The second example shows that he was not above appropriating credit for something that another person had done. In reality, it was at Menon's suggestion that Trivedi had been invited to Delhi to solve the daunting problem of dividing the armed forces.[5] But after Trivedi had succeeded brilliantly, Mountbatten wrote in his report to London, 'All of us had feared that the partition of the Armed Forces...was going to be a major stumbling block...I then had the brain-wave of sending for Trivedi.'[6]

[1] TOP XI, p. 303.
[2] See, p. 485 for a summing up of his character by Philip Ziegler.
[3] See, pp. 531-2.
[4] Pakistan Past and Present, p. 40.
[5] Menon had made this proposal at a staff meeting on 16 June. TOP XI, p. 420.
[6] Ibid., p. 893, see also, p. 520.

Indeed, he did have his share of failures. Campbell-Johnson, his *alter ego,* tells us that the attainment of a united India 'had always been and would remain his first ambition and determination',[1] but his meetings with Jinnah soon made it quite clear that anything short of a decision to divide the country would mean civil war. It was only when Mountbatten adopted as his own the compromise solution which the Congress and Muslim League leaders themselves had already accepted that success came his way.[2]

Mountbatten was also unable to carry out the wishes expressed in Attlee's directive that the Indian Army should remain undivided, that India's defence should continue on an all-India basis and that there should be collaboration in the security of the Indian Ocean area.[3]

He certainly was a trier; he 'could rarely resist giving advice'[4] and even designed flags for India and Pakistan with 'a small Union Jack in the upper canton'[5], although the design was not accepted by either party—Jinnah explained that it would be repugnant to the Muslims to have a Christian cross alongside the crescent, and Nehru said that the general feeling among 'Congress extremists' was that the leaders were pandering far too much to the British and that it would be inadvisable to press the design on them.[6]

As Ziegler has pointed out, 'When the Indians believed that their national interests were involved, then Mountbatten could do little to shift them.'[7]

Mountbatten, as well as the British Government and people, believed that independent India was destined to be one of the great nations of the world and that it would greatly benefit Britain to cultivate good relations with it. In this he succeeded completely; he was able to convert the attitude of the Indians toward the British from one of suspicion and hostility to one of warm goodwill. He was greatly assisted by the fact that, while his predecessors had been suspected of pursuing a policy of divide and rule, he was able to convince the Indians that

---

[1] Campbell-Johnson, op. cit. p. 72.

[2] Congress had agreed to the division of India and the Muslim League had indicated that it would accept a reduction in the territory it demanded as Pakistan. *See*, pp. 479-482.

[3] For the British Chiefs of Staff's view of strategic requirements in the subcontinent *see*, p. 957 of TOP XI, and for Mountbatten's reply pleading that it was difficult to negotiate arrangements for defence for the post-independence period *see*, p. 962, ibid.

[4] Ziegler, op. cit. p. 458.

[5] TOP XI, p. 690.

[6] TOP XII, p.230.

[7] Philip Ziegler, op. cit., p. 436.

his own greatest ambition was to unite and quit, which had long been Congress' own cherished goal.

But to win Indian hearts it was necessary for him also to demonstrate palpably that he was a greater friend of India than of Pakistan. This inevitably hurt Pakistani interests, but the lament of the Pakistanis was swamped by the chorus of approval of his conduct voiced by the British Government and the India leaders.

Lord and Lady Mountbatten finally left India on 21 June 1948. The extent to which they had succeeded in winning the trust and affection of the people and leaders of India is apparent from Nehru's speech at the state banquet on their last evening:

> You came here, Sir, with a high reputation, but many a reputation has foundered in India. You lived here through a period of great difficulty and crisis, and yet your reputation has not foundered.. Used as I am to these vast demonstrations here[1], I was much affected and I wondered how it was that an English man and English woman could become so popular in India during this brief period of time... A period certainly of achievement and success in some measure, but also a period of sorrow and disaster... Obviously this was not connected so much with what had happened, but rather with the good faith, the friendship and love of India that these two possessed... You may have many gifts and presents, but there is nothing more real or precious than the love and affection of the people. You have seen, Sir and Madam, how that love and affection work.

Mountbatten's prejudice against Pakistan was palpable, but Pakistanis do have reason to thank him for restraining India from going to war with Pakistan over Junagarh and Kashmir. His primary motive for doing so, probably, was to protect not Pakistan, but the good name of the 'family of nations', the British Commonwealth, of which India and Pakistan were the new members and Britain the proud founder. But the fact remains that his influence over the Indian leaders may well have saved Pakistan from possible disaster. A Hindu Governor-General could not have restrained Nehru and Patel to the same extent. The poorly-equipped Pakistani army was no match for the Indian forces at that time. 'The position was so bad,' recalled President Ayub Khan, 'that for the first few years we could only allow five rounds of practice ammunition per man a year.'[2]

At a meeting on 27 September, Patel expressed himself in favour of a show of strength in Junagarh. Mountbatten suggested that the question

---

[1] He was referring to the public demonstrations earlier that day.
[2] M. Ayub Khan, *Friends Not Masters*, p. 21.

might be referred to the United Nations but the idea was dropped because Patel and Nehru both opposed it. Mountbatten emphasized the danger of any precipitate action which might lead to war between India and Pakistan. Such a war, he argued, might mean the end of Pakistan altogether, but it would also be the end of India for at least a generation to come. He was anxious that India should not lose its great international position by taking incorrect action.[1]

During a heated and recriminatory discussion between Liaquat and Nehru at Lahore on 9 December, Nehru flared up and declared that the only solution was to clear Kashmir with the sword, and that he would 'throw up his Prime Ministership, and take a rifle himself, and lead the men of India against the invasion'. Mountbatten realized that the deadlock was complete and the only way out was to bring in some third party. For this reason he suggested a reference to the United Nations.[2] Nehru at first was strongly opposed but gradually came round. In a letter to Nehru on Christmas Day, Mountbatten reminded him, 'when first I suggested bringing UNO into this dispute, it was in order to achieve the object I have quoted above—to stop the fighting and to stop it as soon as possible'.[3]

Mountbatten's methods at times were unorthodox: 'Open diplomacy was, so far as possible, the order of the day...Yet openness did not exclude a degree of manipulation, even chicanery, which would have been inconceivable to either of his immediate predecessors.'[4] For example, he told Krishna Menon on 17 April 1947 that he was under 'the strictest instructions not to make any attempt to keep India within the commonwealth' and justified this falsehood as 'tactics'.[5]

Nevertheless, he did succeed in preventing a calamitous collapse of negotiations and managed to transfer power to the two new Dominions with due constitutional propriety. For this at least he deserves the acclamation of Britain, India and Pakistan alike.

---

[1] V. P. Menon, *Integration of the Indian States*, p. 138.

[2] H. V. Hodson, op. cit. p. 465.

[3] Ibid., p. 466. *See also*, the following entry under the date 31 December 1947 in Campbell-Johnson, op. cit. 'Mountbatten has done everything in his power to urge on Nehru what an invasion of Pakistan territory would mean, particularly as the whole problem at India's request is *sub judice*. Quite apart from the catastrophic effect on world opinion, it would involve the automatic departure of British officers serving with both Dominions. This in itself might well, I suppose, work more immediately against Pakistan's interest than India's, but in any case I think Nehru is well aware that any such move would mean that Mountbatten's mission would be at an end.'

[4] Philip Ziegler, op. cit. p. 364.

[5] TOP X, p. 312.

EPILOGUE I

'Why beholdest thou the mote that is in thy brother's eye, but considerest not the beam that is in thine own eye?'

St. Matthew, vii, 3

EPILOGUE I

Before we indulge in throwing stones at British imperialism, let us face the task of looking at our own shortcomings, for it was we South Asians who helped the British to conquer our land and rule over it. When the weight of public opinion turned against them, they left.

After independence, when the British no longer looked quite so evil as they did while they ruled India, Prime Minister Nehru called upon his countrymen to take a more balanced view of the British connection. 'The Industrial Revolution in England was helped tremendously by the original...loot from India,' he said. 'Nevertheless, if the British people went ahead, it was due to their great genius, hard work, organization and discipline and a hundred fine qualities. We do not talk about those qualities; but we talk of the fact that because of our weaknesses they came and conquered India, controlled India and profited by their stay in India. Then we blame them for it while the blame is ours for our failures, stupidity, factions, disruptions in our country.'[1] 'Divide and rule has always been the way of empires, and the measure of their [the British Government's] success in this policy has been also the measure of their superiority over those whom they thus exploit,' he had said upon an earlier occasion, while the British were still in India. 'We cannot complain of this or, at any rate, we ought not to be surprised at it...To ignore it and not provide against it is in itself a mistake in one's thought.'[2]

The British did not divide India. They found India divided and conquered it; India remained divided and they continued to rule over it. As Maulana Muhammad Ali put it: 'It is the old maxim of "divide and rule". But there is a division of labour here. We [Indians] divide and you [British] rule'.[3]

After the death of Aurangzeb, the Mughal Empire began to disintegrate and innumerable chieftains vied with one another for power. In their scramble for overseas exploitation the Portuguese, the Dutch and the French all desired to carve out spheres of influence. The British could scarcely afford to be left behind. Clive's victory at Plassey placed

---

[1] *Indian Parliamentary Debates,* Vol. V, No. 5, 4 August 1950, Col. 375.

[2] Jawaharlal Nehru, *An Autobiography,* p. 136.

[3] *Indian Round Table Conference,* First Session, (1930-1), p. 102.

the resources of the rich province of Bengal at their disposal and set them on the road to piecemeal conquest of the whole of India. They found little difficulty in recruiting Indian sepoys to fight other Indians or in enlisting the support of some Indian princes to defeat other Indian princes.

The Hindustani sepoys had fought for the British against the Gurkhas and the Sikhs: during the Great Rebellion of 1857, the Sikhs and the Gurkhas helped the British in subduing the Hindustani sepoys. At the time of the Rebellion, there were more than seven sepoys to every British soldier, but the insurrection was suppressed because most of the people and princes of India did not side with the rebels. 'There is nothing more true,' concluded John William Kaye in *A History of the Sepoy War in India*, 'than that the calm courage of our Native adherents enabled us to recover India from their own countrymen.'[1] Even in Oudh, the stronghold of the rebellion, the people 'with a few exceptions treated the fugitives of the ruling race with a marked kindness'.[2]

Sir John Seeley, the British historian, correctly concluded that 'India can hardly be said to have been conquered at all by the foreigners. She has rather conquered herself.'

After the Great Rebellion, the disunity of India moved from the battlefield to the political arena. Centuries of invasions and infiltration by foreigners had made Indian society the most variegated mosaic of races, languages, religions, castes and customs in the world. With the pre-Muslim cultures, Hinduism, with its great genius for assimilation, had reached a degree of compatibility but, in the words of the noted Hindu historian, K. M. Panikkar, 'Islam...split Indian society into two sections from top to bottom and what has now come to be known in the phraseology of today as "the two separate nations" came into being from the beginning.'[3] The central clash for political power, therefore, took place between the Hindus and the Muslims. Had these two major communities[4] come to terms, the other minorities would have been forced to come into line.

---

[1] Vol. III, p. 566.

[2] G. W. Forrest, *A History of the Indian Mutiny*, Vol. I, p. xv.

[3] K. M. Panikkar, *A Survey of Indian History*, p. 143.

[4] The Muslims were India's most substantial minority. At the time of the transfer of power they numbered some 90 million out of a population of 400 million. They were thus larger in number than the population of most countries in the world. The next largest minority in India were the Untouchables, totalling 50 million.

Only once in the entire constitutional history of British India did Congress and the Muslim League present an agreed scheme of political reforms—the Lucknow Pact of 1916.[1] Unfortunately, the Nehru Report reneged on the Lucknow Pact when it proposed a constitution for India in 1928; it rejected the principles of separate electorates and provincial autonomy.[2]

The Nehru Report was a landmark in Hindu-Muslim relations and deserves greater attention than it has generally received so far. The rift created by it was deep and abiding. The Muslims began to demand separate electorates and provincial autonomy even more anxiously than before. The experience of 'Hindu raj' by the Congress ministries in 1937-9 dispelled their faith even in the efficacy of constitutional safeguards and inevitably led to the demand for a completely independent state of their own.[3]

The Nehru Report also down-graded the importance of a Hindu-Muslim accord in the fight for freedom. It argued that communal differences were the creation of the British policy of divide and rule and would disappear when India became independent. It made the following sweeping prediction, which became the favourite theme of Congress but which has not been borne out though the country has now been independent for nearly half a century:

> We are certain that as soon as India is free and can face her problems unhampered by alien authority and intervention, the minds of her people will turn to the vital problems of the day...parties will be formed in the country and in the legislature on entirely other grounds, chiefly economic we presume. We shall then find Hindus and Muslims and Sikhs in one party acting together and opposing another party which also consists of Hindus and Muslims and Sikhs. This is bound to happen if we once get going.

At the second session of the Round Table conference, Gandhi echoed the thesis of the Nehru Report:

> This [Hindu-Muslim] quarrel is not old; this quarrel...is coeval with the British advent, and immediately this relationship, the unfortunate, artificial unnatural

---

[1] *See*, pp. 161-3.

[2] For a discussion of the Nehru Report and the effect of its provisions on Muslim opinion *See*, pp. 264-70.

[3] *See*, pp. 306-7 and 315-19. During an informal discussion of the policital situation during the Governors'. Conference (31 August 1944), Wavell observed, 'Pakistan was the creation of Congress, for it was the refusal to establish Coalition Governments in the provinces that alarmed the Muslims and drove them to extremes.' TOP V, p. 2.

relationship, between Great Britain and India is transformed into a natural relationship...you will find that Hindus, Mussalmans, Sikhs, Europeans, Anglo-Indians, Christians, Untouchables, will all live together as one man.

In 1941 the Mahatma said:

I admit that there is unfortunately an unbridgeable gulf between Congress and the Muslim League. But why do not the British statesmen admit that it is, after all, a domestic quarrel? Let them withdraw from India and I promise that Congress and the League and all other parties will find it to their interest to come together and devise a home-made solution for the government of India. It may not be Scientific; it may not be after any Western pattern; but it will be durable.

In the following year, Gandhi asked the British government to 'leave India in God's hands, in modern parlance to anarchy', and admitted that 'anarchy may lead to internecine warfare for a time or to unrestricted dacoities', but argued that 'from these a true India will rise in place of the false one we see'.

To the Muslims, these statements seemed like telling the British, 'Just hand over power to Congress and leave India..the Hindus will then steamroller the minorities by the sheer weight of their superiority in numbers.' The Muslims desired independence no less than Congress, but felt that independence before a communal settlement was like putting the cart before the horse. They stipulated that their status in independent India must be defined before the transfer of power. This was never done to their satisfaction, and in the end they had to be given a separate homeland of their own.[1] The grant of generous constitutional safeguards to the Muslims would have obviated the demand for partition. It would not have deprived the Hindus of the inherent advantages they enjoyed by virtue of being not only the majority community but also the one whose members were better educated, more prosperous and better organized for political action.

It is true that until the British finally fixed the time for leaving India, they believed that it was to their advantage that the Indian communities did not unite against them, but the question remains of why, with the solitary

---

[1] R. C. Majumdar, the leading Hindu historian, writes with refreshing candour, 'It would, perhaps, not be unreasonable to hold that an important contributing factor to the tragic events that took place was the failure of Hindu leaders to make a proper assessment of the feelings and attitudes of the Muslims and a realistic, instead of idealistic, approach to the Hindu-Muslim problem, to which attention has been repeatedly drawn in this volume.' *The Struggle for Freedom*, p. 792.

exception of the Lucknow Pact, Congress and Muslim League leaders never displayed enough political maturity to present united demands to the British Government. Leaders of the calibre of Gandhi, Nehru and Jinnah were not stooges of the British Government and there was nothing to prevent them from coming to a mutual understanding. It reflects poorly upon the extent of their leadership that they spent most of their energy in getting the better of each other, instead of joining forces to seize the initiative from the British, who were constantly challenging them to agree among themselves. They could neither decide to live together amicably nor divide the country sensibly.

After the failure of the Cripps Mission, Secretary of State Amery could truthfully state in the House of Commons that Sir Stafford Cripps 'flew many thousands of miles to meet the Indian leaders in order to arrive at an agreement with them. The Indian leaders in Delhi moved not one step to meet each other, either without him or in his presence. They made no attempt to reach agreement among themselves.'

Having negotiated with the Indian leaders in vain for nearly two months, the Cabinet Mission issued their own proposals. The last part of their Statement of 16 May 1946 read:

> To the leaders and people of India who now have the opportunity of complete independence we would finally say this. We and our Government and countrymen hoped that it would be possible for the Indian people themselves to agree upon the method of framing the new constitution under which they will live. Despite the labours which we have shared with the Indian Parties, and the exercise of much patience and goodwill by all, this has not been possible. We therefore now lay before you proposals which, after listening to all sides and after much earnest thought, we trust will enable you to attain your independence in the shortest time and with the least danger of internal disturbance and conflict. These proposals may not, of course, completely satisfy all parties, but you will recognize with us that at this supreme moment in Indian history statesmanship demands mutual accommodation.

During the debate in the House of Commons on Attlee's statement of 20 February 1947, Sir Stafford Cripps on 5 March replied in the following words to the charge that the statement was vague on the question as to whom power would be handed over to on the due date:

> The only way to remove that uncertainty is to get the agreement of the Indian communities as to what it is they wish us to do. We can hardly be accused of

vagueness and uncertainity when the Indian communities themselves cannot
come to any common agreement upon which we can act.

Gandhi and Nehru did not possess the right attributes for bringing about
Hindu-Muslim unity. Gandhi's style of leadership was essentially Hindu
and his view that Hindu-Muslim differences were simply a creation of the
British and would be automatically cured by driving the foreigners out of
the country inclined him to bypass the problem rather than find a solution
for it. And Nehru, an agnostic-socialist, saw political differences chiefly
in economic terms and failed to gauge the depth of religious feelings
among the people.[1]

Indeed, the basic problem for all the leaders, Hindu and Muslim alike,
was that the masses were illiterate and had not imbibed the same feeling
of nationalism which actuated their Western-educated leaders. Nehru was
a competent exponent of modern political ideas, but the Hindu masses
worshipped Gandhi, who reminded them of the holy men of old. And
Jinnah became a mass Muslim leader only when he raised the cry of 'Islam
in danger'. He had played the role of 'ambassador of Hindu-Muslim unity'
for most of his political life. Before the achievement of Pakistan, his
greatest political triumph had been the making of the Lucknow Pact. He
started to move from the demand for constitutional safeguards in a united
India to that for partition only in the late nineteen-thirties.[2] Nothing
illustrates the governing force of religious passions in the subcontinent
more than the fact that, although the Indian communities readily forgave
their foreign rulers as soon as they were definitely promised freedom,
India and Pakistan have still not forgiven each other. Hindu-Muslim riots
in India are even more frequent than they were before partition, and the

---

[1] Nehru spelled out his views on religion in the chapter, 'What is Religion?' in his
Autobiography. Commenting on Gandhi's fast in September 1932 in disapproval of Ramsay
MacDonald's Communal Award to the Untouchables, Nehru confessed, 'I felt angry with
him at his religious and sentimental approach to a political question, and his frequent
references to God in connectionwith it.' Also, 'I felt lonely and homeless, and India, to whom
I had given my love and for whom I had laboured, seemed a strange and bewildering land to
me. Was it my fault that I could not enter into the spirit and and ways of thinking of my
countrymen?' At another place in the same book (p. 469) he regretted that, 'Stress has been
laid on the "Muslim Nation" in India, on "Muslim culture", on the utter incompatibility of
Hindu and Muslim "cultures"...A few Hindu leaders think exactly on the same lines, with this
difference, however, that they hope that being in a majority their brand of "culture" will
ultimately prevail...To talk of a "Muslim nation"...means...just nothing at all except an
emotional state of mind and a conscious or unconscious desire not to face realities, especially
economic realities.'

[2] For the change in Jinnah's views *see*, pp. 307-20, 327-9 and 348-50.

Sikhs of the Punjab and the Muslims of Kashmir are prosecuting wars of secession.

Most of the major blunders were committed by the Congress leaders[1] due to overconfidence that the British Government would have to recognize that their party represented the whole of India and would be compelled to hand over power to them alone. Not only did they disregard the true nature and depth of Hindu-Muslim religious differences and the genuine fears of the Muslims at the hands of the permanent Hindu majority, but they also made tactical misjudgements which grievously damaged their cause.

The outbreak of World War II proved to be a godsend for the Muslim League. The attitude of Congress towards the forthcoming 'imperialist war' had already alarmed the British Government, and Linlithgow quickly moved to raise the status of the Muslim League to the same level as the Congress party.[2] The angry resignation of Congress ministries soon after the outbreak of the war, and Congress non-co-operation in the war effort, caused most British people to regard that party as their enemy and the Muslim League as their friend.

Congress' refusal to take office at the centre under the Cripps offer was also a serious mistake. Though the central government would have been appointed under the existing constitution, in practice the Viceroy could hardly have dared to interfere unreaonsably in its work and risk a crisis with a popular government in wartime. In vain did Cripps advise Congress that it was not necessary to insist on the legal expansion of the powers of the Viceroy's Executive Council; the force of circumstances would transfer greater responsibility to the Indian political leaders who formed the Council.[3]

An even greater blunder was the Congress decision to launch the 'Quit India' rebellion when Britain had its back to the wall during the war. It compelled the British Government to rely on the Muslims more than ever before. This gave a fillip to the status of the Muslim League and it expanded its authority in the political vacuum created by the incarceration of Congress leaders, although the League was not yet powerful enough to challenge Congress without official goodwill. In a letter to Secretary of State Amery on 10 June 1942, Linlithgow wrote: 'I think he [Jinnah]

---

[1] 'Perhaps the Congress leaders made the worst errors: if so, in the upshot they paid the most dearly in sacrifice of their ideals.' H. V. Hodson, *The Great Divide*, p. 527.

[2] For the attitude of Congress towards the forthcoming war, *see*, pp. 334-7 and for the sudden promotion of Jinnah to the same level as Gandhi by Linlithgow, *see*, Jinnah's statement at p. 343.

[3] *See*, p. 377.

probably looks a little more alarming from London than he does here. I do not however think he wants a row with Government...his threats do not cause me any sleepless nights!...Jinnah is not in as strong a position as Gandhi and Congress, and he is never likely to be, in the near future, since he represents a minority, and a minority that can only effectively hold its own with our assistance. Nor, of course, is his organisation anything like as deep-rooted as is that of Congress.'[1] And at the time of the Simla Conference, Jinnah said to Wavell on 9 July 1945, 'I am at the end of my tether. I ask you not to wreck the League.'[2]

By accepting the Cabinet Mission proposals, Jinnah was, right up to the summer of 1946, prepared to give a trial to the concept of an all-India federation in which Foreign Affairs, Defence and Communications would be administered by the centre.[3] It was only after Congress manoeuvres had caused the death of the Cabinet Mission plan that the Council of the Muslim League at its Bombay session (27-29 July 1946) decided to resort to 'direct action' to achieve Pakistan. This was notice that the Muslims would not shirk from civil war in pursuance of their demand for a separate homeland.

But it was Prime Minister Attlee's statement in the House of Commons on 20 February 1947 that made Pakistan really attainable. The declaration that Britain would hand over power definitely by June 1948, even if it meant the creation of more than one successor state, meant that all Jinnah had to do to win Pakistan was to dig his heels in until the appointed day.

Attlee's statement, moreover, gave a fillip to the Pakistan movement in the Muslim-majority provinces. The Muslims of these provinces, with their Muslim premiers and Muslim-dominated cabinets, had hitherto displayed less enthusiasm for Pakistan than had their co-religionists in the Congress provinces who had tasted Hindu raj. Pakistan having now become a visible reality caused the waverers to jump on the bandwagon. In the key province of the Punjab the Unionist Premier, Khizar Hayat Khan, called Attlee's announcement 'the work of lunatics' and resigned office shortly afterwards, leaving the political field clear for the Muslim League.[4]

The final decision to transfer power to only two successor states, India

---

[1] *TOP* III, p. 1052.

[2] *The Viceroy's Journal*, p. 153.

[3] *See*, p. 433 for the Muslim League's written proposals communicated to the cabinet Mission on 12 May 1946 and p. 452 for the concluding part of Jinnah's address to the All-India Muslim League council.

[4] *See*, p. 477.

and Pakistan, was a compromise between two possibilities, one of which was to transfer power to undivided India and the other to transfer power to the provinces singly or in the shape of voluntarily formed groups.

The movement for a united India appeared first. It was principally the creation of British rule, as the founders of the Indian National Congress acknowledged at their first session in 1885. Subramania Ayer of Madras said that Britain had rescued India from centuries of external aggression and internal strife and that, 'for the first time in the history of the Indian population there is to behold the phenomenon of national unity among them, of a sense of national existance'. When the Muslim League was formed in 1906, it was also an all-India party, and it departed from the concept of One India only in the nineteen-forties.

Provincial autonomy owes its origin to Montagu's statement of 20 August 1917 that the policy of the British Government was that of 'the progressive realisation of responsible government in India'.[1] In their report, Montagu and Chelmsford recommended that the earlier steps toward responsible government should be taken in the provinces and complete responsibility should be given as soon as conditions permitted.[2]

Hitherto, there had been no constitutional division of the functions of the central and provincial governments and no trace of the federal idea: the provinces had been the administrative units of the central government. It was the Act of 1919 that created the division into 'central' and 'provincial' subjects. The portfolios in the Executive Council of the provinces were divided into 'transferred' and 'reserved' subjects.[3] The transferred subjects were entrusted to ministers who were elected members of the legislature; the reserved subjects remained in the charge of persons nominated by the Governor.

The Government of India Act of 1935 contemplated a federation of British India and the princely States. It completed the development of provincial autonomy. There were no reserved subjects; the Governor was assisted by a Council of Ministers responsible to the Legislature.

The Cripps Declaration and the proposals of the Cabinet Mission both recognized the right of the provinces to choose independence either singly or in groups, and Attlee's statement of 20 February 1947 also left open the question whether there would be one or several successor states. Under 'Plan Balkan', which Ismay took to London on 2 May 1947, independence

---

[1] Responsible government, of course, meant that the government was responsible to the elected representatives of the people.

[2] *See*, p. 171 (principle 2).

[3] This system was called 'dyarchy'.

would have been granted to provinces or such confederations as the provinces might have been able to form. 'Plan Balkan' was abandoned after Nehru's protest at Simla on 11 May against the balkanisation of India. It was the plan of 3 June 1947 that finally limited the number of possible successor states to only two. However, it left it to the Indians to decide whether they wished power to be transferred to one or two successor authorities (the plan did not mention the word Pakistan anywhere). It was only after the voting, in accordance with the procedure laid down in the plan of 3 June, had gone in favour of dividing the country, that the birth of a country called Pakistan was constitutionally assured. The Indian Independence Act which was passed on 18 July 1947 declared that as from 15 August of that year two independent Dominions 'shall be set up in India to be known respectively as India and Pakistan'. During the parliamentary debates on Attlee's statement and on the Indian Independence Bill, it was claimed that Britain's greatest gift to India had been national unity and it was regretted by all that the country had to be partitioned.

The principle of granting independence to the provinces was not without its own logic. India was a large country and most of the administrative problems were local in dimension. A large amount of discretion, therefore, was permitted to provincial and district authorities in the day-to-day administration, even when power was constitutionally vested solely in the central government. Indeed, there were feelings of nascent nationalism in the provinces born of a common language and other common interests. The Punjabis, the Bengalis, the Hindustanis, the Marathas, the Tamils, the Biharis and the Oriyas all had a sense of provincial identity.

Of the leaders, Jinnah was the most clear-headed and unflappable. India would have become independent even without Gandhi[1], but it is doubtful whether there would have been a Pakistan without Jinnah. It must be added, however, that even Jinnah could not have won Pakistan without the help provided by Congress blunders. Though Hindu nationalists painted him as the destroyer of Indian unity, he had, in fact, worked harder, longer and more realistically for Hindu-Muslim unity than any Congress leader.

Congress had a team of able politicians but, during the crucial years immediately preceding independence, Jinnah carried the burden of steering the Muslim League practically single-handed. He was able to obtain only

---

[1] The commitment of the British Government to a policy of 'progressive realisation of responsible government in India' had been made by the Secretary of State's announcement on 20 August 1917, before Gandhi became a powerful figure in Indian politics.

a 'moth-eaten' Pakistan, but considering the daunting odds he had to overcome, even he was surprised at his own success. While ascending the steps of the Governor-General's Residence at Karachi on 7 August, he said, 'Do you know, I never expected to see Pakistan in my lifetime. We have to be very grateful to God for what we have achieved.'

Gandhi's chief contribution was to hasten the advent of freedom by giving the movement for independence the weight of mass support. The British Government had prided itself on being the champion of India's dumb cultivators. It was the acquiescence of those millions in British rule that Gandhi shook. He also made world opinion more sympathetic to Indian aspirations by giving a non-violent moral colour to his campaign— a Christ opposing the imperial might of Rome as it were.

Jawaharlal Nehru supplemented Gandhi admirably. Gandhi was an Indian to the core, while Nehru, in Gandhi's words, was 'more English than Indian in his thoughts and make-up'. Gandhi moved the masses; Nehru rallied the Westernized intelligentsia. Gandhi mystified the West; Nehru rationalized India's cause in terms which the West could understand. Nehru's *Autobiography,* written in chaste English and first published in 1936, proved to be an effective testament of Indian nationalism in Britain and America. Unfortunately, his emotionalism sometimes led him astray. His love for Kashmir, his ancestral motherland, caused the still-continuing dispute between India and Pakistan, and his love for the fellow Asian giant, China, led to independent India's biggest foreign policy disaster.

Vallabhbhai Patel was over-shadowed by the Gandhi-Nehru alliance. Had he been allowed greater influence, partition might have taken place more tidily. As a realist, he foresaw the need for an orderly transfer of population.[1] At one stage he was also willing to let Kashmir go to Pakistan.[2] In some ways he resembled Tilak, the orthodox Hindu who had co-operated with Jinnah in making the Lucknow Pact.[3]

Among the Muslim leaders, Sir Syed Ahmed Khan, the Aga Khan and Choudhry Rahmat Ali deserve greater recognition for their contribution to the making of Pakistan than has so far been accorded to them. Sir Syed laid the foundation on which all the others built. He is entitled to the same amount of respect as Quaid-i-Azam Mohammad Ali Jinnah.[4] In the middle period, the Aga Khan played the leading role in securing special constitutional rights for the Muslims and in founding and sustaining the

[1] *See,* p. 547.
[2] *See,* p. 607.
[3] *See,* p. 164.
[4] *See,* pp. 76-89.

Muslim League. And the invention of the self-explanatory magic word
Pakistan by Rahmat Ali did more to inspire the masses to demand a
separate Muslim homeland than the stock arguments advanced by many
other politicians.[1]

---

[1] *See*, pp. 325, 350.

EPILOGUE II

'I have always wondered at and admired the astonishing knack of the British people of making their moral standards correspond with their material interests and of seeing virtue in everything that advances their imperial designs.'

Jawaharlal Nehru, *An Autobiography* p. 340.

EPILOGUE II

Every schoolboy knows that the British originally went to India as traders and that their primary purpose was to make money individually as well as for their employer, the East India Company. So what are we to make of the theory of trusteeship which British statesmen and writers have never tired of advancing with the help of the statements made by some of the men who were sent out to rule India before the Rebellion of 1857?

In 1818 Lord Hastings forecast that

> ...a time not very remote will arrive when England will, on sound principles of policy, wish to relinquish the domination which she has gradually and unintentionally assumed over this country [India] and from which she cannot at present recede.

Thomas Munro stated in 1824 that British rule must be maintained till the people of India

> ...shall in some future age have abandoned most of their superstitions and prejudices, and become sufficiently enlightened to frame a regular government for themselves, and to conduct and preserve it. Whenever such a time shall arrive, it will probably be best for both countries that the British control over India should be gradually withdrawn.

Henry Lawrence prophesied in 1844:

> We cannot expect to hold India for ever. Let us so conduct ourselves...as, when the connexion ceases, it may do so not with convulsions but with mutual esteem and affection, and that England may then have in India a noble ally, enlightened and brought into the scale of nations under her guidance and fostering care.

And ten years later Mountstuart Elphinstone wrote in a similar vein:

> The moral is that we must not dream of perpetual possession, but must apply ourselves to bring the natives into a state that will admit of their governing themselves in a manner that may be beneficial to our interests as well as their own, and that of the rest of the world and to take the glory of the achievement and the sense of having done our duty for the chief reward of our exertions.

The Victorians, as we are well aware, were long on offering pious platitudes but short on the practice of taking care of the disadvantaged: God had made some persons rich and the others poor, they argued conveniently, and they mostly left it to God to look after the poor. One only has to read the works of Charles Dickens to realize how men, women and children of the lower classes fared in the Britain of those days. A trustee is expected to endeavour to leave the affairs of the owner in more prosperous state than that in which he found them. But a striking feature of the recent history of India has been that during the Moghul period it was one of the richest countries in the world, but in the immediately-following British period it became one of the poorest. It is not merely a coincidence that the Industrial Revolution in Britain was born in the second part of the eighteenth century at the same time as Clive and his like were transporting their loot from India to England. At least in the economic sphere of their responsibilities, the trustees defaulted miserably.

However, the early administrators do deserve full praise for recognizing that India was too large a country to be ruled for ever from their small island and that it would be to the advantage of both countries if it was administered in such a way that the parting, when it came, left behind friendly ties instead of ill-feeling.

The self-appointed 'trustees' were also extremely unwilling to restore the property to its rightful owners; they let go only when it became impossible for them to hold on any longer.

In 1916, Hindu-Muslim relations were cordial enough for Congress and the Muslim League to agree on the lines of political advance. India had also made a magnificent contribution to the Allied cause in World War I and was in a loyal mood. And in August 1917, Secretary of State Montagu made the declaration that the policy of the British Government was the 'progressive realization of responsible government in India'.

Altogether it was an ideal time, never to recur, for the British Government to make a bold and generous gesture. But the opportunity to encourage Hindu-Muslim co-operation and benefit Indo-British relations for years to come was lost.[1] The Montagu-Chelmsford Report, the precursor to the niggardly Act of 1919, disappointed both Congress and the Muslim League.[2] It belittled the communal harmony displayed in the Lucknow Pact and concluded that the Indians

[1] *See*, pp. 168-71.
[2] *See*, p. 177.

were not yet ready for self-government. The authors of the report also handled the issue of separate electorates in a patently disingenuous manner.[1]

When the time arrived for the periodic examination of the question of further constitutional reforms promised by the Montagu-Chelmsford Report, a commission under Sir John Simon was duly appointed in November 1927, but it took eight long years for the investigation to reach fruition in the form of the Government of India Act of 1935.

The Cripps Declaration of March 1942 seemed at first glance to promise independence to India directly after the war, but in fact the procedure laid down in it could have taken several years to complete. The Declaration said that 'immediately upon the cessation of hostilities' a constituent assembly would be set up to frame a new constitution for India which the British Government would accept. Having regard to the deep differences between the Indian political parties, it could have taken any length of time for a constitution to emerge; indeed the constituent assembly could have broken up without ever reaching any agreement. Endless controversy could also have resulted from the stipulation in the Declaration that the constitution-making body must sign a treaty with His Majesty's Government covering 'all necessary matters arising out of the complete transfer of responsibility from British to India hands; it will make provision...for the protection of racial and religious minorities'.

The Cabinet Mission proposals of 17 May 1946 were too cumbersome to be practicable.[2] Wavell explained, in his broadcast on 17 May 1946, that the proposals of the Cabinet Mission gave the people of India 'the opportunity of complete independence so soon as the constituent assembly has completed its labours'.[3] This meant that independence was conditional on the production of a constitution by Indians on the labyrinthine lines sketched by the Cabinet Mission. The chances of fulfilling this requirement were almost nil.

It was Attlee's statement of 20 February 1947 that for the first time unconditionally promised freedom by a fixed date. Gone suddenly were the long-standing pre-conditions such as a Hindu-Muslim agreement, the framing of a constitution by the Indians themselves and a guarantee of fair treatment of the minorities, and gone also was the argument that the Indian problem was too complicated to be solved in a hurry. It was a case of 'where there's a will there's a way'.

---

[1] *See*, pp. 169-70.
[2] *See*, p. 450.
[3] TOP VII, p. 612.

The Punjab was a shambles, and the two states to whom power was being transferred were born enemies with any number of disputes to inflame them, but characteristically, the British managed to put a good face on the whole affair. Speaking in the House of Commons on 10 July 1947, Attlee refuted a newspaper allegation that the action which the British Government was taking in India was 'abdication' and claimed: 'It is not the abdication, but the fulfilment of the British mission in India.' In the House of Lords Viscount Samuel, on 16 July 1947, said, 'It may be said of the British Raj, as Shakespeare said of the Thane of Cawdor: "Nothing in his life became him like the leaving it".'

But British statesmen had to concede the reality, at the same time, that it was no longer possible to hold on to India even if they wanted to do so. Secretary of State Lord Pethick-Lawrence admitted in the House of Lords (25 February 1947): 'The advice that we have received from responsible authorities in India has been that, taking all the circumstances into account, British rule cannot be maintained upon its existing basis with adequate efficiency after 1948.' And Prime Minister Attlee told the House of Commons (6 March 1947): 'Nationalist feeling runs right through all the Indian classes. That is the reason why you cannot carry on against the will of the Indian people. All our advice has been to the effect that to strengthen the administration would not get over the difficulties.'

That Britain could not control India any longer was the culmination of a long process influenced by world forces, the changing complexion of British governments in England, and the gradual shifting of power in India from British to Indian hands.

Indian nationalism had been influenced by the growth of nationalism in Europe during and after the Napoleonic Era. It had watched with admiration the defeat of the European colossus, Russia, at the hands of the small Asiatic power, Japan, in 1904-5.

World War I had infused new life into the forces of democracy and equality. In England, suffrage was extended in 1918 to all men of 21 and over, and to all women over 30.[1] The authors of the Montagu-Chelmsford Report had observed that it was on the battlefields of France 'and not in Delhi or Whitehall that the ultimate decision of India's future will be taken'. India's first step toward responsible self-government was taken under the Government of India Act of 1919. And the czardom in Russia as well as the Ottoman and the Austrian empires collapsed in the wake of

---

[1] Women were not given exactly the same voting rights as men until 1928.

the war. World War II had an even greater impact on the fortunes of the
subject races of the world.

At the administrative level in India, the subordinate services, civil as
well as military, had always been manned by the natives. British control
had been exercised by a predominantly British Indian Civil Service and by
an even greater predominance of British officers in the Indian army.
During the Second World War British recruitment to the Indian Civil
Service had been stopped, and on the eve of transfer of power its
membership was 510 Indians and 668 British. Of equal significance was
the fact that the number of Indian commissioned officers had risen to more
than 15,000 and, like other westernized Indians, they too desired the
freedom of their country.[1]

Indian political leaders had also been gaining greater control of the
government. At the provincial level, a start was made in 1919, and provincial
autonomy was granted in 1935. At the centre, the installation of the Interim
Government was a momentous step forward. The Viceroy could scarcely
have overruled a joint demand of the Congress and Muslim League members
of his 'Cabinet'. Henceforth, he was able to influence the decisions of the
Executive Council largely because the council was a house divided against
itself—the Congress and the Muslim League members were at loggerheads
with each other over most of the basic issues. As Secretary of State Lord
Pethick-Lawrence said in the House of Lords on 25 February 1947, 'We have
now reached a new stage...when a large share of power and responsibility has
already been transferred to Indian hands.'

What certainly goes to the immense credit of the British Government
is that they were sagacious enough to accept the inevitable with good
grace and did not resort to the use of force to prolong their imperialism,
as France did in Indo-China and Algeria, the Netherlands did in Indonesia
and Belgium did in the Congo. This was handsomely acknowledged by
both Pakistan and India.

At the state dinner in honour of Lord and Lady Mountbatten at Karachi
on 14 August 1947, Quaid-e-Azam Mohammad Ali Jinnah warmly
praised the British Government, whose decision to transfer power to the
two sovereign Dominions 'marked the fulfilment of the great ideal which
was set forth by the formation of the Commonwealth with the avowed
object to make all nations and countries which formed part of the British
Empire self-governing and independent states, free from the dominion of
any other nation'. Jinnah's remark showed that though Pakistanis were

[1] *See*, pp. 394-5 for the British Government's inability to rely any longer on the Indian
armed forces.

angry with Mountbatten personally for his partiality to the Indians, they retained their admiration for the British people and their political system.

In responding to Mountbatten's address to the Constituent Assembly of India on 15 August 1947, Rajendra Prasad, President of the Assembly, similarly acknowledged that, 'while our achievement is in no small measure due to our own sufferings and sacrifices, it is also the result of world forces and events and, last though not least, it is the consummation and fulfilment of the historic tradition and democratic ideals of the British race.'

The plan of 3 June and the Indian Independence Act were skilfully-drafted documents under which Mountbatten was able to transfer power in such way that all the major decisions were formally taken either jointly by the Congress and Muslim League leaders themselves, or by Mountbatten with their agreement.

That Attlee had replaced Churchill as Prime Minister in 1945 greatly facilitated the quick and smooth transfer of power. Attlee and his cabinet colleague Stafford Cripps had long been friendly to the Indian National Congress and its leaders—in his speech on the Government of India Bill on 4 June 1935, Attlee had protested that the bill had been deliberately framed so as to exclude Congress from power[1] —and the Cripps Mission had been sent out to India by the coalition Prime Minister, Churchill, not only to propitiate the USA, but also because the Deputy Prime Minister, Attlee, had been pressing to break the political deadlock in India.[2]

Had Churchill still been Prime Minister, the transfer of power would have been a more complicated, controversial, and prolonged affair, as indicated by his speech in the House of Commons on 6 March 1947 criticising Attlee's statement of 20 February 1947. He affirmed his adherence to the promises contained in the Cripps Declaration of March 1942, but criticised Attlee's policy on the ground that it had departed from the Cripps offer in three respects:

First, they [His Majesty's Government under Attlee] had eliminated the stage of Dominion Status...The second departure...was the total abandonment by his Majesty's Government of all responsibility for carrying out its pledges to minorities and the depressed classes as well as for fulfilling their treatise with the Indian States. All these are to be left to fend for themselves...The third departure was no less grave. The essence of the Cripps Mission Declaration

[1] *See*, p. 300.
[2] *See*, p. 362.

was that there should be agreement between the principal Indian communities...
That, also, has been thrown overboard.

What were the main characteristics of the British raj in India and what did Britain and India receive from each other during their enforced association for about two centuries?

The British rule in India was far from being a brutal military occupation. The British came to India as traders, not as military conquerors. They had no master plan for the conquest of the country but acquired power and territory because to stand still in the free-for-all situation created by the disintegration of the Mughal Empire was to invite self-destruction. In this process they were greatly helped by the Indians, many of whom welcomed them as more benevolent rulers than the native princes. Though they naturally gave priority to their own commercial and trade interests, they were basically a well-meaning and fair-minded people.

During the debates on the Jallianwala massacres, members of the British parliament made some interesting observations with regard to the character of British rule in India. Secretary of State Montagu said the whole question at issue was: 'Are you going to keep your hold upon India by terrorism, racial humiliation and subordination, and frightfulness, or are you going to rest it upon the goodwill, and the growing goodwill, of the people of India?'[1]

The Secretary of State for War, Churchill, stated that:

Governments who have seized upon power by violence and by usurpation have often resorted to terrorism in their desperate efforts to keep what they have stolen, but the august and venerable structure of the British Empire, where lawful authority descends from hand to hand and generation after generation, does not need such aid. Such ideas are absolutely foreign to the British way of doing things...what we want is co-operation and goodwill...[2]

Another member (Bennett) expostulated:

We have been told that India was conquered by the sword and is being held by the sword. That doctrine is absolutely repudiated by every historical authority of any importance. We began as a trading nation. We did not go as a military nation, and we should have accomplished nothing in India but for the co-operation of Indian agents. Why should we flaunt this doctrine of holding by the sword in the face of a people whom we want to make a free people, and whose liberties we are enlarging?[3]

[1,2,3] 8 July 1920.

In the House of Lords, Lord Meston protested that at Jallianwalla

our British traditions of fair dealing and of humanity and justice to a weaker people were broken, and no casuistry can mend them. It is said that by his ruthlessness General Dyer averted a mutiny. The word is clearly a wrong word, because the Indian Army was as staunch as it ever has been. It was upon Indian troops that he relied for punishment; it was through Indian troops that he executed the punishment at Jallianwallah Bagh, and they obeyed their orders unflinchingly.[1]

The Secretary of State for Foreign Affairs, Lord Curzon, agreed with Lord Meston that if they were to endorse the principles on which General Dyer had acted, 'we shall deal a blow at our reputation in India, we shall lower our own standards of justice and humanity, we shall debase the currency of our national honour'.[2]

The humanity of the British people was acknowledged by Indian Nationalists. 'It is true,' wrote Nehru in his *Autobiography* 'that the average Englishman hates brutality, and I cannot conceive English people openly glorifying in and repeating lovingly the word *Brutalitat* (or its English equivalent) as the Nazis do. Even when they indulge in the deed, they are a little ashamed of it'.[3] He said at another page, 'I write this sitting in a British prison...[but] I do not find any anger against England or the English people. I dislike British imperialism and I resent its imposition on India; I dislike the capitalist system; and I dislike exceedingly and resent the way India is exploited by the ruling classes of Britain. But I do not hold England or the English people as a whole responsible for this...They are as much the victims of circumstances as we are.'[4] Subhas Bose thought that Gandhi's doctrine of non-violence in a country like Russia, Germany or Italy 'would have led him to the cross or to the mental hospital'.[5]

The bitterness of political confrontation was often mitigated by the early release of political prisoners for health and family reasons and by the considerate treatment meted out to them while in detention.

How Britain benefited from its possession of India is best described in the words of British statesmen themselves:

[1,2] 20 July 1920.

[3] P. 400.

[4] Pp. 418-19. Some time after independence Nehru called on Churchill at his home. R. A. Butler, arriving just as the visitior was leaving, found Churchill in tears. 'We put that man in gaol for ten years and he bears us no malice. I could not have been so magnanimous'. H. V. Hodson, *The Great Divide*, p. 401.

[5] Subhas C. Bose, *The Indian Struggle*, p. 327.

It is a commonplace, a truism, to say that there is nothing greater in the life of our empire than the story of our rule in India.[1]

The very association with India added to our prestige and our position in the affairs of the world.[2]

The principal advantage that Britain and the Commonwealth derive from control of India is strategic. The greatest asset is India's manpower. The War of 1939-45 could hardly have been won without India's contribution of two million soldiers, which strengthened the British Empire at its weakest point.

India was also, during this period, a very valuable base of war. Her contribution in material was very considerable; and the potentialities will increase as India's industrial capacity expands.

The naval bases in India and Ceylon have enabled the British navy to dominate the whole of the Indian Ocean region, except for a short interlude in the last war; these bases are of importance for the protection of oil supplies from Persia and the Persian Gulf.

India will also be an indispensable link in the Commonwealth air communications both in peace and war.

Before the war some 60,000 British troops were stationed and trained in India and were paid for by the Government of India, which thus made a very substantial financial contribution to British defence. India also formed a valuable training ground for officers and men.

On the economic side there is a very valuable trade connection between India and the UK. In 1944 India was one of the countries with the largest import and export trade with Britain.

By giving up political power in India, Britain will lose a valuable field of employment for the professional classes in the Indian administrative and technical Services. The earnings of British personnel in these Services are estimated at about £ 2,000,000 a year, and civilian pensions paid by India in the UK amount to £ 3,000,000 a year.[3]

In the House of Lords, Lord Linlithgow said on 16 December 1946, 'We must be prepared to lose the service of the one substantial standing army at the disposal of the Commonwealth. We lose, too, the immense

---

[1] The Archbishop of Canterbury in the House of Lords on 20 July 1920, during the debate on 'The Case of General Dyer'.

[2] Clement Davies in the House of Commons on 15 July 1947, during the debate on the third reading of the Indian Independance Bill.

[3] Lord Wavell in a note dated 13 July 1946. TOP VIII, p. 50.

labour resources of the subcontinent, a potent factor in war, and we abandon a great land base peculiarly well placed for the purpose of maintaining peace and security in the East. India under British rule has stood as a steadying factor for two centuries, the one buttress that has defied the storm and helped to hold together the whole fabric of the Orient from the Red Sea to the Yellow River.'

In short it was India's size, manpower, resources, strategic location and glamour that made small-sized Britain the first super-power in modern times.

What India received from Britain was not material but intangible. The British gave India peace; there were no foreign invasions and the British administrators dispensed justice without favouring the rich against the poor or the Brahmins against the *sudras*. In fact, these aspects of British rule are still recalled nostalgically by all who are old enough to remember them. The British also gave India political unity and a feeling of nationalism, in the development of both of which the English language played no small part. English not only inspired ideas of democracy and liberty but also gave the Indian intelligentsia a common language...after independence, Prime Minister Nehru and President Radhakrishnan could communicate with each other only in English.

This period of peace and efficient administration could have been utilized to halt and reverse the process of economic decline resulting from the dissolution of the Mughal Empire and the excessive greed of the servants of the East India Company. But this did not happen because the overriding objective of British rule in India was to enrich Britain, not India.

Viscount Templewood, the former Sir Samuel Hoare who had been Secretary of State for India during the Round Table Conference, refuted the charge that Britain had divided India and claimed that, in fact, Indian unity had been 'the creation of the British raj'[1] and depended upon the existence of British influence in India, and that, 'whether we like it or not, when the British influence is withdrawn that unity will come to an end'.[2]

Templewood's foreboding was partly fulfilled in 1971 when the eastern wing of Pakistan proclaimed itself the independent state of Bangladesh. Pakistan now forms an easily traversable rectangular geographical unit with the river Indus and a single railway system as its main arteries. It is not free from provincial rivalries, but the linguistic and racial barriers are tolerable, and the almost wholly Muslim population has

[1] In the House of Lords on 16 December 1946.
[2] In the House of Lords on 25 February 1946.

the brotherhood of its religion to hold it together. The land is fertile and its inhabitants are intelligent and energetic. With a reasonable amount of wisdom on the part of its leaders and its people, it should not only survive but be able to thrive. Bangladesh's greatest problems are extreme poverty and periodic devastating storms. Its politics are mercurial, but it is linguistically and culturally homogeneous and is not plagued by regional separatism. India has inherited all the ethnic and religious problems of British India and may have to grant full provincial autonomy to diffuse the tensions. The Indian leaders must realise also, that a lasting improvement in Indo-Pakistani relations can be achieved only after a fair solution of the Kashmir problem. This running haemorrhage is not doing their country any good.

Besides the English language, the most important legacies of British rule in the subcontinent are the parliamentary system of government and the British system of justice. The inherent excellence of these items is undoubted, but whether they will thrive in their original form in a soil foreign to them is another matter. Their progress so far has not been healthy.

The English language is rich in works on all conceivable subjects. It is already more commonly used all over the world than any other language and its popularity is on the increase. In the subcontinent, the most substantial books and newspapers are still published in English. India, Pakistan and Bangladesh would do well to face reality and regularize the status of English. The Nehru Report recognized the usefulness of English and stated that though the language of the commonwealth [of India] would be Hindustani, 'the use of the English language shall be permitted,' and in the provinces, though the official language would be the principal language of a province, 'the use of Hindustani and English shall be permitted'. In practical terms, this placed English on the same footing as the native languages.

The parliamentary system of government, so far, has fared better in India than in the other South Asian countries; all the changes of government in India have taken place through the ballot box. But in India as well as in Pakistan and Bangladesh, governments have been unstable and there has been an excessive proliferation of political parties. All three of them might well consider some constitutional reforms to remedy the situation. They could perhaps adopt a fixed term for a government, say four or five years. During this period the Prime Minister should compulsorily resign or be dismissed by the president only if a no confidence motion against the government is passed by the lower house by a majority of at least 51 per cent of the total number of its members. They could also adopt measures which would prevent members of the legislature from being able to change parties at will. And something might be done to reduce the mushrooming of parties, e.g., denying representation in the legislature to a party which in an election wins votes below a prescribed limit. But the acceptance of democracy is too generally and deeply ingrained to admit of any basic departure from it. Even the military rulers of Pakistan and Bangladesh have had to pay lip-service to it to maintain their position.

The legal system inherited from Britain also clearly needs simplification to speed up the disposal of cases and make litigation less expensive for the largely poor population. Pakistan and Bangladesh are likely to adopt the Islamic system of justice.

It is now universally accepted that good government is no substitute for self-government and no empire is morally justifiable. But if India was destined to suffer foreign domination, it was lucky that it was conquered by Britain. S. Satyamurti of Madras, deputy leader of the Congress party in the central legislative assembly and a member of the All-India Congress Committee, aptly summed up the feelings of most Indians:

> I consider, if by some misfortune we are forced to continue under the control of some alien power for some time yet, it is better to be under the rule of Great Britain than Germany, for the English, in spite of certain drawbacks and the many injustices done to us, are the only people who have a regard for principles and regard for honesty left; unlike Hitler who is the professed enemy of all the black races of the world. If Hitler had been here he would have shot Mahatma Gandhi and all of us by this time. The Hitler regime would be a thousand times worse than the British. What we want is *swaraj*, and it is no use leaving the door open to another alien power to overrun the country.[1]

Mrs Margaret Thatcher, the British Prime Minister, during the Commonwealth Conference at Kuala Lumpur in October 1989, had a difference of opinion with some of her Commonwealth colleagues on the question of sanctions against South Africa. In an interview with Sky Television she said with characteristic bluntness, 'Britain is attacked as exploiting the colonies. I sometimes think they were jolly lucky it was us who colonized them and not other people.'[2] Perhaps it was undiplomatic of her to express herself publicly in this vein but what she stated was right.

---

[1] *Madras Mail*, September 25, 1939, quoted by R. Coupland, *Indian Politics (1936-42)*, p. 214.

[2] *The Times*, 25 October, 1989.

BIBLIOGRAPHY

Abdul Latif, Sayyid, *The Pakistan issue; being the correspondence between Sayyid Abdul Latif and M. A. Jinnah, Azad, Nehru, Etc.*, Lahore, 1943.

Afzal, M. Rafique (ed.), *Quaid-e-Azam Muhammad Ali Jinnah: Speeches in the Legislative Assembly of India, 1924-1930*, Lahore, 1967.

Aga Khan, *India in Transition*, London, 1918.

————,*The Memoirs of Agha Khan*, London, 1954.

Alexander, H. G., *India since Cripps*, London, 1944.

Ali, Chaudhri Muhammad, *The Emergence of Pakistan*, New York, 1967.

All-India Muslim League, *Report of the Inquiry Committee appointed by the Working Committee of the Bihar Provincial Muslim League to inquire into some grievances of Muslims in Bihar*, Patna, 1939.

All India Muslim League, *Report of the Inquiry Committee appointed by the Council of the All India Muslim League to inquire into Muslim grievances in Congress Provinces*, Delhi, 1938.

Allana, G., *Pakistan Movement; Historic Documents*, Lahore, 1977.

Ambedkar, B. R., *Pakistan or the partition of India*, Bombay, 1946.

————*What Congress had done to the Untouchables*, Bombay, 1945.

Ameer Ali, Syed, *Education in India*, London, 1902.

Amery, L. S., *India and Freedom*, London, 1942.

Andrews, C. F., *India and the Simon Report*, London, 1930.

————,*Mahatma Gandhi's Ideas*, London, 1920.

————,and Mookerjee, Girija, *The Rise and Growth of Congress in India*, London, 1938.

Ashraf, Mujeeb, *Muslim Attitude Towards British Rule and Western Culture in India*, Delhi, 1982.

Attlee, Clement R., *Empire into Commonwealth*, London, 1961.

————,and Willams, Francis, *Twilight of Empire: Memoirs of Prime Minister Clement Attlee*, New York, 1962.

Azad, Abul Kalam, *India Wins Freedom*, Madras, 1988.

Azim Husain, *Fazl-i Husain*, Lahore, 1946

Aziz Ahmad and von Grunebaum, G. E., *Muslim Self Statement in India and Pakistan*, Wiesbaden, 1970.

Aziz, K. K, *All-India Muslim Conference: 1928-1933*. Karachi, 1972.

————,*The British in India*, Islamabad, 1976.

————,*The Making of Pakistan*, Lahore, 1976.

————,*Muslims under Congress Rule*, 2 Vols., Islamabad, 1977-1979.

————,*Rahmat Ali: a Biography*, Lahore, 1987.

Bahadur, Lal, *Muslim League, its History, Activities, Achievements*, Lahore, 1979.

Baird, J. G. A., *Private letters of the Marquess of Dalhousie*, London, 1910.

Balabushevich, V. V., and Dyakov, A. M. (ed.), *A Contemporary History of India*, New Delhi, 1964.

Bamford, P. C. *Histories of the Non-co-operation and Khilafat Movements*, Delhi, 1925.

Banerjee, R .C., *Indian Constitutional Documents, 1757-1945*, 2 Vols., Calcutta, 1945.

Banerji, Surendranath, *The Making of Modern India*, London, 1925.

Basham, A. L. (ed.), *A Cultural History of India*, Oxford, 1975.

————,*The Wonder that was India*, London, 1979.

Bazaz, Prem Nath, *The History of Struggle for Freedom in Kashmir*, New Delhi, 1954.

Besant, A., *Annie Besant: An Autobiography*, Adyar, 1939.

————,*How India Wrought for Freedom*, Madras, 1915.

Beveridge, H., *A Complete History of India*, 3 Vols., London, 1862.

Bolitho, Hector, *Jinnah, Creator of Pakistan*, London, 1954.

Bose, S. C.,*The Indian Struggle*, London, 1954.

Brecher, Michael, *Nehru: a Political Biography*, London, 1959.

Brown, J. M., *Gandhi: Prisoner of Hope*, London, 1989.

————,*Gandhi's Rise to Power*, London, 1972.

Bruce, John, *Annals of the East India Company*, 3 Vols., London, 1810.

Buchan, John, *Life of Lord Minto*, London, 1925.

Burke, S. M., *Akbar, the Greatest Mughal*, New Delhi, 1989.

————,*Mainsprings of Indian and Pakistan Foreign Policies*, Minneapolis, 1974

————,and Ziring, Lawrence, *Pakistan's Foreign Policy: an Historical Analysis*, 2nd ed., Karachi, 1990.

Cambridge History of British Foreign Policy, edited by Ward and Gooch. 3 Vols., Cambridge, 1922-3.

Campbell-Johnson, Alan, *Mission with Mountbatten*, London, 1972.

Chelmsford, Sir William, *Allan Octavian Hume*, London, 1913.

Chopra, P. N., *India's Struggle for Freedom: Role of Associated Movements*, New Delhi, 1985.

————,*The Quit India Movement*, New Delhi, 1986.

————,*Towards Freedom, 1937-1947*, New Delhi, 1985.

Churchill, Winston, *The Second World War*, New York, 1962.

Collins, Larry and Lapierre, Dominique, *Freedom at Midnight*, New York, 1975.

————,*Mountbatten and the Partition of India*, New York, 1979.

Connell, John, *Auchinleck*, London, 1959.

Corfield, Conrad, *The Princely India I Knew*, Madras, 1975.

Coupland, R., *The Cripps Mission*, London, 1942.

————,*The Indian Problem, 1933-1935*, (3 parts), London, 1942-3.

Crocker, Walther, *Nehru: a Contemporary's Estimate*, London, 1966.

Curzon, Lord, *Curzon in India, being a selection from his speeches*, edited by R. Raleigh, London, 1906.

————,*The British Government in India*, 2 Vols., London, 1925.

Dalal, M. N., *Whither Minorities*, Bombay, 1940.

Dani, Ahmad Hasan, *World Scholars on Quaid-e Azam Muhammad Ali Jinnah*, Islamabad, 1979.

Das, Manmath Nath, *The End of the British Empire: Select Documents, March-August 1947*, Cuttock, 1983.

de Bary, Wm., Theodore (ed.), *Sources of Indian Tradition*, New York, 1960.

Desai, Bhula Bhai, *The INA Defence*, Delhi, 1945.

Dodwell, H. H., *India*, 2 Vols., London, 1938.

Duff, J. Grant, *History of Maharattas*, 2 Vols., London, 1913.

Durand, Sir M., *Life of Sir Alfred Lyall*, London, 1913.

Elliot, E. H., and Dowson, John, (ed.), *The History of India as told by its own Historians*, 6 Vols., London, 1875.

Elphinstone, M., *The History of India*, 2 Vols., London, 1891.

Embree, A., (ed.), *India in 1857*, Delhi, 1857.

Estorick, Eric, *Stafford Cripps*, Kingswood, 1949.

Farquhar, I. H., *Modern Religious Movements*, London, 1918.

Fazl-e-Hussain, *Letters of Mian Fazl-e Hussain*, Waheed Ahmad (ed.), Lahore, 1976.

Fischer, Louis, *Mahatma Gandhi*, New York, 1954.

Foster, W., (ed.), *Early travels in India*, London, 1878.

Fraser, Lovat, *India Under Curzon and After*, London, 1911.

Gandhi, M. D., *Mahatma Gandhi: His Own Story*: C. F. Andrews (ed.), London, 1930.

————,*Quit India*: R. K. Prabhu and U. R. Rao (ed.) Bombay, 1942.

————,*The Story of my Experiments with Truth*, 2 Vols., Delhi, 1927-9.

————,*Collected Works of M. D. Gandhi*, 85 Vols., New Delhi, 1958.

————,*Jinnah-Gandhi Talks, September 1941*, Delhi, 1944.

Garrett, G. T. (ed.), *The Legacy of India*, Oxford, 1951.

Gilmartin, David, *Empire and Islam: Punjab and the Making of Pakistan*, London, 1988.

Gokhale, G. K., *The Making of the Indian Nation*, Bombay, 1958.

————,*Speeches*, Madras, 1909.

Gordon Walker, Patrick, *The Commonwealth*, London, 1962.

Graham, G. F. I., *The Life and Works of Sir Syed Ahmed Khan*, London, 1909.

Gwyer, Sir Maurice and Appadorai, A., *Speeches and Documents on the Indian Constitution*, 1921-1947, 2 Vols., London, 1957.

Haq, A. K. Fazlul, *Muslim Suffering under Congress*, Calcutta, 1939.

Hardinge, G., Ist Baron Penhurst, *My Indian Years*, London, 1948.

Hasan, K., Sarwar (ed.), *Documents on the Foreign Relations of Pakistan, The Kashmir Question*, Karachi, 1966.

G. R. Markham (ed.), *The Hawkins Voyages*. London. 1878.

————,*History of the Freedom Movement*, A, 4 Vols, Karachi, Pakistan Historical Society, 1957 - 62.

Hoare, Sir Samuel John Gurney, *Speeches, 1933-1935*, London, 1935.

Hodson, H. V., *The Great Divide*, London, 1969.

Hunter, Sir William, *A History of British India*, 2 Vols., London, 1899-1901.

————,*The Indian Mussalmans*, Delhi, 1969.

Ikram, S. M., *Modern Muslim India and the Birth of Pakistan*, London, 1970.

————,*Muslim Rule in India and Pakistan*, Lahore, 1966.

Indian National Congress, *Report of the Commissioners Appointed by the Punjab Sub-Committee of the Indian National Congress* [*President: Motilal Nehru*], 2 Vols., Bombay, 1920.

Iqbal, Sir Muhammad, *Letters of Iqbal to Jinnah*, Lahore, n.d.

————,*The Reconstruction of Religious Thought in Islam*, London, 1960.

Ismay, Lord, *The Memoirs of General the Lord Ismay*, London, 1960.

Jalal, Ayesha, *The Sole Spokesman: Jinnah, The Muslim League and the Demand for Pakistan*, Cambridge, 1985.

Jinnah, M. A., *The Collected Works of Quaid-e-Azam Muhammad Ali Jinnah*, Syed Sharifuddin Pirzada (ed.), 4 Vols., Karachi, 1984.

————,*Jinnah-Irwin Correspondence, 1927-1930*, Waheed Ahmad (ed.), Lahore. 1969.

————,*Quaid-e-Azam Jinnah's Correspondence*, Syed Sharifuddin Pirzada (ed.), Karachi, 1977.

————,*Speeches and Writings of Mr Jinnah,* Jamil-ud-Din Ahmed (ed.), 2 Vols., Lahore, 1968-76.

————,*Speeches as Governor General of Pakistan, 1947-1948*, Karachi, n.d.

Jones, G. E., *Tumult in India*, New York, 1948.

Kanji, Dwarkadas, *India's Fight for Freedom*, Bombay, 1966.

Kaye, Sir John, *The Administration of the East India Company*, London, 1853.

————,and Malleson, G. B., *History of the Sepoy War in India*, 6 Vols., London, 1864-80.

Kaye, Nicholas, *Time Only to Look Forward, Speeches of Rear-Admiral the Earl Mountbatten of Burma*, London, 1949.

Kerr, James Campbell, *Political Trouble in India, 1907-1917*, Calcutta, 1917.

Khaliquzzaman, C., *Pathway to Pakistan*, Lahore, 1961.

Khan, Muhammad Ayub, *Friends Not Masters*, London, 1967.

Khan, Muhammad Zafrullah, *Pakistan's Foreign Relations*, Karachi, 1951.

————,*Servant of God*, London, 1983.

Korbel, Josef, *Danger in Kashmir*, Princeton, 1966.

Lajpat Rai, *Autobiographical Writings*, V. C. Joshi (ed.), Delhi, 1965.

————,*The Political Future of India*, New York, 1919.

Lamb, Alastair, *Kashmir, 1846-1990*, London, 1991.

Lawrence, Sir W. R., *The India We Served*, London, 1928.

Lovett, Sir Verney, *A History of Indian Nationalist Movement*, London, 1920.

Low, Donald Anthony, *Congress and the Raj*, London, 1971.

Lumby, E. W. R., *The Transfer of Power in India*, London, 1954.

Lyall, Sir Alfred, *The Rise and Expansion of British Domination in India*, London, 1905.

MacDonald, J. Ramsay, *The Government of India*, London, 1920.

MacDonell, A. A., *India's Past*, Oxford, 1927.

MacMillan, Margaret, *Women of the Raj*, London, 1988.

Mahajan, Mehr Chand, *Looking Back*, London, 1963.

Majendie, V. D., *Up Among the Pandies*, London, 1859.

Majumdar, R. C., (ed.), *The History and Culture of the Indian People*, 11 Vols., Bombay, 1951-1977.

————,*History of the Freedom Movement in India*, 4 Vols., Calcutta, 1969.

————,(ed.), *Readings in Political History of India*, 1976.

————,*The Sepoy Mutiny and the Revolt of 1857*, Calcutta, 1957.

Malleson, G. B., *The Indian Mutiny of 1857*, London, 1891.

Mansergh, Nicholas (ed.), *The Transfer of Power: Constitutional Relations between Britain and India*, 12 Vols., London, HMSO, 1970-83.

Marx, Karl and Engels, F., *The First Indian War of Independence*, 1857-1959, Moscow, n.d.

————,*Letters on India*, P. L. and Freda Bedi (eds.), Lahore, 1936.

————,*Notes on Indian History*, 1664-1858 Moscow, 1960.

Mason, Philip, *A Matter of Honour: an Account of the Indian Army, its Officers and Men*, London, 1974.

McCrindle, P. W., *Ancient India as Described In Classical Literature,* Westminister, 1901.

McLane, J. R.(ed.), *The Political Awakening in India,* Englewood Cliff, Prentice-Hall, 1970.

Menon, V. P., *The Story of the Integration of the Indian States,* New Delhi, 1985.

————,*The Transfer of Power in India,* Princeton, 1957.

Metcalf, Barbara Daly, *Islamic Revival in British India, Deoband 1860-1900*, Guildford, 1982.

Mill, James, *History of British India,* H. H. Wilson (ed.), 10 Vols., London. 1840-6

Minto, Mary, Countess of India, *Minto and Morley, 1905-1910*, London, 1934.

Muhammad Ali, *My Life*, Afzal Iqbal (ed.), Lahore, 1942.

————,*Select Writings and Speeches of Maulana Muhammad Ali*, Afzal Iqbal (ed.), Lahore, 1963.

Moon. E. P., *The British Conquest and Dominion of India*, London, 1989.

————,*Divide and Quit*, London, 1961.

————,*Strangers in India*, London, 1944.

Moore, R. J., *Churchill, Cripps and India, 1939-1945*, Oxford, 1979.

————,*The Crisis of Indian Unity 1917-1940*, Oxford, 1974.

————,*Escape from Empire*, Oxford, 1983.

Moraes, Frank, *Jawaharlal Nehru*, Bombay, 1962.

Moreland, W. H., *From Akbar to Aurangzeb*, London, 1923.

————,*India at the death of Akbar*, London, 1924.

Morley, J., *Speeches on Indian Affairs*, London, 1909.

Mosley, Henry, *The Last Days of the British Raj*, London, 1961.

Mountbatten, Louis, Rear-Adml. the Earl Mountbatten of Burma, *Reflections on the Transfer of Power and Jawaharlal Nehru*, London, 1968.

————,*Report on the Last Viceroyalty*, 22 March-15 August 1947, London, 1948.

Muhammad, Shan, *Sir Syed Ahmed Khan*, Meerut, 1969.

Mujeeb, M., *The Indian Muslims*, London, 1967.

Nadvi, R.A., (ed.), *Selections from Muhammad Ali's 'Comrade'*, Lahore, 1965.

Natwar Singh, K., (ed.), *The Legacy of Nehru*, New York, 1965.

Nehru, Jawaharlal, *India's Freedom*, London, 1962.

————,*All-India Congress Committee Report. Haripura, February 1938*, Allahbad, 1938.

————,*An Autobiography*, Delhi, 1958.

————,*Discovery of India*, London, 1960.

————,*Eighteen Months in India*, Allahabad, 1938.

————,*Unity of India*, New York, 1942.

Nur Ahmad, Sayyid, *Mian Fazl-e Husain*, Lahore, 1935.

O'Dwyer, Michael, *India As I Knew It*, London, 1925.

Page, David, *Prelude to Partition*, Delhi, 1982.

Pandey, B. N., (ed.), *The Indian Nationalist Movement, 1885-1947: Select Documents*, London, 1979.

Panikkar, K.M., *A Survey of Indian History*, London, 1947.

Panjabi, K. L., *The Indomitable Sardar*, Bombay, 1964.

Philips, C. H., *The Evolution of India and Pakistan*, London, 1962.

————,*Historians of India, Pakistan and Ceylon*, London, 1961.

————,and Wainwright, M. D., *The Partition of India*, London, 1970.

Piggott, S., *Prehistoric India*, London, 1962.

Pirzada, Syed Sharifuddin, *The Foundations of Pakistan. All-India Muslim League Documents, 1906-1947*, 2 Vols., Karachi, 1981-2.

————,*Quaid-e Azam and the Pakistan Resolution*, Islamabad, 1982.

————,*Quaid-e Azam Muhammad Ali Jinnah and Pakistan*, Karachi, 1989.

————,*The Radcliffe Award*, Islamabad, n.d.

Polak, H. S., Brailsford, L.H.N., and Pethick-Lawrence, Lord, *Mahatma Gandhi*, London, 1949.

Pyarelal, *Mahatma Gandhi*, 2 Vols., Ahmedabad, 1956-8.

Quraishi, S. *Quaid-i-Azam Muhammad Ali Jinnah: a bibliography of reviews, news reports,* _editorials etc._ Lahore, 1993.

Qureshi. I. H., _The Administration of the Mughal Empire_, Karachi, 1974.

_____,_The Muslim Community of the Indo-Pakistan Subcontinent_, Karachi, 1977.

_____,_The Struggle for Pakistan_, Karachi, 1965.

_____,_Ulema in Politics_, Karachi, 1974.

Radhakrishna, S., _Eastern Religions and Western Thought_, New York, 1959.

Rahmat Ali, Chaudhri, _Complete Works of Rahmat Ali_, K. K. Aziz (ed.), Vol. 1, Islamabad, 1978.

_____,_The Millat of Islam and the Menance of Indianism_, Cambridge, 1941.

_____,_The Muslim Minority in India and the Sacred Duty of the UNO_, Cambridge, 1948.

_____,_Now or Never_, Cambridge, 1931.

_____,_Pakistan, the Fatherland of Pak Nation_, Cambridge, 1947.

Ratcliffe, S. K., _What the Simon Report Means_, London, 1930.

Rawlinson, H. G., _British Beginnings in Western India_, Oxford, 1920.

Rees, Major-General T. W., _Report of Punjab Boundary Force, 1 August-Midnight 1-2 September 1947_, submitted on 15 November 1947 to the Supreme Commander in Delhi.

Rizvi, Saiyid Ather Abbas, _Religious and Intellectual History of the Muslims in Akbar's Reign_, New Delhi, 1975.

Roe, Sir Thomas, _The Embassy of Sir Thomas Roe to India_, London, 1926.

Russell, Wilfred, _Indian Summer_, Bombay, 1951.

Sadullah, Mian Muhammad, _The Partition of the Punjab, 1947: A Compilation of Official Documents_, 4 Vols., Lahore, 1983.

Sain, Kanwar, _Reminiscences of an Engineer_, New Delhi, 1978.

Saiyid, Matlubul Hasan, _Mohammed Ali Jinnah: a Political Study_, Lahore, 1945.

Savarkar, V. D., _The Indian War of Independence, (The National Rising of 1857)_, Bombay, 1946.

Seal, Anil, _The Emergence of Indian Nationalism_, London, 1968.

Sen, S. P., _Sources for the Study of India_, Calcutta, 1978.

Shafaat Ahmad Khan, _The East India Trade in the Seventeenth Century_, London, 1923.

Shamloo, (Latif Ahmed Sherwani) (ed.), _Speeches and Statements of Iqbal_, Lahore,1948.

Sharif-ul-Mujahid (ed.), _Quaid-e-Azam Jinnah_, Karachi, 1981.

Sheean, Vincent, _Nehru: The Years of Power_, London, 1960.

Sherwani, L. A., _The Partition of India and Mountbatten_, Karachi, 1985.

Singh, Anita Inder, _The Origins of the Partition of India_, Delhi, 1987.

Sitaramayya, P., _History of the Indian National Congress_, 2 Vols., Madras, 1947.

Spate, O. H. E., _The Partition of India and the Prospects of Pakistan_, New York, 1948.

Spear, Percival, _India: a Modern History_, Ann Arbor, 1972.

_____,_The Nabobs_, London, 1980.

_____,_Twilight of the Mughals_, Cambridge, 1951.

Strachey, Sir John, _India, Its Administration_, London, 1909.

Sutherland, John, _Sketches of the Relations Subsisting between the British Government in India and Different Native States_, London, 1837.

Syed Ahmed Khan, Sir, _The Causes of the Indian Revolt_, Benares, 1873.

_____,_Maqalat-i Sir Sayyid_, Muhammad Ismail (ed.), 14 Vols., Lahore, 1963.

_____,_Review on Dr Hunter's Indian Mussalmans_, Lahore, n.d.

Symonds, Richard, _The Making of Pakistan_, London, 1950.

Tavernier, J. B., _Travels in India_, translated and edited by V. Ball, 2 Vols., London, 1925.

Templewood, Viscount, *Nine Troubled Years,* London, 1954.

Tendulkar, D. G., *Mahatma,* 8 Vols., Delhi, 1960-3.

Thapar, Romila, *A History of India,* Vol. 1, London, 1987.

Thompson, E. J. and Garret, G. T., *The Rise and Fulfilment of British Rule in India,* London, 1934.

Tilak, B. G., *Writings and Speeches,* Madras, 1922.

Tinker, H., *Experiment with Freedom,* London, 1967.

Tuker, Sir Francis, *While Memory Serves,* London, 1950.

Twelve Months of War in Kashmir, Washington, Government of India Information Services, 1949.

Wasti, Syed Razi, *Lord Minto and the Indian Nationalist Movement,* London, 1964.

Wavell, Archibald, *The Viceroy's Journal,* P. Moon (ed.), London, 1973.

Wedderburn, Sir William, *Allan Octavian Hume,* London, 1913.

Wheeler, A., *Early Records of British India,* Calcutta, 1878.

Wheeler-Bennett, John W., *King George VI,* New York, 1958.

Williams, L. F. Rushbrook, *The State of Pakistan,* London, 1966.

Wilson, C. H., *Early Annals of the English in Bengal,* 3 Vols., Calcutta, 1895-1917.

Wolf, F., *Life of Lord Rippon,* 2 Vols., London, 1921.

Wolpert, Stanley, *Jinnah of Pakistan,* Oxford, 1984.

_____,*Morley and India,* Berkeley, 1967.

_____,*Tilak and Gokhale,* California, 1962.

Wood, E. F. L., 1st Earl of Halifax, *The Indian Problem,* New York, 1942.

Woodruff, Philip, *The Men who Ruled India.* Vol. 1: *The Founders,* Vol. 2: *The Guardians,* London, 1953-4.

Zaidi, Moin and Zaidi, Shaheda, *The Encyclopaedia of the Indian National Congress,* 26 Vols., Delhi, 1976.

Zakaria, Rafiq, *The Rise of Muslims in Indian Politics,* Bombay, 1970.

Ziegler, Philip, *Mountbatten,* London, 1985.

Zetland, The Marquis, *Steps Towards Indian Home Rule,* London, 1909.

ARTICLES

Abdullah, Sheikh Muhammad, 'Kashmir, India and Pakistan', *Foreign Affairs,* April 1965.

Campbell-Johnson, Alan, 'Reflections on the Transfer of Power', *Asiatic Review,* July 1952.

Jinnah, M. A., 'Two Nations in India', *Time and Tide,* 9 March, 1940.

'The Partition of India' *Indo-British Review,* Special Issue on the Partition of India. Vol. XIV, No. 2, 1988.

Sheean, Vincent, 'The Case for India' *Foreign Affairs,* October 1951.

Spear, P., 'Nehru', *Modern Asian Studies,* January 1967.

Templewood, Viscount, 'Some Reflections on Recent Indian Constitutional History', *Asiatic Review,* October 1952.

Tinker, Hugh, 'Pressure, Persuasion, Decision; Factors in the Partition of the Punjab', *Journal of Asian Studies,* Vol. XXXVI, No. 4, August 1977.

NEWSPAPERS AND PERIODICALS

Aligarh Institute Gazette, Aligarh.

Amrita Bazar Patrika, Calcutta.
Annual Register, London.
Asiatic Review, London.
Comrade, Calcutta.
The Dawn, Delhi/Karachi.
Hamdard, Delhi.
Harijan, Ahmedabad.
The Hindu, Madras.
The Hindustan Times, Delhi.
Indian Annual Register, Calcatta.
The Pakistan Times, Lahore.
The Times, London.
Young India, Ahmedabad.
Also newspaper cutings from major Indian and British newspapers, 1921-46. BL: OIOC
    L/1/2, 148 Vols.

PRIVATE PAPERS

Birkenhead Collection. Papers of the 1st Earl of Birkenhead as Secretary of State for India,
    1924-8.
    MSS Eur D 703
Chelmsford Collection. Papers of the 1st Viscount Chelmsford as Viceroy, 1915-21.
    MSS Eur E 264
Christie Collection. Papers and Diaries of Walter Henry John Christie, ICS, 1928-47.
    MSS Eur D 718
Cunningham Collection. Papers of Sir George Cunningham, Indian Civil Service 1911-
    1946, Governor of the NWFP 1937-46, 1947-8.
    MSS Eur D 670
Curzon Collection. Papers of the Marquess Curzon of Kedleston, Viceroy 1899-1905, Lord
    Privy Seal 1915-9, Foreign Secretary 1919-24.
    MSS Eur F 111
Durand Collection. Papers of Sir Henry Mortimer Durand, Foreign Secretary to the
    Government of India, 1885-94.
    MSS Eur D 727
Hailey Collection. Papers of Sir Malcolm Hailey, 1st Baron Hailey, Governor of the Punjab
    1924-8, Governor of the UP 1928-30.
    MSS Eur E 220
Halifax Collection. Papers of the 1st Baron Irwin (later Ist Earl of Halifax) as Viceroy 1926-
    31.
    MSS Eur C 152
Laithwaite Collection. Papers of Sir Gilbert Laithwaite, Private Secretary to the Viceroy
    1936-43, Permanent Secretary at the Commonwealth Relations Office 1955-9.
    MSS Eur F 138
Lansdowne Collection. Papers of the 5th Marquess of Lansdowne as Viceroy, 1888-94.
    MSS Eur D 558
Morley Collection. Papers of Viscount Morley as Secretary of State for India 1905-10 and
    1911.
    MSS Eur D 573

Mountbatten Collection. Papers of Earl Mountbatten of Burma as Viceroy and Governor General of India 1947-8.
    MSS Eur 10R Neg 15538-15567.
Mudie Collection. Papers of Sir Francis Mudie, Governor of Sindh 1946-7, Governor of West Punjab 1947-9.
    MSS Eur F 164
Reading Collection. Papers of Ist Marques of Reading, Viceroy 1821-60.
    MSS Eur E 238
Zetland Collection. Papers of the 2nd Marquess of Zetland, Governor of Bengal 1917-22, Secretary of State for India 1935-40.
    MSS Eur D 609

PARLIAMENTARY PAPERS

India and the War: communique issued by the Governor-General and resolutions by the Indian National Congress, the All-India Muslim League, and Chambers of Princes.
    Cmd 6196 X 35
Statement published by the Government of India on the Congress Party's responsibility for the disturbances in India, 1942-3.
    Cmd 6430 IX 827
Statement of the finding of H. M. Government made by the Secretary of State for India on 14 June 1945. London, 1945.
    Cmd 6652
India Independence. A Bill to make provision for the setting up in India of two independent Dominions. Government of India Act 1935.
    (Bill 92) II 827
India (Cabinet Mission). Correspondence and documents connected with the conference between the Cabinet Mission and the Viceroy and the representatives of the Congress and the Muslim League. London May 1947.
    Cmd 829 XIX 145
India (Cabinet Mission). Statement by the Mission dated 25 May and memorandum by the Mission on States' treaties and paramountcy.
    Cmd 6835 XIX 165
India (Cabinet Mission). Correspondence with the Congress Party and the Muslim League 20 May-29 June 1946.
    Cmd 6861 XIX 172
East India (Punjab disturbances). Report on the Punjab disturbances April 1919.
    Cmd 534 XIV 931
East India (disturbances in the Punjab, etc.) Report of the Committee appointed by the Government of India to investigate the disturbances in the Punjab. (President Lord Hunter). 7 Vols. (The last two volumes were confidential and not published) 1942-3.
    Cmd 6430 IX 827
Parliamentary debates and Questions (House of Commons and House of Lords) relating to India and Burma, Sessions 1945-6 and 1946-7.
    BL: OIOC V/3/1661
India Round Table Conference, Ist Session, 12 November 1930-19 January 1931. Proceedings of the Sub-committees. Reports, Conference resolutions and Prime Minister's

statement. 2 parts. London, 1931.
Cmd 3772XII 605
_____,Proceedings of the Federal Structure and Minorities Committee, London, 1931-2.
Cmd 3778 XII 91
_____,2nd Session 7 September-1 December 1931. Statement made by the Prime Minister
Cmd 3972 XVIII 957
_____,Proceedings.
Cmd 3997 VIII 1
_____,3rd Session. 17 November-24 December 1932. Reports, Proceedings and Memoranda.
Cmd 4238 XI 169
_____,Proposals for Indian constitutional reforms.
Cmd 4268 XX 997
Jammu and Kashmir Grievances and Complaints (Glancy) Commission, 1931-1932. Jammu, 1932.
BL: O10C V/26/272/8
Punjab Boundary (Radcliffe) Commission 1947.
Bl: OIOC V/26/261/60
Bengal Boundry (Radcliffe) Commission 1947. Report 1947.
BL: OIOC V/26/261/60
India (Cabinet Mission) Correspondence and documents connected with the conference between the Cabinet Mission and HE The Viceroy and representatives of Congress and the Muslim League. May 1946.
Cmd 6829 XIX 145
_____,Correspondence with Congress and the Muslim League 20 May-29 June 1946.
Cmd 686 IXIX 1172
_____,Papers relating to (a) Sikhs: (b) the Indian States; (c) the European community. May-June 1948.
Cmd 6862XIX 137
Indian States (Butler) Committee 1928-9 Report, replies and questionnaire and evidence.
BL: OIOC V/26/272
Report of the India Statutory (Simon) Commission. Vol. 1: Survey London. 1930.
Cmd 3568
_____,Vol. 2: Report and Recommendations.
Cmd 3569 XI
Report on Indian Constitutional Reforms (Montagu-Chelmsford) London, 1918.
Cmd 9109
Sedition Committee Report (Rowlatt), 1918.
White Paper on Jammu and Kashmir. New Delhi, Government of India, 1948.
Constituent Assembly of India Debates.
Constituent Assembly of Pakistan Debates.

OFFICIAL RECORDS

Political and Secret Department Records

Political and Secret Subject Files, 1902-1931   L/P&S/10.
Political and Secret Annual Files, 1912-1930   L/P&S/ 11.

Political Internal/ Indian states files and Collections, 1931-1950. L/P&S/13.
Correspondence with Indian rulers, including Indian Princes, 1796-1920. L/P&S/14
Parliamentary Questions, 1881-1911. L/P&S/17
Political and Secret Memoranda, 1840-1947 L/P&S/18
Political and Secret Miscellaneous Records, 1750-1947 L/P&S/19

Record Department Papers, 1859-1950

Correspondence with India. L/R/3

Public and Judicial Department Records

Correspondence with India, 1795-1950 L/P&J/3
Compilations and Miscellaneous records 1860-1948 L/P&J/5
Departmental Papers: Annual Files. 1880-1939. L/P&J 6-7

Departmental Papers: Collections 1930-1950. L/P&J/8.
Political Constitutional (Transfer of Power) Papers, 1942-1947. L/P&J10.
Public and Judicial Separate Files, including fortnightly reports of the Governors, 1929-1934. L/P&J/12.

Central Government Records

Viceroy's Private Office, 1899-1948. R/3/1

Provincial Government Records, 1932-1947. R/3/2
Private Office papers, (including Constitutional Reforms, Indian Round Table Conference and Transfer of Power Files), 1856-1948.

UNITED NATIONS DOCUMENTS

General Assembly Official Records
Security Council Official Records
Security Council Official Records, Fourth Year, Special Supplement, No 7, UNCIP, Third Report, S/ 1430, 9 December 1949.
Report of the Secretary-General to the Security Council on the situation in Kashmir, S/6651, 3 September 1965.
Introduction to the Report of the Secretary-General on the work of the organisation. New York, 1965.
Report submitted by the United Nations Representative for India and Pakistan, Sir Owen Dixon, to the Security Council, S/ 1791, 15 September 1950.
Reports Submitted by the United Nations Representative for India and Pakistan, Mr F. P. Graham, to the Security Council, S/2375, S/2448, S/2611.S/2783,S/2967,S/3948, dated 15 October 1951, 19 December 1951, 22 April 1952, 19 September 1952, 27 March 1953 and 31 March 1958.
Report submitted by the President of the Security Council for the month of February 1957, Mr Gunnar Jarring, to the Security Council, S/3821, 29 April 1957.

INDEX

Abbott, S.B., 542, 560, 617

Abdul Aziz, Shah, 71, 72

Abdul Ghaffar Khan, Khan (1890-1988), also known as Frontier Gandhi and Bacha Khan, Founder of Khudai Khidmatgar 1930; Member Congress Working Committee 1934; Congress delegate to Simla Conference 1946; Founder of National Awami Party 1957, 277, 281, 292, 302, 352, 432, 465, 466, 493, 514, 515

Abdul Latif, Nawab, 87

Abdul Mejid, 238

Abdul Waheed, 319

Abdul Wahhab, Shaikh Muhammad, 73

Abdullah, Sheikh Muhammad, Founder and President Kashmir Muslim Conference 1932; President, All-India States People's Conference; Prime Minister of Kashmir, 1948-9, 92, 585, 587, 589, 590, 591, 595, 596, 598, 599, 600, 602

Abdur Rahim, Sir Justice, Member, Bengal Legislative Council 1926-30; Indian Legislative Assembly 1930; President, Indian Legislative Assembly 1935-45, 240

Abdur Rashid, 248

Abell, Sir George Edmond Brackenbury, 108, Private Secretary to the Viceroy 1946, 462, 467, 500, 542, 555, 556, 557, 560, 561, 590

Abu Saleh Mohammad Akram, Judge of Calcutta High Court 1940; Member of the Bengali Boundary Commission, 537

Abul Fazl, 77

Abyssinia, 335, 358; Italian attack on, 334

Act of 1773, 13, 44

Act of 1784, 14

Act of 1813, 22

Act of 1833, 22, 44, 56, 58, 59

Act of 1858, 44

Act of 1919, 251, 252, 641, 648, 650

Act of 1935, 252, 299, 300, 306, 328, 344, 345, 346, 413, 499, 500, 504, 517, 526, 532, 567, 641, 649

Addiscombe, 61

Aden, 152, 337

Afghan War, 24, 27, 91, 123

Afghanistan, 24, 27, 144, 212, 221, 231, 239, 351, 498, 584, 597, 604, Amir of, 231; Invasion of, 24

Afghans, 17, 24, 25, 597

Africa, 331; North, 351, 358

Afzal Khan, Mughal General, 69

Aga Khan III Delegation, 85, 126, 127, 130, 131, 132, 169

Aga Khan III, Sir Sultan Muhammad Shah, President, All Parties Muslim Conference 1928-9; Member and Chairman Indian Delegation to RTC 1930-2; Leader, Indian Delegation to League of Nations 1932-6; President, LON 1937, 92, 130, 131, 134, 135, 139, 142, 143, 144, 160, 268, 269, 282, 290, 307, 308, 386, 643

Age of Consent Act, 1891, 68

Agra, 3, 5, 7, 35, 146, 249; Fort, 34

Ahmadabad, 124, 204

Ahmadnagar, 386

A'in-i Akbari, 14

Aix-la-Chapelle, Peace of, 7

Aiyar (Aiyer, Iyer), Sir C. P. Ramaswami, Diwan of Travancore 1936, 576, 577

Ajmal Khan, Hakim, 195, 216, 234

Ajnala, 42

Akali Movement, 257; Party, 619; Sikhs, 428, 476

Akbar, Mughal Emperor, 4, 14

Akbar II, Mughal Emperor, 76

Al-Biruni, 62

Alexander, Albert Victor (later Viscount and Earl Alexander of Hillsborough),

Member, Cabinet Mission to India; Minister of Defence 1946, 425, 427, 439

Algeria, 651

Ali (ibn Abi Talib), 76

Ali brothers, 229, 232, 238

Ali Gauhar, 12

Ali Imam, Syed, 135

Ali Zaheer, Syed, 455, 459

Aligarh, 80, 134, 230, 247; College, 78, 87; Movement, 74

Aligarh Institute Gazette, 79, 82, 129

Aligarh Muslim University; 585; Jinnah's speech to the Union at, 309

Alivardi Khan, Viceroy of Bengal, 9

All Souls College, Oxford, 166

All-India Congress Committee, 122, 192, 275, 276, 278, 295, 301, 302, 303, 337, 384, 387, 512, 658

All-India Convention of Congress Legislators, 312

All-India Federal Constitution, 434

All-India Federal Union, 434

All-India Federation, 282, 283, 324, 325

All-India Hindu Mahasabha, 257

All-India Leaders Manifesto, 261

All-India Liberal Federation, 178, 261

All-India Moderate Conference, 178

All-India Muslim Conference, 286, 312

All-India Muslim League Report on Muslim Grievances in Congress Provinces, 318

All-India Muslim League, 47, 128, 133, 134, 136, 139, 140, 142, 144, 145, 148, 151, 152, 154, 155, 159, 160, 161, 163, 164, 166, 168, 177, 214, 216, 217, 226, 227, 228, 229, 239, 255, 261, 267, 310, 313, 315, 316, 318, 319, 321, 322, 324, 326, 327, 328, 329, 330, 341, 343, 348, 349, 351, 354, 355, 356, 357, 359, 375, 402-06, 408, 410, 413-18, 420, 421, 422, 427, 429, 431-36, 439, 442-47, 450-66, 472-73, 475, 476-80, 482, 511, 519, 525, 529, 531, 536, 538, 548, 550, 551; All-India Muslim League, Aziz Group, 241; Hidayat Group, 241; Jinnah Group, 241, 261, 266; London Branch of, 134; Sir Muhammad Shafi

Group, 241, 261, 266; United Province Group, 316

All-India Radio, 506, 510

All-India States Conference, 480

All-India States People's Conference, 568

All-Jammu and Kashmir Muslim Conference, 585

All-Parties Conference, 218, 263, 264, 267

All-Parties Convention, 268, 270

All-Parties Muslim Conference, 268

Allahabad, 12, 18, 33, 39, 105, 123, 98, 194, 246, 247, 257, 311, 363, 378, 481; Allahabad Bar, 221, High Court, 258

Allied Forces, 149

Alwar, 617

Amanullah Khan, Amir of Afghanistan, 212, 221

Amar Singh Ambalvi, Secretary, Shiromani Akali Dal, 615

Ambala, 323, 430, 481

Ambedkar, Dr Bhimo Ramji, Member, National Defence Council; Leader of Untouchables, 187, 243, 250, 282, 284, 290, 344, 367

Amboyana, massacre of, 5

Ameer Ali, Syed, 87, 134

America (See also, USA) 3, 20, 67, 178, 287, 378, 643,

American(s), 13; colonies, 13; Federation, 264; Injured in riots, 420; Revolution, 90; War of Independence, 13, 15, 22,

Amery, Leopold Charles Maurice Stennett, Colonial Secretary 1924-9; Dominions Secretary 1925-9; Secretary of State for India 1940-5, 352, 362, 374, 378, 389, 394, 396, 399, 400, 405, 411, 415, 416, 417, 418, 637, 639

Amherst, William Pitt, First Earl (1773-1857), Governor-General of India (1823-8), 21

Amrit Kaur, Rajkumari, sometime chairman of the All-India Women's Conference; worked as Secretary to Gandhi, 194

Amritsar, 135, 192, 203, 208, 216, 231, 249, 251, 476, 477, 478, 553, 562, 611, 615, 617, 624; hartal in, 205; Martial Law at, 202

Anand Bhawan, 194

Ananda Math, 67, 317

Andaman, 361

Anderson, John (later Viscount Waverley), Governor of Bengal 1932-7; Home Secretary 1939-40, 398

Andrews, C. F., 89, 113

Aney, Madhao Shrihari, MLA Berar 1924-6; President INC, 1932; Viceroy's Executive Council 1941-7; Governor Bihar 1948-52, 294

Anglo-French rivalry, 8; wars, 53

Anglo-German Naval Treaty, 335

Anglo-Indians, 172, 206, 282, 443, 458, 487

Anglo-native newspapers, 99

Anglo-Oriental Defence Association, 85

Anglo-Russian Entente, 144

Anglo-Saxon race, 105

Ansari, Dr Mukhtar Ahmad, led All-India Medical Mission to Turkey 1912-13; member, Khilafat Deputations 1920, 93, 144, 195, 217, 228, 229, 294

Anti-Untouchability Campaign, 294

Arab States, 574

Arabia, 23, 74; Arabs, 91, 215, 336

Arabian Sea, 6

Arabic Language, 14, 31, 23, 31, 63, 71, 75, 79

Arakan, 21, 395

Arbitral Tribunal, 521, 538, 539, 540

Archbishops, 63

Archbold, W.A.J., 129, 131

Arcot, 8, 19

Arjuna, 185

Armada, 4

Arms Act, 152

Army, Indian, 410, 521, 522, 593, 627, 651, 654

Army, Pakistan, 604, 608, 628

Army, Sikh, 478

Arnold, Sir Edwin, 182

Arya Samaj, 64, 65

Aryans, 63, 90

Asaf Ali, Member, Indian Legislative Assembly, 1935, 1945; Governor of Orissa 1948-52, 366, 455, 640, 529

Asar-ul-Sanadid, 77

Asia, 331

Asia Minor, 215

Asian Relations Conference, 289

Asiatic Society of Bengal, 14

Asquith, Herbert Henry, 141, 159

Assam, 109, 110, 21, 57, 224, 302, 314, 319, 350, 359, 407, 428, 429, 431, 433, 440, 462, 482, 496, 537, 547

Assembly Hall, Peshawar, 479

Atlantic Charter, 368, 386

Attlee, Clement Richard, Secretary of State for Dominion Affairs 1942-3; Deputy Prime Minister 1942-5; Prime Minister 1945-51, 260, 458, 463, 468, 469, 471, 472, 473, 477, 478, 502, 503, 506, 507, 508, 510, 514, 516, 517, 521, 526, 532, 533, 535, 537, 562, 570, 576, 602, 603, 606, 627, 637, 640, 641, 642, 650, 652

Attock, 478

Auchinleck, Field Marshal Sir Claude John Eyre, C-in-C India, January-July 1941 and June 1943, 358, 420, 421, 490, 521, 522, 523, 524, 525, 598, 614, 616

Auckland, Lord, 23

auction, 4

Aurangzeb, Emperor, 6, 7, 71, 93, 633

Australia, 101

Austria, 148, 33; Austrian Empire, 650; Austrian Succession, 7

Autobiography, (Nehru), 111, 154, 191, 288, 643, 645, 654

Ayer, V. D., Assistant Secretary to Boundary Commission, 561

Ayer, Subramania, 641

Ayers, Lt., 69, 98

Ayodhya, 249

Ayub Khan, President of Pakistan, 520, 628

Ayyenger (Aiyangar, Aiyengar, Iengar), Sir Gopalaswami, member, Board of Revenue, Madras 1935-7; Prime Minister of Kashmir 1937-43; Member, Constituent Assembly, 525, 601, 602

Azad, Maulana Abul Kalam (1888-1958), President INC 1923, 1940-6; Education Minister 1947, 86, 111, 151, 185, 195, 218, 219, 266, 305, 315, 339, 346, 352, 356, 358, 359, 361, 366-74, 377, 378, 385-6, 395, 402, 413, 374, 377, 378, 385, 386, 395, 402, 413, 414, 417, 421, 430-2, 438-41, 443-5, 448, 449, 451, 461, 465, 473, 481, 483, 491, 566, 591, 620

Azamgarh, 32, 249

Babar Aaklis, 257
Babur, Emperor, 3
Baden-Powell, Lord, 317
Baghdad, 178
Bahadur Shah II (1775-1862), King of Delhi, 17, 26, 29, 32, 34, 37, 40, 45, 36, 37, 78
Baisakhi, 207
Baji Ro, 21
Bajpai, Sir Girja Shankar, ICS, Agent to the Governor-General in USA 1941-7; Secretary, General Department of External Affairs and Commonwealth Relations 1947, 602
Bakar-Eid festival, 216
Baldev Singh, Sardar, Minister of Development, Punjab 1942-6; Member, Interim Govt. 1946, 430, 455, 457, 460, 463, 464, 501, 503, 506, 507, 511, 520, 525, 547, 569, 595, 596, 618
Baldwin, Stanley, 260, 273
Balfour Declaration, 341
Balkan States, 144; War, 92
Balkan, Plan, 469, 495, 496, 497, 500, 513, 514, 641, 642
Ballia (UP), 249
Baluchistan, 24, 72, 266, 270, 350, 407, 429, 431, 433, 481, 509, 514, 516, 554
Bande Mataram, 67, 111, 135, 316, 317, 322
Banerji, Sir Surendranath (1848-1925) Founder and Editor of Bengali 1879-1921; Member, Bengal Legislative Council 1893-1901, 1913; Member, Indian Legislative Council (1918-20), 49, 94, 95, 102, 103, 112, 119, 123, 128, 153, 178, 196, 256
Bang-i-Islam, 326

Bangistan, 326
Bangladesh, 656, 657, 658
Bankipore, 145
Baramda, 4
Bardoli (Surat), 234, 272, 288
Bardoloi, Gopinath, 428, 462
Bareilly 39; Gaol, 194
Barisal (Bengal), 114
Barkatullah Bhopali, Maulvi, 156
Barlow, Sir George (1762-1847), 19
Barni, Zia-ud-Din, 77
Barrackpore, 21, 27, 28, 30, 38
Barton, Sir William, 597
Basu, Bhupendranath, 153
Batala, 552
Batavia, 5, 10
Battle of Britian, 352, 361
Battle of Plassey, 10, 31
Bay of Bengal, 361
Bayley, E. C., 76
Bazaz, Prem Nath, 591, 594, 599
Beaumont, Sir John William Fisher, Chief Justice of Bombay 1930-43; Member of the Judicial Committee of the Privy Council 1944, 540, 549, 556, 561
Beck, Theodore (1859-99), Principal of MAO College, Aligarh, 78, 87, 88
Belgium, 651
Benares, 17, 32, 79, 93, 120, 249
Bengal, 6, 8, 9, 10, 12, 21, 44, 62, 65, 73, 94, 97, 111, 114, 119, 120, 121, 162, 220, 224, 247, 248, 249, 256, 258, 266, 267, 269, 272, 292, 302, 314, 319, 338, 350, 359, 389, 407, 425, 427, 429, 431, 433, 440, 454, 455, 482, 496, 497, 499, 508, 512, 513, 514, 537, 538, 541, 546, 580; Army, 27, 38, 45; Assembly, 428; Award, 545, 559; Boundary, 559; East, 466, 481, 509, 514, 516, 517, 546, 547, 551; Governor of, 13; Muslims of, 87; nation, 110, 130; Nawab of, 31; partition of, 81, 98, 124, 129, 140, 141, 144, 146, 480, 494; United Independent, 499; West, 424
Bengalis, 61, 642
Bennett, Member of British Govt., 1945, 653
Bentham, Jeremy, 22

Bentinck, Lord William, 21, 22, 23, 54, 62, 100
Berar, 19
Berhampur, 28
Berlin, 156; Radio, 368
Besant, Annie (1847-1933), Member, Theosophical Society 1889-1906, President 1907-33; founder, Central Hindu College, Benares (later Benares Hindu University); founder and editor of *Commonwealth and New India* 1914; founder of Home Rule League 1916, 157, 159, 166, 168, 178, 221, 223
Best, Capt. Thomas, 5
Bethmann-Hollweg, German Chancellor, 156
Bhabha, Coverji Hormusji, Member, Interim Govt. 1946, 455, 461
Bhagalpore, 249
Bhagat Singh, 273, 287, 288
Bhagvad-gita, 196
Bhakata, 65
Bhapolpur, 56
Bharatpur, 617
Bhave, Vinod, 358
Bhonsla, 17
Bhopal, 575, 576; Nawab of, 282, 555, 575, 576, 578, 579
Bibighar, 39
Bible, The, 63.
Bihar, 9, 12, 58, 109, 142, 195, 248, 249, 294, 297, 302, 306, 318, 328, 388, 436, 465, 466, 480; North, 199
Bihar, massacre of Muslims of, 612
Biharis, 110, 642
Bijapur, Sultan of, 3
Bijnor, 77
Bikaner, 543, 558, 561, 617; Canal, 555; State of, 558; Maharaja of, 282, 283, 558, 575
Birkenhead, Lord Frederick Edwin Smith, First Earl of (1872-1930), Secretary of State for India 1924-8, 261, 264, 275, 284
Bishop Cotton School, 206
Bishops, 63
Biswas, C. C., 537

Black Hole of Calcutta, 9, 42
Blavatsky Lodge, 157; Madame, 157
Blunt, W. S., 56, 57, 95
Boer War, 108, 110, 198
Bolan Pass, 24
Bolsheviks, 258
Bombay, 6, 12, 13, 14, 17, 44, 55, 68, 69, 83, 85, 97, 98, 114, 137, 138, 142, 168, 178, 198, 203, 204, 205, 233, 235, 251, 249, 258, 264, 265, 270, 280, 286, 288, 295, 297, 302, 306, 310, 311, 313, 315, 318, 321, 383, 388, 389, 391, 406, 413, 421, 436, 449, 451, 461, 488, 580, 640; Bombay Bar, 136; High Court, 82; INC Session at, 158, 159, 199, 300; Jamia Masjid of, 138; Muslim League Session at, 152, 155, 161, 310; riots, 246; University of, 68, 483
Bombay Resolution, Congress, 358
Bonaparte, Napoleon, 16
Bonnerjee, W. C., 95, 99
Booth, J. B., 516
Borckman, R.V., Personal Secretary to the Viceroy, 617
Bose, Anand Mohan, 102
Bose, Sarat Chandra (1889-1950), Leader of opposition, Central Legislative Assembly 1927 and 1937; Member, Interim Government 1946; founder of Socialist Republican Party, 455, 459, 499
Bose, Subhas Chandra (1897-1945), Member, Indian Legislative Assembly; President, Congress sessions 1938 and 1939; Founder Indian National Army, 158, 189, 191, 192, 196, 225, 254, 256, 262, 263, 271, 274, 275, 289, 293, 295, 329, 335, 336, 369, 393, 420, 499, 654
Boundary Commission, 507, 509, 517, 520, 538, 539, 540, 555, 557, 592
Boundary Commission Award, 535, 536, 542, 546, 547, 548, 560, 621; of Bengal, 537, 538, 540, 541; of Punjab, 537, 541
Boundary Force, 542
Bow, London 291
Bradford, 52
Bradlaugh, Charles, 83, 98, 112, 157

Bradley, Benjamin Francis, 258
Brahmaputra, 21
Brahma Samaj, 64
Brahmanism, 62
Brar, D. S., 520
Bright, John, 321
Bristol East Labour Party, 363
Britain *(See also,* Great Britain and the
    United Kingdom), 5, 20, 22, 112, 148,
    178, 218, 221, 241, 333, 337, 361
British Civil Service, 236; Crown, 43, 44,
    47, 144; Empire, 3, 24, 117, 123, 159,
    167, 168, 175, 193, 200, 221, 228, 276,
    397, 655; Government, 28, 45, 98,
    102; Labour Party, 228; Parliament,
    12, 44, 131, 271; Raj, 219, 653, 656;
    War Cabinet, 378
British India Association, 79
Broomfield, Judge, 235
Brown, Mr, 204
Brussels, 263
Brydon, Dr, 24
Buckingham Palace, 190
Buddha, 182, 296
Buddhist, 182
Budge-Budge (near Calcutta), 156
Bulandshahr, 249
Bulgaria, 148; Bulgarians, 93
Burke, Edmund, 196
Burma, 26, 28, 21, 297, 381, 389, 393,
    395, 397, 418; Indian migration to, 155
Burmese, 21
Burrows, Sir Frederick John, Governor of
    Bengal 1946-7, 453, 454, 54, 546
Butler, Sir Harcourt, 284
Buxar, Battle of, 11, 12
Byron, 400

Cabinet Delegation, 448
Cabinet Mission, 429, 435, 436, 437, 438,
    439, 441, 442, 443, 444, 446, 447, 449,
    453, 456, 461, 462, 475, 482, 491, 493,
    494, 502, 551, 552, 553, 554, 566, 590,
    637; Memorandum, 509, 566, 569, 572;
    Plan, 469, 575; Proposals, 640, 649
Calcutta, 6, 9, 13, 33, 54, 56, 62, 63, 64,
    66, 72, 76, 94, 98, 111, 121, 141, 144,
    177, 218, 219, 224, 225, 226, 227, 233,

234, 241, 246, 247, 253, 266, 267, 268,
    270, 272, 273, 311, 361, 389, 390, 420,
    421, 424, 430, 431, 454, 455, 488, 499,
    541, 544, 548, 550, 551, 552, 610, 619,
    624; Black Hole of, 9, 42; Corporation,
    109; transfer of capital from, 142;
    University, 87, 96
Calcutta Municipal Act, 256
Calicut, 3, 4
Caliphate *(See also,* Khilafat), 217
Cambridge, 74, 79, 262, 322, 327;
    Emanuel College, 324; Gandhi in, 291
Campbell, Sir George, 75
Campbell-Johnson, 493, 514, 540, 544,
    560, 573, 598, 603, 606, 608, 614, 615,
    627
Canada, 101, 102, 123, 124, 156, 256, 288,
    362, 601; West Coast of, 155
Canadian Federation, 264
Candy, General, 399
Cannanore (Madras), 249
Canning, Earl (Charles John Canning,
    1812-62), Governor-General and Ist
    Viceroy of India 1856-62, 26, 45, 564
Canterbury, Archibishop of, 291
Cape, 102
Cape of Good Hope, 3, 5, 64
Carlyle, 80
Carnatic, 8, 9; Nawab of, 7, 8, 17, 26
Caroe, Sir Olaf Kirkpatrick, ICS; Sec-
    retary, External Affairs Dept. 1939-45;
    Governor, NWFP March 1946-7, 465,
    479, 497, 516
Carr, Sir Hubert Winch, president, India-
    Burma Association 1945-7, 282
Carter, Sir (Richard Henry) Archibald,
    Assistant Under-Secretary of State for
    India 1936; Permanent Under-
    Secretary of State for India 1947, 556
cartridges, 28, 38, 77
Casey, Richard Gardiner, Governor of
    Bengal, 1944-6, 424
Catherine of Portugal, 6
Catholic religion, 4; Catholicism, 4;
    Catholics, 325
Cause of the Indian Revolt, 77 78, 88
Cawnpore, 21, 33, 34, 38, 39, 35, 42, 146,
    249; Mosque of, 147

Central Assembly, bomb attack on 273
Central Khilafat Committee, 218
Central Legislative Assembly, 150
Central National Muhammadan Association, 114
Central Provinces, 159, 248, 256, 302, 328, 388, 436
Ceylon, 3, 5, 603, 655
Chailley, Joseph, 60
Chamber of Princes, 173, 251, 571, 572, 576
Chamberlain, Arthur Neville (1869-1940), Minister of Health 1923-9, 31; Chancellor of Exchequer 1923-4, 1931-7; Prime Minister 1937-40, 166, 167, 333, 336, 352
Champaran (North Bihar), 199
Chandernagore, 7, 9
Chandni Chowk, 124
Channel Islands, German occupation of, 352
chapatis, 38
Charkha, 230
Charles II, King, 6
Charlu, Anandu, 99
Charsadda, 280
Charter Bill of 1833, 23
Chatterji, Bankim Chandra, 67, 317
Chauri Chaura, 185, 234, 235, 260, 272
Chelmsford Club, 245
Chelmsford, Ist Viscount (Frederic John Napier Thesiger), Viceroy of India 1916-21, 148, 166, 168, 170, 171, 178, 233, 641
Chenab, River, 430, 585, 615
Chet Singh of Benares, Raja, 13
Chhatari, Nawab of, 359, 582, 583
Chiang Kai-Shek, Generalissimo, President of the Supreme War Council, 339, 361, 362, 381, 383, 384, 386; Madame, 339, 361, 386
child sacrifice, custom of, 22, 23
Child, Sir Josiah, 6, 7
Chillianwala, 25
Chimur, 388
China, 7, 20, 333, 336, 339, 361, 362, 378, 380, 381, 382, 386, 584, 643; Indian migration to, 155; Indian troops in, 263; North, 334

Chinsura, 5
Chirol, Sir Valentine, 180
Chitpavan Brahmin, 625
Chitral, 597
Chittagong, 6, 281; Hill Tracts, 544, 545, 546, 547, 548, 549, 587; Hill Tribes, 546
cholera at Poona, 98
Christ, 182, 191
Christian(s), 3, 4, 19, 28, 66, 172, 182, 232, 308, 309, 312, 443, 444, 458, 477, 636; missionaries, 65; Indian, 415
Christianity, 28, 29, 30, 31, 43, 22, 40, 75, 86, 325
Christie, Walter Henry John, ICS, Deputy Private Secretary to the Viceroy 1939-43; Joint Secretary to the Govt. of India, Food Dept., 1945-7; Joint Private Secretary to the Viceroy 1947, 543, 544, 549, 560
Chundrigar, Ismail Ibrahim, Member, Bombay Legislative Assembly 1939; President, Provincial Muslim League, Bombay 1940-5; Member, Interim Government 1946, 459, 461
Chungking, 339
Churchill, Sir Winston Leonard Spencer, (1874-1965), Malakand Field Force (31st Punjab Infantry) 1897; Secretary of State for Colonies 1906-8; President, Board of Trade 1908-10; Home Secretary 1910-11; Secretary of State for War 1919-21; Prime Minister 1940-5; Leader of the Opposition 1945, 175, 220, 287, 291, 297, 352, 355, 362, 361, 368, 373, 376, 378, 386, 396, 398, 400, 402, 404, 410, 411, 416, 473, 475, 505, 533, 534, 562, 652, 653
Civil and Military Gazette, 240
Civil Disobedience Enquiry Committee, 253
Civil Disobedience Movement, 272, 277, 279, 285, 286, 292, 293, 294, 295
Civilization, Western, 25, 186, 187, 193
Clark, Dr, 273
Clive, 8, 9, 10, 11, 12, 15, 20, 633, 648
Cocanada, 131, 217, 361
Colombia, representative of, 602

Colombo, 3, 361

Columbus, Christopher, 4

Colville, Sir John, Ist Baron Clydesmuir, Governor of Bombay 1943-8, 464

Colvin, Sir Auckland, 105, 107.

Commonweal, The, 157

Commonwealth, 290, 337, 344, 365, 397, 410, 505, 517, 564, 565, 576, 603, 629, 650, 655, 658; of Nations, 167

Commonwealth of India, The 264

Communal Award, 186, 298

communal riots, 93, 247, 288

Communism, 258

Communist Party of Great Britain, 258; of India, 258

Congo, 651

Congress, *see under,* Indian National Congress

Congress Enquiry Committee Report 1920, 203, 212, 213; Working Committee, 289

Congress-Muslim League Coalition, 473; Pact, 329; scheme of reforms, *see,* Lucknow Pact; Treaty of Peace, 267

Congress of the Oppressed Nationalities, 263

Connaught, Duke of, 173, 251

Constantinople, 93, 218, 237

Constitutional Maladies of India, 348

Contai (Midnapore), 390

Cooper, Fredrick, 41, 42

Coorg, annexation of, 23

Corah, 12

Coral Sea, Battle of the, 393

Corfield, Sir Conrad Lawrence, ICS, Political Adviser to Crown Representative 1945-7, 566, 572

Cornwallis, Lord (1738-1805), Governor-General of India 1786-93, 1805, 11, 15, 16, 17, 18, 19, 23, 54

Coromandel, 5

Cotton, Henry, 58

Cow-protection Societies, 85

Craddock, Sir Reginald, 325

Craik, Sir Henry Duffield (1876-1955), Chief Secretary, Punjab 1922-7; Member, Punjab Executive Council 1930-4; Home Member, G.-G.'s Executive Council 1934-8; Governor of Punjab 1934-41; Political Adviser to the Viceroy 1941-3, 317

Crewe, Lord, 141

Crimea, 27

Cripps, Sir (Richard) Stafford (1889-1952), Lord Privy Seal and Leader of House of Commons 1942; Member, Cabinet Mission to India 1942, 305, 355, 361, 363, 364, 366, 367, 368, 370, 371, 372, 373, 374, 375, 376, 377, 378, 384, 390, 395, 396, 402, 410, 414, 418, 424, 425, 426, 427, 438, 439, 447, 450, 451, 456, 458, 469, 474, 475, 487, 565, 566, 567, 637, 639

Cripps Declaration, 565

Cripps Mission, 368, 381, 473, 652; Declaration, 641, 649, 652; failure of, 637

Croft, Sir Frederick, 136

Curzon, Lord George Nathaniel (1859-1925), Viceroy of India, 1899-1905, 55, 57, 59, 92, 107, 108, 109, 110, 123, 127, 141, 150, 256, 321, 654

Czar of Russia, 178

Czech, 339

Czechslovakia, 327, 333, 336

Dacca, 81, 110, 133, 134, 146

Dadu Miyan, *see,* Mohsin-ud-Din

Daily Herald, London, 391

Daily Telegraph, 560

Dalal, Sir Ardeshir, 398

Dalhousie, Lord, 21, 25, 26, 30, 31, 45, 108

Dalip Singh, Maharaja, 25

Dandi, 279

Dar, Bishan Narayan, 52

Dar-ul-aman, 74

Dar-ul-harb, 31, 72, 74

Dar-ul-Islam, 31, 73, 221

Darbhanga, Maharaja of, 105

Dardanelles, 24

Darling, Malcolm, 55

Das, C. R., 214, 224, 233, 234, 235, 253, 255, 256, 263

Datta, Aswini Kumar, 114

Datta, Batukeshwar, 273

Dayanad, Swami, 64, 65, 67

de Suffren, Admiral, 13
Defence of India Act, 152, 202
Defence of India Rules, 410
Dehra Dun, 249
Delhi, 3, 12, 17, 18, 26, 28, 29, 36, 38,
    40, 41, 60, 77, 124, 135, 168, 173,
    194, 200, 202, 203, 215, 246, 247, 249,
    251, 253, 266, 268, 273, 356, 364, 367,
    374, 412, 428, 429, 435, 455, 488, 498,
    503, 511, 518, 520, 526, 543, 546, 550,
    558, 559, 587, 590, 591, 595, 596, 602,
    609, 611, 623, 624, 626, 637, 650;
    Delhi Durbar, 1903 109; *hartal,* 203;
    Manifesto, 274, 275; capture of, 29,
    33; transfer of capital to, 142
Delhi Resolution of Congress, 353, 429
Delhi War Conference, 216
Democratic Swaraj Party, 344
Denmark, German invasion of, 352
Depressed Classes, 284, 367
Desai, Bhulabhai Jivanji (1877-1946),
    Congress Member, Indian Legislative
    Asembly 1934-5; President, Bombay
    Provincial Congress Committee, 292,
    420
Desai, Mahadev, 200
Devanagari script, 79
Dhanabad (Bengal), 249
Dhar, Bishan Narayan, 106
Dharsana, 280
Dholpur, 576, 577, 617; Maharaja of, 577
Dickens, Charles, 90, 648
Digby, John, 63, 64
Digby, William, 83, 112
Din Muhammad, 537
Diwani of Bengal and Bihar, 12
Doctrine of Lapse, 31
Dogra Force, 594
Dosanj, Amar Singh, President, Shiromani
    Akali Dal, 615
Dost Muhammad Khan, 24, 36
Dufferin, Lord Frederick Temple (1826-
    1902), Governor-General of India
    1884-8, 21, 95, 96, 105, 107, 131
Duke of Connaught, visit to India by, 224
Dunkerque, 352
Dupleix, Governor of Pondicherry, 7, 8
Durban, 197

Durga, goddess, 322
Durga Puja, festival of, 111
Durham, Lord, 362
Dutch, 4, 10, 5, 633
Dutt, R. Palme, 258
Dyer, Brigadier-General, 175, 206, 207,
    208, 211, 213, 219-21, 654

East Bengal, 73, 110, 134, 140, 181
East India College, 61
East India Company, 5, 6, 24, 35, 54, 63,
    64, 77, 99, 647, 656
East India Railway Workshop, strike in,
    272
East Indies, 3, 5
East, Sir Hyde, 62
education, female, 30; Western, 16, 26,
    30, 36, 46, 60, 62, 63, 75, 83, 87, 88,
    152, 220
Edward VIII, King, 109, 140, 468
Egypt, 92, 16, 55, 123, 342, 574; Indian
    troops in, 337
Eire, 337
Elgin, Lord, 59
Elizabeth I, Queen, 5
Elphinstone, Mountstuart, 24, 647
Emancipation Act (1850), 3, 30
Emanuel College, Cambridge, 324
Emden, German Cruiser, 148
Enfield rifle, 28
England, 5, 25, 64, 66, 81, 83, 90, 109,
    102, 125, 123, 134, 136, 153, 180, 220,
    241, 334, 339, 344, 367, 396, 420, 447,
    456, 517, 539, 561, 633, 647, 648, 650
English language, 63, 74, 75, 79, 86, 90,
    97, 656, 657; literature, 46
Essays on the Life of Mohammad, 80
Ethiopia, 333, 334; Ethiopians, 110
Europe, Indian troops in, 148; Turks in,
    144
European(s), 15, 27, 29, 39, 39, 54, 59,
    61, 63, 77, 87, 90, 636; languages, 23;
    murder of, 19, 232: powers, 110

Factory Act, 22
Faizpur, 301, 335
Fakhr-ud-din, Prince, 26
famine, 110

famine in Bombay, 98
Far East, 156, 396
Faraizis, 73
Faridkot, 617; Raja of 617
Faridpur, 73
Faruqistan, 326
Fascism, 301, 337, 339, 340, 369, 382,
    327; Fascist, 305, 380
Fatehpur Sikri, 77
Fatima, daughter of the Prophet (PBUH),
    76
fatwa, 72
Fazilka, 558, 559
Fazl-i-Hussain, Sir Mian (1877-1936),
    Member, Punjab Legislative Council
    1916-20; founder, Punjab Nationalist
    Unionist Party 1923; Member,
    Govenor-General's Council 1930-5;
    Minister of Education, Punjab 1936,
    255
Fazlul Haq, 314, 319, 359
Fazlur Rahman, 547
Ferozepore, 543, 555, 556, 557, 558, 559,
    561, 617
Fiji Islands, 102
Firozabad, 249
Fisher, Louis, 370, 449
Formosa, 395
Foster, E. M., 45
France, 5, 13, 23, 109, 148, 149, 150, 218,
    333, 334, 335, 336, 339, 344, 352, 376,
    582, 650
Franco, General, 333, 336
Fraser, Sgt., 204
Free Trade, Doctrine of, 91
French, 6, 7, 8, 9, 10, 16, 17, 21, 25, 633
French East India Company, 7
French Revolution, 21, 16, 22, 64, 90
Frere, Sir Bartle, 44, 45
Frontier Gandhi, *see,* Abdul Ghaffar Khan,
    Khan
Fuller, Sir Bampfylde, 140

Game Birds of India, 96
Ganapati, 70
Ganapati festival, 68, 85
Gandhi, Mohandas Karamchand (1869-
    1948), 51, 52, 88, 89, 104, 105, 114,

120, 135, 136, 145, 148, 154, 157, 158,
164, 165, 180-90, 194-201, 203-5, 210,
213, 214, 216-19, 221, 223-235, 238,
239, 243, 246-8, 250, 252-4, 256-8,
263, 267, 271, 272, 274, 275, 278, 279,
280, 282, 285, 287, 288, 290-6, 302,
303, 307, 309, 316-18, 328, 331, 336,
338, 339, 341-3, 345, 347, 352, 355,
356, 358, 359, 361, 363, 366, 368-70,
374, 377-82, 484, 489, 491-4, 506,
507, 510-12, 514, 515, 565, 568, 587,
589, 591-3, 607, 610, 611, 624, 625,
634, 637, 638, 640, 643, 654
Gandhi cap, 190, 316
Gandhi, Karamchand, 181
Gandhi, Kasturbai, 182, 194
Gandhi, Putlibai, 181
Gandhi-Irwin Pact, 285; truce, 288
Gandhi-Nehru Alliance, 643
Gandhism, 258
Gang Canal, 558
Ganges, 17, 111
Garhmuktesar, 466
Gauhati, 427
Gaya, 253
Gelder, Stuart, 400, 401
Germany, 148, 152, 155, 178, 215, 233,
    334, 336, 352, 393, 654, 658;
    surrender of, 148; German/Germans,
    54, 149, 178, 327, 333, 361, 395;
    German-Russian Pact, 333
George V, King, 140, 173, 291
George VI, King-Emperor 1936, 468, 625
Ghadar Party, 155, 156
Ghazanfar Ali Khan, Raja, Member,
    Indian Legislative Minister of Health
    1946; Minister of Food, Agriculture
    and Health Pakistan 1947; Ambas-
    sador to Iran, Turkey, India, and Italy
    1948-57, 459, 640, 477, 619
Ghazi-ud-din, 11, 12
Ghazni, 72
Ghori, Muhammad, 321
Ghose, Arabindo, 119
Ghosh, Lalmohan, 109
Ghosh, Rasbinhari, 122
Ghulam Abbas, Chaudhri (1901-67),
    Secretary, All-Jammu and Kashmir

Muslim Conference 1932, 585, 586
Ghulam Ali, Shah, 76
Ghulam Muhammad, Bakhshi, 591
Ghulam Qadir, 12
Ghulam Sarwar, 464
Gidney, Lt. Col. Sir Henry Albert John, Member, National Defence Council nominated Non-Official Member; Indian Legislative Assembly; spokesman for Anglo-Indian Community, 282
Gita, 69, 125, 182, 185
Gladstone, W. E., 106, 124
Gladwin, Francis, 14
Goa, 3, 4, 5; Goans, 4
Godse, Nathuram, 624
Gokhale, Gopal Krishna, 98, 104, 107, 110, 119, 124, 136, 138, 147, 152, 157, 198, 199
Gokuldas Tejpal Sanskrit College, Bombay, 99
Gondal, State of, 135
Gorakhpur, 185
Gordon Walker, Patrick, Parliamentary Under-Secretary of State for Commonwealth Relations, 603
Gorga, 17
Government of India Act of 1935, 240, 297, 305, 310, 532
Gracey, General Douglas, 598, 604
Great Britain, 19, 83, 97, 101, 152, 256, 274, 338, 339, 344, 353, 361, 382, 449, 643, 648, 655, 656
Great Divide, The, 535
Great Rebellion of 1857, 17, 21, 27, 46, 54, 59, 59, 74, 76, 77, 78, 90, 97, 125, 143, 216, 220, 553, 634, 647
Greco-Turkish War of 1897, 144
Greece, 90; Greeks, 237
Grenville, Lord, 44
Guam, 393
Gujarat, 5, 183, 234
Gujranwala, *hartal* in, 210, 211; Martial Law at, 202
Gujrat, 25, 64, 181; *hartal* in, 211; Martial Law at, 202
Gulab Singh, Maharaja of Kashmir, 585
Gulbarga, 246
gunpowder, 7

Gurdaspur, 543, 544, 552, 553, 554, 555, 561, 587
Gurdawaras, 615
Gurgaon, 612
Gurkhas, 20, 35, 46, 634
Guru ka bagh, 257
Gwalior, 12, 35, 36, 568; State, 282
Gwyer, Sir Maurice Linford, Chief Justice of India and President of Federal Court 1937, 317, 457

Habibullah, King of Afghanistan, 156
Haidaristan, 326
Haileybury College, 61
Hali, Altaf Hussain, 86, 87
Halifax, 3rd Viscount (Edward Frederick Lindley Wood, 1881-1959), Viceroy of India 1926-31 as Lord Irwin; Delegate to RTC 1932; Member, Joint Parliamentary Committee on Indian Constitutional Reforms 1933-4, 243, 245, 247, 271, 273, 275, 282, 283, 285, 287, 288, 474
Hamed, Syed, 79
Hamilton, Lord George, 57, 59, 107
Hamilton, Sir Fredrick, 56
Hardie, Keir, 273
Hardinge, Lord, 25, 124, 141, 142, 146, 147, 148, 152, 156, 166, 198, 202
Hari Singh, Ruler of Kashmir, (*see also,* Kashmir), 585
Harijan (*see also,* Untouchables), 294
Harijan, 355, 378, 379, 380, 439
Haripur, 335
Harishchandra, 182
Harrow, 262
Hasrat Mohani, 151, 161
Hastings, Warren (1732-1818), Governor of Bengal 1772-4; Governor-General of India 1774-85, 11, 12, 13, 14, 20, 21, 54, 647
Havelock, General, 34, 39
Hawaii, 334
Hawkins, Capt. William, 5, 6
Heber, Reginald, Bishop of Calcutta, 75, 93
Henderson, Arthur, Parliamentary Under Secretary of State for India and Burma 1945, 550, 560

Herat, 24
Hewart, Lord Gordon, 112
Hidayatullah, Sir Ghulam Hussain (1879-1948), Member, Indian Legislative Assembly 1935; Prime Minister of Sind 1937-8; Home Minister, Sind 1941-2; Prime Minister of Sind 1942-7; Governor of Sind 1947-8, 314, 428
Hijrat Movement, 221, 239
Hindi language, 65, 79, 129, 316, 318
Hindi-Urdu agitation, 79; controversy, 79
Hindu, 4, 51, 66, 195, 245; landlords, 74
Hindu College, 62
Hindu Mahasabha, 165, 243, 257, 261, 264, 282, 286, 313, 314, 318, 328, 338, 344, 356, 367, 427, 513
Hindu nation, 165; nationalism, 37; Raj, 315, 328, 390, 391, 498, 634, 640
Hindu Widow Re-Marriage Act of 1856, 30
Hindu-Muslim relations, 132, 138, 143, 146, 160, 163-5, 169, 170, 195, 197, 205, 216, 217, 225, 229, 231-3, 238-40, 243, 246, 247, 250, 254, 255, 265, 267, 286, 288, 318, 322, 343, 391, 409, 418, 454, 473, 634, 638, 642 648, 649; riots, 85, 93, 235, 246, 250, 256; Settlement, 327, 329, 384, 406, 409, 459, 472
Hindu-Sikh community, 478
Hindustan Times, 418
Hindustani language, 657
Hindustani Socialist Army, 273
Hiroshima, 393
Hissar, 130
History of the Congress, 370
History of the Indian National Congress, 131, 294
History of the Sepoy War in India, 18, 634
Hitler, Adolf (1884-45), Leader and Chancellor of Germany 1933-45, 333, 334, 352, 393, 658
Hoare, Sir Samuel, *see,* Templewood
Hodson, Captain, 34, 40
Hodson, Henry Vincent, Reform Commissioner, Govt. of India, 1941, 535, 536, 543, 554, 556, 586, 623
Holkar, 17, 20, 36

Holwell, 42
Home Rule, 135, 157, 216; agitation, 166, 178; League, 157, 158, 168, 227; Special, 164
Hong Kong, Indian migration to, 155
Hooghly River, 6, 65
Hoti Mardan, 41
House of Timur, 18
How Mountbatten bent the rules and the Indian border, 561
Howrah, 280
Humayun's tomb, 40
Hume, Allan Octavian, 94, 95, 96, 97, 99, 105, 131
Hunter Committee Majority Report, 205, 206, 207, 208, 209, 212, 213, 218, 219; *Minority Report,* 208, 212, 218, 217, 219
Hunter, Sir William, 73, 75
Hussain, Sharif of Mecca, 166, 215
Hutchinson, Lester, 574
Hyder Ali of Mysore, 15, 17, 153
Hyderabad, 128, 173, 282, 284, 555, 563, 567, 580, 581, 582, 584, 587, 607
Hyderabad, Sind, 579

Idols, 4
Ikramullah, M., 569
Ilbert Bill, 58, 91, 94
Ilbert, Sir Courtenay, Vice-Chancellor, Calcutta University 1841, 58
Ilm Din, 249
Imperial Civil Service, 59
Imperial Conference, 257
Imperialism, 337, 369
Imphal (Manipur), 395
INA, *see,* Indian National Army
Independence Act of 1947, *see,* Indian Independence Act
Independence Day Celebrations, 610
Independent candidates, 427
India, 246
India (Journal), 112
India and Burma Committee, 533
India Central Committee, 274
India League, 192
India Office, 500, 572
India Wins Freedom, 86, 305, 339, 356, 370

Indian Ambulance Corps, 198, Field Ambulance Training Corps, 198
Indian Annual Register, 257
Indian Association, Calcutta, 94
Indian Chaos, The, 280
Indian Civil Service, 58, 59, 61, 82, 94, 103, 172, 225, 236, 519, 527, 540, 556, 561, 651
Indian Council Act of 1861, 44
Indian Council Act of 1909, 127
Indian Councils Acts, 135
Indian Home Rule League, 159
Indian Independence Act, 516, 526, 535, 560, 642, 652
Indian Independence Act of 1947, 299
Indian Independence Bill, 517, 530, 562, 568, 574
Indian Musalmans, The, 73, 75
Indian National Army, 393, 394, 395, 419, 420, 486, 490
Indian National Congress, 52, 64, 68, 78, 82, 83, 84, 86, 88, 92, 94, 95, 96, 97, 98, 100-9, 112-15, 120-7, 129-31, 133, 136, 137, 139, 142, 143, 146, 148, 151-4, 157-61, 163, 164, 166, 168, 177, 178, 180, 185, 187-9, 191-2, 195, 199, 214, 216, 217, 218, 221, 223, 225, 227-34, 236, 238, 240-1, 243, 247, 248, 251-4, 256, 261-3, 267-8, 271, 273-6, 280-1, 285, 288, 291-2, 295, 296, 299, 300-1, 303-5, 311-12, 316-21, 327-30, 334-5, 337, 341-2, 345, 347, 348, 352-9, 363-4, 366-9, 373-7, 381, 383, 390, 395, 397, 399, 400-5, 408-9, 413-18, 421, 423-4, 427, 429, 431, 432, 434, 439, 440, 442-52, 458, 462-3, 466, 472-3, 476, 483-4, 486, 488, 492-3, 497, 501, 503-4, 507, 514-15, 525, 531, 533, 535-6, 538, 548, 550, 552, 563-67, 575-6, 580, 584, 586, 618-22, 625, 627-8, 634, 636-7, 639-42, 651, 652
Indian Relief Act, 147
Indian Statutory (Simon) Commission, *see,* Simon Commission
Indian States, 563, 567
indigo, 7; planters, 74
Indo-British relations, 546

Indo-China, 21, 651
Indo-German Mission, 156
Indo-Pakistani relations, 657
Indonesia, 651
Indore, Holkar of, 36
Indus, River, 24, 27, 585
Industrial Revolution, 633, 648
Instrument of Accession, 570, 576, 577, 579, 594, 596, 599, 600
Iqbal, Sir Muhammad (1877-1938), Poet; Philosopher; Member, Punjab Legislative Council 1926; President, AIML session, Allahabad 1930; Delegate to RTC 1931-2, 86, 87, 289, 312, 322, 323, 324, 341, 481
Iran, 27, 144
Iraq, 358
Ireland, 104; Home Rule in, 124
Irregular Cavalry, 40
Irwin, Lord, *see,* Halifax
Islamia College, Lahore, 460
Islamic Commonwealth of Nations, 351
Ismail Khan, Nawab Muhammad (1884-1958), Member, UP Legislative Assembly 1937; Member, Constitutional Assembly 1946-7, Vice-Chancellor, Muslim University, Aligarh 1947-8, 316, 432
Ismay, Ist Baron (General Hastings Lionel Ismay), Chief of Staff to Minister of Defence 1940-6; Chief of the Viceroy's Staff 1947, 496, 499, 501, 503, 521, 524, 533, 544, 549, 561, 61, 616
Isna Asharis, 135
Ispahani, Mirza Abul Hassan (1902-81) Member, Bengal Legislative Assembly 1937; Joint Secretary, Bengal Provincial Muslim League 1936-7, Treasurer 1936-47; Member, Constituent Assembly of Pakistan 1947, 530
Italy, 90, 144, 148, 333, 335, 358, 654
Iyer, Subrahmanya, 99, 100

Jafar, Mir, 10, 11
Jagat Seth, 10
Jahangir, Emperor, 5, 6, 77
Jai Kishen Das, Raja, 79

Jakarta, 5

Jalalabad, 24

Jallianwala Bagh Massacre, 166, 175, 184, 206, 207, 211, 217, 219, 233, 261, 279, 653, 654

Jamalpur (Monghyr), 249

Jamia Masjid (Delhi), 204

Jamia Millia Islamia, 230

Jamiat-i-Ulema-i-Hind, 216

Jammu and Kashmir, 552, 593, 596, 604

Jamshedpur, 388

Japan, 110, 148, 358, 361, 362, 368, 378, 379, 380, 381, 393, 397, 412, 418, 650

Jayakar, Dr Mukand Ramrao (1873-1959), Member, Bombay Legislative Council 1923-5; Member, Legislative Assembly 1926-30; Delegate to RTC 1930-2; Member of the Judicial Committee of the Privy Council 1939-41, 178, 282

Jehangir, Sir Cowasji (1879-1962), Member, Revenue, Government of Bombay 1921-2; delegate to RTC 1930-2; Member, Indian Legislative Assembly 1930-47, 344

Jenkins, Sir Evan Meredith, ICS, Private Secretary to the Viceroy 1943-5; Governor of the Punjab 1946-7, 419, 457, 476, 477, 542, 557, 559, 615, 617, 618, 619, 621, 621

Jews, 232, 336, 339, 341

Jhansi, 26, 33, 38; Rani of, 33, 35, 36, 43

Jhelum, 478, 585; Bridge, 604

Jihad, 31, 231, 594

Jindh, Raja of, 36

Jinnah, Mohammad Ali (1876-1948), Founder of Pakistan President, AIML Session 1905; President AIML 1919-30, 1934-47; Governor-General of Pakistan 1947-8, 88, 135-7, 139, 144, 146-7, 158-61, 163, 168, 180, 218, 220-1, 223-4, 226-41, 254, 261, 265, 267-9, 275, 282, 307-22, 324, 326, 328-30, 341, 343-9, 351, 353, 355-7, 359-61, 363, 367, 373-5, 377, 390-403, 405-11, 413-15, 417-19, 421, 423-5, 428, 430, 431, 432, 440-2, 445-8, 451-3, 455, 458-63, 466, 481-2, 487, 489, 491-5, 498-9, 501, 503--7, 510, 511,

513, 516, 519, 520-2, 526-7, 530-2, 534-5, 539, 540, 546, 549, 551, 554, 560, 562, 569-70, 578-81, 584, 595, 598, 606-7, 609, 611, 621, 626, 637, 639-40, 642, 643, 651; Jinnahbhai, 136

Jinnah, Miss Fatimah (1893-1967), sister of Mohammad Ali Jinnah, 138

Jinnah's Fourteen Points, 269

Jinnah, Rutti, 138

Jinnah: a Retrospect, 626

Jiwan Das, 247

Jodhpur, 576, 579; Maharaja of, 579; Prime Minister of, 579; Raja of, 36

Johnson, Col. Frank, 208, 209, 213

Johnson, Louis, 370

Joint Defence Council, 521, 525

Joint Select Committee on Constitutional Reforms, 348

Jones, Sir William, 14, 54

Joshi, M. V., 152

Jubbulpore, 246

Judas, 326

Jullundhur, 430, 476, 478, 613

Jumna River, 17

Junagarh, 575, 580, 581, 600, 607, 628; Nawab of, 581, 606

Justice Party, 255

Kabir, 238

Kabul, 24, 28, 36, 72, 156; Indo-German Mission to, 156

kafir, 80

Kaira (Gujarat), 200

Kaiser of Germany, 156

Kak, Ram Chandra, Prime Minister of Kashmir 1954, 156, 589, 590, 591, 592

Kalat State, 514

Kali, goddess, 67; temple of, 111

Kandhar, 72

Kapurthala, 617, 618

Karachi, 43, 134, 136, 137, 146, 231, 232, 249, 287, 288, 326, 327, 343, 367, 411, 421, 426, 430, 475, 519, 530, 531, 544, 546, 579, 581, 597, 603, 609, 611, 643

Karamat Ali, Maulvi, 74

Karbala, 92

Karnal, 430

Kartar Singh, Giani, Member, Punjab

Legislative Assembly; leader of the Akali Party, 430, 615, 618
Kashi (Benares), 98, 114
Kashmir, 25, 282, 325, 406, 429, 431, 535, 550, 552, 554, 555, 563, 570, 575, 580, 584, 585, 589, 591, 592, 594, 597, 602, 604, 607, 628, 6299, 639, 643; Accession to India, 550; Azad, 598, 604; Maharaja of, 36, 282, 366, 554, 555, 566, 587, 589, 590, 591, 592, 594, 595, 596, 597, 599, 600, 607
Kasur, *hartal* in, 210
Kathiawar, 135, 181; Coast, 580
Kaye, John William, 37, 634
Keene, H. G., 60
Kelkar, 344
Kerno, Ivan, 528
Kesari, 68, 69
Khalifa, 142, 215
Khaliquzzaman, Choudhry (1889-1973), Member, All-India Congress Committee 1917-29; Joint Secretary, AIML, 1919-26; Member, UP Legislative Assembly 1946-7, Member, Indian Constitutional Assembly 1946-7, 229, 316, 350
Khalistan, (*see also,* Sikhistan), 450, 615, 618
Khan brothers, 515, 585, 586, 599
Khan Sahib, Dr (1883-1958), half-brother of Abdul Ghaffar Khan; Congress Member, Indian Legislative Assembly 1935; Congress Chief Minister, NWFP 1937-9, 1945-7; Minister of Communication, Pakistan 1954-5; Chief Minister, West Pakistan 1955-8, 292, 302, 314, 428, 465, 466, 479, 497, 498, 514, 516, 585, 586, 599,
Kher, B. G., 306, 315
Khilafat, 195, 215, 216, 217, 219, 221, 222, 225, 227, 229, 234, 237, 238; Conference, 215, 216, 217, 232, 251; Delegation, 218; Deputation, 217; Movement, 155, 166, 231, 238, 343
Khizar (Khizr) Hayat Khan Tiwana, Malik Sir, Member, Unionist Party; Minister for Public Works, Punjab 1937-42; Premier of Punjab December 1942-

April 1947, 313, 409, 410, 415, 428, 476, 477, 640
Khojas, 135
Khosla, A. N., 543
Khurram, Prince, 5, 6
Khwaja, A.M., 161
Kidwai, Rafi Ahmad (1894-1954), Secretary, UP Congress Committee; Minister of Land Revenue UP; Minister of Information 1947, 461
Kishorganj (Mymensingh District), 249
Kitchlew, Dr Saifuddin (1888-1963), President, All-India Khilafat Committee; General Secretary, Indian National Congress, 203, 205, 218, 229, 232
Kitchener, Lord, 141
Kohala, 604
Kohat, 246, 247
Komagata Maru, 156
Korbel, Joseph, 586, 597
Kripalani, Acharaya J.B., General Secretary, INC 1934-46; President, INC 1946, 352, 589, 494, 495, 506, 507
Krishak Proja Samiti, 314
Krishna, 69, 185
Kuala Lumpur, 658
Kumaon, 20
Kut (Mesopotamia), 178

Lahore, 4, 25, 41, 98, 198, 202, 203, 208, 229, 234, 240, 241, 247, 249, 255, 273, 430, 460, 476, 525, 541, 542, 553, 556, 595, 598, 611, 614, 617, 619, 622, 624; Government College, 322; Martial Law at, 202
Lahore Conspiracy Case, 273
Lahore Resolution, *see,* Pakistan Resolution
Laik Ali, Mir, 583
Lajpat Rai, Lala (1865-1928), Member, Arya Samaj, 111, 113, 119, 120, 122, 125, 126, 164, 221, 224, 231, 233, 262, 321, death of; 272, 273
Lake, Lord, 17, 18, 19
Lakshmi, goddess, 322
Lancashire, 90, 148, 291
Land Reforms, 32

Lascelles, Sir Alan, 448
Law, Islamic, 312
Lawrence, Henry, 34, 647
Leadenhall Street, 18
League Against Imperialism, 263
League of Nations, 257, 333, 335
Lee Commission, 236, 254
Letter to a Hindu, 182
Liaquat Ali Khan, Nawabzada (1895-
    1951), Member, UP Legislative
    Assembly 1926-40; Secretary, AIML
    1936-47; Member, Indian Legislative
    Assembly 1940-7; Finance Member,
    Interim Government 1946-7; Prime
    Minister of Pakistan 1947-51, 51, 459,
    460, 561, 462, 463, 467, 482, 483, 484,
    489, 490, 503, 504, 506, 516, 518, 519,
    520, 522, 523, 525, 532, 544, 547, 551,
    560, 578, 599, 607, 609, 616, 619, 621,
    622, 626, 629
Liberal Federation, 328
Life of Mahomet, 80
Light of Asia, The, 182
Linlithgow, 2nd Marquess of (Victor
    Alexander John Hope), Viceroy and
    Governor-General of India 1936-43,
    297, 304, 305, 306, 337, 344, 346, 351,
    352, 354, 355, 362, 373, 374, 378, 386,
    388, 389, 390, 391, 394, 396, 405, 639,
    655
Listowel, 5th Earl of (William Francis
    Hare), Parliamentary Under-Secretary
    of State for India and Burma, 1944-5;
    Secretary of State for India and Burma
    23 April 1947-14 August 1947, 508,
    510, 519, 528, 538, 539, 540, 567, 568,
    572, 577
Lloyd, George Ambrose (1879-1941),
    Governor of Bombay 1918-23, 215,
    218
Lloyd George, David, 236, 237, 291
Lockhart, Lt. Gen. Sir Rob McGregor
    Macdonald, Military Secretary, India
    Office 1941-3; Deputy Chief of
    General Staff 1944-5; Army Com-
    mander, India 1945-7; Acting
    Governor of NWFP 26 June-13 August
    1947, 516, 523

Lohari Gate, Lahore, 208
London, 60, 77, 113, 181, 190, 198, 219,
    220, 226, 255, 282, 292, 391, 396, 397,
    402, 404, 411, 418, 422, 427, 463, 464,
    469, 496, 497, 501, 502, 503, 505, 512,
    519, 524, 526, 530, 533, 541, 626, 640,
    641; East End of, 291
London Conference, *see,* Round Table
    Conference
Louis XIV, 7
Lower Doab, 17
Loyal Mohamedans of India, The, 78
Lucknow, 33, 40, 34, 39, 81, 82, 83, 129,
    153, 161, 246, 275, 310, 315, 329
Lucknow Pact, 130, 143, 157, 162, 163,
    164, 165, 167, 170, 172, 177, 178, 238,
    266, 267, 343, 634, 637, 638, 643, 648
Luxembourg, German invasion of, 352
Lyallpur, 211, 430; Martial Law at, 202
Lytton, Lord, 58, 59, 88, 91, 96, 97, 106

MAO College, 129
Macao, 3
Macaulay, Thomas Babington (1800-59),
    Head of Law Commission, famous for
    his minute on education, 14, 23, 30,
    54, 62, 63
MacDonald, James Ramsay (1866-1937),
    Prime Minister, 1924, 1929-35;
    Chairman, RTC 1930-2, 186, 273, 275,
    282, 284, 285, 287, 289, 290, 293, 308
MacIlvride, Inspector, 204
Macmillan, (Maurice) Harold, Secretary
    for Air 1945; Prime Minister, 517
MacPherson, John Moleworth, 15, 137
Maddock, Col., 246
Madras, 6, 7, 11, 12, 13, 14, 19, 44, 60,
    82, 97, 98, 127, 142, 158, 201, 231,
    232, 235, 249, 251, 255, 263, 288, 302,
    319, 361, 375, 384, 388, 421, 436,
    641; shelling of, 148
Madras Army, 27
madrassas, 31, 75
Madrid, fall of, 333
Mahabharata, 69
Mahajan, Mehr Chand, Prime Minister of
    Kashmir, 537, 593, 594, 595
Mahavira, 196

Mahendra Pratap of Hathras, Raja, 156
Mahmud Khan, Nawab, 77
Mahmud of Ghazni, 62, 79
Mahmud, Syed, 79
Mahmudabad, Raja of, 155
Mahrashtra, 159
Mainipur, 249
Majendie, Lieut. V. D., 40
Majority Report of 1920, 203, 211
Mujumdar, R. C., 115, 165, 615
Malabar, 3, 5, 232, 239; Coast, 3, 7
Malacca, 3, 5
Malak, H. M., 140
Malaviya, Madan Mohan, 26, 101, 102, 103, 154, 180, 194, 216, 221, 224, 289, 292
Malaya, 155, 381, 393, 394, 397
Malcolm, Sir John, 563
Malwa, 19
Mamdot, Iftikhar Husain Khan, Nawab of, Member, Punjab Legislative Assembly; President, Punjab Provincial Muslim League, Member, Muslim League Working Committee, 477
Manchester, 321
Manchuria, 333
Mandal, Jogindar Nath, Minister, Judicial Works and Buildings, Bengal 1946; Member, Interim Govt. 1946, 459, 461
Mandalay, 125, 159
Mangla Canal, 604
Manipur, 21, 395
Manki Sharif, Pir of, Member, AIML Council, 465
Manu, honorary grand-daughter of Gandhi, 491
Maplistan, 326
Marathas, 12, 13, 15, 16, 18, 21, 36, 568, 625, 642
Mardan, 479
Marshall Islands, 393
Martial Law, 368, 619
Martyn, Mrs How, 194
Marx, Karl, 29
Masulipatam, 6, 7
Matthai, Dr John, Professor of Indian Economics, Madras University 1922-5; Member, later President, Indian Tariff Board 1925-34; Director General, Commercial Intelligence 1935-40; Member, Interim Govt. 1946-7, 455, 457, 460
Matthew, St., 631
Mayo, (Richard Southwell Bourke), 6th Earl of, 75
Mazhar-ul-Haque, 145, 152, 153, 180
Mazzini, 94
McNaughton, General, of Canada, 601
Mecca, 4
Meerut, 19, 27, 28, 29, 37, 33, 38, 41, 77, 82; Conspiracy Case, 258
Mehta, Pherozeshah, 119, 123, 137
Memoirs (Aga Khan), 138
Memoirs (Ismay), 521
Menon, Vengalil Krishna, Secretary, India League 1929-47; High Commissioner for India 1947, 487, 629
Menon, Vapal Pangunni, (V.P.), Rao Bahadur, Reforms Commissioner to the Govt. of India 1942 and Secretary to Governor-General (Public) 1945-6, 427, 481, 491, 492, 496, 497, 499, 500, 501, 502, 503, 505, 506, 511, 513, 544, 545, 548, 549, 550, 551, 552, 560, 561, 566, 569, 570, 570, 571, 573, 583, 584, 586, 587, 593, 594, 595, 596, 623, 629
Merewether, Colonel, 150
Mesopotamia, 148, 157, 178, 218
Messervy, Lieutenant-General Sir Frank Walter, G.O.C.-i-C Northern Command, India 1946, 478, 524
Meston, Lord, 654
Metcalfe, Sir Charles Theophilus (1785-1846), Resident at Delhi 1811-19; Acting Governor-General 1835-6, 23
Middle East, 574
Middle Temple, London, 287
Midnapore, 292, 389, 390
Midway Island, 393
Mieville, Sir Eric Charles, Private Secretary to the Viceroy 1931-6; Principal Secretary to the Viceroy March 1947, 501, 502, 503, 513
Mill, John Stuart, 124
Miller, Webb, 280
Milton, J., 152, 154

Minority Report of 1920, 203, 211
Minto, Lord, 19, 20, 117, 120, 123, 124, 125, 126, 128, 130, 131, 135, 140, 169
Mir Kasim 10, 11
Mira Bahan, 383
Mirzapur, 249
missionaries, 30, 64, 65
Mohammed Akram, 537
Mohamedan All-India Confederacy, 133
Mohammedan Educational Conference, 80, 133
Mohan Singh, Captain, 394
Mohan Singh, Jathedar, 615, 618
Mohani, Hasrat, 229, 234
Mohsin-ud-Din, also called Dadu Miyan, 73
Mohsin-ul-Mulk, Nawab, 87, 129
Moira, Lord (afterwards Marquis of Hastings), 20
Monckton, Sir Walter Turner (later 1st Viscount), Director-General, Ministry of Information 1940-1; Solicitor General 1945; Adviser to Hyderabad State on Constitutional Matters, 582, 583
Mongolia, 334
Montagu, Edwin Samuel, Secretary of State for India, 1917-22, 117, 148, 158, 166, 167, 170, 171, 177, 214, 219, 220, 237, 641, 648, 653
Montagu-Chelmsford Reforms, 150, 214, 266; Report, 168, 171, 172, 177, 178, 648-50; Scheme, 177
Montgomery, Robert, 40
Montgomery, 430
Mookerjee, Girja, 113
Moon, Sir Edward Penderel, ICS 1929-44; Secretary, Development Board, Govt. of India 1946-7; Minister, Bahawalpur State, April 1947, 620
Moonje, B. S., 282
Moors of Spain, 241
Moplah Rebellion, 233, 245; Moplahs, 232, 233, 239
Morley, John, Viscount of Blackburn (1838-1923), Secretary of State for India, 1905-11, 117, 123, 124, 125, 126, 127, 129, 130, 135, 141

Morley-Minto Reforms, 126, 162
Morning Post, 220
Mornington, Lord, 16. *See also,* Wellesley, Marquis of, 16
Moscow, 20, 258, 333, 530
Moses, the Prophet, 136
Mountbatten, Lady Edwina, 472, 485, 486, 497, 498, 609, 628, 651
Mountbatten, Lord Louis, 393, 468-9, 472, 474, 482, 485, 487-507, 510-16, 518-36, 538-40, 542-5, 547-52, 554-5, 557-60, 562, 567-84, 587, 589-600, 603, 607-9, 612, 616-629,651-2
Mountbatten, Pamela, 485, 489, 497
Mountbatten, Patricia, 532
Muddiman, 252; Committee, 254
Mudie, Sir (Robert) Francis, ICS, Chief Secretary, UP 1939; Home Member, Viceroy's Executive Council, 1944-5; Governor of Sind 1946-7, 621
Mudliar, Sir A. Ramaswamy, Member for Commerce, Viceroy's Executive Council 1939-42; for Supply 1943-6; President, UN Economic and Social Council 1946-7; Diwan of Mysore 1946, 398
Mughal dynasty, 3; Empire, 568, 581, 638, 853, 656; Mughals, 9, 24, 53, 54, 62, 70, 74
Muhammad Ali, 131, 132, 151, 160, 217, 218, 228, 230, 231, 235, 243, 247, 268, 282, 383, 286, 322, 433
Muhammad Ali, Chaudhri, 461, 519, 532, 535, 550, 581, 607, 615
Muhammad Ali, Maulana, 633
Muhammad Ali, Nawab of Carnataic, 8
Muhammad bin Qasim, 91
Muhammad Ghori, 91
Muhammad Munir, 537
Muhammad Quresh, 26
Muhammad VI, Caliph, 237, 238
Muhammadan Anglo-Oriental College, Aligarh, 80
Muhammadan Anglo-Oriental Defence Association, 88
Muhammadan Literary Society, 114
Muharram, 246
Munistan, 326

Muir, Sir William, 87

Mukerjee, Shyamprasad, 513

Mukherjee, Bijan Kumar, Judge of the Calcutta High Court 1936; Member, Bengal Boundary Commission, 537

Muller, Max, 67

Multan, 246, 32, 430, 478, 53; uprising in, 25

Munich, 322, 333, 338; Agreement, 336

Munir, Muhammad, Judge of Punjab High Court 1942; Member, Punjab Boundary Commission, Chief Justice of Pakistan, 559

Munro, Major, 11

Munro, Sir Thomas, 60, 647

Musaddas, 87

Muslim Conference, 265, 586, 598

Muslim Herald, 83

Muslim League. *See,* All-India Muslim League

Muslim National Guard, 342, 476

Muslim nationalism, 37

Muslim-Sikh riot, 249

Muslims, East Bengali, 146; massacre of, 612; Nationalist, 428, 444, 445, 446

Mussolini, Benito, Prime Minister of Italy, 291, 352, 393

Mutiny of Fifth Light Infantry, 157

Mutiny of Royal Indian Navy, 421

Muttra, 249

Muzaffarabad, 604

My Indian years, 141, 148, 202

Mysore, 23, 173; State, 682

Nabha House, 133; State, 617; Maharaja of, 617

Nabiullah, Syed, 143

Nadiad, Kaira, 204

Nagasaki, 393

Nagpur, 17, 26, 122, 143, 144, 224, 225, 226, 228, 229, 234, 246, 249, 273, 311

Naidu, P. Rangiah, 100

Naidu, Sarojini, 145, 194, 205, 280, 289, 290, 386

Najaf, 92

Nana Sahib, 21, 26, 31, 33, 34, 35, 36, 39

Nanak, Guru (1469-1539), founder of Sikh religion, 238,257

Nand Kumar, 13, 14

Nankana Sahib, 257

Nanking, 333

Naoroji, Dadabhai, 100, 102, 112, 113, 119, 121, 137, 138

Napoleon, 18, 20

Napoleonic Wars, 7, 20

Nariman, 306

Nasaristan, 326

Nasir Ali, Mir. *See,* Titu Miyan

National Agricultural Party, 315

National Conference, 585, 586, 589, 590, 591, 600

National Defence Council, 359

National Muslim University. *See,* Jamia Millia Islamia

National Paper, The, 164

Nationalist Muslims, 453, 459, 461

Nationalist Party, 159, 254, 413, 427

Native Infantry, 28, 41; 64th Regiment, 27, 238

Native States, 203

Naya Shiwala, 322

Nayar, 4

Nayar, Sushila, 389

Nazars, 54

Nazi Germany, 335, 336; Nazis, 339, 380, 654; Nazism, 301, 340, 382

Nazir Ahmad, Maulvi, 87

Negro, 190

Nehru Committee, 323

Nehru in Retrospect, 606

Nehru Report, 163, 264, 266, 267, 268, 269, 270, 277, 292, 634, 657

Nehru Report, *see,* Congress Enquiry Committee Report

Nehru Report, The (1928), 564

Nehru, Jawaharlal (1889-1964), President, INC 1929, 1936-7, 1946, 1951-4; Prime Minister of India 1947-64, 111, 154, 158, 165, 178, 184-5, 188-97, 214, 229, 230, 233, 259, 262, 263, 264, 271, 272, 274-9, 281-2 286-90, 292-3, 295, 302, 305, 307, 311, 312, 316, 329, 334, 336, 338, 339, 341, 342, 345, 352, 355-9, 361, 363, 366, 367, 371, 373, 375, 379, 380-2, 385, 386, 389, 414, 420, 421, 424, 425, 432, 439, 443-6,

448-51, 453, 455-7, 459-60, 462-3,
465, 466, 473, 475-6, 480, 481, 484
486-7, 489-490, 492-3, 497, 501-4,
511, 513-15, 528-30, 532, 543-7, 558-
61, 573, 580, 586-7, 589-93, 595-6,
598-9, 602, 606, 609, 610, 611, 622-4,
626, 628-9, 633, 638-9, 641, 643, 654,
656; mother of, 279; sister of, 279;
wife of, 279
Nehru, Motilal (1861-1931), Member, UP
Legislative Council 1909; President,
Congress Session 1919, 1928;
Founded *Independent* 1919; founding
member of Swarajya Party; President
and author of Nehru Report, 52, 158,
214, 216, 221, 230, 233, 253, 256, 259,
264, 268, 271, 275, 281, 282, 285, 368
Neill, General, 39, 42
Nepal, 20, 35, 342
Netaji, *see,* Bose, Subhas Chandra
Netherlands, 651; German invasion of,
352
New Delhi, 310, 418, 422, 426, 468, 477,
485, 505, 506, 540, 541, 615, 623
New India, 157
New South Wales, 166
New Testament, The, 182
New World, 4
New York, 602
New Zealand, 256
News Chronicle, 357, 379, 400
Newton, 183
Nichol, Mrs, 423
Nicobar Islands, 562
Nine Troubled Years, 291
Nishtar, Sardar Abdur Rab Khan (1899-
1958), Member, Legislative Assembly
NWFP 1937; Finance Minister, NWFP
1953-45; Member, Interim Govern-
ment 1946; Member, Partition Council
1947, 432, 459, 460, 506, 518, 520,
554, 569
Nizam of Hyderabad, 7, 13, 15, 16, 35,
284, 326, 581-3
Nizamul Mulk, 581
Noakhali, 464, 610, 619, 624; Day, 466
Noel-Baker, Philip, Secretary of State for
Air 1946-7, 550, 560, 602-3.

Non-Co-operation Agitation, 248
Non-co-operation Movement, 155, 260,
279
Noon, Malik Sir Muhammad Firoz
(Feroze) Khan (1893-1970), Unionist
Minister, Local Self-Government,
Punjab 1927-30; Minister of Edu-
cation, Punjab 1931-6; High Commis-
sioner in London 1936-41; Member,
Viceroy's Executive Council 1941-5;
ML Member, Punjab Legislative
Assembly 1946; Governor, East
Pakistan 1950-3; Chief Minister,
Punjab 1953-5; Prime Minister of
Pakistan 1957-8, 378, 394, 395
North-West Frontier, 164
North-West Frontier Province, 322, 323,
325, 330, 387, 388, 407, 420, 428, 429,
431, 433, 479, 488, 497, 502, 507, 509,
511, 514, 516, 522, 529, 530, 554, 599,
619
North-Western Provinces, 27, 32, 44, 85,
105, 99, 109, 221, 247, 266, 269, 270,
277, 290, 292, 302, 305, 314, 319
Norway, German invasion of, 352
Now or Never, 324

O'Dwyer, Sir Michael, 202, 211, 213, 222
Obeidullah Sindhi, 156
Okinawa, 393
Old Vic, 137
Omi Chand, 10
Operation Polo, 584
opium, 20, 254
Orientalists, 23
Orissa, 9, 12, 109, 142, 249, 297, 302, 436
Oriyas, 110, 642
Osmanistan, 326
Ottoman Empire, 341, 650
Oudh, 32, 33, 45, 99, 634; annexation of,
31; Begams of, 13, 35; Nawab of, 12,
13, 17, 26, 33
Oxford, 74, 217; All Souls College, 166

Pabna, 248
Pacific, 393, 395
Pacific War Cabinet, 378
Pakhtuns, 277, 465

Pakistan, 25, 43, 51, 73, 130, 133, 135,
168, 238, 255, 268, 290, 316, 319, 321,
323-6, 350-1, 367, 375-6, 381, 391,
403-5, 408, 411, 416-19, 422-5, 427,
429-31, 433, 435, 436, 440, 442, 443,
446, 448, 452, 455, 460, 473, 480, 481,
488, 490, 491, 494, 495, 496, 498, 499,
504, 505, 506, 511, 512, 514, 516, 517,
518, 519, 522, 523, 524, 526, 527, 528,
529, 531, 532, 534, 535, 543,, 545,
548, 549, 551, 552, 553, 555, 558, 559,
561, 568, 570, 475, 579, 580, 585, 586,
587, 589, 592, 593, 597, 598, 600, 601,
606, 607, 612, 615, 626, 628, 629, 638,
640, 642, 643, 656, 658; East, 548;
West, 517
Pakistan, 325
Pakistan Constituent Assembly, 590
Pakistan Plan, 513
Pakistan Resolution, 313, 348, 351, 353,
377, 585
Pal, Bipin Chandra, 119, 122, 125, 221,
226
Palestine, 148, 218, 335, 341, 342, 343;
Fund, 342
Palwal, 208, 203
Pan-Islamism, 92
Pandit, Vijaya Lakshmi (wife of Ranjit S.
Pandit), sister of Jawaharlal Nehru;
Minister of Local Govt. and Health,
UP, 1937-9 and 1946; leader of Indian
Delegation to UN General Assembly
1946-7, 386, 529, 530
Paneli, 136
Panikkar, Kavalam Madhava, Prime
Minister of Bikaner 1944-7, 51, 558,
634
Panipat, 3
Pant, 414, 422
Paris, 22, 123; Geerman occupation of,
352
Parliament of Religions, Chicago, 66
Parliamentary Delegation, All Parties, 422,
423
Parsees/Parsis, 112, 137, 138, 308, 444
Partition Committee, 518, 519
Partition Council, 519, 520, 523, 621
Partition of Bengal, 107, 109

Pasha, Mustafa Kamal, 237
Patel, Sardar Vallabhbhai Jhaverbhai
(1975-1950), Congress President 1931;
Chairman, Congress Parliamentary
Sub-Committee 1935-9; Home
Member, Interim Government 1946;
Home Minister 1947-50, 189, 200,
256, 273, 275, 292, 295, 306, 352, 421,
422, 432, 445, 446, 449, 455, 457, 460,
461, 475, 481, 483, 489, 490, 491, 500,
501, 503, 506, 507, 513, 518, 519, 520,
550, 545, 546, 547, 550, 551, 552, 560;
569, 570, 573, 574, 577, 579, 580, 583,
591, 592, 593, 607, 611, 618, 621, 623,
624, 628, 643.
Patel, Vithalbhai, 256
Pathan State, 514
Pathanistan, 514
Pathankot, 552
Pathans, 46, 72, 516
Pathway to Pakistan, 229
Patiala, 618; Maharaja of, Pro-Chancellor,
Chamber of Princes 1946-7; officiating
Chancellor June 1947, 282, 589, 617
Patna, 63, 73, 294, 295, 349
Paul, K. T., 282
Peace of Aix-la-Chapelle, 7
Peasants and Tenants Party, 314
Peel, Lord, 308
Permanent Settlement of Bengal, 16
Perron, General, 16
Persia, 655; Persian(s), 14, 23, 24, 31, 63,
71, 75; Gulf, 3, 655; script, 79;
Peshawar, 72, 249, 281, 320, 465, 479,
497, 514
Peshwa, 17, 18 20, 21, 26, 31, 33
Pethick-Lawrence, Frederick William, Ist
Baron (1871-1961), Editor of *Echo,*
Labour MP 1923-31, 1935, Secretary
of State for India and Burma 1945;
Member, Cabinet Mission 1946, 331,
333, 418, 423, 425, 426, 427, 439, 447,
450, 451, 454, 456, 484, 493, 650, 651
Petit, Dinshaw, Sir, 138
Petit, Rutti, 138
Philip II, King of Spain, 4
Philippines, 393
Phoenix, South Africa, 183

Pindaris, 19, 21
Pioneer, The, 96
Pirpur Report, 318
Pitt, 15
Pitt Diamond, 11
Pitt the Younger, William, 18
Pitt, Thomas, 11
plague, 68, 69, 98, 110
Plassey, Battle of, 10; victory at, 633
Poland, 333, 334, 344; German invasion of, 351; Russian invasion of, 351
polygamy, 55, 64
Pondicherry, 7, 10, 125
Poona, 68, 85, 98, 159, 249, 294, 625
Poona Pact of 1932, 187, 293, 298, 386
Poonch, 593; Poonchis, 598, 601, 604
Poor Law, 22
Pope, 63, 291
Porbandar, 181; Rana of, 181
Portuguese, 3, 4, 5, 633
Postal Service, 26, 90
Prasad, Rajendra (1884-1963), President, INC 1934, 1939, 1947-8; Member, Interim Govt. 2 Sept. 1946; President of Constituent Assembly; President of India 1952-62, 185, 199, 238, 306, 317, 345, 352, 445, 455, 460, 518, 519, 520, 509, 652
Presidency College, 87
Press Act, 152, 158
Press, European, 91
Prince of Wales, 107, 120, 233, 468
Princely States, 264, 282, 563
Princestan, 411
Prithvi Raj, 91, 321
Privy Council, 69, 128, 139, 309
Proclamation of 1858, 32, 43, 56, 59, 61, 107
Proclamation of Queen Victoria, 564
Proclamation, Viceroy's, 337
Programme of the Communist International, The, 258
Promised Land, 136
Protestant, 4, 63, 325
Punjab, 28, 34, 40, 41, 44, 65, 72, 73, 99, 109, 111, 125, 155, 162, 179, 180, 202, 203, 212, 217, 221, 222, 225, 234, 236, 248, 249, 255, 257, 258, 266, 267, 269,

302, 313, 319, 321, 322, 323, 324, 325, 338, 350, 359, 407, 409, 414-15, 424-5, 427, 429, 430-1, 433, 436, 457, 465, 476-9, 481-2, 488, 496, 499, 508-9, 512, 521, 535, 537, 538, 542, 546, 553-5, 557, 580, 587, 611, 623, 650; annexation of, 25, 28, 54, 92; atrocities, 219, 220, 227; disturbances, 621; East, 36, 514, 543, 544, 555, 613, 618; Hindu-Muslim troubles in, 612; partition of, 480, 494, 511; West, 164, 313, 516, 614; High Court, 593
Punjab Boundary Award, 512
Punjab Boundary Force, 613
Punjab Hill States, 589
Punjab Muslim League, 255
Punjabis, 156, 231, 642
Pusa (Bihar), 108
Pyarelal, Secretary to Gandhi, 480

Queensland, 166
Quetta, 514, 597
quicksilver, 7
Quit India Demand, 398; Movement, 388, 399, 486; Rebellion, 393, 414, 472, 565, 639; Resolution, 382, 384, 391, 398, 400, 422
Quran, The, 71, 86
Quresh, Muhammad, 26
Qureshi, Shoaib, 530

Radcliffe Boundary Award, 585, 587
Radcliffe, Sir Cyril, 536, 538, 539, 540, 541, 555, 556, 557, 559, 542, 543, 544, 545, 546, 547, 548, 549, 550, 552, 554, 556, 557, 558, 560, 561
Radhakrishnan, 51
Radhakrishnan, Sir Sarvepalli, Vice-Chancellor, Benares Hindu University 1939; President of India, 656
Radical Party of England, 96
Rafi-ud-Din, Maulvi, 160
Rahimtoola, Habib, 530
Rahman, S. A., 532, 537
Rahmat Ali, Choudhary, 324, 325, 326, 350, 351, 643, 644
Raigarh, 68
railways, 30

Rajagopalachari (-riar or -ia, also known as Rajaji) (1879-1972), editor, *Young India;* Secretary INC 1921-2; Prime Minister, Madras 1937-9; Member, Interim Govt., 2, September 1946-13 January 1947, 253, 352, 356, 358, 375, 384, 403, 404, 405, 406, 455, 460, 483, 519, 622

Rajah, 367

Rajkot (Kathiwar), 181

Rajpal, 246, 249

Rajput States, 579

Rajputana, 19, 72

Rajputs, 12, 27; Hindu, 46

rakhi-bandhan, 111, 135

Ram, god, 182

Ram Navami, festival of, 205

Ram, Jagjivan, 455, 460

Rama-rajya, 196

Ramakrishna, 65, 66, 67

Ramayana, 182

Rampur, 576, 578; Nawab of, 36

Rand, Collector of Poona 69, 98

Rangila Rasul, 246, 249

Rangoon, 21, 43, 361, 395, 487

Rani of Jhansi, 35; ballad in praise of, 42

Ranjit Singh, Maharaja (1780-1839), founder of Sikh Kingdom in the Punjab, 20, 24, 25, 72, 153

Rao, Shankar, 352

Rashtriya Swayam Sewak Sang, 476

Rau (Raoo), Sir Benegal Narsingha, ICS, Puisne Judge, High Court, Bengal 1938-44; Prime Minister, Kashmir 1944-5; Constitutional Adviser to Constitutional Assembly July 1946-7, 427, 552

Ravi, River, 275, 614

Rawalpindi, 247, 248, 249, 430, 478, 553, 585

Razakars, 583

Razvi, Kasim, leader of Razakars, 583

Reading, Rufus Daniel Isaacs, Ist Marquis of (1860-1935), Viceroy of India 1921-6, 233, 237, 245, 275, 284

Red Crescent Branch of MNG, 342

Red Fort, Delhi, 419, 420

Red Sea, 3, 55, 656

Red Shirts, 292, 599

Rees, Maj.-Gen. Thomas Wynford, Indian Army, Commander, 4th Indian Division 1945-7, 520, 521, 613

Reforms Act of 1919, 236, 260

Reminiscences (Zafrullah Khan), 602

Reminiscences of an Engineer, 558

Residency, Lucknow, 34

Revolt of 1857, 564

Rewah, Maharajah of, 149

Rhineland, 333

Richards, Professor Robert, Parliamentary Under-Secretary of State for India 1924; leader of the Parliamentary Delegation to India 1946, 423

Rippon, Lord, 58, 81, 88, 91, 106

Rise and Growth of Congress in India, The 113

road building, 26

Roe, Sir Thomas, 6

Rohillas, 13

Roman Empire, 3

Rome, 643

Roosevelt, President of USA, 370, 376, 386

Rose, Sir Hugh, 35

Round Table Conference, 190, 193, 254, 255, 274, 275, 281, 282, 283, 285, 286, 287, 288, 290, 296, 297, 307, 324, 427, 500, 634, 656

Rousseau, 124

Rowlatt Act, 202; Agitation, 201, 216; Committee, 179; reports 179

Rowlatt Bills, 158, 166, 179, 180, 201, 368

Rowlatt, Sir Sidney Arthur Taylor (1962-1945), 85, 179

Roy, Dr Bidhan Chandra, Vice-Chancellor, Calcutta University, 1942-4; Member, Working Committee, INC, 399

Roy, M. N., Member, Bengal Legislative Assembly; Founder of Radical Democratic Party and Indian Federation of Labour, 258

Roy, Raja Ram Mohun, 56, 57, 63, 64, 88

Roy's Weekly (Delhi), 370

Royal Asiatic Soviety, 77

Royal Indian Navy, Mutiny of, 421
Royal Proclamation of 1921, 173
Royal Sussex Regiment, 249
RSSS (Rashtriya Swayam Sewak Sang), 476
Ruskin, 182, 183
Russia, 23, 24, 110, 148, 192, 258, 263, 333, 650, 654; Russian, 97
Russo-Turkish War of 1877, 143

Saadulla, Sir Muhammad, 314, 319, 359
Sabarmati Ashram, 279
sadhus, 158
Safiistan, 326
Sain, Kanwar, 558, 559
Salimullah, Sir Khawaja, Nawab of Dacca (1884-1915), founder member of AIML; President, AIML session at Calcutta 1912, 129, 133, 134
Salisbury, Lord, 130, 297
Salonica, fall of, 144
Salt Tax, 252, 254, 279, 484
Sampuran Singh, 282
San Francisco Charter, 528
San, Aung, 487
Sanatam Dharam College, 209; Sabha, 247
Sanger, Mrs, 194
Sangor Island, 23
Sangthan, 246
Sankey, Lord, 296
Sanskrit, 14, 23, 31, 54, 63
Santanas, 67
sanyasis, 6, 158
Sapru, Tej Bahadur, Law Member, Viceroy's Executive Council 1921-3; President, All-India Liberal Federation 1923, 178, 261, 267, 275, 282, 283, 285, 420
Sarila, Raja of, 296
Sarup Singh 558
Sastri, Sir Srinvas, Vice-President, All-India Liberal Federation, 178, 180, 282, 285
Satara, 26
Satyagraha, 182, 183, 184, 186, 194, 198, 201, 272, 336, 358, 359
Satyamurti, S. (1887-1943), Member, Madras Legislative Council 1923-39; Indian Legislative Assembly 1935, 658

Satyapal, Dr, 203, 205
Satyartha-Prakasa, 65
Saunders, J. P., murder of, 273
Savage, G. R., 621
Savarkar, Vinayak Damodar (1883-1966), President, Hindu Mahasabha 1937-42, 165, 321, 344, 367
Sayyid Ahmad Brelvi, 72, 74
Scheduled Castes, 299, 338, 413, 415, 443, 444, 451, 459, 475, 477, 551
Scientific Society, 79, 86
Scotland, 203
Scott, Sir Ian, Deputy Private Secretary to Mountbatten, 559
Scouting for Boys in India, 317
Secunderabad, 249
Security Council, 584, 600, 601, 602, 603
Sedition Committee Report, 1918, 85
Seeley, Sir John, 634
Separate Communal Electorate, 138
Seringapatam, 17; Treaty of, 15
Sermon on the Mount, 182
Servant of God, 290
Setavald, Chimanlal, 344
Seven Years' War, 7
Seymour, British Ambassador, 386
Shafaat Ahmad Khan, Sir, 455, 459
Shafi, Muhammad, Sir, 144, 147, 268, 282
Shah Alam II, 11, 12, 16, 17, 18
Shah Jahan, Emperor, 5, 6
Shah Nawaz, Begum, Parliamentary Secretary, Education and Public Health, Punjab 1937-43, 283, 359
Shah Shuja, 24
Shahi Mosque, Delhi, 248
Shahidganj Mosque, 249
Shahjahanpur, 246
Shakargarh, 552
Shakespeare, Collector of Bijnor, 77
Shakespeare, William, 152, 154, 560, 650
Shanker Rao, 352
Shariat, 91 228, 231, 312
Shariat-Ullah, Haji, 73
Shaukat Ali, 151, 217, 218, 247
Shaw, Bernard, 291
Sheean, Vincent, 530
Sherwood, Miss, 206, 208
Shias, 71

Shibli, Noamani, 87, 93
Shiromani Akali Dal, 615
Shiromani Gurdwara Prabandhak Committee, 257
Shivaji, 70, 153; festival, 68; utterances of, 69; Walking Staff of, 93
Sholapur, 280
Shore, Sir John, 16
Shradhanand, Swami, 204, 216, 218, 248
shuddhi, 246, 248
Shuja-ud-daula, Nawab of Oudh, 11
Shvernik, President of USSR, 530
Sialkot, 322
Siddiqistan, 326
Sikandar Hayat Khan, Sir (1892-1942), Member, Punjab Legislative Council 1921 and 1926; Unionist Member, Punjab Legislative Assembly 1937; Premier of Punjab 1937-42, 313, 319, 338, 343, 359, 367, 409
Sikandar-Jinnah Pact, 409
Sikh Kingdom, 25, 72, 568; nationalism, 257; rule in Punjab, 41; State, 417, 430, 617
Sikh War, First, 25
Sikh War, Second, 25, 91, 123
Sikh-majority Province, East Punjab as, 618
Sikhistan (*See also*, Khalistan), 533, 617, 618
Sikhs, 7, 24, 25, 35, 36, 41, 45, 72-3, 155-7, 172, 257, 264, 265, 277, 308, 309, 312, 367, 381, 413, 415, 419, 430, 436, 443, 444, 450-1, 458, 463, 477, 488, 506, 511, 547, 548, 553, 584, 593, 612, 615, 616, 621-2, 634, 639; Akali, 428, 476
Simla, 20, 33, 288, 413, 429, 430, 432, 435, 503, 541, 640, 641
Simla Conference, 410, 412, 416, 418, 432, 473
Simon Commission, 171, 248, 250, 253, 255, 261, 264, 272, 273, 274, 281; Report, 283
Simon, Ist Viscount (John Allsebrook Simon), Lord Chancellor 1940-5; Chairman of Indian Statutory Commission 1927-30, 248, 260, 649

Sind, 25, 27, 72, 164, 221, 249, 265, 270, 291, 297, 322, 323, 325, 327, 338, 350, 388, 407, 409, 429, 431, 433, 436, 481, 509, 514, 516, 554; Conquest of, 24
Sind Provincial Muslim League Conference, 240, 326
Sind United Party, 314
Sindhia, 12, 16, 17, 18, 20, 35, 36
Sindhia, Madhaji, 153
Singapore, 155, 157, 361, 381, 487; Indian troops in, 337
Sinha, Sir S. P. 153, 159
Sinha, Sri Krishna, Chief Minister, Bihar 1937-9, 306
Sinn Feinism, 183
Siraj-ud-daula, 9, 10
Sirhind, 321
Sitaramayya, Dr B. Pattabhai Bhagaraja, Member, Working Committee INC 1940-7, 131, 189, 370
Siva Raj, N., 413
Siva, statue of, 64
Sivaji, 625
Slade, Miss, 383
Slade, Sir Edmond, 383
Smith, Colonel Dunlop, 129
Smuts, Feild Marshal Jan Christian, Prime Minister of South Africa 1939, 147
Smyrna, 218, 237
Social Reformer, 80
Socialism, 157
Socotra, 3
Solapur, 247
Solomon Islands, 393
Sorenson, Reginald William, MP (Lab.); Chairman, India League, 423
South Africa, 139, 149, 148, 181, 183, 186, 187, 190, 193, 197, 198, 199, 219, 256, 658; Indians in, 104, 105
South America, 90
South-East Asia, 156, 358
Southall, 52
Soviet Union, 584
Spain, 4, 241, 333, 335, 336; Spaniards, 241
Spencer, Herbert, 196
Spens, Sir William Patrick, Chief Justice of India 1943; 521

Spices, 3, 7
Spratt, Philip, 258
Srinagar, 591, 594, 595, 599
St. Andrew's Day dinner, 105, 107
Standstill Agreement, 570, 576, 583, 584
Stanley, Colonel Oliver Frederick George; Secretary of State for Colonies 1942-5, 304
Star and Crescent, (Muslim League flag), 317
Statement of 3 June 1947, 499
Statutory Commission. See, Simon Commission
Suddhi, 65
Sudras, 656
Suez Canal, 55, 136, 352
Suhrawardy, H. S. (1893-1963), Member, Bengal Legislative Council 1921; Minister of Labour, etc. 1943-5; Chief Minister of Bengal 1946-7; Prime Minister of Pakistan 1956-57, 428, 453, 454, 513, 551, 624
Sukkur, 249
Sultan Ahmad, Sir Sayyid (1880-1963), Delegate to RTC, 1930-1; Law Member, Viceroy's Executive Council, 1941-3; Member for Information and Broadcasting 1943-5; Advisor to the Chamber of Princes 1945-7, 360
Sumatra, 5
Sunnis, 71
Surat, 5, 6, 17, 122, 127, 159, 234
Sutlej, 20, 25, 109
Sutlej Valley canal, 543
suttee, 22, 30, 64
swadeshi, 111, 112, 119, 121, 122, 223, 229
swaraj, 47 68, 69, 121, 193, 217, 223, 224, 225, 226, 228, 229, 230, 231, 233, 234, 239, 240, 243, 276, 336, 459
Swaraj Sabha, 223
Swarajists, 254, 255, 256, 263
Swarajya, 225, 228; Party, 252, 253, 254, 255, 294
Syed Ahmed Khan, Sir (1817-98), social reformer and educationalist; founder of Aligarh Movement, Scientific Society and Aligarh College (which later became Muslim University, Aligarh), 30, 32, 37, 46, 550, 55, 74-83, 88-9, 114, 126, 128-30, 132, 137, 321, 643
Syed Group of Nationalist Muslims, 428
Sylhet, 431, 482, 509, 516, 530, 537, 538, 540; looting in, 454
Sylhet Award, 545
Syria, 218, 342, 358

Tagore, Rabindranath, 195, 199
Tahzib-ul-Akhlaq, 86, 87, 88
Taipei, 395
Taj Mahal, 108, 189
tamasha, 114
Tamils, 642
Tandon, Purushottamdas, 189
Tanjore, Ruler of, 26; annexation of, 17
Tantia Topi, 34, 35
tanzim, 246
tapestries, 7
Tara Singh, Master, leader of Alkali Sikhs, 413, 417, 478, 612, 621
Tarain, Battle of, 321
Teja Singh, 537
telegraph, 26, 30; services, 90
Templewood, Ist Viscount of Chelsea (Sir Samuel John Gurney Hoare, 1880-1959), Secretary of State for India 1931-5, 288, 289, 291, 292, 303, 308, 474, 534, 650, 656
Tenasserim, 21
Terai, 20
Thailand, 389, 393
Thatcher, Margaret, 658
Theosophical Society, 157
Third Cavalary, 28
Thompson, Dr Edward, author and missionary, 323
Thoreau, 183
Thrace, 215, 218, 237
Three Magi, The, 426
Thugs, suppression of, 22
Tibet, 584
Tilak, Lokamanya Gangadhar, 47, 68, 69, 70, 85, 98, 110, 111, 119, 123, 125, 157, 159, 164, 166, 168, 178, 180, 214, 222, 625, 643
Tilak Memorial Swarajiya Fund, 230

Time and Tide, 348
Times, The, 75, 107, 604
Times of India, 506
Timur, House of, 40
Tippera, 464
Tipu Sultan of Mysore, 15, 16, 17
Tiranah-yi Hind, 322
Titu Miyan, 74
Tolstoy, Leo, 182
Tolstoy Farm, 183
Townshend, General, 178
Transfer of Power in India, 481
Transvaal, 182
Travancore, 15, 567, 576, 577
Treaty of Lausanne, 238
Treaty of Seringapatam, 15
Treaty of Sevres, 218, 237
Treaty of Versailles, 333
Tribune, 589
Trichinopoly, 8
Trinity College, Cambridge, 262
Trivedi, Sir Chandulal Madhavlal, Secretary, Govt. of India, War Dept. 1942-6; Governor of Orissa 1946-7, 520, 621, 626
Truman, Harry, President of USA 1945, 529
Tuker, Lt.-Gen. Sir Francis Ivan Simms, G.O.C.-in-C Eastern Command, India 1946-7, 464, 466
Turkey, 24, 92, 144, 155, 156, 178, 215, 216, 237, 238, 342, 351; Sultan of, 166, 226, 237; Turks, 93, 143, 144, 156, 157, 221
Tyabjee, Badruddin, 82, 114, 137, 195

UNO, *see,* United Nations Organization
UP, *see,* United Provinces
Ujjal Singh, 282
ulema, 75, 88, 216, 219, 231
Union Jack, 627; lowering of, 610
Unionist Ministry, Punjab, 409
Unionist Party, 255, 313, 409, 414, 415, 428
Unionists, 476, 477
United Indian Patriotic Association, 83
United Kingdom, 46, 226, 260, 288, 314, 4189, 438, 474, 528, 529, 553, 554,

655; South Asians in, 52
United Nations Organization, 364, 371, 380, 383, 384, 385, 386, 528, 550, 584, 597, 598, 599, 600, 601, 603, 604, 629; Commission on India and Pakistan, 601, 603, 604
United Press, USA, 280
United Provinces, 156, 185, 221, 248, 249, 258, 302, 315, 316, 318, 328, 436, 461, 465, 466, 488, 623
United States, 574, 652
Unity Conference, 247
universities, foundation, 26
Unto this Last, 183
Untouchables, 59, 186, 187, 195, 290, 316, 344, 347, 356, 383, 624, 636
Urdu, 4, 71, 79, 87, 129, 316
Urdu-Hindi Controversy, 143
Uri, 591
USA, 66, 148, 154, 155, 233, 288, 334, 359, 361, 368, 376
Usmanistan, 326
Uzbeg, Abdullah Khan, 4

Vaisa caste, 135, 181
Vakil, C. N., 483
Vankaner, 181
Vasco da Gama 4
Vedanta, 67
Vejononess, 282
Vellore, 27; Mutiny at, 19
Vernacular Press Act of 1878, 91, 94
Viceroy's Conference Papers, 532
Victoria Cross, 150, 153
Victoria, Queen, 35, 43, 45, 59, 106, 564; Diamond Jubilee of, 55
Victorians, 648
Vilayat Ali Khan, Nawab, 56, 57
Viqar-ul-Mulk, Nawab Mushtaq Hosain (1841-1917), Member, Simla Deputation to Lord Minto; founder member of AIML; Secretary, Board of Trustees, Aligarh College, 1907-1912, 128, 129, 133, 145
Virangam (Ahmadabad), 204
Vivekanada, Swami, 66
Vizagapatam, 361
Voltaire, 124

Wacha, D. E., 102
Wadala, (Bombay), 281
Wadia, Dina, 138
Wakf Validating Bill, 147
wakfs, 139
Wales, 25, 615
Wali-Ullah, Shah, 71, 74
War Cabinet, 385, 388, 396, 397, 402, 404, 405
War Council, 354
War of Austrian Succession, 7
War of Independence, American, 13
War Office, 149
Wardha, 304, 306, 337, 339, 352, 356, 374, 381, 388
Wardha Resolution of Congress, 353
Wardha Scheme, 317; of Education, 328
Washington, 404, 530
Waterloo, 7, 54, 20, 25
Watson, Admiral, 9
Watt, James, 22
Wavell, Field Marshal Sir Archibald Percival (1883-1950), Viceroy and Governor-General of India 1943-7, 358, 370, 390, 396, 397, 399, 401, 402, 406, 410, 411, 412, 413, 414, 415, 416, 417, 418, 419, 420, 422, 423, 424, 425, 426, 427, 429, 439, 441, 442, 444, 445, 452, 454-8, 459, 461, 462, 464, 468, 471, 472, 473, 476, 479, 480, 484, 485, 486, 500, 591, 625, 640
Wazir Hasan, Syed, 310
weavers, 32
Webb, Lt.-Col. Wilfred Francis, Resident in Kashmir 1945-7, 590
Wedderburn, Sir William, 97, 98, 83, 112
Wedgwood Benn, 289
Wedwood, Col., 228
Wellesley, Arthur, Marquis of, 17, 18, 19, 20, 54
Wellington, Duke of, 17, 183
Wescott, Bishop, 247
West Sussex Conservative Association, 287
Westminster Hall, 7; Abbey, 339
Westminster, Statute of, 167
Wheeler, Lt.-Gen. Raymond Albert, US Army, Deputy Supreme Allied Com-
mander, S. E. Asia Command 1944, 30, 38
Wheeler, Miss, 38
White Paper, 297, 300
Whitehall, 141, 650
widow's remarriage, 30, 64
Wilberforce, 22
Wilkinson, Miss Ellen, 192
Willingdon, Ist Marquess of (Freeman Freeman-Thomas) (1866-1941), Liberal MP 1900-10; Governor of Bombay 1913-18; Governor of Madras 1919-24; Viceroy of India 1931-6, 288, 292, 294
Wilson, F. W., 280
Wilson, President of USA, 154, 368
Workers and Peasants Parties, 258
World War I, 148, 151, 178, 198, 200, 215, 333, 368, 648
World War II, 171, 299, 330, 331, 342, 593, 639, 651
world wars, 564
Wyllie, Sir Francis Verner, Political Adviser to the Crown Representative 1940-1 and 1943-5; Governor of UP 1945-7, 124

YMCA, 487
yarn, 7
Yellow River, 656
Young India, 184, 214, 217, 235

Zafrullah (Zafrulla) Khan, Sir Muhammad (1893-1985), Member, Punjab Legislative Council 1926-35; Delegate to RTC 1930-2; President, AIML session 1931; Member, Viceroy's Council 1932, 1935-41; Foreign Minister of Pakistan 1947-54; Member, International Court of Justice 1954-61, 1963-70; President, ICJ 1970-2, 290, 308, 362, 550, 601, 602, 604
Zaidi, Bashir Husain, Prime Minister of Bhopal, 578
Zaka Ullah, Maulvi, 87
Zakir Husain, Dr, 445
Zeenat Mahal, Queen of Delhi, 37
Zetland, Lord (1876-1961), Governor of

Bengal 1917-22; Delegate to RTC, 1930-2; Secretary of State for India 1935-40, 303, 304, 306, 318, 351, 352

Ziegler, Philip, 555, 559, 560, 627
Zira, 555, 556, 557, 558, 559, 561
Zulu War, 186, 198, 200